Reading STREET

Grade 5

Scott Foresman
ELL Handbook

PEARSON

Glenview, Illinois
Boston, Massachusetts
Chandler, Arizona
Upper Saddle River, New Jersey

D1511712

ISBN-13: 978-0-328-47643-5
ISBN-10:   0-328-47643-9
3 4 5 6 7 8 9 10   V064   14 13 12 11

Contents

Part 1 English Language Learners: Professional Development Articles

Contents

Resources on Reading Street for English Language Learner Support

All the support you need for your ELL instruction.

The Teacher's Edition has ELL instructional strategies built into the lesson plans at point of use. The lessons provide guidance in using sheltered techniques and routines for teaching academic vocabulary, listening comprehension, phonics, vocabulary, reading comprehension, grammar and conventions, and writing.

Teacher's Edition

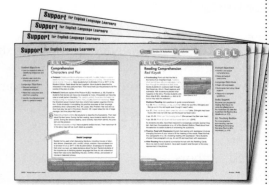

ELL Support pages

ELL Posters contain high-quality illustrations and five days of activities to support key oral vocabulary, selection vocabulary, and lesson concepts.

ELL Poster

High-Frequency Words
break   family   heard
listen   once   pull

Oral Vocabulary
courageous   hazard   rescue

Poster Talk-Through
This **family's** cat is stuck in the tree. The family **heard** the cat meowing loudly. They came out to see what was wrong. The mother went back inside and called 911. Then she came out to wait for help with her family. _Courageous_ firefighters came to _rescue_ the cat. They started to work at **once**. They did not wait. Now one fireman **pulls** the cat from the tree as the branch is about to **break**! The family **listens** as the fireman talks gently to the cat. When they listen, they feel calm. Everything is going to be all right. The _hazard_ is gone.

DAY 1

Check Prior Knowledge
Read the Poster Talk-Through aloud, pointing to images in the art. Check children's knowledge by asking questions.

Beginning Ask children to point to items they recognize on the poster and say what they are. Help them name items if necessary.

Intermediate Have children use short sentences to describe what is happening in the poster.

Advanced/Advanced High Ask children to describe the dangerous situation shown in the poster. Have them explain why it is dangerous.

Develop Concepts and Oral Vocabulary
Reread the Poster Talk-Through to introduce the Oral Vocabulary words. Give visual support by pointing to items on the poster that illustrate _courageous_, _hazard_, and _rescue_. Work with the class on a list of ideas that exemplify the words. Generate examples of hazards, ways to rescue something or someone, and courageous acts. Relate these concepts to the Question of the Week by asking children how they can help each other in dangerous situations.

DAY 2

Use the poster art and question to help children briefly discuss the lesson concept.

Teach High-Frequency Words
Share the Poster Talk-Through again, this time to introduce the tested High-Frequency Words. Label the poster with the High-Frequency Words. Then have the children, one at a time, act out one of the words for the others to guess.

DAY 3

Expand Vocabulary
Give the class examples of possible dangerous situations, such as: _Somebody gets hurt on the playground. Your friend is lost on a busy street._ As you name each situation, give pairs time to discuss and write down or sketch an appropriate way to help. Have pairs share their responses with the class at the end of the allotted time. Tell children that when there is real danger, they should tell an adult or call 911.

DAY 4

Produce Oral Language
Have the class pretend that they are in the poster scene. Have groups act out a television interview with the poster characters. Write _Who?_, _What?_, _When?_, _Where?_, _Why?_, and _How?_ on the board to guide questions.

Beginning/Intermediate Have children act as reporters and ask simple questions of people on the scene.

Advanced/Advanced High Have them play the parts of family members or firefighters.

DAY 5

Check Concepts and Language
Read the Question of the Week aloud. Monitor children's understanding of the lesson concept.

Beginning Provide the children with this sentence prompt: _In a dangerous situation, we can help by _____._ Ask each child to come up with one or two ways to complete the sentence.

Intermediate Ask: _What are two things that we can do to help in dangerous situations?_ Have children write a simple sentence for each response.

Advanced/Advanced High Have children write a very brief paragraph that answers the Question of the Week, _How can we help each other in dangerous situations?_

The ELL Handbook includes phonics and grammar transition lessons, comprehension skill practice, selection vocabulary word cards, study guides for ELL Readers, and multilingual selection summaries and vocabulary charts. Weekly planners provide daily instructional plans.

ELL Handbook

Weekly Planner

Instructional-level fiction and nonfiction books are provided for readers at all proficiency levels. The ELL, ELD, and Concept Literacy Readers relate to weekly concepts and offer students opportunities to read texts and practice target skills and strategies.

ELD/ELL Reader Teaching Guide

ELD Reader

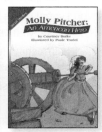

ELL Reader

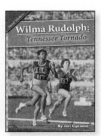

Concept Literacy Reader

Technology

Concept Talk Video

Use the Concept Talk Video to activate an engaging discussion about the weekly concept. Use the Concept Talk Video Routine found in the ELL Handbook to guide students' understanding.

AudioText CD

Use the AudioText CD and the AudioText CD Routine in this ELL Handbook to help students build fluency and comprehension and prepare for reading the main selection.

Grammar Jammer

Grammar Jammer provides additional practice with weekly grammar skills. For suggestions on how to use this learning tool, see the Grammar Jammer Routine in the ELL Handbook.

Language Development Student Outcomes

Language Learning Strategies	• Use prior knowledge and experiences to understand English. • Self-monitor oral or written language to recognize and correct errors or to seek help. • Use strategic learning techniques (such as concept mapping, drawing, memorizing, comparing, contrasting, or reviewing) to learn vocabulary. • Use learning strategies when speaking (request assistance, employ non-verbal cues, or use synonyms and descriptions in place of unknown English words). • Use and reuse newly acquired English words and expressions to improve proficiency and to build concepts. • Learn new essential language by using familiar or accessible language. • Distinguish between formal and informal English and use each language register in appropriate circumstances, in accord with grade-level expectations. • Develop and use language-learning strategies (such as looking for patterns in language or analyzing sayings and expressions), in accord with grade-level expectations.
Listening Skills	• Distinguish sounds and intonation patterns in English words and expressions with increasing clarity. • Distinguish phonetic sounds of English during word learning. • Learn English language structures, expressions, and vocabulary by listening to instruction and talking with peers and teachers. • Self-monitor for understanding of language during instruction and conversations, and seek clarification as needed. • Use visual resources, context, and familiar language to better understand unfamiliar spoken English. • Listen to a variety of media, paying attention to language meaning, to build concepts and acquire language. • Understand the meaning, main points, and important details of spoken language about familiar or unfamiliar topics. • Understand information and implied ideas in complex spoken language, in accord with grade-level expectations. • Demonstrate listening comprehension by following directions, responding to questions and requests, collaborating with peers, taking notes, or retelling and summarizing spoken messages.
Speaking Skills	• Produce phonetic sounds in newly acquired words and expressions in order to pronounce English words in an understandable manner. • Learn and use high-frequency English words to identify and describe people, places, animals, and objects. • Learn English vocabulary by retelling simple stories and information represented or supported by pictures. • Learn and use English words and expressions needed for classroom communication. • Speak using a variety of English grammatical structures, sentence lengths, sentence types, and connecting words with increasing accuracy and ease. • Speak using grade-appropriate content-area vocabulary in context to learn new English words and build academic language proficiency. • Share information interactively with peers and teachers. • Ask for and give information, using high-frequency, concrete words and expressions for basic communication and using abstract and content-based vocabulary during extended speaking assignments.

	• Express opinions, ideas, and feelings, ranging from using words and short phrases to participating in discussions about various grade-appropriate topics. • Explain, narrate, and describe with increasing specificity and detail as more English is acquired. • Adapt spoken language appropriately for formal and informal purposes. • Respond orally to information in print, electronic, audio, and visual media to build concepts and acquire language.
Reading Skills	• Learn relationships between sounds and letters in English, and decode words by recognizing sound-letter relationships and identifying cognates, affixes, roots, and base words. • Recognize the directionality of written English: left to right and top to bottom. • Develop basic English sight vocabulary. • Derive meaning of environmental print. • Comprehend English used routinely in grade-level texts. • Use before-reading strategies such as previewing graphic organizers and illustrations or learning topic-related vocabulary to enhance comprehension of written text. • Read adapted content-area material with a decreasing need for linguistic accommodations as more English is learned. • Use visual resources and context to read grade-appropriate text with understanding and to acquire vocabulary including academic language. • Use support from peers and teachers to read grade-appropriate text with understanding and to acquire vocabulary including academic language. • Demonstrate comprehension of increasingly complex grade-appropriate texts in English by participating in shared reading, retelling, or summarizing; responding to questions; and taking notes. • Read silently with increasing ease and comprehension for sustained periods. • Demonstrate English comprehension by employing and expanding basic reading skills (such as summarizing, understanding supporting ideas and details in text and graphic sources, and distinguishing main ideas from details) in accord with grade-level needs. • Demonstrate English comprehension by employing and expanding inferential skills (such as predicting, making connections between ideas, drawing conclusions from text and graphic sources, and finding supporting text evidence) in accord with grade-level needs. • Demonstrate English comprehension by employing and expanding analytical skills (such as evaluating written information and critically examining texts) in accord with grade-level needs.
Writing Skills	• Represent the sounds of the English language with letters when writing words in English. • Write using newly acquired basic English vocabulary and grade-level academic vocabulary. • Spell common English words with increasing accuracy, and use spelling patterns correctly as more English is acquired. • Edit writing for standard grammar and usage, including subject-verb agreement, pronoun agreement, and appropriate verb tenses, in accord with grade-level expectations as more English is acquired. • Use grammatical structures (such as verbs in different tenses, pronouns, possessive nouns, contractions, and negatives) correctly in writing, in accord with grade-level expectations. • Write using a variety of grade-appropriate sentence lengths, patterns, and connecting words to combine phrases, clauses, and sentences in increasingly accurate ways. • Narrate, describe, and explain with increasing detail to fulfill grade-appropriate writing needs as more English is acquired.

Grade 5 Readers on Reading Street

Every week there are a variety of readers to choose from to target instruction and meet the language development needs and reading levels of all learners. Every reader supports weekly grade-level concept development and the Question of the Week.

Leveled Readers

Weekly fiction and nonfiction readers are provided for students at the On-Level, Strategic Intervention, and Advanced levels.

On-Level

Strategic Intervention

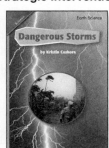

Advanced

Build Concepts

The Concept Literacy Reader builds concepts and language.

Concept Literacy

Build Language

Scaffolded versions build vocabulary and comprehension skills each week at different proficiency levels.

ELD Reader

ELL Reader

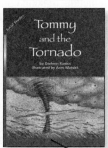

Beginning • Intermediate	Intermediate • Advanced • Advanced High
• Contains the same high-quality art as the ELL Reader.	• Contains the same high-quality art as the ELD Reader.
• Text adapted for Beginning and Intermediate proficiency levels.	• Text adapted for Intermediate to Advanced High proficiency levels.
• High-frequency and concept words are emphasized.	• Concept words that students need to know to understand the text are highlighted and defined.
• Graphic elements are simplified.	• Graphic elements such as captions, diagrams, maps, flow charts, and signs are included.
• Captions for photos are simple, then progress to either phrases or short sentences.	• Captions for photos are complete sentences.

Scott Foresman ELL Authors

Elena Izquierdo, Ph.D.
Associate Professor
University of Texas at El Paso

Jim Cummins, Ph.D.
Professor
Department of Curriculum,
Teaching and Learning
University of Toronto

Lily Wong Fillmore, Ph.D.
Professor Emerita
Graduate School of Education
University of California, Berkeley

Georgia Earnest García, Ph.D.
Professor
Language and Literacy Division
Department of Curriculum
and Instruction
University of Illinois at
Urbana-Champaign

George A. González, Ph.D.
Professor (Retired)
School of Education
University of Texas-Pan American,
Edinburg

The Three Pillars of English Language Learning

Dr. Jim Cummins, the University of Toronto

In order to understand how English learners develop second-language literacy and reading comprehension, we must distinguish between three different aspects of language proficiency:

Conversational fluency This dimension of proficiency represents the ability to carry on a conversation in face-to-face situations. Most native speakers of English have developed conversational fluency by age 5. This fluency involves use of high-frequency words and simple grammatical constructions. English learners generally develop fluency in conversational English within a year or two of intensive exposure to the language in school or in their neighborhood environments.

Discrete language skills These skills reflect specific phonological, literacy, and grammatical knowledge that students can acquire in two ways— through direct instruction and through immersion in a literacy-rich and language-rich environment in home or in school. The discrete language skills acquired early include:

- knowledge of the letters of the alphabet
- knowledge of the sounds represented by individual letters and combinations of letters
- the ability to decode written words

Children can learn these specific language skills concurrently with their development of basic English vocabulary and conversational fluency.

Academic language proficiency This dimension of proficiency includes knowledge of the less frequent vocabulary of English as well as the ability to interpret and produce increasingly complex written language. As students progress through the grades, they encounter:

- far more low-frequency words, primarily from Greek and Latin sources
- complex syntax (for example, sentences in passive voice)
- abstract expressions

Acquiring academic language is challenging. Schools spend at least 12 years trying to teach all students the complex language associated with academic success. It is hardly surprising that research has repeatedly shown that English language learners, on average, require *at least* 5 years of exposure to academic English to catch up to native-speaker norms.

Effective instruction for English language learners is built on three fundamental pillars.

English Language Learners

Activate Prior Knowledge/ Build Background	Access Content	Extend Language

Activate Prior Knowledge/ Build Background

No learner is a blank slate. Each person's prior experience provides the foundation for interpreting new information. In reading, we construct meaning by bringing our prior knowledge of language and of the world to the text. The more we already know about the topic in the text, the more of the text we can understand. Our prior knowledge enables us to make inferences about the meaning of words and expressions that we may not have come across before. Furthermore, the more of the text we understand, the more new knowledge we can acquire. This expands our knowledge base (what cognitive psychologists call *schemata*, or underlying patterns of concepts). Such comprehension, in turn, enables us to understand even more concepts and vocabulary.

It is important to *activate* students' prior knowledge because students may not realize what they know about a particular topic or issue. Their knowledge may not facilitate learning unless that knowledge is brought to consciousness.

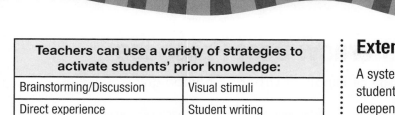

Teachers can use a variety of strategies to activate students' prior knowledge:	
Brainstorming/Discussion	Visual stimuli
Direct experience	Student writing
Dramatization	Drawing

When students don't already have knowledge about a topic, it is important to help them acquire that knowledge. For example, in order to comprehend texts such as *The Midnight Ride of Paul Revere,* students need to have background knowledge about the origin of the United States.

Access Content

How can teachers make complex academic English comprehensible for students who are still in the process of learning English?

We can *scaffold* students' learning by modifying the input itself. Here are a variety of ways of modifying the presentation of academic content to students so that they can more effectively gain access to the meaning.

Using visuals Visuals enable students to "see" the basic concepts we are trying to teach much more effectively than if we rely only on words. Among the visuals we can use are:

- pictures/diagrams
- graphic organizers
- vocabulary cards
- maps
- real objects

Dramatization/Acting out For beginning English learners, physical response, in which they follow commands such as "Turn around," can be highly effective. The meanings of words can be demonstrated through *gestures* and *pantomime*.

Language clarification This category of teaching methods includes language-oriented activities that clarify the meaning of new words and concepts. *Use of dictionaries,* either bilingual or English-only, is still the most direct method of getting access to meaning.

Making personal and cultural connections We should constantly search for ways to link academic content with what students already know or what is familiar to them from their family or cultural experiences. This not only validates children's sense of identity, but it also makes the learning more meaningful.

Extend Language

A systematic exploration of language is essential if students are to develop a curiosity about language and deepen their understanding of how words work. Students should become *language detectives* who investigate the mysteries of language and how it has been used throughout history to shape and change society.

Students also can explore the building blocks of language. A large percentage of the less frequently heard academic vocabulary of English derives from Latin and Greek roots. Word formation follows predictable patterns. These patterns are very similar in English and Spanish.

When students know rules or conventions of how words are formed, it gives them an edge in extending vocabulary. It helps them figure out the meanings of words and how to form different parts of speech from words. The exploration of language can focus on meaning, form, or use.

Focus on meaning Categories that can be explored within a focus on meaning include:

- home language equivalents or cognates
- synonyms, antonyms, and homonyms
- meanings of prefixes, roots, and suffixes

Focus on form Categories that can be explored within a focus on form include:

- word families
- grammatical patterns
- words with same prefixes, roots, or suffixes

Focus on use Categories that can be explored within a focus on use include:

- general uses
- proverbs
- idioms
- advertisements
- metaphorical use
- puns and jokes

The Three Pillars

- Activate Prior Knowledge/Build Background,
- Access Content,
- Extend Language,

establish a solid structure for the effective instruction of English language learners.

English Learners and Literacy: Best Practices

Dr. Georgia Earnest García, the University of Illinois at Urbana-Champaign

Like other children, English language learners come to school with much oral language knowledge and experience. Their knowledge and experience in languages other than English provide skills and world knowledge that teachers can build on.

Making literacy instruction comprehensible to English language learners is essential. Many of the teaching strategies developed for children who are proficient in English can be adapted for English learners, and many strategies from an English language learner curriculum are also useful in "mainstream" reading education.

Building on Children's Knowledge

It is vital to learn about each student's literacy development and proficiency in the home language. School personnel should ask parents:

- How many years of school instruction has the child received in the home language?
- Can the child read and write in that language?
- Can the child read in any other language?

Students can transfer aspects of home-language literacy to their English literacy development, such as phonological awareness and reading (or listening) comprehension strategies. If they already know key concepts and vocabulary in their home languages, then they can transfer that knowledge to English. For the vocabulary concepts they already know in their home languages, they only need to learn the English labels. Not all English learners automatically transfer what they have learned in the home language to their reading in English. Teachers can help facilitate relevant transfer by explicitly asking English learners to think about what they have learned about a topic in the home language.

A teacher need not speak each student's home language to encourage English language learners to work together and benefit from one another's knowledge. Students can communicate in their home languages and English, building the content knowledge, confidence, and English skills that they need to participate fully in learning. Devising activities in which students who share home languages can work together also allows a school to pool resources, such as bilingual dictionaries and other books, as well as home-language tutors or aides.

Sheltering Instruction in English

Often, beginning and intermediate English language learners may not understand what their classroom teachers say or read aloud in English. These students benefit when teachers shelter, or make comprehensible, their literacy instruction.

Sheltered techniques include using:

- consistent, simplified, clearly enunciated, and slower-paced oral language to explain literacy concepts or activities
- gestures, photos, illustrations, drawings, real objects, dramatization, and/or physical action to illustrate important concepts and vocabulary
- activities that integrate reading, writing, listening, and speaking, so students see, hear, read, and write new vocabulary, sentence structures, and content

When it is clear from students' actions and responses that they understand what is being said, teachers can vary their strategies. As students' comprehension expands, teachers can gradually curtail their use of adapted oral language and of gestures, illustrations, and dramatizations.

Adapting Literacy Activities

Teachers can use many instructional activities developed for native English speakers with English language learners. For example, teacher read-alouds, shared reading, and paired reading can allow an English learner to follow the text during a reading. Such techniques greatly improve students' learning skills and comprehension.

Similarly, interactive journal writing, in which the teacher and student take turns writing entries, allows students to explore topics and ask questions. It also allows teachers to engage in ongoing authentic assessment of student proficiency and to pinpoint areas of misunderstanding.

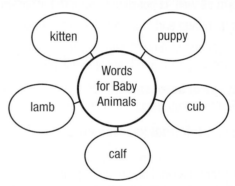

Small group instruction and discussion also are helpful. Beginning English language learners benefit from the repeated readings of predictable texts with illustrations, especially when the teacher has provided a brief preview of each text to introduce the topic of the story and preview new vocabulary.

Repeated reading aloud of such predictable, patterned, illustrated texts provides English language learners with multiple opportunities to match the text they read with the words they hear. When students participate in shared reading and echo the spoken text or read the words aloud chorally, anxiety about pronunciation or decoding errors is reduced. When teachers choose texts that are culturally familiar and ask English language learners personal questions related to the text, the result is a lower-risk learning environment and an increased opportunity for students to make accurate inferences.

Examples of Teaching Strategies

Before students read content material, provide them with hands-on or visual experience directly related to the content. Then have them use a graphic organizer to map what they have learned or seen about the topic. Let pairs or small groups of students brainstorm for words that are related to the concept. Then introduce other related words, including vocabulary from the reading. Illustrate new concepts or vocabulary with drawings,

photographs, or artifacts that represent the concepts. The hands-on experience and graphic organizer that precede the reading help introduce students to new concepts. Students will thus be familiar with the selection's subject before they begin to read.

Semantic Mapping Working with graphic organizers can help teach vocabulary and concepts in subject areas.

For example, before a reading on the subject of baby animals, have students help you to complete a semantic map showing pictures of animals and the names of baby animals. Ask them to volunteer the names for animal babies in their home language and transcribe their responses. Then show students examples of the different forms of writing. Ask students to meet in small groups to identify the examples. They may do this in English or their home language. If they use the home language, the teacher needs to write the English labels on the board for each form of writing. Then students need to enter the words for the different forms of writing, with drawings or home language equivalents, into a vocabulary notebook.

```
        kitten          puppy

                Words
   lamb        for Baby        cub
                Animals

            calf
```

Summarizing After reading, students can dictate what they remember from their reading to the teacher. Students can then illustrate their summaries, and label the illustrations with vocabulary from the reading.

Preparing English Language Learners for Assessment

Dr. Lily Wong Fillmore, the University of California, Berkeley

Under federal and state law, all students—including English learners—must be assessed annually on their progress toward mastery of academic standards in reading, math, and science. Many questions arise when certain assessments are used with ELLs because their test scores are never easy to interpret when they are assessed in English. The most critical question is this: What do test scores mean when they are based on instruction and assessments given in a language students have not yet mastered? Although difficult to interpret, assessments are required of all students, so we must consider how to help ELLs perform as well as possible.

Addressed in this essay

- What can teachers do to fast-track their ELL students' mastery of the language and content needed to perform as well as possible in required assessments?
- What language and literacy skills are needed?
- What learning strategies can teachers promote to facilitate language and literacy development?

Three types of assessments are vital to reading instruction for all students, including ELLs.

1. Ongoing informal assessments

The assessments that provide teachers the most useful and important information about English learners are those used as part of the instructional process. How well do children understand the materials they are working with, and what needs adjustment or modification in instruction? These are built into these instructional materials and help teachers keep an ongoing record of student progress over time. Such assessments do not need to be elaborate. Asking children what they think is happening in a text can reveal how well they comprehend what they are reading. Asking children what they think words or phrases mean can show

whether they are trying to make sense of text. These types of questions are highly useful to teachers since they allow them to monitor participation levels and help them discover who understands the materials and who needs more attention and support.

2. Diagnostic assessments

A second type of assessment that some ELLs may require is diagnostic, and it is needed when individuals are not making the progress expected of them. The school must determine where student problems lie (e.g., skill development, or perception or awareness of English sounds, vocabulary, or grammar) before teachers can provide the corrective help needed.

3. Standardized assessments

The type of assessments that causes teachers of ELLs the greatest concern are the standards-based tests of English Language Arts and content area tests (especially in Math). These state tests are required of all students and are recognized as "high stakes" tests for students and for schools. They are often used to evaluate the effectiveness of a curriculum, the teacher, or the instructional approach used.

What's involved in reading?

Reading skills are built on several types of knowledge: linguistic, symbolic, experiential, and strategic. Each is crucial and is linked with the others. *Language is fundamental;* it is the medium through which meaning—information, story, knowledge, poetry, and thought—is communicated from writer to reader. Unlike speech, what is communicated by written language is indirect and *encoded in symbols* that must be deciphered before access to meaning is possible.

But reading goes beyond mere decoding. Texts call for readers to apply what they know about how language is used to convey thought and ideas to interpret what they are reading. Having *experienced reading as a sense-making activity,* readers will seek meaning as they learn to read. This calls for *special strategies:* They look for meaning if they assume it is to be found in texts. If they do not know

the language in which the texts are written, they will recognize that learning the code is the key to unlocking meaning. They will pay attention to the language and ask: *What is this saying? What does this mean? How does this relate to what I already know about the way the language works?*

English learners have an easier time learning to read in English if they have already learned to read in their first language. Without question, a language barrier makes learning to read a more difficult task. But if students have already learned to read in their primary language, they know what is involved, what to expect, and thus they are in a better position to deal with learning to read in the new language in order to access meaning.

Can children learn to read in a language before they are fully proficient in that language?

Can they in fact learn the language through reading? *Yes, but only with ample instructional assistance that supports the development of both.* Ideally, reading instruction in English comes after ELLs have gained some familiarity with the sounds and patterns of spoken English. Children need to hear the sounds of the new language before they can connect symbols to those sounds. For example, in order for children to gain confidence relating the many vowel sounds of English to the five vowel symbols used to "spell them," they need help hearing them and differentiating them in words.

Similarly, many ELLs need help dealing with the ways consonants pile up at the beginning and at the ends of syllables and words in English, which may be quite different than the way consonants are used in their primary language. Most crucially, ELLs need help in connecting the words they are learning to decode from the text to their referents. Using pictures, demonstrations, diagrams, gestures, and enactments, teachers can help ELLs see how the words, phrases, and sentences in the reading selections have meaning that can be accessed through the language they are learning.

Helping ELLs become successful readers

The most important way to help ELLs perform well in mandated reading assessments is by giving them the instructional support they need to become successful readers. This involves help in:

- Learning English
- Discovering the purpose of reading
- Becoming active learners
- Gaining access to academic language

Learning English

The more proficient children are in the language they are reading, the more readily they learn to read. For ELLs, support for learning English is support for learning to read. The most effective kind of help comes in content-focused language instruction, where learners are engaged in grade-level-appropriate instructional activities and their participation is scaffolded and supported as needed.

The most effective activities provide ELLs ample opportunity to hear English and to use it productively in meaningful communication. Teachers play a vital role in creating a supportive classroom environment. ELLs must be able to participate to the extent possible (again, with as much support as needed) in discussions with classmates who are more proficient in English. Peers can offer practice and support, but only teachers can ensure that ELLs get access to the kind of language needed for literacy development.

Purpose of reading

The greatest dangers ELLs face in learning to read in English before they are proficient in that language is that the effort involved in decoding takes precedence in their minds over all else. Connections between words and referents, between words and structures, and between text and meaning are overlooked when children focus on sounding out, figuring out symbols, and figuring out sounds. This is especially likely to happen when there is too little emphasis placed on reading as a sense-making activity in instructional programs. If meaning— no matter how difficult it is to come by—is not constantly emphasized in reading instruction, children end up believing that decoding is reading, and that there is nothing missing when they read without understanding.

Decoding becomes an end in itself, and the real purpose of reading is lost. Unfortunately, this is the outcome for many ELLs, who even after having learned English do not perform well in reading assessments.

Literacy in English begins as deciphering for ELLs; they must first figure out how the code in which the text is written works. It is not until the reader engages in an interpretive process in which the thoughts, information, concepts, situations, and relations encoded in the texts are manifested as meanings that there is real reading. This is true for both ELLs and for native English speakers. ELLs, however, will need a lot of guidance and instructional support from teachers to do that. Once children have gained enough familiarity with English to participate even at a rudimentary level in discussions about reading selections and content, they begin to learn that the materials they are reading have something to say to them and that hearing what they have to say is the real purpose of learning to read.

Active readers

Helping children become active learners of English and users of the literacy skills they are acquiring is a key to their becoming successful students and performing well in the assessments they have to take. This is accomplished by encouraging children to take an active role in instructional activities, asking questions, seeking answers, and trying to make sense of what they are studying in school.

Both teachers and students can have many preconceived ideas about the roles they play as teachers and learners. Children sometimes come to school believing that learning is something that will be done to them, rather than something they must take an active role in doing. In their view, the role of the teacher is active and the role they play as learners is passive. When teachers share that belief, there is little likelihood of active or independent learning. Instruction is most effective when teachers are knowledgeable about the subject matter they are teaching, and they create a classroom environment in which learners can take an active role in discovering how things work, what things mean, and how to get and make sense of information.

Academic English

Teachers are aware that the language used in written texts is sufficiently different from everyday spoken language to constitute a barrier to children who are not already familiar with it. Academic English is not just another name for "standard English." It is, instead, the special forms of standard English used in academic discourse and in written texts. It makes use of grammatical constructions, words, and rhetorical conventions that are not often used in everyday spoken language.

Paradoxically, academic language is both a prerequisite for full literacy and the outcome of it. Some children arrive at school with a running start in acquiring it. Children who come from homes where family members engage in frequent discussions of books and ideas are already familiar with it, and thus have an advantage learning to read.

It should be noted that the language used at home does not have to be English for children to benefit from such experiences. Teachers can provide their students, irrespective of background, experiences with academic language by reading to them and discussing readings, instructional activities, and experiences. By drawing children into instructional conversations focused on the language they encounter in their school texts and other materials, teachers get children to notice language itself and to figure out how it works.

Supporting language and literacy development for ELLs

Teachers support language development by engaging children as active participants in making sense of the texts they are working on. They do it by drawing the English learners into discussions relating to the texts. Even relative newcomers are able to participate in these discussions as long as ample scaffolding is provided:

> It says here, "Her teacher picked up the paper and studied it carefully."

> Hector, what does the text tell us Vashti's teacher did first?

Yes, she picked up the paper first.

Take a look at the picture. Marta, can you show us which part of the sentence tells us what the teacher is doing?

Can you tell us what she is doing?

Yes! She is studying the paper carefully.

Teachers draw attention to words, phrases, and sentences, by asking: "Let's see if we can figure out what that means!" By relating language to meaning, they help students gain access to meaning by demonstrating, referring to illustrations and diagrams, and paraphrasing in simpler language.

Instructional conversations about the texts they are reading are as essential for newcomers as they are for ELLs who have already gained some proficiency in English. It is vital to their literacy development to realize that what they are "reading" can be understood, even if its meaning is not immediately available to them as it would be to readers who are fully proficient in English. Without such help, ELLs sometimes come to believe that decoding without access to meaning is an empty exercise one does in school, and except for that, it has little relevance to their lives.

Teachers can help students discover how the language works and how to extract meaning from texts by considering how the language they encounter can convey information, ideas, stories, feelings, and images. This cannot wait until the learners are fully proficient in the language they are reading. It can enhance language development if done from the start, as soon as ELLs are introduced to English reading.

Strategies for supporting language and literacy development and preparing ELLs for assessment

The most effective support comes in the form of instructional conversations in which ELLs are drawn into discussions of reading selections and content. By hearing their teachers and other classmates discuss the materials they are reading, they gradually learn how the language works in texts and in conversation.

- Draw attention to the language used in reading selections and other text materials—words, phrases, and sentences—and relate them to meaning that is discussed and commented on, both locally and globally, to help ELLs learn how to get at meaning in texts.

- Provide students ample opportunity to use the language of texts in speaking (during discussions of the reading selections, for example) and in writing (in response to writing prompts).

- Teach English learners to be strategic readers by guiding them to assume that the text should make sense and that meaning can be accessed by figuring out what the words, phrases, and sentences mean.

- Teach students to ask questions about meaning as it unfolds in the text. Help them recognize that some parts of texts provide background knowledge while other parts reveal new information.

- Teach children how to relate new information presented in a text to what is already known. Train students to make inferences about meaning based on the words and phrases used in a text.

- Expect ELLs to make progress, and then ensure it by providing ample grade-level discussion of content. At the same time, recognize that it takes time to learn English, and that learners may differ in the amount and kind of help they need in order to make progress.

- Recognize that the most crucial kind of preparation for assessment is in helping children develop the *language and literacy skills* that are essential to successful performance in tests and for academic progress itself.

- Call children's attention to words, phrases, and constructions that often figure in text items. For example, words such as *both, not,* and *best* may not seem to be noteworthy, but their uses in test questions prove otherwise. ELLs need help in seeing how such words frame and constrain the ideas expressed in sentences in which they appear.

- Teach children the logic of test questions. Use released test items or models of test items (both of which are likely to be available online from your state department of education or district Web sites). Show children, for example, that the question, "Which of the following is NOT a sentence?" entails that all of the listed options except one *are* sentences.

- Teach children to read carefully. Children who are fully proficient in English may occasionally benefit

from test-taking strategies such as reading the test question and answer options first and then skimming the test passage to find information that will aid in the selection of the correct answer to the question. This tactic does not serve English learners well. They need to read and understand the passage carefully, and then consider how to answer the questions asked.

- Teach children when the text calls for activation of prior knowledge. All children have such knowledge, but English learners need help in deciding where it is called for and how they should bring what they already know to interpret the texts they are reading.

- Expand children's horizons by reading them texts that may be too difficult to handle on their own. Help them make sense of such materials by commenting on meaning, drawing attention to how language is used in them, and engaging children in discussions about aspects of the texts.

The texts that are read to children, and the ones they read themselves, provide reliable access to the academic language they need for literacy and for assessment, provided teachers call their attention to language and help children see how it works. Teachers do this by identifying interesting (not just new) phrases and commenting on them, inviting children to try using the phrases, and providing scaffolds as needed; they model the uses of language from texts in subsequent instructional activities; they encourage children to remember and keep records of words they learn from texts; they remind them when words and phrases encountered earlier show up again in different contexts.

The Concept of Transfer

Dr. Elena Izquierdo, the University of Texas at El Paso

Research continues to support the critical role of the child's first language (L1) in literacy development and its effect on literacy in (L2) English. Strong L1 literacy skills facilitate the transfer into English literacy, and students ultimately progress rapidly into learning in English. In reality, the concept of transfer refers to the child's facility in appropriating knowledge from one language to the other. Children do not know they know, but they know. They are constantly and indirectly, unconsciously and automatically, constructing the knowledge that is inherent in the contexts for which each of these languages can function. Reasearch by Jim Cummins has shown that the effective transfer of skills transpires as students develop their metalinguistic and metacognitive skills and as they engage in a contrastive analysis of the two languages.

Matters of transfer occur within essentials of language that are (1) common to L1 and L2; (2) similar, but not exact in both languages; and (3) specific to each language and not applicable to the other language. In essence, children develop a special awareness of language and its function;

learn that some sounds are the same in both languages; and also learn that there are certain boundaries for specific sounds depending on the language.

Children who have developed an awareness for phonemes, phonics, vocabulary building, and reading comprehension skills, can transfer these skills to English. They develop an enhanced awareness of the relationship between their L1 and English, which leads them to successfully appropriate strategies of transfer in similar types of word recognition processing; searching for cognates; making reference to prior knowledge, inferencing, questioning, and monitoring. Facilitating these cognitive skills in children will support their success in English literacy and their learning in English.

English Language Learner Profiles

English Language Learners—ELLs—are a quickly growing population in U.S. schools. While some are children of recent immigrants, many more were born in the United States but have spoken other languages in their homes. ELLs may come to classrooms with knowledge of other places as well as diverse cultures and customs. As you work with ELLs, you will want to consider how proficient your students are and how you can make the academic content accessible. You will be integrating language and content instruction, most likely within the context of a classroom of students with many abilities and proficiencies. As you consider how to best meet the needs of ELLs in your classroom, think about their characteristics, patterns of development, and literacy challenges.

General Characteristics of English Language Learners

- ELLs have a first language—also called a home language, primary language, or native language—other than English and are in the process of acquiring English.

- Some ELLs have newly arrived in the United States, while others were born in the United States but have lived for many years in households where family members do not speak English.

- Some ELLs have already acquired and developed literacy skills in their native languages, while others have not learned the academic vocabulary and background knowledge necessary for continued success in school.

- ELLs vary in that some have primary languages that resemble English in word order, sound system, and in the patterns of forming words. Spanish, French, and Portuguese, for example, are languages that share alphabets and left-to-right directionality with English. Some words in English and Spanish are cognates. Some languages, such as Swahili or Vietnamese, do not have as much in common with English. For children who speak these languages, initial learning of English is more difficult.

Types of English Language Learners

- **Newly Arrived English Language Learners** may come with adequate or limited schooling. Those with adequate schooling will make steady academic progress, although they may have difficulty on standardized tests in English. Those with limited formal schooling may lack a sense of school culture and routines. Their limited literacy development may lead to poor academic achievement until both their background knowledge and English proficiency grow.

- **Long Term English Language Learners** have been in the United States for some time, but they have had limited exposure to English in their communities and little reason to learn or know English. As they begin to acquire English, they may lose proficiency in their native languages and have difficulty grasping new content.

- **Older English Language Learners** may be more capable of quickly learning academic concepts even though they have not developed the language proficiency of other students their age. Curriculum challenges will help these students bridge their academic gaps while they gain English proficiency. Provide scaffolds for instruction and organize collaborative activities to help these students gain success.

Literacy Challenges for ELLs

1. **Phonemic Awareness** ELLs may find it difficult to differentiate between certain phonemes in English. Some children may find it difficult to separate groups of phonemes into words.

2. **Phonics** ELLs need to be able to match sounds to letters and letters to sounds in order to read and write English successfully. They need to develop both oral vocabularies of frequently used words and written vocabularies of sight words.

3. **Vocabulary Development** Some ELLs are able to repeat, pronounce, decode, and produce words in English without really knowing what these words mean. ELLs need opportunities to link vocabulary words to meaning through routines, concrete objects, pictures and gestures, physical movement, and experiences. These students need multiple exposures to words through explanation, discussion, and repeated readings.

4. **Fluency** Fluent reading involves reading quickly, accurately, and expressively. This can be challenging for ELLs, who need many opportunities to listen and speak English before they can feel comfortable and successful with fluent reading. In large groups, ELLs may be reluctant to read orally. They need opportunities to listen and follow along with read-alouds.

5. **Comprehension** Help ELLs gain comprehension in reading by choosing reading materials with familiar topics, settings, and concepts. Use nonfiction materials, such as photographs and science experiments. Use anticipation guides and graphic organizers to prepare ELLs for reading and allow them to comprehend more of what they read.

Best Practices

Scaffolding instruction for ELLs allows them to access content while gaining proficiency in English. Most strategies that help ELLs access content and language are appropriate for struggling readers in your classroom whose native language is English, so these strategies can be used with the whole class. Some best practices for teaching ELLs include:

- using questioning techniques to elicit experiences that relate to students' native cultures;

- using visual aids, including photographs, graphic organizers, and real objects;

- linking learning to a physical response, such as raising hands, doing a "thumbs up," nodding, and moving to a different part of the room;

- actively engaging students in the lesson by including less teacher talk and down time and keeping students involved;

- using scaffolding techniques, such as think-alouds, paraphrasing, partnering, and reciprocal teaching; and

- building background with such activities as cloze sentences, creating word walls, and working with students to make personal dictionaries.

English language learners are generally divided into proficiency levels. The chart below describes what you might expect from students at each level, and it compares different proficiency levels used across the United States. It also includes teaching strategies for your classroom. *Reading Street* provides systematic leveled support to meet the needs of all students.

	LEVELS OF PROFICIENCY		BEHAVIORS	TEACHING STRATEGIES
I	Beginning		• may be unfamiliar with sounds, rhythms, or patterns in English • respond by pointing, gesturing, or drawing • can use simple yes/no responses or one- to two-word answers • read simple language that they have already heard • write labels, patterned sentences, or short cloze sentences	• provide opportunities for active listening and visuals • model language with songs and chants • pair students with more proficient speakers • ask yes/no questions; require responses of one or two words • use manipulatives and pictures • provide writing frames
II	Early Intermediate	Intermediate	• may understand more details in spoken English • use longer phrases and sentences with better grammar • write for a variety of purposes using models • can read independently after oral previews	• allow students to make personal connections with the material • structure group discussion time • ask open-ended questions and then model, expand, restate, and enrich student language • allow students opportunities to create language for a variety of purposes and audiences
III	Intermediate		• participate in discussions about academic content • can use higher-order language to describe or persuade • write narratives and expository text • use vocabulary with more accuracy and correctness	• use graphic organizers to prepare students for reading and to discuss selections • promote academic concepts and vocabulary with nonfictional texts, magazines, newspapers, and so on • conference with students about writing to point out areas of progress and areas for improvement
IV	Early Advanced	Advanced	• have a deeper understanding of everyday language, including idioms • use more extensive vocabulary and produce language with fewer grammatical errors • use standard forms when writing • produce writing about varied topics	• structure discussion for the group • provide reference materials for students and guide them with the research • introduce more variety of literary forms • provide opportunities for more variation in writing assignments
V	Advanced	Advanced High	• use more complex and varied grammatical structures and vocabulary • read texts appropriate for grade level • write about a variety of topics on grade level • begin to self-monitor and correct as they read and write	• provide opportunities for students to publish their writing for others to read • increase students' production of language through drama and music • continue to make strong links between content-area materials and literacy activities

Essentials of ELL Instruction in *Reading Street*

Imagine students from diverse language backgrounds communicating in English on the playground. It's easy to think that they are fluent English speakers, but they may still be at the beginning stage of using English for learning purposes. Research proves that it takes at least five years of exposure to academic English to catch up with native-speaker proficiency in school.

How Do English Language Learners Differ from Other Learners?

ELLs face challenges because they have not acquired academic English. Student's reading and language skills may seem deficient because their language experiences have lacked academic instruction. ELLs need targeted instruction to participate fully in reading/language arts lessons with their peers. Helping ELLs achieve academically is critically important because they must meet the same state and federal grade-level standards as other students. Their academic success depends on learning to read well, and this depends on rich language knowledge.

> **Academic Language** is the language of the classroom. It's used for academic purposes, not social or personal ones.

Essentials of ELL Instruction

These five essential practices take into account language and academic needs of English language learners. They are incorporated into *Reading Street* as common-sense, everyday strategies that help you build an effective learning relationship between you and your ELL students.

Identify and Communicate Content Objectives and Language Objectives English language learners need instruction for the same grade-level skills and strategies as students whose first language is English. Deliver your instruction with clear, simple language. Provide extra support for academic vocabulary. Provide direct instruction for the academic language that students need to use to complete classroom tasks successfully.

Frontload the Lesson When new information arrives as a blur to ELL students, they are lost at the beginning of a lesson. Taking time to frontload, or preteach lesson elements, will bring them into mainstream instruction. Activating prior knowledge, building background, previewing, and setting a purpose for reading are frontloading methods that remove learning obstacles. Asking students to make personal connections helps them see relationships and gives you insight into their experiences and backgrounds.

Provide Comprehensible Input The instruction and content you present to ELL students may be unclear because of language barriers. Use visual supports, multimedia, examples of real items, and demonstrations to provide comprehensible instruction. Communicating with methods such as gestures, props, and dramatization can be an effective approach. Hands-on activities and multiple exposures to new concepts can lessen confusion.

Enable Language Production The listening, speaking, reading, and writing ELLs do for school is different from the language they use in everyday conversation. In school, ELLs need ample opportunities to demonstrate their use of English. Two critical methods for enabling student's English language production are direct instruction and modeling the use of a skill in a comprehensible way. Create scaffolds so that students can read and hear English language patterns and build on them to express their own thoughts. Paraphrasing, restatements, cloze sentences, writing prompts, and templated forms for note-taking are useful supports. Responding to student's strengths and needs by modifying instruction gives them opportunities to express themselves in an academic setting and gain proficiency in English.

Assess for Content and Language Understanding ELLs are required to achieve the same high standards as mainstream students. Keep in mind that children are at different stages for learning English language and literacy skills. Asking these questions frequently and using assessments will help you determine how to modify your instruction for different proficiency levels.

- Where are ELL students in their acquisition of English language proficiency?

- Where are they in their acquisition of literacy skills?

Just as for all students, you will rely on diagnostic, formative, and summative assessments for ELLs. Consistently integrate informal assessment into your lessons to target specific problem areas for learning, adapt your instruction, and intervene earlier rather than later.

You can modify both formal and informal assessments so that ELLs show their proficiency in literacy skills with a minimal amount of negative impact. These modifications include time extensions, use of bilingual dictionaries and glossaries, repeated readings of listening passages, use of dual-language assessments, and allowing written responses in the first language.

To meet ELLs at their own levels of English acquisition, teachers use instructional supports and tools. Through scaffolding and modifying instruction you can lead ELLs to achieve the same instructional goals that mainstream students do. The ELL strategies and supports in *Reading Street* have the five essential principles of ELL as their foundation. Use them throughout your instruction to modify or scaffold core instruction. With *Reading Street* ELL Leveled Support activities, you meet students where they are—from beginning to advanced levels of English proficiency.

Other English language learner resources include:

Student Edition The Student Edition builds every student's reading and language skills.

Teacher's Edition The Teacher's Edition has ELL instructional strategies built into the lesson plans. The ELL weekly lessons have pacing plans to help you carefully integrate instruction. The ELL Support lessons guide you in using sheltered techniques and routines for teaching concept development, academic vocabulary, listening comprehension, phonics, phonemic awareness, vocabulary, comprehension, and writing.

ELD/ELL Readers ELD/ELL Readers develop English learners' vocabulary and comprehension skills. Study guides support comprehension and provide writing and take-home activities.

ELL Posters ELL Posters contain high-quality illustrations and five days of activities supporting key oral vocabulary, selection vocabulary, and lesson concepts.

Essentials of ELL Instruction in *Reading Street*

- Identify and Communicate Content Objectives and Language Objectives
- Frontload the Lesson
- Provide Comprehensible Input
- Enable Language Production
- Assess for Content and Language Understanding

ELL Handbook The ELL Handbook supports teachers' professional development and the transition to advanced levels of English proficiency for all ELLs. The Handbook contains comprehension skill practice, selection vocabulary word cards, multilingual summaries of Student Edition literature, study guides for ELL Readers, and multilingual vocabulary charts. The English selection summaries and vocabulary charts are accompanied by translations in Spanish and in several other languages. The flexible bank of Phonics and Grammar Transition Lessons provides differentiated practice.

Ten Important Sentences The Ten Important Sentences reproducibles help students focus on comprehension while they expand their English proficiency.

English Language Proficiency-What, Why, and How The next section, English Language Proficiency-What, Why, and How, provides ideas for how to use *Reading Street* across language proficiency levels and instructional strands. Using research from Dr. Jim Cummins, this section explains why and how *Reading Street* promotes literacy attainment for English language learners at all levels.

English Language Proficiency—What, Why, and How

Concept Development

 "No learner is a blank slate. The more we know about the topic in the text, the more of the text we can understand."—Dr. Jim Cummins

Why

Organizing concept development around big question themes is essential for ELLs. Through the use of themes, it is easier to connect the curriculum to students' lives and backgrounds. Themes help to make sense of the curriculum because students know what the topic is, even if the instruction is in English. By learning more about the topic through concept development, students will increase their social and academic vocabulary production and be more engaged when reading the text.

How

Reading Street promotes literacy attainment through Concept Development activities in the core and ELL Support lessons that encourage literacy engagement. These activities activate prior knowledge and build background, scaffold meaning, affirm identity, and extend language.

Activate Prior Knowledge/Build Background

Frontload the Lesson Build background and scaffold meaning to prepare for the core Anchored Talk lesson. In a small group, use Preteach Concepts from the Concept Development section of the ELL Support pages and the Poster Talk Through to frontload the lesson.

Access Content

Provide Comprehensible Input Use the linguistically accommodated questions in the Concept Development section of the ELL Support pages to reach all language proficiency levels and make personal and cultural connections that validate identity and link academic content with what students already know.

Scaffold Meaning Give visual support that students need to access academic content with the photographs in the Anchored Talk section in the Student Edition, the concept graphic organizer created during the week's discussion, the Concept Talk Video from the digital path, and the daily Poster Activities. The activities in the ELL Support pages for Concept Development and the ELL Support notes throughout the Teacher Edition give ideas to scaffold meaning for all language proficiency levels.

Extend Language

Enable Language Production Use the daily activities on the ELL Poster and the Anchored Talk questions in the core to build concept attainment and encourage oral language production. The Team-Talk Routine in the core instruction and the Poster Talk, Concept Talk activities from the *ELL Handbook* provide nonthreatening small group oral practice with social and academic vocabulary related to the concept. The Concept Literacy Reader builds both concepts and language.

	Student Behaviors	Teacher Behaviors	Examples
Beginning	• Actively listens • Responds nonverbally • Can follow one-step oral directions • Answers in one- or two-word phrases • May not seek clarification Student can: point, move, choose, match, mime, draw.	• Use gestures, repetition, slower speech, visuals, and simple language. *Point to the _____.* *Find the _____.* *Is this a _____?*	How does city life compare to life in the country? Use the *Let's Talk About It* photographs in the Student Edition to activate prior knowledge and build background. .... *Point to the city. Find the picture of the country.* *Are they the same or different?* *Is this a building?* *Is this a farm?* *Where is the cow?*
Intermediate	• Actively listens with greater understanding • Needs processing time • Uses short phrases • Identifies people and objects • Begins to seek clarification Student can: name, list, say, tell, restate.	• Model correct responses. • Don't call attention to grammar errors. • Ask general questions to encourage production. • Ask questions for two-word responses. *Is this a _____ or a _____?* *What is this?*	*Is this a building or a farm?* *Is this the city or the country?* *What do you see in the city?* *What do you see in the country?* *Are they the same or different?*
Advanced	• Actively listens to longer questions and directions • Uses language more freely • Sometimes needs more processing time and depends on visuals • Will seek clarification Student can: describe, restate, compare, contrast.	• Ask open-ended questions to encourage language production. • Check comprehension frequently. *Why?* *How?* *Tell me about _____.* *Describe _____.*	*Describe the city.* *Tell me about the country.* *How are they the same?* *How are they different?*
Advanced High	• Understands longer, elaborated discussions • Occasionally needs more processing time • Understands details and information comparable to a native speaker • Rarely seeks clarification • Produces a variety of sentence lengths Student can: explain, define, support, describe, summarize.	• Make lessons interactive and comprehensible. • Structure group discussions. *Describe/compare _____.* *How are these similar or different?* *What would happen if _____?* *What is your opinion of _____?*	*Compare the pictures of the city and country.* *How are they the same and different?* *Which place do you like better? Why?*

Listening Comprehension

 "How can teachers make complex academic English comprehensible for children who are still in the process of learning English? We can scaffold students' learning by modifying the input itself." –Dr. Jim Cummins

Why

English language learners must be able to comprehend newly acquired language in all content areas. They must listen to a variety of speakers, including teachers and peers, along with understanding the language they hear in electronic media. In order for English language learners to meet grade-level learning expectations and have access to the core curriculum, all instruction delivered in English must be linguistically accommodated for all levels of English language proficiency.

How

Reading Street promotes literacy attainment with listening comprehension activities in the core lessons and ELL Support lessons that encourage literacy engagement. These activities activate prior knowledge, build background, scaffold meaning, affirm identity, and extend language.

Activate Prior Knowledge/Build Background

Frontload the Lesson Each adapted Read Aloud in the Listening Comprehension section of the ELL Support pages covers the same concept and information as the Read Aloud in the core curriculum. Use it with a small group to build background and scaffold meaning before listening to the core Read Aloud. Each adapted Read Aloud has frontloading activities that build background to improve comprehension before listening to the selection. In the core Teacher Edition, ELL Notes give ideas for frontloading the regular Read Aloud at point of use.

Access Content

Provide Comprehensible Input For Beginning and Intermediate levels, use the grade-appropriate adapted Read Aloud in place of the regular Read Aloud until children no longer need the linguistic support and modification.

First Listening: Listen to Understand gives children a purpose for listening. The questions are designed to generate interest and help children understand the general meaning of the adapted Read Aloud so that all proficiency levels can achieve success without cognitive overload.

Language Clarification Second Listening: Listen to Check Understanding allows children to clarify what they have heard. Once children have understood the main idea of the adapted Read Aloud, they can listen again on subsequent days to clarify understanding of important details of spoken language. The graphic organizers provide visual support for organizing information and taking notes.

Extend Language

Enable Language Production Discussing the adapted Read Aloud in a small group setting provides a nonthreatening environment, lowering the affective filter and facilitating increased language production.

The AudioText CD of the main reading selection and the digital products provide more opportunities for listening practice throughout each week, building and reinforcing children's concept and language attainment.

	Student Behaviors	Teacher Behaviors	Examples
Beginning	• Needs accommodations to understand grade-appropriate stories • Responds nonverbally • Can follow one-step oral directions • Answers in one or two words • Can match oral statements to illustrations or objects Student can: point, move, choose, match, mime, draw, label.	• Use gestures, repetition, slower speech, visuals, and simple language. *Point to the _____.* *Find the _____.* *Is this a _____?*	In a small group, use the modified Read Aloud. Build background and scaffold comprehension by reviewing the concept or showing a visual. Read the text clearly. Stop at intervals to check for understanding and clarify language. Use gestures to scaffold meaning. Children may need to hear the text repeated multiple times.
Intermediate	• Needs accommodations to understand grade-appropriate stories. • Actively listens with greater understanding • Uses short phrases • Understands simple directions • Identifies people and objects • Identifies key words and phrases • Begins to seek clarification Student can: name, list, say, tell, restate, describe.	• Model correct responses. • Use visuals, gestures, and preteaching to preview topic-related vocabulary. • Don't call attention to grammar errors. • Ask general questions to encourage production. • Ask questions that elicit two-word responses. *(Where did he go? To work.)* *Is this a _____ or a _____?* *What is this?*	In a small group, use the modified Read Aloud. Preview topic-related vocabulary and then read the text clearly. Stop at intervals to check for understanding and clarify language. Then use the Anchored Talk photographs to build vocabulary and concepts and encourage more discussion.
Advanced	• Actively listens and understands longer questions • Understands multistep oral directions • Understands main points and most important details • Uses language more freely • Can categorize or sequence oral information using objects or pictures • Can analyze and apply oral information • Will seek clarification Student can: describe, restate, compare, contrast, retell.	• Ask open-ended questions to encourage language production. • Check comprehension frequently. • Give more time to process information and provide visual support as needed. *Why?* *How?* *Tell me about _____.* *Describe _____.*	In a small group, use the modified Read Aloud to prepare for listening to the oral reading in the core text. Stop at intervals to check for understanding. Then have partners restate some of the important points and share with the class.
Advanced High	• Understands longer, elaborated discussions • Understands details and information comparable to a native speaker • Can draw conclusions from oral information • Rarely seeks clarification • Produces a variety of sentence lengths Student can: explain, define, support, describe, summarize.	• Make lessons interactive and comprehensible. • Structure group discussions. • Give more processing time if needed. *Describe/compare _____.* *How are these similar or different?* *What would happen if _____?* *What is your opinion of _____?*	In a small group, use the modified Read Aloud to prepare for listening to the oral reading in the core text. Then have children summarize the selection and explain something new that they learned.

Phonics, Spelling, and Word Analysis

 "A systematic exploration of language is essential if students are to develop a curiosity about language and deepen their understanding of how words work. Children should become language detectives who investigate the mysteries of language and how it has been used throughout history to shape and change society."— Dr. Jim Cummins

Why

Discrete language skills that English language learners need to develop second language literacy and comprehension include:

- knowledge of the letters of the alphabet
- knowledge of the sounds represented by individual letters and combinations of letters
- the ability to decode words
- knowledge of the rules and conventions of how words are formed

Students can learn these skills at the same time they are developing basic English vocabulary. While letter-sound correspondences in numerous languages are relatively simple, the relationships of letters to sounds in English can be complicated. The challenges of written English affect spelling, word recognition, comprehension of text, and confidence in language learning. *Reading Street* addresses these challenges in both the core curriculum and in the ELL Support pages.

How

Reading Street promotes literacy attainment through engaging phonics, spelling, and word analysis activities in the core lessons and ELL Support lessons. These activities activate prior knowledge and build background, scaffold meaning, affirm identity, and extend language.

Activate Prior Knowledge/Build Background

Frontload the Lesson Use the Phonics and Spelling and Word Analysis lessons in the ELL Support pages with a small group to preteach the skill before the core lesson. Then use the Reteach activities from the ELL Support pages to provide more practice and help students internalize language.

Affirm Identity Use the Transfer Skills Notes throughout the core Teacher Edition, on the ELL Support pages, and in the Phonics Transition Lessons in the *ELL Handbook,* to activate prior knowledge about a phonics or word analysis skill before the core lesson or for reteaching the skill to a small group to scaffold meaning.

Access Content

Provide Comprehensible Input Use the Sound-Spelling Cards and the Envision it! Words to Know from the Student Edition to provide visual support and scaffold meaning for the phonics and spelling lessons at all proficiency levels. Choose appropriate Phonics Transition Lessons and reproducible practice pages from the bank of lessons in the *ELL Handbook* to provide instruction on consonant sounds and blends, varying English vowel sounds, and other phonics challenges for all proficiency levels. The *Words! Vocabulary Handbook* in the Student Edition provides visual support for explaining the Word Analysis skill. Use it to preteach or reteach the skill. Use the leveled ideas in the Word Analysis section of the ELL Support pages to differentiate instruction and reach all students. The Word Analysis lessons focus on word endings, contractions, prefixes, suffixes, compound words, cognates, and other vocabulary builders.

Extend Language

Enable Language Production Guide small groups of students in exploring the rules and conventions of how words are formed using the leveled Word Analysis lessons from the ELL Support pages. When students learn the patterns of English word formation, students will become more engaged in literacy activities, and oral and written production will increase.

Focus on Meaning and Form Use the Word Analysis lessons from the ELL Support pages to teach home language equivalents, synonyms, antonyms, and the meaning of prefixes, roots, and suffixes. This knowledge engages students in figuring out meanings of new words, increasing their comprehension and language production.

	Student Behaviors	Teacher Behaviors	Examples
Beginning	• Actively listens and responds non-verbally • Can follow one-step oral directions • Answers in one- to two-word phrases • Uses high-frequency words, concrete words, and phrases Student can: point, move, choose, match, mime, draw label.	• Use gestures, repetition, slower speech, visuals, and simple language. *Point to the _____.* *Find the _____.* *Is this a _____?*	prefixes *un-* and *in-* .... Give students a piece of cloth and model the difference between *cover* and *uncover*. Use Student Edition *Words! Vocabulary Handbook* to provide more visual support for meaning. Have students draw pictures to show *lock/unlock* and *happy/unhappy*. Use the *ELL Handbook* reproducible pages to provide more practice with prefixes.
Intermediate	• Actively listens with greater understanding • Needs more processing time • Uses short phrases • Identifies people and objects • Begins to seek clarification if he or she doesn't understand Student can: name, list, say, tell, restate.	• Model correct responses. • Don't call attention to grammar errors. • Ask general questions to encourage production. • Ask questions that elicit two-word responses. *Is this a _____ or a _____?* *What is this?*	Use the Student Edition *Words! Vocabulary Handbook* to provide visual support for meaning. Ask questions about the picture to clarify meaning. Provide more practice using *in-* with words *expensive* and *inexpensive*. Use the *ELL Handbook* reproducible pages to provide more practice with prefixes.
Advanced	• Actively listens to longer questions and directions • Uses language more freely • Sometimes needs more processing time and depends on visuals • Will seek clarification Student can: describe, restate, compare, contrast.	• Ask open-ended questions to encourage language production. • Check comprehension frequently. *Why? How?* *Tell me about _____.*	Use the Student Edition *Words! Vocabulary Handbook* to provide visual support for meaning. *Tell me about the first picture. Compare it to the second picture. Look at the chart. What does the prefix un- mean? Where do we find prefixes?* Repeat with prefix *in-*. Use the *ELL Handbook* reproducible pages to provide more practice with prefixes.
Advanced High	• Understands longer, elaborated discussions • Occasionally needs more processing time • Understands details and information comparable to a native speaker • Rarely seeks clarification Student can: explain, define, support, describe, summarize.	• Make lessons interactive and comprehensible. • Structure group discussions. *Describe/compare _____.* *How are these similar or different?* *What would happen if _____?* *What is your opinion of _____?*	Use the Student Edition *Words! Vocabulary Handbook* to provide visual support for meaning. *Compare the two pictures. Look at the chart. What do the prefixes un- and in- mean? Explain what else you know about prefixes.* Write the words *lock, happy, complete,* and *action* on the board. Have pairs add the appropriate prefix and then write sentences using the words. Use the *ELL Handbook* reproducible pages to provide more practice with prefixes.

Vocabulary

"We should constantly search for ways to link academic content with what students already know or what is familiar to them from their family or cultural experiences. This not only validates children's sense of identity, but it also makes the learning more meaningful."— Dr. Jim Cummins

Why

Vocabulary development is critically important for English language learners, even more so than for their English-speaking peers. English learners need explicit instruction to acquire both social and academic language for literacy attainment. Research indicates that a broad knowledge of academic vocabulary is critical to student achievement and distinguishes students who experience academic success from those who struggle in school. Instruction in social and academic vocabulary should be explicit and systematic. Students need multiple exposures to new vocabulary through frequent listening, reading, writing, and oral language activities.

How

Reading Street promotes literacy attainment through interactive vocabulary activities in the core lessons and ELL Support pages that encourage literacy engagement. These activities activate prior knowledge and build background, scaffold meaning, affirm identity, and extend language.

Activate Prior Knowledge/Build Background

Frontload the Lesson The Concept Development activities from the ELL Support lessons, the Vocabulary Routines in the core and in the ELL Support pages, the ELL Poster, and the word cards from the *ELL Handbook* can be used to activate prior knowledge and build background for reading the selection. Use them in a small group to preteach, practice, and reinforce the grade-level lesson vocabulary. By using and reusing the words in meaningful interactions, students will internalize the words and be more engaged in reading the selection.

Access Content

Provide Comprehensible Input The Vocabulary Activities in the ELL Support lessons provide ideas for giving visual, contextual, and linguistic support so students can access grade-level lesson vocabulary. The activities are designed so students reuse the vocabulary using different modalities to confirm and enhance understanding. Give visual support that students need to access academic content vocabulary with the Anchored Talk photos and illustrations in the Student Edition, the Poster illustrations, Envision It! Words to Know in the Student Edition, and the digital vocabulary activities.

Affirm Identity Multilingual vocabulary lists in the *ELL Handbook* translate the selection vocabulary words from English into Spanish, Chinese, Vietnamese, Hmong, and Korean. Use the lists to preview the words or to check understanding.

Language Clarification Throughout the core and ELL Support pages, there are a variety of ideas for teachers to use to help students clarify meaning of language. Ideas range from activities using bilingual and English dictionaries to leveled questioning examples. In the core Teacher Edition, helpful ELL notes are located at point of use. These notes give language transfer support and a variety of ideas to clarify meaning for students.

Extend Language

Enable Language Production Use the Concept Talk and vocabulary activities on the ELL Support pages and the daily activities on the ELL Poster for ideas to give repeated exposure to social and academic vocabulary to build concept and language attainment.

The leveled vocabulary activities in the ELL Support lessons and the reproducible word cards in the *ELL Handbook* actively engage students in producing and reusing grade-level vocabulary in different contexts through spoken and written communication, so vocabulary becomes internalized.

	Student Behaviors	Teacher Behaviors	Examples
Beginning	• Actively listens • Answers in one- to two-word phrases • Uses and reads some high-frequency words, concrete words, and phrases represented by pictures Student can: point, move, choose, match, mime, draw, label, copy.	• Activate prior knowledge. • Use gestures, repetition, slower speech, and visuals. • Preteach topic-related vocabulary. *Point to the* _____. *Find the* _____. *Is this a* _____?	Use a word grid or word cards to preteach vocabulary. .... Students can write the new word in the circle in the middle and then draw or find a picture to illustrate the meaning of the word. Students can point to the squares while the other students describe the card to the class.
Intermediate	• Actively listens with greater understanding • Uses short phrases • Understands simple directions • Identifies people and objects • Begins to seek clarification if he or she doesn't understand Student can: name, list, say, tell, restate.	• Model correct responses. • Use visuals, gestures, and preteaching to preview topic-related vocabulary. • Ask general questions to encourage production. • Ask questions that elicit two-word responses. *Is this a* _____ *or a* _____? *What is this?*	Students can write a synonym or antonym for the word. They can assist beginners with creating a visual of the word. When sharing with the class, these students can list the synonyms and antonyms.
Advanced	• Understands longer, more elaborate directions and conversations • Understands main points and most important details • Sometimes needs more processing time; depends on more visuals • Will seek clarification Student can: describe, restate, compare, contrast.	• Ask open-ended questions to encourage language production. • Check comprehension frequently. • Give more time to process information. *Why?* *How?* *Tell me about* _____. *Describe* _____.	Students can write sentences with the word and identify cognates. They can describe their cards to the class when they are finished.
Advanced High	• May need more processing time • Understands details and information comparable to a native speaker • Rarely seeks clarification • Produces a variety of sentence lengths Student can: explain, define, support, describe, summarize.	• Make lessons interactive and comprehensible. • Structure group discussions. • Give extra processing time. *Describe/compare* _____. *How are these similar or different?* *What would happen if* _____? *What is your opinion of* _____?	Students can check the work of others and edit and revise the sentences so they are correct. They can describe the cards to the class when they are finished.

Reading Comprehension

"The more of the text we understand, the more new knowledge we can acquire. This expands our knowledge base, what cognitive psychologists call *schemata*, or underlying patterns of concepts. Such comprehension, in turn, enables us to understand even more concepts and vocabulary."— Dr. Jim Cummins

Why

English learners need guidance to become active readers who engage with texts on multiple levels before, during, and after reading. Comprehension instruction in *Reading Street* focuses on *metacognition*, a good reader's ability to independently reflect on the purpose of reading, select appropriate approaches to texts, ask questions as he or she reads, and actively resolve areas of confusion.

How

Core Comprehension Skill
Activate Prior Knowledge/Build Background
Frontload the Lesson Use the Preteach activities in the Guide Comprehension section of the ELL Support lessons with a small group to build background for the main Comprehension Skill. The Envision It! Visual Skills Handbook in the Student Edition and Envision It! Animations from the digital path provide visual support to fully engage students in the core skill instruction.

Access Content and Scaffold Meaning
Provide Comprehensible Input The leveled Reteach activities in the Guide Comprehension section of the ELL Support pages provide visual, contextual, and linguistic support for the grade-level Comprehension Skill. The interactive activities are designed so students reuse the academic vocabulary related to each Comprehension Skill using different modalities to enhance understanding. Topics range from basic reading skills, such as understanding supporting ideas and details in text, to expanded skills, such as making inferences.

Language Clarification The leveled support notes in the Reteach activities of the Guide Comprehension section of the ELL Support pages provide ideas for clarifying meaning for all proficiency levels.

Extend Language
Enable Language Production and Affirm Identity
The mini-lessons in the Guide Comprehension section of the ELL Support pages focus on the Comprehension Skill. Use them to encourage students to express ideas and participate in discussions using social and academic vocabulary.

Comprehension of Core Selection
Sheltered Reading
Activate Prior Knowledge/Build Background
Frontload the Lesson Use the Before Reading activities in the Sheltered Reading section in the ELL Support pages for ideas to preview the text and set a purpose for reading. The Multilingual Summaries in the *ELL Handbook* activate prior knowledge, affirm identity, and build background before reading the main selection.

Access Content and Scaffold Meaning
Provide Comprehensible Input Use the Sheltered Reading questions and the graphic organizer on the ELL Support pages to guide comprehension and clarify understanding of the selection.

Extend Language
Enable Language Production The Sheltered Reading section on the ELL Support pages has questions that encourage students to use oral language during reading to demonstrate understanding. The Fluency and the After Reading sections have ideas for shared reading, summarizing, and organizing information for each selection.

ELD and ELL Readers
There is an ELD and an ELL Reader for each week of instruction. Each Reader has a topic that supports grade-level concept development, tying into the Question of the Week. The ELD Readers are written for Beginning and Intermediate language proficiency levels, and the ELL Readers are designed for Intermediate to Advanced High levels. The rich language and information, sentence patterns, repetition, and visual support will unlock new words for students and give them models for using English words, phrases, and sentence structures.

Activate Prior Knowledge/Build Background
Frontload the Lesson Use the Before Reading section in the ELL Support pages for the ELL and ELD Readers for ideas to preview the text and set a purpose for reading.

Access Content and Scaffold Meaning
Provide Comprehensible Input Use the During Reading Routine along with the sheltered questions in the ELL/ELD Reader Support pages and visuals in the Readers to build background, model, and guide comprehension.

Extend Language
Enable Language Production and Affirm Identity Use the Anchored Talk and Let's Write About It activities on the inside back cover of each ELL Reader to have students apply the lesson's target comprehension skill. The reproducible Study Guide found in the ELL Handbook supports students' comprehension and provides writing and take-home activities.

	Student Behaviors	Teacher Behaviors	Examples
Beginning	• Uses vocabulary that includes environmental print, some high-frequency and concrete words represented by pictures • Depends on visuals and prior knowledge • Able to apply comprehension skills when reading texts at his or her level • May recognize a few letter-sound relationships • Reads word by word	• Use gestures, repetition, slower speech, visuals, and simple language. • Assess prior knowledge, build background, and frontload extensively before reading text. • Make sure text is linguistically accommodated for level or provide teacher/peer support for grade-level text.	Use gestures to explain first, next, and last. Hold up one finger as you say *first* and put on a shoe. Hold up two fingers as you say *next* and tie the shoe. Hold up three fingers as you say *last* and take a step forward. Then use the Envision It! Visual Skills Handbook picture in the Student Edition to identify sequence words *first, next,* and *last.* Use the Picture It! activity from the *ELL Handbook* to practice and assess sequence.
Intermediate	• Reads some everyday oral language, knows literal meanings of common words, and uses routine academic language • Reads slowly and in short phrases and may need to reread to clarify meaning • Can locate and classify information • Understands simple sentences but is dependent on visual cues, topic familiarity, prior knowledge, or pre-taught vocabulary • Can apply basic and higher-order thinking skills in texts that are linguistically accommodated	• Use gestures, repetition, slower speech, visuals, and simple language. • Assess prior knowledge, build background, and frontload extensively before reading text. • Make sure text is linguistically accommodated for level or provide support for grade-level text.	Use gestures to explain *first, next,* and *last.* As you tie your shoe, have students describe what you do first, next, and last. Then use the Envision It! Visual Skills Handbook in the Student Edition to have students identify sequence words *first, next,* and *last* and then describe the sequence in the pictures. Use the Picture It! activity from the *ELL Handbook* to practice and assess sequences.
Advanced	• Reads with greater ease • Uses a variety of comprehension strategies • Can understand words and phrases beyond their literal meanings • Able to apply basic and higher-order comprehension skills • Occasionally dependent on visuals and teacher/peer assistance with unfamiliar topics	• Frontload text and build background before reading. • Preteach unfamiliar concepts and related vocabulary. • Use visuals to clarify meanings of new topics. • Provide support for grade-level text.	Use the Envision It! Visual Skills Handbook in the Student Edition to preteach sequence. Students can describe what is happening in each picture and identify sequence words. After using the Routine to frontload the ELL Reader, guide students to find words that show sequence. Use the graphic organizer to fill in the sequence of events. Use the organizer to retell the sequence of events with a partner and then share with the class.
Advanced High	• Reads and understands vocabulary nearly comparable to native English-speaking peers • Can infer meaning, draw conclusions, and use context to infer meanings of new words • Can interpret information and find details that support main ideas	• Frontload text and build background before reading. • Preteach unfamiliar concepts and related vocabulary. • Use visuals to clarify meanings of new topics. • Provide support for grade-level text as needed.	Use the Envision It! Visual Skills Handbook in the Student Edition to preteach sequence. Students can describe what is happening in each picture and identify other sequence words they may know. After using the routine to frontload the ELL Reader, pairs can find words that show sequence. Use a graphic organizer to fill in the sequence of events and then retell the story. Use the organizer if needed.

Conventions and Writing

 "Writing helps solve problems, affirms students' identities, and generates linguistic feedback from teachers that can increase language awareness and academic language proficiency."— Dr. Jim Cummins

Why

Research shows that students acquire language most readily when they are fully involved in all learning activities in the classroom. Activities should integrate listening, speaking, reading, and writing, since these language skills develop interdependently. Teachers can facilitate language learning and literacy development by ensuring that students hear language in natural ways, in real and practical contexts, and write it in structured formats.

Each English language learner comes from a unique background of language, literacy, and culture. Because students are at varying levels of English proficiency, it is important that each student has challenging work, appropriate for his or her level of English proficiency and literacy. The conventions and writing lessons in the ELL Support pages of *Reading Street* provide the systematic instruction that students need at each language proficiency level to scaffold use of increasingly complex grammatical structures in content area writing.

How

Reading Street promotes literacy attainment through engaging Conventions and Writing activities in the core Teacher Edition and ELL Support lessons. These activities activate prior knowledge and build background, scaffold meaning, affirm identity, and extend language.

Activate Prior Knowledge/Build Background

Frontload the Lesson Use the Preteach activities in the Conventions and Writing sections of the ELL Support pages with a small group of students before the lesson to introduce the concepts. Each Conventions lesson contains a helpful chart to convey grammatical forms and has ideas for addressing the functions of the grammatical structure to students. The Writing section contains a simple model to use when guiding instruction for beginning and intermediate levels.

Affirm Identity Use the Language Transfer notes in the core Teacher Edition, the Language Transfer Charts in the *ELL Handbook*, and the *ELL Handbook* Grammar Transition Lessons to lead students in transferring knowledge from their home languages to English.

Access Content and Scaffold Meaning

Provide Comprehensible Input Use the leveled Conventions practice activities in the ELL Support pages for contextual and linguistic support for each grade-level grammar skill. The interactive activities are designed so students reuse the language related to each core convention using different modalities to enhance understanding. For more practice on a core skill, or to meet the needs of beginners and intermediate students, use the Grammar Transition bank of flexible activities in the *ELL Handbook* or the Grammar Jammer from the digital path during small group time. Use the leveled writing ideas and the simplified writing models in the ELL Support pages to scaffold meaning for all students.

Language Clarification The leveled support notes throughout the Teacher Edition pages and the Grammar Transition Lessons in the *ELL Handbook* contain ideas for clarifying meaning for all proficiency levels.

Extend Language

Enable Language Production The Conventions and Writing sections of the ELL Support pages have practice activities for students to actively use grammar and writing skills. The sentence frames and leveled writing prompts guide and encourage oral and written language production for all levels of English proficiency. Use the ELL Notes throughout the core Teacher Edition Language Arts pages for ideas to support all levels of English language learners in prewriting, editing, revising, and publishing writing pieces.

References for English Language Proficiency— What, Why, and How

Gottlieb, Margo, M. Elizabeth Cranley, and Andrea R. Oliver. (2007). *The WIDA English Language Proficiency Standards and Resource Guide, Pre-Kindergarten through Grade 12*. Board of Regents of the University of Wisconsin on behalf of the WIDA Consortium.

Peregoy, Suzanne F., and Owen F. Boyle (2008). *Reading, Writing, and Learning in ESL: A Resource Book for Teaching K–12 English Learners*. New York: Pearson.

	Student Behaviors	Teacher Behaviors	Examples
Beginning	• Can label, list, copy, and use basic punctuation and capitalization • Uses some standard word order • Uses high-frequency words phrases and short sentences in present tense • May recognize a few letter-sound relationships • Responds to pictured events using words or phrases based on models	• Allow extra time for prewriting and build background before writing. • Use language experience stories. • Help students turn words and phrases into sentences. • Accept phonetic spelling, but show corrections. • Give a checklist for revising that has visual cues and help students use dictionaries or word walls.	Descriptive paragraph about a family member. ••••••••••••••••••••••••• Students can produce words or phrases about a family member using a drawing or photograph. Guide production of supporting details on a graphic organizer. Write out sentences and have students copy the sentences and read them to you or a partner.
Intermediate	• Communicates best when topics are familiar and concrete • Produces short phrases and simple sentences • May use simple future and past tenses inconsistently • Can compare and contrast • Can describe events, people, processes, and procedures with limited details	• Allow extra time for building background and prewriting. • Help students turn phrases into sentences. • Accept phonetic spelling, but show corrections. • Give a checklist for revising that has written cues and help students use dictionaries or word walls.	Students can write short sentences about a family member. Guide students to use a graphic organizer to add details. Have partners work together to write at least three interesting details describing the family member. Share their sentences with the class.
Advanced	• Can engage in grade-appropriate writing tasks with support • Can write phrases, sentences, and paragraphs with some errors • Can edit and revise using a checklist with a written description • Has a basic grasp of basic verb tenses, grammar features, sentence patterns, and cohesive devices • Provides increased detail and can summarize information from graphics and notes	• Allow extra time for prewriting. • Use brainstorming, concept mapping, peer conferencing, interviewing, and reading. • Help students with correct spelling, capitalization, and punctuation. • Clarify error correction by peers or teachers to make changes.	Use a graphic organizer to develop ideas and details about a family member. Students can develop a paragraph based on the graphic organizer.
Advanced High	• Can express ideas in writing and engage meaningfully in grade-level writing assignments with minimal support • Writes comparable to native English speaker • Makes minor errors that rarely interfere with communication	• Use brainstorming, concept mapping, peer conferencing, interviewing, and reading. • Help students with correct spelling, capitalization, and punctuation if needed. • Clarify error correction by peers or teachers to make changes.	Use a graphic organizer to develop ideas about a family member. Students can develop a paragraph based on the graphic organizer. Share the details they find most interesting.

 **Language Development Routine**

Hear It!   See It!   Say It!   Use It!

Use this flexible routine with all levels of English language learners to guide their language development as they learn new basic and academic vocabulary, increase conceptual knowledge, and improve their reading comprehension. The following instructional sequence will encourage production and guide language development.

Start with choral work (Whole Group), and then move to partners or small groups, followed by "on your own" activities. Because choral, partner, and small group practice activities are nonthreatening, the affective filter is lowered, increasing language production.

Academic Vocabulary Routine

Hear It!

Model the word so that students can hear the correct pronunciation. Provide a student-friendly definition and relate it to something that students know, affirming their identity.

See It!

Display the word, and use a picture or pantomime to visually clarify meaning. Ask questions, and have students respond to show their understanding of the word.

Say It!

Have students repeat the word chorally and then with a partner. Students will be able to use the word with more confidence and accuracy.

Use It!

Engage students in activities that encourage language production. Have them create their own definitions and use the word multiple times orally and in writing to internalize vocabulary and concept knowledge.

ELL Use the Academic Vocabulary Routine

This example shows how to use the Academic Vocabulary Routine to pre-teach the word *noun*.

How to Teach the Word *Noun*

	Say the word **noun**. A **noun** is a naming word for people, places, animals, or things. Point to a desk. Say: *This is a desk. A desk is a thing, so the word* desk *is a* **noun**.
	Write the word **noun** on the board and word wall. To clarify meaning, point to other items in the classroom. Ask: *What is this?* (a chair) *Is this a person?* (no) *Is this a place?* (no) *Is this a thing?* (yes) *So, the word* chair *must be a* **noun**.
	Have students repeat the word **noun**. In pairs, have them say the word **noun** and the definition, *a* **noun** *is a naming word for people, places, animals, or things.*
	Have pairs work together to identify more **nouns** for people and things they see in the classroom. Then have them write and illustrate their own definition of **noun**. Pairs can then share their definitions orally with the class.

LS Leveled Support

Beginning Pair students with more proficient speakers or students who speak the same language. Use more gestures and repetition. Allow students to answer by pointing, gesturing, or giving one-word responses.

Intermediate Continue to use visuals and gestures. Model correct responses. Ask questions that elicit two-word responses.

Advanced Continue to provide visual support. Give students more time to process information. Questions can be more open-ended, but be sure to check comprehension frequently.

Advanced High Provide visual support as needed. Have students work with beginners who speak the same language to clarify meaning.

Contents

Professional Development

Introduction: How to Use This Book

Across the United States, teachers are welcoming increasing numbers of English language learners (ELLs) into their classrooms. English language learners make up the fastest growing K–12 student population in the United States.

While English language learners share many characteristics with other students, they need support and scaffolding specific to their needs. They represent a highly diverse population. They come from many home language backgrounds and cultures, and they have a wide range of prior educational and literacy experiences acquiring in their home languages.

This Handbook is designed to help you identify and support the needs of ELLs in your classroom. The strategies and activities will allow you to scaffold and support instruction so that all students can learn in ways that are comprehensible and meaningful, and in ways that promote their academic success and achievement.

Carefully crafted **professional development articles** assist you in understanding and planning for the unique needs of English language learners in your classroom.

Weekly Planners outline all activities in a "week at a glance" format and include objectives for each instructional strand.

Each reading selection is supported by a set of reproducibles. **Word Cards** allow students to use key vocabulary for speaking, writing, and content acquisition. Each **Picture It!** focuses on a reading comprehension skill with leveled instruction targeted to English language learners. **Multilingual Selection Summaries,** in English, Spanish, Chinese, Vietnamese, Korean, and Hmong, allow students to access selection content and share their reading with their families. **Study Guides** for ELL Readers allow you to assess comprehension of content and the use of key reading strategies. All of these resources provide access to core content material, each unit and week of the year. Detailed instructions for using these resources are provided in the ELL Support pages of the Teacher's Edition.

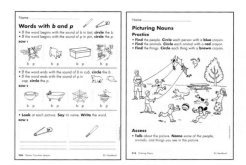

Phonics pages target instruction with consonants, vowels, and syllable patterns that may be challenging for English language learners. **Grammar** lessons supplement core instruction in speaking and writing. Use these lessons as students need additional support.

English Language Learner Workshops provide direct and explicit instruction in such topics as using transactional language, retelling or summarizing in English, asking for assistance, giving and following directions, and using formal and informal English. A teacher-driven lesson as well as a student worksheet is provided for a model/teach/practice/assess progression as students gradually master these skills.

Teaching Routines for English language learners allow for a systematic approach to learning that yields results. Routines are tied to instruction, allowing students to master the skills needed to succeed.

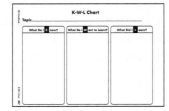

Graphic Organizers give students visual support to assist them in accessing the content. ELL teaching ideas are provided for each graphic organizer.

Multilingual Vocabulary charts translate the lesson words into Spanish, Korean, Hmong, Vietnamese, and Chinese to allow the frontloading of important vocabulary and concepts that ensures greater comprehension.

Poster Talk, Concept Talk leveled activities encourage language production using the poster visuals and vocabulary related to the weekly concept.

Identifying Language Proficiency Levels

To differentiate both instruction and assessment for the English language learners in your classroom, it is important to identify their various levels of language proficiency across the four domains of listening, speaking, reading, and writing. Language proficiency is a collection of interdependent components. Fundamentally, language proficiency requires phonemic awareness and awareness of phonological relationships. It requires knowledge of vocabulary, grammar, syntax, and pronunciation. More subtle and sophisticated skills also apply. For instance, can a student switch his or her usage to match either a conversational or academic setting? The interplay of these abilities determines a student's linguistic competency.

Four or five levels of English proficiency are generally used to describe learners at various stages of language acquisition: **Beginning** (or preproduction), **Intermediate** (or early production), **Advanced** (or intermediate fluency), and **Advanced High** (or near proficient). The table below shows some responses you can expect from students at each level. The Comparative Oral Language Proficiency Chart on p. 6 provides more in-depth descriptions of what you might expect from students at each stage of oral language development, and it compares different proficiency levels used across the United States. Use the chart to plan instruction for your class.

	Listening	Speaking	Reading	Writing
Beginning	Can respond to simple commands or questions nonverbally.	Uses only single words or phrases and may be prone to echo others.	May match pictures to words or recognize a few letter-sound relationships.	May write single words and attempt to copy statements.
Intermediate	Understands short sentences and simple conversational language and can follow simple directions. Beginning to grasp concrete details and a few abstract concepts.	Learns common social phrases by heart and can communicate simple information. Begins to speak in complete sentences, and vocabulary increases.	Understands simple texts and can group words such as synonyms and antonyms. Comprehends texts on familiar topics and may be able to summarize a simple passage or identify its sequence of events.	Writing is error-prone, but can use correct word order in simple sentences. Begins to use basic rules of grammar and mechanics to write statements and questions.
Advanced	Grasps most conversational and some academic language.	Speaks in more complex sentences and uses a wider range of vocabulary.	Reads with greater ease and uses a variety of comprehension strategies, but may stumble over texts with unfamiliar concepts or vocabulary.	Can write multi-sentence paragraphs organized logically.
Advanced High	Follows multistep directions and grasps speech with complex syntax and academic vocabulary.	Uses both conversational and academic language with ease and can speak on a range of topics, using idioms.	Reads grade-level appropriate texts, can infer meaning, draw conclusions, and use context to infer meanings of words.	Writes organized texts with few errors, sufficient detail, and specific vocabulary.

How can you differentiate instruction for the different proficiency levels?

You can use a variety of instructional techniques, activities, and assessment tools to support English language learners at different levels of proficiency—all within the same lesson. For example, to teach sequence of events, you might choose to adapt your instruction as follows:

Teach/Model

Read a short passage to the whole class, showing pictures of each event in the story as you do so. When you have finished reading, review the events in the story. Model using sequence words.

- Use gestures to explain "first," "next," and "last" to students at the **Beginning** level. For example, hold up one finger as you say "first" and put on a shoe. Hold up two fingers as you say "next" and lace up the shoe. Hold up three fingers as you say "last" and take a step.

- Have students at the **Intermediate** level echo you as you say "first," "next," and "last" and then add a detail to each to make a phrase or short sentence.

- Have students at the **Advanced** level answer questions about sequence of events as you read aloud.

- Have students at the **Advanced High** level answer questions about the sequence of inferred events as you read aloud. (For example, "What must have happened before Jack slipped in the paint?" "The paint can fell.")

Practice

- After you read, have students at the **Beginning** level arrange the pictures in the story in the correct order.

- Have students at the **Intermediate** level answer the questions, "What happened first?" "What happened next?" "What happened last?"

- Have students at the **Advanced** level verbally describe the events in the story using sequence words.

- Have students at the **Advanced High** level write the sequence of events in the story using complete sentences.

Assess

- Have students at the **Beginning** level arrange a new series of pictures in the correct order.

- Have students at the **Intermediate** level look at a new series of pictures and then answer the questions, "What happened first?" "What happened next?" "What happened last?"

- Have students at the **Advanced** level read a new passage and then verbally describe its events using sequence words.

- Have students at the **Advanced High** level read a new passage and answer questions about the sequence of inferred events.

Comparative Oral Language Proficiency Chart

Levels of Proficiency	Level I Entering	Level II Beginning	Level III Developing	Level IV Expanding	Level V Bridging
	Beginning	Early Intermediate	Intermediate	Early Advanced	Advanced
	Beginning	Intermediate	Intermediate	Advanced	Advanced High
Characteristics of the English Language Learner	• Minimal comprehension • May be very shy • No verbal production • Non-English speaker • Silent period (10 hours to 3 months) • Uses gestures and actions to communicate	• Limited comprehension • Gives one- or two-word responses • May use two- or three-word phrases • Stage may last 6 months to 2 years	• Comprehension increases • Errors still occur in speech • Simple sentences • Stage may last 2 to 4 years	• Good comprehension • Sentences become more complex • Engages in conversation • Errors in speech are more complex	• Few errors in speech • Orally proficient • Near-native vocabulary • Uses complex sentences
What They Can Do: Performance Indicators	• Listen • Point • Illustrate • Match • Choose	• Name • List and group • Categorize • Label • Demonstrate	• Compare and contrast • Recall and retell • Summarize • Explain	• Higher-order thinking skills • Analyze, debate, justify	• All performance indicators
Instructional Ideas for Teachers	• Visual cues • Tape passages • Pair students • Total Physical Response activities • Concrete objects • Graphic organizers	• Short homework assignments • Short-answer quizzes • Open-ended sentences	• Graphs • Tables • Group discussions • Student-created books • Cloze activities	• Group panels • Paraphrasing • Defending and debating	• Lessons on writing mechanics • Free reading of appropriate books • Cooperative learning groups

What Reading Teachers
Should Know About Language

Why do reading teachers need to know about the structure of language?

English language learners are entering U.S. classrooms in steadily increasing numbers. The demands on teachers are also surging. To communicate effectively with these students, teachers need to know how to make their instructional talk more comprehensible. All teachers need to better understand their students' attempts at written and spoken language. To improve students' literacy skills in English, teachers must understand how language works *in education.* What should we know about English and other languages? What truths about language help teachers as communicators, as guides, and as evaluators?

Knowledge about the structure of languages—and particularly of English—is vital not only to linguists and ELL teachers. Reading and content-area teachers, too, can make practical, everyday use of the concepts that are posed and explored by the following questions.

What are the basic units of language?

Spoken language consists of units of different sizes:

Phonemes

Phonemes are the individual sounds in a word that affect meaning. The word *cat* consists of these three phonemes: /k/ /a/ /t/.

Different languages use different sets of phonemes. English language learners may not be familiar with some English phonemes and may need help recognizing and producing these sounds.

Phonemes signal different word meanings. For example, the different vowel sounds in the words *hit* and *heat* indicate that these are two different words.

Morphemes

Morphemes are the smallest units of meaning in a language. Some morphemes are **free** (or independent) units. Words such as *dog, jump,* and *happy* are free morphemes. Other morphemes are **bound** (or attached), such as inflected endings, prefixes, and suffixes:

- the noun ending *-s* in *dogs*
- the verb ending *-ed* in *jumped*
- the prefix *un-* in *unhappy*
- the adjective ending *-er* in *happier*
- the suffix *-ness* in *happiness*

These bound morphemes add meaning and, in fact, form new words.

Words

A word consists of one or more morphemes. A word also can be defined as a meaningful group of morphemes. Native English speakers may pronounce words in ways that make it difficult for English language learners to hear word boundaries. For example, in conversation, an English speaker may ask, "Did you eat?"—but pronounce it like "Jeet?"

Some languages use bound morphemes (for example, word endings) to convey the meanings of certain functional English words such as the prepositions *in, on,* and *between.* English language learners may need explicit instruction in order to use these functional words correctly. On the other hand, an English word such as *in* may seem familiar to a Spanish speaker who uses the similar preposition *en.*

Phrases

A phrase is a group of words that have meaning together but do not include a subject and a predicate. Since some languages allow the subject or verb to be understood, students may believe that certain phrases in English are equivalent to sentences.

Sentences

A sentence is a meaningful group of words that includes a subject and a predicate. English language learners may understand the concept of sentences, but they may apply word order conventions from their home languages. They also may struggle with the dense sentence structures of academic English.

Discourses

Discourses include speeches, essays, and many other kinds of communication made up of sentences. One kind of discourse frequently heard in U.S. classrooms involves the teacher asking questions and students responding aloud. Depending on their home cultures, some English language learners may find the question-and-answer form of discourse unfamiliar.

Why do English language learners need to learn about basic units of language?

It helps teachers to understand that units, such as bound and free morphemes, words, phrases, and sentences or clauses, operate differently in different languages. For example:

- In Chinese, the past tense is not expressed with verb endings, but by separate words that indicate the time of the action (similar to *yesterday* and *already*).
- In Spanish, verb endings indicate the person and number of sentence subjects, so the subject may not be stated in some sentences.
- In Arabic, related words share three-consonant roots. Speakers form related verbs, nouns, and adjectives by applying fixed patterns to these roots and sometimes adding prefixes and suffixes.

English language learners are working mentally to determine how units of English work—as they also try to understand texts and acquire content knowledge.

What is academic English?

Academic English might be described as the language of teachers, literature, textbooks, and content areas, such as science and social studies. Unlike conversational English, academic English is language of a cognitively demanding register, or range. Academic English does not depend as much upon the gestures and circumstances of speech as conversational English does.

Academic English includes content-area vocabulary embedded in complex grammatical structures. It features words about abstract ideas. Understanding this language requires knowledge of content, as well as experience with written materials and classroom discussions. Many English language learners can carry on conversations in English with their native-English-speaking classmates. But they still struggle with reading and writing English—and even understanding their teachers in class. They have acquired social English skills used in personal communication, but they have not yet mastered the academic English used at their grade level.

How do English language learners learn vocabulary?

English language learners must learn much more than the selected vocabulary words in a lesson. They also must make sense of the other unfamiliar words in the lesson—and thousands of other words they continually encounter in school.

Knowing a word involves much more than hearing it and learning its definition. Students must learn how each word relates to its other forms. They gradually learn how it relates to other words and concepts. Knowledge of a word grows during many encounters.

Students learn words in meaningful groups more effectively than in unrelated lists. Look for opportunities to group words in meaningful ways. For example, as students learn the word *invite*, they also can learn *invited, uninvited, invitation, inviting,* and other words in this family.

What is "regular" to English language learners?

Proficient English speakers often take for granted irregularities in English that can puzzle younger and less fluent learners.

For example, a student who learns the plural forms *dogs, cats,* and *turtles* may wonder why *mouses, mooses,* and *childs* meet with disapproval. A student who masters these past tense forms—*jumped, walked,* and *stopped*—may try to use *throwed, catched,* or *taked.* In both cases, the child demonstrates an awareness of English conventions, and a teacher should acknowledge this in a positive way. The teacher also should gradually help each student master the many exceptions to the rules. Teachers who are aware of the principles of word formation in English can help students acquire vocabulary. English has many helpful patterns for new speakers, readers, and writers to learn. Savvy teachers break up the instruction into manageable chunks so that students are not overwhelmed by the many English word patterns they encounter.

What characteristics of written words might challenge English language learners?

- Written English is an alphabetic language, and letters represent sounds in words. Languages such as Chinese and Japanese are not alphabetic; written symbols can represent larger parts of words than just individual sounds. For students whose home languages are not alphabetic, learning the alphabetic system is an early and continuing challenge.

- The home languages of many English language learners—including Spanish, Vietnamese, Hmong, Haitian Creole, and others—are alphabetic. Yet the letter-sound correspondences in these languages are different from those of English. Students can use literacy skills they may have in their home languages, but much new learning is needed to master English.

- While letter-sound correspondences in numerous languages are relatively simple, the relationships of letters to sounds in English can be complicated. In Spanish, for example, the vowel *a* has one sound. In English, *a* can represent many different sounds.

- Even in related English words, the same letters can stand for different sounds. Consider *c* in the words *electric, electricity,* and *electrician.* The spellings of these words may challenge English language learners.

- The challenges of written English affect not only spelling but also word recognition, comprehension of text, and confidence in language learning.

Welcoming Newcomers
to the Mainstream Classroom

The teacher's first concern when welcoming newcomers to the mainstream classroom must be to help each student learn the basic concepts and vocabulary needed to participate in school life.

Prepare

Learn as much as possible about your newcomer students in order to tailor instruction to their individual needs.

Find out from parents or other sources about educational practices in the student's home country or culture. For example, if the student is accustomed to memorizing and reciting material in a group, he or she may feel anxious about independent work or homework, particularly if the family is not able to help the child in English.

Newcomers who are acquiring English may experience identifiable stages of adjustment and adaptation.

- **A Silent Period** For a student quite new to an English-language environment, a "silent period" is normal. The student may be learning classroom routine and acquiring basic vocabulary by watching and listening.

- **Culture Shock** In this phase, newcomers may prefer to spend much of their time with family or friends from the home culture and to temporarily reject the new language and culture. Help children to cope with this phase by providing extra help and attention when possible. A bilingual friend or classroom aide can help to make the environment feel more navigable to the child and can help to alleviate any feeling of anxiety or sadness.

Getting Started in the Classroom

Before classes begin, you may wish to plan a small reception for newcomers. Invite the students' parents or other family members, and include someone who can translate.

- **Orient the newcomer to the classroom.** Have students help you to label the classroom and the objects in it with self-stick notes. Pronounce the name of each item as you do, and use the word in a short sentence. *"Desk. This is your desk."*

- **Show interest in and respect for each child's home culture.** Create opportunities for the class to learn more about the newcomer's home country and culture. Learn a few phrases in the student's home language. Correctly pronounce the student's name.

- **Demonstrate crucial skills.** Have students tour the school with older students who speak the same home language. Post seating charts and go through assigned textbooks with newcomers to help them understand what content is presented in each.

- **Try to provide a risk-free learning environment.** Create opportunities for students to practice speaking English in small groups or with a partner without worrying about errors they may make. Accept errors in speech without comment and model the correct phrasing.

- **Provide a "buddy."** A buddy system helps students feel more secure in their environment. Buddies need not speak the same home language, but pairing up buddies with the same home language can allow buddies to serve as tutors.

- **Include newcomers in classroom routines.** Assign newcomers their share of regular classroom chores. Such responsibilities can help them feel they are part of the group. Students can be shown how to successfully carry out routine tasks without using or needing extensive English.

Teaching Strategies

Educational strategies should assist students to learn in content areas at the same time that they acquire the new language. Remember that students' skills in the home language can be transferred to English learning. Encourage students to continue to speak and read in the home language.

- **Build on students' prior knowledge.** Newcomers often have knowledge bases that are much greater than their skill levels in English. Find ways to gauge students' familiarity with the topics of upcoming lessons. Regularly using visual aids, such as semantic maps, K-W-L charts, or time lines, can help you determine how much each student already knows or needs to learn about a topic.

- **Encourage students to use learning resources.** Teach students how to use a picture dictionary or a children's dictionary, and encourage them to use it frequently to find the words they need. Ask them to start their own word banks by listing frequently used vocabulary in a notebook. Provide bilingual dictionaries for extra support.

- **Use environmental print to teach.** Put up posters and other materials from periodicals and magazines. If possible, provide students with parallel texts about the same topic in English and in the home language.

- **Invite the families of newcomers to participate in school life.** Find ways to communicate information about homework and class projects in English and the home language. Make families aware that literacy skills in the home language can help students transfer those skills to English.

- **Build a support network.** Bilingual tutors or classroom aides can clarify assignments or lesson content for English language learners without disrupting the day's activities. Similarly, family members who volunteer to help in the classroom can greatly lessen students' anxiety levels.

- **Help students transfer their writing skills.** For English language learners who have developed any emergent writing skills in their home languages, build on these skills by occasionally having them write in both languages. Short sentences and picture labels written in a home language and English help students with writing and English acquisition.

- **Include culturally relevant assignments.** Try to find readings for students that refer to their home cultures. If writing skills are limited, encourage learners to show their understanding by talking about the stories and creating illustrations.

While it may take some time for English language learners to gain proficiency in academic English, newcomers need not feel like outsiders for very long.

Sheltering Instruction for English Language Learners

What is sheltered instruction?

Sheltered instruction is a combination of strategies for teaching academic content to English language learners at the same time that they are developing proficiency in the English language. This approach to instruction is called *sheltered* because it offers a haven, or refuge, for students who must comprehend subject matter presented in a language they are still learning. Sheltered instruction supports English language learners who do not have grade-level academic vocabulary or the familiarity with the American school system that their English speaking classmates have. It provides extended English language support that English language learners receive as they learn subject-area concepts.

How does sheltered instruction help students and teachers?

Sheltered instruction offers practical, easy-to-implement strategies that teachers can use in a mainstream classroom to extend and scaffold instruction about the English language. Sheltered instruction helps English language learners find the keys they need to make sense of instruction in English about the concepts and processes they need to perform grade-level work in all subjects.

Teachers can help students build mental bridges to new concepts and learning in English by encouraging them to connect their prior knowledge—the diverse skills, experiences, language, and cultural knowledge that they bring to the classroom—to their new learning activities. Finding ways for students to draw on their home language, cultural background, and prior experience can facilitate each English language learner's ability to grasp and retain abstract ideas and grade-level vocabulary. Finding connections between what they are learning and what they already know in their home language can motivate students to read, write, listen, and speak in English. As comprehension and vocabulary

increase, students can transfer more and more concepts from their home languages into English.

This knowledge transfer can work for teachers, too. As teachers tap into students' prior knowledge, the teachers will discover when they need to supply background about American events, customs, and idioms that may be new to English language learners. At the same time, they will be expanding their knowledge about English language learners' backgrounds and traditions.

Some Basics

1. Use Appropriate Speech (Comprehensible Input)

   ✓ **Enunciate.** Speak slowly and clearly, especially when introducing new content and vocabulary.

   ✓ **Provide wait time.** English language learners often need extra time to process questions in English and to formulate responses.

   ✓ **Explain and demonstrate the meanings of complex terms.** Use activities that help students practice speaking, hearing, writing, and reading key words and phrases.

Complex term	Activities to clarify meaning
weather	Write and say: weather Write and say: hot, cold Say: *The weather is hot today.* (Fan yourself to show you are hot.) Then say: *The weather is cold today.* (Hug yourself and shiver to show you are cold.) Have volunteers repeat each sentence with gestures. Then fan yourself and ask: *What is the weather like today?* (hot) Hug yourself and shiver and ask: *Is the weather hot or cold today?* (cold) Have partners take turns using gestures and asking and answering the questions. Start a wall chart of weather words with pictures.

✓ **Allow students to show comprehension at their levels of language proficiency.** Ask questions that can be answered with "yes" or "no," by choosing one of two words as the answer (*Is ice hot or cold?*), by pointing to a picture or object (*Point to the tree.*), or by following simple oral directions.

2. Develop Academic Concepts

✓ **Link concepts explicitly to students' prior knowledge and background.** For example, if you introduce a unit on weather, ask students to describe, illustrate, and share what they know about weather. Create and display a class chart that tells about weather in places where students have lived.

✓ **Use hands-on activities to build background for new information.** For example, introduce the idea of touch (The Five Senses) by having students touch objects with different textures and learn a word or words to describe how each object feels.

✓ **Use supplementary materials.** Picture books can clarify and support concept learning. Use picture books that show terms that are hard to explain, such as *covered wagons, rations,* or the *Pony Express.*

3. Emphasize and Develop Key Vocabulary

✓ **Repeat key words, phrases, and concepts, and have students practice using them.**

✓ **Provide feedback on students' language use.** Use gestures to indicate understanding, as well as supportive questions to prompt students to provide more details.

✓ **Make the development of proficiency in English an explicit goal in all of your teaching. To learn new academic vocabulary, students need to use it.** Provide situations that challenge students to push themselves to a higher level of proficiency.

4. Connect Written and Oral Language

✓ **Say and write new vocabulary.** When teaching new words or phrases, such as idioms, write the word or phrase where everyone can see it. Say it slowly as you point to it. Have students repeat the word or phrase. Use gestures, role play, or drawings to demonstrate what the word means. Have students practice saying, reading, and writing the word or phrase in sentences.

✓ **Use word and picture cards to explain vocabulary and content.**

✓ **Have students build personal word files.** Have them write a word on one side of a card and draw a picture to represent its meaning on the other side. The files can include target words for different content areas as well as words that students find interesting or important. Have students use the cards for sorting and categorizing activities (e.g., color words, animal names, weather words, math words, action words).

✓ **Provide letter and phoneme cards for phonics activities.** Pair English language learners with native English speakers to use cards in order to build and say words that contain target sounds and spelling patterns. Give English language learners extra time and support to hear, say, and practice sounds and to build words using those sounds.

5. Use Visuals, Dramatization, and Realia (Real Things)

✓ **Use picture walks to preview text, concepts, and vocabulary—and to build background knowledge.** Use pictures to introduce characters and the setting and to give a simple summary of a story. You can use this same strategy with nonfiction text, having students preview illustrations, captions, boldfaced words, and other text features.

✓ **Use realia and graphic organizers.** Whenever possible, show objects and pictures that will help students understand concepts and speak about them in English. Use graphic organizers, diagrams, drawings, charts, and maps to help students conceptualize abstract information.

✓ **Use Total Physical Response (TPR) for active learning, so that students can show comprehension through physical movement.** For example, have students hear and follow instructions: *Clap your hands for Carla. Go to the board and circle the noun with a red piece of chalk.*

✓ **Use role play, drama, rhymes, songs, and movement.** All students need opportunities to be active learners. For English language learners, participating in a small group reenactment of a story, for example, can allow them to show comprehension and personal responses beyond what their language abilities may allow them to express.

6. Ongoing Formal and Informal Assessment

✓ **Assess early to understand a student's language level and academic preparedness. Use your assessment to plan and guide instruction.**

✓ **Set personal goals for each student and monitor progress regularly.** A student who uses phrases might be pushed to say and write complete sentences. A student who uses simple sentences might be pushed to add clauses to the sentences.

✓ **Provide various ways to demonstrate knowledge, including acting, singing, retelling, demonstrating, and illustrating.**

✓ **Use a variety of formal assessments such as practice tests, real tests, and oral and written assessments.** Use multiple choice, cloze, and open-response formats to help students become familiar with various assessment formats.

Sheltered instruction provides English language learners with opportunities to understand and access content-area learning. Within this framework, teachers provide activities that integrate reading, writing, listening, and speaking. Teachers can address the range of cultural, linguistic, and literary experiences that English language learners bring to the classroom. Sheltered instruction provides English language learners with many opportunities to understand and access content-area learning. Within this kind of instruction, teachers support English language learners by providing activities that integrate reading, writing, listening, and speaking. Teachers use students' experiences and prior knowledge as the key to unlock doors to content and language learning.

Vocabulary Knowledge and Strategies

Knowing how to organize vocabulary instruction around a few key areas will go a long way toward ensuring that students achieve both language proficiency and overall academic success. The new vocabulary that you teach should be carefully selected. As you consider the vocabulary you will teach in your classroom, you'll need to be aware of both survival language and academic language.

Survival Language

Think of survival language as a useful toolkit for new English language learners—a practical store of words and phrases that can be used to navigate new environments and accomplish everyday tasks in the classroom and at home. Survival language not only involves teaching students labels for common objects, places, and people, but includes giving students instruction in how to understand and follow directions, ask for help, and function appropriately in social situations. While it is valuable to reinforce this type of vocabulary acquisition throughout the day, as spontaneous interactions with students arise, it is also important to offer structured and intentional instruction in survival language. Consider organizing related words and phrases under the heading of a topic such as "School," as in the following table.

People	Places	Objects	Phrases
principal	cafeteria	desk	May I have...?
teacher	classroom	chair	Please show
nurse	bathroom	chalkboard	me....
student	library	worksheet	I want to...
coach	gym	ruler	What is a ...?
			I need help
			with....

Teachers Support Vocabulary Learning

English language learners come to school with a wide range of home language literacy, English language proficiency, and previous educational experiences. All of these factors impact their learning in English.

Teachers can use various strategies to support vocabulary development. Students need multiple exposures to words. Understanding deepens over time through gradually increased and varied experiences with the words.

English language learners need opportunities to learn vocabulary through activities that integrate reading, writing, speaking, and listening skills in the context of meaningful literacy experiences. Language learning is an exploration. Students have a curiosity about learning, and effective teachers nurture this quality through engaging and meaningful activities. Teachers can use what students already know to help them extract meaning from text by teaching them ways to learn and think about words.

Strategies for Exploring Words

Use these strategies to build vocabulary.

Related Words

Provide opportunities for English language learners to learn new words by grouping words that are related to a specific theme, quality, or activity. Help students classify English words in meaningful categories.

Use word walls, graphic organizers, and concept maps to group related words and create visual references that can be used in future lessons. Teachers can help students group and relate words in different ways, depending on what they can notice and understand, as well as how students will use the vocabulary.

Color names are one example of related words that can be the focus of a lesson.

✓ Write the word *colors* at the top of a wall chart.

✓ With colored markers, make a column of squares under the heading: red, blue, yellow, green.

✓ Point to the word *colors* and tell students they are going to learn the names of colors.

✓ Point to the first square and say, *This color is red.* Write *red* and repeat it clearly as you underline it with your finger.

✓ Show a familiar red object, such as a block, and say: *This is a red block. The color of this block is red. What color is this block?* (red)

Repeat this process with the other colors, making sure that students hear, say, and read each color name, and connect it to the color itself.

Have students create other sections in their personal word card files such as "family names," "numbers," "days and months," "weather," and "time."

Whenever you introduce a new topic or concept, take time to teach English language learners words they will need to understand the lesson. Keep in mind that they may need to learn some words and phrases in the lesson—including idioms and background references—that may already be common knowledge to native speakers. Encourage native speakers to act as resources for English language learners when they encounter a word, phrase, or concept that puzzles them.

Charts such as the one here can help students learn how words change form, depending on their function.

Naming Word	Describing Word	Action Word
rain	rainy	rain, rains, rained, raining
dance, dancer	dancing	dance, dances, danced, dancing
sleep, sleeper	sleepy	sleep, sleeps, slept, sleeping

Cognates

When students hear or see a word that looks or sounds similar to a word they know in their home language, encourage them to explore the connection. For example, a Russian speaker hearing the word *music* may recognize its connection to the Russian word *musika.* Many words that sound similar in two or more languages are cognates—they have the same or similar meaning in both languages. Record cognates on a wall chart and add to it during the year.

Multiple-meaning Words

Many English words have multiple meanings. Illustrating and creating examples of the ways words are used can build English language learners' experiences and understanding of the multiple meanings that words may have. Teachers can help students expand their understanding of multiple meanings by sharing sentences, definitions, and pictures that demonstrate the different meanings. For example, contrasting *The pitcher is full of water* with *The pitcher threw the ball,* with illustrations, will help English language learners remember the two meanings of *pitcher.*

Academic Language

Research indicates that acquiring a strong grasp of academic vocabulary is perhaps the most vital factor that distinguishes successful students from those who struggle in school. Becoming fluent in academic language will enable English language learners to understand and analyze texts, write clearly about their ideas, and comprehend subject-area material. Academic vocabulary differs from conversational English. It is the language of classroom discourse, and it is used to accomplish academic, not social or personal, purposes. Academic vocabulary also includes words, phrases, and sentence structures not commonly found in oral language but used frequently in academic texts such as textbooks, reports, essays, articles, and test materials. Instruction in academic vocabulary should be explicit and systematic. Give students multiple exposures to academic terms through frequent reading, writing, and oral language activities. Because academic vocabulary involves the use of language that is not commonly encountered in conversational contexts, English language learners need structured opportunities to practice this vocabulary in formal settings where teachers and peers are modeling the use of effective academic language.

Below is a partial list of types of academic vocabulary to which students should be exposed:

- **Transition words**

  therefore; thus; however; similarly; alternatively

- **Content-specific words**

  cell (science); *era* (social studies); *graph* (math)

- **Difficult verb and tense forms**

  was written by (passive voice); *have voted* (present perfect); *had ended* (past perfect)

- **The language of written instructions**

  compare; define; analyze; calculate; summarize

<u>Home Language Activities</u>

Teachers can use home language activities to help students reinforce their learning of the concepts and meanings of vocabulary and literacy activities. English language learners can participate in a variety of activities such as discussion, telling or reading stories, listening to songs and music, hearing radio or television weather or sports reports, and interviewing family members, and then use those experiences as topics for discussion and sharing in the classroom. Students can transfer their understanding of a word or concept from their home language to English when they have experiences that illustrate meaning. Teachers can find ways to use the home environment as an educational resource by planning activities that involve reading, writing, listening, and speaking about students' family histories, cultures, and experiences.

<u>Technology</u>

Teachers can use various forms of technology (computer, Internet, audio, video recording) to meet the specific and varied needs of English language learners.

For example, you might choose target words and have students use computers to find images that illustrate their meanings.

Creating and Adapting Strategies

A great deal of reading in English, listening to selections read aloud, and conversing in English will help learners acquire thousands of words per year if they are engaged in learning. Continue using the instructional strategies that work, adapt (or discontinue) the ones that are not effective, and try new approaches as needed.

References

August, Diane (Principal Investigator), and T. Shanahan (Panel Chair) (2006). *Developing Literacy in Second-Language Learners: Report of the National Literacy Panel on Language-Minority Children and Youth.* Mahwah, New Jersey: Lawrence Erlbaum Associates.

Blachowicz, Camille L. Z., and Peter Fisher. *Teaching Vocabulary in All Classrooms.* Upper Saddle River, NJ: Prentice Hall, 2002.

Vocabulary Development for Reading Success. Scott Foresman Professional Development Series, Module 6. Glenview, IL: Scott Foresman, 2004.

Effective Comprehension Instruction for English Language Learners

Clear and explicit comprehension instruction is a key component of successful English language development. Traditionally, the main purpose of comprehension instruction has been limited to having students answer assigned questions related to a passage they have read. As a result, what can and should be a complex, analytical process has been diminished by a narrow focus on products. A greater benefit to English language learners, as for all students, is guidance in becoming active readers who are engaged in texts on multiple levels before, during, and after reading.

Jim Cummins identifies conditions that promote engaging with literacy for English language learners and, in fact, for all students. To attain literacy, students must be fully engaged in their reading and writing. Students need to read a variety of texts that reflect children's cultures and languages. Teachers must use strategies that promote a deep understanding of the text. Through engaging students by activating prior knowledge, frontloading to build background, affirming identity, scaffolding the language, and extending language through various experiences, students move from engagement in literacy to achievement in literacy.

Comprehension instruction that will achieve this more sophisticated goal focuses on *metacognition*, the name we give to a good reader's ability to independently reflect on the purpose of reading, select appropriate approaches to texts, ask questions as he or she reads, and actively resolve areas of confusion. Metacognitive strategies such as predicting, questioning, self-monitoring, summarizing, and making inferences should be transferable from one type of text to another. For this reason it is important to introduce these strategies to students using a variety of fiction and nonfiction texts. The following comprehension instruction techniques will help you encourage literacy engagement and the development of metacognition in your students.

What Is Frontloading?

Imagine that you are teaching someone how to bake a cake. If you knew that your pupil had no experience in the kitchen, you would not jump right into the recipe and instructions. Instead, you would start by naming and explaining the key ingredients in the cake—the flour, sugar, baking powder, eggs, and so on. You would demonstrate how to use measuring cups. You might explain how baking differs from frying or boiling. In other words, you would anticipate the knowledge that your budding baker requires in order to be successful at this new task and make sure to introduce that knowledge first. This is the essence of frontloading.

Frontloading for English language learners involves preteaching the vital vocabulary, background concepts, and sometimes the text structures that students need to know before they can understand an upcoming lesson. Prior to a lesson in which students will be reading a story from *Aesop's Fables*, for example, you might choose to frontload the following vocabulary using a graphic organizer.

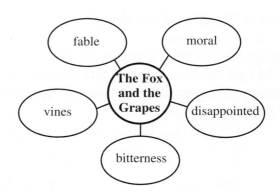

What Is Shared Reading?

Shared reading is reading that is rich with interactions between teacher and students. When using the shared reading model, the goal is to invite students to actively participate in the reading process. This is an excellent opportunity to encourage English language learners to use oral language in a relaxed and informal setting. Use an enlarged text as the central focus as you conduct a shared reading session, so that everyone in the group can clearly see the text. The basic elements of shared reading include:

✓ **Think Alouds:** Model making predictions, asking questions, and drawing conclusions about the text by thinking aloud as you read.

✓ **Guided Discussions:** Using open-ended questions, encourage students to respond to, analyze, and summarize the text.

✓ **Active Participation:** Students can contribute to the reading of the text by chorusing repetitive words or phrases or reading sight words that you point to.

✓ **Multiple Readings:** Return to the same text several times over a few days. Set a focus for each reading such as enjoyment, decoding, comprehension, or vocabulary.

What Is Reciprocal Teaching?

"Reciprocal teaching is best represented as a dialogue between teachers and students in which participants take turns assuming the role of teacher."

— *Annemarie Sullivan Palincsar, instructional researcher*

Reciprocal teaching is an instructional model that focuses on four key comprehension strategies: predicting, question generating, clarifying, and summarizing. First, you explain, discuss, and model the strategies. Then, while working in small groups, students gradually take responsibility for strategies while making their way through a text.

- **Predicting:** Make predictions about what an author will discuss next.
- **Question Generating:** Pose "teacher-like" questions about main ideas in the text.
- **Clarifying:** Notice potential areas of confusion and take steps to clarify them (e.g., reread, identify the definition of a word).
- **Summarizing:** Identify and recap the most important information.

Reciprocal teaching has proven to be of great help in developing the skills of English language learners. Although it can be used with a variety of text types, this technique is especially useful for deepening comprehension of expository text.

References

Cummins, Jim. *Reading Instruction and Reading Achievement Among EL Students* (Research Into Practice monograph). Glenview, IL: Pearson, 2009.

Drucker, M. J. "What Reading Teachers Should Know About ESL Learners." *The Reading Teacher,* 57(1) (2003), pp. 22–29.

Francis, D. J., et al. "Practical Guidelines for the Education of English Language Learners: Research-Based Recommendations for Instruction and Academic Interventions." Houston, TX: Center on Instruction, 2006.

Institute of Education Sciences, National Center for Educational Evaluation and Regional Assistance. "Effective Literacy and English Language Instruction for English Learners in the Elementary Grades." IES Practice Guide, 2007.

Effective Writing Instruction for English Language Learners

The Role of Writing in Language and Literacy Development

Research shows that students acquire language most readily when they are fully involved in all learning activities in the classroom. Classroom activities should integrate reading, writing, listening, and speaking, as these language skills develop interdependently. This approach supports English language development in the context of meaningful instructional content. That is, students will learn to write (in English) about real ideas and things.

Teachers can facilitate students' language learning and literacy development by ensuring that:

- students hear language in natural ways, in real and practical contexts—and write it in structured formats

- activities in which students participate regularly provide opportunities for listening and speaking so students can internalize the language

- opportunities for acquiring new vocabulary are always present in reading activities and environmental print, and are related to the content areas of the curriculum

- opportunities are always available for interesting conversations with English-speaking peers

- mistakes are accepted as part of learning

- students understand why they are being asked to complete various oral communication, reading, and writing tasks

English language learners who are already literate, or are emergent readers and writers in their home languages, no doubt have been influenced by their backgrounds and experiences with writing genres, writing styles, and cultural discourse. By learning more about the characteristics of English language learners' literacy experiences, teachers can recognize when students are transferring what they already know

to their new, early literacy learning in English, and teachers can support these efforts. It is helpful to seek information about students in sensitive ways, appropriately respecting families' privacy and regarding home languages and cultures with respect.

Such efforts to find out students' strengths and needs are worthwhile. For example, teachers who compare spelling patterns between a home language and English will better understand the efforts students make to acquire and write English words. Teachers can point out the differences and similarities so that students can learn to compare the languages and develop metalinguistic understanding about how both languages work. This will help them sort out the ways they can use language in their writing.

ENGLISH	rose
SPANISH	rosa

Young English language learners also are emergent writers. For most children, the line between emergent writing and drawing (that is, art) is not a bold border. It helps learners to write in both words and pictures. Experts in English language learning advise, however, that English language learners who draw too often without writing any words are missing vital opportunities to practice writing in English. Encourage students to write about their pictures.

Scaffolding the Steps of the Writing Process

Writing, whether in a home language or especially in a new language, is the most difficult mode of language use to master (Collier and Ovando, 1998). Each English language learner has a unique background and set of experiences with language, literacy, and culture. Students access writing instruction at varying levels of English proficiency. It is important for teachers to provide each student with challenging work that is appropriate for his or her level of English proficiency and literacy.

By understanding the specific kinds of support English language learners need at each stage of the writing process, teachers can tailor their instruction to fit individual needs. The chart below provides suggestions to help you do this.

	Level I	Level II & III	Level IV & V
	Beginning (little experience in English)	**Intermediate** (conversational but not academic English)	**Advanced/ Advanced High** (gaining skills in academic English)
Prewrite	Allow extra time for prewriting. Use brainstorming. Have student draw or act out ideas. Map, or illustrate and label, words that the student needs.	Allow extra time for prewriting. Use brainstorming. Have student draw and label, or act out and describe, ideas. Help student learn and write the words he or she needs.	Allow extra time for prewriting. Use brainstorming, drawing, word mapping, and story mapping. Help student learn and write the words he or she needs.
Draft	Allow student to dictate, as appropriate. As skills emerge, student writes words and phrases. Accept phonetic invented spelling, but model correct spelling, capitalization, and punctuation.	Student writes words, phrases, and simple sentences. Help student turn phrases into sentences. Accept phonetic invented spelling, but show correct spelling, capitalization, and punctuation.	Student writes words, phrases, and simple sentences. Help student add details to sentences and create paragraphs. Accept phonetic invented spelling, but show correct spelling, capitalization, and punctuation.
Revise	With help, student revises work with the aid of a checklist that has visual clues about each task.	Student revises work with the aid of a checklist that has visual and written clues about each task. Help student incorporate written or oral commentary from teacher in revisions.	Student revises work with the aid of a checklist that has visual and written clues about each task—and asks for clarification. Help student incorporate written or oral comments from teacher in revisions.
Edit	Student sees teacher model how to correct errors and begins to correct errors.	Student corrects errors with help from the teacher.	Student corrects errors with help from the teacher and incorporates teacher's suggestions into writing.
Publish	Student creates final product of writing with teacher's guidance.	Student creates final product of writing with teacher's guidance.	Student creates final product of writing with teacher's guidance.

Structured Writing

Teachers can use **structured writing** to scaffold writing instruction. Structured writing aids include writing/sentence frames and graphic organizers, which help students record and organize their ideas.

Writing Assignments for English Language Learners

There are various kinds of assignments and activities that encourage English language learners to use their background knowledge and previous experiences to connect with the writing process. Establishing a daily or weekly **routine** for these assignments and activities helps cue students about what to expect and provides extra support for participating in classroom instruction.

Teachers can compile a **writing portfolio** to show progress and to facilitate home communication and teacher/student dialogue about writing.

Writing Products

While there are varieties of authentic writing assignments that encourage students to write about their interests and experiences, there are specific genres with which students must become familiar in order to build an understanding of text structures that reflect district and state standards/curriculum frameworks. The following examples suggest ways to approach each genre in relation to English language learners' needs.

Language Experience Approach

Students dictate stories to the teacher (or aide), who writes them down. Students then copy the words that the teacher wrote. In this way, reading and writing become processes directly related to children's experiences. They read and write to express themselves and communicate their experiences.

Dialogue Journals

Dialogue journals develop writing skills and provide authentic communication between a student and teacher. This writing is informal and may include pictures. It allows students to choose topics for writing. The teacher may suggest topics, but the choice is the writer's. The student writes as in conversation with the teacher. The teacher responds to the content of the writing, also in a conversational manner. Writing errors are not explicitly corrected, but the teacher's writing serves as a model (Collier and Ovando, 1998).

Home Literacy Activities

Home literacy activities encourage conversation between students and their families as they read together in their home language and/or in English. If parents are not literate, students can practice reading aloud and discussing stories with them. Teachers can plan activities such as interviewing family members in the home language and then sharing the responses with the class in English.

Students learning to write will benefit from writing in their home language as well as the new language, English. Bilingual parents, staff members, and students can help children write in home languages.

Rubrics to Evaluate Writing

Teachers can use school, district, state, or national standards for English language learners (which are aligned with English Language Arts standards) to create rubrics that adjust expectations for English language learners based on their individual English proficiency levels.

The sample rubric on the following page focuses on one of the traits of good writing: rules (or conventions) of English. It describes what English language learners at various levels (beginning, intermediate, advanced, and advanced high) would be expected to write. Teachers can develop similar evaluation forms that reflect the needs of the school, the grade, and the students involved. Other examples of traits of good writing may include Focus/Ideas, Order, Writer's Voice, Word Choice, and Sentences.

Traits of Good Writing: Rules (English Language Learners)

	Level	Capitalization	Punctuation	Sentence Structure and Grammar	Spelling
Beginning (little experience in English)	1	Uses capitalization when writing one's own name.	Adds a period to the end of a sentence and a question mark to the end of a question.	Begins to use some standard word order, with mostly inconsistent grammatical forms (for example, subject/verb agreement).	Produces some independent writing that includes inconsistent spelling.
Intermediate/ Advanced (conversational but not academic English)	2–4	Uses capitalization to begin sentences and proper nouns.	Produces independent writing that may include some inconsistent use of periods and question marks.	Uses standard word order but may use inconsistent grammatical forms.	Produces independent writing that includes some misspellings.
Advanced High (gaining skills in academic English)	5	Produces independent writing with consistent use of correct capitalization.	Produces independent writing with generally consistent use of correct punctuation.	Uses complete sentences and generally correct word order.	Produces independent writing with consistent use of correct spelling.

References

August, Diane (Principal Investigator), and T. Shanahan (Panel Chair) (2006). *Developing Literacy in Second-Language Learners: Report of the National Literacy Panel on Language-Minority Children and Youth.* Mahwah, New Jersey: Lawrence Erlbaum Associates.

Collier, V. P., and C. J. Ovando (1998). *Bilingual and ESL Classrooms: Teaching in Multicultural Contexts.* Boston, MA: McGraw Hill.

Echevarria, J.; M. Vogt; and D. Short (2004). *Making Content Comprehensible for English Learners: The SIOP Model.* Boston: Allyn & Bacon.

Fillmore, L. W., and C. E. Snow (2000). "*What Teachers Need to Know About Language.*" Washington, DC: ERIC Clearinghouse on Languages and Linguistics.

English Language Learners and Assessment

Assessment Needs of Diverse Learners

Because English language learners make up a dynamic group of learners who enter school with a wide range of linguistic, cultural, and learning experiences, it is important for teachers to learn about the unique background of each individual learner. Overall, assessment can provide important information about students' learning that can be used to plan appropriate and meaningful instruction. However, the kinds of assessment, the purposes for which they are used, and how the results are evaluated can directly impact how meaningful the assessments are (Cummins, 1981).

High-stakes Testing vs. Authentic Assessment

While so-called "high-stakes" testing has become increasingly influential, high-profile tests can be difficult for English language learners because they require proficiency in academic English, understanding of grade-level subject matter, and an understanding of cultural contexts. While high-stakes test results in the United States influence instructional decisions made in schools, these results often do not reflect what English language learners know. Consequently, the instructional decisions based on test results often do not reflect the specific learning needs of English language learners (Bielenberg and Fillmore, 2005).

It is important to find a variety of ways to assess English language learners that show what each learner is able to do. Focusing on what students already know—and what they are learning but have not mastered—helps teachers identify specific educational needs and enables educators to build their ongoing instruction upon all the resources, experiences, and abilities that English language learners bring to school. Authentic assessment, or ongoing classroom-

based (often informal) assessment of students by teachers, allows students to show their strengths. Ongoing assessment also provides teachers with an accurate, dynamic picture of how to plan instruction and provide feedback in ways that meet the changing learning needs of each student (García, 1994).

Outcome-based/norm-referenced tests are different from ongoing authentic assessment because they evaluate, or make a judgment about, the performance of a student at a given time, while authentic assessment informs both teachers and students about day-to-day learning and provides feedback about how to proceed in order to meet the needs of individual learners.

English language learners must be taught test-taking strategies and must build background about the language and procedures of test taking. Use the suggestions below when preparing English language learners, who may not be experienced with the specialized language and implications of standardized tests. (Bielenberg and Fillmore, 2005):

- Point out text structures and conceptual references used in tests.
- Point out difficult language structures, and provide sufficient practice before the test.
- Preteach basic and content-area vocabulary.
- Build background and knowledge about test taking and procedural language.

Preteach Vocabulary and Question Types

- Make a T-chart to show examples of the question types students will find on tests. Explain what the structures mean and what they ask test-takers to do.
- Make a short list of test vocabulary, phrases, and instructions found on tests—such as *choose, write, fill in the circle, less than,* and *greater than.* Illustrate what these expressions ask students to do.

Example:

TEST DIRECTIONS	WHAT SHOULD I DO?
<u>Choose</u> the word that goes in the <u>blank</u>. <u>Mark</u> your answer. 1. Nancy rides her _____. O book O bike O store O gloves	• **Choose** = pick, decide on one • **Blank** = the line 1. Nancy rides her _____. • **Mark** = use pencil to fill in the circle

Example:

INSTRUCTIONS	WHAT SHOULD I DO?		
Find the **sum.**	Add numbers, + 10 + 1 = 11		
Compare the numbers using **>** , **<** , or **=**	<	less than	1 < 10
	>	greater than	9 > 2
	=	equals	3 = 3

Reading Fluency and Comprehension Assessment

Authentic assessment focuses on teachers making informed decisions based on authentic literacy tasks within the classroom context that reflect individual student's progress and learning (García, 1994). Finding ways to help English language learners develop reading fluency means finding out if students really comprehend what they read, rather than just decode words.

Student's English language proficiency levels, the kinds of literacy and learning experiences students have had, and how familiar they are with the topic of the reading passage will affect how much they struggle with understanding what they read. Literature also can be challenging for English language learners because of the use of figurative language, including metaphors, similes, and symbolism. Check students' reading comprehension and understanding of concepts such as *setting, characters, plot, beginning, middle,* and *end.*

When assessing fluency and comprehension, it is helpful for teachers to learn how students' home literacy and languages affect their learning in English. English language learners may draw on what they already know; for example, an English language learner whose home language is Spanish may use Spanish spelling patterns and/or phonetics when reading or writing words in English. Recognizing the influence of the home language, and the student's reliance upon the literacy skills and strategies he or she knows in the home language, will help teachers not only assess more accurately, but know how to point out similarities and differences between English and the home language as a way to develop awareness about how different languages are related. This helps develop metalinguistic awareness, or thinking about how language works.

Teachers must ultimately use all they know about each student's English proficiency and literacy skills in order to:

- monitor progress
- organize students in groups for effective learning
- differentiate instruction

Assessing English language learners and learning about their cultural, linguistic, and learning experiences can help teachers plan instruction that is comprehensible and challenging.

Scaffolding High-stakes Testing

While "high-stakes" testing presents various challenges for English language learners, there are various test-taking strategies that teachers can use to support students in preparing for eventual mastery of standardized testing. Showing students ways in which they can recognize test formats and decode the questions of a test will help them figure out what each question is asking them to do.

Assessment Accommodations for English Language Learners

While English language learners need time to acquire the academic language necessary to be able to practice and perform well on standardized tests in English, there are some accommodations that may support their attempts at extracting meaning from test language, questions, and passages. Accommodations for English language learners may include the following:

- Provide English language learners with extra time to complete the test.
- Allow the use of a bilingual dictionary or a picture dictionary to clarify words that may hinder comprehension.
- Read the question aloud in some cases.

References

August, D., and K. Hakuta. *Improving Schooling for Language Minority Children: A Research Agenda.* Washington, DC: National Academy Press, 1997.

Bielenberg, B., and L. W. Fillmore. "The English They Need for the Test." *Educational Leadership,* 62(4) (2004/2005), pp. 45–49.

Cummins, J. "The Role of Primary Language Development in Promoting Educational Success for Language Minority Students." *Schooling and Language Minority Students: A Theoretical Framework.* Sacramento, CA: California Department of Education, 1981.

García, G. E. "Assessing the Literacy Development of Second Language Students: A Focus on Authentic Assessment" in K. Spangenbergk-Urbschat and R. Pritchard, eds. *Kids Come in All Languages: Reading Instruction for ESL Students,* pp. 180–205. Newark, DE: International Reading Association, 1994.

Scott Foresman Reading Street
Overview of Weekly Support for English Language Learners

The ELL Handbook provides weekly lesson materials to support English language learners with scaffolded and leveled comprehension and vocabulary instruction for language development. It builds on the Student Edition and on literacy instruction in the Teacher's Edition. Each strand contains a wide variety of activities that promote literacy attainment for your English language learners.

Weekly Planners offer a quick reference to the ELL Support materials for each lesson of the year.

Weekly Resources Guide for English Language Learner Support

Unit 2, Week 1 **At the Beach**

For this week's content and language objectives, see p. 59e.

This symbol indicates leveled instruction to address language proficiency levels.

Instructional Strand	Day 1	Day 2	Day 3	Day 4	Day 5
Concept Development/Academic Language	**TEACHER'S EDITION** • Academic Language, p. DI•16 • Concept Development, p. DI•16 • Anchored Talk, pp. 176j—176–177 • Preteach Academic Vocabulary, p. 179a • Concept Talk Video **ELL HANDBOOK** • Hear It, See It, Say It, Use It, pp. xxxvi–xxxvii • ELL Poster Talk, Concept Talk, p. 59c **ELL POSTER 6** • Day 1 Activities	**TEACHER'S EDITION** • Academic Language, p. DI•16 • Concept Development, p. DI•16 • Anchored Talk, p. 180a • Concept Talk Video **ELL HANDBOOK** • ELL Poster Talk, Concept Talk, p. 59c • Concept Talk Video Routine, p. 477 **ELL POSTER 6** • Day 2 Activities	**TEACHER'S EDITION** • Academic Language, p. DI•16 • Concept Development, p. DI•16 • Anchored Talk, p. 190a • Concept Talk Video **ELL HANDBOOK** • ELL Poster Talk, Concept Talk, p. 59c **ELL POSTER 6** • Day 3 Activities	**TEACHER'S EDITION** • Academic Language, p. DI•16 • Concept Development, p. DI•16 • Anchored Talk, p. 198a • Concept Talk Video **ELL HANDBOOK** • ELL Poster Talk, Concept Talk, p. 59c **ELL POSTER 6** • Day 4 Activities	**TEACHER'S EDITION** • Academic Language, p. DI•16 • Concept Development, p. DI•16 • Concept Talk Video **ELL HANDBOOK** • ELL Poster Talk, Concept Talk, p. 59c **ELL POSTER 6** • Day 5 Activities
Phonics and Spelling	**TEACHER'S EDITION** • Phonics and Spelling, p. DI•20	**TEACHER'S EDITION** • Phonics and Spelling, p. DI•20	**ELL HANDBOOK** • Phonics Transition Lesson, pp. 224, 227	**ELL HANDBOOK** • Phonics Transition Lesson, pp. 224, 227	**TEACHER'S EDITION** • Phonics and Spelling, p. DI•20
Listening Comprehension	**TEACHER'S EDITION** • Modified Read Aloud, p. DI•19 • Read Aloud, p. 177b • Concept Talk Video **ELL HANDBOOK** • Concept Talk Video Routine, p. 477	**TEACHER'S EDITION** • Modified Read Aloud, p. DI•19 • AudioText of At the Beach • Concept Talk Video **ELL HANDBOOK** • AudioText CD Routine, p. 477 • Venn Diagram, p. 488	**TEACHER'S EDITION** • AudioText of At the Beach • Concept Talk Video **ELL HANDBOOK** • AudioText CD Routine, p. 477	**TEACHER'S EDITION** • Concept Talk Video	**TEACHER'S EDITION** • Concept Talk Video
Reading Comprehension	**TEACHER'S EDITION** • Preteach Compare and Contrast, p. DI•21	**TEACHER'S EDITION** • Reteach Compare and Contrast, p. DI•21 • Frontloading Reading, p. DI•22 **ELL HANDBOOK** • Picture It! Skill Instruction, pp. 60–60a • Multilingual Summaries, pp. 61–63	**TEACHER'S EDITION** • Sheltered Reading, p. DI•22 **ELL HANDBOOK** • Multilingual Summaries, pp. 61–63	**TEACHER'S EDITION** • ELL/ELD Reader Guided Reading, p. DI•23 **ELL HANDBOOK** • ELL Study Guide, p. 64	**TEACHER'S EDITION** • ELL/ELD Reader Guided Reading, p. DI•23 **ELL HANDBOOK** • ELL Study Guide, p. 64
Vocabulary Basic and Lesson Vocabulary Word Analysis: Compound Words	**TEACHER'S EDITION** • Basic Vocabulary, p. DI•17 • Preteach Lesson Vocabulary, p. DI•17 • Compound Words, p. DI•20 **ELL HANDBOOK** • Word Cards, p. 59 • ELL Vocabulary Routine, p. 471 **ELL POSTER 6** • Day 1 Activities	**TEACHER'S EDITION** • Basic Vocabulary, p. DI•17 • Reteach Lesson Vocabulary, p. DI•18 • Compound Words, p. DI•20 **ELL HANDBOOK** • Word Cards, p. 59 • Multilingual Vocabulary List, p. 433 **ELL POSTER 6** • Day 2 Activities	**TEACHER'S EDITION** **ELL HANDBOOK** • High-Frequency Words Activity Bank, p. 446 **ELL POSTER 6** • Day 3 Activities	**TEACHER'S EDITION** **ELL HANDBOOK** • High-Frequency Words Activity Bank, p. 446	**TEACHER'S EDITION** • Spanish Word Origins, p. 201l **ELL HANDBOOK** • High-Frequency Words Activity Bank, p. 446
Grammar and Conventions	**TEACHER'S EDITION** • Preteach Regular and Irregular Plural Nouns, p. DI•24	**TEACHER'S EDITION** • Reteach Regular and Irregular Plural Nouns, p. DI•24	**TEACHER'S EDITION** • Grammar Jammer **ELL HANDBOOK** • Grammar Transition Lesson, pp. 316, 322 • Grammar Jammer Routine, p. 478	**TEACHER'S EDITION** • Grammar Jammer **ELL HANDBOOK** • Grammar Transition Lesson, pp. 316, 322	**TEACHER'S EDITION** • Grammar Jammer **ELL HANDBOOK** • Grammar Transition Lesson, pp. 316, 322
Writing	**TEACHER'S EDITION** • Descriptive Language, p. DI•25 • Introduce Description, pp. 179e–179f	**TEACHER'S EDITION** • Writing Trait: Focus/Ideas, pp. 189d–189e	**TEACHER'S EDITION** • Let's Write It!, p. 196–197 • Writing Trait: Descriptive Language: The Five Senses, pp. 197a–197b	**TEACHER'S EDITION** • Revising Strategy, pp. 201d–201e	**TEACHER'S EDITION** • Plural Nouns and Quotations, pp. 201p–201q

Copyright © Pearson Education, Inc., or its affiliates. All Rights Reserved. 5

59a *At the Beach* Unit 2, Week 1   *ELL Handbook*

ELL Handbook   Unit 2, Week 1   *At the Beach* **59b**

Weekly Planner

27a Research into Practice

ELL Handbook

Copyright © Pearson Education, Inc., or its affiliates. All Rights Reserved. 5

The daily Concept Development activities activate prior knowledge and build background, scaffold meaning, affirm identity, and develop and extend language.

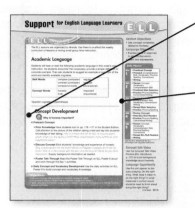

Use the linguistically accommodated questions to reach all language proficiency levels and make personal and cultural connections that validate identity and link academic content with what students already know.

Use the Concept Development section and the Poster in a small group prior to the core lesson to build background and scaffold meaning.

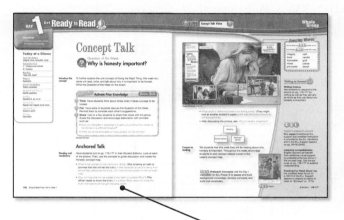

Use the daily activities on the ELL Poster and the Anchored Talk questions in the core lesson to build concept attainment and encourage oral language development and production.

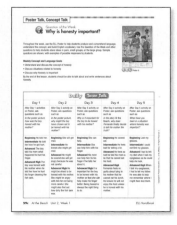

- Use the daily, leveled Poster Talk, Concept Talk in the ELL Handbook and the Team Talk activities in the core lesson to encourage oral language production.

Listening Comprehension

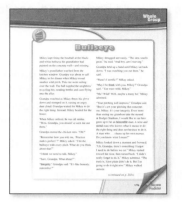

The adapted Read Aloud in the Listening Comprehension section of the ELL Support pages covers the same concept and information as the Read Aloud in the core curriculum.

In order for English language learners to meet grade-level learning expectations, have access to the core curriculum, and develop language, all instruction delivered in English must be linguistically accommodated for all levels of English language proficiency.

For Beginning and Intermediate levels, use the grade-appropriate adapted Read Aloud in place of the regular Read Aloud until students no longer need the linguistic support and modification.

- **First Listening: Listen to Understand** gives students a purpose for listening. The questions are designed to generate interest and help students get the gist of the adapted Read Aloud, so all proficiency levels can achieve success.

- **Second Listening: Listen to Check Understanding** Once students understand the main idea of the adapted Read Aloud, they can listen on subsequent days to clarify understanding of important details of spoken language.

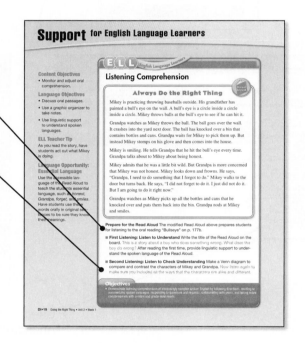

Additional Products

Concept Talk Video

Concept Talk Video Routine

AudioText CD

AudioText Routine

Discrete language skills that English language learners need include knowledge of the letters of the alphabet, familiarity with the sounds represented by letters, the ability to decode words, and the rules and conventions of how words are formed.

The Phonics support lessons work along with the Phonics Transition Lessons to help students learn phonics skills at the same time they are developing basic English vocabulary.

Language Transfer Notes activate prior knowledge about a phonics skill. Relating the skill being taught to a student's home language helps students build on what they already know and affirm their identities.

The flexible bank of Phonics Transition Lessons provides practice for developing and internalizing language at all proficiency levels. The Practice Pages provide visual support and context for the skills.

Additional Products

The Modeled Pronunciation Audio CD and routine offers additional practice with sound-spelling correspondence.

Modeled Pronunciation
Audio CD

English learners need explicit and systematic instruction to acquire both social and academic language for literacy attainment. Students need multiple exposures to new vocabulary through frequent listening, reading, writing, and oral language activities.

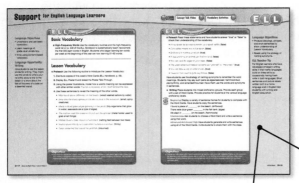

- Vocabulary activities in the ELL Support pages and in the core lessons provide ideas for giving visual, contextual, and linguistic support so students can access grade-level lesson vocabulary.

- Word Analysis lessons from the ELL Support and core lesson pages engage students in figuring out meanings of new words, thereby increasing their comprehension and language production.

- Daily activities in the Poster increase oral and written production of newly acquired vocabulary.

- The Poster Talk, Concept Talk provides leveled support to meet the needs of all students.

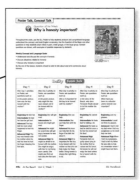

Engaging activities in the core lessons, the ELL Handbook, and the three Comprehension sections of the ELL Support lessons activate prior knowledge, build background, scaffold meaning, affirm identity, and develop and extend language.

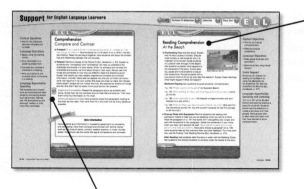

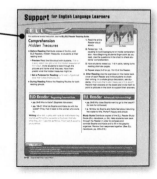

Comprehension activities provide questions that encourage students to use oral language during reading to demonstrate understanding of text and to employ inferential skills.

- The leveled notes in the ELL Support and Picture It! instruction pages provide ideas for differentiating instruction at all proficiency levels.

- The ELD Readers are written for Beginning and Intermediate language proficiency levels, and the ELL Readers are designed for Advanced to Advanced High levels, allowing you to meet the needs of a diverse classroom.

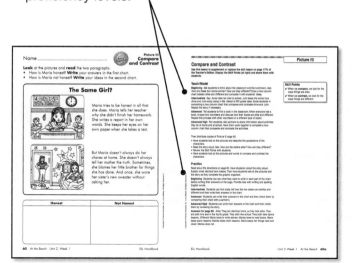

Additional Products

Multilingual Summaries

AudioText CD

AudioText CD Routine

Language Arts

The Grammar and Conventions and Writing lessons provide the systematic instruction that students need at each language proficiency level to scaffold use of increasingly complex grammatical structures in content area reading and writing.

Grammar and Conventions

- The interactive activities are designed so students reuse the language related to each core convention, using different modalities to enhance understanding.

- The flexible bank of Grammar Transition Lessons leads students in transferring knowledge from their home languages to English and guides language development.

Writing

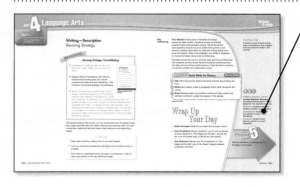

- ELL Notes throughout the core Language Arts pages provide ideas to support all levels of English language learners in prewriting, editing, revising, and publishing writing pieces.

- The writing model, sentence frames, and leveled writing prompts guide and encourage oral and written language production for all levels of English proficiency.

Concept Talk Video

- Use the Concept Talk Video to activate an engaging discussion about the weekly concept. Use the Concept Talk Video Routine found in the ELL Handbook to guide students' understanding.

AudioText CD

- Students can build fluency and comprehension and prepare for reading the main selection by using the AudioText CD and the AudioText CD Routine.

I love my dog Thunder.

Grammar Jammer

- Use the Grammar Jammer for additional practice with the target skill. For suggestions on how to use this learning tool, see the Grammar Jammer Routine in the ELL Handbook.

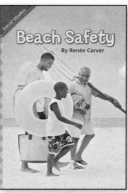

Concept Literacy Reader

- Use the Concept Literacy Reader for additional support to develop the weekly concept.

Part 2
English Language Support

Contents

Unit 1

Unit 2

Unit 3

Unit 4

Unit 5

Unit 6

Weekly Resources Guide for English Language Learner Support

For this week's content and language objectives, see p. 29e.

Instructional Strand	Day 1	Day 2
Concept Development/Academic Language	TEACHER'S EDITION • Academic Language, p. DI•16 • Concept Development, p. DI•16 • Anchored Talk, pp. 20j—20–21 • Preteach Academic Vocabulary, p. 23a • Concept Talk Video ELL HANDBOOK • Hear It, See It, Say It, Use It, pp. xxxvi–xxxvii • ELL Poster Talk, Concept Talk, p. 29c ELL POSTER 1 • Day 1 Activities	TEACHER'S EDITION • Academic Language, p. DI•16 • Concept Development, p. DI•16 • Anchored Talk, p. 24a • Concept Talk Video ELL HANDBOOK • ELL Poster Talk, Concept Talk, p. 29c • Concept Talk Video Routine, p. 477 ELL POSTER 1 • Day 2 Activities
Phonics and Spelling	TEACHER'S EDITION • Phonics and Spelling, p. DI•20	TEACHER'S EDITION • Phonics and Spelling, p. DI•20
Listening Comprehension	TEACHER'S EDITION • Modified Read Aloud, p. DI•19 • Read Aloud, p. 21b • Concept Talk Video ELL HANDBOOK • Concept Talk Video Routine, p. 477	TEACHER'S EDITION • Modified Read Aloud, p. DI•19 • AudioText of *Red Kayak* • Concept Talk Video ELL HANDBOOK • AudioText CD Routine, p. 477 • Story Map A, p. 483
Reading Comprehension	TEACHER'S EDITION • Preteach Characters and Plot, p. DI•21	TEACHER'S EDITION • Reteach Characters and Plot, p. DI•21 • Frontloading Reading, p. DI•22 ELL HANDBOOK • Picture It! Skill Instruction, pp. 30–30a • Multilingual Summaries, pp. 31–33
Vocabulary **Basic and Lesson Vocabulary** **Word Analysis: Suffix -*ly***	TEACHER'S EDITION • Basic Vocabulary, p. DI•17 • Preteach Lesson Vocabulary, p. DI•17 • Suffix -*ly*, p. DI•20 ELL HANDBOOK • Word Cards, p. 29 • ELL Vocabulary Routine, p. 471 ELL POSTER 1 • Day 1 Activities	TEACHER'S EDITION • Basic Vocabulary, p. DI•17 • Reteach Lesson Vocabulary, p. DI•18 • Suffix -*ly*, p. DI•20 ELL HANDBOOK • Word Cards, p. 29 • Multilingual Vocabulary List, p. 431 ELL POSTER 1 • Day 2 Activities
Grammar and Conventions	TEACHER'S EDITION • Preteach Four Kinds of Sentences, p. DI•24	TEACHER'S EDITION • Teach Four Kinds of Sentences, p. DI•24
Writing	TEACHER'S EDITION • Sequence/Order, p. DI•25 • Introduce Directions, pp. 23e–23f	TEACHER'S EDITION • Writing Trait: Organization, pp. 33d–33e

This symbol indicates leveled instruction to address language proficiency levels.

Day 3	Day 4	Day 5
TEACHER'S EDITION • Academic Language, p. DI•16 • Concept Development, p. DI•16 • Anchored Talk, p. 34a • Concept Talk Video **ELL HANDBOOK** • ELL Poster Talk, Concept Talk, p. 29c **ELL POSTER 1** • Day 3 Activities	**TEACHER'S EDITION** • Academic Language, p. DI•16 • Concept Development, p. DI•16 • Anchored Talk, p. 46a • Concept Talk Video **ELL HANDBOOK** • ELL Poster Talk, Concept Talk, p. 29c **ELL POSTER 1** • Day 4 Activities	**TEACHER'S EDITION** • Academic Language, p. DI•16 • Concept Development, p. DI•16 • Concept Talk Video **ELL HANDBOOK** • ELL Poster Talk, Concept Talk, p. 29c **ELL POSTER 1** • Day 5 Activities
		TEACHER'S EDITION • Phonics and Spelling, p. DI•20
ELL HANDBOOK • Phonics Transition Lesson, pp. 232, 236, 246–252	**ELL HANDBOOK** • Phonics Transition Lesson, pp. 232, 236, 246–252	
TEACHER'S EDITION • AudioText of *Red Kayak* • Concept Talk Video **ELL HANDBOOK** • AudioText CD Routine, p. 477	**TEACHER'S EDITION** • Concept Talk Video	**TEACHER'S EDITION** • Concept Talk Video
TEACHER'S EDITION • Sheltered Reading, p. DI•22 **ELL HANDBOOK** • Multilingual Summaries, pp. 31–33	**TEACHER'S EDITION** • ELL/ELD Reader Guided Reading, p. DI•23 **ELL HANDBOOK** • ELL Study Guide, p. 34	**TEACHER'S EDITION** • ELL/ELD Reader Guided Reading, p. DI•23 **ELL HANDBOOK** • ELL Study Guide, p. 34
		TEACHER'S EDITION • Suffix -*ly*, p. 49i
ELL HANDBOOK • High-Frequency Words Activity Bank, p. 446 **ELL POSTER 1** • Day 3 Activities	**ELL HANDBOOK** • High-Frequency Words Activity Bank, p. 446	**ELL HANDBOOK** • High-Frequency Words Activity Bank, p. 446
TEACHER'S EDITION • Grammar Jammer **ELL HANDBOOK** • Grammar Transition Lesson, pp. 342–343, 352–354 • Grammar Jammer Routine, p. 478	**TEACHER'S EDITION** • Grammar Jammer **ELL HANDBOOK** • Grammar Transition Lesson, pp. 342–343, 352–354	**TEACHER'S EDITION** • Grammar Jammer **ELL HANDBOOK** • Grammar Transition Lesson, pp. 342–343, 352–354
TEACHER'S EDITION • Let's Write It!, p. 44–45 • Writer's Craft: Sequence, pp. 45a–45b	**TEACHER'S EDITION** • Revising Strategy, pp. 49d–49e	**TEACHER'S EDITION** • Sentences, pp. 49p–49q

Question of the Week
What inspires people to act courageously?

Throughout the week, use the ELL Poster to help students produce and comprehend language, understand the concept, and build English vocabulary. Use the Question of the Week and other questions to help students share ideas in pairs, small groups, or the large group. Sample questions are shown, with examples of possible responses by students.

Weekly Concept and Language Goals

• Explain why people act courageously

• Discuss how courageous people act in emergencies

• Name emergency service jobs

By the end of the lesson, students should be able to talk about and write sentences about something courageous.

E L L Poster 1

Daily Team Talk

Day 1	Day 2	Day 3	Day 4	Day 5
After Day 1 activities on Poster, ask questions such as *In the poster picture, why was the situation the park ranger remembers an emergency?*	After Day 2 activity on Poster, ask questions such as *In the poster picture, how did the park ranger save the man drowning in the river?*	After Day 3 activity on Poster, ask questions such as *Why do you think the park ranger acted so courageously in the emergency situation?*	After Day 4 activity on Poster, ask questions such as *Why doesn't the park ranger want the boaters to launch their boat here?*	After Day 5 activity on Poster, ask questions such as *Besides park ranger, what other emergency service jobs do you know about?*
Beginning He fell in. **Intermediate** He fell into the river. **Advanced** The man fell into the river. She had to save him. **Advanced High** The park ranger had to save the man who had fallen into the river. He might have drowned if she had not saved him.	**Beginning** She got him out. **Intermediate** She swam to him and got him out. **Advanced** She saved him by swimming in the river and pulling him out. **Advanced High** The park ranger jumped into the river, swam over to the man, and pulled him out. She gave him chest compressions to help him breathe.	**Beginning** To help him. **Intermediate** She wanted to save him. **Advanced** She wanted to do what she could to save his life. **Advanced High** The park ranger acted courageously because she wanted to save the man from drowning.	**Beginning** She remembers. **Intermediate** She does not want them falling in. **Advanced** She does not want the boaters to get hurt. **Advanced High** The park ranger does not want the boaters to get hurt, like the man she rescued.	**Beginning** Police and fireman. **Intermediate** Firefighters and police help people. **Advanced** Ambulance workers, firefighters, and the police all help save people. **Advanced High** Some emergency service jobs are police officer, paramedic, and firefighter.

This Week's Materials

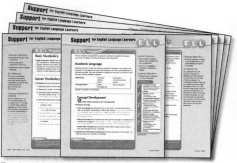

Teacher's Edition pages 20j–49q

See the support for English language learners throughout the lesson, including ELL strategies and scaffolded activities at points of use.

Teacher's Edition pages DI•16–DI•25

Differentiated Instruction for English language learners provides daily group activities that "frontload," or preteach, core instruction.

ELL Handbook pp. 29a–34

Find additional lesson materials that support the core lesson and the ELL instructional pages.

Poster 1

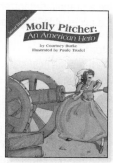

ELL Reader 5.1.1

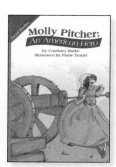

ELD Reader 5.1.1

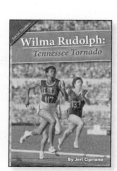

Concept Literacy Reader

ELD, ELL Reader Teaching Guide

Concept Literacy Reader Teaching Guide

Technology

Online Teacher's Edition Use the digital version of the core Teacher's Edition for planning and instruction.

eReaders
This week's ELL and ELD Readers and Concept Literacy Reader are also available in digital format.

This Week's Content and Language Objectives by Strand

Concept Development/ Academic Language What inspires people to act courageously?	**Content Objectives** • Use concept vocabulary related to how people can act courageously. • Use prior knowledge to understand meanings in English. **Language Objective** • Express ideas in response to art and discussion.
Phonics and Spelling Short Vowel VCCV, VCV	**Content Objective** • Identify and define words with short vowel sounds in the patterns VCCV and VCV. **Language Objectives** • Distinguish sounds of short and long vowels. • Monitor oral language production and self-correct.
Listening Comprehension Modified Read Aloud: "Kate to the Rescue"	**Content Objective** • Monitor and adjust oral comprehension. **Language Objectives** • Discuss oral passages. • Use a graphic organizer to take notes. • Use accessible language and learn essential language.
Reading Comprehension Characters and Plot	**Content Objectives** • Use the analytical skills of identifying characters and plot. • Monitor and clarify the characters and plot. **Language Objectives** • Retell the characters and plot from a reading. • Identify the characters and plot in a personal event. • Summarize text using visual support. • Respond to complex questions.
Vocabulary Basic and Lesson Vocabulary	**Language Objectives** • Understand and use basic vocabulary. • Learn meanings of grade-level vocabulary. • Understand ideas in spoken language. • Produce drawings, phrases, or short sentences to show understanding of Lesson Vocabulary.
Word Analysis Suffix: –ly	**Content Objective** • Identify words with the suffix –ly. **Language Objective** • Discuss the meaning of words with the suffix –ly.
Grammar and Conventions Four Kinds of Sentences	**Content Objective** • Decode and use the four kinds of sentences. **Language Objectives** • Read and distinguish between the four kinds of sentences. • Write and speak using the four types of sentences.
Writing Sequence/Order	**Content Objective** • Identify the sequence of events in a text. **Language Objectives** • Monitor understanding of spoken language. • Write a paragraph with specificity and detail that explains a sequence.

compressions

grumbled

insistently

intentionally

minute

neutral

normally

Teacher Note: Beginning Teach two to three words. **Intermediate** Teach three to four words. **Advanced** Teach four to five words. **Advanced High** Teach all words.

Name _____

Look at the pictures. **Read** the story.
- **Think** about the characters. **Think** about the plot. What is the problem? What is the solution?
- **Complete** the chart at the bottom of the page.

Last-Minute Drama

It was the night of the school play. Ana had worked hard. Everything was ready. Then Mr. Lopez told her the bad news. Mai was sick! And Mai was the star of the show!

"What are we going to do?" Ana said. "Who can learn Mai's part right now?"

"I think I know one person who can play the part," Mr. Lopez said. "You."

Ana did know the lines. "But who will be the stage manager?" she asked. "I will," said Mr. Lopez. "You already did most of the work. It will be easy."

Mr. Lopez was wrong about one thing: his new job was not easy. But he and Ana made it through. The play was saved!

Characters	Problem	Solution

ELL Handbook

Plot and Character

Use this lesson to supplement or replace the skill lesson on page 21c of the Teacher's Edition. Display the Skill Points (at right) and share them with students.

Teach/Model

Beginning Say: *Listen to the beginning of a story: Abby needs a job. She wants to earn money to buy a new bike. She looks in the paper, but she doesn't find any jobs for kids. What can she do?* Ask students to identify the character and Abby's problem. Have them tell something about Abby based on her actions.

Intermediate Say: *Reva's piano recital is in one week. Every night after she finishes her homework, she practices for two hours. The night before her recital, Reva can't find her music.* Ask: *What is Reva's problem? What do Reva's actions tell you about her?* Then have students decide how to end the story by suggesting a solution to her problem.

Advanced Say: *James makes an announcement to his class. He says that he can help anyone with his or her math homework. Hannah is relieved to hear this. She asks James for help.* Ask: *What do James's and Hannah's actions tell about them?* (James likes to help others. Hannah is not good at math.)

Advanced High Create a group story. Write the first sentence on the board. For example: *Jesse knew today was going to be a good day.* Ask students to continue the story. Remind them to include a problem and solution.

Then distribute copies of Picture It! page 30.

- Tell students to look at and describe each picture. Ask them to use the pictures to make a guess about the problem at the beginning of the story.
- Review the Skill Points with students.
- Read the story. Ask: *What was the problem? What was the solution?*

Practice

Read aloud the directions on page 30. Have volunteers reread each part aloud. Explain what a stage manager does. Then have students look at the pictures and the story as they complete the graphic organizer.

Beginning Students can first say what they want to write and then write words and phrases in the boxes. Provide help with English words and writing.

Intermediate Students can first say their answers and then write sentences in the boxes. Provide help with English words and writing.

Advanced Students can write their answers in the boxes and then check them by discussing them with a partner.

Advanced High Students can write their answers in the boxes and then tell what a character is like based on what the character says or does.

Answers for page 30: *Characters:* Ana, Mr. Lopez, Mai; *Problem:* Mai was sick, so Ana must play her part in the show. *Solution:* Mr. Lopez takes the role of stage manager, and Ana plays Mai's part.

> ### Skill Points
> ✔ The **plot** of a story is what happens. A story usually has a problem and a solution.
> ✔ **Characters** are the people in the story. You can tell what characters are like from what they do and say.

Multilingual Summaries

Red Kayak

Brady scans the shoreline for a red kayak and Mr. DiAngelo's wife and son. Brady's mom calls and tells him they found Mrs. DiAngelo. They haven't found Ben.

Ben is somewhere in the water with only a life jacket. It is cold. Brady and Tilly continue their search. Tilly begins to bark towards the riverbank. They find Ben caught on a piling in the water.

Brady remembers the emergency ABC's. Brady checks Ben's airway and checks his breathing. Ben isn't breathing. Brady does CPR and heads his boat downstream. They reach the landing. Carl and Jimmy get Ben into the ambulance. Ben has a pulse. Brady heads home. He knows that he will never be the same person.

Spanish

El kayac rojo

Brady busca en la costa un kayak rojo y a la esposa e hijo del señor DiAngelo. La madre de Brady llama y le cuenta que encontraron a la señora DiAngelo. Ellos no han encontrado a Ben.

Ben se encuentra bajo el agua con un salvavidas solamente. Hace frío. Brady y Tilly continúan su búsqueda. Tilly comienza a ladrar hacia el banco de arena. Luego encontraron a Ben en una parte profunda del agua.

Brady recuerda los primeros auxilios. Brady revisa las vías respiratorias de Ben y también su respiración. Ben no está respirando. Brady le da resucitación cardio-pulmonar y dirige su bote río abajo. Llegan a tierra. Carl y Jimmy meten a Ben dentro de la ambulancia. Ben todavía tiene pulso. Brady se dirige a su casa. Él sabe que jamás volverá a ser el mismo.

Multilingual Summaries

Chinese

紅色小船

布萊迪沿著河岸尋找一艘紅色小船與迪安吉羅先生的太太和兒子。 布萊迪的媽媽打電話給他，跟他說他們已經找到了迪安吉羅太太，但是他們沒找到班。

不知道班身在水上何處，而且他身上只穿了一件救生衣。 天氣很冷。布萊迪和提利繼續尋找班。 提利開始對著河岸大叫起來。 他們發現班被困在了水裡的椿材上。

布萊迪想起了急救口訣。他檢查班的氣道和呼吸。 班沒有呼吸。 布萊迪幫班進行 CPR 急救，並把他的船往下游開。 他們到達了岸邊。 卡爾和吉米把班送上了救護車。 班還有脈搏。 布萊迪回家了。 他知道他不再是以前的布萊迪了。

Vietnamese

Chiếc Thuyền Chèo Màu Đỏ

Brady quét một vòng bờ sông để tìm chiếc thuyền chèo màu đỏ có vợ và con của ông DiAngelo trong đó. Mẹ Brady gọi và cho nó biết là đã tìm được bà DiAngelo. Nhưng họ vẫn chưa tìm được Ben.

Ben có thể đang ở nơi nào trên mặt nước với vỏn vẹn cái áo phao trong mình. Trời đang lạnh. Brady và Tilly tiếp tục tìm kiếm. Chợt Tilly la to về hướng bờ sông. Họ tìm thấy Ben bị vướng trên đống đá trong nước.

Brady nhớ đến trình tự cấp cứu ABC đã học. Brady xem xét đường hô hấp của Ben và nhịp thở của em. Ben không còn thở. Brady vội vã làm hô hấp nhân tạo và chèo xuồng xuôi dòng nước. Họ đến được bờ. Carl và Jimmy để Ben vào xe cứu thương. Mạch của Ben đập trở lại. Brady quay về nhà. Em biết rằng em sẽ không bao giờ còn là con người như trước nữa.

Multilingual Summaries

빨간 카약

브래디가 빨간 카약과 디안젤로 씨의 부인과 아들을 찾아 강변을 뒤진다. 브래디의 엄마가 그를 불러서 디안젤로 씨의 아들을 찾았다고 말한다. 아직 벤은 찾지 못했다.

벤은 구명조끼만을 입은 채 물 속 어딘가에 있다. 물이 차다. 브래디와 틸리가 탐색을 계속한다. 틸리가 강둑을 향해 짖기 시작한다. 그들은 물 속의 말뚝에 매달려 있는 벤을 발견한다.

브래디가 응급 구조 순서를 기억해낸다. 브래디는 벤의 기도를 살피고 숨을 쉬는지 살펴본다. 벤이 숨을 쉬지 않는다. 브래디가 심폐소생술을 하고 하류로 배를 향한다. 상륙한 후 칼과 지미가 벤을 구급차에 싣는다. 벤의 맥박이 뛴다. 브래디는 집으로 간다. 그는 자신이 앞으로 달라질 거라고 생각한다.

Lub Kayak Liab

Brady saib taug tus ntug dej puas pom lub kayak liab liab thiab Mr. DiAngelo tus poj niam thiab tus tub. Brady niam hu thiab qhia rau nws hais tias lawv nriav tau Mrs. DiAngelo lawm. Lawv tsis tau pom Ben.

Ben yeej tseem nyob hauv hav dej nrog nws lub tsho ntab. Nws no heev. Brady thiab Tilly tseem pheej nriav mus. Tilly pib tom mus rau tim sab ntug dej. Nkawd thiaj pom Ben raug ib co khib nyiab mus tsuam tas lawm.

Brady nco qab txog nws cov kev pab cawm neeg ABC. Brady khuaj Ben txoj thiab khuaj saib nws puas ua pa lawm. Ben tsis ua pa lawm. Brady pib ua CPR thiab nws lub tob hau tso nris hav. Lawv los txog tim ntug. Carl thiab Jimmy nqa Ben mus rau hauv lub luv hoo maum. Ben cov leeg tseem ntoj. Brady mus tsev lawm. Nws paub hais tias nws yuav tsis yog tus neeg qub lawm.

Name_____

- **Read** *Molly Pitcher* again.
- Use the information from the story to **complete** the chart below. The first one has been done for you.

Who?	Molly Pitcher or Mary Hays
What?	
When?	
Where?	
Why?	

Family Link

The hero of this story is Molly Pitcher. Who is your hero? Talk to family members about your heroes.

Weekly Resources Guide for English Language Learner Support

For this week's content and language objectives, see p. 35e.

Instructional Strand	Day 1	Day 2
Concept Development/Academic Language	**TEACHER'S EDITION** • Academic Language, p. DI•41 • Concept Development, p. DI•41 • Anchored Talk, pp. 50j—50–51 • Preteach Academic Vocabulary, p. 53a • Concept Talk Video **ELL HANDBOOK** • Hear It, See It, Say It, Use It, pp. xxxvi–xxxvii • ELL Poster Talk, Concept Talk, p. 35c **ELL POSTER 2** • Day 1 Activities	**TEACHER'S EDITION** • Academic Language, p. DI•41 • Concept Development, p. DI•41 • Anchored Talk, p. 54a • Concept Talk Video **ELL HANDBOOK** • ELL Poster Talk, Concept Talk, p. 35c • Concept Talk Video Routine, p. 477 **ELL POSTER 2** • Day 2 Activities
Phonics and Spelling	**TEACHER'S EDITION** • Phonics and Spelling, p. DI•45	**TEACHER'S EDITION** • Phonics and Spelling, p. DI•45
Listening Comprehension	**TEACHER'S EDITION** • Modified Read Aloud, p. DI•44 • Read Aloud, p. 51b • Concept Talk Video **ELL HANDBOOK** • Concept Talk Video Routine, p. 477	**TEACHER'S EDITION** • Modified Read Aloud, p. DI•44 • AudioText of *Thunder Rose* • Concept Talk Video **ELL HANDBOOK** • AudioText CD Routine, p. 477 • K-W-L Chart, p. 480
Reading Comprehension	**TEACHER'S EDITION** • Preteach Cause and Effect, p. DI•46	**TEACHER'S EDITION** • Reteach Cause and Effect, p. DI•46 • Frontloading Reading, p. DI•47 **ELL HANDBOOK** • Picture It! Skill Instruction, pp. 36–36a • Multilingual Summaries, pp. 37–39
Vocabulary **Basic and Lesson Vocabulary** **Word Analysis: Latin Roots**	**TEACHER'S EDITION** • Basic Vocabulary, p. DI•42 • Preteach Lesson Vocabulary, p. DI•42 • Latin Roots, p. DI•45 **ELL HANDBOOK** • Word Cards, p. 35 • ELL Vocabulary Routine, p. 471 **ELL POSTER 2** • Day 1 Activities	**TEACHER'S EDITION** • Basic Vocabulary, p. DI•42 • Reteach Lesson Vocabulary, p. DI•43 • Latin Roots, p. DI•45 **ELL HANDBOOK** • Word Cards, p. 35 • Multilingual Vocabulary List, p. 431 **ELL POSTER 2** • Day 2 Activities
Grammar and Conventions	**TEACHER'S EDITION** • Teach Subjects and Predicates, p. DI•49	**TEACHER'S EDITION** • Reteach Subjects and Predicates, p. DI•49
Writing	**TEACHER'S EDITION** • Sensory Details, p. DI•50 • Writing for Tests: Tall Tale, pp. 53e–53f	**TEACHER'S EDITION** • Writing for Tests: Tall Tale, pp. 65d–65e

This symbol indicates leveled instruction to address language proficiency levels.

Day 3	Day 4	Day 5
TEACHER'S EDITION • Academic Language, p. DI•41 • Concept Development, p. DI•41 • Anchored Talk, p. 66a • Concept Talk Video **ELL HANDBOOK** • ELL Poster Talk, Concept Talk, p. 35c **ELL POSTER 2** • Day 3 Activities	**TEACHER'S EDITION** • Academic Language, p. DI•41 • Concept Development, p. DI•41 • Anchored Talk, p. 78a • Concept Talk Video **ELL HANDBOOK** • ELL Poster Talk, Concept Talk, p. 35c **ELL POSTER 2** • Day 4 Activities	**TEACHER'S EDITION** • Academic Language, p. DI•41 • Concept Development, p. DI•41 • Concept Talk Video **ELL HANDBOOK** • ELL Poster Talk, Concept Talk, p. 35c **ELL POSTER 2** • Day 5 Activities
		TEACHER'S EDITION • Phonics and Spelling, p. DI•45
ELL HANDBOOK • Phonics Transition Lesson, pp. 232, 236, 253–259	**ELL HANDBOOK** • Phonics Transition Lesson, pp. 232, 236, 253–259	
TEACHER'S EDITION • AudioText of *Thunder Rose* • Concept Talk Video **ELL HANDBOOK** • AudioText CD Routine, p. 477	**TEACHER'S EDITION** • Concept Talk Video	**TEACHER'S EDITION** • Concept Talk Video
TEACHER'S EDITION • Sheltered Reading, p. DI•47 **ELL HANDBOOK** • Multilingual Summaries, pp. 37–39	**TEACHER'S EDITION** • ELL/ELD Reader Guided Reading, p. DI•48 **ELL HANDBOOK** • ELL Study Guide, p. 40	**TEACHER'S EDITION** • ELL/ELD Reader Guided Reading, p. DI•48 **ELL HANDBOOK** • ELL Study Guide, p. 40
		TEACHER'S EDITION • Greek and Latin Roots, p. 81i
ELL HANDBOOK • High-Frequency Words Activity Bank, p. 446 **ELL POSTER 2** • Day 3 Activities	**ELL HANDBOOK** • High-Frequency Words Activity Bank, p. 446	**ELL HANDBOOK** • High-Frequency Words Activity Bank, p. 446
TEACHER'S EDITION • Grammar Jammer **ELL HANDBOOK** • Grammar Transition Lesson, pp. 340, 348 • Grammar Jammer Routine, p. 478	**TEACHER'S EDITION** • Grammar Jammer **ELL HANDBOOK** • Grammar Transition Lesson, pp. 340, 348	**TEACHER'S EDITION** • Grammar Jammer **ELL HANDBOOK** • Grammar Transition Lesson, pp. 340, 348
TEACHER'S EDITION • Let's Write It!, p. 76–77 • Writing for Tests: Evaluation, pp. 77a–77b	**TEACHER'S EDITION** • Writing for Tests, p. 81d	**TEACHER'S EDITION** • Writing for Tests, pp. 81p–81q

Question of the Week
How can nature challenge us?

ELL Poster 2

Throughout the week, use the ELL Poster to help students produce and comprehend language, understand the concept, and build English vocabulary. Use the Question of the Week and other questions to help students share ideas in pairs, small groups, or the large group. Sample questions are shown, with examples of possible responses by students.

Weekly Concept and Language Goals

• Understand the concept of a challenge in nature

• Discuss tornadoes, floods, and other challenges in nature

• Connect cause and effect to challenges in nature

By the end of the lesson, students should be able to talk about and write sentences about how people survive challenges in nature.

Daily Team Talk

Day 1	Day 2	Day 3	Day 4	Day 5
After Day 1 activities on Poster, ask questions such as *In the poster picture, what kind of storm do you think caused so much damage?*	After Day 2 activity on Poster, ask questions such as *In the poster picture, what is the man on the ladder repairing? Why?*	After Day 3 activity on Poster, ask questions such as *Why do the families have a tent in their backyard?*	After Day 4 activity on Poster, ask questions such as *How do the families respond to the challenge caused by nature?*	After Day 5 activity on Poster, ask questions such as *What challenge caused by nature have you faced?*
Beginning A big storm. **Intermediate** A big storm caused it. **Advanced** A strong storm, such as a tornado, caused the damage. **Advanced High** The damage might have been caused by a tornado, a flood, or another kind of strong storm.	**Beginning** The roof. **Intermediate** He is fixing the roof. **Advanced** The man is repairing the roof. The storm blew it off. **Advanced High** The man on the ladder is repairing the roof of his house. The storm blew off some of the shingles.	**Beginning** They stay there. **Intermediate** They need a place to stay. **Advanced** They need a safe place to stay while they fix their houses after the storm. **Advanced High** The families use the tent as a shelter while they repair the damage to their houses caused by the storm.	**Beginning** They work. **Intermediate** They work hard to fix things. **Advanced** They are working together to clean and fix their homes. **Advanced High** The families respond by working together. They are fixing the damage to one house and cleaning up the mess in their yards.	**Beginning** No power. **Intermediate** The power went out from a storm. **Advanced** Once, a storm caused the electricity to go out for hours. **Advanced High** One time, a huge storm caused the electricity to go out for five hours. My family and I had to come up with things to do so we would not get bored.

This Week's Materials

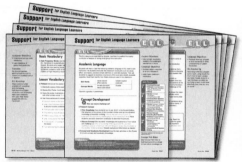

Teacher's Edition pages 50j–81q

See the support for English language learners throughout the lesson, including ELL strategies and scaffolded activities at points of use.

Teacher's Edition pages DI•41–DI•50

Differentiated Instruction for English language learners provides daily group activities that "frontload," or preteach, core instruction.

ELL Handbook pp. 35a–40

Find additional lesson materials that support the core lesson and the ELL instructional pages.

ELL Poster 2

ELL Reader 5.1.2

ELD Reader 5.1.2

Concept Literacy Reader

ELD, ELL Reader Teaching Guide

Concept Literacy Reader Teaching Guide

Technology

Online Teacher's Edition Use the digital version of the core Teacher's Edition for planning and instruction.

eReaders
This week's ELL and ELD Readers and Concept Literacy Reader are also available in digital format.

This Week's Content and Language Objectives by Strand

Concept Development/ Academic Language How can nature challenge us?	**Content Objective** • Use concept vocabulary related to the challenges people find in nature. **Language Objectives** • Express ideas in response to art and discussion. • Learn basic classroom vocabulary.
Phonics and Spelling Long Vowel VCV Patterns	**Content Objectives** • Identify VCV patterns. • Review long vowel VCV patterns. **Language Objective** • Monitor written language production.
Listening Comprehension Modified Read Aloud: "Tornado"	**Content Objective** • Monitor and adjust oral comprehension. **Language Objectives** • Discuss oral passages. • Use accessible language to learn new language. • Use a graphic organizer to take notes. • Use linguistic support to understand spoken language.
Reading Comprehension Cause and Effect	**Content Objectives** • Distinguish between cause and effect. • Identify causes and effects to aid comprehension. • Monitor and adjust comprehension. **Language Objectives** • Internalize academic language relating to causes and effects. • Read grade-level text at an acceptable rate. • Summarize text using visual support.
Vocabulary Basic and Lesson Vocabulary	**Language Objectives** • Understand and use basic vocabulary. • Learn meanings of grade-level vocabulary. • Produce drawings, phrases, or short sentences to show understanding of Lesson Vocabulary.
Word Analysis Latin Roots	**Language Objectives** • Decode words. • Use contextual support to grasp language structures.
Grammar and Conventions Subjects and Predicates	**Content Objective** • Identify subjects and predicates. **Language Objectives** • Write sentences with subjects and predicates. • Edit for subject-verb agreement.
Writing Sensory Details	**Content Objective** • Identify sensory details in text. **Language Objectives** • Use sensory details in writing. • Share feedback for editing and revising. • Speak using a variety of sentence lengths. • Describe with increasing detail and specificity.

Copyright © Pearson Education, Inc., or its affiliates. All Rights Reserved. 5

Word Cards for Vocabulary Activities

branded	**constructed**
daintily	**devastation**
lullaby	**pitch**
resourceful	**thieving**
veins	

Teacher Note: Beginning Teach three to four words. **Intermediate** Teach four to six words. **Advanced** Teach six to seven words. **Advanced High** Teach all words.

Name _____

Look at the pictures and **read** the paragraph. Then **complete** the table.
- For each effect shown, **write** its cause.
- For each cause shown, **write** its effect.

The Terrible Effects of a Drought

When the rain stops for a long time, a drought happens. Water dries up and disappears. Without water, plants begin to die. Insects and fish cannot live without plants and water. They disappear too. When that happens, there is no more food for the birds. Soon, the birds move away. A drought has a long chain of effects.

Cause	Effect
	A drought happens.
The water in the pond dries up.	
	Birds move away.

Cause and Effect

Use this lesson to supplement or replace the skill lesson on page 51c of the Teacher's Edition. Display the Skill Points (at right) and share them with students.

Teach/Model

Beginning Say: *The water in the pond splashes because I drop a rock in the pond. What happens?* (The water splashes.) *This is the effect. Why does this happen?* (I drop a rock in the pond.) *This is the cause.*

Intermediate Display a picture of a plant. Say: *A plant needs sunlight, water, and nutrients from soil to grow. This plant is growing. What happens?* (The plant grows.) *This is the effect. Why does the plant grow?* (It gets sunlight, water, and nutrients.) *Sunlight, water, and nutrients* <u>cause</u> *the plant to grow.*

Advanced Provide a cause. For example: *It rains for two days.* Say: *This rain can cause many things. What are some effects of it raining for two days?* Have students write their responses. (Plants get water. Rivers rise. There could be floods.)

Advanced High Have students think about nature. Say: *There are many cause-and-effect relationships in nature. For example: When the sun goes down, the blooms close. What are some other causes and effects in nature?* Ask students to write their examples.

Then distribute copies of Picture It! page 36.

• Have students compare the two pictures. The pictures show a pond before and after a drought. Explain that a drought is a long period of time without water. Then read the paragraph aloud.
• Review the Skill Points with students.
• Ask: *What are some of the effects of the drought?* (The water dries up. The plants die. The insects and fish die. The birds move away.)

Practice

Read aloud the directions on page 36. Have students reread the paragraph aloud. Then have them look at the pictures and the paragraph as they fill in the cause-and-effect table.

Beginning Students can first orally answer and then write their answers in the table. Provide help with English words and writing.

Intermediate Students can first say the causes and effects before writing them in the table. Provide help with English words and writing.

Advanced Students can write their answers in the table and then check them by comparing them with a partner's.

Advanced High Students can write simple sentences to complete the table and then use a clue word to say each cause-and-effect relationship.

Answers for page 36: *Cause:* The rain stops for a long time. *Effect:* Plants, insects, and fish die. *Cause:* There is no more food.

Skill Points
✔ A **cause** is why something happens. The **effect** is what happens.
✔ An effect may become the cause of another effect.
✔ Words such as *because* and *why* are clues. They tell you that you are reading about a cause-and-effect relationship.

Multilingual Summaries

Thunder Rose

Rose was born in a thunderstorm. She could sit up and talk the day she was born. Rose had the power of thunder in her. She drank milk straight from the cows. She could bend metal when she was two years old. When Rose was twelve, she stopped a herd of cattle from stampeding. She jumped on the biggest bull's back. She grabbed his horns, and she stopped him.

Rose decided to take the herd to market. She rode on the big bull. There was no rain on the trail. The cattle were tired and thirsty. Rose tried to lasso the clouds. She tried to squeeze rain out of them.

But a tornado came instead. Rose tried to tame it. The tornado became two tornadoes. Rose began to sing. Her voice sounded like thunder. Rose's song calmed the tornadoes. It began to rain.

Spanish

Rosa Trueno

Rosa nació en medio una gran tormenta. Ella podía hablar desde el día que nació. Rosa tenía el poder de los truenos dentro de ella. Bebía leche directamente de las vacas. A los dos años podía doblar metales. Cuando cumplió doce años, detuvo una manada de ganado que salía en estampida. Saltó sobre el lomo del toro más grande. Sujetó sus cuernos y lo hizo detener.

Rosa decidió llevar la manada al mercado. Iba montaba sobre el toro grande. No se vislumbraba lluvia en camino. El ganado estaba cansado y sediento. Rosa trató de enlazar las nubes. Trató de exprimirles algo de lluvia.

Pero lo que llegó fue un tornado. Rosa trató de amansarlo. El tornado se convirtió en dos tornados. Rosa comenzó a cantar. Su voz era como el sonido de los truenos. La canción de Rosa logró que los tornados se calmaran. Entonces comenzó a llover.

Multilingual Summaries

雷之女羅絲

　　羅絲出生的那一天，外頭正下著大雷雨。她一出生就會坐起來講話，她擁有雷所賜予的超能力，可以直接從母牛身上喝牛奶，兩歲的時候可以把金屬弄彎，十二歲時能夠使驚慌亂竄的牛群安靜下來，她跳上那隻體積最大的公牛背上，抓住他頭上的角，成功地讓牠停了下來。

　　羅絲決定把牛群趕到市場上賣。她騎在大公牛身上，一路上都沒有下雨，每隻牛都又累又渴。羅絲試著召來一些雲，想從雲裡面擠出一點雨來。

　　結果，雲沒有來，反而是龍捲風出現了。羅絲想把龍捲風平息下來，但是沒想到龍捲風竟然從一個變成兩個。羅絲看到情況不對，於是開始唱歌，她的歌聲聽起來就像雷聲。羅絲的歌聲平息了龍捲風，天空這時候也開始下雨了。

Vietnamese

Nàng Rose Sấm Sét

　　Rose sanh ra trong một cơn mưa bão. Cô ấy có thể thức cả đêm để kể chuyện ngày cô ra đời. Rose có sức mạnh sấm sét trong mình. Cô bé uống sữa trực tiếp từ những con bò. Cô bé có thể uốn cong kim loại khi mới hai tuổi. Khi Rose mười hai tuổi, cô ngăn được đàn bò không cho chúng chạy tán loạn. Cô nhảy lên lưng con bò đực to lớn nhất. Cô nắm lấy sừng của nó và làm nó phải dừng lại.

　　Rose quyết định đưa đàn bò ra chợ. Cô cõi con bò đực to. Trên đường đi không có mưa. Đàn bò mỏi mệt và khát nước. Rose cố bắt những cụm mây bằng dây thòng lọng. Cô bé cố vắt mây để lấy mưa.

　　Nhưng một cơn lốc xoáy đến. Rose cố gắng làm cho nó thuần phục. Cơn lốc xoáy trở thành hai. Rose bắt đầu hát. Tiếng hát của cô nghe giống như sấm vang. Bài hát của Rose làm lắng dịu những cơn lốc. Trời bắt đầu mưa.

Multilingual Summaries

천둥 로즈

폭우 속에서 태어난 로즈는 태어나자마자 일어나 앉고 말을 할 수 있었다. 로즈는 천둥의 힘을 갖고 있었고 젖소로부터 직접 우유를 마셨다. 로즈가 두 살이 되었을 때는 쇠를 구부릴 수 있었고 열두 살이던 때에는 달아나던 소떼를 멈추기도 했다. 덩치가 가장 큰 소의 등에 뛰어올라 뿔을 움켜잡고 소를 멈춘 것이다.

로즈는 소떼를 시장으로 몰고 가기로 하고 큰 소 위에 올라탄다. 가는 길에 비가 오지 않아 소떼가 피곤해하고 목말라하자 로즈는 올가미 밧줄로 구름을 낚아채 비를 짜내려 한다.

하지만 비 대신 회오리바람이 불어 온다. 로즈는 회오리바람을 꺾으려고 애쓰지만 회오리바람은 두 개가 되어 버린다. 그러자 로즈가 천둥 같은 목소리로 노래를 부르기 시작한다. 로즈의 노래는 회오리바람을 잠재운다. 그리고 곧 비가 내린다.

Xob Quaj Rose

Rose yug los thaum los nag xob nag cua. Hnub nws yug los ntawd nws sawv hais lus. Rose muaj xob quaj lub hwj chim nyob rau hauv nws. Nws haus kua mis nyuj. Thaum nws muaj ob xyoo xwb, nws muab hlau chom kom nkhaus li. Thaum Rose muaj kaum ob xyoo, nws ua kom ib pawg nyuj kom txhob khiav lwj khiav liam ub no. Nws dhia mus rau saum tus txiv nyuj loj tshaj nruab qaum. Nws tsuab tus txiv nyuj kub txwm kom nws tsum kiag.

Rose txiav txim siab tias nws yuav coj pawg nyuj nawd mus tom kiab khw. Nws caij tus txiv nyuj loj. Lawv mus kev ntev heev mas nag tsis los li. Cov nyuj nkeeg heev thiab nqhis dej. Rose sim muab txoj hlua ntes huab cua. Nws sim nyem huab cua ntawd kom los nag.

Tab sis ua cas muaj khaub zeeg cua tuaj xwb. Rose sim tua khuab zeeg cua ntawd tab sis khaub zeeg cua faib ua ob qhov. Rose pib hu nkauj. Nws lub suab zoo li xob quaj. Qhov Rose hu nkauj no ua kom khaub zeeg cua tus tus lawm. Ces nws pib los nag.

Name _____

- **Read** *Tommy and the Tornado* again.
- Use the information in the book to **fill in** the cause-and-effect boxes below.

Cause	**Effect**
Tommy's parents were going to a wedding.	
	Tex started whining when Tommy and Christopher were in the barn.
Tex knew where they had to go for protection from the tornado. He led the way to the storm cellar.	

Family Link

Has anyone in your family been through a storm? What was it like? Ask family members to share what they know about storms.

Weekly Resources Guide for English Language Learner Support

For this week's content and language objectives, see p. 41e.

Instructional Strand	Day 1	Day 2
Concept Development/Academic Language	**TEACHER'S EDITION** • Academic Language, p. DI•66 • Concept Development, p. DI•66 • Anchored Talk, pp. 82j—82–83 • Preteach Academic Vocabulary, p. 85a • Concept Talk Video **ELL HANDBOOK** • Hear It, See It, Say It, Use It, pp. xxxvi–xxxvii • ELL Poster Talk, Concept Talk, p. 41c **ELL POSTER 3** • Day 1 Activities	**TEACHER'S EDITION** • Academic Language, p. DI•66 • Concept Development, p. DI•66 • Anchored Talk, p. 86a • Concept Talk Video **ELL HANDBOOK** • ELL Poster Talk, Concept Talk, p. 41c • Concept Talk Video Routine, p. 477 **ELL POSTER 3** • Day 2 Activities
Phonics and Spelling	**TEACHER'S EDITION** • Phonics and Spelling, p. DI•70	**TEACHER'S EDITION** • Phonics and Spelling, p. DI•70
Listening Comprehension	**TEACHER'S EDITION** • Modified Read Aloud, p. DI•69 • Read Aloud, p. 83b • Concept Talk Video **ELL HANDBOOK** • Concept Talk Video Routine, p. 477	**TEACHER'S EDITION** • Modified Read Aloud, p. DI•69 • AudioText of *Island of the Blue Dolphins* • Concept Talk Video **ELL HANDBOOK** • AudioText CD Routine, p. 477 • Story Map A, p. 483
Reading Comprehension	**TEACHER'S EDITION** • Preteach Theme and Setting, p. DI•71	**TEACHER'S EDITION** • Reteach Theme and Setting, p. DI•71 • Frontloading Reading, p. DI•72 **ELL HANDBOOK** • Picture It! Skill Instruction, pp. 42–42a • Multilingual Summaries, pp. 43–45
Vocabulary **Basic and Lesson Vocabulary** **Word Analysis: Compound Words**	**TEACHER'S EDITION** • Basic Vocabulary, p. DI•67 • Preteach Lesson Vocabulary, p. DI•67 • Compound Words, p. DI•70 **ELL HANDBOOK** • Word Cards, p. 41 • ELL Vocabulary Routine, p. 471 **ELL POSTER 3** • Day 1 Activities	**TEACHER'S EDITION** • Basic Vocabulary, p. DI•67 • Reteach Lesson Vocabulary, p. DI•68 • Compound Words, p. DI•70 **ELL HANDBOOK** • Word Cards, p. 41 • Multilingual Vocabulary List, pp. 431–432 **ELL POSTER 3** • Day 2 Activities
Grammar and Conventions	**TEACHER'S EDITION** • Preteach Independent and Dependent Clauses, p. DI•74	**TEACHER'S EDITION** • Reteach Independent and Dependent Clauses, p. DI•74
Writing	**TEACHER'S EDITION** • Include Important Information, p. DI•75 • Introduce Invitation, pp. 85e–85f	**TEACHER'S EDITION** • Writing Trait: Focus/Ideas, pp. 95d–95e

This symbol indicates leveled instruction to address language proficiency levels.

Day 3	Day 4	Day 5
TEACHER'S EDITION • Academic Language, p. DI•66 • Concept Development, p. DI•66 • Anchored Talk, p. 96a • Concept Talk Video **ELL HANDBOOK** • ELL Poster Talk, Concept Talk, p. 41c **ELL POSTER 3** • Day 3 Activities	**TEACHER'S EDITION** • Academic Language, p. DI•66 • Concept Development, p. DI•66 • Anchored Talk, p. 104a • Concept Talk Video **ELL HANDBOOK** • ELL Poster Talk, Concept Talk, p. 41c **ELL POSTER 3** • Day 4 Activities	**TEACHER'S EDITION** • Academic Language, p. DI•66 • Concept Development, p. DI•66 • Concept Talk Video **ELL HANDBOOK** • ELL Poster Talk, Concept Talk, p. 41c **ELL POSTER 3** • Day 5 Activities
ELL HANDBOOK • Phonics Transition Lesson, pp. 253, 255	**ELL HANDBOOK** • Phonics Transition Lesson, pp. 253, 255	**TEACHER'S EDITION** • Phonics and Spelling, p. DI•70
TEACHER'S EDITION • AudioText of *Island of the Blue Dolphins* • Concept Talk Video **ELL HANDBOOK** • AudioText CD Routine, p. 477	**TEACHER'S EDITION** • Concept Talk Video	**TEACHER'S EDITION** • Concept Talk Video
TEACHER'S EDITION • Sheltered Reading, p. DI•72 **ELL HANDBOOK** • Multilingual Summaries, pp. 43–45	**TEACHER'S EDITION** • ELL/ELD Reader Guided Reading, p. DI•73 **ELL HANDBOOK** • ELL Study Guide, p. 46	**TEACHER'S EDITION** • ELL/ELD Reader Guided Reading, p. DI•73 **ELL HANDBOOK** • ELL Study Guide, p. 46
ELL HANDBOOK • High-Frequency Words Activity Bank, p. 446 **ELL POSTER 3** • Day 3 Activities	**ELL HANDBOOK** • High-Frequency Words Activity Bank, p. 446	**TEACHER'S EDITION** • Compound Words, p. 109i **ELL HANDBOOK** • High-Frequency Words Activity Bank, p. 446
TEACHER'S EDITION • Grammar Jammer **ELL HANDBOOK** • Grammar Transition Lesson, pp. 345, 358 • Grammar Jammer Routine, p. 478	**TEACHER'S EDITION** • Grammar Jammer **ELL HANDBOOK** • Grammar Transition Lesson, pp. 345, 358	**TEACHER'S EDITION** • Grammar Jammer **ELL HANDBOOK** • Grammar Transition Lesson, pp. 345, 358
TEACHER'S EDITION • Let's Write It!, p. 102–103 • Writing: Invitation, p. 103a • Writer's Craft: Include Important Information, p. 103b	**TEACHER'S EDITION** • Revising Strategy, pp. 109d–109e	**TEACHER'S EDITION** • Independent and Dependent Clauses, pp. 109p–109q

Question of the Week
How do people survive in the wilderness?

Throughout the week, use the ELL Poster to help students produce and comprehend language, understand the concept, and build English vocabulary. Use the Question of the Week and other questions to help students share ideas in pairs, small groups, or the large group. Sample questions are shown, with examples of possible responses by students.

Weekly Concept and Language Goals

• Identify things you need to survive

• Understand some challenges of the wilderness

• Discuss life in the wilderness

By the end of the lesson, students should be able to talk about and write sentences about survival.

ELL Poster 3

Daily Team Talk

Day 1	Day 2	Day 3	Day 4	Day 5
After Day 1 activities on Poster, ask questions such as *In the poster picture, how can the man's supplies help him survive?*	After Day 2 activity on Poster, ask questions such as *In the poster picture, what can the man find on the island that will help him survive?*	After Day 3 activity on Poster, ask questions such as *What challenge might the man face on the island?*	After Day 4 activity on Poster, ask questions such as *How can the man protect himself from the wild dog?*	After Day 5 activity on Poster, ask questions such as *Besides the supplies shown in the poster, what else can help you survive in the wilderness?*
Beginning He has food. **Intermediate** He can eat the food to live. **Advanced** He has enough to eat and drink because of the food, water, and fishing poles. **Advanced High** With the fishing poles, he can catch fish to eat with the canned food. He can drink the water and use the bottles to get more. The first-aid kit will keep him safe.	**Beginning** Fish and water. **Intermediate** He can get fish and fresh water. **Advanced** He can catch fish from the ocean. He can get fresh water. **Advanced High** He can catch fish from the ocean and gather kelp to eat. He can collect fresh water from the ravine.	**Beginning** There is a dog. **Intermediate** A dog lives on the island. **Advanced** A wild dog is living on the island. It does not look nice. **Advanced High** There is a wild dog that does not seem friendly living on the island. It might become a challenge for the man.	**Beginning** Make a home. **Intermediate** He can build a house. **Advanced** The man can build a shelter to protect himself. **Advanced High** The man can protect himself and his supplies by building a shelter that the wild dog cannot get into.	**Beginning** Warm clothes. **Intermediate** It would help to have warm clothes. **Advanced** Having a jacket or other warm clothes would help me survive. **Advanced High** It might get cold at night, so warm clothes such as a jacket or gloves would help me survive. It would also help to have matches to start a fire.

This Week's Materials

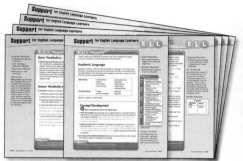

Teacher's Edition pages 82j–109q

See the support for English language learners throughout the lesson, including ELL strategies and scaffolded activities at points of use.

Teacher's Edition pages DI•66–DI•75

Differentiated Instruction for English language learners provides daily group activities that "frontload," or preteach, core instruction.

ELL Handbook pp. 41a–46

Find additional lesson materials that support the core lesson and the ELL instructional pages.

 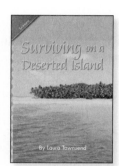

ELL Poster 3

ELL Reader 5.1.3

ELD Reader 5.1.3

Concept Literacy Reader

ELD, ELL Reader
Teaching Guide

Concept Literacy Reader
Teaching Guide

Technology

Online Teacher's Edition Use the digital version of the core Teacher's Edition for planning and instruction.

eReaders
This week's ELL and ELD Readers and Concept Literacy Reader are also available in digital format.

This Week's Content and Language Objectives by Strand

Concept Development/ Academic Language How do people survive in the wilderness?	**Content Objective** • Use concept vocabulary related to surviving in the wilderness. **Language Objective** • Express ideas in response to art and discussion.
Phonics and Spelling Long Vowel Digraphs	**Content Objectives** • Learn the relationship between spellings and sound for /ā/. • Spell words with long vowel digraphs. **Language Objectives** • Apply phonics and decoding skills to vocabulary. • Produce sounds in vocabulary.
Listening Comprehension Modified Read Aloud: "Light the Fire!"	**Content Objective** • Monitor and adjust oral comprehension. **Language Objectives** • Discuss oral passages. • Use a graphic organizer to take notes.
Reading Comprehension Theme and Setting	**Content Objectives** • Understand theme and setting. • Monitor and adjust comprehension. **Language Objectives** • Use routine language in classroom communication. • Retell theme and setting from a reading. • Build background with visual support.
Vocabulary Basic and Lesson Vocabulary	**Language Objectives** • Acquire, understand and use basic vocabulary. • Learn meanings of grade-level vocabulary. • Produce drawings, phrases, or short sentences to show understanding of Lesson Vocabulary.
Word Analysis Compound Words	**Content Objective** • Identify and define words in compound words. **Language Objective** • Discuss meanings of compound words.
Grammar and Conventions Independent and Dependent Clauses	**Content Objectives** • Identify dependent and independent clauses. • Add independent clauses to express a complete thought. **Language Objectives** • Say and write dependent and independent clauses. • Speak using a variety of sentence lengths.
Writing Include Important Information	**Content Objective** • Include important information in a written text. **Language Objectives** • Share feedback for editing and revising. • Take notes.

Word Cards for Vocabulary Activities

gnawed	**headland**
kelp	**lair**
ravine	**shellfish**
sinew	

Teacher Note: Beginning Teach two to three words. **Intermediate** Teach three to four words. **Advanced** Teach four to five words. **Advanced High** Teach all words.

Name _____

Look at the picture and **read** the story. Then **answer** the questions that follow.

Emergency!

The pilot was in trouble. He was flying over the wilderness when, suddenly, a storm hit. The winds were too strong. It was dangerous to keep flying. So the pilot made an emergency landing. The plane was wrecked. What could the pilot do now? How would he stay alive?

Read each question. **Circle** the letter of the correct answer.

1. Where does the story take place?
   A. in a desert
   B. over the ocean
   C. in a forest
   D. in the mountains

2. When does the story take place?
   A. during a drought
   B. during a storm
   C. in the middle of the night
   D. in the future

3. What is the theme of the story?
   A. the challenges of survival
   B. the beauty of nature
   C. the fun of traveling
   D. the pleasures of everyday life

Theme and Setting

Use this lesson to supplement or replace the skill lesson on page 83c of the Teacher's Edition. Display the Skill Points (at right) and share them with students.

Teach/Model

Talk about a familiar story such as the fable "The Hare and the Tortoise." In it, a hare makes fun of a slow-moving tortoise, and one day they race across the land. The hare is so confident that he naps during the race, planning to sprint and win. The tortoise, slow but steady, wins the race.

Beginning Ask: *Where and when does this story take place?* (during the day, outside) *This is the setting. What does the author want you to learn from this story?* (Possible answer: Don't underestimate others.) *This is the story's theme.*

Intermediate Ask students to write a sentence that describes the setting of "The Hare and the Tortoise." Then together decide what the theme of the story is. Discuss how you used what happens in the story to figure out the theme.

Advanced Have students write a sentence that tells the theme of "The Hare and the Tortoise." Ask: *How do the events in the story help you identify the theme?* (They explain what the characters learn, which is the theme.)

Advanced High Together think of a theme. For example: *It is never too late to do the right thing.* Make up a story based on the theme. Have students write sentences that tell the plot. Remind them to include details that tell about the setting.

Then distribute copies of Picture It! page 42.

- Tell students to look at the picture, and explain that the picture goes with the story. Remind students that pictures often help tell part of the story.
- Ask students to use the picture to guess when and where the story takes place. Then read the story aloud.
- Review the Skill Points with students.

Practice

Read aloud the directions on page 42. Have students reread the story with a partner. Have them look at the picture and the story as they answer the questions.

Beginning Students can answer orally before circling their answers. Provide help with circling the correct answers.

Intermediate Students can first orally answer and then circle the letters of their answers. Provide help with circling the correct answers.

Advanced Students can circle the letters of their answers and then check their answers by comparing them with a partner's.

Advanced High Students can circle the letters of their answers and then check them by rereading the story and underlining the details that answer the questions.

Answers for page 42: 1. c; 2. b; 3. a

Skill Points

✔ The **setting** of a story is when and where it happens.

✔ The **theme** is the message or underlying meaning of the story. Often the theme is not stated. You can figure out the theme from events in the story.

Multilingual Summaries

Island of the Blue Dolphins

Karana lived alone on the Island of the Blue Dolphins. She needed to find a place to build a shelter. One place was too close to the wild dogs. Another place was too noisy. The sea elephants' barking would keep her awake. Then Karana found a safe place near some big rocks.

First, Karana used branches to make a place to sleep. Then, she used whale ribs to build a fence next to a big rock. The fence would keep animals away from the food she gathered.

Then, she gathered wooden poles and big leaves. She tied these together to make the walls and roof of her house. Karana made bowls for cooking and shelves to hold her food. Now she had food and shelter. She was alone but she had what she needed.

Spanish

La isla de los delfines azules

Karana vivía sola en la isla de los delfines azules. Necesitaba encontrar un lugar para construir su refugio. Uno de los lugares estaba muy cerca de los perros salvajes. En otro había mucho ruido. Los ladridos de los elefantes marinos la despertarían. Luego, Karana encontró un lugar seguro cerca de unas rocas grandes.

Primero usó ramas para hacer un lugar donde dormir. Luego, usó costillas de ballena para hacer una cerca al lado de una roca grande. La cerca mantendría a los animales alejados de la comida que recolectara.

Después buscó palos y hojas grandes. Amarró todas esas cosas juntas para hacer las paredes y el techo de su casa. Karana hizo ollas para cocinar y armarios para guardar su comida. Ya tenía comida y refugio. Estaba sola, pero tenía lo que necesitaba.

Multilingual Summaries

藍色海豚島

　　卡拉娜自己一個人住在藍色海豚島上。她需要找個可以遮風避雨的地方住，原本她找到兩個地方，但是一個太接近野狗，而另一個又太吵了，海象的叫聲老是把她吵醒。後來，卡拉娜終於在一堆大岩石旁邊找到了一個安全的地方。

　　剛開始的時候，卡拉娜用樹枝鋪了一個地方睡覺，後來，又用鯨魚肋骨在一塊大岩石旁邊建了圍欄，這樣動物就不能偷吃她辛苦採集的食物。

　　然後，她又收集很多木椿和大片樹葉，把它們綁在一起，當作房子的屋頂和外牆。卡拉娜還做了煮東西的大碗和放食物的架子。現在，她有吃的東西，也有住的地方。她還是一個人，不過所有需要的東西她都有了。

Đảo Cá Heo Xanh

　　Karana sống một mình trên Đảo Cá Heo Xanh. Cô cần tìm một nơi để làm một chỗ ẩn náu. Một nơi thì quá gần với những con chó hoang. Một nơi khác thì quá ồn. Tiếng sủa của những con voi biển làm cô không ngủ được. Rồi Karana tìm được một nơi an toàn gần những hòn đá lớn.

　　Đầu tiên Karana dùng những cành cây để làm chỗ ngủ. Rồi cô dùng xương sườn của cá voi để làm hàng rào bên cạnh một hòn đá lớn. Hàng rào sẽ ngăn không cho các con thú đến gần thức ăn mà cô đã thu nhặt được.

　　Rồi cô đi lượm gậy gọc và những chiếc lá to. Cô cột chúng lại để làm vách và mái nhà. Karana làm tô chén để nấu ăn và ngăn kệ để giữ thức ăn. Bây giờ cô có thức ăn và chỗ ở. Cô ấy chỉ có một mình nhưng cô có những thứ mình cần.

Multilingual Summaries

푸른 돌고래 섬

푸른 돌고래 섬에 혼자 살고 있는 카라나는 집 지을 장소를 찾아 다니는데 어떤 곳은 야생 개들과 너무 가까이 있고 어떤 곳은 너무 시끄럽다. 바다 코끼리가 내는 소리 때문에 계속 잠을 못 잘 것 같기도 하다. 곧 카라나는 큰 바위들 근처에 있는 안전한 장소를 찾아낸다.

카라나는 먼저 나뭇가지를 이용해 잠잘 곳을 만들고 나서 고래 갈비뼈로 큰 바위 옆에 울타리를 만든다. 이 울타리는 카라나가 모아둔 음식을 동물들이 가져가지 못하게 할 것이다.

다음에 카라나는 나무 막대기와 큰 잎사귀들을 모은 다음 이것들을 함께 묶어 벽과 지붕을 만든다. 요리할 그릇과 음식을 넣어둘 선반도 만든 카라나는 이제 음식도 있고 집도 있다. 카라나는 혼자이지만 필요한 것들을 가지고 있다.

Hmong

Pov Txwv Ntses Ntov Fis Xim Xiav

Karana nyob nws ib leeg xwb nyob ntawm Pov Txwv Ntses Ntov Fis (Dolphin) Xim Xiav. Nws nrhiav ub nrhiav no ib qhov chaw ua tsev nyob. Ib qhov chaw nyob ze ze ib pawg dev qus. Lwm qhov chaw nrov nrov heev. Cov dej hiav txwv ntxhwv tsem heev ces nws pw tsis tau li. Ces nws ho nrhiav ib qhov chaw zoo nyob ze ib co pob zeb loj loj heev.

Karana xub thawj siv ceg ntoo los ua ib thaj chaw pw. Tom qab ntawd nws siv ib tug ntses whale loj loj cov tav los xov laj kab nyob ze ib lub pob zeb loj. Txoj laj kab no yuav tiv thaiv cov tsiaj txhu kom lawv cuag tsis tau cov mov nws sau lawm.

Ua li ntawd tas ces nws nrhiav cov ncej ntoo thiab nplooj loj loj. Nws muab cov no los khi ua ke los ua phab ntsa thiab lub ru tsev. Karana ua lub ntim los ua mov noj thiab txua txee los khaws cia nws cov mov. Ces nws thiaj li muaj mov noj thiab muaj tsev nyob. Nws haj tseem nyob nws ib leeg xwb tab sis nws muaj txhua yam nws xav tau.

- **Read** *Finding Home* again. **Look** at the illustrations and pay attention to the descriptions of the settings.
- **Draw** a map that shows Anacapa's village, the forest, the beach, and the path that Anacapa followed. **Label** each part of your map.

Family Link

Have you or has anybody in your family gone on a camping trip? What was it like? Talk to family members about a camping trip you took or would like to take.

Weekly Resources Guide for English Language Learner Support

For this week's content and language objectives, see p. 47e.

Instructional Strand	Day 1	Day 2
Concept Development/Academic Language	TEACHER'S EDITION • Academic Language, p. DI•91 • Concept Development, p. DI•91 • Anchored Talk, pp. 110j—110–111 • Preteach Academic Vocabulary, p. 113a • Concept Talk Video ELL HANDBOOK • Hear It, See It, Say It, Use It, pp. xxxvi–xxxvii • ELL Poster Talk, Concept Talk, p. 47c ELL POSTER 4 • Day 1 Activities	TEACHER'S EDITION • Academic Language, p. DI•91 • Concept Development, p. DI•91 • Anchored Talk, p. 114a • Concept Talk Video ELL HANDBOOK • ELL Poster Talk, Concept Talk, p. 47c • Concept Talk Video Routine, p. 477 ELL POSTER 4 • Day 2 Activities
Phonics and Spelling	TEACHER'S EDITION • Phonics and Spelling, p. DI•95	TEACHER'S EDITION • Phonics and Spelling, p. DI•95
Listening Comprehension	TEACHER'S EDITION • Modified Read Aloud, p. DI•94 • Read Aloud, p. 111b • Concept Talk Video ELL HANDBOOK • Concept Talk Video Routine, p. 477	TEACHER'S EDITION • Modified Read Aloud, p. DI•94 • AudioText of *Satchel Paige* • Concept Talk Video ELL HANDBOOK • AudioText CD Routine, p. 477 • Cause and Effect, p. 489
Reading Comprehension	TEACHER'S EDITION • Preteach Fact and Opinion, p. DI•96	TEACHER'S EDITION • Reteach Fact and Opinion, p. DI•96 • Frontloading Reading, p. DI•97 ELL HANDBOOK • Picture It! Skill Instruction, pp. 48–48a • Multilingual Summaries, pp. 49–51
Vocabulary **Basic and Lesson Vocabulary** **Word Analysis: Shades of Meaning**	TEACHER'S EDITION • Basic Vocabulary, p. DI•92 • Preteach Lesson Vocabulary, p. DI•92 • Shades of Meaning, p. DI•95 ELL HANDBOOK • Word Cards, p. 47 • ELL Vocabulary Routine, p. 471 ELL POSTER 4 • Day 1 Activities	TEACHER'S EDITION • Basic Vocabulary, p. DI•92 • Reteach Lesson Vocabulary, p. DI•93 • Shades of Meaning, p. DI•95 ELL HANDBOOK • Word Cards, p. 47 • Multilingual Vocabulary List, p. 432 ELL POSTER 4 • Day 2 Activities
Grammar and Conventions	TEACHER'S EDITION • Teach Compound and Complex Sentences, p. DI•99	TEACHER'S EDITION • Practice Compound and Complex Sentences, p. DI•99
Writing	TEACHER'S EDITION • Answer the 5Ws and How, p. DI•100 • Introduce Newsletter Article, pp. 113e–113f	TEACHER'S EDITION • Writer's Craft: Answer the 5Ws & How, pp. 125d–125e

This symbol indicates leveled instruction to address language proficiency levels.

Day 3	Day 4	Day 5
TEACHER'S EDITION • Academic Language, p. DI•91 • Concept Development, p. DI•91 • Anchored Talk, p. 126a • Concept Talk Video **ELL HANDBOOK** • ELL Poster Talk, Concept Talk, p. 47c **ELL POSTER 4** • Day 3 Activities	**TEACHER'S EDITION** • Academic Language, p. DI•91 • Concept Development, p. DI•91 • Anchored Talk, p. 134a • Concept Talk Video **ELL HANDBOOK** • ELL Poster Talk, Concept Talk, p. 47c **ELL POSTER 4** • Day 4 Activities	**TEACHER'S EDITION** • Academic Language, p. DI•91 • Concept Development, p. DI•91 • Concept Talk Video **ELL HANDBOOK** • ELL Poster Talk, Concept Talk, p. 47c **ELL POSTER 4** • Day 5 Activities
		TEACHER'S EDITION • Phonics and Spelling, p. DI•95
ELL HANDBOOK • Phonics Transition Lesson, pp. 269, 271	**ELL HANDBOOK** • Phonics Transition Lesson, pp. 269, 271	
TEACHER'S EDITION • AudioText of *Satchel Paige* • Concept Talk Video **ELL HANDBOOK** • AudioText CD Routine, p. 477	**TEACHER'S EDITION** • Concept Talk Video	**TEACHER'S EDITION** • Concept Talk Video
TEACHER'S EDITION • Sheltered Reading, p. DI•97 **ELL HANDBOOK** • Multilingual Summaries, pp. 49–51	**TEACHER'S EDITION** • ELL/ELD Reader Guided Reading, p. DI•98 **ELL HANDBOOK** • ELL Study Guide, p. 52	**TEACHER'S EDITION** • ELL/ELD Reader Guided Reading, p. DI•98 **ELL HANDBOOK** • ELL Study Guide, p. 52
		TEACHER'S EDITION • Shades of Meaning, p. 139i
ELL HANDBOOK • High-Frequency Words Activity Bank, p. 446 **ELL POSTER 4** • Day 3 Activities	**ELL HANDBOOK** • High-Frequency Words Activity Bank, p. 446	**ELL HANDBOOK** • High-Frequency Words Activity Bank, p. 446
TEACHER'S EDITION • Grammar Jammer **ELL HANDBOOK** • Grammar Transition Lesson, pp. 344–345, 355, 357 • Grammar Jammer Routine, p. 478	**TEACHER'S EDITION** • Grammar Jammer **ELL HANDBOOK** • Grammar Transition Lesson, pp. 344–345, 355, 357	**TEACHER'S EDITION** • Grammar Jammer **ELL HANDBOOK** • Grammar Transition Lesson, pp. 344–345, 355, 357
TEACHER'S EDITION • Let's Write It!, p. 132–133 • Writing Trait: Word Choice, pp. 133a–133b	**TEACHER'S EDITION** • Revising Strategy, pp. 139d–139e	**TEACHER'S EDITION** • Compound and Complex Sentences, pp. 139p–139q

Question of the Week
How do we face personal challenges?

Throughout the week, use the ELL Poster to help students produce and comprehend language, understand the concept, and build English vocabulary. Use the Question of the Week and other questions to help students share ideas in pairs, small groups, or the large group. Sample questions are shown, with examples of possible responses by students.

ELL Poster 4

Weekly Concept and Language Goals
- Participate in a discussion about personal challenges
- Discuss types of personal challenges
- Tell about overcoming personal challenges

By the end of the lesson, students should be able to talk about and write sentences about personal challenges.

Daily Team Talk

Day 1	Day 2	Day 3	Day 4	Day 5
After Day 1 activities on Poster, ask questions such as *In the poster picture, what challenge does the batter face?*	After Day 2 activity on Poster, ask questions such as *In the poster picture, how might the batter overcome the challenge of hitting the ball?*	After Day 3 activity on Poster, ask questions such as *After the batter hits the ball, what challenge does the other team face?*	After Day 4 activity on Poster, ask questions such as *What challenge do you think the person dressed up as a chicken faces?*	After Day 5 activity on Poster, ask questions such as *How have you overcome a personal challenge?*
Beginning The ball is fast. **Intermediate** The ball she has to hit is fast. **Advanced** The pitcher threw the ball fast. She must try to hit it. **Advanced High** The batter must try to hit a fastball. The pitcher also made the ball curve, so it will be hard to hit.	**Beginning** Watch it. **Intermediate** She can watch the ball. **Advanced** She can concentrate on watching the ball. **Advanced High** She will have to keep her eye on the ball so she knows when to swing. She must concentrate and not get distracted.	**Beginning** Get her out. **Intermediate** They have to try to get her out. **Advanced** They have to work together to get the batter out. **Advanced High** The other team must work together quickly to get the batter and the other runner out.	**Beginning** It is hot. **Intermediate** It is hot inside. **Advanced** I think it is hot inside the chicken costume. **Advanced High** The person dressed up as a chicken mascot may be hot inside the costume or embarrassed to be dressed like a chicken.	**Beginning** I practice. **Intermediate** I practiced playing drums. **Advanced** I had to practice a lot to learn to play the drums. **Advanced High** At first, I was not good at playing drums. I had to practice a lot, and now I can play drums well.

This Week's Materials

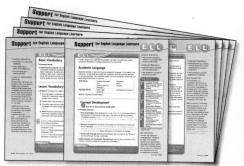

Teacher's Edition pages 110j–139q

See the support for English language learners throughout the lesson, including ELL strategies and scaffolded activities at points of use.

Teacher's Edition pages DI•91–DI•100

Differentiated Instruction for English language learners provides daily group activities that "frontload," or preteach, core instruction.

ELL Handbook pp. 47a–52

Find additional lesson materials that support the core lesson and the ELL instructional pages.

ELL Poster 4

ELL Reader 5.1.4

ELD Reader 5.1.4

Concept Literacy Reader

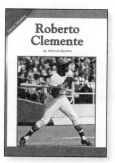

ELD, ELL Reader Teaching Guide

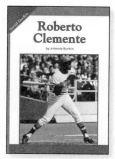

Concept Literacy Reader Teaching Guide

Technology

Online Teacher's Edition Use the digital version of the core Teacher's Edition for planning and instruction.

eReaders
This week's ELL and ELD Readers and Concept Literacy Reader are also available in digital format.

This Week's Content and Language Objectives by Strand

Concept Development/ Academic Language How do we face personal challenges?	**Content Objective** • Use concept vocabulary related to how people face personal challenges. **Language Objectives** • Express ideas in response to art and discussion. • Use academic language in speaking activities.
Phonics and Spelling Adding *–ed, -ing*	**Content Objectives** • Identify word endings. • Review how to add *–ed* and *–ing* endings. **Language Objectives** • Distinguish intonation patterns of English. • Discuss how and when to choose words with similar meanings.
Listening Comprehension Modified Read Aloud: "Two Great Men"	**Content Objective** • Monitor and adjust oral comprehension. **Language Objectives** • Discuss oral passages. • Use a graphic organizer to take notes.
Reading Comprehension Fact and Opinion	**Content Objectives** • Distinguish between facts and opinions. • Identify facts and opinions as an aid to comprehension. • Monitor and adjust comprehension. **Language Objectives** • Discuss evidence for facts and opinions. • Use visual and contextual support to aid comprehension.
Vocabulary Basic and Lesson Vocabulary	**Language Objectives** • Acquire, understand, and use basic vocabulary. • Learn meanings of grade-level vocabulary. • Produce drawings, phrases, or short sentences to show understanding of Lesson Vocabulary.
Word Analysis Shades of Meaning	**Content Objective** • Identify and define words with different shades of meaning. **Language Objectives** • Apply phonics and decoding skills to vocabulary. • Discuss how and when to choose words with similar meanings.
Grammar and Conventions Compound and Complex Sentences	**Content Objectives** • Differentiate compound and complex sentences. • Create compound and complex sentences. **Language Objectives** • Speak using a variety of sentence lengths. • Use correct punctuation when writing compound and complex sentences.
Writing Answer the 5Ws and How	**Content Objective** • Use the 5Ws and How to answer questions in a text. **Language Objective** • Give information using the 5Ws and How as a guide.

confidence

fastball

mocking

outfield

unique

weakness

windup

Teacher Note: Beginning Teach two to three words. **Intermediate** Teach four to five words. **Advanced** Teach five to six words. **Advanced High** Teach all words.

Name _____

Read the story of Wilma Rudolph's life.

• **Underline** the sentences that are facts. **Circle** the sentences that are opinions.

• In the boxes below, **write** a fact and an opinion.

Wilma Rudolph

Wilma Rudolph was a great athlete. In 1960, she won three gold medals. Wilma started life as a sickly child, though. She was born in 1940. When she was five, she became very ill. It was hard for her to walk. She kept trying. In 1956, she won a bronze medal at the Olympic Games. People called her "the fastest woman alive." The story of her life is more interesting than any other athlete's story. If she were alive today, she would be able to win more gold medals.

Facts	**Opinions**
_____	_____
_____	_____
_____	_____
_____	_____
_____	_____

Fact and Opinion

Use this lesson to supplement or replace the skill lesson on page 111c of the Teacher's Edition. Display the Skill Points (at right) and share them with students.

Teach/Model

Beginning Point to Italy on a map. Say: *In 1960, the Summer Olympics were played in Rome, Italy. Is this a fact or an opinion?* (a fact) *How can you prove it is true?* (look in a book or on the Internet) Say: *The 100 meter running race is the most exciting event. Is this a fact or opinion?* (an opinion) *How do you know?* (It tells someone's feelings.)

Intermediate Write and read aloud these sentences: *The world's best athletes compete in the Olympics. The winners receive a gold medal.* Ask students to copy the fact. (the statement about a gold medal) Have them write a sentence that tells how they can prove the statement is true.

Advanced Read aloud these statements: *Most athletes have great and interesting stories to tell. The library has a section of sports biographies and autobiographies.* Have students explain how they can tell which statement is a fact and which is an opinion.

Advanced High Ask students to write one fact and one opinion. Pair students. One partner reads aloud his or her statements, and the other partner identifies the fact and the opinion. Then the partners trade roles.

Then distribute copies of Picture It! page 48.

- Have students look at the picture. Read the story aloud.
- Ask: *What is one fact?* (Possible answer: In 1960, she won three gold medals.) *Where can you check to see if it is true?* (Possible answers: in an encyclopedia or on the Internet)
- Review the Skill Points with students.
- Ask students to find clue words that tell that a statement is an opinion.

Practice

Read aloud the directions on page 48. Have students reread the story aloud. Then have them use the picture and the story as they fill in the boxes.

Beginning Students can find the facts and opinions in the story before writing them in the boxes. Provide help with English writing.

Intermediate Students can first say what they will write and then write their answers on the lines.

Advanced Students can write their answers in the boxes and then check their answers by comparing them with a partner's.

Advanced High Students can write their answers in the boxes and then orally explain how they decided whether each statement was a fact or an opinion.

Answers for page 48: *Facts:* She was born in 1940. In 1960, she won three gold medals. When she was five, she became very ill. In 1956, she won a bronze medal. *Opinions:* Wilma was a great athlete. The story of her life is more interesting than any other athlete's story. If she were alive today, she would be able to win more gold medals.

Skill Points

✔ A statement of **fact** tells something that can be proven true or false. To prove a fact, you can look in a book, check the Internet, or ask an expert.

✔ An **opinion** tells someone's ideas or feelings. These clue words tell you a statement is an opinion: *more interesting, great, best, like.*

Multilingual Summaries

Satchel Paige

Satchel Paige was a great baseball pitcher. He started playing on professional teams when he was nineteen. Many people came to see him strike batters out. After one year, he started playing in the Negro major leagues. He played on different teams for seventeen years.

Satchel got married in 1941. He thought he would stay home and not play baseball. But he could not stay away from baseball. After a year, he was playing again.

In 1942, Satchel's team was in the league championship. Satchel had to pitch to Josh Gibson. Gibson was the best batter in the league. Satchel said he would strike him out, and he did.

Spanish

Satchel Paige

Satchel Paige fue un gran lanzador de béisbol. Comenzó a jugar en equipos profesionales cuando tenía diecinueve años. Mucha gente iba a los partidos a verlo ponchar bateadores. Después de un año, comenzó a lanzar en las Ligas Mayores Negras. Jugó en diferentes equipos por diecisiete años.

Satchel se casó en 1941. Pensó que podría quedarse en casa y no jugar más béisbol. Pero no podía mantenerse lejos de este juego. Después de un año, estaba jugando de nuevo.

En 1942, el equipo de Satchel estaba en el campeonato de la liga. Satchel tenía que lanzarle a Josh Gibson. Gibson era el mejor bateador de la liga. Satchel dijo que podía poncharlo y así fue.

Multilingual Summaries

薩裘．派吉

薩裘．派吉是個偉大的棒球投手。他在 19 歲時加入職業棒球隊開始了棒球生涯，很多人都專程來看他投出使擊球員連續出局的好球。一年後，他又轉到黑人大聯盟裡打球。他在那裡總共待了 17 年，期間換過幾次球隊。

薩裘在 1941 年結婚，他覺得自己要多點時間跟家人共處，所以決定不打棒球了。但是他實在沒有辦法抵抗棒球的誘惑，一年後，他又開始打了。

1942 年，薩裘在聯盟冠軍賽中遇上了喬許．吉布森，他是棒球聯盟裡最厲害的擊球手。薩裘說他要使吉布森出局，結果，他真的辦到了。

Satchel Paige

Satchel Paige là một cầu thủ ném bóng chày xuất sắc. Ông bắt đầu chơi cho những đội chuyên nghiệp khi ông mười chín tuổi. Nhiều người đến xem ông đánh bại những cầu thủ đánh bóng chày. Sau một năm, ông bắt đầu chơi cho các liên đoàn bóng chày quan trọng của Người Mỹ Đen. Ông ấy chơi cho nhiều đội khác nhau trong 17 năm.

Satchel lập gia đình vào năm 1941. Ông ấy nghĩ là mình sẽ nghỉ ở nhà và không chơi bóng chày nữa. Nhưng ông không thể không chơi bóng chày. Sau một năm, ông trở lại chơi tiếp.

Vào năm 1942, đội của Satchel tranh giải vô địch liên đoàn. Satchel phải ném bóng chày cho Josh Gibson. Gibson là người đánh bóng chày giỏi nhất trong liên đoàn. Satchel nói là sẽ đánh bại ông ấy, và ông đã làm vậy.

Multilingual Summaries

사첼 페이지

사첼 페이지는 훌륭한 야구 투수로 열 아홉 살에 프로 야구팀에서 뛰기 시작했는데 많은 사람들이 그가 타자를 삼진 아웃시키는 것을 보러 왔다. 1년 후 그는 니그로 메이저리그에서 뛰기 시작했으며 그 후 17년 동안 여러 팀에서 선수 생활을 했다.

1941년에 결혼한 사첼은 야구를 하지 않고 계속 집에서 지내겠다고 생각했지만 야구를 떠나서 살 수 없었던 그는 결국 1년 후 다시 야구를 시작했다.

1942년 사첼의 팀이 리그 결승전에 올랐는데 경기 중에 사첼은 리그 최고의 타자인 조시 깁슨을 상대로 공을 던져야 했다. 사첼은 그를 삼진 아웃시키겠다고 말했고 사첼의 말대로 이루어졌다.

Satchel Paige

Satchel Paige txawj pov pob baseball. Nws pib ua si rau cov pawg uas them nyiaj thaum nws muaj kaum cuaj xyoo xwb. Neeg coob coob tuaj saib nws pov pob dhau cov neeg uas sim ntaus pob. Nws ua si ib xyoo xwb ces nws pib ua si rau hauv ib lub koom haum ua si rau cov Miskas Dub. Nws ua si 17 xyoo nrog ntau pawg.

Satchel yuav poj niam xyoo 1941. Nws xav zoj tias nws yuav tso baseball tseg thiab nyob tsev xwb. Tab sis nws tso tsis tau tseg kiag. Tom qab ib xyoo, nws rov ua si dua.

Xyoo 1942, Satchel pawg yog ib lub pawg ntawm ob lub uas zoo tshaj nyob rau hauv koom haum ua si baseball. Yog li ntawd ob lub pawg ntawd yuav ua si ua ke seb leej twg mam li yeej. Satchel tau pov pob baseball rau Josh Gibson. Gibson yog tus ntaus baseball zoo tshaj nyob hauv koom haum ua si ntawd. Satchel hais tias nws yuav pov peb lub pob dhau Gibson kom nws ntaus tsis tau, ces nws ua li ntawd thiab tiag.

Name _____

- **Read** *Roberto Clemente* again.
- Which event happened first? Which happened next? **Number** the events in order from 1 to 6.

___ In 1954, he joins the Pittsburgh Pirates.

___ Roberto Clemente dies in a plane crash on December 31, 1972.

___ He plays for the Puerto Rican Winter League.

___ Roberto Clemente is born on August 18, 1934, in Carolina, Puerto Rico.

___ The Dodgers offer him $10,000 to join their team.

___ Roberto helps the Pirates win the World Series.

Family Link
What is your favorite sport? Talk to your family about it. Ask family members what sports they liked when they were your age.

Weekly Resources Guide for English Language Learner Support

For this week's content and language objectives, see p. 53e.

Instructional Strand	Day 1	Day 2
Concept Development/Academic Language	**TEACHER'S EDITION** • Academic Language, p. DI•116 • Concept Development, p. DI•116 • Anchored Talk, pp. 140j—140–141 • Preteach Academic Vocabulary, p. 143a • Concept Talk Video **ELL HANDBOOK** • Hear It, See It, Say It, Use It, pp. xxxvi–xxxvii • ELL Poster Talk, Concept Talk, p. 53c **ELL POSTER 5** • Day 1 Activities	**TEACHER'S EDITION** • Academic Language, p. DI•116 • Concept Development, p. DI•116 • Anchored Talk, p. 144a • Concept Talk Video **ELL HANDBOOK** • ELL Poster Talk, Concept Talk, p. 53c • Concept Talk Video Routine, p. 477 **ELL POSTER 5** • Day 2 Activities
Phonics and Spelling	**TEACHER'S EDITION** • Phonics and Spelling, p. DI•120	**TEACHER'S EDITION** • Phonics and Spelling, p. DI•120
Listening Comprehension	**TEACHER'S EDITION** • Modified Read Aloud, p. DI•119 • Read Aloud, p. 141b • Concept Talk Video **ELL HANDBOOK** • Concept Talk Video Routine, p. 477	**TEACHER'S EDITION** • Modified Read Aloud, p. DI•119 • AudioText of *Ten Mile Day* • Concept Talk Video **ELL HANDBOOK** • AudioText CD Routine, p. 477 • Story Map B, p. 484
Reading Comprehension	**TEACHER'S EDITION** • Preteach Cause and Effect, p. DI•121	**TEACHER'S EDITION** • Reteach Cause and Effect, p. DI•121 • Frontloading Reading, p. DI•122 **ELL HANDBOOK** • Picture It! Skill Instruction, pp. 54–54a • Multilingual Summaries, pp. 55–57
Vocabulary **Basic and Lesson Vocabulary** **Word Analysis: Suffix *-ing***	**TEACHER'S EDITION** • Basic Vocabulary, p. DI•117 • Preteach Lesson Vocabulary, p. DI•117 • Suffix *-ing*, p. DI•120 **ELL HANDBOOK** • Word Cards, p. 53 • ELL Vocabulary Routine, p. 471 **ELL POSTER 5** • Day 1 Activities	**TEACHER'S EDITION** • Basic Vocabulary, p. DI•117 • Reteach Lesson Vocabulary, p. DI•118 • Suffix *-ing*, p. DI•120 **ELL HANDBOOK** • Word Cards, p. 53 • Multilingual Vocabulary List, p. 432 **ELL POSTER 5** • Day 2 Activities
Grammar and Conventions	**TEACHER'S EDITION** • Preteach Common and Proper Nouns with Appositives, p. DI•124	**TEACHER'S EDITION** • Practice Common and Proper Nouns with Appositives, p. DI•124
Writing	**TEACHER'S EDITION** • Problem and Solution, p. DI•125 • Introduce Expository Composition, pp. 143e–143f	**TEACHER'S EDITION** • Writing Trait: Organizing Ideas, pp. 153d–153e

This symbol indicates leveled instruction to address language proficiency levels.

Day 3	Day 4	Day 5
TEACHER'S EDITION • Academic Language, p. DI•116 • Concept Development, p. DI•116 • Anchored Talk, p. 154a • Concept Talk Video **ELL HANDBOOK** • ELL Poster Talk, Concept Talk, p. 53c **ELL POSTER 5** • Day 3 Activities	**TEACHER'S EDITION** • Academic Language, p. DI•116 • Concept Development, p. DI•116 • Anchored Talk, p. 164a • Concept Talk Video **ELL HANDBOOK** • ELL Poster Talk, Concept Talk, p. 53c **ELL POSTER 5** • Day 4 Activities	**TEACHER'S EDITION** • Academic Language, p. DI•116 • Concept Development, p. DI•116 • Concept Talk Video **ELL HANDBOOK** • ELL Poster Talk, Concept Talk, p. 53c **ELL POSTER 5** • Day 5 Activities
		TEACHER'S EDITION • Phonics and Spelling, p. DI•120
ELL HANDBOOK • Phonics Transition Lesson, pp. 280, 283 **TEACHER'S EDITION** • AudioText of *Ten Mile Day* • Concept Talk Video **ELL HANDBOOK** • AudioText CD Routine, p. 477	**ELL HANDBOOK** • Phonics Transition Lesson, pp. 280, 283 **TEACHER'S EDITION** • Concept Talk Video	**TEACHER'S EDITION** • Concept Talk Video
TEACHER'S EDITION • Sheltered Reading, p. DI•122 **ELL HANDBOOK** • Multilingual Summaries, pp. 55–57	**TEACHER'S EDITION** • ELL/ELD Reader Guided Reading, p. DI•123 **ELL HANDBOOK** • ELL Study Guide, p. 58	**TEACHER'S EDITION** • ELL/ELD Reader Guided Reading, p. DI•123 **ELL HANDBOOK** • ELL Study Guide, p. 58
ELL HANDBOOK • High-Frequency Words Activity Bank, p. 446 **ELL POSTER 5** • Day 3 Activities	**ELL HANDBOOK** • High-Frequency Words Activity Bank, p. 446	**TEACHER'S EDITION** • Suffix *-ing*, p. 169i **ELL HANDBOOK** • High-Frequency Words Activity Bank, p. 446
TEACHER'S EDITION • Grammar Jammer **ELL HANDBOOK** • Grammar Transition Lesson, pp. 314, 318–319, 346 • Grammar Jammer Routine, p. 478	**TEACHER'S EDITION** • Grammar Jammer **ELL HANDBOOK** • Grammar Transition Lesson, pp. 314, 318–319, 346	**TEACHER'S EDITION** • Grammar Jammer **ELL HANDBOOK** • Grammar Transition Lesson, pp. 314, 318–319, 346
TEACHER'S EDITION • Let's Write It!, p. 162–163 • Writer's Craft: Paragraphs, pp. 163a–163b	**TEACHER'S EDITION** • Revising Strategy, pp. 169d–169e	**TEACHER'S EDITION** • Common and Proper Nouns, pp. 169p–169q

Question of the Week

What challenges do immigrants encounter?

Throughout the week, use the ELL Poster to help students produce and comprehend language, understand the concept, and build English vocabulary. Use the Question of the Week and other questions to help students share ideas in pairs, small groups, or the large group. Sample questions are shown, with examples of possible responses by students.

Weekly Concept and Language Goals

• Understand the concept of immigration

• Talk about the experiences of immigrants

• Identify challenges immigrants have in a new country

By the end of the lesson, students should be able to talk about and write sentences about challenges immigrants have in a new country.

ELL Poster 5

Daily Team Talk

Day 1	Day 2	Day 3	Day 4	Day 5
After Day 1 activities on Poster, ask questions such as *Where did the people in the poster picture come from?*	After Day 2 activity on Poster, ask questions such as *In the poster picture, what challenges do the immigrants have?*	After Day 3 activity on Poster, ask questions such as *Besides the hard work, why else is it hard for the immigrants to live in a new country?*	After Day 4 activity on Poster, ask questions such as *Why do you think the immigrants moved to America?*	After Day 5 activity on Poster, ask questions such as *If you moved to a new country, what challenges would you face?*
Beginning Other places. **Intermediate** They came from other countries. **Advanced** The people came from other countries to live in America. **Advanced High** The people are immigrants from other countries. They all moved from different countries and now live together in America.	**Beginning** They work. **Intermediate** They are working hard. **Advanced** They have to work hard on the railroad. They do not get much money. **Advanced High** The work they do on the railroad is very difficult, and they do not get paid much money for their work.	**Beginning** It is different. **Intermediate** People do things differently. **Advanced** The culture is different. It will take time to adjust. **Advanced High** Life in a new country might be hard for immigrants because it is difficult to adjust to a new culture. The language and what they eat might be different.	**Beginning** To get work. **Intermediate** They wanted to get jobs. **Advanced** They probably needed to get jobs to make money for their families. **Advanced High** Life was hard in their old countries. They moved to America so they could get jobs to support their families.	**Beginning** I miss home. **Intermediate** I would miss my home and friends. **Advanced** I would miss my old home. I would also feel lonely without my friends. **Advanced High** If I moved to a new country, I would miss my old house. I would also feel lonely because I miss my friends. It might take a while to make new friends.

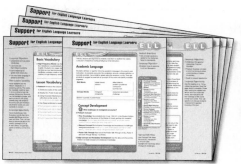

Teacher's Edition pages 140j–173a

Teacher's Edition pages DI•116–DI•125

ELL Handbook pp. 53a–58

See the support for English language learners throughout the lesson, including ELL strategies and scaffolded activities at points of use.

Differentiated Instruction for English language learners provides daily group activities that "frontload," or preteach, core instruction.

Find additional lesson materials that support the core lesson and the ELL instructional pages.

ELL Poster 5

ELL Reader 5.1.5

ELD Reader 5.1.5

Concept Literacy Reader

ELD, ELL Reader
Teaching Guide

Concept Literacy Reader
Teaching Guide

Technology

Online Teacher's Edition Use the digital version of the core Teacher's Edition for planning and instruction.

eReaders
This week's ELL and ELD Readers and Concept Literacy Reader are also available in digital format.

This Week's Content and Language Objectives by Strand

Concept Development/ Academic Language What challenges do immigrants encounter?	**Content Objective** • Use concept vocabulary related to the challenges faced by immigrants. **Language Objective** • Express ideas in response to art and discussion.
Phonics and Spelling Contractions	**Content Objectives** • Identify words that are contractions. • Review word structure. **Language Objective** • Apply phonics and decoding skills to vocabulary.
Listening Comprehension Modified Read Aloud: "Yehuda and the Wait"	**Content Objective** • Monitor and adjust oral comprehension. **Language Objectives** • Discuss oral passages. • Use a graphic organizer to take notes.
Reading Comprehension Cause and Effect	**Content Objectives** • Guide students in understanding cause and effect. • Monitor and adjust comprehension. **Language Objectives** • Discuss importance of cause and effect. • Identify causes and effects in text. • Read grade-level text with accuracy.
Vocabulary Basic and Lesson Vocabulary	**Language Objectives** • Acquire, understand and use basic, grade-level and high frequency vocabulary. • Understand the general measuring of spoken language. • Produce drawings, phrases, or short sentences to show understanding of Lesson Vocabulary. • Speak to request assistance.
Word Analysis Suffix -ing	**Content Objective** • Use suffix –ing. **Language Objective** • Discuss how the suffix –ing affects meaning.
Grammar and Conventions Common and Proper Nouns with Appositives	**Content Objective** • Decode and correctly use proper nouns. **Language Objective** • Spell words using proper nouns correctly.
Writing Problem and Solution	**Content Objective** • Understand how to write about problems and solutions. **Language Objective** • Use the language structure of problems and solutions.

Word Cards for Vocabulary Activities

barren

deafening

lurched

previous

prying

surveying

Teacher Note: Beginning Teach two to three words. **Intermediate** Teach three to four words. **Advanced** Teach five to six words. **Advanced High** Teach all words.

Name _____

Read the story. **Complete** the word webs below.

Emilio's Road to Success

When Emilio came to the United States, he didn't understand English. But he wanted to learn. He studied and practiced every day. In a few years, he could speak English very well. In high school, Emilio got good grades. He graduated at the top of his class. Next year, Emilio is going to college.

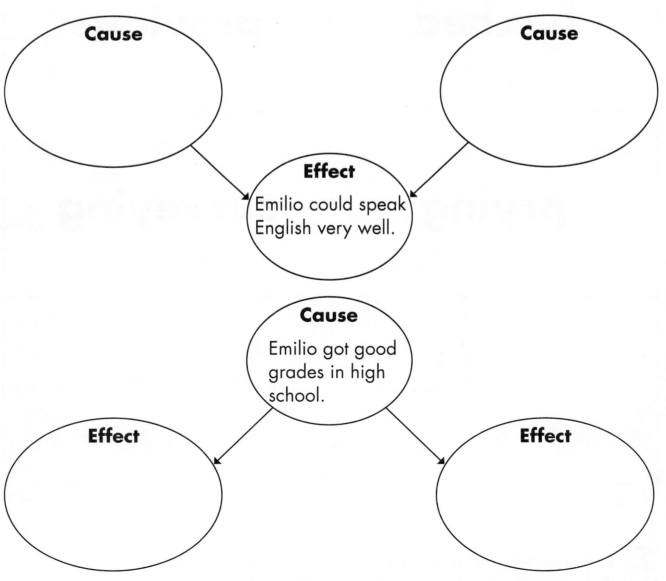

Cause

Cause

Effect
Emilio could speak English very well.

Cause
Emilio got good grades in high school.

Effect

Effect

ELL Handbook

Cause and Effect

Use this lesson to supplement or replace the skill lesson on page 141c of the Teacher's Edition. Display the Skill Points (at right) and share them with students.

Teach/Model

Beginning Say and write on the board: *The fire alarm rings. The class lines up.* *What happens after the alarm rings?* (The class lines up.) *This is the effect. Why does the class line up?* (The fire alarm rings.) *This is the cause.*

Intermediate Say and write on the board: *I overslept and was late for school.* Ask students to copy the sentence, underline the cause (I overslept), and circle the effect (was late for school).

Advanced Make a word web on the board. Label the center circle *Cause* and write *going to school* in the center. Ask students to think about the effects of going to school. Write those effects in the outer circles. Explain that some causes have more than one effect.

Advanced High Write on the board: *You stayed up late last night.* Ask: *What are some possible effects of staying up late last night?* (Possible answer: I nap on the school bus.) *What are some causes for you staying up late last night?* (Possible answer: I was reading a good book.)

Then distribute copies of Picture It! page 54.
- Have students read the title and predict what the paragraph might be about.
- Review the Skill Points with students.
- Read the story aloud. Guide students to identify some of the causes and effects from the story.

Practice

Read aloud the directions on page 54. Have students reread the story with a partner. Then have them use the picture and the story as they fill in the cause-and-effect web.

Beginning Students can first say the causes and effects they want to write before writing their answers in the circles. Provide help with English words and writing.

Intermediate Students can first orally answer and then write simple sentences in the webs.

Advanced Students can write their answers in the organizers and then check them by comparing them with a partner's.

Advanced High Students can write their answers in the organizers and then explain how the completed organizer helps them understand the story.

Answers for page 54: *Causes:* He studied every day. He practiced every day. *Effects:* He graduated at the top of his class. He is going to college.

Skill Points
- ✔ A **cause** is why something happens. The **effect** is what happens.
- ✔ Words such as *because* and *why* are clues. They tell you that you are reading about a cause-and-effect relationship.
- ✔ Sometimes a cause has more than one effect. Sometimes an effect has more than one cause.

Multilingual Summaries

Ten Mile Day

On April 28, 1869, Charles Crocker and James Strobridge called for volunteers to meet the challenge of laying 10 miles of railroad track in one day. Fourteen hundred Central Pacific laborers were selected.

At 7 a.m. the race began and laborers began to work. Well organized teams completed special jobs. Tired workers were replaced. However, the eight "iron men" did not stop. By 9:00 a.m. two miles of track were spiked. At 1:30 p.m. six miles of track were laid.

Work slowed as the tracks climbed the mountains. No one stopped. At 7:00 p.m. there was a final blast of the train whistle. Work stopped. The railhead was ten miles and fifty-six feet farther than it had been the night before.

El día de las diez millas

El 28 de abril de 1869 Charles Crocker y James Strobridge solicitaron voluntarios para que trataran de cumplir la hazaña de colocar 10 millas de rieles en un solo día. Mil cuatrocientos trabajadores de la compañía Central Pacific fueron seleccionados.

A las 7 a.m. la carrera inició y los trabajadores comenzaron su labor. Cuadrillas bien organizadas completaban las labores especiales. Los trabajadores agotados eran reemplazados. Sin embargo, el octavo "hombre de hierro" no dejó de trabajar en ningún momento. Hacia las 9:00 a.m. dos millas de rieles ya despuntaban. A la 1:30 p.m. seis millas de rieles se habían colocado.

Las labores se hicieron más lentas mientras los rieles subían las montañas. Nadie se detuvo. A las 7:00 p.m. sonó el silbato del tren por última vez. Los trabajos habían terminado. Las vías del tren medían ahora diez millas y cincuenta y seis pies más que la noche anterior.

Multilingual Summaries

Chinese

十英里日

　　1869 年 4 月 28 日那一天，查爾斯　克羅克和詹姆斯　史特比吉召集了一群志工，挑戰在一天之內鋪設 10 英里軌道的壯舉。　他們挑選了 1400 名「中太平洋鐵路公司」的員工參加。

　　早上 7 點計時開始，員工們開始工作。　組織良好的團隊完成了特殊的任務。　疲累的員工休息換班。　不過，有八個「鐵人」一直沒有停止工作。　早上 9 點時，鋪設完成了 2 英里長的軌道。　下午 1:30 時，鋪設好了 6 英里長的軌道。

　　鋪軌道的工作在爬坡時慢了下來。　但沒有人停止工作。　到了晚上 7 點，時間終了的火車汽笛聲響起。　大家放下了工作。　軌道比前一晚的長度長了十英里 56 英呎。

Vietnamese

Một Ngày Mười Dặm

　　Vào ngày 28 tháng Tư, 1869, Charles Crocker và James Strobridge kêu gọi mọi người tình nguyện ghi danh làm đường rầy để đạt thử thách đặt được mười dặm đường trong một ngày. Một ngàn bốn trăm lao công của Central Pacific được chọn.

　　Cuộc đua bắt đầu lúc 7:00 giờ sáng và người lao công bắt tay vào việc. Những đội có tổ chức trước đã hoàn thành xong các công việc đặc biệt. Lao công nào mỏi mệt thì được người khác thế. Mặc dầu vậy, có tám "người sắt" vẫn không ngừng nghỉ. Đến 9:00 sáng thì hai dặm đường rầy đã được hoàn tất. Lúc 1:30 trưa thì sáu dặm đường sắt đã được đặt xuống.

　　Công việc chậm lại khi đường bắt đầu lên dốc núi. Nhưng vẫn không ai ngừng. Đến 7:00 chiều thì có tiếng còi xe lửa cuối cùng hú lên. Mọi việc đều ngừng lại. Đường rầy đã dài được mười dặm, và năm mươi sáu bộ hơn đêm trước.

Multilingual Summaries

하루에 십 마일

　1869년 4월 28일에 찰스 크로커와 제임스 스트로브리지는 하루 만에 철도 선로 10마일을 놓는 것에 도전할 지원자를 모집한다. 천 사백 명의 중앙 태평양 노동자들이 선발되었다.

　오전 7시에 도전이 시작되고 노동자들이 일하기 시작했다. 그들은 조직적으로 작업을 수행했다. 지친 노동자들은 교대했지만, 여덟 명의 "철인"은 멈추지 않았다. 오전 9시에 철도 선로 2마일이 고정되었고, 오후 1시 30분에는 6마일의 선로가 놓였다.

　선로가 산으로 올라가면서 작업 속도가 느려졌다. 아무도 멈추지 않았다. 오후 7시에는 기차의 경적 소리가 울렸다. 일이 끝났다. 철도는 전날에 비해 10마일, 즉 56피트나 더 길어졌다.

Hnub 10 Mile

　Nyob rau lub 4 Hli, hnub 28, xyoo 1869 Charles Crocker thiab James Strobridge raug caw mus sib tw nyob rau qhov kev sib tw 10 miles rau hnub ntawd. 1400 Central Pacific raug xaiv.

　Thaum 7 moo sawv ntxov, kev sib tw pib thiab cov neeg ua hauj lwm pib ua hauj lwm mus. Pab neeg uas raug xaiv tshwj xeeb ua tau tes hauj lwm txhwj xeeb kawg. Cov neeg uas nkees ces raug pauv lawm. Tsis tas li ntawm, muaj 8 tus "iron men" tsis nres li. Thaum 9:00 moo sawv ntxov muaj 2 miles rau caw.　Nyob rau thaum 1:30 tsaus ntuj 6 miles tiav lawm.

　Cov hauj lwm qeeb ib yam li pab ntawd nce lub roob. Tsis muaj neeg nres. Thaum 7:00 moo tsaus ntuj thiaj hnov lub tsheb nqaj lub suab nrov los. Tej hauj nres tas. Txoj kev tsheb tiav lawm 10 miles, 56 feet ntau tshaj li thawj hmo dhau los lawm.

Name _____

- **Read** *Love, Enid* again.
- Use the information in the book to **fill in** the cause-and-effect boxes below.

Cause	Effect
	Enid was very nervous.
Enid's mom is always tired after work.	
	Enid and her mom are saving money so that they can buy Enid a warm coat and hat.

Family Link

Has anyone in your family moved a long distance, from one region to another? Ask family members to talk about moving.

Weekly Resources Guide for English Language Learner Support

For this week's content and language objectives, see p. 59e.

Instructional Strand	Day 1	Day 2
Concept Development/Academic Language	**TEACHER'S EDITION** • Academic Language, p. DI•16 • Concept Development, p. DI•16 • Anchored Talk, pp. 176j—176–177 • Preteach Academic Vocabulary, p. 179a • Concept Talk Video **ELL HANDBOOK** • Hear It, See It, Say It, Use It, pp. xxxvi–xxxvii • ELL Poster Talk, Concept Talk, p. 59c **ELL POSTER 6** • Day 1 Activities	**TEACHER'S EDITION** • Academic Language, p. DI•16 • Concept Development, p. DI•16 • Anchored Talk, p. 180a • Concept Talk Video **ELL HANDBOOK** • ELL Poster Talk, Concept Talk, p. 59c • Concept Talk Video Routine, p. 477 **ELL POSTER 6** • Day 2 Activities
Phonics and Spelling	**TEACHER'S EDITION** • Phonics and Spelling, p. DI•20	**TEACHER'S EDITION** • Phonics and Spelling, p. DI•20
Listening Comprehension	**TEACHER'S EDITION** • Modified Read Aloud, p. DI•19 • Read Aloud, p. 177b • Concept Talk Video **ELL HANDBOOK** • Concept Talk Video Routine, p. 477	**TEACHER'S EDITION** • Modified Read Aloud, p. DI•19 • AudioText of *At the Beach* • Concept Talk Video **ELL HANDBOOK** • AudioText CD Routine, p. 477 • Venn Diagram, p. 488
Reading Comprehension	**TEACHER'S EDITION** • Preteach Compare and Contrast, p. DI•21	**TEACHER'S EDITION** • Reteach Compare and Contrast, p. DI•21 • Frontloading Reading, p. DI•22 **ELL HANDBOOK** • Picture It! Skill Instruction, pp. 60–60a • Multilingual Summaries, pp. 61–63
Vocabulary **Basic and Lesson Vocabulary** **Word Analysis: Compound Words**	**TEACHER'S EDITION** • Basic Vocabulary, p. DI•17 • Preteach Lesson Vocabulary, p. DI•17 • Compound Words, p. DI•20 **ELL HANDBOOK** • Word Cards, p. 59 • ELL Vocabulary Routine, p. 471 **ELL POSTER 6** • Day 1 Activities	**TEACHER'S EDITION** • Basic Vocabulary, p. DI•17 • Reteach Lesson Vocabulary, p. DI•18 • Compound Words, p. DI•20 **ELL HANDBOOK** • Word Cards, p. 59 • Multilingual Vocabulary List, p. 433 **ELL POSTER 6** • Day 2 Activities
Grammar and Conventions	**TEACHER'S EDITION** • Preteach Regular and Irregular Plural Nouns, p. DI•24	**TEACHER'S EDITION** • Reteach Regular and Irregular Plural Nouns, p. DI•24
Writing	**TEACHER'S EDITION** • Descriptive Language, p. DI•25 • Introduce Description, pp. 179e–179f	**TEACHER'S EDITION** • Writing Trait: Focus/Ideas, pp. 189d–189e

This symbol indicates leveled instruction to address language proficiency levels.

Day 3	Day 4	Day 5
TEACHER'S EDITION • Academic Language, p. DI•16 • Concept Development, p. DI•16 • Anchored Talk, p. 190a • Concept Talk Video **ELL HANDBOOK** • ELL Poster Talk, Concept Talk, p. 59c **ELL POSTER 6** • Day 3 Activities	**TEACHER'S EDITION** • Academic Language, p. DI•16 • Concept Development, p. DI•16 • Anchored Talk, p. 198a • Concept Talk Video **ELL HANDBOOK** • ELL Poster Talk, Concept Talk, p. 59c **ELL POSTER 6** • Day 4 Activities	**TEACHER'S EDITION** • Academic Language, p. DI•16 • Concept Development, p. DI•16 • Concept Talk Video **ELL HANDBOOK** • ELL Poster Talk, Concept Talk, p. 59c **ELL POSTER 6** • Day 5 Activities
		TEACHER'S EDITION • Phonics and Spelling, p. DI•20
ELL HANDBOOK • Phonics Transition Lesson, pp. 224, 227	**ELL HANDBOOK** • Phonics Transition Lesson, pp. 224, 227	
TEACHER'S EDITION • AudioText of *At the Beach* • Concept Talk Video **ELL HANDBOOK** • AudioText CD Routine, p. 477	**TEACHER'S EDITION** • Concept Talk Video	**TEACHER'S EDITION** • Concept Talk Video
TEACHER'S EDITION • Sheltered Reading, p. DI•22 **ELL HANDBOOK** • Multilingual Summaries, pp. 61–63	**TEACHER'S EDITION** • ELL/ELD Reader Guided Reading, p. DI•23 **ELL HANDBOOK** • ELL Study Guide, p. 64	**TEACHER'S EDITION** • ELL/ELD Reader Guided Reading, p. DI•23 **ELL HANDBOOK** • ELL Study Guide, p. 64
		TEACHER'S EDITION • Spanish Word Origins, p. 201i
ELL HANDBOOK • High-Frequency Words Activity Bank, p. 446 **ELL POSTER 6** • Day 3 Activities	**ELL HANDBOOK** • High-Frequency Words Activity Bank, p. 446	**ELL HANDBOOK** • High-Frequency Words Activity Bank, p. 446
TEACHER'S EDITION • Grammar Jammer **ELL HANDBOOK** • Grammar Transition Lesson, pp. 316, 322 • Grammar Jammer Routine, p. 478	**TEACHER'S EDITION** • Grammar Jammer **ELL HANDBOOK** • Grammar Transition Lesson, pp. 316, 322	**TEACHER'S EDITION** • Grammar Jammer **ELL HANDBOOK** • Grammar Transition Lesson, pp. 316, 322
TEACHER'S EDITION • Let's Write It!, p. 196–197 • Writing Trait: Descriptive Language: The Five Senses, pp. 197a–197b	**TEACHER'S EDITION** • Revising Strategy, pp. 201d–201e	**TEACHER'S EDITION** • Plural Nouns and Quotations, pp. 201p–201q

Question of the Week
Why is honesty important?

Throughout the week, use the ELL Poster to help students produce and comprehend language, understand the concept, and build English vocabulary. Use the Question of the Week and other questions to help students share ideas in pairs, small groups, or the large group. Sample questions are shown, with examples of possible responses by students.

ELL Poster 6

Weekly Concept and Language Goals

• Discuss the concept of honesty

• Explain situations related to honesty

• Tell why honesty is important

By the end of the lesson, students should be able to talk about and write sentences about the importance of honesty.

Daily Team Talk

Day 1	Day 2	Day 3	Day 4	Day 5
After Day 1 activities on Poster, ask questions such as *In the poster picture, how was the boy honest with his mother?*	After Day 2 activity on Poster, ask questions such as *In the poster picture, why might the boy not be honest with his mother?*	After Day 3 activity on Poster, ask questions such as *Why is it important for the boy to be honest with his mother?*	After Day 4 activity on Poster, ask questions such as *In the story At the Beach, why does Fernando finally decide to tell his mother the truth?*	After Day 5 activity on Poster, ask questions such as *Tell about a time when honesty was important.*
Beginning He tells her. **Intermediate** He tells her how he got hurt. **Advanced** The boy told his mom what happened to hurt his finger. **Advanced High** The boy was honest with his mother when he told her how he hurt his finger cleaning the fish tank.	**Beginning** She will get mad. **Intermediate** He knows she might get mad. **Advanced** He might be scared she will get angry because he was not careful. **Advanced High** He might be afraid to be honest with his mother. She might be angry with him for not being more careful. She might also find out how dirty the fish tank was.	**Beginning** She can help. **Intermediate** She can help him with his finger. **Advanced** His mom can help him fix his finger if he tells her about it. **Advanced High** It is important for the boy to be honest with his mother so that she can help make his finger better. Being honest is always the right thing to do.	**Beginning** He cannot eat. **Intermediate** He feels bad for telling a lie. **Advanced** He feels so bad he told his mom a lie that he cannot eat his food. **Advanced High** Fernando feels so guilty about lying to his mother that he cannot eat his lunch. He knows he will not enjoy the food unless he is honest with his mother.	**Beginning** Lost my glasses. **Intermediate** I could not find my glasses. **Advanced** I had to tell my dad when I lost my glasses so he could help me look. **Advanced High** When I lost my glasses, I had to tell my father. He was able to help me remember where I might have lost them.

This Week's Materials

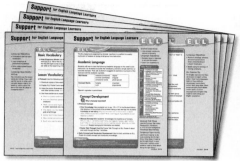

Teacher's Edition pages 176j–201q

See the support for English language learners throughout the lesson, including ELL strategies and scaffolded activities at points of use.

Teacher's Edition pages DI•16–DI•25

Differentiated Instruction for English language learners provides daily group activities that "frontload," or preteach, core instruction.

ELL Handbook pp. 59a–64

Find additional lesson materials that support the core lesson and the ELL instructional pages.

ELL Poster 6

ELL Reader 5.2.1

ELD Reader 5.2.1

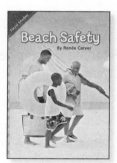

Concept Literacy Reader

ELD, ELL Reader Teaching Guide

Concept Literacy Reader Teaching Guide

Technology

Online Teacher's Edition Use the digital version of the core Teacher's Edition for planning and instruction.

eReaders
This week's ELL and ELD Readers and Concept Literacy Reader are also available in digital format.

This Week's Content and Language Objectives by Strand

Concept Development/ Academic Language Why is honesty important?	**Content Objective** • Use concept vocabulary related to honesty. **Language Objectives** • Express ideas in response to art and discussion. • Learn new expressions.
Phonics and Spelling Digraphs *ch, sh*	**Content Objective** • Identify digraphs *ch* and *sh*. **Language Objectives** • Apply phonics and decoding skills to vocabulary. • Monitor and self-correct. • Distinguish and practice producing sounds of English.
Listening Comprehension Modified Read Aloud: "Always Do the Right Thing"	**Content Objective** • Monitor and adjust oral comprehension. **Language Objectives** • Discuss oral passages. • Use a graphic organizer to take notes. • Use linguistic support to understand spoken languages.
Reading Comprehension Compare and Contrast	**Content Objectives** • Identify the difference between compare and contrast. • Monitor and adjust comprehension. **Language Objectives** • Speak using connecting words. • Compare and contrast a character in a reading. • Write comparisons and contrasts about a character in a reading. • Read grade-level text with expression.
Vocabulary Basic and Lesson Vocabulary	**Language Objectives** • Understand and use basic vocabulary. • Write using content-based vocabulary. • Understand the general measuring of spoken language. • Produce drawings, phrases, or short sentences to show understanding of Lesson Vocabulary. • Speak using the strategy of naming synonyms.
Word Analysis Compound Words	**Content Objective** • Identify and define words in compound words. **Language Objective** • Discuss meanings of compound words.
Grammar and Conventions Regular and Irregular Plural Nouns	**Content Objective** • Decode and correctly use regular and irregular plural nouns. **Language Objective** • Speak and write using the patterns of regular and irregular plural nouns.
Writing Descriptive Language	**Content Objective** • Understand the purpose of descriptive language in writing. **Language Objective** • Write sentences using descriptive language.

Word Cards for Vocabulary Activities

algae

concealed

driftwood

hammocks

lamented

sea urchins

sternly

tweezers

Teacher Note: Beginning Teach three to four words. **Intermediate** Teach four to six words. **Advanced** Teach six to seven words. **Advanced High** Teach all words.

Name _____

Look at the pictures and **read** the two paragraphs.
- How are Maria and Marisa alike? **Write** your answers in the first column.
- How are they different? **Write** your answers in the second column.

Maria And Marisa

Maria is nine years old and in the fourth grade. She likes school because she likes learning new things. She loves to write stories. After school, Maria takes dance and piano lessons. At home, she always keeps her side of the bedroom neat and clean.

Marisa is Maria's twin sister. Marisa likes school too. She takes violin and dance lessons after school. Marisa loves to read books. When she is reading, she doesn't even hear Mama calling her. Marisa also doesn't make her bed or put away her things.

Alike	Different

Compare and Contrast

Use this lesson to supplement or replace the skill lesson on page 177c of the Teacher's Edition. Display the Skill Points (at right) and share them with students.

Teach/Model

Beginning Ask students to think about the classroom and the lunchroom. Ask: *How are these two rooms similar? How are they different?* Draw a two-column chart labeled *Alike* and *Different* and complete it with students' ideas.

Intermediate Say: *Anna rides her bike to school. Julio takes the school bus. Anna and Julio enjoy being in Ms. Nelson's fifth grade class.* Guide students in completing a two-column chart that compares and contrasts Anna and Julio. Repeat the story if necessary.

Advanced Tell students to find a book in the classroom. When everyone has a book, choose two volunteers and discuss how their books are alike and different. Repeat this process with other volunteers or a different type of object.

Advanced High Pair students. Ask partners to share information about activities they do at home and at school. Have them work together to complete a two-column chart that compares and contrasts the activities.

Then distribute copies of Picture It! page 60.

- Have students look at the pictures and describe the appearance of the characters.
- Read the story aloud. Ask: *How are the sisters alike? How are they different?*
- Review the Skill Points with students.
- Have students look at the pictures and words to compare and contrast the characters.

Practice

Read aloud the directions on page 60. Have students reread the story aloud. Explain what *identical twin* means. Then have students look at the pictures and the story as they complete the graphic organizer.

Beginning Students can say what they want to write in each part of the chart before writing their answers on the page. Provide help with writing and spelling English words.

Intermediate Students can first orally tell how the two sisters are similar and different and then write their answers in the chart.

Advanced Students can write their answers in the chart and then check them by comparing their chart with a partner's.

Advanced High Students can write their answers in the chart and then check them by reviewing the story.

Answers for page 60: *Alike:* They are twins, so they look alike. They are both nine and in the fourth grade. They both like school. They both take dance lessons. *Different:* Maria loves to write stories; Marisa loves to read books. Maria takes piano lessons; Marisa takes violin lessons. Maria keeps her things neat and clean; Marisa does not.

Skill Points

✔ When we **compare,** we look for the ways things are alike.

✔ When we **contrast,** we look for the ways things are different.

Multilingual Summaries

At the Beach

One day Fernando goes to the beach with his family. They all go in Papi's car. The children run into the water as soon as they get there. The adults sit in the shade. The men play dominoes.

Fernando wants to go to the reef. The other children go with him. Their parents had told them not to go. Fernando's little cousin Javi steps on a sea urchin. Sea urchins have sharp spines. Javi is hurt. The children will be in trouble if their parents find out that they went to the reef. Fernando tells a lie when they go back for lunch.

Fernando feels bad about lying. He tells the truth. He thinks Mami will not give him lunch. But Mami thanks him for telling the truth, and Fernando eats his lunch.

Spanish

En la playa

Un día, Fernando va a la playa con su familia. Todos van en el auto de Papi. Los niños corren hacia el agua tan pronto llegan allí. Los adultos se sientan en la sombra. Los hombres juegan dominó.

Fernando quiere ir al arrecife. Los otros niños van con él. Sus padres les han dicho que no vayan allí. El primo pequeño de Fernando, Javi, pisa un erizo de mar. El erizo de mar tiene espinas afiladas. Javi se hace daño. Los niños tendrán problemas si sus padres descubren que ellos fueron al arrecife. Fernando dice una mentira cuando regresan a almorzar.

Fernando se siente mal porque ha mentido y finalmente dice la verdad. Él piensa que Mami no le dará el almuerzo. Pero Mami le da las gracias por decirle la verdad, y Fernando se come su almuerzo.

Multilingual Summaries

Chinese

在海邊

一天，費爾南多和家人一起去海邊，爸爸開車帶他們去。孩子們一到海邊，就跑去游泳。大人們坐在遮陽傘下，男人們在玩多米諾牌。

費爾南多想去珊瑚礁，雖然父母親不讓去，小朋友們還是跟著他。小表弟加維不小心踩到海膽，被尖銳的刺扎傷了。為了不讓父母發現他們去珊瑚礁玩了，費爾南多回來吃午餐時，沒有說實話。

撒謊之後，費爾南多心裏總發慌，最後還是說了實話。他想媽咪肯定不會給他吃午餐。可為了獎勵他的誠實，媽咪還是讓費爾南多吃了午餐。

Vietnamese

Trên Bãi Biển

Ngày nọ Fernando đi ra bãi biển với gia đình. Cả gia đình đi trên xe của Papi. Các đứa trẻ chạy xuống nước ngay khi đến nơi. Người lớn ngồi dưới bóng râm. Các ông thì chơi cờ đô-mi-nô.

Fernando muốn đi ra dãy đá ngầm. Các đứa trẻ khác muốn đi với cậu ấy. Cha mẹ chúng đã bảo chúng đừng đi. Đứa em họ của Fernando là Javi đạp trúng một con nhím biển. Những con nhím biển có các gai nhọn. Javi bị đau. Các đứa trẻ sẽ bị rầy rà nếu cha mẹ chúng biết được chúng đã đi ra dãy đá ngầm. Fernando đã nói dối khi chúng quay về ăn trưa.

Fernando cảm thấy ân hận vì đã nói dối. Cậu nói lên sự thật. Cậu bé nghĩ là Mami sẽ không cho cậu ăn trưa. Nhưng Mami cám ơn cậu bé đã nói thật, và Fernando được ăn bữa ăn trưa của mình.

Multilingual Summaries

해변에서

어느 날 페르난도는 아빠의 차를 타고 가족과 함께 바다에 간다. 아이들은 도착하자마자 물로 뛰어들고 어른들은 그늘에 앉는다. 남자들은 도미노 게임을 한다.

페르난도는 암초에 가고 싶어해서 다른 아이들과 함께 암초에 간다. 하지만 아이들 부모님들은 암초에 가지 말라고 미리 주의를 주었다. 페르난도의 어린 사촌인 하비가 성게를 밟는다. 성게 표면에 뾰족한 가시가 있어 하비는 상처를 입는다. 아이들이 암초에 갔었다는 걸 부모님들이 알게 된다면 아이들은 벌을 받게 될 것이다. 페르난도는 아이들과 점심을 먹으러 돌아갔을 때 거짓말을 한다.

페르난도는 거짓말한 것을 뉘우치며 사실을 말하고 엄마가 점심을 주지 않을 것이라고 생각한다. 하지만 엄마는 사실을 말해 준 것에 대해 고마워하고 페르난도는 점심을 먹는다.

Tom Ntug Dej Hiav Txwv

Muaj ib hnub Fernando thiab nws tsev neeg mus tom ntug dej ntawm cov dej hiav txwv. Sawvdaws huv tib si mus rau hauv Papi ib lub tshevb. Thaum mus txog ntug dej lawm ces cov menyuam txawm khiav mus nkag rau hauv cov dej. Cov tiav hlob zaum hauv qhov chaw uas ntxoov ntxoo li. Cov txiv neej ua si dominoes.

Fernando xav mus tom cov pob zeb ntse uas nyob ntug dej. Luag lwm cov menyuam nrogg nws mus thiab. Sawvdaws cov niam thiav txiv qhia tias tsis txhob mus qhov ntawd. Fernando tus kwvtij yau Javi, tsuj nthi ib tug ntses Urchin uas nyob lub hiav txwv. Cov ntses Urchin uas nyob lub hiav txwv, muaj cov koob ntse uas nyob ntawm lawv txoj nqaj qaum. Javi raug mob. Cov niam, txiv yuav chim siab yog alwv paub tias lawv cov menyuam mus xyuas cov pob zeb ntse nyob ntug dej hiav txwv. Thaum cov menyuam rov qab mus noj su, ces Fernando hais lus dag.

Fernando nyob tsis zoo hauv lub siab rau qhov nws hais lus dag. Nws cia li rov qab hai lus tseeb. Fernando xav tias Mami yuav tsis pub su rau nws noj. Tiamsis Mami ua Fernando tsaug vim rau qhov nws hais lus tseeb, Fernando cia li noj nws cov mov.

Name _____

- **Read** *Hidden Treasures* again.
- **Answer** the questions to show how Sophie and Katie are alike and different.
- **Write** words and phrases under each heading.

Pages	Sophie	Katie
pages 2–3 **What does she look like?**		
pages 3–4 **What does she like to do on the beach?**		
page 5 **What did she find on the beach?**		
page 6 **At first, what did she want to do with the money?**		
pages 7–9 **What did she do with the wallet?**		

Family Link

Ask family members if they have ever lost something. How did they feel? Was it returned to them?

Weekly Resources Guide for English Language Learner Support

For this week's content and language objectives, see p. 65e.

Instructional Strand	Day 1	Day 2
Concept Development/Academic Language	**TEACHER'S EDITION** • Academic Language, p. DI•41 • Concept Development, p. DI•41 • Anchored Talk, pp. 202j—202–203 • Preteach Academic Vocabulary, p. 205a • Concept Talk Video **ELL HANDBOOK** • Hear It, See It, Say It, Use It, pp. xxxvi–xxxvii • ELL Poster Talk, Concept Talk, p. 65c **ELL POSTER 7** • Day 1 Activities	**TEACHER'S EDITION** • Academic Language, p. DI•41 • Concept Development, p. DI•41 • Anchored Talk, p. 206a • Concept Talk Video **ELL HANDBOOK** • ELL Poster Talk, Concept Talk, p. 65c • Concept Talk Video Routine, p. 477 **ELL POSTER 7** • Day 2 Activities
Phonics and Spelling	**TEACHER'S EDITION** • Phonics and Spelling, p. DI•45	**TEACHER'S EDITION** • Phonics and Spelling, p. DI•45
Listening Comprehension	**TEACHER'S EDITION** • Modified Read Aloud, p. DI•44 • Read Aloud, p. 203b • Concept Talk Video **ELL HANDBOOK** • Concept Talk Video Routine, p. 477	**TEACHER'S EDITION** • Modified Read Aloud, p. DI•44 • AudioText of *Hold the Flag High* • Concept Talk Video **ELL HANDBOOK** • AudioText CD Routine, p. 477 • Story Map A, p. 483
Reading Comprehension	**TEACHER'S EDITION** • Preteach Sequence, p. DI•46	**TEACHER'S EDITION** • Reteach Sequence, p. DI•46 • Frontloading Reading, p. DI•47 **ELL HANDBOOK** • Picture It! Skill Instruction, pp. 66–66a • Multilingual Summaries, pp. 67–69
Vocabulary **Basic and Lesson Vocabulary** **Word Analysis: Inflected Endings** *-ed, -ing*	**TEACHER'S EDITION** • Basic Vocabulary, p. DI•42 • Preteach Lesson Vocabulary, p. DI•42 • Inflected Endings *-ed, -ing*, p. DI•45 **ELL HANDBOOK** • Word Cards, p. 65 • ELL Vocabulary Routine, p. 471 **ELL POSTER 7** • Day 1 Activities	**TEACHER'S EDITION** • Basic Vocabulary, p. DI•42 • Reteach Lesson Vocabulary, p. DI•43 • Inflected Endings *-ed, -ing*, p. DI•45 **ELL HANDBOOK** • Word Cards, p. 65 • Multilingual Vocabulary List, p. 433 **ELL POSTER 7** • Day 2 Activities
Grammar and Conventions	**TEACHER'S EDITION** • Preteach Possessive Nouns, p. DI•49	**TEACHER'S EDITION** • Reteach Possessive Nouns, p. DI•49
Writing	**TEACHER'S EDITION** • Characterization, p. DI•50 • Introduce Informal Letter, pp. 205e–205f	**TEACHER'S EDITION** • Writer's Craft: Characterization, pp. 213d–213e

Copyright © Pearson Education, Inc., or its affiliates. All Rights Reserved. 5

This symbol indicates leveled instruction to address language proficiency levels.

Day 3	Day 4	Day 5
TEACHER'S EDITION • Academic Language, p. DI•41 • Concept Development, p. DI•41 • Anchored Talk, p. 214a • Concept Talk Video **ELL HANDBOOK** • ELL Poster Talk, Concept Talk, p. 65c **ELL POSTER 7** • Day 3 Activities	**TEACHER'S EDITION** • Academic Language, p. DI•41 • Concept Development, p. DI•41 • Anchored Talk, p. 224a • Concept Talk Video **ELL HANDBOOK** • ELL Poster Talk, Concept Talk, p. 65c **ELL POSTER 7** • Day 4 Activities	**TEACHER'S EDITION** • Academic Language, p. DI•41 • Concept Development, p. DI•41 • Concept Talk Video **ELL HANDBOOK** • ELL Poster Talk, Concept Talk, p. 65c **ELL POSTER 7** • Day 5 Activities
		TEACHER'S EDITION • Phonics and Spelling, p. DI•45
ELL HANDBOOK • Phonics Transition Lesson, pp. 268, 270	**ELL HANDBOOK** • Phonics Transition Lesson, pp. 268, 270	
TEACHER'S EDITION • AudioText of *Hold the Flag High* • Concept Talk Video **ELL HANDBOOK** • AudioText CD Routine, p. 477	**TEACHER'S EDITION** • Concept Talk Video	**TEACHER'S EDITION** • Concept Talk Video
TEACHER'S EDITION • Sheltered Reading, p. DI•47 **ELL HANDBOOK** • Multilingual Summaries, pp. 67–69	**TEACHER'S EDITION** • ELL/ELD Reader Guided Reading, p. DI•48 **ELL HANDBOOK** • ELL Study Guide, p. 70	**TEACHER'S EDITION** • ELL/ELD Reader Guided Reading, p. DI•48 **ELL HANDBOOK** • ELL Study Guide, p. 70
		TEACHER'S EDITION • French Word Origin, p. 229i
ELL HANDBOOK • High-Frequency Words Activity Bank, p. 446 **ELL POSTER 7** • Day 3 Activities	**ELL HANDBOOK** • High-Frequency Words Activity Bank, p. 446	**ELL HANDBOOK** • High-Frequency Words Activity Bank, p. 446
TEACHER'S EDITION • Grammar Jammer **ELL HANDBOOK** • Grammar Transition Lesson, pp. 317, 323 • Grammar Jammer Routine, p. 478	**TEACHER'S EDITION** • Grammar Jammer **ELL HANDBOOK** • Grammar Transition Lesson, pp. 317, 323	**TEACHER'S EDITION** • Grammar Jammer **ELL HANDBOOK** • Grammar Transition Lesson, pp. 317, 323
TEACHER'S EDITION • Let's Write It!, p. 222–223 • Writing Trait: Voice, pp. 223a–223b	**TEACHER'S EDITION** • Revising Strategy, pp. 229d–229e	**TEACHER'S EDITION** • Informal Letter, pp. 229p–229q

Question of the Week
What are the risks in helping others?

Throughout the week, use the ELL Poster to help students produce and comprehend language, understand the concept, and build English vocabulary. Use the Question of the Week and other questions to help students share ideas in pairs, small groups, or the large group. Sample questions are shown, with examples of possible responses by students.

Weekly Concept and Language Goals
- Discuss the concept of taking risks
- Talk about the value of helping others
- Share ideas about taking risks to help other people

By the end of the lesson, students should be able to talk about and write sentences about taking risks to help others.

E L L Poster 7

Daily Team Talk

Day 1	Day 2	Day 3	Day 4	Day 5
After Day 1 activities on Poster, ask questions such as *In the poster picture, how have the brothers helped others?*	After Day 2 activity on Poster, ask questions such as *Why are the brothers in the poster picture taking a risk by fighting in a war?*	After Day 3 activity on Poster, ask questions such as *How do we know each brother took risk?*	After Day 4 activity on Poster, ask questions such as *What good came out of the risks the brothers took?*	After Day 5 activity on Poster, ask questions such as *Besides soldiers, who else do you know that takes risks to help others?*
Beginning They fight. **Intermediate** They fight for things they believe in. **Advanced** They fought for what their half of the country believed. **Advanced High** The brothers helped others by fighting to defend their half of the country and the things they believed in.	**Beginning** They can get hurt. **Intermediate** People can get hurt in a war. **Advanced** It is a risk to go to war because people can get injured. **Advanced High** The brothers are taking a risk by fighting in a war because people can get injured when they fight.	**Beginning** They are hurt. **Intermediate** They are hurt. One broke his arm. **Advanced** One brother has broken his arm. The other has a cane. **Advanced High** The brother in blue has a sling on his arm, so it must be broken. The brother in gray has a cane, so he must have injured his leg.	**Beginning** Stop the war. **Intermediate** The war ended. They came home. **Advanced** The war in the country ended. The brothers saw each other again. **Advanced High** The country stopped fighting, and the Civil War ended. The brothers came home and saw each other again.	**Beginning** Firefighters do. **Intermediate** Firefighters take risks to help. **Advanced** Firefighters risk their lives to help save people. **Advanced High** Firefighters take risks to help others. They run into dangerous fires to save people who are trapped.

This Week's Materials

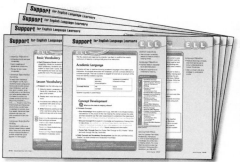

Teacher's Edition pages 202j–229q

See the support for English language learners throughout the lesson, including ELL strategies and scaffolded activities at points of use.

Teacher's Edition pages DI•41–DI•50

Differentiated Instruction for English language learners provides daily group activities that "frontload," or preteach, core instruction.

ELL Handbook pp. 65a–70

Find additional lesson materials that support the core lesson and the ELL instructional pages.

ELL Poster 7

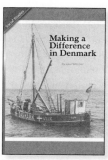

ELL Reader 5.2.2

ELD Reader 5.2.2

Concept Literacy Reader

ELD, ELL Reader Teaching Guide

Concept Literacy Reader Teaching Guide

Technology

Online Teacher's Edition Use the digital version of the core Teacher's Edition for planning and instruction.

eReaders
This week's ELL and ELD Readers and Concept Literacy Reader are also available in digital format.

This Week's Content and Language Objectives by Strand

Concept Development/ Academic Language What are the risks in helping others?	**Content Objective** • Use concept vocabulary related to risks involved in helping others. **Language Objectives** • Express ideas in response to art and discussion. • Use prior experience to understand meaning.
Phonics and Spelling Irregular Plurals	**Content Objective** • Identify words with irregular plurals. **Language Objectives** • Apply phonics and decoding skills to vocabulary. • Use contexted support to develop vocabulary.
Listening Comprehension Modified Read Aloud: "The Photograph"	**Content Objective** • Monitor and adjust oral comprehension. **Language Objectives** • Discuss oral passages. • Use a graphic organizer to take notes.
Reading Comprehension Sequence	**Content Objectives** • Describe the sequence of a text. • Identify sequence to aid comprehension. • Monitor and adjust comprehension. **Language Objectives** • Employ and expand the skill of determining sequence to comprehend text. • Retell the sequence in a reading. • Write a sequence of events.
Vocabulary Basic and Lesson Vocabulary	**Language Objectives** • Understand and use basic and grade-level vocabulary. • Review to learn basic vocabulary. • Produce drawings, phrases, or short sentences to show understanding of Lesson Vocabulary. • Use a concept web as a strategy to understand words.
Word Analysis Inflected Endings –ed, -ing	**Content Objective** • Identify words with inflected endings –ed and ing. **Language Objective** • Spell words with inflected endings with increasing accuracy.
Grammar and Conventions Possessive Nouns	**Content Objective** • Decode and use possessive nouns. **Language Objective** • Speak and write using possessive nouns.
Writing Characterization	**Content Objective** • Identify characterization in text. **Language Objectives** • Distinguish between formal and informal English. • Adapt spoken language for informal purposes. • Write paragraphs that include characterization.

Word Cards for Vocabulary Activities

canteen	**confederacy**
glory	**quarrel**
rebellion	**stallion**
union	

Teacher Note: Beginning Teach two to three words. **Intermediate** Teach three to four words. **Advanced** Teach four to five words. **Advanced High** Teach all words.

Name _____

Look at the poster and **read** the paragraph.

- Put the sentences in order. **Write** a 1 by the event that happens first. **Write** a 2 by the event that happens second. **Write** a 3 by the event that happens third.

HELP REFUGEES TODAY!

The Refugee Center needs your help. There are many refugees from all over the world at the center. They are trying to start a new life. Won't you please help?

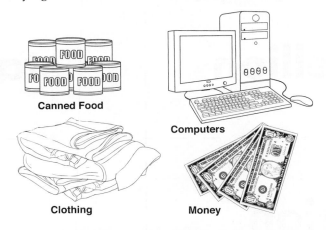

Canned Food

Computers

Clothing

Money

Please make a donation today!
You will help make the world a better place.

Please use our Web site to donate money for refugees. We send that money directly to the refugee center. Once the money is there, the volunteers use the money. They buy clothing and food for refugees in need.

The money goes to the refugee center. _____

A person makes a donation online. _____

Volunteers buy clothing and food. _____

Sequence

Use this lesson to supplement or replace the skill lesson on page 203c of the Teacher's Edition. Display the Skill Points (at right) and share them with students.

Teach/Model

Beginning Say: *I make sandwiches. I put each sandwich in a bag. I add carrots and an apple to each bag. I give the bags to friends.* Have students retell the events of the story in the correct sequence using the clue words *first, next, then,* and *last.*

Intermediate Write on the board: *I look through my closet. I take out clothes that I no longer wear. Volunteers from a charity pick up the clothes. They give the clothes to people in need.* Have students copy the sentences and add sequence clue words *(first, next, then, last).*

Advanced Describe what happens at a food pantry from donation to distribution. Do not use sequence clue words. Ask: *How can we use clue words to make the sequence easier to understand and follow?* Have volunteers use clue words to write sentences telling the events in order.

Advanced High Have students think of a simple snack that they can prepare in at least four steps. Have them write sentences about the steps using sequence words *first, next, then,* and *last.* Pair students. Have partners take turns reading their directions aloud.

Then distribute copies of Picture It! page 66.

- Have students look at the poster and tell what they see in the pictures.
- Review the Skill Points with students.
- Read the poster aloud. Ask: *What happens to the money people give to the refugee center?* Encourage children to use *first, then, last.* Ask for clarification if students give answers without sequence words.

Practice

Read aloud the directions on page 66. Reread the poster aloud, providing definitions of the words *refugee, donation,* and *volunteers.* Have students look at the pictures and the information on the poster as they number the events listed beneath the poster.

Beginning Students can describe the order in which the events take place before numbering them. Provide help with English words.

Intermediate Students can number the order of events to complete the activity.

Advanced Students can write their answers and then check them by rereading the paragraph and making necessary changes.

Advanced High Students can write their answers and then read the sentences in order, adding sequence words *first, next,* and *last* to indicate sequence.

Answers for page 66: 2, 1, 3

Skill Points

✔ **Sequence** is the order in which things happen.
✔ Look for clue words such as *first, next, then,* and *last.*
✔ Sometimes a story will not have clue words.

Multilingual Summaries

Hold the Flag High

In the American Civil War, the Union army of the North fought the Confederate army of the South. The Fifty-Fourth was an African American regiment in the Union army.

Ned was a drummer boy in the Fifty-Fourth. The night before a battle, he was scared. Carney was an officer. He told Ned to follow the Stars and Stripes flag if he got lost.

During the battle, the soldier carrying the flag was shot. Carney picked up the flag. He held the flag high. Ned and the other soldiers followed the flag to safety. The soldiers were honored for their brave actions.

Sostén la bandera en alto

En la Guerra Civil Norteamericana, el ejército de la Unión del Norte luchó contra el Confederado del Sur. El regimiento 54 del ejército de la Unión estaba formado por afroamericanos.

Ned era un tamborilero del regimiento. La noche anterior a la batalla, tenía miedo. Carney era un oficial. Le dijo a Ned que siguiera a la bandera de las Barras y las Estrellas si se perdía.

Durante la batalla, el soldado que llevaba la bandera recibió un disparo. Carney tomó la bandera. Él la sostuvo en alto. Ned y otros soldados siguieron la bandera hasta un lugar seguro. Los soldados recibieron honores por sus valientes acciones.

Multilingual Summaries

高举旗子

　　美国内战期间，北方联盟军和南方联盟军开战，北方联盟军内的第五十四团全由美国黑人组成。

　　耐德是第五十四团的鼓手。有一个晚上，一场战斗即将爆发，耐德很害怕。卡尼是团里的军官，他告诉耐德如果他迷失方向，向着星条旗走过去就可以。

　　战斗期间，拿着星条旗的士兵中枪倒下，卡尼拾起并高举旗子，耐德和其他士兵跟随旗子到达安全的地方。第五十四团的士兵都得到英勇勋章。

Vietnamese

Giương Cao Ngọn Cờ

Trng Cuộc Nội Chiến Mỹ, quân đội Union của miền Bắc đánh nhau với quân đội Confederate của miền Nam. Fifty-Fourth là một Trung Đoàn trong Quân đội Union.

Ned là người đánh trống của Fifty-Fourth. Trong đêm trước trận đánh, anh ta khiếp sợ. Camey là một sĩ quan trong trung đoàn Fifty-Fourth. Ông bảo Ted nếu lạc đường thì cứ theo ngọn cờ Sao và Sọc.

Trong trận đánh, người lính cầm cờ bị trúng đạn. Camey cầm cây cờ lên. Ông giương cao lá cờ. Ned và những người lính khác an toàn đi theo lá cờ. Binh sĩ Trung đoàn Fifty-Four được tuyên dương về hành vi dũng cảm của họ.

Multilingual Summaries

깃발을 높이 들어라

미국 남북전쟁 때 북부연합군은 남부연합군에 맞서 싸웠다. 연합군내 54연대는 흑인연대였다.

네드는 54연대의 고수(북 연주자)였다. 전투 전날 밤, 네드는 두려웠다. 카니는 54연대의 장교였다. 그는 네드에게 길을 잃으면 별과 줄무늬의 깃발을 따르라고 했다.

전투 중, 깃발을 들고가던 병사가 총에 맞았다. 카니는 깃발을 들었다. 그는 깃발을 높이 들었다. 네드와 다른 병사들은 그 깃발을 안전하게 따라갔다. 54연대의 병사들은 용감한 행동으로 칭송받았다.

Tuav tus Chij Siab Siab

Thaus lub sijhawm American Civil War, cov tubrog Union nyob qaum teb sis tua rog nrog cov tubrog Confederate nyob qab teb. Pawg tubrog Tsibcaug-Plaub yog ib pab tubrog Asmiskas Dub rau cov tubrog Union.

Ned yog ib tus tub ntaus nruag rau pawg Tsibcaug-Plaub. Mo ua ntej yuav mus sis tua, nwg mag raug caus npliav. Carney yob ib tug tubrog hauv pawg Tsibcaug-Plaub. Nwg hais rau Ned kom caum tus chij uas muaj nub qub thiab tej kab txaij yog tias nwg poob zoo.

Thaus lawv sis tua rog, tus tubrog uas nqa tus chij mag tua raug. Carney khaw loo tus chij. Nwg tuav tus chij siab siab. Ned thiab cov tubrog ntawd caum tus chij twb ywm txog chaw nyab xeeb. Cov tubrog ntawm pawg Tsibcaug-Paub raug hawm foom zoo rau lawv txoj kev uas muaj siab tawv.

Name _____

- **Read** *Making a Difference in Denmark* again.
- **Read** the answers. **Write** a question for each answer. Follow the example.

Page	Question	Answer
2	**1.** What did the citizens of Denmark do during World War II?	They saved thousands of Jewish people.
3	**2.** _____	The Danes could rule themselves if they did not fight.
4	**3.** _____	He was a German diplomat who helped the Danish government.
5–6	**4.** _____	Many hid in people's homes, barns, office buildings, and churches.
7	**5.** _____	Over 7,000 Jewish Danes went to Sweden.
8	**6.** _____	Denmark was one of the only European countries to protect these homes.

Family Link

Tell your family what you have learned about Denmark during World War II. Ask family members to tell what they know about that war.

Weekly Resources Guide for English Language Learner Support

For this week's content and language objectives, see p. 71e.

Instructional Strand	Day 1	Day 2
Concept Development/Academic Language	**TEACHER'S EDITION** • Academic Language, p. DI•66 • Concept Development, p. DI•66 • Anchored Talk, pp. 230j—230–231 • Preteach Academic Vocabulary, p. 233a • Concept Talk Video **ELL HANDBOOK** • Hear It, See It, Say It, Use It, pp. xxxvi–xxxvii • ELL Poster Talk, Concept Talk, p. 71c **ELL POSTER 8** • Day 1 Activities	**TEACHER'S EDITION** • Academic Language, p. DI•66 • Concept Development, p. DI•66 • Anchored Talk, p. 234a • Concept Talk Video **ELL HANDBOOK** • ELL Poster Talk, Concept Talk, p. 71c • Concept Talk Video Routine, p. 477 **ELL POSTER 8** • Day 2 Activities
Phonics and Spelling	**TEACHER'S EDITION** • Phonics and Spelling, p. DI•70	**TEACHER'S EDITION** • Phonics and Spelling, p. DI•70
Listening Comprehension	**TEACHER'S EDITION** • Modified Read Aloud, p. DI•69 • Read Aloud, p. 231b • Concept Talk Video **ELL HANDBOOK** • Concept Talk Video Routine, p. 477	**TEACHER'S EDITION** • Modified Read Aloud, p. DI•69 • AudioText of *The Ch'i-lin Purse* • Concept Talk Video **ELL HANDBOOK** • AudioText CD Routine, p. 477 • Venn Diagram, p. 488
Reading Comprehension	**TEACHER'S EDITION** • Preteach Compare and Contrast, p. DI•71	**TEACHER'S EDITION** • Reteach Compare and Contrast, p. DI•71 • Frontloading Reading, p. DI•72 **ELL HANDBOOK** • Picture It! Skill Instruction, pp. 72–72a • Multilingual Summaries, pp. 73–75
Vocabulary **Basic and Lesson Vocabulary** **Word Analysis: Suffixes *-tion, -ion***	**TEACHER'S EDITION** • Basic Vocabulary, p. DI•67 • Preteach Lesson Vocabulary, p. DI•67 • Suffixes *-tion, -ion*, p. DI•70 **ELL HANDBOOK** • Word Cards, p. 71 • ELL Vocabulary Routine, p. 471 **ELL POSTER 8** • Day 1 Activities	**TEACHER'S EDITION** • Basic Vocabulary, p. DI•67 • Reteach Lesson Vocabulary, p. DI•68 • Suffixes *-tion, -ion*, p. DI•70 **ELL HANDBOOK** • Word Cards, p. 71 • Multilingual Vocabulary List, pp. 433–434 **ELL POSTER 8** • Day 2 Activities
Grammar and Conventions	**TEACHER'S EDITION** • Preteach Action and Linking Verbs, p. DI•74	**TEACHER'S EDITION** • Reteach Action and Linking Verbs, p. DI•74
Writing	**TEACHER'S EDITION** • Poetic Techniques, p. DI•75 • Introduce Poem, pp. 233e–233f	**TEACHER'S EDITION** • Writing Trait: Organization, pp. 243d–243e

This symbol indicates leveled instruction to address language proficiency levels.

Day 3	Day 4	Day 5
TEACHER'S EDITION • Academic Language, p. DI•66 • Concept Development, p. DI•66 • Anchored Talk, p. 244a • Concept Talk Video **ELL HANDBOOK** • ELL Poster Talk, Concept Talk, p. 71c **ELL POSTER 8** • Day 3 Activities	**TEACHER'S EDITION** • Academic Language, p. DI•66 • Concept Development, p. DI•66 • Anchored Talk, p. 254a • Concept Talk Video **ELL HANDBOOK** • ELL Poster Talk, Concept Talk, p. 71c **ELL POSTER 8** • Day 4 Activities	**TEACHER'S EDITION** • Academic Language, p. DI•66 • Concept Development, p. DI•66 • Concept Talk Video **ELL HANDBOOK** • ELL Poster Talk, Concept Talk, p. 71c **ELL POSTER 8** • Day 5 Activities
		TEACHER'S EDITION • Phonics and Spelling, p. DI•70
ELL HANDBOOK • Phonics Transition Lesson, pp. 262–265	**ELL HANDBOOK** • Phonics Transition Lesson, pp. 262–265	
TEACHER'S EDITION • AudioText of *The Ch'i-lin Purse* • Concept Talk Video **ELL HANDBOOK** • AudioText CD Routine, p. 477	**TEACHER'S EDITION** • Concept Talk Video	**TEACHER'S EDITION** • Concept Talk Video
TEACHER'S EDITION • Sheltered Reading, p. DI•72 **ELL HANDBOOK** • Multilingual Summaries, pp. 73–75	**TEACHER'S EDITION** • ELL/ELD Reader Guided Reading, p. DI•73 **ELL HANDBOOK** • ELL Study Guide, p. 76	**TEACHER'S EDITION** • ELL/ELD Reader Guided Reading, p. DI•73 **ELL HANDBOOK** • ELL Study Guide, p. 76
		TEACHER'S EDITION • Suffixes *-tion, -ion,* p. 257i
ELL HANDBOOK • High-Frequency Words Activity Bank, p. 446 **ELL POSTER 8** • Day 3 Activities	**ELL HANDBOOK** • High-Frequency Words Activity Bank, p. 446	**ELL HANDBOOK** • High-Frequency Words Activity Bank, p. 446
TEACHER'S EDITION • Grammar Jammer **ELL HANDBOOK** • Grammar Transition Lesson, pp. 324–325, 327, 330–331, 336 • Grammar Jammer Routine, p. 478	**TEACHER'S EDITION** • Grammar Jammer **ELL HANDBOOK** • Grammar Transition Lesson, pp. 324–325, 327, 330–331, 336	**TEACHER'S EDITION** • Grammar Jammer **ELL HANDBOOK** • Grammar Transition Lesson, pp. 324–325, 327, 330–331, 336
TEACHER'S EDITION • Let's Write It!, p. 252–253 • Writer's Craft: Poetic Style, pp. 253a–253b	**TEACHER'S EDITION** • Revising Strategy, pp. 257d–257e	**TEACHER'S EDITION** • Action and Linking Verbs, pp. 257p–257q

Question of the Week
What are the rewards in helping others?

Throughout the week, use the ELL Poster to help students produce and comprehend language, understand the concept, and build English vocabulary. Use the Question of the Week and other questions to help students share ideas in pairs, small groups, or the large group. Sample questions are shown, with examples of possible responses by students.

Weekly Concept and Language Goals

• Understand the rewards in helping others

• Offer examples of ways to help others

• Explain the value of helping others

By the end of the lesson, students should be able to talk about and write sentences about the rewards in helping others.

ELL Poster 8

Daily Team Talk

Day 1	Day 2	Day 3	Day 4	Day 5
After Day 1 activities on Poster, ask questions such as	After Day 2 activity on Poster, ask questions such as	After Day 3 activity on Poster, ask questions such as	After Day 4 activity on Poster, ask questions such as	After Day 5 activity on Poster, ask questions such as
In the poster picture, what does the couple at the door do to help the girl?	*In the poster picture, what reward does the couple get for helping the little girl?*	*How is the family helping the couple at the door?*	*What reward does the family get for sharing their culture?*	*Did you ever get a reward for helping others?*
Beginning Give her things.	**Beginning** She is happy.	**Beginning** They share things.	**Beginning** They are happy.	**Beginning** Yes. Some chocolate.
Intermediate They give her presents.	**Intermediate** Their presents make her happy.	**Intermediate** They share their holiday with them.	**Intermediate** They are proud to share it.	**Intermediate** When I help, I get chocolate.
Advanced They give her gifts, such as the red envelope.	**Advanced** The gifts they give make her happy. She is thankful.	**Advanced** The family shares their culture with them. They experience new things.	**Advanced** The family is proud of their culture. Sharing it makes them happy.	**Advanced** I helped my neighbor rake her leaves. She made me hot chocolate.
Advanced High The couple at the door give her gifts, such as the red envelope filled with money.	**Advanced High** She is grateful for the gifts and advice they give her. The couple is rewarded by making the little girl happy.	**Advanced High** The family shares the Chinese New Year with the couple. This helps them experience new things and learn about a different culture.	**Advanced High** The family is proud of Chinese culture. They enjoy the Chinese New Year, and it makes them happy to be able to share it with others.	**Advanced High** Last week, I helped my neighbor rake the leaves in her yard. Then she invited me inside for hot chocolate and told me stories of when she was a kid.

This Week's Materials

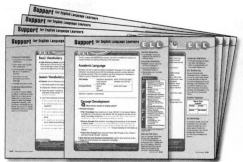

Teacher's Edition pages 230j–257q

See the support for English language learners throughout the lesson, including ELL strategies and scaffolded activities at points of use.

Teacher's Edition pages DI•66–DI•75

Differentiated Instruction for English language learners provides daily group activities that "frontload," or preteach, core instruction.

ELL Handbook pp. 71a–76

Find additional lesson materials that support the core lesson and the ELL instructional pages.

ELL Poster 8

ELL Reader 5.2.3

ELD Reader 5.2.3

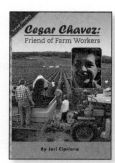

Concept Literacy Reader

ELD, ELL Reader
Teaching Guide

Concept Literacy Reader
Teaching Guide

Technology

Online Teacher's Edition Use the digital version of the core Teacher's Edition for planning and instruction.

eReaders
This week's ELL and ELD Readers and Concept Literacy Reader are also available in digital format.

This Week's Content and Language Objectives by Strand

Concept Development/ Academic Language What are the rewards in helping others?	**Content Objective** • Use concept vocabulary related to the rewards of helping others. **Language Objectives** • Express ideas in response to art and discussion. • Use prior experience to understand meaning. • Derive meaning of concept from media.
Phonics and Spelling Vowel Sounds with *r*	**Content Objective** • Use English spelling patterns. **Language Objectives** • Distinguish sounds of English. • Recognize the sound element of *r*-controlled vowels. • Produce sounds in English.
Listening Comprehension Modified Read Aloud: "Joseph and the Mermaid"	**Content Objective** • Monitor and adjust oral comprehension. **Language Objectives** • Seek clarification of spoken language. • Discuss oral passages. • Use a graphic organizer to take notes.
Reading Comprehension Compare and Contrast	**Content Objectives** • Identify the difference between compare and contrast. • Monitor and adjust comprehension. **Language Objectives** • Use academic language on a writing activity. • Compare and contrast a character in a reading. • Write comparisons and contrasts about a character in a reading.
Vocabulary Basic and Lesson Vocabulary	**Language Objectives** • Understand and use basic and grade-level vocabulary. • Learn basic vocabulary. • Internalize basic language by using it in speaking activities. • Understand the general meaning of spoken language. • Produce drawings, phrases, or short sentences to show understanding of Lesson Vocabulary.
Word Analysis Suffixes *–tion, -ion*	**Content Objective** • Identify words with suffixes *–tion* and *–ion*. **Language Objective** • Discuss meaning of words with suffixes *–tion* and *–ion*.
Grammar and Conventions Action and Linking Verbs	**Content Objective** • Decode and use action and linking verbs. **Language Objectives** • Recognize patterns in English. • Write sentences with action and linking verbs.
Writing Poetic Techniques	**Content Objective** • Identify poetic techniques in a text. **Language Objectives** • Speak using a variety of sentence lengths. • Use poetic techniques to write sentences.

Word Cards for Vocabulary Activities

astonished	**behavior**
benefactor	**distribution**
gratitude	**procession**
recommend	**sacred**
traditions	

Teacher Note: Beginning Teach three to four words. **Intermediate** Teach four to six words. **Advanced** Teach six to seven words. **Advanced High** Teach all words.

Name _____

Read the passages. Then **complete** the chart.
- **Write** the similarities and differences about New Year celebrations that are in the text.
- Then, **write** any additional similarities and differences you know about.

New Year Celebrations

The Chinese New Year begins in late January or early February. During the celebration, people march in parades. They carry long, colorful dragon puppets and light fireworks. Many of the dragons are red because the color red is considered good luck.

In the United States and many other countries, **New Year's Eve** is on December 31. On that night, thousands of people go to Times Square in New York City. Just before midnight, a ball drops from the top of a tower. When the ball reaches the bottom, fireworks burst in the sky. Everybody sings and shouts. The next day, there is a big parade.

Similarities in Text	Differences in Text	Compared with What I Know

Compare and Contrast

Use this lesson to supplement or replace the skill lesson on page 231c of the Teacher's Edition. Display the Skill Points (at right) and share them with students.

Teach/Model

Beginning Draw a three-column chart on the board. Label the columns *Watch and Clock, Watch,* and *Clock.* Display a wristwatch and point to the wall clock. Have students tell how the timepieces are alike (they tell time, they show numbers) and different (Watch: movable, digital; Clock: does not move, large). Record their responses in the chart.

Intermediate Say: *Veterans Day and Martin Luther King, Jr., Day are American holidays. Both holidays honor people who fought for freedom. On Veterans Day, we honor those who served in the armed forces. On Martin Luther King, Jr., Day, we think of Dr. King.* Ask students to write sentences telling how the holidays are similar and different.

Advanced Write: *Thanksgiving is a U.S. holiday in November. On Thanksgiving, people eat a big meal and give thanks.* Draw a chart with columns labeled *Similarities, Differences, Compared with What I Know.* Have students copy and complete the chart to compare and contrast Thanksgiving and another holiday.

Advanced High Have students write short paragraphs describing their favorite holidays. Pair students and have them compare and contrast the information in their paragraphs. Have pairs use a chart or Venn diagram to record the similarities and differences.

Then distribute copies of Picture It! page 72.

- Tell students that the two pictures show New Year celebrations. Ask students to share what they know about these celebrations.
- Read the passages aloud. Ask: *What other information do you know about New Year's celebrations?*
- Review the Skill Points with students.
- Tell students to use the pictures to help them compare and contrast.

Practice

Read aloud the directions on page 72. Have students reread the paragraph silently. Then have them look at the pictures and the paragraph as they complete the graphic organizer.

Beginning Students can first tell what they want to write in the boxes before writing their ideas. Provide help with writing and spelling.

Intermediate Students can describe the similarities and differences between the holidays before filling in the boxes.

Advanced Students can write their ideas in the chart. They can check their ideas by rereading the paragraphs and recording any other similarities and differences.

Advanced High Students can write their ideas to complete the chart. Then they can describe their own New Year's traditions and compare and contrast them with the information in the paragraphs.

Answers for page 72: *Similarities in Text:* fireworks, parades; *Differences in Text:* dragons, the color red, the ball drop, the date of New Year's celebrations; *Compared with What I Know:* Possible answers: A similarity between Chinese New Year and New Year's Eve is the season of the celebration, winter. A difference would be the special foods eaten on the holidays.

> ### Skill Points
> ✔ When writers **compare and contrast,** they show how things are similar and how they are different.
> ✔ You can use a chart or a diagram to keep track of the similarities and differences.
> ✔ You can compare the information in a text to information you already know.

Multilingual Summaries

The Ch'i-lin Purse

Hsiang-ling was a spoiled child. She always got what she wanted. When she was sixteen, she married. Her mother gave her a Ch'i-lin purse and told her to open it later. But on her wedding day, Hsiang-ling gave her purse to another bride who was poor. She gave it away before she knew what was inside.

Hsiang-ling was happily married. She and her husband had a son. Six years later, the family was separated by a flood.

Hsiang-ling went to work for a man and his wife. She took care of their little son.

Hsiang-ling saw her old Ch'i-lin purse at her new house. The man's wife had been the poor bride! The purse had had valuable things in it. The poor bride and her husband had become wealthy. The wife was very happy to have found Hsiang-ling. She gave Hsiang-ling half of everything she owned. Hsiang-ling's family was found. The two families became friends.

Spanish

El bolso Ch'i-lin

Hsiang-ling era una niña malcriada. Siempre conseguía lo que quería. Cuando tenía dieciséis años se casó. Su madre le dio un bolso Ch'i-lin y le dijo que lo abriera después. Pero el día de su boda, ella le regaló el bolso a otra novia que era pobre. Se lo regaló antes de saber qué tenía adentro.

Hsiang-ling estaba felizmente casada. La pareja tuvo un niño. Seis años después, la familia fue separada por una inundación.

Hsiang-ling se fue a trabajar con un matrimonio. Ella se hizo cargo de su niño.

Hsiang-ling vio su bolso Ch'i-lin en su nuevo hogar. ¡La mujer era aquella novia pobre! El bolso tenía adentro cosas muy valiosas. La novia pobre y su esposo se habían vuelto ricos. La mujer estaba muy feliz de haber encontrado a Hsiang-ling. Ella le dio a Hsiang-ling la mitad de lo que poseía. Después, encontraron a la familia de Hsiang-ling. Las dos familias se hicieron amigas.

Multilingual Summaries

Copyright © Pearson Education, Inc., or its affiliates. All Rights Reserved. 5

Chinese

麒麟囊

香玲一直受到家人的嬌慣溺愛，總是能夠得到想要的一切。16歲出嫁時，母親交給她一個麒麟囊，囑咐她不要馬上打開。可是結婚那天，香玲隨便就把它送給另一個貧窮的新娘。她一點也不知道裏面到底裝了什麼。

結婚後，香玲生活得很快樂，不久就有了個兒子。六年時間一晃而過，一家人在意外的洪災中失散了。

香玲只好去別人家作傭人，幫忙照顧他們的小兒子。

有一天香玲在主人家看見自己的麒麟囊，女主人原來就是那個貧窮的新娘！麒麟囊裏藏有珍寶，令他們一家變得非常富有。女主人很高興找到香玲，把一半財產分給她。香玲也終於和家人團聚，兩家人成了好朋友。

Vietnamese

Cái Ví Ch'i-lin

Hsiang-ling là một đứa trẻ được nuông chiều. Cô bé lúc nào cũng có được điều mình muốn. Khi cô lên mười sáu tuổi, cô lấy chồng. Mẹ của cô cho cô một cái ví Ch'i-lin và bảo cô chờ sau này hãy mở ví. Nhưng vào ngày cưới, Hsiang-ling tặng ví này cho một cô dâu nghèo. Cô cho ví này trước khi cô biết được có gì ở trong ví.

Hsiang-ling có chồng được hạnh phúc. Cô và chồng có được một đứa con trai. Sáu năm sau, gia đình phân ly vì một cơn lũ lụt.

Hsiang-ling đi làm mướn cho một người đàn ông và vợ của ông. Cô chăm sóc đứa con trai nhỏ của họ.

Hsiang-ling thấy cái ví Ch'i-lin của mình ở căn nhà mới này. Vợ của người đàn ông là cô dâu nghèo thuở trước! Cái ví có những vật quý báu trong đó. Cô dâu nghèo và chồng của cô trở nên giàu có. Người vợ rất vui mừng đã tìm gặp Hsiang-ling. Cô ấy cho Hsiang-ling phân nửa tài sản mà cô có. Gia đình của Hsiang-ling được tìm ra. Hai gia đình trở thành bạn.

Multilingual Summaries

Korean

기린 지갑

샹링은 버릇없는 아이로 항상 원하는 것은 손에 넣었다. 16살이 되자 그녀는 결혼을 했다. 그녀의 어머니는 그녀에게 기린 지갑을 주며 나중에 열어보라고 말했다. 하지만 결혼식 날 샹링은 그녀의 지갑을 가난한 다른 신부에게 주었다. 그녀는 지갑 안에 무엇이 있는지도 알기 전에 남에게 줘버린 것이다.

샹링은 행복해하며 결혼식을 올렸고 남편과의 사이에 아들을 하나 두었다. 6년 뒤 샹링 가족은 홍수로 인해 흩어지게 되었다.

샹링은 한 부부 밑에서 그들의 어린 아들을 돌보게 되었다.

샹링은 그 새 집에서 자신의 지갑을 보았다. 남자의 아내가 바로 그 가난한 신부였던 것이다! 지갑 안에는 귀중한 물건들이 있었고 그 가난한 신부와 남편은 부자가 되어있었다. 그 아내는 샹링을 찾게 되어서 매우 기뻐했다. 그녀는 샹링에게 자신이 가진 것의 반을 주었고 샹링의 가족은 한자리에 모이게 되었다. 그 두 가족은 곧 친구가 되었다.

Hmong

Lub Hnab Ch'i-lin

Hsiang-ling yog ib tug menyuam uas tau txhua yam rau li nws lub siab ntsaw. Nws yeej ib txwm tau txhua yam uas nws xav yuav. Thaum nws muaj hnub nyoog kaum rau xyoo, nws mus yuav txiv. Nws niam muab ib lub hnab Ch'i-lin rau nws thiab hais rau nws kom tsis txhob rawm maj qheb. Tiamsis txog hnub uas yog nws rooj tshoob, Hsiang-ling tau muab lub hnab no rau ib tug nkauj nyab uas txom txomnyem. Nws cia li muab lub hnab no rau tus nkauj nyab ntawm ua ntej nws paub seb dab tsi nyob rau hauv.

Hsiang-ling tau ua lub neej nrog txoj kev zoo siab. Nws thiab nws tus txiv nkawd yug tau ib tug me tub. Rau xyoo tom ntej, dej los nyab ua rau lawv tsevneeg thiaj sib cais.

Hsiang-ling mus ua haujlwm rau ib tug pojniam thiab nws tus txiv. Nws tu nkawd tus tub.

Hsiang-ling pom lub hnab nyob rau hauv nkawd lub tsev. Tus pojniam ntawd txawm yog tus nkauj nyab uas txom txomnyem. Lub hnab no muaj ntau yam khoom uas muaj nuj nqes tshaj plaws nyob rau hauv. Tus nkauj nyab no thiab nws tus txiv nkawd thiaj li muaj nyiaj nplua nuj. Tus pojniam no zoo siab uas nws tseem nrhiav tau Hsiang-ling. Hsiang-ling los kuj mus nrhiav tau nws tsevneeg lawm. Nkawd ob tse neeg thiaj li los ua phooj ua ywg zoo.

- **Read** *Kids Helping Kids* again.
- **Think** about how the lives of people in New Orleans were before and after Hurricane Katrina. **Write** your answers in the chart below.

Before Katrina	After Katrina
1. _____	1. _____
2. _____	2. _____
3. _____	3. _____
4. _____	4. _____

Family Link
Ask family members if they have experienced a terrible storm like a hurricane or blizzard. How did they survive the storm?

Weekly Resources Guide for English Language Learner Support

For this week's content and language objectives, see p. 77e.

Instructional Strand	Day 1	Day 2
Concept Development/Academic Language	**TEACHER'S EDITION** • Academic Language, p. DI•91 • Concept Development, p. DI•91 • Anchored Talk, pp. 258j—258–259 • Preteach Academic Vocabulary, p. 261a • Concept Talk Video **ELL HANDBOOK** • Hear It, See It, Say It, Use It, pp. xxxvi–xxxvii • ELL Poster Talk, Concept Talk, p. 77c **ELL POSTER 9** • Day 1 Activities	**TEACHER'S EDITION** • Academic Language, p. DI•91 • Concept Development, p. DI•91 • Anchored Talk, p. 262a • Concept Talk Video **ELL HANDBOOK** • ELL Poster Talk, Concept Talk, p. 77c • Concept Talk Video Routine, p. 477 **ELL POSTER 9** • Day 2 Activities
Phonics and Spelling	**TEACHER'S EDITION** • Phonics and Spelling, p. DI•95	**TEACHER'S EDITION** • Phonics and Spelling, p. DI•95
Listening Comprehension	**TEACHER'S EDITION** • Modified Read Aloud, p. DI•94 • Read Aloud, p. 259b • Concept Talk Video **ELL HANDBOOK** • Concept Talk Video Routine, p. 477	**TEACHER'S EDITION** • Modified Read Aloud, p. DI•94 • AudioText of *A Summer's Trade* • Concept Talk Video **ELL HANDBOOK** • AudioText CD Routine, p. 477 • Story Map B, p. 484
Reading Comprehension	**TEACHER'S EDITION** • Preteach Author's Purpose, p. DI•96	**TEACHER'S EDITION** • Reteach Author's Purpose, p. DI•96 • Frontloading Reading, p. DI•97 **ELL HANDBOOK** • Picture It! Skill Instruction, pp. 78–78a • Multilingual Summaries, pp. 79–81
Vocabulary **Basic and Lesson Vocabulary** **Word Analysis: Prefixes *in-, con-***	**TEACHER'S EDITION** • Basic Vocabulary, p. DI•92 • Preteach Lesson Vocabulary, p. DI•92 • Prefixes *in-, con-*, p. DI•95 **ELL HANDBOOK** • Word Cards, p. 77 • ELL Vocabulary Routine, p. 471 **ELL POSTER 9** • Day 1 Activities	**TEACHER'S EDITION** • Basic Vocabulary, p. DI•92 • Reteach Lesson Vocabulary, p. DI•93 • Prefixes *in-, con-*, p. DI•95 **ELL HANDBOOK** • Word Cards, p. 77 • Multilingual Vocabulary List, p. 434 **ELL POSTER 9** • Day 2 Activities
Grammar and Conventions	**TEACHER'S EDITION** • Preteach Main and Helping Verbs, p. DI•99	**TEACHER'S EDITION** • Reteach Main and Helping Verbs, p. DI•99
Writing	**TEACHER'S EDITION** • Using Powerful Verbs, p. DI•100 • Introduce Personal Narrative, pp. 261e–261f	**TEACHER'S EDITION** • Writing: Story Sequence, pp. 271d–271e

This symbol indicates leveled instruction to address language proficiency levels.

Day 3	Day 4	Day 5
TEACHER'S EDITION • Academic Language, p. DI•91 • Concept Development, p. DI•91 • Anchored Talk, p. 272a • Concept Talk Video **ELL HANDBOOK** • ELL Poster Talk, Concept Talk, p. 77c **ELL POSTER 9** • Day 3 Activities	**TEACHER'S EDITION** • Academic Language, p. DI•91 • Concept Development, p. DI•91 • Anchored Talk, p. 282a • Concept Talk Video **ELL HANDBOOK** • ELL Poster Talk, Concept Talk, p. 77c **ELL POSTER 9** • Day 4 Activities	**TEACHER'S EDITION** • Academic Language, p. DI•91 • Concept Development, p. DI•91 • Concept Talk Video **ELL HANDBOOK** • ELL Poster Talk, Concept Talk, p. 77c **ELL POSTER 9** • Day 5 Activities
		TEACHER'S EDITION • Phonics and Spelling, p. DI•95
ELL HANDBOOK • Phonics Transition Lesson, pp. 235, 239	**ELL HANDBOOK** • Phonics Transition Lesson, pp. 235, 239	
TEACHER'S EDITION • AudioText of *A Summer's Trade* • Concept Talk Video **ELL HANDBOOK** • AudioText CD Routine, p. 477	**TEACHER'S EDITION** • Concept Talk Video	**TEACHER'S EDITION** • Concept Talk Video
TEACHER'S EDITION • Sheltered Reading, p. DI•97 **ELL HANDBOOK** • Multilingual Summaries, pp. 79–81	**TEACHER'S EDITION** • ELL/ELD Reader Guided Reading, p. DI•98 **ELL HANDBOOK** • ELL Study Guide, p. 82	**TEACHER'S EDITION** • ELL/ELD Reader Guided Reading, p. DI•98 **ELL HANDBOOK** • ELL Study Guide, p. 82
		TEACHER'S EDITION • Spanish Word Origin, p. 287i
ELL HANDBOOK • High-Frequency Words Activity Bank, p. 446 **ELL POSTER 9** • Day 3 Activities	**ELL HANDBOOK** • High-Frequency Words Activity Bank, p. 446	**ELL HANDBOOK** • High-Frequency Words Activity Bank, p. 446
TEACHER'S EDITION • Grammar Jammer **ELL HANDBOOK** • Grammar Transition Lesson, pp. 324, 327, 330, 335 • Grammar Jammer Routine, p. 478	**TEACHER'S EDITION** • Grammar Jammer **ELL HANDBOOK** • Grammar Transition Lesson, pp. 324, 327, 330, 335	**TEACHER'S EDITION** • Grammar Jammer **ELL HANDBOOK** • Grammar Transition Lesson, pp. 324, 327, 330, 335
TEACHER'S EDITION • Let's Write It!, p. 280–281 • Writer's Craft: Powerful Verbs, pp. 281a–281b	**TEACHER'S EDITION** • Revising Strategy, pp. 287d–287e	**TEACHER'S EDITION** • Main and Helping Verbs, pp. 287p–287q

Question of the Week
Why do people make sacrifices for others?

Throughout the week, use the ELL Poster to help students produce and comprehend language, understand the concept, and build English vocabulary. Use the Question of the Week and other questions to help students share ideas in pairs, small groups, or the large group. Sample questions are shown, with examples of possible responses by students.

Weekly Concept and Language Goals
- Describe sacrifices people make for others
- Understand how teamwork takes sacrifice
- Talk about the value of helping others

By the end of the lesson, students should be able to talk about and write sentences about making sacrifices for others.

ELL Poster 9

Daily Team Talk

Day 1	Day 2	Day 3	Day 4	Day 5
After Day 1 activities on Poster, ask questions such as *In the poster picture, how are the people building the house making a sacrifice?*	After Day 2 activity on Poster, ask questions such as *In the poster picture, what sacrifice are the people preparing lunch making?*	After Day 3 activity on Poster, ask questions such as *Why do you think the people work together to build the house?*	After Day 4 activity on Poster, ask questions such as *What sacrifices do people have to make to work together as a team?*	After Day 5 activity on Poster, ask questions such as *What sacrifice did you make to help others?*
Beginning It is hot. **Intermediate** It is hard work and hot out. **Advanced** The people are working hard and it is hot outside, but they want to help. **Advanced High** The people building the house are working hard in the hot sun. They are probably uncomfortable, but they want to help build the house for a family.	**Beginning** They cook for them. **Intermediate** They spend time cooking for them. **Advanced** The people spend time preparing the food instead of doing other things. **Advanced High** The people spend time preparing lunch for the people working. They might have other things they need to do, but they spend time making food instead.	**Beginning** To help them. **Intermediate** They want to help the family. **Advanced** They want to help build a house for the family. They can get it done quickly. **Advanced High** The people in the tribe want to help build the house for the family. They know if they work together, it will get done quickly.	**Beginning** They help each other. **Intermediate** They can't do what they want. **Advanced** People working together have to help out and do what is best for everyone. **Advanced High** When people work together as a team, they have to think about what is best for everyone. They help everyone instead of doing what is best for themselves.	**Beginning** I helped clean. **Intermediate** I help a friend clean his room. **Advanced** I spent my afternoon helping my friend clean his room. **Advanced High** My friend needed to clean his bedroom by Saturday night. I spent my afternoon helping him clean.

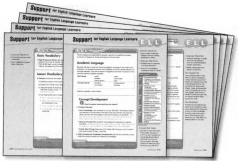

Teacher's Edition pages 258j–287q

See the support for English language learners throughout the lesson, including ELL strategies and scaffolded activities at points of use.

Teacher's Edition pages DI•91–DI•100

Differentiated Instruction for English language learners provides daily group activities that "frontload," or preteach, core instruction.

ELL Handbook pp. 77a–82

Find additional lesson materials that support the core lesson and the ELL instructional pages.

ELL Poster 9

ELL Reader 5.2.4

ELD Reader 5.2.4

Concept Literacy Reader

ELD, ELL Reader Teaching Guide

Concept Literacy Reader Teaching Guide

Technology

Online Teacher's Edition Use the digital version of the core Teacher's Edition for planning and instruction.

eReaders
This week's ELL and ELD Readers and Concept Literacy Reader are also available in digital format.

This Week's Content and Language Objectives by Strand

Concept Development/ Academic Language How do people make sacrifices for others?	**Content Objective** • Use concept vocabulary related to people making sacrifices for others. **Language Objectives** • Express ideas in response to art and discussion. • Use prior experience to understand meaning.
Phonics and Spelling Final Syllables *–en, -an, -el, -le, -il*	**Content Objective** • Identify final syllables *–en, -an, -el, -le, -il.* **Language Objectives** • Apply phonics and decoding skills to spelling. • Distinguish intonation patterns of English. • Employ English spelling patterns.
Listening Comprehension Modified Read Aloud: "Christie Makes a Sacrifice"	**Content Objective** • Monitor and adjust oral comprehension. **Language Objectives** • Discuss oral passages. • Use a graphic organizer to take notes.
Reading Comprehension Author's Purpose	**Content Objectives** • Understand author's purpose. • Monitor and adjust comprehension. **Language Objectives** • Have students use the inferential and analytical skills of determining author's purpose. • Discuss evidence for author's purpose.
Vocabulary Basic and Lesson Vocabulary	**Language Objectives** • Understand and use basic vocabulary. • Learn meanings of grade-level vocabulary. • Speak using grade-level content vocabulary. • Produce drawings, phrases, or short sentences to show understanding of Lesson Vocabulary.
Word Analysis Prefixes *in-, con-*	**Content Objective** • Identify prefixes *in-, con-* in words. **Language Objective** • Discuss meaning of words with prefixes.
Grammar and Conventions Main and Helping Verbs	**Content Objectives** • Identify main and helping verbs. • Modify main verbs to match the tense of the helping verbs. **Language Objectives** • Speak using the grammatical structure of main and helping verbs. • Edit writing for verb tenses.
Writing Using Powerful Verbs	**Content Objective** • Identify powerful verbs that express feeling. **Language Objective** • Write sentences using powerful verbs.

Word Cards for Vocabulary Activities

bandana

bracelet

hogan

jostled

mesa

Navajo

turquoise

 Teacher Note: Beginning Teach two to three words. **Intermediate** Teach three to four words. **Advanced** Teach four to five words. **Advanced High** Teach all words.

Name _____

Read the paragraph. **Look** at the picture.

- **Read** each question and the three answer choices given.
- **Circle** the letter of the correct answer for each question.

Keep Falcons in the City

More cities should protect falcons that nest on their buildings. Falcons are beautiful birds. They have very powerful eyesight. They usually live in the wild. They can be important to cities too. They nest on the ledges of buildings. People living in the cities are lucky to be able to see the wild birds up close. Falcons eat mice, so I would like a falcon in my neighborhood!

Answer these questions.

1. What is the author's purpose?
   a. to persuade or try to convince the reader
   b. to make the reader laugh
   c. to frighten the reader

2. How does the author meet this purpose?
   a. by telling interesting stories
   b. by writing about her emotions
   c. by providing opinions

Author's Purpose

Use this lesson to supplement or replace the skill lesson on page 259c of the Teacher's Edition. Display the Skill Points (at right) and share them with students.

Teach/Model

Beginning Write: *The bald eagle is our national bird. Adult eagles are brown with white head feathers. They mostly eat fish.* Ask: *Is this paragraph written to persuade or to inform?* (to inform) Have students explain how they know this is an informative paragraph.

Intermediate Say: *I am reading a funny play about a family who adopts a wild bird. Make a prediction about the author's purpose.* (The author's purpose is to entertain.) Ask: *Why did you predict this purpose?* (The piece is funny. It is a play.)

Advanced Write on the board: *Protect Sea Life—Keep the Oceans Clean.* Say: *This is the title of a pamphlet. What do you think is the author's purpose for writing this pamphlet?* (to persuade) Have each student write a sentence for the pamphlet that supports the author's purpose to persuade.

Advanced High Ask students to write a short paragraph about a bird. Tell them to write with a specific purpose in mind: to inform, to entertain, to persuade, or to express feelings. Have students read their paragraphs aloud in a manner that suits their purposes. For example, expressive paragraphs should be read with emotion.

Then distribute copies of Picture It! page 78.

- Have students read the title and predict what the paragraph might be about.
- Review the Skill Points with students.
- Read the paragraph aloud. Ask: *What is the author's purpose? Why does the author write this paragraph?*
- Have students look at the picture and words to identify author's purpose.

Practice

Read aloud the directions on page 78. Have students reread the paragraph with partners. Have them look at the picture and the paragraph as they answer the questions.

Beginning Students can orally answer before circling their answers on the page. Provide help with circling.

Intermediate Students can circle their answers on the page.

Advanced Students can circle their answers and check the paragraph to confirm that their answers are correct.

Advanced High Students can circle their answers and identify details that helped them determine the author's purpose.

Answers for page 78: 1. a; 2. c

> ### Skill Points
> ✔ The **author's purpose** is the reason an author writes something.
> ✔ An author could write to entertain, to inform, to express feelings, or to persuade.
> ✔ Sometimes the title helps you predict the author's purpose.

Multilingual Summaries

A Summer's Trade

Tony lives on the Navajo Indian Reservation. He needs a saddle so he can ride horses with his father. He saves his money to buy a saddle.

Tony's uncle breaks his leg. He cannot work to support his family. Tony's grandmother has a beautiful silver bracelet. She sells it to get money for Tony's Uncle. Tony's grandmother is very sad.

Tony buys the bracelet. He uses the money he was saving for the saddle. He gives the bracelet back to his grandmother. Tony's grandmother is happy! She agrees to make a rug to trade for the saddle. Tony is now happy to ride horses with his father.

Spanish

Intercambio de verano

Tony vive en una reservación de indios Navajo. Él necesita una silla de montar para cabalgar con su padre. Él ahorra para comprar la silla.

El tío de Tony se rompe una pierna. El no puede trabajar para sostener a su familia. La abuela de Tony vende un hermoso brazalete de plata para obtener dinero para el tío de Tony. La abuela está muy triste.

Tony compra el brazalete. Usa el dinero que había ahorrado para la silla y le devuelve el brazalete a su abuela. La abuela está feliz. Ella decide hacer una alfombra para intercambiarla por la silla. Tony está feliz ahora puede cabalgar con su padre.

Multilingual Summaries

一个夏天的交易

　　托尼住在纳瓦霍印地安保留区。他想要一个马鞍，好让自己可以和爸爸一起骑马；为了买一个马鞍，他开始储蓄。

　　托尼的叔叔摔断了一条腿，因为不能工作，所以家庭的经济有困难。托尼的祖母有一条很漂亮的银手镯，为了帮助她的儿子，她要把手镯卖掉，但她很舍不得，所以很难过。

　　托尼用他储的钱把手镯买了，并把手镯还给他祖母。祖母得回自己的手镯，就很高兴，并答应编织一张地毯来帮助托尼买马鞍，托尼也很高兴可以和爸爸去骑马。

Một Cuộc Trao Đổi Mùa Hè

Tony sống trong Vùng dành riêng cho người Da đỏ Navajo Indian Reservation. Tony cần yên ngựa để cõi ngựa theo cha. Nó để dành tiền để mua yên ngựa.

Chú của Tony bị gãy chân. Với cái chân gãy, ông ta không thể làm việc để nuôi gia đình. Bà nội của Tony có một chiếc vòng bạc đẹp. Bà bán chiếc vòng để lấy tiền cho chú của Tony. Bà nội Tony rất buồn vì phải bán chiếc vòng.

Tony mua lại chiếc vòng. Nó dùng số tiền để dành định mua yên ngựa. Nó đưa lại chiếc vòng cho bà nội. Bà nội của Tony sung sướng nhận lại chiếc vòng. Bà nhận làm một tấm thảm để đổi lấy cái yên ngựa. Tony sung sướng có được cái yên để cõi ngựa theo cha.

Multilingual Summaries

여름 장사

토니는 나바호 인디언 보호지역에 삽니다. 토니는 아버지와 함께 말을 타기 위해서 안장이 필요합니다. 그래서 안장을 사려고 저축했습니다.

토니의 삼촌이 다리를 다쳤습니다. 부러진 다리로는 삼촌은 식구들을 먹여 살릴 수 없습니다. 토니의 할머니는 예쁜 은팔찌를 가지고 계십니다. 할머니는 삼촌에게 줄 돈을 마련하기 위해 팔찌를 팔기로 했습니다. 할머니께선 팔찌를 파는 것에 무척 슬퍼하셨습니다.

토니가 그 팔찌를 샀습니다. 안장을 사려로 모았던 돈을 썼던거지요. 토니는 팔찌를 할머니께 되돌려 드렸습니다. 할머니께선 다시 팔찌를 갖게 되셔서 아주 기뻐하셨습니다! 할머니는 안장이랑 맞바꿀 양탄자를 만들어 주시기로 하셨습니다. 토니는 아버지와 함께 말을 탈 수 있게 안장을 얻게 된 것이 마냥 기쁩니다.

Sis Pauv Khoom Thaus Caij Ntuj Kub

Tony ua neej nyob ntawm cov khab Navajo thaj av nyob. Nwg yuav tsum tau lub eeb nees nwg thiaj caij nees tau nrog nwg txiv. Nwg tseg nwg cov nyiaj mus yuav lub eeb nees.

Tony tus txiv ntxawm ua lov nwg txhais ceg. Thaus txhais ceg lov lawm, nwg mus ua tsi taug haujlwm nrhiav noj haus rau nwg tsevneeg. Tony pog muaj ib lub paug teg nyiaj uas zoo nkauj heev. Nwg muab coj mus muag kom tau nyiaj rau Tony tus txiv ntxawm. Tony pog tu tu siab vim nwg tau muag nwg lub paug teg.

Tony mus yuav lub paug teg. Nwg siv cov nyiaj uas nwg tseg yuav lub eeb nees. Nwg muab lub paug teg rov qab rau nwg pog. Tony pog zoo siab heev tias nwg tau nwg lub paug rov qab! Nwg txaus siab ua daim ntaub pua av coj mus pauv yuav lub eeb nees. Tony zoo siab tau lub eeb nees coj mus caij nees nrog nwg txiv.

- **Read** *Havens for Horses* again.
- Use the information in the book to **answer** the questions.

pages 2–5

1. What do abandoned horses need?

_____

_____

pages 6–9

2. How are havens, sanctuaries, and refuges alike?

_____

_____

pages 10–11

3. What is the difference between sponsoring a horse and adopting a horse?

_____

_____

4. What is the author's purpose for writing the article?

_____

Family Link

Tell your family what you learned about horse havens. Talk to your family members about how they might be able to help abandoned animals.

Weekly Resources Guide for English Language Learner Support

For this week's content and language objectives, see p. 83e.

Instructional Strand	Day 1	Day 2
Concept Development/Academic Language	**TEACHER'S EDITION** • Academic Language, p. DI•116 • Concept Development, p. DI•116 • Anchored Talk, pp. 288j—288–289 • Preteach Academic Vocabulary, p. 291a • Concept Talk Video **ELL HANDBOOK** • Hear It, See It, Say It, Use It, pp. xxxvi–xxxvii • ELL Poster Talk, Concept Talk, p. 83c **ELL POSTER 10** • Day 1 Activities	**TEACHER'S EDITION** • Academic Language, p. DI•116 • Concept Development, p. DI•116 • Anchored Talk, p. 292a • Concept Talk Video **ELL HANDBOOK** • ELL Poster Talk, Concept Talk, p. 83c • Concept Talk Video Routine, p. 477 **ELL POSTER 10** • Day 2 Activities
Phonics and Spelling	**TEACHER'S EDITION** • Phonics and Spelling, p. DI•120	**TEACHER'S EDITION** • Phonics and Spelling, p. DI•120
Listening Comprehension	**TEACHER'S EDITION** • Modified Read Aloud, p. DI•119 • Read Aloud, p. 289b • Concept Talk Video **ELL HANDBOOK** • Concept Talk Video Routine, p. 477	**TEACHER'S EDITION** • Modified Read Aloud, p. DI•119 • AudioText of *The Midnight Ride of Paul Revere* • Concept Talk Video **ELL HANDBOOK** • AudioText CD Routine, p. 477 • Story Map B, p. 484
Reading Comprehension	**TEACHER'S EDITION** • Preteach Author's Purpose/Background Knowledge, p. DI•121	**TEACHER'S EDITION** • Reteach Author's Purpose/Background Knowledge, p. DI•121 • Frontloading Reading, p. DI•122 **ELL HANDBOOK** • Picture It! Skill Instruction, pp. 84–84a • Multilingual Summaries, pp. 85–87
Vocabulary **Basic and Lesson Vocabulary** **Word Analysis: Word Families**	**TEACHER'S EDITION** • Basic Vocabulary, p. DI•117 • Preteach Lesson Vocabulary, p. DI•117 • Word Families, p. DI•120 **ELL HANDBOOK** • Word Cards, p. 83 • ELL Vocabulary Routine, p. 471 **ELL POSTER 10** • Day 1 Activities	**TEACHER'S EDITION** • Basic Vocabulary, p. DI•117 • Reteach Lesson Vocabulary, p. DI•118 • Word Families, p. DI•120 **ELL HANDBOOK** • Word Cards, p. 83 • Multilingual Vocabulary List, p. 434 **ELL POSTER 10** • Day 2 Activities
Grammar and Conventions	**TEACHER'S EDITION** • Preteach Subject-Verb Agreement, p. DI•124	**TEACHER'S EDITION** • Reteach Subject-Verb Agreement, p. DI•124
Writing	**TEACHER'S EDITION** • Imagery, p. DI•125 • Writing for Tests: Historical Fiction, pp. 291e–291f	**TEACHER'S EDITION** • Writing for Tests: Historical Fiction, pp. 301d–301e

Leveled LS Support

This symbol indicates leveled instruction to address language proficiency levels.

Day 3	Day 4	Day 5
TEACHER'S EDITION • Academic Language, p. DI•116 • Concept Development, p. DI•116 • Anchored Talk, p. 302a • Concept Talk Video **ELL HANDBOOK** • ELL Poster Talk, Concept Talk, p. 83c **ELL POSTER 10** • Day 3 Activities	**TEACHER'S EDITION** • Academic Language, p. DI•116 • Concept Development, p. DI•116 • Anchored Talk, p. 312a • Concept Talk Video **ELL HANDBOOK** • ELL Poster Talk, Concept Talk, p. 83c **ELL POSTER 10** • Day 4 Activities	**TEACHER'S EDITION** • Academic Language, p. DI•116 • Concept Development, p. DI•116 • Concept Talk Video **ELL HANDBOOK** • ELL Poster Talk, Concept Talk, p. 83c **ELL POSTER 10** • Day 5 Activities
ELL HANDBOOK • Phonics Transition Lesson, pp. 266–267	**ELL HANDBOOK** • Phonics Transition Lesson, pp. 266–267	**TEACHER'S EDITION** • Phonics and Spelling, p. DI•120
TEACHER'S EDITION • AudioText of *The Midnight Ride of Paul Revere* • Concept Talk Video **ELL HANDBOOK** • AudioText CD Routine, p. 477	**TEACHER'S EDITION** • Concept Talk Video	**TEACHER'S EDITION** • Concept Talk Video
TEACHER'S EDITION • Sheltered Reading, p. DI•122 **ELL HANDBOOK** • Multilingual Summaries, pp. 85–87	**TEACHER'S EDITION** • ELL/ELD Reader Guided Reading, p. DI•123 **ELL HANDBOOK** • ELL Study Guide, p. 88	**TEACHER'S EDITION** • ELL/ELD Reader Guided Reading, p. DI•123 **ELL HANDBOOK** • ELL Study Guide, p. 88
ELL HANDBOOK • High-Frequency Words Activity Bank, p. 446 **ELL POSTER 10** • Day 3 Activities	**ELL HANDBOOK** • High-Frequency Words Activity Bank, p. 446	**TEACHER'S EDITION** • Word Families, p. 317i **ELL HANDBOOK** • High-Frequency Words Activity Bank, p. 446
TEACHER'S EDITION • Grammar Jammer **ELL HANDBOOK** • Grammar Transition Lesson, pp. 340, 349 • Grammar Jammer Routine, p. 478	**TEACHER'S EDITION** • Grammar Jammer **ELL HANDBOOK** • Grammar Transition Lesson, pp. 340, 349	**TEACHER'S EDITION** • Grammar Jammer **ELL HANDBOOK** • Grammar Transition Lesson, pp. 340, 349
TEACHER'S EDITION • Let's Write It!, p. 310–311 • Writing for Tests: Evaluation, pp. 311a–311b	**TEACHER'S EDITION** • Writing for Tests, p. 317d	**TEACHER'S EDITION** • Writing for Tests, pp. 317p–317q

Question of the Week
How can people promote freedom?

ELL Poster 10

Throughout the week, use the ELL Poster to help students produce and comprehend language, understand the concept, and build English vocabulary. Use the Question of the Week and other questions to help students share ideas in pairs, small groups, or the large group. Sample questions are shown, with examples of possible responses by students.

Weekly Concept and Language Goals

• Discuss the meaning of freedom

• Share ideas about heroes who have promoted freedom

• Tell how people can promote freedom

By the end of the lesson, students should be able to talk about and write sentences about promoting freedom.

Daily Team Talk

Day 1	Day 2	Day 3	Day 4	Day 5
After Day 1 activities on Poster, ask questions such as *In 1775, why did the people of Massachusetts think they were not free?*	After Day 2 activity on Poster, ask questions such as *In the poster picture, where do you think the people are going?*	After Day 3 activity on Poster, ask questions such as *The people in the poster picture are going to fight in the Revolutionary War. Why are Revolutionary War soldiers heroes?*	After Day 4 activity on Poster, ask questions such as *In the story* The Midnight Ride of Paul Revere, *how did Paul Revere promote freedom?*	After Day 5 activity on Poster, ask questions such as *Besides fighting in a war, what is another way to promote freedom?*
Beginning No control. **Intermediate** They had no control. **Advanced** They were a colony. The British controlled them. **Advanced High** Massachusetts was a British colony, which means the British controlled it. The people wanted to be in control of themselves.	**Beginning** To fight. **Intermediate** They are going to fight. **Advanced** The people are going to fight the British for their freedom. **Advanced High** The people of the colony are going off to fight in a war. They want to gain their freedom from the British.	**Beginning** We are free. **Intermediate** Our country is free because of them. **Advanced** They fought the British. America is free because of them. **Advanced High** The Revolutionary War soldiers fought the British to gain freedom. People in America enjoy freedom because the soldiers fought for it.	**Beginning** Warned them. **Intermediate** He warned them about the British. **Advanced** He rode and warned the people that the British were coming. **Advanced High** He rode his horse through all the villages to warn people that the British were coming. The people were ready when the British came.	**Beginning** You can vote. **Intermediate** People can vote for leaders. **Advanced** People who vote for President and other leaders promote freedom. **Advanced High** People can promote freedom by being active in the government. One way to do that is by voting for President or other leaders.

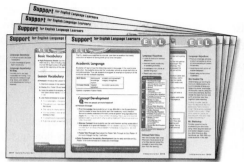

Teacher's Edition pages 288j–321a

See the support for English language learners throughout the lesson, including ELL strategies and scaffolded activities at points of use.

Teacher's Edition pages DI•116–DI•125

Differentiated Instruction for English language learners provides daily group activities that "frontload," or preteach, core instruction.

ELL Handbook pp. 83a–88

Find additional lesson materials that support the core lesson and the ELL instructional pages.

ELL Poster 10

ELL Reader 5.2.5

ELD Reader 5.2.5

Concept Literacy Reader

ELD, ELL Reader Teaching Guide

Concept Literacy Reader Teaching Guide

Technology

Online Teacher's Edition Use the digital version of the core Teacher's Edition for planning and instruction.

eReaders
This week's ELL and ELD Readers and Concept Literacy Reader are also available in digital format.

This Week's Content and Language Objectives by Strand

Concept Development/ Academic Language How can people promote freedom?	**Content Objective** • Use concept vocabulary related to how people promote freedom. **Language Objectives** • Use new basic vocabulary in speaking activities. • Understand main points of spoken language.
Phonics and Spelling Final Syllables *–er, -ar, -or*	**Content Objective** • Identify final unstressed syllables *–er, -ar, -or.* **Language Objectives** • Apply phonics and decoding skills to spelling. • Distinguish intonation patterns of English.
Listening Comprehension Modified Read Aloud: "Fighting for Freedom"	**Content Objective** • Monitor and adjust oral comprehension. **Language Objectives** • Discuss oral passages. • Use contextual support to confirm understanding.
Reading Comprehension Author's Purpose	**Content Objectives** • Understand author's purpose. • Use visual support to understand language. **Language Objectives** • Summarize text using visual support. • Discuss author's purpose.
Vocabulary Basic and Lesson Vocabulary	**Language Objectives** • Understand and use basic vocabulary. • Learn meanings of grade-level vocabulary. • Speak using content-area vocabulary.
Word Analysis Word Families	**Content Objective** • Identify word families. **Language Objectives** • Understand concept of word families. • Learn new language structures.
Grammar and Conventions Subject-Verb Agreement	**Content Objectives** • Understand subject-verb agreement. • Modify verbs to match subjects. **Language Objectives** • Practice subject-verb agreement in speaking. • Write sentences using subject-verb agreement.
Writing Imagery	**Content Objectives** • Identify imagery in poetry. • Understand the meaning and purpose of images in writing. **Language Objectives** • Write sentences explaining imagery. • Describe with increasing specificity and detail.

Word Cards for Vocabulary Activities

fate

fearless

glimmer

lingers

magnified

somber

steed

Teacher Note: Beginning Teach two to three words. **Intermediate** Teach three to four words. **Advanced** Teach four to five words. **Advanced High** Teach all words.

Name _____

Read the paragraph. **Look** at the pictures.

- **What** is the author's purpose? **Circle** the letter of the correct answer.
- How did the author meet his or her purpose? **Write** a short answer on the lines below.

The Boston Tea Party

In 1768, British soldiers moved into Boston. They took control of the city. In 1773, ships from Great Britain came to Boston Harbor. The ships were loaded with tea. On December 16 of that year, colonists climbed on the ships. They were dressed like Native Americans. The colonists threw all the tea into the harbor. This event is called the Boston Tea Party.

Answer these questions.

1. What is the author's purpose?
   a. to persuade or try to convince the reader
   b. to inform or explain something to the reader
   c. to entertain or make the reader enjoy the paragraph
   d. to write ideas and feelings

2. How does the author meet his or her purpose?

   _____

   _____

   _____

Author's Purpose

Use this lesson to supplement or replace the skill lesson on page 289c of the Teacher's Edition. Display the Skill Points (at right) and share them with students.

Teach/Model

Beginning Say: *I am writing a report about the American Revolution. What is my purpose in writing?* Have students write their answer. (to inform) Continue the activity by asking the purpose of a poem you are writing about freedom. (to express feelings)

Intermediate Play a recording or read the first verse of "My Country, 'Tis of Thee." Say: *An author may write a poem or song to entertain or to express feelings.* Ask: *What do you think the author's purpose was in writing this song?* (to express feelings) Have students explain their answers.

Advanced Tell students the myth of George Washington and the cherry tree. Have them identify the author's purpose. (to entertain or to persuade) Ask: *What kind of book would have factual information about Washington's life?* (a history book, a biography, a reference book)

Advanced High Ask students to select a fiction or nonfiction book about U.S. history from the library. Have them read a chapter or section and look for details that suggest the author's purpose. Ask students to write a sentence that identifies the author's purpose and a sentence that explains their reasoning.

Then distribute copies of Picture It! page 84.

- Have students read the title and predict what the paragraph might be about.
- Review the Skill Points with students.
- Read the paragraph aloud. Ask: *What is the author's purpose? Why does the author write this paragraph?*

Practice

Read aloud the directions on page 84. Have students reread the paragraph silently. Provide a definition of the word *colonist*. Have students look at the pictures and the paragraph as they answer the questions.

Beginning Students can first orally answer and then circle and write their answers on the page. Provide help with writing and spelling English words.

Intermediate Students can circle and write their answers to the questions.

Advanced Students can circle and write their answers and check their answers by locating support within the paragraph.

Advanced High Students can circle and write their answers. They can describe how the paragraph would be different if it had been written to entertain or to express feelings.

Answers for page 84: 1. b; 2. The author gives facts and information about the Boston Tea Party. The author does not give opinions or use persuasive language.

Skill Points

✔ The **author's purpose** is the reason an author writes something.

✔ An author could write to entertain, to inform, to express feelings or ideas, or to persuade.

✔ Sometimes the title helps you to predict the author's purpose.

Multilingual Summaries

The Midnight Ride of Paul Revere

On April 18, 1775, Paul Revere made a famous ride. British soldiers were coming to fight with Revolutionary soldiers. Paul Revere wanted to warn people.

The British troops had two ways to reach the towns. They could march by land, or they could sail on the sea. That night, Revere told his friend to hang one lantern in the church tower if the British went by land. He asked the friend to hang two lanterns if they went by sea. If he knew how the British were coming, he could tell the people in the towns.

When it got dark, Revere saw two lanterns in the church tower. He rode his horse to tell the people to get ready to fight the British. He got to the first town at midnight. He rode through many towns on the way to Concord. The next morning was the first battle of the American Revolution.

Spanish

El viaje nocturno de Paul Revere

El 18 de abril de 1775, Paul Revere hizo un recorrido glorioso. Los soldados británicos llegarían a luchar contra los soldados revolucionarios. Paul Revere quería alertar a la gente.

Las tropas británicas tenían dos caminos para llegar a los pueblos. Podían marchar por tierra o podían llegar navegando. Esa noche, Revere le dijo a su amigo que pusiera un farol encendido en la torre de la iglesia si los británicos venían por tierra. Revere le dijo a su amigo que pusiera dos faroles si los británicos llegaban por mar. Si sabía cómo llegaban los británicos, él podía avisarle a la gente en los pueblos.

Cuando oscureció, Revere vio dos faroles en la torre de la iglesia. Montó en su caballo y se fue a decirle a la gente que estuviera preparada para luchar contra los británicos. Llegó al primer pueblo a la medianoche. Atravesó muchos pueblos en su camino a Concord. A la mañana siguiente, ocurrió la primera batalla de la Guerra de Independencia.

Multilingual Summaries

保羅・瑞維爾午夜報信

　　保羅・瑞維爾騎馬報信的故事家喻戶曉。1775年4月18日那天，英軍要去鎮壓起義者，保羅想通知同胞們早做準備。

　　英軍有兩條路綫可選：或者從陸上進攻，或者從海上入侵。那天晚上，保羅對朋友說，如果英軍從陸上來，就在教堂鐘樓上挂一盞燈，如果從海上過，就挂兩盞燈。事先知道英軍的路綫，好給村民們報信。

　　天色漸漸黑了，保羅看見鐘樓上有兩盞燈。他騎馬飛奔去通知人們，做好迎擊英軍的準備。到達第一個村莊時，已經是午夜。他一路飛馳報信，穿過許多村莊，來到康科德城。第二天早上，打響了美國獨立革命的第一槍。

Chuyến Cưỡi Ngựa Vào Lúc Nửa Đêm của Paul Revere

　　Vào ngày 18 tháng Tư, năm 1775, Paul Revere đã làm một chuyến đi lừng danh. Binh lính Anh sắp đến đánh với binh lính Cách Mạng. Paul Revere muốn báo trước cho mọi người biết.

　　Quân đội Anh có hai cách để đến các thành phố. Họ có thể hành quân bằng đường bộ. Hoặc họ có thể đến bằng thuyền buồm trên biển. Tối hôm đó, Revere dặn bạn của ông treo một ngọn đèn lồng trên tháp nhà thờ nếu quân Anh đến bằng đường bộ. Ông kêu người bạn này treo hai ngọn đèn lồng nếu họ đến bằng đường biển. Nếu ông biết cách quân Anh đến, ông có thể nói cho người trong các thành phố biết.

　　Khi trời tối, Paul thấy hai ngọn đèn lồng trên tháp ngôi nhà thờ. Ông cưỡi ngựa đi kêu mọi người chuẩn bị chiến đấu với quân Anh. Ông đến thành phố đầu tiên vào lúc nửa đêm. Ông cưỡi ngựa qua nhiều thành phố trên đường đến Concord. Sáng hôm sau là trận chiến đầu tiên của cuộc Cách Mạng Hoa Kỳ.

Multilingual Summaries

한 밤중에 말을 탄 폴 리비어

1775년 4월 18일 폴 리비어는 말을 타고 유명해졌다. 그 당시 영국군은 독립군과 싸우기 위해 오고 있는 중이었다. 폴 리비어는 사람들에게 위험을 알리고 싶었다.

영국군이 마을에 도착할 수 있는 방법은 두 가지로 육지로 행군하거나 바다로 항해하는 것이었다. 그날 밤 리비어는 자신의 친구에게 만약 영국군이 육지로 가게 되면 교회 탑에 랜턴 하나를 걸어두고 바다로 가면 랜턴 두 개를 걸어달라고 부탁했다. 만약 영국군이 어떻게 오는지를 알게 된다면 마을 사람들에게 말을 해 줄 수 있을 것이었다.

어두워지자 폴은 교회 탑에 랜턴 두 개가 걸린 것을 보았다. 그는 영국군과 싸울 준비를 하도록 사람들에게 알려주기 위해 자신의 말을 몰았다. 그는 자정에 첫 번째 마을에 도착했고 콩코드까지 여러 마을들을 지나며 말을 달렸다. 그 다음날 아침이 바로 미국 독립전쟁의 첫 전투가 시작된 날이었다.

Paul Revere Kev Caij Tshej Thaum Ib Tag Hmo

Hnub tim kaum yim lub plaub hlis ntuj xyoo ib txhiab xya pua xya caum tsib, Paul Revere tau caij ib kev tshej ua tau nto npe heev. Tub rog Askiv yuav tuaj tua cov tub rog Revolutionary. Paul Revere xav mus ceeb toom neeg sawvdaws.

Cov tub rog Askiv thaug tau ob txoj kev tuaj rau pem zos. Lawv tuaj tau kaw taw saum av tuaj. Lossis lawv kuj caij tau nkoj tuaj thiab. Hmo ntawd, Revere qhia nws tus phooj ywg kom nws dai ib lub teeb rau saum lub tshawj tus pejthuam yog cov tub rog Askiv tuaj kaw taw tuaj. Nws nug kom nws tus phooj ywg dai ob lub teeb yog lawv tuaj nkoj tuaj. Yog nws paub tias cov tub rog Askiv tuaj li cas tuaj ces nws thiaj li qhia tau zej zog sawvdaws.

Thaum tsaus ntuj lawm, Paul pom ob lub teeb dai rau saum lub tshawj tus pejthuam. Nws caij nws tus nees mus qhia neeg sawvdaws kom lawv npaj mus tuaj rog norg cov Askiv. Nws mus txog thawj lub zos thaum ib tag hmo. Nws caij nees dhau zos ntau kawg thiaj li mus txog Concord. Tag kis sawv ntxov tom qab ntawd yog thawj ntsug rog ntawm kev ua rog American Revolution.

Name _____

- **Read** *After the Midnight Ride* again.
- Which event happened first? Which happened next?
  Number the events in order from 1 to 6.

____ Somebody fires a shot on the Lexington village green.

____ The British decide to go back to Boston.

____ Minutemen attack British soldiers on the North Bridge of Concord.

____ Samuel Prescott warns colonists that the British are coming.

____ Minutemen shoot at the British as they retreat to Boston.

____ British Regulars arrive at Lexington on their way to Concord.

Family Link

Tell your family what you learned about the American Revolution. Ask them to tell you what they know about the Revolution.

Weekly Resources Guide for English Language Learner Support

For this week's content and language objectives, see p. 89e.

Instructional Strand	Day 1	Day 2
Concept Development/Academic Language	**TEACHER'S EDITION** • Academic Language, p. DI•16 • Concept Development, p. DI•16 • Anchored Talk, pp. 324j—324–325 • Preteach Academic Vocabulary, p. 327a • Concept Talk Video **ELL HANDBOOK** • Hear It, See It, Say It, Use It, pp. xxxvi–xxxvii • ELL Poster Talk, Concept Talk, p. 89c **ELL POSTER 11** • Day 1 Activities	**TEACHER'S EDITION** • Academic Language, p. DI•16 • Concept Development, p. DI•16 • Anchored Talk, p. 328a • Concept Talk Video **ELL HANDBOOK** • ELL Poster Talk, Concept Talk, p. 89c • Concept Talk Video Routine, p. 477 **ELL POSTER 11** • Day 2 Activities
Phonics and Spelling	**TEACHER'S EDITION** • Phonics and Spelling, p. DI•20	**TEACHER'S EDITION** • Phonics and Spelling, p. DI•20
Listening Comprehension	**TEACHER'S EDITION** • Modified Read Aloud, p. DI•19 • Read Aloud, p. 325b • Concept Talk Video **ELL HANDBOOK** • Concept Talk Video Routine, p. 477	**TEACHER'S EDITION** • Modified Read Aloud, p. DI•19 • AudioText of *The Fabulous Perpetual Motion Machine* • Concept Talk Video **ELL HANDBOOK** • AudioText CD Routine, p. 477 • K-W-L Chart, p. 480
Reading Comprehension	**TEACHER'S EDITION** • Preteach Sequence, p. DI•21	**TEACHER'S EDITION** • Reteach Sequence, p. DI•21 • Frontloading Reading, p. DI•22 **ELL HANDBOOK** • Picture It! Skill Instruction, pp. 90–90a • Multilingual Summaries, pp. 91–93
Vocabulary **Basic and Lesson Vocabulary** **Word Analysis: Shades of Meaning**	**TEACHER'S EDITION** • Basic Vocabulary, p. DI•17 • Preteach Lesson Vocabulary, p. DI•17 • Shades of Meaning, p. DI•20 **ELL HANDBOOK** • Word Cards, p. 89 • ELL Vocabulary Routine, p. 471 **ELL POSTER 11** • Day 1 Activities	**TEACHER'S EDITION** • Basic Vocabulary, p. DI•17 • Reteach Lesson Vocabulary, p. DI•18 • Shades of Meaning, p. DI•20 **ELL HANDBOOK** • Word Cards, p. 89 • Multilingual Vocabulary List, p. 435 **ELL POSTER 11** • Day 2 Activities
Grammar and Conventions	**TEACHER'S EDITION** • Preteach Past, Present, and Future Tenses, p. DI•24	**TEACHER'S EDITION** • Reteach Past, Present, and Future Tenses, p. DI•24
Writing	**TEACHER'S EDITION** • Write Dialogue, p. DI•25 • Introduce Play, pp. 327e–327f	**TEACHER'S EDITION** • Writing Trait: Organization, pp. 337d–337e

The Fabulous Perpetual Motion Machine

This symbol indicates leveled instruction to address language proficiency levels.

Day 3	Day 4	Day 5
TEACHER'S EDITION • Academic Language, p. DI•16 • Concept Development, p. DI•16 • Anchored Talk, p. 338a • Concept Talk Video **ELL HANDBOOK** • ELL Poster Talk, Concept Talk, p. 89c **ELL POSTER 11** • Day 3 Activities	**TEACHER'S EDITION** • Academic Language, p. DI•16 • Concept Development, p. DI•16 • Anchored Talk, p. 348a • Concept Talk Video **ELL HANDBOOK** • ELL Poster Talk, Concept Talk, p. 89c **ELL POSTER 11** • Day 4 Activities	**TEACHER'S EDITION** • Academic Language, p. DI•16 • Concept Development, p. DI•16 • Concept Talk Video **ELL HANDBOOK** • ELL Poster Talk, Concept Talk, p. 89c **ELL POSTER 11** • Day 5 Activities
		TEACHER'S EDITION • Phonics and Spelling, p. DI•20
ELL HANDBOOK • Phonics Transition Lesson, pp. 266, 267	**ELL HANDBOOK** • Phonics Transition Lesson, pp. 266, 267	
TEACHER'S EDITION • Audio Text of *The Fabulous Perpetual Motion Machine* • Concept Talk Video **ELL HANDBOOK** • AudioText CD Routine, p. 477	**TEACHER'S EDITION** • Concept Talk Video	**TEACHER'S EDITION** • Concept Talk Video
TEACHER'S EDITION • Sheltered Reading, p. DI•22 **ELL HANDBOOK** • Multilingual Summaries, pp. 91–93	**TEACHER'S EDITION** • ELL/ELD Reader Guided Reading, p. DI•23 **ELL HANDBOOK** • ELL Study Guide, p. 94	**TEACHER'S EDITION** • ELL/ELD Reader Guided Reading, p. DI•23 **ELL HANDBOOK** • ELL Study Guide, p. 94
		TEACHER'S EDITION • Shades of Meaning, p. 353i
ELL HANDBOOK • High-Frequency Words Activity Bank, p. 446 **ELL POSTER 1** • Day 3 Activities	**ELL HANDBOOK** • High-Frequency Words Activity Bank, p. 446	**ELL HANDBOOK** • High-Frequency Words Activity Bank, p. 446
TEACHER'S EDITION • Grammar Jammer **ELL HANDBOOK** • Grammar Transition Lesson, pp. 324–325, 330–332 • Grammar Jammer Routine, p. 478	**TEACHER'S EDITION** • Grammar Jammer **ELL HANDBOOK** • Grammar Transition Lesson, pp. 324–325, 330–332	**TEACHER'S EDITION** • Grammar Jammer **ELL HANDBOOK** • Grammar Transition Lesson, pp. 324–325, 330–332
TEACHER'S EDITION • Let's Write It!, p. 346–347 • Writing Trait: Word Choice, pp. 347a–347b	**TEACHER'S EDITION** • Revising Strategy, pp. 353d–353e	**TEACHER'S EDITION** • Past, Present, and Future Tenses, pp. 353p–353q

Poster Talk, Concept Talk

Question of the Week
How do inventors inspire our imaginations?

Throughout the week, use the ELL Poster to help students produce and comprehend language, understand the concept, and build English vocabulary. Use the Question of the Week and other questions to help students share ideas in pairs, small groups, or the large group. Sample questions are shown, with examples of possible responses by students.

ELL Poster 11

Weekly Concept and Language Goals

• Participate in a discussion about the value of inventors and inventions

• Name inventions

• Describe how inventions are useful

By the end of the lesson, students should be able to talk about and write sentences about how inventors inpire us.

Daily Team Talk

Day 1	Day 2	Day 3	Day 4	Day 5
After Day 1 activities on Poster, ask questions such as *In the poster picture, what does the queen ask the inventor to do?*	After Day 2 activity on Poster, ask questions such as *In the poster picture, what is the inventor's idea?*	After Day 3 activity on Poster, ask questions such as *How does the inventor's idea inspire the queen?*	After Day 4 activity on Poster, ask questions such as *Do you think the inventor's and the queen's ideas are useful? Why or why not?*	After Day 5 activity on Poster, ask questions such as *What is one invention you think is useful? Why do you think it is useful?*
Beginning Invent something. **Intermediate** She asks him to invent something. **Advanced** The queen asks him to invent a new way to get around. **Advanced High** The queen tells the inventor to invent a new way for her to travel.	**Beginning** A wheel. **Intermediate** It is a wheel she can ride. **Advanced** His idea is to make a wheel the queen can ride. **Advanced High** The inventor's idea was to create a wheel that a person can ride on. His invention looks like a unicycle.	**Beginning** She has an idea. **Intermediate** She thinks of another idea. **Advanced** The queen thinks of a way to make his idea better. **Advanced High** The queen is inspired by the inventor's idea of riding on a wheel, and she thinks of a way to make it better. Her idea is a bicycle.	**Beginning** Yes. They help. **Intermediate** Yes, because they help people get around. **Advanced** Yes. Their ideas are useful because they help people travel easily. **Advanced High** The inventor's and the queen's ideas are useful to people. People can use bicycles and unicycles to travel more easily.	**Beginning** A phone. **Intermediate** A phone is useful. People talk. **Advanced** A cell phone is useful because it helps people talk easily. **Advanced High** One useful invention is the cell phone. People can use a cell phone to talk to people whenever they need to.

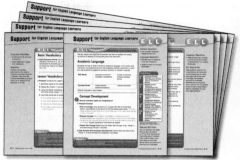

Teacher's Edition pages 324j–353q

See the support for English language learners throughout the lesson, including ELL strategies and scaffolded activities at points of use.

Teacher's Edition pages DI•16–DI•25

Differentiated Instruction for English language learners provides daily group activities that "frontload," or preteach, core instruction.

ELL Handbook pp. 89a–94

Find additional lesson materials that support the core lesson and the ELL instructional pages.

 Poster 11

ELL Reader 5.3.1

Scientific Methods in Action

ELD Reader 5.3.1

Concept Literacy Reader

ELD, ELL Reader Teaching Guide

Concept Literacy Reader Teaching Guide

Technology

Online Teacher's Edition Use the digital version of the core Teacher's Edition for planning and instruction.

eReaders
This week's ELL and ELD Readers and Concept Literacy Reader are also available in digital format.

This Week's Content and Language Objectives by Strand

Concept Development/ **Academic Language** How do inventors inspire our imaginations?	**Content Objective** • Use concept vocabulary related to inventors. **Language Objectives** • Listen to media for concept attainment. • Express ideas in response to art and discussion.
Phonics and Spelling Words with Schwa	**Content Objective** • Identify words with schwa. **Language Objectives** • Apply phonics and decoding skills to spelling. • Distinguish vowel sounds of English. • Learn relationships between sounds and letters of English.
Listening Comprehension Modified Read Aloud: "Ben Franklin, Inventor"	**Content Objective** • Monitor and adjust oral comprehension. **Language Objectives** • Discuss sequence words. • Use sequence words to identify the order in which events occurred.
Reading Comprehension Sequence	**Content Objectives** • Order the sequence of events in a text. • Monitor and adjust comprehension. **Language Objectives** • Summarize text using visual support. • Retell the sequence of events in a reading. • Express opinions.
Vocabulary Basic and Lesson Vocabulary	**Language Objectives** • Understand and use basic vocabulary. • Learn meanings of grade-level vocabulary. • Produce drawings, phrases, or short sentences to show understanding of Lesson Vocabulary.
Word Analysis Shades of Meaning	**Content Objective** • Identify and define words with shades of meaning. **Language Objective** • Discuss shades of meaning for words with similar meanings.
Grammar and Conventions Past, Present, and Future Tenses	**Content Objective** • Decode and use past, present, and future verb tenses. **Language Objectives** • Speak using the correct verb tense. • Write phrases and sentences with past, present, and future verb tenses.
Writing Write Dialogue	**Content Objective** • Identify dialogue in a text. **Language Objectives** • Write dialogue. • Know when to use informal language.

Word Cards for Vocabulary Activities

applauds	**browsing**
fabulous	**inspecting**
project	

Teacher Note: Beginning Teach two to three words. **Intermediate** Teach three to four words. **Advanced** Teach four to five words. **Advanced High** Teach all words and review two words from an earlier lesson.

Look at the two pictures. **Read** the paragraphs.

- Put the sentences in order. **Write** a 1 by the event that happened first. **Write** a 2 by the event that happened second. **Write** a 3 by the event that happened third.

From Model Ts to T-birds

Henry Ford built the first Model T in 1908. At first, Ford simply wanted to build a car most people could afford. Then, in 1914, he created the assembly line. This new way of building things made the work much faster. The speed of building made the price of the car drop. Ford spent nineteen years building the same basic design of the Model T. He sold 15,000,000 Model Ts.

In 1955, Ford Motor Company built another popular car, the Thunderbird. People called them T-birds. The car had only a front seat, so no more than two or three people could ride. The next year Ford designed a T-bird with front and back seats. The company built thirteen different types of T-birds over the years. In 2005, Ford stopped producing T-birds.

---

1. Henry Ford created the assembly line. _____

Ford Motor Company sold 15,000,000 Model Ts. _____

Henry Ford built the first Model T in 1908. _____

2. Ford Motor Company made the last T-bird. _____

Ford Motor Company made the first T-bird. _____

Ford designed a T-bird with front and back seats. _____

Sequence

Use this lesson to supplement or replace the skill lesson on page 325c of the Teacher's Edition. Display the Skill Points (at right) and share them with students.

Teach/Model

Write on the board: *In 1903, the Wright brothers flew the first airplane. It flew 120 feet in twelve seconds. Other people already knew about wings and engines. The Wright brothers put everything together and made a way to control the plane. They tested their ideas in 1900.*

Beginning Read the sentences aloud. Ask: *What did the Wright brothers do before the airplane flew?* (They tested it.) *How do you know that is the order of events?* (The dates help tell the order.)

Intermediate Read the sentences aloud. Ask students to tell where they can add clue words such as *before, then, next,* or *last*.

Advanced Ask volunteers to read the sentences. Have students copy the sentences and number them in order. Then have them use sequence words to tell the events to a partner.

Advanced High Ask students to think of the sequence of steps to make something such as a sandwich or a bed. Have them write three sentences using sequence words that tell the order of the steps.

Then distribute copies of Picture It! page 90.

- Have students look at the pictures and title and tell what they think the paragraphs will be about.
- Review the Skill Points with students.
- Read the paragraphs aloud. Ask: *How did Henry Ford's Model T car change?* Encourage children to use *first, next, then,* and *last.* Ask for clarification if students give answers without sequence words.

Practice

Read aloud the directions on page 90. Reread the first paragraph aloud, explaining how an assembly line works. Then have students use the pictures and paragraphs as they put the sentences beneath the box in order.

Beginning Students can first say which numbers they want to write by each sentence before writing them. Provide help with English words.

Intermediate Students can first orally answer and then write the correct numbers on the lines. Provide help with English words.

Advanced Students can write their answers and then check the numbers by comparing them with a partner's.

Advanced High Students can write their answers and then read the sentences in sequential order using sequence words *first, next,* and *finally*.

Answers for page 90: 1. 2, 3, 1; **2.** 3, 1, 2

Skill Points

✔ **Sequence** is the order in which things happen.

✔ Look for clue words such as *first, next, then,* and *last.*

✔ Sometimes a story will not have clue words.

Multilingual Summaries

The Fabulous Perpetual Motion Machine

Carla, Carlos, Effie and Larry are in the basement. They talk about the Science Fair. Everyone is trying to come up with a project that hasn't been done before.

Joyce unveils Carlos and Carla's project. It is a perpetual motion machine. It does not have a power source and can run forever. Carlos and Carla's brother Domingo comes down. He doesn't believe the machine can work.

Mr. Pérez comes home with Lee who is a reporter. Larry and Joyce notice that their watches have stopped. Mrs. Pérez says that the oven is not cooking the chicken. Lee's camera does not work. Domingo explains the law of thermodynamics. Carlos and Carla realize their machine is borrowing energy. They need a new science project.

Spanish

La fabulosa máquina de movimiento perpetuo

Carla, Carlos, Effie y Larry están en el sótano. Hablan acerca de la Feria Científica. Todos están tratando de lograr un proyecto que no se haya inventado antes.

Joyce descubre el proyecto de Carlos y Carla. Es una máquina de movimiento perpetuo. Ella no tiene una fuente de poder y puede funcionar por siempre. Domingo, el hermano de Carlos y Carla, llega a casa. Él no cree que la máquina pueda funcionar.

El señor Pérez llega a casa con Lee que es reportero. Larry y Joyce descubren que sus relojes se han detenido. Domingo les explica la ley de la termodinámica. Carlos y Carla se dan cuenta de que su máquina está absorbiendo energía. Ahora necesitan un nuevo proyecto científico.

Multilingual Summaries

Chinese

傑出的培瑞茲雙胞胎，神奇的永動機

　　卡拉、卡羅斯、艾非和賴瑞聚在地下室。　他們正在討論科學比賽的事。　每個人都試著想出一個沒有人做過的計劃。

　　喬依絲說出了卡羅斯和卡拉的計劃。　他們打算做一台永動機。　永動機不使用能源，卻可以永遠運轉下去。　卡羅斯和卡拉的哥哥多明哥也來到地下室。　他不相信永動機可以運轉。

　　培端茲先生帶著記者李先生回家了。　賴瑞和喬依絲發現他們的錶停了。培瑞茲太太說烤箱壞了，沒辦法烤雞。　李先生的相機出故障了。　多明哥向大家解釋熱力學定律。　卡羅斯和卡拉明白了，他們的機器在借用能量。　他們需要想出新的科學計劃。

Vietnamese

Cái Máy Thần Kỳ Chuyển Động Không Ngừng của Hai Cậu Sinh Đôi Thần Kỳ Họ Pérež

　　Carla, Carlos, Effie và Larry đang ở tầng hầm dưới đất. Chúng đang bàn với nhau về ngày Hội Chợ Khoa Học. Mọi người đang suy nghĩ để chế tạo ra vật gì chưa từng có trước đây.

　　Joyce kéo màn xuống phơi bày ra cái máy của Carlos và Carla. Đây là một cái máy chuyển động không ngừng. Nó không có năng lượng và có thể chạy mãi mãi. Domingo là anh của Carla và Carlos đi xuống. Anh không tin cái máy có thể chạy được.

　　Ông Pérez về nhà cùng với một nhà báo tên Lee. Larry và Joyce nhận thấy cái đồng hồ không còn chạy nữa. Bà Pérez thì nói cái lò không nấu gà được. Máy chụp hình của ông Lee cũng không xài được. Domingo giải thích về định luật Nhiệt Động Học. Carlos và Carla biết được cái máy của chúng là máy hút năng lượng. Chúng cần tìm đề án khoa học mới khác.

Multilingual Summaries

전설적인 페레즈 쌍둥이의 전설적인 영구기관

카를라, 카를로스, 에피와 래리는 지하실에서 과학박람회에 대해 얘기하고 있다. 모두들 이전에는 아무도 하지 않았던 연구 과제를 해보려 한다.

조이스가 카를로스와 카를라의 과제를 공개한다. 그건 영구기관이다. 동력이 없이 영원히 움직일 수 있는 기계이다. 카를로스와 카를라의 형 도밍고가 내려온다. 그는 그게 작동할 거라고 믿지 않는다.

페레즈 씨가 리 기자와 함께 집에 온다. 래리와 조이스는 시계가 멈춘 것을 알아챈다. 페레즈 부인은 오븐에서 닭 요리가 되지 않았다고 말한다. 리의 사진기가 작동하지 않는다. 도밍고가 열역학 법칙에 대해 설명한다. 카를로스와 카를라는 자기네 영구기관이 에너지를 쓰고 있었다는 걸 깨닫는다. 그들은 새로운 과학 연구 과제를 찾아야 한다.

Ob Tug Pérez Ntxaib Lub Cav Nti Zoo Zoo

Carla, Carlos, Effie thiab Larry nyob hauv qab daus. Lawv tham txog qhov Science Fair. Txhua tus nriav ua yam uas tsis tau neeg ua dua los li.

Joyce qhia rau Carlos thiab Carla qhov uas nws yuav ua. Nws yogib lub cav txawj nti. Nws tsis muaj qhov txuas fais fab li thiab thiaj khiav tau tas mus li. Carlos thiab Carla tus kwv tij Domingo tuaj xyuas lawv. Nws tsis ntseeg hais tias lub cav ntawd ua hauj lwm.

Mr. Pérez los tsev nrog Lee uas yog tus neeg sau ntawv. Larry thiab Joyce xam pom hais tias lawv lub moo nres lawm. Mrs. Pérez hais tias lub qhov cub ci qaib tsis ua hauj lwm lawm. Lee lub koob thaij duab los tsis ua hauj lwm lawm. Domingo piav txog txoj cai rau thermodynamics. Carlos thiab Carla pom tau hais tias nkawd lub cav qiv lub zog los siv xwb. Nkawd yuav tau ua dua lwm qhov science project.

Name _____

- **Read** *Scientific Methods in Action* again.
- Use the information in the book to **answer** the questions. Use complete sentences if you can.

page 2
1. What did Al-Razi use the scientific method for?

_____

_____

pages 3–4
2. What was the problem Ben Franklin wanted to solve?

_____

_____

pages 5–6
3. According to Ben's hypothesis, what would happen if lightning were the same thing as electricity?

_____

_____

pages 7–8
4. Why did most colonists choose pointed lightning rods instead of blunt ones?

_____

_____

Family Link

Tell your family what you learned about the scientific method and Benjamin Franklin. Ask family members to tell you about another scientist they know.

Weekly Resources Guide for English Language Learner Support

For this week's content and language objectives, see p. 95e.

Instructional Strand	Day 1	Day 2
Concept Development/Academic Language	**TEACHER'S EDITION** • Academic Language, p. DI•41 • Concept Development, p. DI•41 • Anchored Talk, pp. 354j—354–355 • Preteach Academic Vocabulary, p. 357a • Concept Talk Video **ELL HANDBOOK** • Hear It, See It, Say It, Use It, pp. xxxvi–xxxvii • ELL Poster Talk, Concept Talk, p. 95c **ELL POSTER 12** • Day 1 Activities	**TEACHER'S EDITION** • Academic Language, p. DI•41 • Concept Development, p. DI•41 • Anchored Talk, p. 358a • Concept Talk Video **ELL HANDBOOK** • ELL Poster Talk, Concept Talk, p. 95c • Concept Talk Video Routine, p. 477 **ELL POSTER 12** • Day 2 Activities
Phonics and Spelling	**TEACHER'S EDITION** • Phonics and Spelling, p. DI•45	**TEACHER'S EDITION** • Phonics and Spelling, p. DI•45
Listening Comprehension	**TEACHER'S EDITION** • Modified Read Aloud, p. DI•44 • Read Aloud, p. 355b • Concept Talk Video **ELL HANDBOOK** • Concept Talk Video Routine, p. 477	**TEACHER'S EDITION** • Modified Read Aloud, p. DI•44 • AudioText of *Leonardo's Horse* • Concept Talk Video **ELL HANDBOOK** • AudioText CD Routine, p. 477 • K-W-L Chart, p. 480
Reading Comprehension	**TEACHER'S EDITION** • Preteach Main Idea and Supporting Details, p. DI•46	**TEACHER'S EDITION** • Reteach Main Idea and Supporting Details, p. DI•46 • Frontloading Reading, p. DI•47 **ELL HANDBOOK** • Picture It! Skill Instruction, pp. 96–96a • Multilingual Summaries, pp. 97–99
Vocabulary **Basic and Lesson Vocabulary** **Word Analysis: Greek and Latin Roots**	**TEACHER'S EDITION** • Basic Vocabulary, p. DI•42 • Preteach Lesson Vocabulary, p. DI•42 • Greek and Latin Roots, p. DI•45 **ELL HANDBOOK** • Word Cards, p. 95 • ELL Vocabulary Routine, p. 471 **ELL POSTER 12** • Day 1 Activities	**TEACHER'S EDITION** • Basic Vocabulary, p. DI•42 • Reteach Lesson Vocabulary, p. DI•43 • Greek and Latin Roots, p. DI•45 **ELL HANDBOOK** • Word Cards, p. 95 • Multilingual Vocabulary List, p. 435 **ELL POSTER 12** • Day 2 Activities
Grammar and Conventions	**TEACHER'S EDITION** • Preteach Principal Parts of Regular Verbs, p. DI•49	**TEACHER'S EDITION** • Reteach Principal Parts of Regular Verbs, p. DI•49
Writing	**TEACHER'S EDITION** • Detailed and Relevant Evidence, p. DI•50 • Writing for Tests: Persuasive Speech, pp. 357e–357f	**TEACHER'S EDITION** • Writing for Tests: Persuasive Speech, pp. 371d–371e

ELL Handbook

This symbol indicates leveled instruction to address language proficiency levels.

Day 3	Day 4	Day 5
TEACHER'S EDITION • Academic Language, p. DI•41 • Concept Development, p. DI•41 • Anchored Talk, p. 372a • Concept Talk Video **ELL HANDBOOK** • ELL Poster Talk, Concept Talk, p. 95c **ELL POSTER 12** • Day 3 Activities	**TEACHER'S EDITION** • Academic Language, p. DI•41 • Concept Development, p. DI•41 • Anchored Talk, p. 382a • Concept Talk Video **ELL HANDBOOK** • ELL Poster Talk, Concept Talk, p. 95c **ELL POSTER 12** • Day 4 Activities	**TEACHER'S EDITION** • Academic Language, p. DI•41 • Concept Development, p. DI•41 • Concept Talk Video **ELL HANDBOOK** • ELL Poster Talk, Concept Talk, p. 95c **ELL POSTER 12** • Day 5 Activities
		TEACHER'S EDITION • Phonics and Spelling, p. DI•45
ELL HANDBOOK • Phonics Transition Lesson, pp. 278, 281 **TEACHER'S EDITION** • AudioText of *Leonardo's Horse* • Concept Talk Video **ELL HANDBOOK** • AudioText CD Routine, p. 477	**ELL HANDBOOK** • Phonics Transition Lesson, pp. 278, 281 **TEACHER'S EDITION** • Concept Talk Video	**TEACHER'S EDITION** • Concept Talk Video
TEACHER'S EDITION • Sheltered Reading, p. DI•47 **ELL HANDBOOK** • Multilingual Summaries, pp. 97–99	**TEACHER'S EDITION** • ELL/ELD Reader Guided Reading, p. DI•48 **ELL HANDBOOK** • ELL Study Guide, p. 100	**TEACHER'S EDITION** • ELL/ELD Reader Guided Reading, p. DI•48 **ELL HANDBOOK** • ELL Study Guide, p. 100
		TEACHER'S EDITION • Greek and Latin Roots, p. 387i
ELL HANDBOOK • High-Frequency Words Activity Bank, p. 446 **ELL POSTER 12** • Day 3 Activities	**ELL HANDBOOK** • High-Frequency Words Activity Bank, p. 446	**ELL HANDBOOK** • High-Frequency Words Activity Bank, p. 446
TEACHER'S EDITION • Grammar Jammer **ELL HANDBOOK** • Grammar Transition Lesson, pp. 326, 333 • Grammar Jammer Routine, p. 478	**TEACHER'S EDITION** • Grammar Jammer **ELL HANDBOOK** • Grammar Transition Lesson, pp. 326, 333	**TEACHER'S EDITION** • Grammar Jammer **ELL HANDBOOK** • Grammar Transition Lesson, pp. 326, 333
TEACHER'S EDITION • Let's Write It!, p. 380–381 • Writing for Tests: Evaluation, pp. 381a–381b	**TEACHER'S EDITION** • Writing for Tests, pp. 387d–387e	**TEACHER'S EDITION** • Writing for Tests, pp. 387p–387q

Question of the Week
How do artists inspire future generations?

Throughout the week, use the ELL Poster to help students produce and comprehend language, understand the concept, and build English vocabulary. Use the Question of the Week and other questions to help students share ideas in pairs, small groups, or the large group. Sample questions are shown, with examples of possible responses by students.

Weekly Concept and Language Goals

• Understand the meaning of art and artists

• Discuss what artists can do

• Describe how artists inspire people

By the end of the lesson, students should be able to talk about and write sentences about how artists inspire people.

ELL Poster 12

Daily Team Talk

Day 1	Day 2	Day 3	Day 4	Day 5
After Day 1 activities on Poster, ask questions such as *Why do you think designing a building, as they do in the poster picture, is a kind of art?*	After Day 2 activity on Poster, ask questions such as *In the poster picture, is Benjamin Banneker an artist? Why or why not?*	After Day 3 activity on Poster, ask questions such as *How did Benjamin Banneker inspire people by planning the U.S. Capitol?*	After Day 4 activity on Poster, ask questions such as *Think about the story Leonardo's Horse. What are some of the different ways Leonardo Da Vinci was an artist?*	After Day 5 activity on Poster, ask questions such as *How has an artist inspired you?*
Beginning People draw it.	**Beginning** Yes. He makes it.	**Beginning** A new building.	**Beginning** He can paint.	**Beginning** I like the piano.
Intermediate People draw a picture of the building.	**Intermediate** Yes, because he helps make a building.	**Intermediate** He helped make a new building.	**Intermediate** He painted and made a horse.	**Intermediate** I like hearing my piano teacher play.
Advanced It is art because people have to be creative to make a building.	**Advanced** Yes. Benjamin uses creativity to help make a building.	**Advanced** The old Capitol building burned. He helped rebuild it.	**Advanced** Leonardo painted pictures, made statues, and played music.	**Advanced** Hearing my piano teacher play music is inspiring. I want to play like her.
Advanced High Creating a building is art because the person who designs it must think creatively. Artists are people who use creativity to make things.	**Advanced High** Benjamin Banneker is an artist because he uses his creativity to design a building, which is a kind of art.	**Advanced High** When the British burned the old Capitol, people were sad. By helping to rebuild it, Benjamin Banneker helped people believe in our country again.	**Advanced High** Leonardo Da Vinci was an artist in many ways, including painting, designing statues, playing music, and inventing things.	**Advanced High** Listening to my piano teacher play music is inspiring because the music sounds so pretty. It makes me want to play well too.

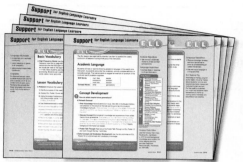

Teacher's Edition pages 354j–387q

See the support for English language learners throughout the lesson, including ELL strategies and scaffolded activities at points of use.

Teacher's Edition pages DI•41–DI•50

Differentiated Instruction for English language learners provides daily group activities that "frontload," or preteach, core instruction.

ELL Handbook pp. 95a–100

Find additional lesson materials that support the core lesson and the ELL instructional pages.

ELL Poster 12

ELL Reader 5.3.2

ELD Reader 5.3.2

Concept Literacy Reader

ELD, ELL Reader Teaching Guide

Concept Literacy Reader Teaching Guide

Technology

Online Teacher's Edition Use the digital version of the core Teacher's Edition for planning and instruction.

eReaders
This week's ELL and ELD Readers and Concept Literacy Reader are also available in digital format.

This Week's Content and Language Objectives by Strand

Concept Development/ Academic Language How do artists inspire future generations?	**Content Objective** • Use concept vocabulary related to artists and their achievements. **Language Objective** • Express ideas in response to art and discussion.
Phonics and Spelling Compound Words	**Content Objective** • Identify words in compound words. **Language Objectives** • Apply phonics and decoding skills to vocabulary. • Monitor oral language production.
Listening Comprehension Modified Read Aloud: "A New Way"	**Content Objective** • Monitor and adjust oral comprehension. **Language Objectives** • Discuss oral passages. • Use a graphic organizer to take notes.
Reading Comprehension Main Idea and Details	**Content Objectives** • Identify the main idea and details. • Monitor and adjust comprehension. **Language Objectives** • Write the main idea of familiar stories. • Use the new academic language: main idea and details. • Understand main points of spoken languages.
Vocabulary Basic and Lesson Vocabulary	**Language Objectives** • Understand and use basic vocabulary. • Learn meanings of grade-level vocabulary. • Produce drawings, phrases, or short sentences to show understanding of Lesson Vocabulary.
Word Analysis Greek and Latin Roots	**Content Objective** • Identify Greek and Latin roots in words. **Language Objective** • Discuss meanings of Greek and Latin roots.
Grammar and Conventions Principal Parts of Regular Verbs	**Content Objective** • Identify principal parts of regular verbs. **Language Objective** • Speak using correct forms of regular verbs.
Writing Detailed and Relevant Evidence	**Content Objective** • Identify evidence to support the main idea in writing. **Language Objectives** • Write complete paragraphs. • Express ideas. • Know when to use formal English and adapt language for formal purposes.

Word Cards for Vocabulary Activities

achieved	**architect**
bronze	**cannon**
depressed	**fashioned**
midst	**philosopher**
rival	

Teacher Note: Beginning Teach three to four words. **Intermediate** Teach four to six words. **Advanced** Teach six to seven words. **Advanced High** Teach all words.

Name _____

Look at the picture. **Read** the paragraph.

• Which sentence tells the main idea of the paragraph? **Write** that sentence in the *Main Idea* box.

• Which sentences give details? **Write** them in the *Detail* boxes.

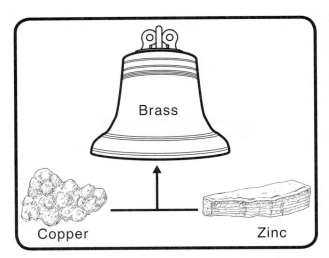

Brass

Brass is not a metal that comes from nature. It is a mixture of two metals that uses the good qualities of both of them. One of the metals is copper; the other is zinc. To make brass, copper and zinc are melted. Then they are combined. Brass is used to make many things, including jewelry and musical instruments.

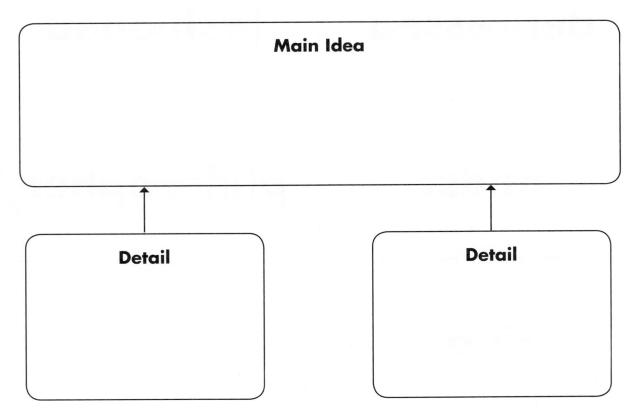

Main Idea

Detail

Detail

Main Idea and Details

Use this lesson to supplement or replace the skill lesson on page 355c of the Teacher's Edition. Display the Skill Points (at right) and share them with students.

Teach/Model

Beginning Display a collection of art supplies. For example: crayons, markers, pencil, construction paper, modeling clay. Ask: *What are these things used for? What is the main idea of showing these objects?* (Possible answer: There are many kinds of art supplies.) *What details tell about the main idea?* (Crayons are art supplies. Markers can be art supplies.)

Intermediate Say: *Many artists make art in their homes. People hang art in their offices. An art museum has a big collection of rare and expensive art.* Work with students to decide a main idea that the three details tell about. (Possible answer: Art is used in many different places.)

Advanced Write and read aloud these details: *Artists paint on canvas. Artists draw on paper. Artists use spray paint on bricks. Artists sculpt clay into statues.* Ask students to write a main idea that all the details tell about. (Possible answer: Artists use different materials to make art.)

Advanced High Discuss art with students. Together think of a main idea such as *Art comes in many forms.* Write it on the board and circle it. Have students write supporting details in circles around the main idea.

Then distribute copies of Picture It! page 96.

- Have students look at the picture and ask them what they know about metal.
- Read the paragraph aloud. Ask: *What is this paragraph about?* (how brass is created)
- Review the Skill Points with students.

Practice

Read aloud the directions on page 96. Have students reread the paragraph with a partner. Then have them use the picture and the paragraph as they fill in the graphic organizer.

Beginning Students can first say what they will write in each box and then write words or phrases to complete the organizer. Provide help with English spelling and writing.

Intermediate Students can first orally answer before writing their answers in the boxes. Provide help with English spelling.

Advanced Students can write their answers in the organizer and then check their answers by comparing them with a partner's.

Advanced High Students can write their answers in the boxes and then explain how the details support the main idea.

Answers for page 96: *Main Idea:* Brass is a mixture of two metals. *Detail:* One of the metals is copper. *Detail:* The other metal is zinc.

Skill Points

✔ The **main idea** is the most important idea in a paragraph. It usually comes at the beginning of the paragraph.

✔ **Details** are pieces of information that tell more about the main idea.

Multilingual Summaries

Leonardo's Horse

As a boy, Leonardo da Vinci was curious about everything. As a teenager, he went to study art in Florence, Italy. He became a famous artist. He made a silver flute shaped like a horse's head. The ruler of Florence sent Leonardo to give the flute to the duke of Milan as a gift.

In Milan, the duke asked Leonardo to make a statue of a horse. It would be three times bigger than a real horse. Leonardo studied other statues and real horses. He made a clay model that was twenty-four feet tall.

France was threatening to invade Milan. The duke used the metal intended for the statue to make a cannon. The clay model became a pile of mud. Leonardo was sad about his horse. In the 1990s, two artists made a statue of a horse like Leonardo's. More than 450 years after Leonardo died, the horse was brought to Milan.

Spanish

El caballo de Leonardo

Cuando era niño, Leonardo da Vinci sentía curiosidad por todo. De adolescente, fue a estudiar arte a Florencia, Italia. Se convirtió en un artista famoso. Hizo una flauta de plata con la forma de una cabeza de caballo. El gobernador de Florencia envió a Leonardo con la flauta de regalo para el duque de Milán.

En Milán, el duque le pidió a Leonardo que hiciera la estatua de un caballo. Debería ser tres veces más grande que un caballo real. Leonardo estudió otras estatuas y caballos reales. Hizo un modelo de arcilla que tenía veinticuatro pies de alto.

Francia amenazaba con invadir Milán. El duque usó el metal de la estatua para hacer un cañón. El modelo de arcilla se convirtió en un montón de barro. Leonardo estaba muy triste por su caballo. Pero en la década de 1990, dos artistas hicieron una estatua de un caballo como el de Leonardo. Más de 450 años después de la muerte de Leonardo, el caballo fue llevado a Milán.

Multilingual Summaries

Chinese

達芬奇的馬

　　達芬奇小時候就對萬事萬物充滿好奇。青少年時，他前往意大利佛羅倫薩學習藝術，成為著名的藝術家。他創作了一隻銀笛，形狀就像馬頭。佛羅倫薩王公派他去米蘭，把銀笛送給公爵。

　　米蘭公爵請達芬奇做一個馬雕像，要求比真馬整整大三倍。達芬奇仔細研究了許多雕像與真馬，做了一個泥馬模型，足有24英尺高。

　　此時法國威脅入侵米蘭，公爵只好把做雕像的金屬造大炮。泥馬模型變成了一堆泥漿，達芬奇傷心極了。二十世紀90年代時，兩個藝術家特意仿製達芬奇的馬雕像。在紀念達芬奇逝世450多年時，送給了米蘭。

Vietnamese

Con Ngựa Của Leonardo

　　Khi còn là một đứa bé, Leonardo da Vinci tò mò về mọi thứ. Khi là một thanh thiếu niên, ông ấy đi học nghệ thuật ở Florence, nước Ý. Ông trở nên một họa sĩ nổi tiếng. Ông làm một ống sáo bằng bạc có hình dạng đầu ngựa. Nhà cai trị ở Florence sai Leonardo đi trao ống sáo này cho vị Công Tước ở Milan để làm quà.

　　Ở Milan, vị công tước yêu cầu Leonardo làm một bức tượng ngựa. Tượng này lớn hơn gấp ba lần một con ngựa thật. Leonardo nghiên cứu các bức tượng khác và những con ngựa thật. Ông làm một mô hình bằng đất sét cao hai mươi bốn bộ.

　　Pháp đang hăm he xâm lăng Milan. Vị công tước dùng kim loại làm bức tượng để làm ra súng đại bác. Mô hình đất sét trở thành một đống bùn. Leonardo buồn về con ngựa của mình. Vào thập niên 1990, có hai họa sĩ làm bức tượng ngựa giống như của Leonardo. Hơn 450 năm sau khi Leonardo qua đời, ngựa này được mang đến Milan.

Multilingual Summaries

Korean

레오나르도의 말

레오나르도 다빈치는 소년 시절 호기심이 아주 많았다. 청소년 시절 그는 이탈리아 피렌체로 예술 공부를 하러 떠났고 유명한 예술가가 되었다. 그는 말의 머리처럼 생긴 은색 플루트를 만들었다. 피렌체의 군주는 레오나르도를 시켜 밀라노의 공작에게 그 플루트를 선물로 보냈다.

밀라노의 공작은 레오나르도에게 말 동상을 만들어달라고 요청했는데 그것은 실제 말보다 세 배나 더 큰 것이었다. 레오나르도는 다른 동상들과 실제 말에 대해 공부한 후 24피트 높이의 점토 모형을 만들었다.

프랑스가 밀라노를 침략하겠다고 위협하고 있었다. 공작은 말 동상에 쓸 금속으로 대포를 만들었다. 점토로 만든 말 모형은 진흙 더미가 되었고 레오나르도는 자기 작품이 그렇게 된 것에 슬퍼했다. 1990년대 들어 두 명의 예술가가 레오나르도의 것과 같은 말 동상을 만들었다. 레오나르도가 죽은 지 450년이 지나 그 말 동상은 밀라노로 돌려 보내졌다.

Hmong

Leonardo tus Nees

Thaum nws yog menyuam tub, Leonardo da Vinci xav paub txog txhua yam. Thaum ib yog ib tug tub hluas, nws mus kawm teeb duab nyob rau Florence, Italy. Nws los ua ib tug neeg teeb duab uas nto npe heev. Nws txua tau ib lub raj nyiaj zoo li ib tug nees lub taub hau. Tus tswv nyob Florence xa Leonardo mus muab lub raj ntawd ua ib qhov khoom plig rau tus tswv lub lav Milan.

Nyob Milan, tus tswv ntawd nug Leonardo kom nws puab ib tug nees kom loj tshaj ib tug nees tiag lawm li peb zaug. Leonardo kawm txog tej mlom uas tau puab lawm thiab kawm txog nees. Nws sim av nplaum puas tau ib tug qauv ua siab li nees nkaum plaub fiv (feet).

Fabkis phem tawm tsam tias lawv yuav tuaj tua Milan. Tus tswv ntawd siv cov hlau yuav los ua tus nees ntawd coj los ua phom. Cov av nplaum ua puas tau tus qauv ntawd cia li los ua ib phawg av nkos lawm xwb. Leonardo tu siab txog nws tus nees ntawd. Nyob rau lub caij ib txhiab cuaj puas cuaj caum ntawd, ob tug neeg teeb duab tau ua tau ib tug nees zoo li Leonardo tus. Tshaj plaub puas tsib caug xyoo tom qab Leonardo tuag lawm, luag coj tau tus nees ntawd tuaj rau Milan.

Name _____

- **Read** *The Renaissance* again.
- What did you learn about the people of the Renaissance?
  Write the main thing that each person did below his picture.

Michelangelo

_____
_____
_____
_____

Copernicus

_____
_____
_____
_____

Descartes

_____
_____
_____
_____

Leonardo da Vinci

_____
_____
_____
_____

Shakespeare

_____
_____
_____
_____

Family Link

Tell your family what you learned about these people. Ask them to tell you about other famous scientists, thinkers, or artists.

For this week's content and language objectives, see p. 101e.

Instructional Strand	Day 1	Day 2
Concept Development/Academic Language	TEACHER'S EDITION • Academic Language, p. DI•66 • Concept Development, p. DI•66 • Anchored Talk, pp. 388j—388–389 • Preteach Academic Vocabulary, p. 391a • Concept Talk Video ELL HANDBOOK • Hear It, See It, Say It, Use It, pp. xxxvi–xxxvii • ELL Poster Talk, Concept Talk, p. 101c ELL POSTER 13 • Day 1 Activities	TEACHER'S EDITION • Academic Language, p. DI•66 • Concept Development, p. DI•66 • Anchored Talk, p. 392a • Concept Talk Video ELL HANDBOOK • ELL Poster Talk, Concept Talk, p. 101c • Concept Talk Video Routine, p. 477 ELL POSTER 13 • Day 2 Activities
Phonics and Spelling	TEACHER'S EDITION • Phonics and Spelling, p. DI•70	TEACHER'S EDITION • Phonics and Spelling, p. DI•70
Listening Comprehension	TEACHER'S EDITION • Modified Read Aloud, p. DI•69 • Read Aloud, p. 389b • Concept Talk Video ELL HANDBOOK • Concept Talk Video Routine, p. 477	TEACHER'S EDITION • Modified Read Aloud, p. DI•69 • AudioText of *The Dinosaurs of Waterhouse Hawkins* • Concept Talk Video ELL HANDBOOK • AudioText CD Routine, p. 477 • Story Map A, p. 483
Reading Comprehension	TEACHER'S EDITION • Preteach Fact and Opinion, p. DI•71	TEACHER'S EDITION • Reteach Fact and Opinion, p. DI•71 • Frontloading Reading, p. DI•72 ELL HANDBOOK • Picture It! Skill Instruction, pp. 102–102a • Multilingual Summaries, pp. 103–105
Vocabulary **Basic and Lesson Vocabulary** **Word Analysis: Suffixes -*tion*, -*sion***	TEACHER'S EDITION • Basic Vocabulary, p. DI•67 • Preteach Lesson Vocabulary, p. DI•67 • Suffixes -*tion*, -*sion*, p. DI•70 ELL HANDBOOK • Word Cards, p. 101 • ELL Vocabulary Routine, p. 471 ELL POSTER 13 • Day 1 Activities	TEACHER'S EDITION • Basic Vocabulary, p. DI•67 • Reteach Lesson Vocabulary, p. DI•68 • Suffixes -*tion*, -*sion*, p. DI•70 ELL HANDBOOK • Word Cards, p. 101 • Multilingual Vocabulary List, pp. 435–436 ELL POSTER 13 • Day 2 Activities
Grammar and Conventions	TEACHER'S EDITION • Preteach Principle Parts of Irregular Verbs, p. DI•74	TEACHER'S EDITION • Reteach Principle Parts of Irregular Verbs, p. DI•74
Writing	TEACHER'S EDITION • Making Word Choices, p. DI•75 • Introduce Advertising Brochure, pp. 391e–391f	TEACHER'S EDITION • Writing Trait: Word Choice, pp. 401d–401e

The Dinosaurs of Waterhouse Hawkins

Day 3	Day 4	Day 5
TEACHER'S EDITION • Academic Language, p. DI•66 • Concept Development, p. DI•66 • Anchored Talk, p. 402a • Concept Talk Video **ELL HANDBOOK** • ELL Poster Talk, Concept Talk, p. 101c **ELL POSTER 13** • Day 3 Activities	**TEACHER'S EDITION** • Academic Language, p. DI•66 • Concept Development, p. DI•66 • Anchored Talk, p. 416a • Concept Talk Video **ELL HANDBOOK** • ELL Poster Talk, Concept Talk, p. 101c **ELL POSTER 13** • Day 4 Activities	**TEACHER'S EDITION** • Academic Language, p. DI•66 • Concept Development, p. DI•66 • Concept Talk Video **ELL HANDBOOK** • ELL Poster Talk, Concept Talk, p. 101c **ELL POSTER 13** • Day 5 Activities
		TEACHER'S EDITION • Phonics and Spelling, p. DI•70
ELL HANDBOOK • Phonics Transition Lesson, pp. 272, 275	**ELL HANDBOOK** • Phonics Transition Lesson, pp. 272, 275	
TEACHER'S EDITION • AudioText of *The Dinosaurs of Waterhouse Hawkins* • Concept Talk Video **ELL HANDBOOK** • AudioText CD Routine, p. 477	**TEACHER'S EDITION** • Concept Talk Video	**TEACHER'S EDITION** • Concept Talk Video
TEACHER'S EDITION • Sheltered Reading, p. DI•72 **ELL HANDBOOK** • Multilingual Summaries, pp. 103–105	**TEACHER'S EDITION** • ELL/ELD Reader Guided Reading, p. DI•73 **ELL HANDBOOK** • ELL Study Guide, p. 106	**TEACHER'S EDITION** • ELL/ELD Reader Guided Reading, p. DI•73 **ELL HANDBOOK** • ELL Study Guide, p. 106
		TEACHER'S EDITION • Suffixes *-tion, -ion*, p. 423i
ELL HANDBOOK • High-Frequency Words Activity Bank, p. 446 **ELL POSTER 13** • Day 3 Activities	**ELL HANDBOOK** • High-Frequency Words Activity Bank, p. 446	**ELL HANDBOOK** • High-Frequency Words Activity Bank, p. 446
TEACHER'S EDITION • Grammar Jammer **ELL HANDBOOK** • Grammar Transition Lesson, pp. 326, 334 • Grammar Jammer Routine, p. 478	**TEACHER'S EDITION** • Grammar Jammer **ELL HANDBOOK** • Grammar Transition Lesson, pp. 326, 334	**TEACHER'S EDITION** • Grammar Jammer **ELL HANDBOOK** • Grammar Transition Lesson, pp. 326, 334
TEACHER'S EDITION • Let's Write It!, p. 414–415 • Writer's Craft: Sound Reasoning, pp. 415a–415b	**TEACHER'S EDITION** • Revising Strategy, pp. 423d–423e	**TEACHER'S EDITION** • Principal Parts of Irregular Verbs, pp. 423p–423q

Question of the Week

How can paleontologists help us understand the past?

Throughout the week, use the ELL Poster to help students produce and comprehend language, understand the concept, and build English vocabulary. Use the Question of the Week and other questions to help students share ideas in pairs, small groups, or the large group. Sample questions are shown, with examples of possible responses by students.

Weekly Concept and Language Goals

• Understand and use words related to dinosaurs and paleontologists

• Describe dinosaurs

• Talk about the work of paleontologists

By the end of the lesson, students should be able to talk about and write sentences about paleontologists.

ELL Poster 13

Daily Team Talk

Day 1	Day 2	Day 3	Day 4	Day 5
After Day 1 activities on Poster, ask questions such as *In the poster picture, what is special about what the paleontologist found?*	After Day 2 activity on Poster, ask questions such as *In the poster picture, what does the paleontologist do with the dinosaur fossil?*	After Day 3 activity on Poster, ask questions such as *What will happen after the paleontologist finishes the fossil's mold?*	After Day 4 activity on Poster, ask questions such as *What does the dinosaur at the top of the poster picture look like?*	After Day 5 activity on Poster, ask questions such as *Why do you think it might be important for paleontologists to study dinosaurs?*
Beginning It is old. **Intermediate** She finds a fossil. **Advanced** The scientist finds a fossil in the ground. It is from a dinosaur. **Advanced High** The paleontologist finds a dinosaur fossil buried in the ground. She can use it to learn more about the dinosaur.	**Beginning** Makes a frame. **Intermediate** She makes a frame for a mold. **Advanced** She is using modeling clay to make a mold of the fossil. **Advanced High** The paleontologist is making a mold of the dinosaur fossil. First, she makes a frame. Then she presses modeling compound around the fossil.	**Beginning** She will copy it. **Intermediate** She will make a copy of the fossil. **Advanced** Her assistant will use the mold to make a model of the fossil out of plaster. **Advanced High** The paleontologist's assistant will pour plaster into the mold. When the plaster dries, it will make a model of the fossil that the paleontologist can use.	**Beginning** It is big. **Intermediate** It is big and has a long tail. **Advanced** The dinosaur is large, with a thick tail and horns on its head. **Advanced High** The triceratops has a long, thick tail and two horns on top of its head. It also has a long nose with a horn on top. The dinosaur looks very large.	**Beginning** To know about them. **Intermediate** It is important to know about the past. **Advanced** Learning about the past is important. It helps us know more about our world. **Advanced High** Dinosaurs are a link to the past. Learning about the past helps us to understand the world we live in.

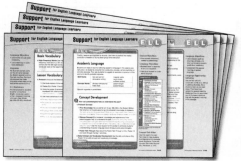

Teacher's Edition pages 388j–423q

See the support for English language learners throughout the lesson, including ELL strategies and scaffolded activities at points of use.

Teacher's Edition pages DI•66–DI•75

Differentiated Instruction for English language learners provides daily group activities that "frontload," or preteach, core instruction.

ELL Handbook pp. 101a–106

Find additional lesson materials that support the core lesson and the ELL instructional pages.

Poster 13

ELL Reader 5.3.3

ELD Reader 5.3.3

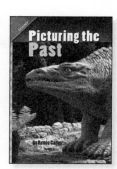

Concept Literacy Reader

ELD, ELL Reader Teaching Guide

Concept Literacy Reader Teaching Guide

Technology

Online Teacher's Edition Use the digital version of the core Teacher's Edition for planning and instruction.

eReaders
This week's ELL and ELD Readers and Concept Literacy Reader are also available in digital format.

This Week's Content and Language Objectives by Strand

Concept Development/ Academic Language How can paleontologists help us understand the past?	**Content Objective** • Use concept vocabulary related to paleontology. **Language Objectives** • Express ideas in response to art and discussion. • Use visual support to understand language.
Phonics and Spelling Consonant Sounds /j/ and /s/	**Content Objective** • Identify consonant sounds /j/ and /s/. **Language Objectives** • Apply phonics and decoding skills to vocabulary. • Learn relationships between sounds and letters of English.
Listening Comprehension Modified Read Aloud: "Finding Dinosaurs"	**Content Objective** • Monitor and adjust oral comprehension. **Language Objectives** • Discuss oral passages. • Use a graphic organizer to take notes.
Reading Comprehension Fact and Opinion	**Content Objectives** • Identify facts and opinions to aid comprehension. • Monitor and adjust comprehension. **Language Objectives** • Expand inferential skills to differentiate fact from opinion. • Discuss facts and opinions from personal experience. • Read grade-level text with appropriate phrasing.
Vocabulary Basic and Lesson Vocabulary	**Language Objectives** • Understand and use basic vocabulary. • Learn meanings of grade-level vocabulary. • Understand the general meaning of spoken language.
Word Analysis Suffixes –tion and –sion	**Content Objective** • Identify suffixes –tion and –sion in words. **Language Objective** • Discuss meanings of words with suffixes.
Grammar and Conventions Principal Parts of Irregular Verbs	**Content Objective** • Correctly form past tense form of irregular verbs. **Language Objectives** • Correctly pronounce irregular past tense verb forms. • Say and write sentences with irregular past tense verbs.
Writing Making Word Choices	**Content Objective** • Use sound reasoning when making word choices. **Language Objectives** • Write persuasive paragraphs. • Express opinions.

Word Cards for Vocabulary Activities

erected	**foundations**
mold	**occasion**
proportion	**tidied**
workshop	

Teacher Note: Beginning Teach two to three words. **Intermediate** Teach three to four words. **Advanced** Teach four to five words. **Advanced High** Teach all words.

Name _____

Read the paragraph. Then **complete** the chart.
- **Find** information that can be proved. **Write** it in the *Facts* column.
- **Find** information that expresses the writer's thoughts or feelings. **Write** it in the *Opinions* column.

The "King" of Dinosaurs

Tyrannosaurus rex was the "king" of dinosaurs. It was 18 feet tall, and it weighed 6 tons or more. Its teeth were sharp and pointed. They could cut through bone and meat. No other dinosaur can compare to T. rex. People will always think of T. rex as the biggest and scariest dinosaur of all time.

Facts	Opinions

Fact and Opinion

Use this lesson to supplement or replace the skill lesson on page 389c of the Teacher's Edition. Display the Skill Points (at right) and share them with students.

Teach/Model

Beginning Say: *Dinosaurs were animals. Is this a fact or an opinion?* (fact) *How do you know?* (It can be proven true.) *The T. rex is my favorite dinosaur. Is this a fact or opinion?* (opinion) *What makes it an opinion?* (It tells how you feel about dinosaurs.)

Intermediate Say: *Scientists use fossils to learn about dinosaurs. Digging up fossils is really serious work.* Ask students to identify the fact and the opinion. Then have them explain how they can prove the fact.

Advanced Ask: *What do you know about dinosaurs?* Have students share facts they know about dinosaurs. Ask: *How can you find information or evidence for those facts?* Then have students share their opinions about dinosaurs. Ask: *What makes these opinions and not facts?*

Advanced High Pair students. Have one partner tell a fact and opinion about dinosaurs. Have the other partner identify each and explain how he or she decided. Then have partners trade roles.

Then distribute copies of Picture It! page 102.

- Tell students to look at the picture of Tyrannosaurus rex. Tell them they are going to read a paragraph about it.
- Ask: *Do you think you will be reading facts, opinions, or both?* Check predictions after reading.
- Review the Skill Points with students.
- Have students share one fact they learned about the Tyrannosaurus rex or their opinion about the dinosaur.

Practice

Read aloud the directions on page 102. Have students reread the paragraph with a partner. Then have them use the picture and the paragraph as they complete the chart.

Beginning Students can first orally answer before writing facts and opinions in the chart. Provide help with English writing and spelling.

Intermediate Students can first say the facts and opinions from the paragraph and then write them in the chart.

Advanced Students can write their answers in the chart and then check them by comparing their answers to a partner's.

Advanced High Students can write their answers in the chart and then orally explain how they determined which statements were facts and which statements were opinions.

Answers for page 102: *Fact:* T. rex was 18 feet tall, and it weighed 6 tons or more. Its teeth were sharp and pointed. They could cut through bone and meat. *Opinion:* T. rex was the "king" of dinosaurs. No other dinosaur can compare to T. rex. People will always think of T. rex as the biggest and scariest dinosaur of all time.

Skill Points

- ✔ A **fact** is something that is true. It can be proven.
- ✔ An **opinion** shows what somebody thinks or feels.
- ✔ A single sentence can contain both a fact and an opinion.

Multilingual Summaries

English

The Dinosaurs of Waterhouse Hawkins

Waterhouse Hawkins had a workshop. He created models of animals. His biggest project was to create life-sized models of dinosaurs. In 1853, people had discovered dinosaur bones. However, no one really knew what a dinosaur looked like. Hawkins asked a scientist to help. The scientist compared dinosaur bones with the bones of modern reptiles.

Hawkins saw that the bones were very much alike. He decided that dinosaurs must have looked like giant lizards. He used fossil bones to estimate how big the dinosaurs must have been. Then he made life-sized models of the dinosaurs.

Queen Victoria and Prince Albert admired Hawkins's models. Prince Albert wanted to display the dinosaurs in his new museum.

First, Hawkins wanted scientists to accept his work. He held a party on New Year's Eve. He had the dinner table inside one of his models. The guests loved Hawkins's creations.

Spanish

Los dinosaurios de Waterhouse Hawkins

Waterhouse Hawkins tenía un taller. Él creaba modelos de animales. Su mayor proyecto fue crear modelos del tamaño real de los dinosaurios. En 1853, la gente había descubierto huesos de dinosaurios. Sin embargo, nadie sabía realmente cómo era un dinosaurio. Hawkins le pidió ayuda a un científico. El científico comparó los huesos de los dinosaurios con los huesos de los reptiles modernos.

Hawkins vio que los huesos eran muy parecidos. Él decidió que los dinosaurios parecían grandes lagartos. Usó huesos fósiles para estimar qué tan grandes eran los dinosaurios. Luego hizo modelos del tamaño real de los dinosaurios.

La reina Victoria y el príncipe Alberto admiraron los modelos de Hawkins. El príncipe Alberto quería exhibir los dinosaurios en su nuevo museo.

Primero, Hawkins quiso que los científicos aceptaran su trabajo. Hizo una fiesta la víspera del Año Nuevo. Tenía la mesa con la cena dentro de uno de sus modelos. Los invitados admiraron las creaciones de Hawkins.

Multilingual Summaries

Chinese

霍金斯的恐龍

　　霍金斯有一個工場，專門製做動物模型。他最遠大的計劃，就是做 出與真恐龍大小一樣的恐龍模型。1853年，人們發現恐龍骨頭化石。然而，當時沒有人知道恐龍究竟長得什麼樣。霍金斯向科學家請教，將恐龍骨頭與現代爬行動物的骨頭進行對比。

　　霍金斯發現這些骨頭非常相像，心裏想恐龍肯定像現在的巨蜥。他用骨頭化石估算恐龍大小，然後製做出恐龍模型，與真的一般大小。

　　維多利亞女王與阿爾伯特王子很喜歡霍金斯的恐龍模型。王子想在新建的博物館裏，向公眾展示這些模型。

　　但是，霍金斯希望科學家們能夠首先接受他的作品，於是在新年前夕舉辦了一個晚會，請客人在他的恐龍模型裏就餐。大家都非常喜歡他的恐龍。

Vietnamese

Những Con Khủng Long của Waterhouse Hawkins

　　Waterhouse Hawkins có một xưởng nhỏ. Ông làm những mô hình thú vật. Dự án lớn nhất của ông là làm những mô hình khủng long to như thật. Vào năm 1853, người ta đã tìm ra xương khủng long. Tuy nhiên, không ai thật sự biết một con khủng long trông như thế nào. Hawkins nhờ một nhà khoa học giúp đỡ. Nhà khoa học này so sánh các xương của khủng long với các xương của loài bò sát cận đại.

　　Hawkins thấy là các xương đều rất giống nhau. Ông quyết định là những con khủng long chắc hẳn là trông giống như những con thần lằn khổng lồ. Ông ấy dùng những xương đã hóa thạch để phỏng đoán xem các con khủng long này đã to đến cỡ nào. Tiếp đó ông làm những mô hình khủng long to như thật.

　　Nữ Vương Victoria và Hoàng Tử Albert hâm mộ những mô hình của Hawkins. Hoàng Tử Albert muốn trưng bày những con khủng long này ở viện bảo tàng mới của ông.

　　Trước hết, Hawkins muốn các nhà khoa học chấp nhận công trình của mình. Ông tổ chức một buổi tiệc vào hôm Giao Thừa. Ông cho đặt bàn ăn bên trong một trong những mô hình của mình. Các quan khách đều yêu thích những sáng tác của Hawkins.

Multilingual Summaries

워터하우스 호킨스의 공룡

워터하우스 호킨스는 작업장을 하나 갖고 있었다. 그는 동물 모형들을 만들었는데 그의 가장 큰 계획은 실제 크기의 공룡 모형을 만드는 것이었다. 1853년 사람들은 공룡의 뼈를 발견했지만 공룡의 모습을 알고 있는 사람은 아무도 없었다. 호킨스는 어느 과학자에게 도움을 요청했고 그 과학자는 공룡과 현대 파충류의 뼈를 비교해 주었다.

호킨스는 공룡과 파충류의 뼈가 아주 유사하다는 점을 발견하고 공룡이 거대한 도마뱀 같이 생겼을 것이라고 생각했다. 그는 화석 뼈를 이용해 공룡의 크기를 어림잡아 실제 크기의 공룡 모형을 만들었다.

빅토리아 여왕과 알버트 왕자는 호킨스의 모형을 보고 감탄했다. 알버트 왕자는 그 공룡 모형을 자신의 새 박물관에 전시하고 싶어했다.

먼저 호킨스는 과학자들이 자신의 업적을 인정해 주길 바랬다. 그는 새해 전날 밤 파티를 열었는데 자신이 만든 공룡 모형 중 한 개의 내부에 저녁 식탁을 차렸다. 손님들은 호킨스의 작품을 아주 좋아했다.

Cov Tsiaj Daisnausxauj (dinosaurs) Ntawm Waterhouse Hawkins

Waterhouse Hawkins muaj ib lub lab ua hauj lwm. Nws txua ib cov tsiaj coj los ua qauv piv txwv. Nws txoj hauj lwm loj tshaj plaws yog txua kom tau ib cov qauv ua luaj li cov tsiaj uas muaj siab. Thaum xyoo ib txhiab yim puas tsib caug peb, neeg tau nrhiav pom ib cov pob txha daisnausxauj. Tiam sis, tsis muaj leej twg uas paub tias ib tug daisnausxauj zoo li cas tiag tiag. Hawkins tau nug ib tug xib hwb kawm txog cov tsiaj ntawd pab nws. Tus xibhwm ntawd muaj cov pob txha daisnausxauj coj los piv nrog cov pob txha ntawm tej tsiaj niaj hnub niam no.

Hawkins pom tau tias cov pob txha ntawd muaj tsis zoo ib yam. Nws tau txiav txim siab tias daisnausxauj yuav tsum muaj tsis zoo li ib cov dev nab qa uas loj kawg li. Nws siv cov pob txha qub uas qhuav rau hauv av lawm coj los kuaj xyuas seb cov daisnausxauj ntawd tau luaj li cas tiag. Ces nws tseem ua tau ib cov qauv daisnausxauj uas luaj li thaum tiag.

Tus pob huabtais Queen Victoria thiab tub nom Prince Albert nyiam Hawkins cov qauv ntawd kawg. Prince Albert xav muab cov daisnausxauj ntawd rau sawv daws saib nyob rau hauv nws tsev khaws khoom qub uas nws txua tshiab.

Hawkins xav kom sawv daws lees nws txoj hauj lwm ntawd. Nws thiaj tau ua ib pluag mov noj hmo ua ntej xyoo tshiab. Nws tau teeb lub rooj noj mov rau hauv ib tug qauv ntawd. Nws cov qhua tau nyiam nws tej khoom uas nws tau tsim kawg.

- **Read** *Dinosaur Time Line* again.
- Next to each sentence below, **write** *F* for *Fact* or *O* for *Opinion*.

1. Paleontologists are always learning things about dinosaurs.

_____

2. Dinosaurs were cold-blooded.

_____

3. Dinosaurs are the most interesting animals that ever lived on Earth.

_____

4. Diplodocus was a plant-eating dinosaur.

_____

5. Scientists do not know why all dinosaurs died long ago.

_____

6. It is better for people that dinosaurs no longer live on Earth.

_____

Family Link
Give your family members a quiz. Ask them questions about dinosaurs. Then give them the answers.

Weekly Resources Guide for English Language Learner Support

For this week's content and language objectives, see p. 107e.

Instructional Strand	Day 1	Day 2
Concept Development/Academic Language	TEACHER'S EDITION • Academic Language, p. DI•91 • Concept Development, p. DI•91 • Anchored Talk, pp. 424j—424–425 • Preteach Academic Vocabulary, p. 427a • Concept Talk Video ELL HANDBOOK • Hear It, See It, Say It, Use It, pp. xxxvi–xxxvii • ELL Poster Talk, Concept Talk, p. 107c ELL POSTER 14 • Day 1 Activities	TEACHER'S EDITION • Academic Language, p. DI•91 • Concept Development, p. DI•91 • Anchored Talk, p. 428a • Concept Talk Video ELL HANDBOOK • ELL Poster Talk, Concept Talk, p. 107c • Concept Talk Video Routine, p. 477 ELL POSTER 14 • Day 2 Activities
Phonics and Spelling	TEACHER'S EDITION • Phonics and Spelling, p. DI•95	TEACHER'S EDITION • Phonics and Spelling, p. DI•95
Listening Comprehension	TEACHER'S EDITION • Modified Read Aloud, p. DI•94 • Read Aloud, p. 425b • Concept Talk Video ELL HANDBOOK • Concept Talk Video Routine, p. 477	TEACHER'S EDITION • Modified Read Aloud, p. DI•94 • AudioText of *Mahalia Jackson* • Concept Talk Video ELL HANDBOOK • AudioText CD Routine, p. 477 • Main Idea, p. 487
Reading Comprehension	TEACHER'S EDITION • Preteach Main Idea and Details, p. DI•96	TEACHER'S EDITION • Reteach Main Idea and Details, p. DI•96 • Frontloading Reading, p. DI•97 ELL HANDBOOK • Picture It! Skill Instruction, pp. 108–108a • Multilingual Summaries, pp. 109–111
Vocabulary **Basic and Lesson Vocabulary** **Word Analysis: Suffix *-ous***	TEACHER'S EDITION • Basic Vocabulary, p. DI•92 • Preteach Lesson Vocabulary, p. DI•92 • Suffix *-ous*, p. DI•95 ELL HANDBOOK • Word Cards, p. 107 • ELL Vocabulary Routine, p. 471 ELL POSTER 14 • Day 1 Activities	TEACHER'S EDITION • Basic Vocabulary, p. DI•92 • Reteach Lesson Vocabulary, p. DI•93 • Suffix *-ous*, p. DI•95 ELL HANDBOOK • Word Cards, p. 107 • Multilingual Vocabulary List, p. 436 ELL POSTER 14 • Day 2 Activities
Grammar and Conventions	TEACHER'S EDITION • Preteach Troublesome Verbs, p. DI•99	TEACHER'S EDITION • Reteach Troublesome Verbs, p. DI•99
Writing	TEACHER'S EDITION • Elaborate, p. DI•100 • Introduce Description, pp. 427e–427f	TEACHER'S EDITION • Writing Trait: Word Choice, pp. 433d–433e

This symbol indicates leveled instruction to address language proficiency levels.

Day 3	Day 4	Day 5
TEACHER'S EDITION • Academic Language, p. DI•91 • Concept Development, p. DI•91 • Anchored Talk, p. 434a • Concept Talk Video **ELL HANDBOOK** • ELL Poster Talk, Concept Talk, p. 107c **ELL POSTER 14** • Day 3 Activities	**TEACHER'S EDITION** • Academic Language, p. DI•91 • Concept Development, p. DI•91 • Anchored Talk, p. 442a • Concept Talk Video **ELL HANDBOOK** • ELL Poster Talk, Concept Talk, p. 107c **ELL POSTER 14** • Day 4 Activities	**TEACHER'S EDITION** • Academic Language, p. DI•91 • Concept Development, p. DI•91 • Concept Talk Video **ELL HANDBOOK** • ELL Poster Talk, Concept Talk, p. 107c **ELL POSTER 14** • Day 5 Activities
		TEACHER'S EDITION • Phonics and Spelling, p. DI•95
ELL HANDBOOK • Phonics Transition Lesson, pp. 302, 307	**ELL HANDBOOK** • Phonics Transition Lesson, pp. 302, 307	
TEACHER'S EDITION • AudioText of *Mahalia Jackson* • Concept Talk Video **ELL HANDBOOK** • AudioText CD Routine, p. 477	**TEACHER'S EDITION** • Concept Talk Video	**TEACHER'S EDITION** • Concept Talk Video
TEACHER'S EDITION • Sheltered Reading, p. DI•97 **ELL HANDBOOK** • Multilingual Summaries, pp. 109–111	**TEACHER'S EDITION** • ELL/ELD Reader Guided Reading, p. DI•98 **ELL HANDBOOK** • ELL Study Guide, p. 112	**TEACHER'S EDITION** • ELL/ELD Reader Guided Reading, p. DI•98 **ELL HANDBOOK** • ELL Study Guide, p. 112
		TEACHER'S EDITION • Suffix *-ous*, p. 447i
ELL HANDBOOK • High-Frequency Words Activity Bank, p. 446 **ELL POSTER 14** • Day 3 Activities	**ELL HANDBOOK** • High-Frequency Words Activity Bank, p. 446	**ELL HANDBOOK** • High-Frequency Words Activity Bank, p. 446
TEACHER'S EDITION • Grammar Jammer **ELL HANDBOOK** • Grammar Transition Lesson, pp. 329, 338–339 • Grammar Jammer Routine, p. 478	**TEACHER'S EDITION** • Grammar Jammer **ELL HANDBOOK** • Grammar Transition Lesson, pp. 329, 338–339	**TEACHER'S EDITION** • Grammar Jammer **ELL HANDBOOK** • Grammar Transition Lesson, pp. 329, 338–339
TEACHER'S EDITION • Let's Write It!, p. 440–441 • Writer's Craft: Elaboration, pp. 441a–441b	**TEACHER'S EDITION** • Revising Strategy, pp. 447d–447e	**TEACHER'S EDITION** • Troublesome Verbs, pp. 447p–447q

Question of the Week
How does an artist use music to inspire others?

Throughout the week, use the ELL Poster to help students produce and comprehend language, understand the concept, and build English vocabulary. Use the Question of the Week and other questions to help students share ideas in pairs, small groups, or the large group. Sample questions are shown, with examples of possible responses by students.

Weekly Concept and Language Goals

• Discuss the role of music and musicians in society

• Identify how musicians make music

• Describe how musicians inspire them

By the end of the lesson, students should be able to talk about and write sentences about musicians.

ELL Poster 14

Daily Team Talk

Day 1	Day 2	Day 3	Day 4	Day 5
After Day 1 activities on Poster, ask questions such as *In the poster picture, how do the musicians make music?*	After Day 2 activity on Poster, ask questions such as *In the poster picture, how do you think the musicians inspire the audience?*	After Day 3 activity on Poster, ask questions such as *Why do you think the town has a music festival to celebrate black history and culture?*	After Day 4 activity on Poster, ask questions such as *How is music a part of the history of our country?*	After Day 5 activity on Poster, ask questions such as *How have musicians inspired you?*
Beginning They sing. **Intermediate** They use their voices. **Advanced** The musicians make music by using their voices to sing. **Advanced High** The musicians in the church choir use their voices to sing. The musician on the mural is using an instrument to make music.	**Beginning** They sing. **Intermediate** They are singing their music. **Advanced** They are singing music from their culture. **Advanced High** The musicians inspire the audience because they are singing gospel music, which is part of their background.	**Beginning** It is part of it. **Intermediate** Music is part of their history. **Advanced** Music is an important part of black history and culture. **Advanced High** The town uses music to celebrate black history and culture because in the past, African Americans often used music to express themselves.	**Beginning** We like it. **Intermediate** We use it to tell stories. **Advanced** People like to use music to tell stories and to tell how they feel. **Advanced High** People like to tell stories or express their feelings through music. Listening to music from the past tells about how people felt and thought.	**Beginning** In the parade. **Intermediate** I like the music in the parade. **Advanced** The musicians who play in the parade make me feel proud. **Advanced High** The musicians who play in the Fourth of July parade make me feel proud of our country.

This Week's Materials

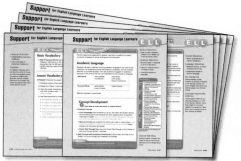

Teacher's Edition pages 424j–447q

See the support for English language learners throughout the lesson, including ELL strategies and scaffolded activities at points of use.

Teacher's Edition pages DI•91–DI•100

Differentiated Instruction for English language learners provides daily group activities that "frontload," or preteach, core instruction.

ELL Handbook pp. 107a–112

Find additional lesson materials that support the core lesson and the ELL instructional pages.

ELL Poster 14

ELL Reader 5.3.4

ELD Reader 5.3.4

Concept Literacy Reader

ELD, ELL Reader Teaching Guide

Concept Literacy Reader Teaching Guide

Technology

Online Teacher's Edition Use the digital version of the core Teacher's Edition for planning and instruction.

eReaders
This week's ELL and ELD Readers and Concept Literacy Reader are also available in digital format.

This Week's Content and Language Objectives by Strand

Concept Development/ Academic Language How does an artist use music to inspire others?	**Content Objective** • Use concept vocabulary related to how artists use music to inspire others. **Language Objectives** • Express ideas in response to art and discussion. • Use prior experiences to understand ideas. • Internalize academic language.
Phonics and Spelling One Consonant or Two	**Content Objective** • Identify and use words with one or two consonants. **Language Objectives** • Apply phonics and decoding skills to vocabulary. • Monitor oral language production.
Listening Comprehension Modified Read Aloud: "Sounds of a Storm"	**Content Objective** • Monitor and adjust oral comprehension. **Language Objectives** • Discuss oral passages. • Use a graphic organizer to take notes.
Reading Comprehension Main Idea and Details	**Content Objectives** • Identify and distinguish between the main idea and details. • Monitor and adjust comprehension. **Language Objectives** • Employ the basic reading skill of determining main idea and details. • Write the main idea and details in a personal event. • Understand the main points of spoken language.
Vocabulary Basic and Lesson Vocabulary	**Content Objective** • Show understanding of Lesson Vocabulary. **Language Objectives** • Understand and use basic vocabulary. • Produce drawings, phrases, or short sentences to acquire grade-level vocabulary. • Understand details of spoken language.
Word Analysis Suffix –ous	**Content Objective** • Identify suffix –ous. **Language Objective** • Discuss meanings of words with –ous suffix.
Grammar and Conventions Troublesome Verbs	**Content Objective** • Decode and use troublesome verbs. **Language Objective** • Read and write sentences with troublesome verbs.
Writing Elaborate	**Content Objective** • Identify precise words and vivid adjectives. **Language Objectives** • Describe with increasing specificity. • Write using connecting words.

Copyright © Pearson Education, Inc., or its affiliates. All Rights Reserved. 5

Word Cards for Vocabulary Activities

appreciate

barber

choir

released

religious

slavery

teenager

Teacher Note: Beginning Teach two to three words. **Intermediate** Teach three to four words. **Advanced** Teach four to five words. **Advanced High** Teach all words.

Name _____

Read the paragraph. Then **complete** the chart.
- **Write** the main idea of the paragraph in the *Main Idea* box.
- **Write** three details that support the main idea in the *Detail* boxes.

The Rhythm of Soul

Rhythm is an important part of soul music. A good drumbeat starts the rhythm. The bass builds on that rhythm. Then the guitar player creates a melody to go with it. Even the singer must have a good sense of rhythm. When people listen to soul music, the rhythm makes them feel like dancing.

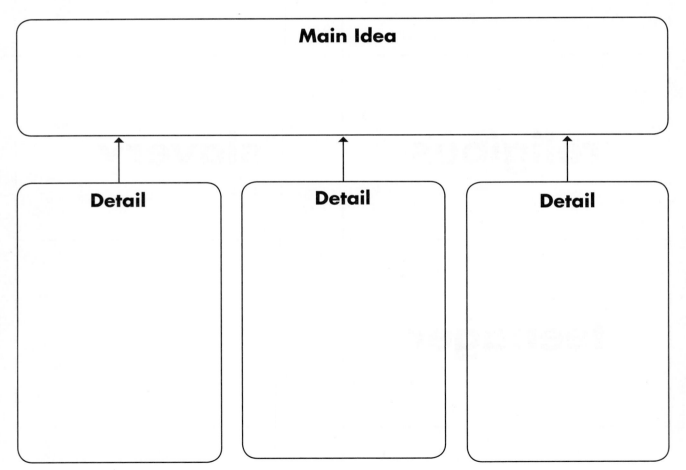

Main Idea

Detail

Detail

Detail

Main Idea and Details

Use this lesson to supplement or replace the skill lesson on page 425c of the Teacher's Edition. Display the Skill Points (at right) and share them with students.

Teach/Model

Beginning Display pictures of a rock band, a marching band, and an orchestra. Ask: *What do these pictures show? What is the main idea of these pictures?* (Possible answer: Different groups of people can play instruments together.) Identify the types of groups in the pictures and explain that these are the details that support the main idea.

Intermediate Say: *Bands use all types of instruments. Drums and guitars are popular instruments in rock bands. A marching band has tubas. Which sentence tells the main idea?* (the first one) *What are details that support the main idea?* (Drums, guitars, and tubas can be played in a band.)

Advanced Say: *The sound from a printer or another machine can make music. People tap their fingers on a table to make a beat. They also stomp their feet on the ground.* Ask students to write possible main idea sentences for the details. (Possible answer: Music is made with many things around us.)

Advanced High Discuss music with students. As a group, think of a main idea such as *Songs are similar to poetry.* Write it on the board. Have each student write one supporting detail and share it with the rest of the group.

Then distribute copies of Picture It! page 108.

- Tell students they are going to read a paragraph about a special kind of music called soul music. Point to the picture. Tell students that it will help them understand the text.
- Ask: *How does the title of the paragraph help you better understand the main idea?* (The title mentions rhythm, which is an important part of soul music.)
- Review the Skill Points with students.

Practice

Read aloud the directions on page 108. Have volunteers reread the paragraph aloud. Then have students use the picture and the paragraph as they complete the chart.

Beginning Students can say what they want to write in each box before writing words in the appropriate boxes. Provide help filling in the chart and writing.

Intermediate Students can first orally tell the main idea and details and then write their answers in the appropriate boxes. Provide help with writing.

Advanced Students can write their answers in the chart and then check them by silently rereading the paragraph and making any necessary corrections.

Advanced High Students can write their answers in the chart and then use it to orally identify the main idea and details.

Answers for page 108: *Main Idea:* Rhythm is an important part of soul music. *Detail:* The drumbeat starts the rhythm. *Detail:* The bass builds the rhythm. *Detail:* Even the singer must have rhythm.

Skill Points

- ✔ The **main idea** is the most important idea in a paragraph. It often comes at the beginning of the paragraph.
- ✔ **Details** are pieces of information that tell more about the main idea.

Multilingual Summaries

Mahalia Jackson

"Having the blues" is a way to describe feeling sad. Blues is also a kind of music. The blues started with slavery. Slaves sang about their sadness. Since then, there have been many great blues singers. Mahalia Jackson was a great blues singer.

Mahalia was born in New Orleans. When she was five years old, her mother died. Mahalia went to live with an aunt. Mahalia loved music. She wanted to sing like Bessie Smith, another great singer. Mahalia's aunt took her to church every Sunday. She heard gospel music there. Mahalia learned to love gospel music. It sounded like the blues.

Mahalia moved to Chicago. She joined a gospel group. Mahalia's singing became popular. She recorded albums. Martin Luther King, Jr., asked her to sing before he gave a famous speech. She had a powerful voice. Mahalia became the most famous gospel singer in the world.

Spanish

Mahalia Jackson

En inglés, "having the blues" es una manera de describir la tristeza. Los blues son también un tipo de música. Los blues comenzaron en la época de la esclavitud. Los esclavos cantaban sobre sus tristezas. Desde entonces, han habido muchos y grandes cantantes de blues. Mahalia Jackson fue una gran cantante de blues.

Mahalia nació en Nueva Orleáns. Cuando tenía cinco años, su madre murió. Mahalia se fue a vivir con una tía. Mahalia amaba la música. Quería cantar como Bessie Smith, otra gran cantante. La tía de Mahalia la llevaba a la iglesia todos los domingos. Ella escuchaba allí la música gospel. Mahalia aprendió a amar la música gospel. Esa música sonaba como los blues.

Mahalia se fue a vivir a Chicago. Se unió a un grupo de música gospel. Su manera de cantar se volvió popular. Grabó álbumes. Martin Luther King, Jr., le pidió que cantara antes de que él diera un discurso famoso. Ella tenía una voz potente. Mahalia se convirtió en la cantante de música gospel más famosa del mundo.

Multilingual Summaries

Chinese

瑪哈莉雅 • 杰克森

英語裏"藍色"通常表示憂傷。有一種樂曲叫做藍調音樂，起源於黑人奴隸的歌唱，他們用音樂渲泄自己的悲傷。從那以後，出現過許多偉大的藍調歌唱家，瑪哈莉雅•杰克森就是其中之一。

杰克森出生在新奧爾良，5歲時，媽媽就死了。她和姑姑住在一起。杰克森非常喜歡音樂，歌后貝西•史密斯是她的偶像。每個星期天，姑姑都帶她去教堂。她在那聆聽福音音樂，漸漸地越來越喜歡，因為它聽起來和藍調音樂非常像。

杰克森後來到了芝加哥，成為福音團體的成員。她唱了許多有名的歌曲，錄了很多唱片。馬丁路德金發表著名演說前，還請她唱過歌。杰克森的嗓音很有穿透力，她是全世界最著名的福音歌唱家。

Vietnamese

Mahalia Jackson

Câu nói "Having the blues" là một cách diễn tả cảm giác buồn. "Blues" cũng là một loại nhạc. Nhạc blues bắt đầu từ thời nô lệ. Những người nô lệ hát về nỗi buồn của họ. Từ đó, có nhiều ca sĩ nhạc blues tài giỏi. Mahalia Jackson là một ca sĩ nhạc blues nổi bật.

Mahalia sanh ở New Orleans. Khi cô lên năm, mẹ cô qua đời. Mahalia đến ở với người cô. Cô bé yêu âm nhạc. Cô bé muốn hát như Bessie Smith, một ca sĩ xuất sắc khác. Cô của Mahalia dẫn cô đến nhà thờ vào mỗi Chủ Nhật. Cô bé nghe nhạc đạo ở đó. Mahalia bắt đầu yêu thích nhạc đạo. Nhạc này nghe giống như nhạc blues.

Mahalia dọn đến Chicago. Cô gia nhập một nhóm hát nhạc đạo. Tài ca hát của Mahalia được nhiều người ưa chuộng. Cô thu thanh vào đĩa hát. Martin Luther King, Jr. mời cô hát trước khi ông đọc bài diễn văn nổi tiếng. Cô có giọng hát ngân vang. Mahalia trở nên một ca sĩ nhạc đạo nổi tiếng nhất thế giới.

Multilingual Summaries

Korean

마할리아 잭슨

'우울하다(blue)' 는 말은 마음이 울적한 것을 표현하는 한 가지 방법으로 블루스는 음악의 한 종류이기도 하다. 블루스는 노예 제도와 함께 시작되었다. 노예들은 자신들의 슬픈 처지를 노래로 불렀고 시간이 흘러 훌륭한 블루스 가수들이 많이 나왔다. 마할리아 잭슨도 그들 중 한 명이었다.

잭슨은 뉴올리언스에서 태어났다. 다섯 살 때 어머니가 돌아가시자 잭슨은 숙모와 함께 살았다. 그녀는 음악을 좋아해서 베시 스미스같은 훌륭한 가수처럼 노래를 하고 싶어했다. 마할리아의 숙모는 매주 일요일마다 그녀를 교회에 데려갔는데 그녀는 그곳에서 가스펠 뮤직을 듣고 가스펠을 무척 좋아하게 되었다. 그것은 블루스와 같은 느낌이었다.

마할리아는 시카고로 이사를 갔고 한 가스펠 단체에 가입했다. 그녀의 노래 솜씨가 유명해지자 음반 녹음을 했고 마틴 루터 킹 2세는 유명한 연설을 하기 전에 그녀에게 노래를 불러달라고 부탁하기도 했다. 그녀의 목소리에는 힘이 있었다. 곧 마할리아는 세계에서 가장 유명한 가스펠 가수가 되었다.

Hmong

Mahalia Jackson

Lus Miskas hais tias "having the blues" no txhais tau tias yus tsis zoo siab lossis ntxhov siab. Blues kuj yog ib yam nkauj thiab. Cov qhe pib hu cov nkauj blues ntawd. Txij thaum ntawd los, tau muaj coob tus neeg txawj hu nkauj blues zoo heev los. Mahalia Jackson yog ib tug uas txawj hu nkauj blues heev.

Mahalia yug nyob rau New Orleans. Thaum nws muaj tsib xyoos, nws niam tau tuag lawm. Mahalia tau mus nrog nws tu phauj nyob. Mahalia nyiam phee heev. Nws xav hu nkauj kom tau li Bessie Smith, ib tug ua hu nkauj zoo tshaj plaws thiab. Mahalia tus phauj coj nws mus tshawj (church) txhua hnub vas thiv. Nws tau mloog nkauj gospel ntawd. Mahalia tau los nyiam phee gospel heev. Yus hu cov nkauj ntawd muaj tsis zoo li cov nkauj blues.

Mahalia tsiv mus nyob rau Chicago. Nws tau mus hu nkauj nrog ib pab hu nkauj tshawj. Mahalia kev txawj hu nkauj pib nrov heev. Nws kaw tau ib co nkauj. Martin Luther King, Jr. nug nws kom nws pab tuaj hu nkauj ua ntej thaum nws yuav los hais lus rau sawvdaws. Nws lub suab muaj ceem heev. Mahalia tau los ua tus neeg hu nkauj gospel uas nto npe tshaj plaws thoob qab ntuj no.

　　　　　　　　　　　ELL Handbook

- **Read** *Willie Dixon's Blues* again.
- Use the information in the book to **answer** the questions.

pages 2–5
1. How did the author get the information for this book?

_____

_____

2. How did Marie and Willie meet?

_____

_____

pages 6–7
3. Why did many musicians leave the South in the 1930s?

_____

_____

4. Why did Willie go to Paris in 1960?

_____

_____

pages 8–12
5. What do gospel and the blues have in common?

_____

_____

6. Why do you think Keshia is so good at music?

_____

_____

Family Link

Tell your family what you learned about the blues. Talk to your family members about their favorite kinds of music.

Weekly Resources Guide for English Language Learner Support

For this week's content and language objectives, see p. 113e.

Instructional Strand	Day 1	Day 2
Concept Development/Academic Language	**TEACHER'S EDITION** • Academic Language, p. DI•116 • Concept Development, p. DI•116 • Anchored Talk, pp. 448j—448–449 • Preteach Academic Vocabulary, p. 451a • Concept Talk Video **ELL HANDBOOK** • Hear It, See It, Say It, Use It, pp. xxxvi–xxxvii • ELL Poster Talk, Concept Talk, p. 113c **ELL POSTER 15** • Day 1 Activities	**TEACHER'S EDITION** • Academic Language, p. DI•116 • Concept Development, p. DI•116 • Anchored Talk, p. 452a • Concept Talk Video **ELL HANDBOOK** • ELL Poster Talk, Concept Talk, p. 113c • Concept Talk Video Routine, p. 477 **ELL POSTER 15** • Day 2 Activities
Phonics and Spelling	**TEACHER'S EDITION** • Phonics and Spelling, p. DI•120	**TEACHER'S EDITION** • Phonics and Spelling, p. DI•120
Listening Comprehension	**TEACHER'S EDITION** • Modified Read Aloud, p. DI•119 • Read Aloud, p. 449b • Concept Talk Video **ELL HANDBOOK** • Concept Talk Video Routine, p. 477	**TEACHER'S EDITION** • Modified Read Aloud, p. DI•119 • AudioText of *Special Effects in Film and Television* • Concept Talk Video **ELL HANDBOOK** • AudioText CD Routine, p. 477 • Problem and Solution, p. 490
Reading Comprehension	**TEACHER'S EDITION** • Preteach Graphic Sources, p. DI•121	**TEACHER'S EDITION** • Reteach Graphic Sources, p. DI•121 • Frontloading Reading, p. DI•122 **ELL HANDBOOK** • Picture It! Skill Instruction, pp. 114–114a • Multilingual Summaries, pp. 115–117
Vocabulary **Basic and Lesson Vocabulary** **Word Analysis: Compound Words**	**TEACHER'S EDITION** • Basic Vocabulary, p. DI•117 • Preteach Lesson Vocabulary, p. DI•117 • Compound Words, p. DI•120 **ELL HANDBOOK** • Word Cards, p. 113 • ELL Vocabulary Routine, p. 471 **ELL POSTER 15** • Day 1 Activities	**TEACHER'S EDITION** • Basic Vocabulary, p. DI•117 • Reteach Lesson Vocabulary, p. DI•118 • Compound Words, p. DI•120 **ELL HANDBOOK** • Word Cards, p. 113 • Multilingual Vocabulary List, p. 436 **ELL POSTER 15** • Day 2 Activities
Grammar and Conventions	**TEACHER'S EDITION** • Preteach Prepositions and Prepositional Phrases, p. DI•124	**TEACHER'S EDITION** • Teach Prepositions and Prepositional Phrases, p. DI•124
Writing	**TEACHER'S EDITION** • Write Introductions and Conclusions, p. DI•125 • Introduce Expository Text, pp. 451e–451f	**TEACHER'S EDITION** • Writing Trait: Organization, pp. 459d–459e

This symbol indicates leveled instruction to address language proficiency levels.

Day 3	Day 4	Day 5
TEACHER'S EDITION • Academic Language, p. DI•116 • Concept Development, p. DI•116 • Anchored Talk, p. 460a • Concept Talk Video **ELL HANDBOOK** • ELL Poster Talk, Concept Talk, p. 113c **ELL POSTER 15** • Day 3 Activities	**TEACHER'S EDITION** • Academic Language, p. DI•116 • Concept Development, p. DI•116 • Anchored Talk, p. 468a • Concept Talk Video **ELL HANDBOOK** • ELL Poster Talk, Concept Talk, p. 113c **ELL POSTER 15** • Day 4 Activities	**TEACHER'S EDITION** • Academic Language, p. DI•116 • Concept Development, p. DI•116 • Concept Talk Video **ELL HANDBOOK** • ELL Poster Talk, Concept Talk, p. 113c **ELL POSTER 15** • Day 5 Activities
ELL HANDBOOK • Phonics Transition Lesson, pp. 284, 291	**ELL HANDBOOK** • Phonics Transition Lesson, pp. 284, 291	**TEACHER'S EDITION** • Phonics and Spelling, p. DI•120
TEACHER'S EDITION • AudioText of *Special Effects in Film and Television* • Concept Talk Video **ELL HANDBOOK** • AudioText CD Routine, p. 477	**TEACHER'S EDITION** • Concept Talk Video	**TEACHER'S EDITION** • Concept Talk Video
TEACHER'S EDITION • Sheltered Reading, p. DI•122 **ELL HANDBOOK** • Multilingual Summaries, pp. 115–117	**TEACHER'S EDITION** • ELL/ELD Reader Guided Reading, p. DI•123 **ELL HANDBOOK** • ELL Study Guide, p. 118	**TEACHER'S EDITION** • ELL/ELD Reader Guided Reading, p. DI•123 **ELL HANDBOOK** • ELL Study Guide, p. 118
ELL HANDBOOK • High-Frequency Words Activity Bank, p. 446 **ELL POSTER 15** • Day 3 Activities	**ELL HANDBOOK** • High-Frequency Words Activity Bank, p. 446	**TEACHER'S EDITION** • Compound Words, p. 473i **ELL HANDBOOK** • High-Frequency Words Activity Bank, p. 446
TEACHER'S EDITION • Grammar Jammer **ELL HANDBOOK** • Grammar Transition Lesson, pp. 379–380 • Grammar Jammer Routine, p. 478	**TEACHER'S EDITION** • Grammar Jammer **ELL HANDBOOK** • Grammar Transition Lesson, pp. 379–380	**TEACHER'S EDITION** • Grammar Jammer **ELL HANDBOOK** • Grammar Transition Lesson, pp. 379–380
TEACHER'S EDITION • Let's Write It!, p. 466–467 • Writer's Craft: Introduction and Conclusion, pp. 467a–467b	**TEACHER'S EDITION** • Revising Strategy, pp. 473d–473e	**TEACHER'S EDITION** • Prepositions, pp. 473p–473q

Question of the Week

How do artists create special effects to entertain us?

Throughout the week, use the ELL Poster to help students produce and comprehend language, understand the concept, and build English vocabulary. Use the Question of the Week and other questions to help students share ideas in pairs, small groups, or the large group. Sample questions are shown, with examples of possible responses by students.

Weekly Concept and Language Goals

• Share ideas about special effects

• Explain how filmmakers create special effects

• Provide examples of special effects they have seen in movies

By the end of the lesson, students should be able to talk about and write sentences about special effects in movies.

ELL Poster 15

Daily Team Talk

Day 1	Day 2	Day 3	Day 4	Day 5
After Day 1 activities on Poster, ask questions such as *In the poster picture, what is the artist doing?*	After Day 2 activity on Poster, ask questions such as *Why do you think filmmakers use storyboards when they make a movie?*	After Day 3 activity on Poster, ask questions such as *How can filmmakers use special effects to create the explosion the artist drew?*	After Day 4 activity on Poster, ask questions such as *In* Special Effects in Film and Television, *how do filmmakers use miniature models of a scene?*	After Day 5 activity on Poster, ask questions such as *What other special effect did you see in a movie?*
Beginning He is drawing. **Intermediate** He is drawing pictures for a movie. **Advanced** The artist is making a storyboard of a movie. **Advanced High** The artist is drawing a storyboard, which shows what will happen in a scene in a movie.	**Beginning** To see pictures. **Intermediate** They want to see how it will look. **Advanced** They use storyboards to help them picture how a scene will turn out. **Advanced High** Filmmakers use storyboards because the storyboards help them picture the scene they are filming. It is easier to see how a scene will look.	**Beginning** Use a computer. **Intermediate** They can use a computer to make it. **Advanced** They can create the explosion using a special computer program. **Advanced High** Filmmakers can create the explosion using special computer programs and effects. They can also build a model of the scene.	**Beginning** To plan it. **Intermediate** They use them to plan. **Advanced** They use models to figure out how things and actors in a scene should look. **Advanced High** Filmmakers use miniature models to plan a scene. They figure out how the scenery should look and what the actors should do in the scene.	**Beginning** A flood. **Intermediate** I saw a street flood with water. **Advanced** There was a flood. The water rushed through the streets. **Advanced High** In one scene, water flooded the streets. As the water rushed through, it knocked down trees and carried away cars. It looked real.

This Week's Materials

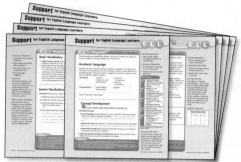

Teacher's Edition pages 448j–477a

See the support for English language learners throughout the lesson, including ELL strategies and scaffolded activities at points of use.

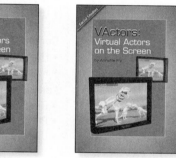

Teacher's Edition pages DI•116–DI•125

Differentiated Instruction for English language learners provides daily group activities that "frontload," or preteach, core instruction.

ELL Handbook pp. 113a–118

Find additional lesson materials that support the core lesson and the ELL instructional pages.

ELL Poster 15

ELL Reader 5.3.5

ELD Reader 5.3.5

Concept Literacy Reader

ELD, ELL Reader Teaching Guide

Concept Literacy Reader Teaching Guide

Technology

Online Teacher's Edition Use the digital version of the core Teacher's Edition for planning and instruction.

eReaders
This week's ELL and ELD Readers and Concept Literacy Reader are also available in digital format.

This Week's Content and Language Objectives by Strand

Concept Development/ Academic Language How do artists create special effects to entertain us?	**Content Objective** • Use concept vocabulary related to artists and entertainment. **Language Objectives** • Express ideas in response to art and discussion. • Use media to build concept attainment.
Phonics and Spelling Prefixes *un-* and *dis-*	**Content Objectives** • Identify and define words in compound words. • Identify prefixes in words. **Language Objectives** • Apply phonics and decoding skills to vocabulary. • Employ English spelling rules. • Discuss meanings of compound words.
Listening Comprehension Modified Read Aloud: "The Magic of Middle Earth"	**Content Objective** • Monitor and adjust oral comprehension. **Language Objectives** • Discuss oral passages. • Use a graphic organizer to take notes.
Reading Comprehension Graphic Sources	**Content Objectives** • Have students use graphics to aid in comprehension. • Monitor and adjust comprehension. **Language Objectives** • Discuss importance of graphic sources. • Predict content based on graphic sources. • Use graphic sources to aid in comprehension of text.
Vocabulary Basic and Lesson Vocabulary	**Content Objective** • Show understanding of Lesson Vocabulary. **Language Objectives** • Understand and use basic vocabulary. • Learn meanings of grade-level vocabulary. • Produce drawings, phrases, or short sentences to acquire grade-level vocabulary.
Word Analysis Compound Words	**Content Objective** • Identify and define words in compound words. **Language Objective** • Discuss meanings of compound words.
Grammar and Conventions Prepositions and Prepositional Phrases	**Content Objective** • Decode and use prepositions and prepositional phrases. **Language Objective** • Speak and write using prepositional phrases.
Writing Write Introductions and Conclusions	**Content Objective** • Understand the role of the introduction and conclusion. **Language Objectives** • Write paragraphs using an introduction and conclusion. • Know when to use formal English.

Copyright © Pearson Education, Inc., or its affiliates. All Rights Reserved. 5

Word Cards for Vocabulary Activities

background

landscape

miniature

prehistoric

reassembled

Teacher Note: Beginning Teach two to three words. **Intermediate** Teach three to four words. **Advanced** Teach four to five words. **Advanced High** Teach all words and review two words from an earlier lesson.

Name _____

Look at the picture. What do you think the paragraph is going to be about?

1. Write your guess.

_____

Read the paragraph. **Answer** the questions that follow.

Making Faces

In film and television, makeup is a kind of special effect. It can totally change the way you look. It can even make a young man look old. Masks and wigs are part of the makeup department. These are the props that help actors and actresses "make faces." Props can also help them act better.

2. What is this paragraph about?

_____

3. What items shown in the picture are also mentioned in the paragraph?

_____

ELL Handbook

Graphic Sources

Use this lesson to supplement or replace the skill lesson on page 449c of the Teacher's Edition. Display the Skill Points (at right) and share them with students.

Teach/Model

Beginning Display a map of your state. Say: *This is a graphic source. What can we learn from this?* (the names of cities, rivers, distances between cities, etc.) Ask students to tell about a time they have used or should use a map.

Intermediate Show the list of movie showings in a newspaper or other resource. Say: *This table tells what times you can see movies. What else can we learn from this table?* (how long a movie is, which theaters are playing the movie)

Advanced Display a graph or chart from a newspaper. Ask: *What kind of information does this graphic source tell us? How does the title help you to know what information is in this graph (chart)?* Have students write a sentence that tells something they learned from the graphic source.

Advanced High Make a diagram of a theater stage on the board. Draw a rectangle and label *stage left, stage right, up stage,* and *down stage.* Say: *This is a diagram of a theater stage. It tells what the parts of a stage are called. What other things can we put on a diagram of a stage?* (where actors should stand, where scenery or props should be)

Then distribute copies of Picture It! page 114.

- Point to the picture. Tell students that it is a graphic source.
- Ask students to use the picture to make a prediction about what the paragraph will be about.
- Review the Skill Points with students.
- Ask: *How does the picture help you better understand the paragraph?* (It shows some of the things mentioned in the paragraph.)

Practice

Read aloud the directions on page 114. Have students reread the paragraph with a partner. Then have them use the picture and the paragraph as they answer the questions.

Beginning Students can answer the questions orally and then write their answers. Provide help with writing.

Intermediate Students can orally answer the questions before writing their answers.

Advanced Students can write their answers and then check them by comparing their answers with a partner's.

Advanced High Students can write their answers and then explain how each part of the picture is explained in the paragraph.

Answers for page 114: 1. Answers will vary. Possible answer: costumes or makeup; 2. special effects makeup; 3. masks, wigs, and makeup

Skill Points

✔ **Graphic sources** are pictures, diagrams, maps, and time lines.
✔ A graphic source helps you to better understand written text.
✔ Preview graphic sources before you read. Predict what the text is about, based on the graphic source.

Multilingual Summaries

Special Effects
in Film and Television

Special effects help movies and television shows seem real. One special effect is to create imaginary landscapes. To do this, technicians make small models of landscapes.

First, the script or director describes a setting. Next, the special effects team decides how to build it. The team makes a small model of the scene. The team makes changes to the small model to make it more realistic. Then, the team makes a full-sized model.

This model is sprayed with foam to make the surface smooth. Then the model is cut into pieces and reassembled in the studio. Technicians use pictures of the small model as a guide. In the studio, little trees, rocks, and plants are added. The team makes the landscape look as real as possible. Everything is painted in detail. When the scene is filmed, the landscape will seem real to the audience.

Spanish

Efectos especiales en el cine
y la televisión

Los efectos especiales permiten que las películas y los programas de televisión parezcan reales. Uno de los efectos especiales es hacer paisajes imaginarios. Para lograr esto, los técnicos hacen modelos pequeños de paisajes.

Primero, el guionista o director describe una escena. Después, el equipo de efectos especiales decide cómo construirla. El equipo hace un modelo pequeño de la escena. Hacen cambios al pequeño modelo para hacerlo más realista. Después, el equipo hace un modelo de tamaño natural.

El modelo es rociado con espuma para hacer la superficie más suave. Luego, se corta en pedazos y es reensamblada en el estudio. Los técnicos usan fotos del modelo pequeño como guía. En el estudio, se agregan árboles pequeños, rocas y plantas. El equipo hace que el paisaje parezca lo más real posible. Todo se pinta hasta en los más mínimos detalles. Cuando se filma la escena, el paisaje les parecerá real a los espectadores.

Multilingual Summaries

Chinese

電影電視的特效

特效讓電影和電視更加真實。做特效首先要有假想的場景。為此，技術人員要做許多縮小的場景模型。

首先，編劇或導演會描述場景，接著特效工作人員商談如何建造。他們先做一個縮小模型，然後做一些改動，讓它看上去更加真實。最後工作人員才會製做實物大小的模型。

模型表面要噴上泡沫，使它平滑。接著場景分成幾個部分，在攝影棚裏重新組裝。技術人員還要不時參照小模型照片。他們在攝影棚里加上小樹、小石頭和其它植物，讓場景儘量與真的一模一樣。每個地方都要仔細繪製。觀眾看到影片時，就會覺得和真的一樣。

Vietnamese

Các Kỹ Thuật Ấn Tượng Đặc Biệt Trong Phim Ảnh và Truyền Hình

Các kỹ thuật ấn tượng đặc biệt giúp cho phim và các chương trình truyền hình có vẻ như thật. Một kỹ thuật ấn tượng đặc biệt là tạo ra những phong cảnh tưởng tượng. Để làm điều này, các kỹ thuật viên làm những mô hình nhỏ của các phong cảnh này.

Đầu tiên, kịch bản hoặc nhà đạo diễn miêu tả một khung cảnh. Kế đến, đội chuyên trách về các kỹ thuật ấn tượng đặc biệt sẽ quyết định cách xây nên khung cảnh này. Đội này sẽ làm một mô hình nhỏ về cảnh này. Họ thay đổi mô hình nhỏ này để nó trông giống như thật hơn. Rồi đội này sẽ làm một mô hình với kích thước như thật.

Mô hình này được phủ bằng một chất bọt để làm cho bề mặt được trơn phẳng. Rồi cảnh này được cắt ra làm nhiều miếng và được ráp lại ở phim trường. Các kỹ thuật viên dùng những bức ảnh của mô hình nhỏ làm bản chỉ dẫn. Trong phim trường, các cây cối nhỏ, đá, và thảo mộc được thêm vào. Đội này làm phong cảnh trông càng giống như thật càng tốt. Mọi thứ được sơn phết thật chi tiết. Khi cảnh này lên phim, phong cảnh này sẽ trông giống như thật đối với khán giả.

Multilingual Summaries

영화와 텔레비전의 특수 효과

특수 효과는 영화와 텔레비전의 장면이 실제처럼 보일 수 있도록 해 준다. 특수 효과 중의 하나는 가상 풍경을 만드는 것으로 기술자들은 먼저 작은 풍경 모형을 만든다.

먼저 대본이나 감독이 배경을 결정한다. 그 다음으로 특수 효과팀이 그 배경을 어떻게 만들 지 결정하고 작은 장면 모형을 만든다. 이들은 좀더 현실감 있도록 모형에 변화를 준다. 그리고 나서 실제 크기의 모형을 만들게 된다.

이 모형에 거품을 뿌려 표면을 매끄럽게 만든 다음 장면을 조각조각으로 나누고 스튜디오에서 재조립한다. 이때 기술자들은 작은 모형 그림을 참고한다. 스튜디오에서는 작은 나무와 바위, 그리고 식물을 추가한다. 특수 효과팀은 풍경을 최대한 실제처럼 보이도록 만들며 모든 것에 세밀하게 색을 입힌다. 장면이 촬영되면 관객들은 실제 풍경인 것처럼 착각하게 될 것이다.

Hmong

Special Effects Nyob Hauv Moosvim thiab Tisvis

Special effects pab moosvim thiab tisvis kom tej yeeb yam ntawd ntxim muaj tiag. Ib qhov special effect yog kev tsim kom ntxim li muaj teb muaj chaws. Kom ua li ntawd, cov neeg technicians txua ib cov qauv teb chaws me me.

Ua ntej tshaj plaws, daim ntawv nyeem lossis tus coj piav kom tau se bib qhov chaws zoo li cas. Ces, pab neeg ua special effects txiav txim siab ua kom tau. Pab neeg ua hauj lwm uake los txua kom tau ib tug qauv ntawm qhov chaws ntawd. Lawm hloov tej yam me me kom ua ntxim li muaj tiag. Ces pab neeg ua hauj lwm uake mam li txua ib tug qauv loj zoo li teb chaws tiag.

Ces lawv mam li tsuag foam rau tus qauv ntawd kom tej nplaim khoom ntawd yaig heev. Ces lawv muab tus qauv loj ntawd txiav ua tej daim tej daim kom thiab li rov muab tso tau uake hauv hoom thaij duab. Cov neeg technician siv cov duab ntawm tus qauv me me los pab coj lawv kev. Hauv hoom thaij duab, lawv mam li ntxiv menyuam ntoo, pobzeb thiab pab ntoo rau. Pab neeg ua hauj lwm uake ua kom tus qauv ntawd txim li muaj tiag kom zoo li zoo tau. Lawv muab txhua yam tha kom zoo zoo. Thaum thaij duab, tus qauv ntawd thiaj li zoo li muaj tseeb tiag tiag.

Name _____

- **Read** *Virtual Actors on the Screen* again.
- **Complete** the chart. Use information from the text. You may also include your own ideas.

What is special or unique about animated characters?	What is special or unique about real actors?
_____	_____
_____	_____
_____	_____
_____	_____
_____	_____
_____	_____
_____	_____
_____	_____

Family Link

Tell your family what you learned about computer animation. Talk with family members about their favorite animated movie.

Weekly Resources Guide for English Language Learner Support

For this week's content and language objectives, see p. 119e.

Instructional Strand	Day 1	Day 2
Concept Development/Academic Language	**TEACHER'S EDITION** • Academic Language, p. DI•16 • Concept Development, p. DI•16 • Anchored Talk, pp. 20j—20–21 • Preteach Academic Vocabulary, p. 23a • Concept Talk Video **ELL HANDBOOK** • Hear It, See It, Say It, Use It, pp. xxxvi–xxxvii • ELL Poster Talk, Concept Talk, p. 119c **ELL POSTER 16** • Day 1 Activities	**TEACHER'S EDITION** • Academic Language, p. DI•16 • Concept Development, p. DI•16 • Anchored Talk, p. 24a • Concept Talk Video **ELL HANDBOOK** • ELL Poster Talk, Concept Talk, p. 119c • Concept Talk Video Routine, p. 477 **ELL POSTER 16** • Day 2 Activities
Phonics and Spelling	**TEACHER'S EDITION** • Phonics and Spelling, p. DI•20	**TEACHER'S EDITION** • Phonics and Spelling, p. DI•20
Listening Comprehension	**TEACHER'S EDITION** • Modified Read Aloud, p. DI•19 • Read Aloud, p. 21b • Concept Talk Video **ELL HANDBOOK** • Concept Talk Video Routine, p. 477	**TEACHER'S EDITION** • Modified Read Aloud, p. DI•19 • AudioText of *Weslandia* • Concept Talk Video **ELL HANDBOOK** • AudioText CD Routine, p. 477 • Story Map B, p. 484
Reading Comprehension	**TEACHER'S EDITION** • Preteach Draw Conclusions, p. DI•21	**TEACHER'S EDITION** • Reteach Draw Conclusions, p. DI•21 • Frontloading Reading, p. DI•22 **ELL HANDBOOK** • Picture It! Skill Instruction, pp. 120–120a • Multilingual Summaries, pp. 121–123
Vocabulary **Basic and Lesson Vocabulary** **Word Analysis: Inflected Endings -s, -ed, -ing**	**TEACHER'S EDITION** • Basic Vocabulary, p. DI•17 • Preteach Lesson Vocabulary, p. DI•17 • Inflected Endings -s, -ed, -ing, p. DI•20 **ELL HANDBOOK** • Word Cards, p. 119 • ELL Vocabulary Routine, p. 471 **ELL POSTER 16** • Day 1 Activities	**TEACHER'S EDITION** • Basic Vocabulary, p. DI•17 • Reteach Lesson Vocabulary, p. DI•18 • Inflected Endings -s, -ed, -ing, p. DI•20 **ELL HANDBOOK** • Word Cards, p. 119 • Multilingual Vocabulary List, p. 431 **ELL POSTER 16** • Day 2 Activities
Grammar and Conventions	**TEACHER'S EDITION** • Preteach Subject and Object Pronouns, p. DI•24	**TEACHER'S EDITION** • Reteach Subject and Object Pronouns, p. DI•24
Writing	**TEACHER'S EDITION** • Dialogue p. DI•25 • Introduce Picture Book, pp. 23e–23f	**TEACHER'S EDITION** • Writer's Craft: Organization, pp. 33d–33e

Leveled LS Support

This symbol indicates leveled instruction to address language proficiency levels.

Day 3	Day 4	Day 5
TEACHER'S EDITION • Academic Language, p. DI•16 • Concept Development, p. DI•16 • Anchored Talk, p. 34a • Concept Talk Video **ELL HANDBOOK** • ELL Poster Talk, Concept Talk, p. 119c **ELL POSTER 16** • Day 3 Activities	**TEACHER'S EDITION** • Academic Language, p. DI•16 • Concept Development, p. DI•16 • Anchored Talk, p. 42a • Concept Talk Video **ELL HANDBOOK** • ELL Poster Talk, Concept Talk, p. 119c **ELL POSTER 16** • Day 4 Activities	**TEACHER'S EDITION** • Academic Language, p. DI•16 • Concept Development, p. DI•16 • Concept Talk Video **ELL HANDBOOK** • ELL Poster Talk, Concept Talk, p. 119c **ELL POSTER 16** • Day 5 Activities
ELL HANDBOOK • Phonics Transition Lesson, pp. 269, 271	**ELL HANDBOOK** • Phonics Transition Lesson, pp. 269, 271	**TEACHER'S EDITION** • Phonics and Spelling, p. DI•20
TEACHER'S EDITION • AudioText of *Weslandia* • Concept Talk Video **ELL HANDBOOK** • AudioText CD Routine, p. 477	**TEACHER'S EDITION** • Concept Talk Video	**TEACHER'S EDITION** • Concept Talk Video
TEACHER'S EDITION • Sheltered Reading, p. DI•22 **ELL HANDBOOK** • Multilingual Summaries, pp. 121–123	**TEACHER'S EDITION** • ELL/ELD Reader Guided Reading, p. DI•23 **ELL HANDBOOK** • ELL Study Guide, p. 124	**TEACHER'S EDITION** • ELL/ELD Reader Guided Reading, p. DI•23 **ELL HANDBOOK** • ELL Study Guide, p. 124
ELL HANDBOOK • High-Frequency Words Activity Bank, p. 446 **ELL POSTER 16** • Day 3 Activities	**ELL HANDBOOK** • High-Frequency Words Activity Bank, p. 446	**TEACHER'S EDITION** • Word Endings *-ing, -ed, -s*, p. 45i **ELL HANDBOOK** • High-Frequency Words Activity Bank, p. 446
TEACHER'S EDITION • Grammar Jammer **ELL HANDBOOK** • Grammar Transition Lesson, pp. 362, 365–366 • Grammar Jammer Routine, p. 478	**TEACHER'S EDITION** • Grammar Jammer **ELL HANDBOOK** • Grammar Transition Lesson, pp. 362, 365–366	**TEACHER'S EDITION** • Grammar Jammer **ELL HANDBOOK** • Grammar Transition Lesson, pp. 362, 365–366
TEACHER'S EDITION • Let's Write It!, p. 40–41 • Writing Trait: Focus/Ideas, pp. 41a–41b	**TEACHER'S EDITION** • Revising Strategy, pp. 45d–45e	**TEACHER'S EDITION** • Subject and Object Pronouns, pp. 45p–45q

Question of the Week
How do people adapt to difficult situations?

Throughout the week, use the ELL Poster to help students produce and comprehend language, understand the concept, and build English vocabulary. Use the Question of the Week and other questions to help students share ideas in pairs, small groups, or the large group. Sample questions are shown, with examples of possible responses by students.

ELL Poster 16

Weekly Concept and Language Goals

• Understand how people adapt

• Identify difficult situations

• Describe ways people adapt to face a difficult situation

By the end of the lesson, students should be able to talk about and write sentences about ways people adapt to a difficult situation.

Daily Team Talk

Day 1	Day 2	Day 3	Day 4	Day 5
After Day 1 activities on Poster, ask questions such as *In the poster picture, what difficult situation do the students try to solve in the game?*	After Day 2 activity on Poster, ask questions such as *What can the students in the poster picture do to save the temple from flooding?*	After Day 3 activity on Poster, ask questions such as *If the situation in the computer game happened in real life, how would people react?*	After Day 4 activity on Poster, ask questions such as *In the story* Weslandia, *what difficult situation does Wesley face?*	After Day 5 activity on Poster, ask questions such as *Did you ever adapt to a difficult situation? Tell about it.*
Beginning The river gets high. **Intermediate** The river is rising and will flood. **Advanced** The river is quickly rising and is going to flood the temple. **Advanced High** The river is rising quickly. The students have to find a way to save the temple from flooding.	**Beginning** They can move it. **Intermediate** They can move the temple away. **Advanced** The students can move the temple away from the bank before it floods. **Advanced High** The students can move the temple one block at a time to high ground, where it will not get flooded.	**Beginning** Run away. **Intermediate** They will run away to stay safe. **Advanced** The people could run away or they could try to protect the temple. **Advanced High** The people might choose to be safe by running away or they might choose to protect the temple by making a wall to block the water from coming in.	**Beginning** He has no friends. **Intermediate** He is sad and has no friends. **Advanced** Wesley is sad because he has no friends. People make fun of him. **Advanced High** Wesley is miserable because he is an outcast. He has no friends, and people torment him all the time.	**Beginning** We moved. New friends. **Intermediate** I had to make friends at a new school. **Advanced** When my family moved, I had to make friends at my new school. **Advanced High** When my family moved last year, I had no friends at my new school. I had to learn how to make new friends.

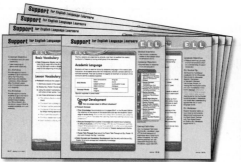

Teacher's Edition pages 20j–45q

See the support for English language learners throughout the lesson, including ELL strategies and scaffolded activities at points of use.

Teacher's Edition pages DI•16–DI•25

Differentiated Instruction for English language learners provides daily group activities that "frontload," or preteach, core instruction.

ELL Handbook pp. 119a–124

Find additional lesson materials that support the core lesson and the ELL instructional pages.

ELL Poster 16

ELL Reader 5.4.1

ELD Reader 5.4.1

Concept Literacy Reader

ELD, ELL Reader Teaching Guide

Concept Literacy Reader Teaching Guide

Technology

Online Teacher's Edition Use the digital version of the core Teacher's Edition for planning and instruction.

eReaders
This week's ELL and ELD Readers and Concept Literacy Reader are also available in digital format.

This Week's Content and Language Objectives by Strand

Concept Development/ Academic Language How do people adapt to difficult situations?	**Content Objective** • Use concept vocabulary related to how people adapt to difficult situations. **Language Objective** • Express ideas in response to art and discussion.
Phonics and Spelling Words Ending in –ed, -ing	**Content Objective** • Identify final syllables –ed and –ing. **Language Objective** • Apply phonics and decoding skills to vocabulary.
Listening Comprehension Modified Read Aloud: "A Baseball Man"	**Content Objective** • Monitor and adjust oral comprehension. **Language Objectives** • Discuss oral passages. • Use a graphic organizer to take notes.
Reading Comprehension Draw Conclusions	**Content Objectives** • Understand how to draw conclusions. • Monitor and adjust comprehension. **Language Objectives** • Discuss how to draw a conclusion. • Use commas as clues to pause in oral reading.
Vocabulary Basic and Lesson Vocabulary	**Language Objectives** • Understand and use basic vocabulary. • Learn meanings of grade-level vocabulary. • Produce drawings, phrases, or short sentences to show an understanding of Lesson Vocabulary.
Word Analysis Inflected Endings –s, -ed, -ing	**Content Objective** • Identify inflected endings –s, -ed, -ing. **Language Objective** • Understand use of verb endings.
Grammar and Conventions Subject and Object Pronouns	**Content Objective** • Identify subject and object pronouns. **Language Objectives** • Practice using subject and object pronouns in speaking. • Write sentences using subject and object pronouns.
Writing Dialogue	**Content Objectives** • Identify dialogue in fiction. • Understand idioms. **Language Objectives** • Write a short dialogue. • Share feedback for editing and revising.

Word Cards for Vocabulary Activities

blunders	**civilization**
complex	**envy**
fleeing	**inspired**
rustling	**strategy**

Teacher Note: Beginning Teach three to four words. **Intermediate** Teach four to six words. **Advanced** Teach six to seven words. **Advanced High** Teach all words.

Name _____

Read the story. Then fill in the four boxes that follow to show what the story is about.

- **Write** details from the text in the first two boxes.
- **Write** something from your own knowledge in the third box.
- **Write** a conclusion telling what the story is about in the fourth box.

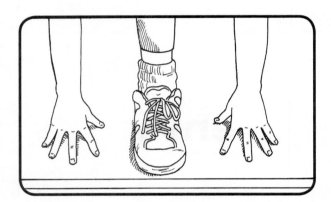

The Moment of Truth

Veronique stood at the starting line. She had prepared for this moment all summer.

"Ready!" She knelt down.

"Set!" She straightened out her back leg.

"Go!" At the sound of the horn, Veronique took off like a rocket.

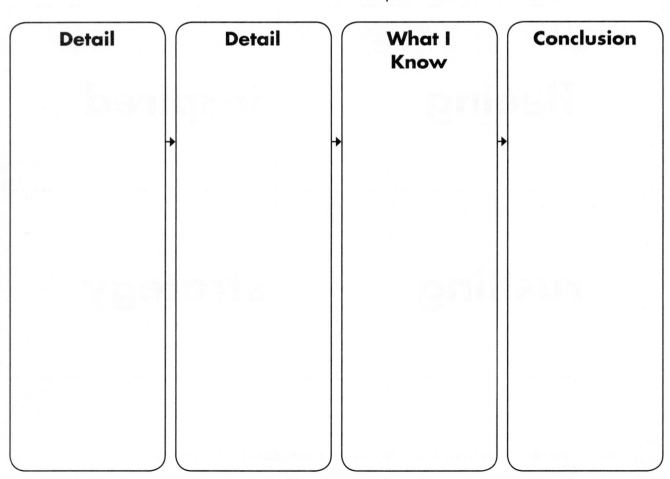

Detail	Detail	What I Know	Conclusion

Draw Conclusions

Use this lesson to supplement or replace the skill lesson on page 21c of the Teacher's Edition. Display the Skill Points (at right) and share them with students.

Teach/Model

Beginning Display a newspaper photo of a winning sports team celebrating on the field. Tell students details about the game without explicitly saying that the pictured team won. Ask: *What conclusion can you draw about this team?* (They won the game.)

Intermediate Say: *Maria crouches down and watches the ball. A player on the other team kicks the soccer ball toward her. Maria jumps to her left and catches the ball. Her teammates cheer. She throws the ball back.* Ask students to use details from the story and what they know about soccer to write a conclusion about Maria. (Maria is the goalie.)

Advanced Write: *I run fast, but my friend runs faster. After the race, we shake hands. "You tried your best!" she says.* Draw four boxes on the board, labeled *Detail, Detail, What I Know,* and *Conclusion.* Ask students to copy the graphic organizer and fill it in to draw a conclusion about the story. (You lost the race to your friend.)

Advanced High Have students write a brief story about a sport or game they played. Pair students and have them share their stories. Have each partner draw a conclusion about the other person's story.

Then distribute copies of Picture It! page 120.

- Have students look at the picture and read the title. Have them predict what the story might be about.
- Review the Skill Points with students.
- Read the story aloud. Ask: *What happens in this story? What are some details?*

Practice

Read aloud the directions on page 120. Have students reread the story with a partner. Have them look at the picture and the story as they complete the graphic organizer.

Beginning Students can tell what they want to write before filling in the boxes. Provide help with spelling English words.

Intermediate Students can orally answer before writing sentences to fill in the boxes.

Advanced Students can write sentences to complete the graphic organizer and check their work by rereading the paragraph for details.

Advanced High Students can write sentences to complete the graphic organizer and orally explain how their prior knowledge helped them reach their conclusions.

Answers for page 120: Possible answers: *Detail:* Veronique is at the starting line. *Detail:* Somebody says, "Ready! Set! Go!" *What I Know:* A horn is sometimes used to start a race. *Conclusion:* Veronique must be in a race.

Skill Points

✔ When you **draw conclusions,** you combine what you know with details in the text.

✔ You can think of a conclusion as an idea or decision you make after combining your knowledge with information from the text.

Multilingual Summaries

Weslandia

Wesley was different. The other children did not like him. They did not like the same things. He did not have any friends. The other children chased Wesley.

One summer, Wesley decided to grow his own garden. He decided to found his own civilization. He would do everything his way. He called his civilization Weslandia. Soon his plants were taller than he was. Wesley ate their fruit and roots. He used their bark and fibers to make clothes.

After that, the neighborhood children who had teased Wesley wanted to be his friends. Wesley invented new games. The other children came to play with him. Wesley used the sun to tell time. He even made up his own language and alphabet. He went back to school with many friends.

Weslandia

Wesley era diferente. A los otros niños no les gustaba Wesley. No les gustaban las mismas cosas. Él no tenía amigos. Los otros niños lo perseguían para burlarse.

Un verano, Wesley decidió plantar su propio jardín. Decidió fundar su propia civilización. Haría todo a su manera. Llamó a su civilización Weslandia. Muy pronto, sus plantas eran más altas que él. Wesley se comió sus frutos y raíces. También usó sus cortezas y fibras para hacer ropa.

Después de esto, los niños del barrio que se habían burlado de él querían ser sus amigos. Wesley inventó nuevos juegos. Los niños empezaron a jugar con él. Wesley usaba el sol para saber qué hora era. Hasta inventó su propio lenguaje y alfabeto. Regresó a la escuela con muchos amigos.

Multilingual Summaries

威斯利王國

　　威斯利是個異類，其他小孩都不喜歡他，他們不喜歡像威斯利那樣的怪人。威斯利沒有朋友，大家都排斥他。

　　某年夏天，威斯利決定開墾一個花園，他要創造一個屬於自己的文明，用自己喜歡的方式過日子，他管這個文明世界叫做「威斯利王國」。很快地，他在花園裡種的植物已經長得比他高了，威斯利吃這些植物的果實和根，還用樹皮和纖維來做衣服。

　　以前曾經嘲笑過威斯利的鄰居小孩看到他的花園後，都想要和他做朋友了。威斯利發明了新遊戲，其他小孩覺得很有趣也跑來跟他玩。威斯利很聰明會利用太陽來知道時間，他甚至創造了自己的語言和文字。後來，威斯利再回到學校的時候，身邊多了好多朋友。

Weslandia

　　Wesley khác thường. Những đứa trẻ khác không thích cậu bé. Chúng không có cùng sở thích. Cậu không có bạn. Những đứa trẻ khác rượt đuổi Wesley.

　　Vào một mùa hè, Wesley quyết định làm một mảnh vườn riêng cho mình. Cậu quyết định thành lập một nền văn minh của riêng mình. Cậu sẽ làm mọi điều theo cách của mình. Cậu gọi nền văn minh của cậu là Weslandia. Không bao lâu các cây cối trong vườn cao hơn cậu. Wesley ăn trái cây và rễ của những cây đó. Cậu dùng vỏ cây và chất sợi trong cây để làm quần áo.

　　Sau đó, các đứa trẻ trong khu phố đã từng trêu ghẹo Wesley lại muốn làm bạn với cậu. Wesley phát minh những trò chơi mới. Các đứa trẻ khác đến chơi với cậu. Wesley dùng mặt trời để biết giờ giấc. Cậu bé thậm chí còn tạo ra mẫu tự và ngôn ngữ riêng. Cậu bé trở lại trường học có được nhiều bạn.

Multilingual Summaries

웨슬랜디아

웨슬리는 특별하다. 그 점 때문에 다른 아이들은 그를 싫어한다. 그들은 서로 다른 것을 좋아한다. 아이들은 아무 친구도 없는 웨슬리를 뒤쫓아 다닌다.

어느 여름날 웨슬리는 자기만의 정원과 자기만의 세계를 만들기로 마음먹는다. 무엇이든 자기 마음대로 할 생각이었다. 그는 자기만의 세계를 웨슬랜디아라고 이름 붙인다. 정원에서 곧 웨슬리가 심은 식물들이 그보다 더 크게 자란다. 그는 정원에서 자란 과일과 식물 뿌리를 먹으며 나무껍질과 섬유로 옷을 만든다.

그러자 웨슬리를 괴롭혔던 주변의 아이들이 그와 친구가 되고 싶어한다. 웨슬리가 새로운 게임을 만들어내자 다른 아이들도 와서 함께 어울려 논다. 웨슬리는 시간을 알아보는데 해를 이용하고 자기만의 언어와 알파벳까지 만들어낸다. 결국 그는 많은 친구들과 함께 학교로 돌아간다.

Wesley Thaj Av

Wesley yog ib tug txawv. Lwm cov menyuam tsis nyiam nws. Lawv tsis nyiam tej yam Wesley nyiam. Nws tsis muaj cov phoojywg. Luag lwm cov menyuam caum Wesley.

Muaj ib lub caij ntuj sov, Wesley txiav txim siab pib nws ib lub vaj. Nws txiav txim siab pib nws ib lub teb lub chaws. Txhua yam nws yuav ua yuav yog raws li nws lub siab nyiam. Nws tis ib lub npe rau nws lub teb lub chaws hu ua "Wesley Thaj Av". Tsis ntev tom qab, nws cov zaub siab tshaj nws. Wesley noj nws cov txiv ntoo thiab lawv cov cag. Nws siv cov tawv ntoo kom ua khaubncaws.

Tom qab ntawd cov menyuam uas tau thuam Wesley xav ua nws ib tug phoojywg. Wesley tau tsim tej kev ua si tshiab. Luag lwm cov menyuam twb tuaj nrog nws ua si. Wesley tau siv lub hnub kom paub saib pestsawg moo lawm. Nws twb tau tsim nws ib yam lus thiab cov tsiaj ntawv tshiab. Nws rov qab mus tom lub tsev kawm ntawv thiab muaj cov phooj ywg coob.

Name _____

- **Read** *The Anasazi: The Ancient Builders* again.
- **Draw** a picture of an Anasazi pueblo. **Include** and **label** a *mesa, plaza, kiva,* and *courtyard.* Use the pictures in the book for help.

Family Link

Share your drawing with family members. Talk with them about Anasazi pueblos. How are the dwellings like towns today?

Weekly Resources Guide for English Language Learner Support

For this week's content and language objectives, see p. 125e.

Instructional Strand	Day 1	Day 2
Concept Development/Academic Language	**TEACHER'S EDITION** • Academic Language, p. DI•41 • Concept Development, p. DI•41 • Anchored Talk, pp. 46j—46–47 • Preteach Academic Vocabulary, p. 49a • Concept Talk Video **ELL HANDBOOK** • Hear It, See It, Say It, Use It, pp. xxxvi–xxxvii • ELL Poster Talk, Concept Talk, p. 125c **ELL POSTER 17** • Day 1 Activities	**TEACHER'S EDITION** • Academic Language, p. DI•41 • Concept Development, p. DI•41 • Anchored Talk, p. 50a • Concept Talk Video **ELL HANDBOOK** • ELL Poster Talk, Concept Talk, p. 125c • Concept Talk Video Routine, p. 477 **ELL POSTER 17** • Day 2 Activities
Phonics and Spelling	**TEACHER'S EDITION** • Phonics and Spelling, p. DI•45	**TEACHER'S EDITION** • Phonics and Spelling, p. DI•45
Listening Comprehension	**TEACHER'S EDITION** • Modified Read Aloud, p. DI•44 • Read Aloud, p. 47b • Concept Talk Video **ELL HANDBOOK** • Concept Talk Video Routine, p. 477	**TEACHER'S EDITION** • Modified Read Aloud, p. DI•44 • AudioText of *Tripping Over the Lunch Lady* • Concept Talk Video **ELL HANDBOOK** • AudioText CD Routine, p. 477 • T-Chart, p. 493
Reading Comprehension	**TEACHER'S EDITION** • Preteach Generalize, p. DI•46	**TEACHER'S EDITION** • Reteach Generalize, p. DI•46 • Frontloading Reading, p. DI•47 **ELL HANDBOOK** • Picture It! Skill Instruction, pp. 126–126a • Multilingual Summaries, pp. 127–129
Vocabulary **Basic and Lesson Vocabulary** **Word Analysis: Suffixes**	**TEACHER'S EDITION** • Basic Vocabulary, p. DI•42 • Preteach Lesson Vocabulary, p. DI•42 • Suffixes, p. DI•45 **ELL HANDBOOK** • Word Cards, p. 125 • ELL Vocabulary Routine, p. 471 **ELL POSTER 17** • Day 1 Activities	**TEACHER'S EDITION** • Basic Vocabulary, p. DI•42 • Reteach Lesson Vocabulary, p. DI•43 • Suffixes, p. DI•45 **ELL HANDBOOK** • Word Cards, p. 125 • Multilingual Vocabulary List, p. 431 **ELL POSTER 17** • Day 2 Activities
Grammar and Conventions	**TEACHER'S EDITION** • Preteach Pronouns and Antecedents, p. DI•49	**TEACHER'S EDITION** • Reteach Pronouns and Antecedents, p. DI•49
Writing	**TEACHER'S EDITION** • Simple and Compound Sentences, p. DI•50 • Introduce Friendly Letter, pp. 49e–49f	**TEACHER'S EDITION** • Writing Trait: Sentences, pp. 61d–61e

Tripping Over the Lunch Lady

This symbol indicates leveled instruction to address language proficiency levels.

Day 3	Day 4	Day 5
TEACHER'S EDITION • Academic Language, p. DI•41 • Concept Development, p. DI•41 • Anchored Talk, p. 62a • Concept Talk Video **ELL HANDBOOK** • ELL Poster Talk, Concept Talk, p. 125c **ELL POSTER 17** • Day 3 Activities	**TEACHER'S EDITION** • Academic Language, p. DI•41 • Concept Development, p. DI•41 • Anchored Talk, p. 72a • Concept Talk Video **ELL HANDBOOK** • ELL Poster Talk, Concept Talk, p. 125c **ELL POSTER 17** • Day 4 Activities	**TEACHER'S EDITION** • Academic Language, p. DI•41 • Concept Development, p. DI•41 • Concept Talk Video **ELL HANDBOOK** • ELL Poster Talk, Concept Talk, p. 125c **ELL POSTER 17** • Day 5 Activities
		TEACHER'S EDITION • Phonics and Spelling, p. DI•45
ELL HANDBOOK • Phonics Transition Lesson, pp. 285–286, 292–293	**ELL HANDBOOK** • Phonics Transition Lesson, pp. 285–286, 292–293	
TEACHER'S EDITION • AudioText of *Tripping Over the Lunch Lady* • Concept Talk Video **ELL HANDBOOK** • AudioText CD Routine, p. 477	**TEACHER'S EDITION** • Concept Talk Video	**TEACHER'S EDITION** • Concept Talk Video
TEACHER'S EDITION • Sheltered Reading, p. DI•47 **ELL HANDBOOK** • Multilingual Summaries, pp. 127–129	**TEACHER'S EDITION** • ELL/ELD Reader Guided Reading, p. DI•48 **ELL HANDBOOK** • ELL Study Guide, p. 130	**TEACHER'S EDITION** • ELL/ELD Reader Guided Reading, p. DI•48 **ELL HANDBOOK** • ELL Study Guide, p. 130
		TEACHER'S EDITION • Suffixes *-ly, -ian*, p. 75i
ELL HANDBOOK • High-Frequency Words Activity Bank, p. 446 **ELL POSTER 17** • Day 3 Activities	**ELL HANDBOOK** • High-Frequency Words Activity Bank, p. 446	**ELL HANDBOOK** • High-Frequency Words Activity Bank, p. 446
TEACHER'S EDITION • Grammar Jammer **ELL HANDBOOK** • Grammar Transition Lesson, pp. 363, 368 • Grammar Jammer Routine, p. 478	**TEACHER'S EDITION** • Grammar Jammer **ELL HANDBOOK** • Grammar Transition Lesson, pp. 363, 368	**TEACHER'S EDITION** • Grammar Jammer **ELL HANDBOOK** • Grammar Transition Lesson, pp. 363, 368
TEACHER'S EDITION • Let's Write It!, p. 70–71 • Writing Trait: Sentences, pp. 71a–71b	**TEACHER'S EDITION** • Revising Strategy, pp. 75d–75e	**TEACHER'S EDITION** • Conventions, pp. 75p–75q

Question of the Week
How do people overcome obstacles?

Throughout the week, use the ELL Poster to help students produce and comprehend language, understand the concept, and build English vocabulary. Use the Question of the Week and other questions to help students share ideas in pairs, small groups, or the large group. Sample questions are shown, with examples of possible responses by students.

ELL Poster 17

Weekly Concept and Language Goals

• Participate in a discussion about overcoming obstacles

• Name obstacles people face

• Discuss ways people overcome obstacles

By the end of the lesson, students should be able to talk about and write sentences about overcoming obstacles.

Daily Team Talk

Day 1	Day 2	Day 3	Day 4	Day 5
After Day 1 activities on Poster, ask questions such as	After Day 2 activity on Poster, ask questions such as	After Day 3 activity on Poster, ask questions such as	After Day 4 activity on Poster, ask questions such as	After Day 5 activity on Poster, ask questions such as
In the poster picture, what obstacle does the boy who is sitting face?	*In the poster picture, how do the boy's parents help him overcome his sprained ankle?*	*What obstacle do you think the girl in the pink skirt will face if she wants to become a champion skater?*	*The little boy in the red jacket used to be afraid to skate. How do you think he overcame this obstacle?*	*What obstacles do you think the people faced to make a skating rink?*
Beginning He is hurt. **Intermediate** He hurt his ankle. **Advanced** He sprained his ankle while skating. **Advanced High** The boy had an accident while he was skating and sprained his ankle.	**Beginning** They use snow. **Intermediate** They put snow on his ankle. **Advanced** His parents are putting snow on his ankle so it does not swell. **Advanced High** The boy's parents are putting snow on his sprained ankle to keep it from swelling so that it can get better soon.	**Beginning** Practice a lot. **Intermediate** She will have to practice a lot. **Advanced** She will have to work hard and practice a lot. **Advanced High** The girl will have to learn to work hard and practice constantly.	**Beginning** He learned how. **Intermediate** He learned how to skate. **Advanced** His brother helped him learn how to skate. **Advanced High** The boy's brother taught him how to skate. His brother holds his hand so he does not fall.	**Beginning** All the snow. **Intermediate** There is a lot of snow. **Advanced** They had to clear the snow off the pond. **Advanced High** It looks like there is a lot of snow on the ground. They probably had to clear the snow off the pond before they could skate on it.

This Week's Materials

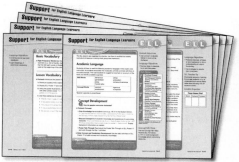

Teacher's Edition pages 46j–75q

See the support for English language learners throughout the lesson, including ELL strategies and scaffolded activities at points of use.

Teacher's Edition pages DI•41–DI•50

Differentiated Instruction for English language learners provides daily group activities that "frontload," or preteach, core instruction.

ELL Handbook pp. 125a–130

Find additional lesson materials that support the core lesson and the ELL instructional pages.

ELL Poster 17

ELL Reader 5.4.2

ELD Reader 5.4.2

Concept Literacy Reader

ELD, ELL Reader Teaching Guide

Concept Literacy Reader Teaching Guide

Technology

Online Teacher's Edition Use the digital version of the core Teacher's Edition for planning and instruction.

eReaders
This week's ELL and ELD Readers and Concept Literacy Reader are also available in digital format.

This Week's Content and Language Objectives by Strand

Concept Development/ Academic Language How do people overcome obstacles?	**Content Objective** • Use concept vocabulary related to overcoming obstacles. **Language Objective** • Express ideas in response to art and discussion.
Phonics and Spelling Prefixes *over-, under-, sub-, super-, out-*	**Content Objective** • Identify and discuss the meanings of the prefixes *over-, under-, sub-, super-, out-*. **Language Objective** • Apply phonics and decoding skills to vocabulary.
Listening Comprehension Modified Read Aloud: "Beautiful Music"	**Content Objective** • Monitor and adjust oral comprehension. **Language Objectives** • Discuss oral passages. • Use a graphic organizer to take notes.
Reading Comprehension Generalize	**Content Objectives** • Generalize to aid comprehension. • Identify details that support generalizations. • Monitor and adjust comprehension. **Language Objectives** • Write sentences that show generalizations. • Learn and use routine language for classroom communication. • Read with accuracy.
Vocabulary Basic and Lesson Vocabulary	**Language Objectives** • Understand and use basic vocabulary. • Learn meanings of grade-level vocabulary. • Produce drawings, phrases, or short sentences to show an understanding of Lesson Vocabulary. • Use strategies to acquire new vocabulary.
Word Analysis Suffixes	**Content Objective** • Identify the suffixes *–ly* and *-ian*. **Language Objective** • Discuss meanings of words with the suffixes.
Grammar and Conventions Pronouns and Antecedents	**Content Objectives** • Decode and use pronouns and antecedents. • Correctly form pronouns and antecedents. **Language Objectives** • Write using a variety of sentence patterns. • Speak using a pattern of pronouns and antecedents. • Write phrases and sentences with pronouns and antecedents.
Writing Simple and Compound Sentences	**Content Objective** • Identify simple and compound sentences. **Language Objectives** • Write simple and compound sentences. • Write using connecting words. • Edit for subject-verb agreement.

Dalmatian

frilly

promenading

sprained

substitute

Teacher Note: Beginning Teach two words. **Intermediate** Teach three words. **Advanced** Teach four to five words. **Advanced High** Teach all words and review words from an earlier lesson.

Name _____

Read the story. Then **complete** the graphic organizer.

- Write a generalization about the people who helped others through the Underground Railroad.
- Write the information from the text that supports that generalization.

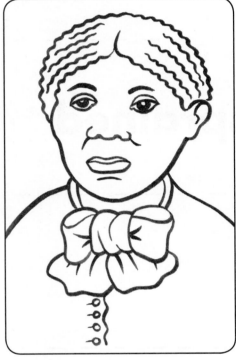

The Underground Railroad

Harriet Tubman was a formerly enslaved person. She helped rescue others from slavery. Tubman was just one member of the Underground Railroad. The Underground Railroad was a network of heroes who helped to free enslaved people. They acted as guides or gave enslaved people food, supplies, and shelter. The helpers were men and women. They included formerly enslaved people, free African Americans, and white abolitionists. They were business owners, farmers, and members of different churches.

Support from Text

Generalization

Support from Text

Support from Text

Generalize

Use this lesson to supplement or replace the skill lesson on page 47c of the Teacher's Edition. Display the Skill Points (at right) and share them with students.

Teach/Model

Beginning Say: *You need a passport to visit a different country. Many people have passports. Which sentence tells how many people are alike?* (the second sentence) *This sentence is a generalization.* Point out that the word *many* is a clue word for recognizing a generalization.

Intermediate Write on the board: *Most children like to ride bicycles.* Read the sentence aloud. Ask: *How do you know this is a generalization?* (It tells a way most children are alike. It has the word *most*.)

Advanced Write on the board: *There are landmarks in all the states.* Ask students why this is a generalization. Then have them write a sentence that supports the generalization. Explain that telling a landmark and which state has that landmark supports the generalization: *The Statue of Liberty is in New York.*

Advanced High Pair students. Have partners write a generalization about vacations. Remind students to use clue words such as *most, many, all,* or *always* in their generalizations. Have them write a sentence that supports their generalization.

Then distribute copies of Picture It! page 126.

- Tell students they are going to read a paragraph about the Underground Railroad. Discuss what students know about slavery and the Underground Railroad, providing background information if necessary.
- Review the Skill Points with students.
- Read the paragraph aloud. Ask: *What can you say about the people who helped others through the Underground Railroad?* (They were heroes. They came from many backgrounds.)

> ## Skill Points
> ✔ A **generalization** is a broad statement that applies to many examples.
> ✔ A good generalization uses details and examples for support.
> ✔ Authors may use clue words such as *all, most, many,* and *always* to let readers know they are making generalizations.

Practice

Read aloud the directions on page 126. Reread the paragraph aloud. Provide background for the words *underground* and *abolitionist.* Have students look at the picture and the paragraph as they complete the graphic organizer.

Beginning Students can say what they want to write before writing words or phrases in the graphic organizer. Provide help with English words and writing.

Intermediate Students can first orally respond and then write sentences to complete the graphic organizer. Provide help with writing.

Advanced Students can write sentences to complete the graphic organizer and then check their answers by silently rereading the paragraph.

Advanced High Students can write sentences to complete the graphic organizer and then orally explain how the details support their generalization.

Answers for page 126: *Possible generalization:* Many kinds of people helped enslaved people through the Underground Railroad. *Support from Text:* Possible answers: Some were formerly enslaved people. Some were free African Americans. Some were white abolitionists.

Multilingual Summaries

Tripping Over the Lunch Lady

Jinx is very clumsy. He has a lot of accidents! Jinx does not like gym class, because she has accidents there.

Jinx sees people square dancing on television. She decides that she would like to try square dancing. It looks like fun. She asks the gym teacher if the students can square dance during gym class. He does not really like the idea.

One day, the gym teacher is absent. He has an injury. A substitute teacher comes to gym class. She lets the class square dance. While dancing, Jinx is injured! Jinx goes to the hospital. She sees her gym teacher at the hospital. Jinx laughs. She cannot believe she got hurt square dancing!

Spanish

Tropiezo con la señora del almuerzo

Jinx es muy torpe. Ella tiene muchos accidentes. Por eso, no le gusta la clase de educación física.

Jinx ve a a la personas bailando en la televisión. Le gustaría intentar el baile de figuras. Parece divertido. Le pregunta al profesor de educación física, el señor Deimeister, si los estudiantes pueden practicar el baile de figuras en la clase de educación física. A él no le gusta la idea.

Un día, el profesor no asiste a la clase. Tiene una lesión. Hay un profesor sustituto. Practican el baile. Mientras baila, ¡Jinx se lastima! Va al hospital. Ve al profesor de educación física, el señor Deimeister, en el hospital. Jinx se ríe. ¡No puede creer que se haya lastimado con el baile!

Multilingual Summaries

绊倒饭堂女工

金克斯很笨拙，所以常常发生意外。她不喜欢体育课，因为她在体育课有过意外。

金克斯看见电视上的人跳方块舞，就想试试。她请求体育老师德民斯特先生让学生在体育课跳方块舞，可是德民斯特不赞成。

一天，因为德民斯特受了伤，所以不能来学校，体育课由代课老师来上；代课老师让学生跳方块舞。金克斯跳的时候，意外受伤，而且被送去医院。在医院里她一看见德民斯特老师，就哈哈大笑；她不能相信她会因跳方块舞而受伤。

Ngã Nhào Vào Bà Bếp.

Jinx rất vụng về. Cô ta vụng về đến nỗi đã gặp nhiều tai nạn. Jinx không thích học lớp thể thao vì cô từng gặp tai nạn tại đó.

Jinx thấy người ta nhảy tay tư trên truyền hình. Cô quyết định thích thử nhảy tay tư. Hình như môn này vui lắm. Cô hỏi Ộ. Deimeister, giáo viên thể thao xem học sinh có thể nhảy tay tư trong lớp thể thao không. Ông này thật không thích ý kiến đó.

Một hôm giáo viên thể thao vắng mặt. Ông ta bị thương. Một cô giáo dạy thế đến lớp. Cô này để cho cả lớp nhảy tay tư. Trong lúc nhảy, Jinx bị thương! Jinx đi bệnh viện. Cô thấy Ộ Deimeister, giáo viên thể thao ở bệnh viện. Jinx cười lớn. Cô không tin cô bị thương vì nhảy tay tư!

Multilingual Summaries

춤추다 넘어지다!

징크스는 참 일에 서툽니다. 너무 서툴러서 많은 사고를 치지요! 징크스는 자꾸 사고가 나는 체육시간을 싫어합니다.

징크스는 텔레비전에서 사람들이 스퀘어춤을 스퀘어댄스를 추는 걸 보았습니다. 그녀는 스퀘어댄스에 도전해보기로 마음먹었습니다. 춤이 재미있어 보였거든요. 체육 담당 데이메이스터 선생님께 체육 시간에 학생들이 스퀘어댄스를 출 수 있는 지 물어보았습니다. 선생님은 별로 달가워하지 않으셨습니다.

어느 날 체육 선생님이 결근하셨습니다. 선생님은 부상을 당하셨습니다. 대리 선생님이 체육 시간에 오셨습니다. 선생님은 스퀘어댄스를 추게 허락하셨습니다. 춤추는 동안, 징크스는 부상을 당했지 뭐에요! 징크스는 병원에 갔습니다. 병원에서 데이메이스터 선생님을 만났습니다. 징크는 키득키득 웃었습니다. 스퀘어댄스를 추다가 다친 것이 믿기지가 않았지요.

Pheej Dawm tug Pojniam Ua Su

Jinx peej dawm ub dawm no. Nwg pheej feeb tsi meej rau txoj kev taug kev mas nwg huam yuaj ntau heev. Jinx tsi nyiam hoob khiav uasi, rau qhov nwg pheej raug huam yuaj hauv.

Jinx pom tibneeg seev cev square dance hauv thisvis. Nwg txiav txim tias nwg xav sim seev cev square dance thiab. Zoo li lomzem kawg. Nwg thov tus xibhwb qhia uasi, Mr. Deimeister, saib cov menyuam kawm ntawv puas seev cev square dance tau rau lub caij kawm uasi hauv hoob. Mr. Deimeister tsi tshuam nyiam lub tswvyim ntawd.

Ib nub, tus xibhwb qhia uasi tsi tuaj. Nwg raug mob lawm. Ib tus xibhwb hloov tuaj rau hauv hoob qhia uasi. Nwg cia lub hoob seev cev square dance. Thaum uas lawv seev cev, Jinx ciali raug mob! Jinx mus tim tsev kho mob. Nwg pom nwg tug xibhwb qhia uasi, Mr. Deimeister, tom tsev kho mob. Jinx luag. Nwg ntseeg tsi tau tias nwg raug mob vim seev cev square dance!

- **Read** *Strength of Spirit* again.
- **Complete** the chart. **Write** about the challenges and achievements of Helen Keller and Franklin Delano Roosevelt.

	Challenges	Achievements
Helen Keller		
Franklin Delano Roosevelt		

Family Link

Share what you learned about Helen Keller and Franklin Delano Roosevelt with your family. Ask family members about other people they know who have disabilities.

Weekly Resources Guide for English Language Learner Support

For this week's content and language objectives, see p. 131e.

Instructional Strand	Day 1	Day 2
Concept Development/Academic Language	**TEACHER'S EDITION** • Academic Language, p. DI•66 • Concept Development, p. DI•66 • Anchored Talk, pp. 76j—76–77 • Preteach Academic Vocabulary, p. 79a • Concept Talk Video **ELL HANDBOOK** • Hear It, See It, Say It, Use It, pp. xxxvi–xxxvii • ELL Poster Talk, Concept Talk, p. 131c **ELL POSTER 18** • Day 1 Activities	**TEACHER'S EDITION** • Academic Language, p. DI•66 • Concept Development, p. DI•66 • Anchored Talk, p. 80a • Concept Talk Video **ELL HANDBOOK** • ELL Poster Talk, Concept Talk, p. 131c • Concept Talk Video Routine, p. 477 **ELL POSTER 18** • Day 2 Activities
Phonics and Spelling	**TEACHER'S EDITION** • Phonics and Spelling, p. DI•70	**TEACHER'S EDITION** • Phonics and Spelling, p. DI•70
Listening Comprehension	**TEACHER'S EDITION** • Modified Read Aloud, p. DI•69 • Read Aloud, p. 77b • Concept Talk Video **ELL HANDBOOK** • Concept Talk Video Routine, p. 477	**TEACHER'S EDITION** • Modified Read Aloud, p. DI•69 • AudioText of *Exploding Ants* • Concept Talk Video **ELL HANDBOOK** • AudioText CD Routine, p. 477 • Outline Form, p. 495
Reading Comprehension	**TEACHER'S EDITION** • Preteach Graphic Sources, p. DI•71	**TEACHER'S EDITION** • Reteach Graphic Sources, p. DI•71 • Frontloading Reading, p. DI•72 **ELL HANDBOOK** • Picture It! Skill Instruction, pp. 132–132a • Multilingual Summaries, pp. 133–135
Vocabulary **Basic and Lesson Vocabulary** **Word Analysis: Suffix -ize**	**TEACHER'S EDITION** • Basic Vocabulary, p. DI•67 • Preteach Lesson Vocabulary, p. DI•67 • Suffix -ize, p. DI•70 **ELL HANDBOOK** • Word Cards, p. 131 • ELL Vocabulary Routine, p. 471 **ELL POSTER 18** • Day 1 Activities	**TEACHER'S EDITION** • Basic Vocabulary, p. DI•67 • Reteach Lesson Vocabulary, p. DI•68 • Suffix -ize, p. DI•70 **ELL HANDBOOK** • Word Cards, p. 131 • Multilingual Vocabulary List, p. 431 **ELL POSTER 18** • Day 2 Activities
Grammar and Conventions	**TEACHER'S EDITION** • Preteach Possessive Pronouns, p. DI•74	**TEACHER'S EDITION** • Reteach Possessive Pronouns, p. DI•74
Writing	**TEACHER'S EDITION** • Writing with a Sense of Closure, p. DI•75 • Introduce Formal Letter, pp. 79e–79f	**TEACHER'S EDITION** • Writing Strategy: Choose a Topic, pp. 89d–89e

This symbol indicates leveled instruction to address language proficiency levels.

Day 3	Day 4	Day 5
TEACHER'S EDITION • Academic Language, p. DI•66 • Concept Development, p. DI•66 • Anchored Talk, p. 90a • Concept Talk Video **ELL HANDBOOK** • ELL Poster Talk, Concept Talk, p. 131c **ELL POSTER 18** • Day 3 Activities	**TEACHER'S EDITION** • Academic Language, p. DI•66 • Concept Development, p. DI•66 • Anchored Talk, p. 98a • Concept Talk Video **ELL HANDBOOK** • ELL Poster Talk, Concept Talk, p. 131c **ELL POSTER 18** • Day 4 Activities	**TEACHER'S EDITION** • Academic Language, p. DI•66 • Concept Development, p. DI•66 • Concept Talk Video **ELL HANDBOOK** • ELL Poster Talk, Concept Talk, p. 131c **ELL POSTER 18** • Day 5 Activities
		TEACHER'S EDITION • Phonics and Spelling, p. DI•70
ELL HANDBOOK • Phonics Transition Lesson, pp. 279, 282	**ELL HANDBOOK** • Phonics Transition Lesson, pp. 279, 282	
TEACHER'S EDITION • AudioText of *Exploding Ants* • Concept Talk Video **ELL HANDBOOK** • AudioText CD Routine, p. 477	**TEACHER'S EDITION** • Concept Talk Video	**TEACHER'S EDITION** • Concept Talk Video
TEACHER'S EDITION • Sheltered Reading, p. DI•72 **ELL HANDBOOK** • Multilingual Summaries, pp. 133–135	**TEACHER'S EDITION** • ELL/ELD Reader Guided Reading, p. DI•73 **ELL HANDBOOK** • ELL Study Guide, p. 136	**TEACHER'S EDITION** • ELL/ELD Reader Guided Reading, p. DI•73 **ELL HANDBOOK** • ELL Study Guide, p. 136
		TEACHER'S EDITION • Suffix *-ize*, p. 103i
ELL HANDBOOK • High-Frequency Words Activity Bank, p. 446 **ELL POSTER 18** • Day 3 Activities	**ELL HANDBOOK** • High-Frequency Words Activity Bank, p. 446	**ELL HANDBOOK** • High-Frequency Words Activity Bank, p. 446
TEACHER'S EDITION • Grammar Jammer **ELL HANDBOOK** • Grammar Transition Lesson, pp. 363, 367 • Grammar Jammer Routine, p. 478	**TEACHER'S EDITION** • Grammar Jammer **ELL HANDBOOK** • Grammar Transition Lesson, pp. 363, 367	**TEACHER'S EDITION** • Grammar Jammer **ELL HANDBOOK** • Grammar Transition Lesson, pp. 363, 367
TEACHER'S EDITION • Let's Write It!, p. 96–97 • Writing: Evaluation, p. 97a • Writer's Craft: Formal Letter, p. 97b	**TEACHER'S EDITION** • Revising Strategy, pp. 103d–103e	**TEACHER'S EDITION** • Possessive Nouns, pp. 103p–103q

Poster Talk, Concept Talk

Question of the Week
How do animals adapt to survive?

Throughout the week, use the ELL Poster to help students produce and comprehend language, understand the concept, and build English vocabulary. Use the Question of the Week and other questions to help students share ideas in pairs, small groups, or the large group. Sample questions are shown, with examples of possible responses by students.

Weekly Concept and Language Goals

- Explain animal adaptations
- Name animal body parts that help them survive
- Describe how body parts enable animals to live in a habitat

By the end of the lesson, students should be able to talk about and write sentences about animal adaptations.

ELL Poster 18

Daily Team Talk

Day 1	Day 2	Day 3	Day 4	Day 5
After Day 1 activities on Poster, ask questions such as *In the poster picture, what does a snail have that helps it move?*	After Day 2 activity on Poster, ask questions such as *What body parts do the birds in the poster picture have that help them survive?*	After Day 3 activity on Poster, ask questions such as *How do the different birds use their beaks to help them survive?*	After Day 4 activity on Poster, ask questions such as *How does the ants' saliva help the ants live in their habitat?*	After Day 5 activity on Poster, ask questions such as *In Exploding Ants, what special feature do snakes have that help them eat their prey?*
Beginning It is wet. **Intermediate** The snail has mucus. **Advanced** The snail has mucus that helps it move along the ground. **Advanced High** A snail's body is covered in mucus, which helps it glide along the ground.	**Beginning** They have wings. **Intermediate** Birds have wings to fly. **Advanced** The birds have wings, which help them fly. **Advanced High** All of the birds have wings, which help them fly. They also have beaks, which help them get food.	**Beginning** They pick things up. **Intermediate** They pick up food with their beaks. **Advanced** The birds use their beaks to pick up food, such as bugs or flowers. **Advanced High** One bird uses its beak to pick up an ant, and another uses its beak to get food from inside a flower. The peahen is picking food out of a shell.	**Beginning** It makes food safe. **Intermediate** It makes their food safe to eat. **Advanced** Their saliva cleans the food so it is safe to eat. **Advanced High** The ants' saliva makes their food sterile as they chew it, which makes the food safe to eat.	**Beginning** Big mouths. **Intermediate** Their mouths open wide. **Advanced** Snakes can open their mouths wide to swallow big animals. **Advanced High** Snakes have special jaws that stretch wide so they can swallow large animals whole.

This Week's Materials

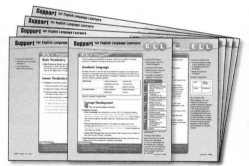

Teacher's Edition pages 76j–103q

See the support for English language learners throughout the lesson, including ELL strategies and scaffolded activities at points of use.

Teacher's Edition pages DI•66–DI•75

Differentiated Instruction for English language learners provides daily group activities that "frontload," or preteach, core instruction.

ELL Handbook pp. 131a–136

Find additional lesson materials that support the core lesson and the ELL instructional pages.

ELL Poster 18

ELL Reader 5.4.3

ELD Reader 5.4.3

Concept Literacy Reader

ELD, ELL Reader Teaching Guide

Concept Literacy Reader Teaching Guide

Technology

Online Teacher's Edition Use the digital version of the core Teacher's Edition for planning and instruction.

eReaders
This week's ELL and ELD Readers and Concept Literacy Reader are also available in digital format.

This Week's Content and Language Objectives by Strand

Concept Development/ Academic Language How do animals adapt to survive?	**Content Objective** • Use concept vocabulary related to adaption. **Language Objectives** • Express ideas in response to art and discussion. • Use basic vocabulary in classroom interactions.
Phonics and Spelling Homophones	**Content Objectives** • Identify homophones • Review synonyms. **Language Objectives** • Apply phonics and decoding skills to vocabulary. • Use linguistic and contextual support to understand spoken language.
Listening Comprehension Modified Read Aloud: "Animal Disguises"	**Content Objective** • Monitor and adjust oral comprehension. **Language Objectives** • Discuss oral passages. • Use a graphic organizer to take notes.
Reading Comprehension Graphic Sources	**Content Objectives** • Identify graphic sources to aid comprehension. • Monitor and adjust comprehension. **Language Objectives** • Demonstrate and expand reading skills. • Use graphic sources to discuss information from a reading. • Use information from a reading to label a diagram. • Use visual and contextual support to read text.
Vocabulary Basic and Lesson Vocabulary	**Language Objectives** • Understand and use basic vocabulary. • Learn meanings of grade-level vocabulary. • Produce drawings, phrases, or short sentences to show an understanding of Lesson Vocabulary. • Speak using content vocabulary.
Word Analysis Suffix -ize	**Content Objective** • Identify and define words with suffix -ize. **Language Objective** • Discuss the meaning of words with suffix -ize.
Grammar and Conventions Possessive Pronouns	**Content Objective** • Decode and correctly form possessive pronouns. **Language Objectives** • Speak using the pattern of possessive pronouns. • Write phrases and sentences with possessive pronouns.
Writing Writing with a Sense of Closure	**Content Objective** • Identify strong conclusions that provide a sense of closure. **Language Objectives** • Write concluding paragraphs providing a sense of closure. • Know when to use formal English.

Word Cards for Vocabulary Activities

critical	**enables**
mucus	**scarce**
specialize	**sterile**

Teacher Note: Beginning Teach two to three words. **Intermediate** Teach three to four words. **Advanced** Teach four to five words. **Advanced High** Teach all words.

Read the paragraph and **study** the diagram.
Label the diagram using information from the paragraph.

Metamorphosis

The life cycle of a butterfly starts with an egg. A caterpillar hatches from the egg. The caterpillar turns into a pupa. When the pupa becomes an adult butterfly, it emerges transformed from its protective cocoon. This stage of the life cycle is known as *metamorphosis*. Later, the female butterfly will lay eggs, and the whole cycle starts again.

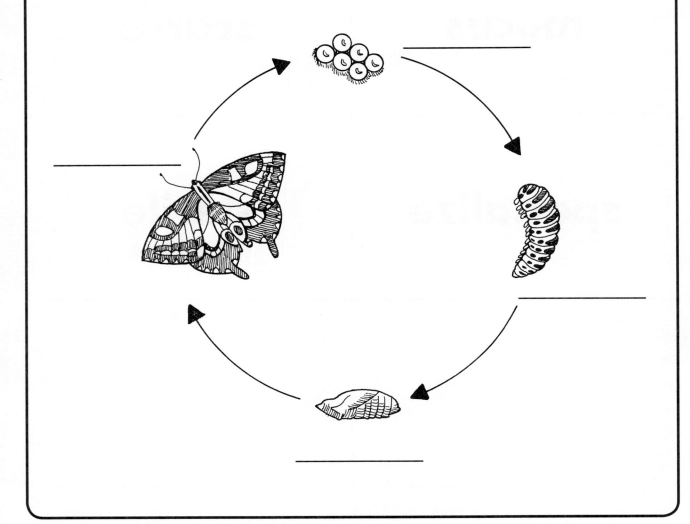

Graphic Sources

Use this lesson to supplement or replace the skill lesson on page 77c of the Teacher's Edition. Display the Skill Points (at right) and share them with students.

Teach/Model

Beginning Provide a diagram of the life cycle of a frog. Ask: *What does the diagram tell you about?* (the life cycle of a frog) *Where do you think you would find this graphic source?* (a science book or nature magazine or the Internet)

Intermediate Preview the graphic sources contained in a chapter from a life science textbook. Ask: *How can these graphic sources help you predict what this chapter will be about?* Have students write their responses. Read portions of the chapter to confirm their predictions.

Advanced Say: *I am writing a report about snakes. I want to show where different snake species can be found in our state.* Ask: *What graphic source should I make?* (a map) Continue the activity, asking how to visually show descriptions of snakes (pictures) and how to visually show the number of snake sightings by county or area (chart).

Advanced High Pair students. Have one partner write a paragraph about a familiar insect. Have the other partner use the paragraph to make a graphic source that shows part of the information. Then have the partners trade roles.

Then distribute copies of Picture It! page 132.

- Point to the graphic. Ask students what they think the paragraph is going to be about, based on the diagram.
- Review the Skill Points with students.
- Tell students they are going to label the diagram with words from the paragraph. Then read the paragraph aloud.

Practice

Read aloud the directions on page 132. Reread the paragraph aloud, explaining the words *metamorphosis, pupa,* and *cocoon.* Have students look at the diagram and the paragraph as they write their labels.

Beginning Students can tell what they want to write for each part of the diagram before writing the labels. Provide help with labeling.

Intermediate Students can orally describe the diagram before writing the labels.

Advanced Students can write labels to complete the diagram and then check their labels by comparing them to a partner's.

Advanced High Students can write labels to complete the diagram and then explain how the diagram helps them understand the life cycle of a butterfly.

Answers for page 132: Students should label the diagram with these words, starting at the top and going clockwise: *egg, caterpillar, cocoon, butterfly.*

Skill Points

✔ **Graphic sources** include pictures, diagrams, maps, and time lines.
✔ A graphic source helps you to better understand written text.
✔ Preview graphic sources before you read. Predict what the text is about, based on the graphic sources.

Multilingual Summaries

Exploding Ants

Animals do things that seem gross. They eat things that people would not eat. They live in all kinds of places, even inside other animals. They use their bodies in strange ways.

Honey ants swell up and keep honey in their bodies. They feed other ants with it. Some soldier ants explode if they are attacked. They spray chemicals that kill the attacker.

Owls eat small animals whole. Later, they spit out pellets of bones and fur. Snakes also eat their food whole. Their mouths can expand. A snake can eat something bigger than its own head.

Spanish

Hormigas que explotan

Algunos animales hacen cosas que parecen repugnantes. Comen cosas que las personas no comerían. Viven en todo tipo de lugares, hasta dentro de otros animales. Otros usan sus cuerpos de maneras muy extrañas.

Las hormigas de miel se hinchan y mantienen miel en sus cuerpos. Con esta miel alimentan a otras hormigas. Algunas hormigas soldado explotan si son atacadas. Ellas lanzan químicos que matan al atacante.

Los búhos se comen enteros a los pequeños animales. Después arrojan bolas con los huesos y la piel. Las serpientes también se comen los animales enteros. Su boca se puede expandir. Una serpiente puede comerse algo más grande que su propia cabeza.

Multilingual Summaries

Chinese

會爆炸的螞蟻

　　動物會做一些看起來很噁心的事情，他們吃人類不吃的東西，住在各式各樣的地方，包括其他動物的身體裡。他們會用很奇怪的方式對待自己的身體。

　　蜜蟻會膨脹身體好將蜂蜜存放在裡面，然後再將身體裡的蜂蜜提供給其他同伴吃。有些兵蟻如果遭遇到攻擊，身體會爆炸，噴出有毒的化學物質殺死入侵者。

　　貓頭鷹會把小動物整個吃下去，然後再吐出骨頭和毛皮混雜而成的小球。蛇也能把食物整個吞下去，牠們的嘴巴可以張很大很大，吞下比自己的頭還要大的食物。

Vietnamese

Kiến Nổ

　　Thú vật làm những chuyện có vẻ kinh tởm. Chúng ăn những thứ mà con người không ăn. Chúng sống trong đủ loại chỗ, thậm chí ở trong những con thú khác. Chúng dùng thân thể của mình trong nhiều cách lạ thường.

　　Các kiến mật căng người ra và giữ mật trong cơ thể chúng. Chúng nuôi những con kiến khác từ mật này. Có loại kiến lính bùng nổ nếu chúng bị tấn công. Chúng phun chất hóa học để giết kẻ tấn công mình.

　　Những con chim cú nuốt trửng các con thú nhỏ. Sau đó chúng nhổ ra những viên xương và lông. Rắn cũng nuốt trửng thức ăn của chúng. Miệng rắn có thể giãn nở. Một con rắn có thể ăn một vật to hơn cả cái đầu của chính nó.

Multilingual Summaries

스스로 몸을 터뜨리는 개미

동물들은 지독해 보이는 일들을 한다. 사람들이 먹지 않는 것들도 먹고 다른 동물의 몸 속을 포함한 모든 종류의 장소에서 살기도 한다. 동물들은 이상한 방법으로 자신의 몸을 사용한다.

꿀개미는 몸을 부풀려 몸 안에 꿀을 보관하고 그 꿀을 다른 개미들에게 먹인다. 어떤 병정개미들은 공격을 받으면 몸을 터뜨리는데 이때 화학 성분을 뿌려 공격자를 죽인다.

올빼미는 작은 동물들을 통째로 먹고 나중에 뼈와 털로 된 작은 덩어리를 뱉어낸다. 뱀도 먹이를 통째로 먹는데 뱀의 입은 늘어나기 때문에 자기 머리보다 더 큰 것도 먹을 수 있다.

Cov Ntsaum Raug Tawg

Cov tsiaj txhu ua tej yam txawv. Lawv noj tej yam cov neeg yuav tsis noj. Lawv nyob txhua txhia qhov chaw, twb nyob rau hauv lwm cov tsiaj txhu. Nyias siv nyias lub cev txawv.

Cov ntsaum zib lub cev su, kom ceev zib tseg. Lawv pub zib rau lwm cov ntsaum noj. Thaum ib txhia cov ntsaum tub rog ntsib txoj kev tawm tsam, ces lawv lub cev tawg. Lawv tsuag tshuaj rau tus tawm tsam kom tuag.

Cov plas noj cov menyuam tsiaj txhu kom tas. Ib mentsis tom qab, lawv nti cov plaub thiab pob txha. Cov nab kuj noj lawv cov mov keev hlo. Lawv cov ncauj muaj peevxwm nthuav ntxiv kom dav. Ib lub nab noj tau ib qhov loj tshaj tus nab ntawd lub taub hau.

Name _____

- **Read** *Masters of Disguise* again.
- **Write** about these insects. Tell what they look like. Follow the example.

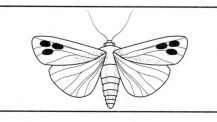

1. Moth
A moth looks like a scary animal.

_____

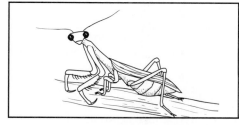

2. Praying Mantis

_____

_____

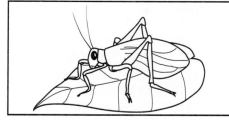

3. Katydid

_____

_____

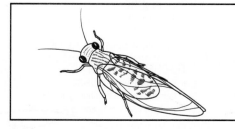

4. Syrphid Fly

_____

_____

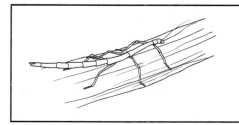

5. Walking Stick

_____

_____

Family Link
Talk with family members about how the insects are disguised in nature. Ask them if they have ever seen one of the insects named on this page.

Weekly Resources Guide for English Language Learner Support

For this week's content and language objectives, see p. 137e.

Instructional Strand	Day 1	Day 2
Concept Development/Academic Language	**TEACHER'S EDITION** • Academic Language, p. DI•91 • Concept Development, p. DI•91 • Anchored Talk, pp. 104j—104–105 • Preteach Academic Vocabulary, p. 107a • Concept Talk Video **ELL HANDBOOK** • Hear It, See It, Say It, Use It, pp. xxxvi–xxxvii • ELL Poster Talk, Concept Talk, p. 137c **ELL POSTER 19** • Day 1 Activities	**TEACHER'S EDITION** • Academic Language, p. DI•91 • Concept Development, p. DI•91 • Anchored Talk, p. 108a • Concept Talk Video **ELL HANDBOOK** • ELL Poster Talk, Concept Talk, p. 137c • Concept Talk Video Routine, p. 477 **ELL POSTER 19** • Day 2 Activities
Phonics and Spelling	**TEACHER'S EDITION** • Phonics and Spelling, p. DI•95	**TEACHER'S EDITION** • Phonics and Spelling, p. DI•95
Listening Comprehension	**TEACHER'S EDITION** • Modified Read Aloud, p. DI•94 • Read Aloud, p. 105b • Concept Talk Video **ELL HANDBOOK** • Concept Talk Video Routine, p. 477	**TEACHER'S EDITION** • Modified Read Aloud, p. DI•94 • AudioText of *The Stormi Giovanni Club* • Concept Talk Video **ELL HANDBOOK** • AudioText CD Routine, p. 477 • Story Map A, p. 483
Reading Comprehension	**TEACHER'S EDITION** • Preteach Generalize, p. DI•96	**TEACHER'S EDITION** • Reteach Generalize, p. DI•96 • Frontloading Reading, p. DI•97 **ELL HANDBOOK** • Picture It! Skill Instruction, pp. 138–138a • Multilingual Summaries, pp. 139–141
Vocabulary **Basic and Lesson Vocabulary** **Word Analysis: Prefixes *com-*, *pro-*, and *epi-***	**TEACHER'S EDITION** • Basic Vocabulary, p. DI•92 • Preteach Lesson Vocabulary, p. DI•92 • Prefixes *com-*, *pro-*, and *epi-*, p. DI•95 **ELL HANDBOOK** • Word Cards, p. 137 • ELL Vocabulary Routine, p. 471 **ELL POSTER 19** • Day 1 Activities	**TEACHER'S EDITION** • Basic Vocabulary, p. DI•92 • Reteach Lesson Vocabulary, p. DI•93 • Prefixes *com-*, *pro-*, and *epi-*, p. DI•95 **ELL HANDBOOK** • Word Cards, p. 137 • Multilingual Vocabulary List, p. 431 **ELL POSTER 19** • Day 2 Activities
Grammar and Conventions	**TEACHER'S EDITION** • Teach Indefinite and Reflexive Pronouns, p. DI•99	**TEACHER'S EDITION** • Teach Indefinite and Reflexive Pronouns, p. DI•99
Writing	**TEACHER'S EDITION** • Graphic Elements: Capital Letters and Line Length, p. DI•100 • Introduce Narrative Poetry, pp. 107e–107f	**TEACHER'S EDITION** • Writing Trait: Word Choice, pp. 117d–117e

This symbol indicates leveled instruction to address language proficiency levels.

Day 3	Day 4	Day 5
TEACHER'S EDITION • Academic Language, p. DI•91 • Concept Development, p. DI•91 • Anchored Talk, p. 118a • Concept Talk Video **ELL HANDBOOK** • ELL Poster Talk, Concept Talk, p. 137c **ELL POSTER 19** • Day 3 Activities	**TEACHER'S EDITION** • Academic Language, p. DI•91 • Concept Development, p. DI•91 • Anchored Talk, p. 130a • Concept Talk Video **ELL HANDBOOK** • ELL Poster Talk, Concept Talk, p. 137c **ELL POSTER 19** • Day 4 Activities	**TEACHER'S EDITION** • Academic Language, p. DI•91 • Concept Development, p. DI•91 • Concept Talk Video **ELL HANDBOOK** • ELL Poster Talk, Concept Talk, p. 137c **ELL POSTER 19** • Day 5 Activities
ELL HANDBOOK • Phonics Transition Lesson, pp. 288, 295	**ELL HANDBOOK** • Phonics Transition Lesson, pp. 288, 295	**TEACHER'S EDITION** • Phonics and Spelling, p. DI•95
TEACHER'S EDITION • AudioText of *The Stormi Giovanni Club* • Concept Talk Video **ELL HANDBOOK** • AudioText CD Routine, p. 477	**TEACHER'S EDITION** • Concept Talk Video	**TEACHER'S EDITION** • Concept Talk Video
TEACHER'S EDITION • Sheltered Reading, p. DI•97 **ELL HANDBOOK** • Multilingual Summaries, pp. 139–141	**TEACHER'S EDITION** • ELL/ELD Reader Guided Reading, p. DI•98 **ELL HANDBOOK** • ELL Study Guide, p. 142	**TEACHER'S EDITION** • ELL/ELD Reader Guided Reading, p. DI•98 **ELL HANDBOOK** • ELL Study Guide, p. 142
ELL HANDBOOK • High-Frequency Words Activity Bank, p. 446 **ELL POSTER 19** • Day 3 Activities	**ELL HANDBOOK** • High-Frequency Words Activity Bank, p. 446	**TEACHER'S EDITION** • Prefixes *com-, pro-, epi-,* p. 135i **ELL HANDBOOK** • High-Frequency Words Activity Bank, p. 446
TEACHER'S EDITION • Grammar Jammer **ELL HANDBOOK** • Grammar Transition Lesson, pp. 364, 369 • Grammar Jammer Routine, p. 478	**TEACHER'S EDITION** • Grammar Jammer **ELL HANDBOOK** • Grammar Transition Lesson, pp. 364, 369	**TEACHER'S EDITION** • Grammar Jammer **ELL HANDBOOK** • Grammar Transition Lesson, pp. 364, 369
TEACHER'S EDITION • Let's Write It!, p. 128–129 • Writing Trait: Word Choice, pp. 129a–129b	**TEACHER'S EDITION** • Revising Strategy, pp. 135d–135e	**TEACHER'S EDITION** • Indefinite and Reflexive Pronouns, pp. 135p–135q

Question of the Week
How do people adapt to new places?

Throughout the week, use the ELL Poster to help students produce and comprehend language, understand the concept, and build English vocabulary. Use the Question of the Week and other questions to help students share ideas in pairs, small groups, or the large group. Sample questions are shown, with examples of possible responses by students.

E L L Poster 19

Weekly Concept and Language Goals

• Explain how people adapt to a new place

• Talk about the challenges of adapting to a new school

• Name ways people can adapt to new places

By the end of the lesson, students should be able to talk about and write sentences about ways people adapt to a new place.

Daily Team Talk

Day 1	Day 2	Day 3	Day 4	Day 5
After Day 1 activities on Poster, ask questions such as *In the poster picture, which students are new to the school? How can you tell?*	After Day 2 activity on Poster, ask questions such as *In the poster picture, how do the three new students adapt in different ways?*	After Day 3 activity on Poster, ask questions such as *Why do you think the two new students to the right would like to join the football team?*	After Day 4 activity on Poster, ask questions such as *Why do you think the student on the bench waits before getting involved in the school?*	After Day 5 activity on Poster, ask questions such as *If you were the coach, how would you help the new students adapt?*
Beginning The ones in front. **Intermediate** The boys in front are new. **Advanced** The students in front are new. They do not know anyone. **Advanced High** The three students in front are new to the school. It seems like they do not know anyone, and they are not involved in the school yet.	**Beginning** They want to join. **Intermediate** Two want to join the team. One does not. **Advanced** Two of them want to get involved right away. One waits to get involved. **Advanced High** The two new students on the right want to get involved and join the football team. The new student on the bench wants to wait before getting involved.	**Beginning** To meet people. **Intermediate** They want to make friends. **Advanced** The two students want to make friends and get involved in the school. **Advanced High** The two new students want to make friends at their new school, so they want to get involved in school activities.	**Beginning** He is scared. **Intermediate** He looks scared to meet people. **Advanced** It looks like he is nervous to meet people at his new school. **Advanced High** The student looks shy. He is probably nervous about meeting new people.	**Beginning** Let them play. **Intermediate** I would let them join the team. **Advanced** I would help the students get involved by letting them join the team. **Advanced High** I would help the new students get involved in the school and make new friends by letting them join the football team.

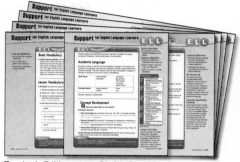

Teacher's Edition pages 104j–135q

See the support for English language learners throughout the lesson, including ELL strategies and scaffolded activities at points of use.

Teacher's Edition pages DI•91–DI•100

Differentiated Instruction for English language learners provides daily group activities that "frontload," or preteach, core instruction.

ELL Handbook pp. 137a–142

Find additional lesson materials that support the core lesson and the ELL instructional pages.

ELL Poster 19

ELL Reader 5.4.4

ELD Reader 5.4.4

Concept Literacy Reader

ELD, ELL Reader Teaching Guide

Concept Literacy Reader Teaching Guide

Technology

Online Teacher's Edition Use the digital version of the core Teacher's Edition for planning and instruction.

eReaders
This week's ELL and ELD Readers and Concept Literacy Reader are also available in digital format.

This Week's Content and Language Objectives by Strand

Concept Development/ Academic Language How do people adapt to new places?	**Content Objective** • Use concept vocabulary related to adapting to new places. **Language Objectives** • Express ideas in response to art and discussion. • Use prior knowledge to understand word meanings. • Listen to media for concept attainment.
Phonics and Spelling Suffixes *–ible, -able*	**Content Objective** • Identify and use words containing suffixes *-ible* and *-able*. **Language Objectives** • Apply phonics and decoding skills to vocabulary. • Decode words using various skills. • Use patterns in spelling.
Listening Comprehension Modified Read Aloud: "A Brave Woman"	**Content Objective** • Monitor and adjust oral comprehension. **Language Objectives** • Discuss oral passages. • Use a graphic organizer to take notes.
Reading Comprehension Generalize	**Content Objectives** • Identify and make generalizations. • Monitor and adjust comprehension. **Language Objectives** • Discuss characteristics of generalizations. • Write details of generalizations. • Summarize text using visual support.
Vocabulary Basic and Lesson Vocabulary	**Language Objectives** • Understand and use basic vocabulary. • Learn meanings of grade-level vocabulary. • Produce drawings, phrases, or short sentences to show an understanding of Lesson Vocabulary. • Understand the general meaning and main points of spoken language.
Word Analysis Prefixes *com-, pro-,* and *epi-*	**Content Objective** • Identify and define words using prefixes *com-, pro-* and *epi-*. **Language Objectives** • Discuss meaning of words with prefixes *com-* and *pro-*. • Develop sight vocabulary.
Grammar and Conventions Indefinite and Reflexive Pronouns	**Content Objective** • Identify and use indefinite and reflexive pronouns. **Language Objectives** • Speak and write phrases and sentences using the patterns of indefinite and reflexive pronouns. • Edit writing for pronoun agreement.
Writing Graphic Elements: Capital Letters and Line Length	**Content Objective** • Identify graphic elements. **Language Objective** • Write paragraphs using graphic elements.

Word Cards for Vocabulary Activities

cavities

combination

demonstrates

episode

profile

strict

Teacher Note: Beginning Teach two to three words. **Intermediate** Teach three to four words. **Advanced** Teach four to five words. **Advanced High** Teach all words.

Name _____

Read the story. Then **complete** the graphic organizer.
- **Write** a generalization about the students at Hugo's school.
- **Write** the information from the text that supports that generalization.

New Boy at School

Today was Hugo's first day at school. He was nervous. "Will the other students be nice or mean?" he wondered.

When he got to school, somebody showed Hugo to the office. Another student took him to all his classes. At lunch, a girl offered to share her sandwich with him.

"This isn't going to be too bad after all," Hugo thought.

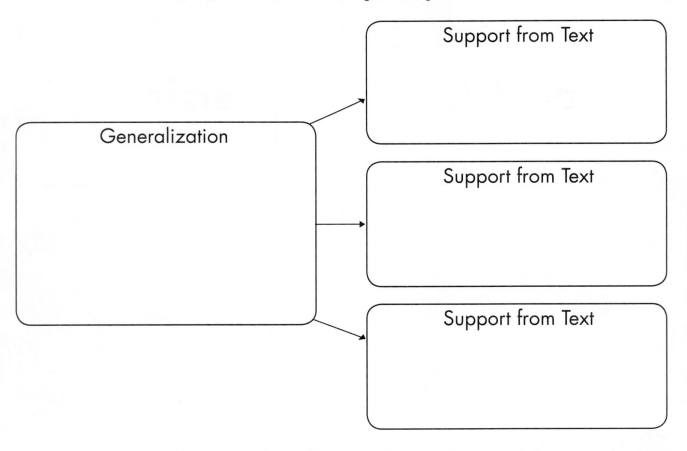

Support from Text

Generalization

Support from Text

Support from Text

Generalize

Use this lesson to supplement or replace the skill lesson on page 105c of the Teacher's Edition. Display the Skill Points (at right) and share them with students.

Teach/Model

Beginning Say: *Many students buy school lunches. This year my sister can eat school lunches or bring lunches from home. Which sentence tells a way that most students are alike?* (the first sentence) *Which sentence is a generalization?* (the first sentence) Point out that the word *many* is a clue word for recognizing a generalization.

Intermediate Write and read aloud this sentence: *Most middle school students join an after-school club or sports team.* Ask: *What makes this sentence a generalization?* (It tells a way most middle school students are alike. It uses the word *most.*)

Advanced Write: *All classrooms in our school have boards.* Ask students why this is a generalization. Have them copy the generalization and write sentences that support the generalization.

Advanced High Pair students. Have one partner write a generalization about a common classroom object. Say: *Remember to use a clue word such as* most, many, all, *or* always *in your generalization.* Have the other partner write a fact that supports the generalization. Then have partners trade roles.

Then distribute copies of Picture It! page 138.

- Tell students they will read a story about a boy's first day at a new school.
- Read the story aloud. Ask: *What do you think about the people at Hugo's new school?*
- Review the Skill Points with students.

Practice

Read aloud the directions on page 138. Have students reread the story with a partner. Then have them look at the picture and the story as they complete the graphic organizer.

Beginning Students can say what they want to write before writing words or phrases in the graphic organizer. Provide help with English words and writing.

Intermediate Students can first orally respond and then write sentences to complete the graphic organizer. Provide help with English words and writing.

Advanced Students can write sentences to complete the graphic organizer and then check their answers by silently rereading the paragraph.

Advanced High Students can write sentences to complete the graphic organizer and then orally explain how they made their generalization.

Answers for page 138: Possible answers: *Generalization:* Many students at Hugo's school are nice. *Support from Text:* Somebody showed Hugo the way to the office. Another student took him to all his classes. At lunch, a girl offered to share her sandwich.

Skill Points

✔ A **generalization** is a broad statement that applies to many examples.

✔ A generalization may not be true all the time, but it is true most of the time.

✔ A good generalization uses details and examples for support.

✔ Authors may use clue words such as *all, most, many,* and *always* to let readers know they are making generalizations.

Multilingual Summaries

The Stormi Giovanni Club

Stormi Giovanni Green has just moved to a new city. She misses her friends back in Chicago. She decides that she will be happier if she does not make new friends. She says that she will start the Stormi Giovanni Club, and she will be the only member.

Stormi meets a girl named Hannah at school. Hannah invites Stormi to sit with her and her friends at lunch. Stormi wants to sit alone.

The next day, the cafeteria is full. Stormi sits with Hannah and her friends. The new people remind Stormi of her friends in Chicago. Stormi decides that she will be happier now that she has made some new friends.

Spanish

El club Stormi Giovanni

Stormi Giovanni Green se acaba de mudar a una nueva ciudad. Extraña a sus amigos de Chicago. Ella decide que será más feliz si no hace nuevos amigos. Dice que va a crear el club Stormi Giovanni y ella será su única socia.

En la escuela, Stormi conoce a una niña llamada Hannah. Hannah invita a Stormi a sentarse con ella y con sus amigos a la hora del almuerzo. Stormi quiere sentarse sola.

Al día siguiente, la cafetería está llena. Stormi se sienta con Hannah y sus amigos. Ellos le recuerdan a sus amigos de Chicago. Stormi decide que será más feliz ahora que ha hecho algunos nuevos amigos.

Multilingual Summaries

史托蜜俱樂部

史托蜜・喬凡妮格林剛剛搬到一個新城市，她很想念以前在芝加哥的朋友，希望他們能回到她身邊。她覺得不交新朋友的話自己會比較快樂，所以她就決定不交新朋友了。她說她要成立史托蜜俱樂部，裡面唯一的會員就是她自己。

史托蜜在學校遇到一個名叫漢娜的女孩，漢娜邀請史托蜜和她們一起吃午餐，史托蜜拒絕了，她想自己吃。

隔天午餐時，餐廳竟然客滿，史托蜜只好跟漢娜還有她的朋友一起吃飯。結果，這群新同學讓史托蜜想起她在芝加哥的朋友。史托蜜覺得如果交些新朋友自己會比較快樂，所以她決定敞開心門去交新朋友了。

Câu Lạc Bộ Stormi Giovanni

Stormi Giovanni Green vừa mới dọn đến một thành phố mới. Cô bé nhớ các bạn của mình ở Chicago. Cô quyết định mình sẽ vui hơn nếu không có bạn mới. Cô nói là sẽ lập ra Câu Lạc Bộ Stormi Giovanni, và cô sẽ là thành viên duy nhất.

Stormi gặp một cô gái tên Hannah ở trường. Hannah rủ Stormi đến ngồi với mình và các bạn của cô ở buổi ăn trưa. Stormi lại muốn ngồi một mình.

Hôm sau, phòng ăn ở trường có đông người. Stormi ngồi chung với Hannah và các bạn của cô. Các người mới làm Stormi nhớ đến các bạn của mình ở Chicago. Stormi quyết định là mình sẽ vui hơn vì bây giờ cô đã có vài bạn mới.

Multilingual Summaries

스토미의 지오반니 클럽

이제 막 새 도시로 이사온 스토미 지오반니 그린은 시카고에 있는 친구들을 그리워한다. 그녀는 새 친구를 만들지 않으면 더 행복해 질 것이라고 마음먹는다. 그녀는 스토미 지오반니 클럽을 만들고 자신만이 유일한 회원이 될 것이라고 말한다.

스토미는 학교에서 한나라는 친구를 만난다. 한나는 점심시간에 자기와 자기 친구들과 함께 앉자고 스토미를 초대하지만 스토미는 혼자 앉고 싶어한다.

다음 날 학교 식당은 사람들로 가득하다. 한나와 한나 친구들과 함께 앉아 있는 스토미는 새 친구들을 보자 시카고에 있는 친구들이 생각난다. 스토미는 이제 새 친구가 있어서 더 행복해질 것이라고 생각한다.

Stormi Giovanni lub Pawg Ua Si

Stormi Giovanni Green nyuam qhuav tsiv rau lub zog tshiab. Nws nco nco nws cov phoojywg uas tseem nyob hauv lub zog Chicago. Nws txiav txim siab tias nws yuav zoo siab dua yog nws tsis ntsib cov phoojywg tshiab. Nws qhia tias nws yuav pib Stormi Giovanni lub Pawg Ua Si, thiab nws yuav yog tib tug mej zeej xwb.

Stormi ntsib Hannah, ib tug mentxhais, tom lub tsev kawm ntawv. Hannah caw Stormi los tuaj noj su nrog nws thiab nws cov phoojywg. Stormi xav zaum nws ib leeg xwb.

Hnub tom qab ntawd, hoob noj mov muaj cov neeg puv npo. Stormi zaum nrog Hannah thiab Hannah cov phoojywg. Cov neeg tshiab kom Stormi nco txog nws cov phoojywg nyob hauv Chicago. Stormi txiav txim siab tias nws yuav zoo siab dua rau qhov nws ntsib cov phoojywg tshiab.

Name _____

- **Read** *In This New Place* again.
- **Write** one or two sentences about each poem.

1. Questions

_____

_____

2. Where Am I From?

_____

_____

3. In This New Place

_____

_____

4. Cafeteria Menu, First Time Around

_____

_____

5. Supply List for a New Student

_____

_____

Family Link

Read one of these poems for your family. Ask family members to read or recite other poems that they know.

Weekly Resources Guide for English Language Learner Support

For this week's content and language objectives, see p. 143e.

Instructional Strand	Day 1	Day 2
Concept Development/Academic Language	**TEACHER'S EDITION** • Academic Language, p. DI•116 • Concept Development, p. DI•116 • Anchored Talk, pp. 136j—136–137 • Preteach Academic Vocabulary, p. 139a • Concept Talk Video **ELL HANDBOOK** • Hear It, See It, Say It, Use It, pp. xxxvi–xxxvii • ELL Poster Talk, Concept Talk, p. 143c **ELL POSTER 20** • Day 1 Activities	**TEACHER'S EDITION** • Academic Language, p. DI•116 • Concept Development, p. DI•116 • Anchored Talk, p. 140a • Concept Talk Video **ELL HANDBOOK** • ELL Poster Talk, Concept Talk, p. 143c • Concept Talk Video Routine, p. 477 **ELL POSTER 20** • Day 2 Activities
Phonics and Spelling	**TEACHER'S EDITION** • Phonics and Spelling, p. DI•120	**TEACHER'S EDITION** • Phonics and Spelling, p. DI•120
Listening Comprehension	**TEACHER'S EDITION** • Modified Read Aloud, p. DI•119 • Read Aloud, p. 137b • Concept Talk Video **ELL HANDBOOK** • Concept Talk Video Routine, p. 477	**TEACHER'S EDITION** • Modified Read Aloud, p. DI•119 • AudioText of *The Gymnast* • Concept Talk Video **ELL HANDBOOK** • AudioText CD Routine, p. 477 • Story Map A. p. 483
Reading Comprehension	**TEACHER'S EDITION** • Preteach Draw Conclusions, p. DI•121	**TEACHER'S EDITION** • Reteach Draw Conclusions, p. DI•121 • Frontloading Reading, p. DI•122 **ELL HANDBOOK** • Picture It! Skill Instruction, pp. 144–144a • Multilingual Summaries, pp. 145–147
Vocabulary **Basic and Lesson Vocabulary** **Word Analysis: Idioms**	**TEACHER'S EDITION** • Basic Vocabulary, p. DI•117 • Preteach Lesson Vocabulary, p. DI•117 • Idioms, p. DI•120 **ELL HANDBOOK** • Word Cards, p. 143 • ELL Vocabulary Routine, p. 471 **ELL POSTER 20** • Day 1 Activities	**TEACHER'S EDITION** • Basic Vocabulary, p. DI•117 • Reteach Lesson Vocabulary, p. DI•118 • Idioms, p. DI•120 **ELL HANDBOOK** • Word Cards, p. 143 • Multilingual Vocabulary List, p. 431 **ELL POSTER 20** • Day 2 Activities
Grammar and Conventions	**TEACHER'S EDITION** • Preteach Using *Who* and *Whom*, p. DI•124	**TEACHER'S EDITION** • Reteach Using *Who* and *Whom,* p. DI•124
Writing	**TEACHER'S EDITION** • Writing an Autobiographical Sketch, p. DI•125 • Writing for Tests: Autobiographical Sketch, pp. 139e–139f	**TEACHER'S EDITION** • Writing for Tests: Autobiographical Sketch, pp. 147d–147e

This symbol indicates leveled instruction to address language proficiency levels.

Day 3	Day 4	Day 5
TEACHER'S EDITION • Academic Language, p. DI•116 • Concept Development, p. DI•116 • Anchored Talk, p. 148a • Concept Talk Video **ELL HANDBOOK** • ELL Poster Talk, Concept Talk, p. 143c **ELL POSTER 20** • Day 3 Activities	**TEACHER'S EDITION** • Academic Language, p. DI•116 • Concept Development, p. DI•116 • Anchored Talk, p. 156a • Concept Talk Video **ELL HANDBOOK** • ELL Poster Talk, Concept Talk, p. 143c **ELL POSTER 20** • Day 4 Activities	**TEACHER'S EDITION** • Academic Language, p. DI•116 • Concept Development, p. DI•116 • Concept Talk Video **ELL HANDBOOK** • ELL Poster Talk, Concept Talk, p. 143c **ELL POSTER 20** • Day 5 Activities
		TEACHER'S EDITION • Phonics and Spelling, p. DI•120
ELL HANDBOOK • Phonics Transition Lesson, pp. 285, 292 **TEACHER'S EDITION** • AudioText of *The Gymnast* • Concept Talk Video **ELL HANDBOOK** • AudioText CD Routine, p. 477	**ELL HANDBOOK** • Phonics Transition Lesson, pp. 285, 292 **TEACHER'S EDITION** • Concept Talk Video	**TEACHER'S EDITION** • Concept Talk Video
TEACHER'S EDITION • Sheltered Reading, p. DI•122 **ELL HANDBOOK** • Multilingual Summaries, pp. 145–147	**TEACHER'S EDITION** • ELL/ELD Reader Guided Reading, p. DI•123 **ELL HANDBOOK** • ELL Study Guide, p. 148	**TEACHER'S EDITION** • ELL/ELD Reader Guided Reading, p. DI•123 **ELL HANDBOOK** • ELL Study Guide, p. 148
		TEACHER'S EDITION • Idioms, p. 161i
ELL HANDBOOK • High-Frequency Words Activity Bank, p. 446 **ELL POSTER 20** • Day 3 Activities	**ELL HANDBOOK** • High-Frequency Words Activity Bank, p. 446	**ELL HANDBOOK** • High-Frequency Words Activity Bank, p. 446
TEACHER'S EDITION • Grammar Jammer **ELL HANDBOOK** • Grammar Transition Lesson, pp. 362, 365–366 • Grammar Jammer Routine, p. 478	**TEACHER'S EDITION** • Grammar Jammer **ELL HANDBOOK** • Grammar Transition Lesson, pp. 362, 365–366	**TEACHER'S EDITION** • Grammar Jammer **ELL HANDBOOK** • Grammar Transition Lesson, pp. 362, 365–366
TEACHER'S EDITION • Let's Write It!, p. 154–155 • Writing for Tests: Evaluation, pp. 155a–155b	**TEACHER'S EDITION** • Writing for Tests, pp. 161d–161e	**TEACHER'S EDITION** • Writing for Tests, pp. 161p–161q

Question of the Week
Why do people try to change themselves?

Throughout the week, use the ELL Poster to help students produce and comprehend language, understand the concept, and build English vocabulary. Use the Question of the Week and other questions to help students share ideas in pairs, small groups, or the large group. Sample questions are shown, with examples of possible responses by students.

ELL Poster 20

Weekly Concept and Language Goals

• Identify ways that people try to change themselves

• Discuss why people try to change themselves

• Share personal examples of trying to change

By the end of the lesson, students should be able to talk about and write sentences about why people try to change themselves.

Daily Team Talk

Day 1	Day 2	Day 3	Day 4	Day 5
After Day 1 activities on Poster, ask questions such as *In the poster picture, what are the boys learning to do?*	After Day 2 activity on Poster, ask questions such as *In the poster picture, how are the boys changing themselves?*	After Day 3 activity on Poster, ask questions such as *How can the boy who is hesitating adapt to get better at gymnastics?*	After Day 4 activity on Poster, ask questions such as *Why do you think the boys want to change themselves by getting better at gymnastics?*	After Day 5 activity on Poster, ask questions such as *How have you tried to change yourself?*
Beginning Gymnastics. **Intermediate** They learn gymnastics. **Advanced** The boys are learning to do handstands and somersaults. **Advanced High** The boys are learning to do different things in gymnastics, such as handstands, somersaults, and cartwheels.	**Beginning** They are working. **Intermediate** They are getting stronger. **Advanced** The boys are building muscles and getting stronger. **Advanced High** Gymnastics helps to build muscles. The boys are changing themselves by getting stronger.	**Beginning** He can practice. **Intermediate** He can get better if he practices. **Advanced** The boy can practice his handstands until he is better. **Advanced High** The boy can ask his coach to help him practice handstands to get better.	**Beginning** To get strong. **Intermediate** They want to exercise and get strong. **Advanced** It is important to exercise and be healthy, so the boys do gymnastics. **Advanced High** The boys want to get better at gymnastics because it is a fun way to exercise and stay healthy and strong.	**Beginning** Learn about animals. **Intermediate** I learned about animals by reading. **Advanced** I wanted to learn more about animals, so I read some books about them. **Advanced High** I love animals and wanted to learn more about them, so I studied about animals in books and by going to the zoo.

This Week's Materials

Teacher's Edition pages 136j–165a

See the support for English language learners throughout the lesson, including ELL strategies and scaffolded activities at points of use.

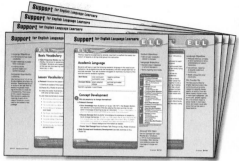

Teacher's Edition pages DI•116–DI•125

Differentiated Instruction for English language learners provides daily group activities that "frontload," or preteach, core instruction.

ELL Handbook pp. 143a–148

Find additional lesson materials that support the core lesson and the ELL instructional pages.

ELL Poster 20

ELL Reader 5.4.5

ELD Reader 5.4.5

ELD, ELL Reader Teaching Guide

Concept Literacy Reader Teaching Guide

Concept Literacy Reader

Technology

Online Teacher's Edition Use the digital version of the core Teacher's Edition for planning and instruction.

eReaders
This week's ELL and ELD Readers and Concept Literacy Reader are also available in digital format.

This Week's Content and Language Objectives by Strand

Concept Development/ Academic Language Why do people try to change themselves?	**Content Objective** • Use concept vocabulary related to changes. **Language Objectives** • Express ideas in response to art and discussion. • Derive meaning from media.
Phonics and Spelling Negative Prefixes *in-*, *im-*	**Content Objectives** • Identify prefixes in words. • Explain how negative prefixes change the meaning of words. **Language Objective** • Apply phonics and decoding skills to vocabulary.
Listening Comprehension Modified Read Aloud: "The Winner"	**Content Objective** • Monitor and adjust oral comprehension. **Language Objectives** • Discuss oral passages. • Use a graphic organizer to take notes.
Reading Comprehension Draw Conclusions	**Content Objectives** • Form opinions and make decisions about text. • Monitor and adjust comprehension. **Language Objectives** • Use inferential skills to comprehend text. • Identify text and visual support for conclusions. • Use details from text to write a conclusion.
Vocabulary Basic and Lesson Vocabulary	**Language Objectives** • Understand and use basic vocabulary. • Learn meanings of grade-level vocabulary. • Produce drawings, phrases, or short sentences to show an understanding of Lesson Vocabulary. • Understand the general meaning of spoken language.
Word Analysis Idioms	**Content Objective** • Identify idioms. **Language Objectives** • Discuss meaning of idioms. • Understand language patterns of idioms.
Grammar and Conventions Using *Who* and *Whom*	**Content Objectives** • Identify the use of *who* and *whom*. • Use *who* and *whom* correctly in sentences. **Language Objective** • Speak and write phrases and sentences with *who* or *whom*.
Writing Writing an Autobiographical Sketch	**Content Objective** • Identify the writer's personality in a text. **Language Objectives** • Narrate with increased specificity. • Write an autobiographical sketch about a personal experience.

Word Cards for Vocabulary Activities

bluish	**cartwheels**
gymnastics	**hesitation**
limelight	**skidded**
somersault	**throbbing**
wincing	

Teacher Note: Beginning Teach three to four words. **Intermediate** Teach four to six words. **Advanced** Teach six to seven words. **Advanced High** Teach all words.

Name _____

Read the paragraph, and then complete the graphic organizer.
- In the *Detail* boxes, **write** information from the paragraph.
- In the *Conclusion* box, **write** a conclusion you have made about gymnasts.

Gymnastics

Gymnastics is a difficult sport. To be a gymnast, you must be flexible. You must be able to bend over backward. You have to be able to touch the floor. But that's not all. You also need to be strong. You have to be able to hang from bars and lift your own weight. Good gymnasts have all these skills.

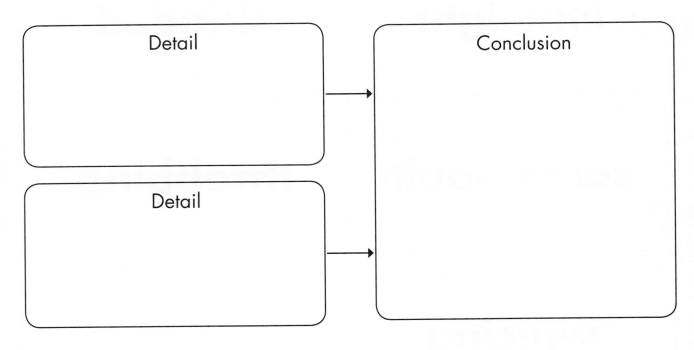

Detail

Detail

Conclusion

Draw Conclusions

Use this lesson to supplement or replace the skill lesson on page 137c of the Teacher's Edition. Display the Skill Points (at right) and share them with students.

Teach/Model

Beginning Display a photo of a runner. Provide background information about runners and ask students to name details from the photo. Ask: *What are some conclusions we can draw about this runner?* (Possible answer: She (He) has strong legs.)

Intermediate Say: *I am learning to skateboard. I practice every weekend. At first, I fell a lot. Skating is hard work. Now, I love to glide and do simple tricks.* Ask students to use details from the story to write a conclusion. (Possible answer: You never give up.)

Advanced Write: *I slide into the pool. I swim laps for thirty minutes! I am out of breath at the end.* Have students write a conclusion they can draw from the details and then explain how the details helped them make that conclusion. (Swimming is an activity that makes you tired.)

Advanced High Have students write a brief story about learning a new skill. Pair students and have them share stories. Have each partner draw a conclusion about the other partner's story.

Then distribute copies of Picture It! page 144.

- Have students look at the picture and read the title of the paragraph. Read the paragraph aloud.
- Review the Skill Points with students.
- Say: *This paragraph tells about the qualities of a good gymnast. What conclusion can you draw about the sport, based on details about people who practice it?* Discuss students' ideas.

Practice

Read aloud the directions on page 144. Have students reread the paragraph silently. Have them look at the picture and the paragraph as they complete the graphic organizer.

Beginning Students can tell what they want to write in the boxes before filling in the boxes. Provide help writing in the boxes.

Intermediate Students look for the details in the paragraph and then write sentences to fill in the graphic organizer.

Advanced Students can write sentences to fill in the graphic organizer and then check them by silently rereading the story and making any necessary corrections.

Advanced High Students can write sentences to fill in the graphic organizer and then orally explain how information from the paragraph helped them draw the conclusions.

Answers for page 144: *Details:* Gymnasts must be flexible enough to bend over backward and touch the floor. Gymnasts must be strong enough to hang from bars and lift their own weight. *Conclusion:* Possible answer: Gymnasts must work hard to be flexible and strong.

> ## Picture It!

> ### Skill Points
> ✔ When you **draw conclusions,** you combine details in the text. Together, the details tell you something that might not be actually said in the text.
> ✔ A conclusion is an idea or decision you make after combining details and your personal knowledge.

Multilingual Summaries

The Gymnast

Gary's cousin, Issac, was a gymnast. Gary was jealous of his cousin. He liked his cousin's special shoes. Gary also liked the tape around his cousin's wrists. Gary wanted to do cartwheels and back flips like his cousin.

Gary's cousin let him try on the special shoes and the tape. The shoes came off when Gary tried to do a cartwheel. Gary went home. The next day he found old slippers and put them on. He practiced doing cartwheels.

Gary got hurt when he tried to do a back flip. He landed on his head. His feet were sore and his neck hurt. Later, Gary tried to do a back flip again. He landed on his neck. Gary rested and thought about his cousin the gymnast.

Spanish

El gimnasta

Isaac, el primo de Gary, era gimnasta. Gary estaba celoso de su primo. Le gustaban las zapatillas especiales que él usaba. También le gustaba la cinta que se ponía en sus muñecas. Gary quería dar volteretas laterales y saltos mortales como su primo.

El primo de Gary lo dejó probarse las zapatillas especiales y la cinta. Las zapatillas se le salieron cuando trató de dar una voltereta lateral. Gary se fue a su casa. Al día siguiente se encontró unas zapatillas viejas y se las puso. Practicó las volteretas laterales.

Gary se lastimó cuando trató de hacer un salto mortal. Cayó de cabeza. Tenía los pies adoloridos y le dolía el cuello. Más tarde, Gary trató nuevamente de dar un salto mortal. Cayó y se torció el cuello. Gary descansó y pensó en su primo gimnasta.

Multilingual Summaries

Chinese

體操選手

　　蓋瑞的表哥—伊薩克是個體操選手。蓋瑞嫉妒他的表哥，因為他喜歡表哥那雙特別的鞋子，也喜歡表哥手腕上的包紮貼布。蓋瑞想學表哥做側手翻和後空翻。

　　蓋瑞的表哥讓他試穿鞋子、試綁包紮貼布，可是當蓋瑞試著做側手翻時，鞋子卻飛出去了。蓋瑞回家後第二天發現一雙舊拖鞋，於是穿上他們練習做側手翻。

　　蓋瑞在做後空翻的時候不小心頭先著地受傷了，他覺得腳和脖子都很痛。蓋瑞休息一下之後又想再試一次，結果這次是他的脖子先著地。蓋瑞只得躺在床上好好養傷，他覺得表哥真是個屬害的體操選手。

Vietnamese

Vận Động Viên Thể Dục

　　Anh họ của Gary, Issac, là một vận động viên thể dục. Gary ghen tỵ với anh họ của mình. Gary thích đôi giày đặc biệt của anh họ. Gary cũng thích miếng băng vải quấn ở cổ tay của người anh họ. Gary muốn lộn nhào và lộn ngược như anh họ của mình.

　　Người anh họ cho Gary thử đôi giày đặc biệt và miếng băng quấn của mình. Đôi giày tuột ra khi Gary thử lộn nhào. Gary về nhà. Ngày hôm sau cậu tìm được đôi dép cũ và mang vào. Cậu tập lộn nhào.

　　Gary bị đau khi cậu thử lộn ngược. Cậu ngã đập đầu xuống. Chân cậu ê ẩm và cổ bị đau. Sau đó Gary thử lộn ngược lần nữa. Cậu ngã đập vào cổ. Gary nghỉ ngơi và suy nghĩ về người anh họ, nhà vận động viên thể dục của mình.

Multilingual Summaries

체조 선수

게리의 사촌인 아이작은 체조 선수이다. 게리는 사촌을 부러워해서 사촌이 체조할 때 신는 특수 신발이나 손목 주변에 감는 테이프를 좋아한다. 게리는 사촌처럼 옆으로 재주넘기나 뒤로 재주넘기를 하고 싶어 한다.

게리의 사촌은 게리에게 특수 신발과 테이프를 빌려준다. 게리가 옆으로 재주넘기를 하려고 하는데 신발이 벗겨지고 게리는 집으로 돌아간다. 다음 날 게리는 낡은 슬리퍼를 찾아서 신고는 옆으로 재주넘는 연습을 한다.

게리가 뒤로 재주넘기를 하려다 머리로 착지해 다친다. 발이 따끔거리고 목도 아프다. 게리는 나중에 뒤로 재주넘기를 다시 해보지만 이번에는 목으로 착지한다. 게리는 쉬면서 체조선수인 사촌을 생각해 본다.

Tus Gymnast

Gary ib tug kwvtij Isaac, yog ib tug gymnast. Gary khib siab ntawm nws tus kwvtij. Nws nyiam nws tus kwvtij nkawm khau. Gary kuj nyiam cov ntawv nplaum nyob ib ncig nws tus kwvtij cov dab teg. Gary twb xav ua gymnastics zoo li nws tus kwvtij.

Gary tus kwvtij los pub nws siv nkawm khau, thiab cov ntawv nplaum. Thaum Gary sim ua gymnastics ces nkawm khau hle mus ub mus no. Gary tau mus tsev. Hnub tom qab ntawd nws tau nrhiav lwm nkawm khau, thiab muab lawv siv. Nws xyaum ua gymnastics.

Gary raug mob thaum nws sim ua gymnastics. Nws taubhau tsaws ua ntej nws cov kotaw. Nws cov kotaw thiab caj dab mob mob li. Ib chim Gary tau sim ua gymnastics ib zaug ntxiv. Nws caj dab raug av ua ntej nws cov kotaw. Gary zaum los so thiab xav txog nws ib tug kwvtij txawj ua gymnastics.

- **Read** *Fast as Lightning* again.
- Use the information in the book to **write** details that support the conclusion shown below.

> **Conclusion:** Betty Robinson showed the whole world that she was a champion.

Detail

Detail

Detail

Family Link
Tell family members what you learned about Betty Robinson. Ask them to tell you about another famous athlete.

Weekly Resources Guide for English Language Learner Support

For this week's content and language objectives, see p. 149e.

Instructional Strand	Day 1	Day 2
Concept Development/Academic Language	**TEACHER'S EDITION** • Academic Language, p. DI•16 • Concept Development, p. DI•16 • Anchored Talk, pp. 168j—168–169 • Preteach Academic Vocabulary, p. 171a • Concept Talk Video **ELL HANDBOOK** • Hear It, See It, Say It, Use It, pp. xxxvi–xxxvii • ELL Poster Talk, Concept Talk, p. 149c **ELL POSTER 21** • Day 1 Activities	**TEACHER'S EDITION** • Academic Language, p. DI•16 • Concept Development, p. DI•16 • Anchored Talk, p. 172a • Concept Talk Video **ELL HANDBOOK** • ELL Poster Talk, Concept Talk, p. 149c • Concept Talk Video Routine, p. 477 **ELL POSTER 21** • Day 2 Activities
Phonics and Spelling	**TEACHER'S EDITION** • Phonics and Spelling, p. DI•20	**TEACHER'S EDITION** • Phonics and Spelling, p. DI•20
Listening Comprehension	**TEACHER'S EDITION** • Modified Read Aloud, p. DI•19 • Read Aloud, p. 169b • Concept Talk Video **ELL HANDBOOK** • Concept Talk Video Routine, p. 477	**TEACHER'S EDITION** • Modified Read Aloud, p. DI•19 • AudioText of *The Skunk Ladder* • Concept Talk Video **ELL HANDBOOK** • AudioText CD Routine, p. 477 • Story Map B, p. 484
Reading Comprehension	**TEACHER'S EDITION** • Preteach Character and Plot, p. DI•21	**TEACHER'S EDITION** • Reteach Character and Plot, p. DI•21 • Frontloading Reading, p. DI•22 **ELL HANDBOOK** • Picture It! Skill Instruction, pp. 150–150a • Multilingual Summaries, pp. 151–153
Vocabulary **Basic and Lesson Vocabulary** **Word Analysis: Prefix *im-***	**TEACHER'S EDITION** • Basic Vocabulary, p. DI•17 • Preteach Lesson Vocabulary, p. DI•17 • Prefix *im-*, p. DI•20 **ELL HANDBOOK** • Word Cards, p. 149 • ELL Vocabulary Routine, p. 471 **ELL POSTER 21** • Day 1 Activities	**TEACHER'S EDITION** • Basic Vocabulary, p. DI•17 • Reteach Lesson Vocabulary, p. DI•18 • Prefix *im-*, p. DI•20 **ELL HANDBOOK** • Word Cards, p. 149 • Multilingual Vocabulary List, p. 431 **ELL POSTER 21** • Day 2 Activities
Grammar and Conventions	**TEACHER'S EDITION** • Teach Contractions and Negatives, p. DI•24	**TEACHER'S EDITION** • Reteach Contractions and Negatives, p. DI•24
Writing	**TEACHER'S EDITION** • Rhythm, p. DI•25 • Introduce Rhyming Poem, pp. 171e–171f	**TEACHER'S EDITION** • Writer's Craft: Rhyme, pp. 181d–181e

This symbol indicates leveled instruction to address language proficiency levels.

Day 3	Day 4	Day 5
TEACHER'S EDITION • Academic Language, p. DI•16 • Concept Development, p. DI•16 • Anchored Talk, p. 182a • Concept Talk Video **ELL HANDBOOK** • ELL Poster Talk, Concept Talk, p. 149c **ELL POSTER 21** • Day 3 Activities	**TEACHER'S EDITION** • Academic Language, p. DI•16 • Concept Development, p. DI•16 • Anchored Talk, p. 192a • Concept Talk Video **ELL HANDBOOK** • ELL Poster Talk, Concept Talk, p. 149c **ELL POSTER 21** • Day 4 Activities	**TEACHER'S EDITION** • Academic Language, p. DI•16 • Concept Development, p. DI•16 • Concept Talk Video **ELL HANDBOOK** • ELL Poster Talk, Concept Talk, p. 149c **ELL POSTER 21** • Day 5 Activities
ELL HANDBOOK • Phonics Transition Lesson, pp. 302, 307	**ELL HANDBOOK** • Phonics Transition Lesson, pp. 302, 307	**TEACHER'S EDITION** • Phonics and Spelling, p. DI•20
TEACHER'S EDITION • AudioText of *The Skunk Ladder* • Concept Talk Video **ELL HANDBOOK** • AudioText CD Routine, p. 477	**TEACHER'S EDITION** • Concept Talk Video	**TEACHER'S EDITION** • Concept Talk Video
TEACHER'S EDITION • Sheltered Reading, p. DI•22 **ELL HANDBOOK** • Multilingual Summaries, pp. 151–153	**TEACHER'S EDITION** • ELL/ELD Reader Guided Reading, p. DI•23 **ELL HANDBOOK** • ELL Study Guide, p. 154	**TEACHER'S EDITION** • ELL/ELD Reader Guided Reading, p. DI•23 **ELL HANDBOOK** • ELL Study Guide, p. 154
ELL HANDBOOK • High-Frequency Words Activity Bank, p. 446 **ELL POSTER 21** • Day 3 Activities	**ELL HANDBOOK** • High-Frequency Words Activity Bank, p. 446	**TEACHER'S EDITION** • Prefix *im-*, p. 197i **ELL HANDBOOK** • High-Frequency Words Activity Bank, p. 446
TEACHER'S EDITION • Grammar Jammer **ELL HANDBOOK** • Grammar Transition Lesson, pp. 328, 337 • Grammar Jammer Routine, p. 478	**TEACHER'S EDITION** • Grammar Jammer **ELL HANDBOOK** • Grammar Transition Lesson, pp. 328, 337	**TEACHER'S EDITION** • Grammar Jammer **ELL HANDBOOK** • Grammar Transition Lesson, pp. 328, 337
TEACHER'S EDITION • Let's Write It!, p. 190–191 • Writing Trait: Word Choice, pp. 191a–191b	**TEACHER'S EDITION** • Revising Strategy, pp. 197d–197e	**TEACHER'S EDITION** • Contractions and Negatives, pp. 197p–197q

Question of the Week
How can we find adventure in ordinary events?

Throughout the week, use the ELL Poster to help students produce and comprehend language, understand the concept, and build English vocabulary. Use the Question of the Week and other questions to help students share ideas in pairs, small groups, or the large group. Sample questions are shown, with examples of possible responses by students.

Weekly Concept and Language Goals

• Understand the concept of adventure

• Explain how adventures can happen

• Share examples of adventures

By the end of the lesson, students should be able to talk about and write sentences about ordinary adventures.

E L L Poster 21

Daily Team Talk

Day 1	Day 2	Day 3	Day 4	Day 5
After Day 1 activities on Poster, ask questions such as *What adventure are the students in the poster picture having?*	After Day 2 activity on Poster, ask questions such as *Who do you think planned the adventure in the poster?*	After Day 3 activity on Poster, ask questions such as *What do you think the two students in front are enjoying most about their adventure?*	After Day 4 activity on Poster, ask questions such as *What do you think is the most exciting thing about the students' adventure in the cavern?*	After Day 5 activity on Poster, ask questions such as *What adventure have you had on a day that you expected to be ordinary?*
Beginning Going on a field trip. **Intermediate** They are on a field trip in a cavern. **Advanced** The students are taking a field trip inside a cavern. **Advanced High** The students are having an adventure exploring inside a cavern.	**Beginning** The teacher. **Intermediate** The teacher planned a field trip. **Advanced** The teacher planned a field trip to the cavern, and it turned into an adventure. **Advanced High** The teacher's plan for a field trip to the cavern became an exciting adventure.	**Beginning** They like the bats. **Intermediate** I think they like the bats most. **Advanced** The boy is pointing to the bat, so I think they enjoy the bats most. **Advanced High** The students in front seem to be enjoying the bats and cave formations.	**Beginning** The bats are cool. **Intermediate** I like the old tools. **Advanced** I think the most exciting thing is the bats or the echo you can hear in a cave. **Advanced High** I think the most exciting thing about the students' adventure is that they get to see stalagmites and stalactites up close.	**Beginning** I saw people making chocolate. **Intermediate** We went to a chocolate factory. **Advanced** My class went to a chocolate factory and got to see how chocolate is made. **Advanced High** On a field trip to a huge candy factory, my classmates and I learned how chocolate is made.

This Week's Materials

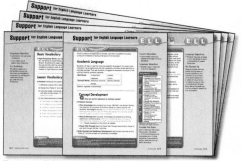

Teacher's Edition pages 168j–197q

See the support for English language learners throughout the lesson, including ELL strategies and scaffolded activities at points of use.

Teacher's Edition pages DI•16–DI•25

Differentiated Instruction for English language learners provides daily group activities that "frontload," or preteach, core instruction.

ELL Handbook pp. 149a–154

Find additional lesson materials that support the core lesson and the ELL instructional pages.

ELL Poster 21

ELL Reader 5.5.1

ELD Reader 5.5.1

Concept Literacy Reader

ELD, ELL Reader
Teaching Guide

Concept Literacy Reader
Teaching Guide

Technology

Online Teacher's Edition Use the digital version of the core Teacher's Edition for planning and instruction.

eReaders
This week's ELL and ELD Readers and Concept Literacy Reader are also available in digital format.

This Week's Content and Language Objectives by Strand

Concept Development/ Academic Language How can we find adventure in ordinary events?	**Content Objective** • Use concept vocabulary related to the idea of finding adventure. **Language Objective** • Express ideas in response to art and discussion.
Phonics and Spelling Multisyllabic Words	**Content Objective** • Identify and understand multisyllabic words. **Language Objectives** • Apply phonics and decoding skills to vocabulary. • Decode (sound out) words by chunking.
Listening Comprehension Modified Read Aloud: "Animals in the Desert"	**Content Objective** • Monitor and adjust oral comprehension. **Language Objectives** • Discuss oral passages. • Use a graphic organizer to take notes.
Reading Comprehension Character and Plot	**Content Objectives** • Identify the plot and characters of a story. • Monitor and adjust comprehension. **Language Objectives** • Give examples to identify the characters and plot. • Retell the story using visual support.
Vocabulary Basic and Lesson Vocabulary	**Language Objectives** • Understand and use basic vocabulary. • Learn meanings of grade-level vocabulary. • Produce drawings, phrases, or short sentences to show an understanding of Lesson Vocabulary.
Word Analysis Prefix *im-*	**Content Objective** • Understand the prefix *im-*. **Language Objective** • Correctly use words that contain the prefix *im-*.
Grammar and Conventions Contractions and Negatives	**Content Objective** • Use contractions and negatives correctly. **Language Objectives** • Speak using contractions and negatives. • Write sentences using contractions and negatives correctly. • Use spelling rules for contractions.
Writing Rhythm	**Content Objectives** • Identify rhythm in poetry. • Use rhymes and rhythm in writing couplets. **Language Objectives** • Write couplets with predictable rhythm. • Speak using a variety of sentence types. • Narrate with increasing specificity.

Word Cards for Vocabulary Activities

abandoned

attempt

bellow

cavern

feat

immensely

savage

Teacher Note: Beginning Teach two to three words. **Intermediate** Teach three to four words. **Advanced** Teach four to five words. **Advanced High** Teach all words.

Name _____

Read the story. Complete the character map. **Write** words that show what Sonja is like. **Write** the plot of the story.

Sonja Makes It to the Top

At last! Sonja was climbing Mount Washington. All the members of her group were excited too. But after two hours, three people quit. They were too tired. After two more hours, another person quit. Sonja was the last person. She was tired too. But she had an idea. She took off her backpack. The only thing she kept was her water bottle. Now it was easier. She had new energy. Sonja reached the top, just as she knew she would.

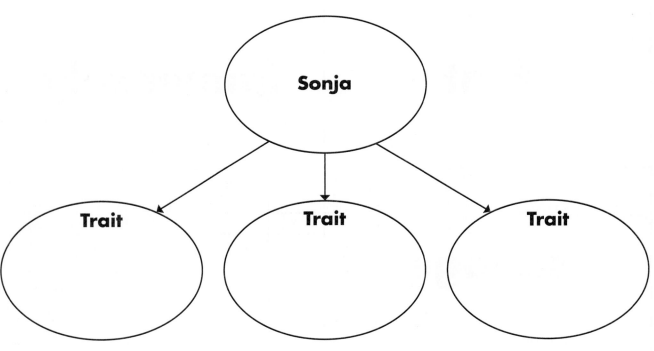

Sonja

Trait

Trait

Trait

What is the plot of the story? _____

_____

_____

Character and Plot

Use this lesson to supplement or replace the skill lesson on page 169c of the Teacher's Edition. Display the Skill Points (at right) and share them with students.

Teach/Model

Beginning Say: *Amos has to write a report for school. He misses a baseball game. He stops watching his favorite TV shows. He spends every free moment working on the report. His earns the top grade. What do these actions tell about Amos?* (He cares about school.) Ask students to retell the plot.

Intermediate Say and write on the board: *Kevin walks his dog every morning before school. Sometimes Jen finishes her homework right before class. Which sentence shows a character that is responsible?* (the first one) *What does the second sentence tell about Jen?* (She waits to finish things.)

Advanced Tell a short story: *Kai wants to go to her cousin's birthday party, but she is asked to babysit. She decides to babysit to earn money for a new bike. She is sad to miss the party but happy to get a new bike sooner than she thought.* Ask students to retell the plot. Have them explain something they know about Kai based on her actions.

Advanced High Write three character traits on the board: *kind, shy, hardworking.* Ask students to choose a character trait and write one sentence about a made-up character that shows the trait. Then pair students. Ask one partner to use his or her character to tell a short story. Have the other partner retell the plot. Then have partners trade roles.

Then distribute copies of Picture It! page 150.

- Have students look at the picture and tell what they think the story is about.
- Read the story aloud. Ask: *Who is this story about? What happens in this story?* Have students identify the characters and plot.
- Review the Skill Points with students.

Practice

Read aloud the directions on page 150. Have students reread the story with a partner. Then have them use the picture and the events in the story as they fill in the character map and answer the question.

Beginning Students can first tell what they will write in each circle before writing the traits and answering the question. Provide help with writing.

Intermediate Students can first orally answer and then complete the organizer and answer the question.

Advanced Students can complete the character map and answer the question and check their responses by rereading the story.

Advanced High Students can complete the organizer and answer the question and then explain the parts of the story that support the character traits.

Answers for page 150: *Traits:* focused, determined, smart; *Plot:* Sonja and some others were climbing to the top of Mount Washington. The other people quit, but Sonja took off her backpack and made it to the top.

> ### Skill Points
> ✔ **Characters** are the people or animals in a story. You can tell what characters are like from what they do and say.
> ✔ The **plot** of a story is what happens. It tells the important events in the story.

Multilingual Summaries

The Skunk Ladder

Eddie Muldoon and his friend try to think of something to do. Eddie's father tells them not to build anything.

Eddie and his friend dig a hole. The hole is so big, they have to use ropes to climb out. They decide to fill in the hole the next day in case a cow falls into it.

During the night, a skunk gets into the hole. The boys don't want to go into the hole with a skunk. They build a ladder for the skunk to use. Mr. Muldoon falls into the hole. The skunk climbs out. Eddie throws him back into the hole with Mr. Muldoon. Mr. Muldoon races up the skunk ladder.

Spanish

La escalera del Zorrillo

Eddie Muldoon y su amigo tratan de pensar en algo que hacer. El padre de Eddie les dice que no construyan nada.

Eddie y su amigo cavan un agujero. El agujero es tan grande, que necesitan usar cuerdas para poder salir de él. Ellos deciden tapar el agujero el día siguiente para evitar que una vaca caiga en él.

Durante la noche, un zorrillo cae dentro del agujero. Los chicos no quieren entrar al agujero con ese zorrillo. Así es que construyen una escalera para que el zorrillo pueda salir. El señor Muldoon cae dentro del agujero. El zorrillo logra salir. Eddie lo lanza otra vez al agujero con el señor Muldoon dentro y el señor Muldoon corre para salir de ese agujero.

Multilingual Summaries

Chinese

臭鼬的梯子

　　艾迪　莫爾頓和他的朋友試著找點事來做。艾迪的爸爸要他們別蓋任何東西。

　　艾迪和他的朋友挖了個洞。　那個洞很大，他們必須用繩索才能爬出來。　他們決定隔天就把洞填平，以免牛掉進去。

　　半夜裡，一隻臭鼬掉進了洞裡。　男孩們不想下到有臭鼬的洞裡。　他們做了一個梯子給臭鼬用。後來莫爾頓先生也掉到了洞裡。　臭鼬爬了出來。艾迪又把臭鼬扔回洞裡去，此時莫爾頓先生也在洞裡。莫爾頓先生飛快地衝上了為臭鼬做的梯子。

Vietnamese

Cái Thang cho Con Chồn Hôi

　　Eddie Muldoon và bạn của nó đang tính xem có việc gì làm. Cha của Eddie không muốn chúng toan tính xây cất gì hết.

　　Eddie và bạn của nó đi đào một cái lổ. Chúng đào cái lổ quá lớn đến đổi phải dùng dây để trèo lên. Chúng định ngày hôm sau sẽ lấp cái lổ lại để con bò khỏi bị rớt xuống.

　　Tối hôm đó, có một con chồn hôi bị rớt xuống lổ. Hai em này không muốn đi xuống cái lổ có con chồn trong đó. Vì vậy nên chúng làm một cái thang cho con chồn leo lên. Tình cờ ông Muldoon bị rớt xuống lổ. Lúc đó thì con chồn hôi đã leo được ra ngoài. Eddie mới phá bắt con chồn thảy vào cái lổ có ông Muldoon đang ở trong đó. Ông Muldoon hoảng hốt trèo nhanh lên cái thang của con chồn.

Multilingual Summaries

Korean

스컹크 사다리

에디 멀둔과 그의 친구가 뭘 할 지 생각한다. 에디의 아버지가 아무 것도 만들지 말라고 한다.

에디와 친구는 구멍을 판다. 구멍이 아주 커서 빠져 나오기 위해 밧줄을 써야 한다. 그들은 소가 떨어질 것을 염려하여 다음날 구멍을 메우기로 한다.

밤중에 스컹크 한 마리가 구멍에 들어간다. 아이들은 스컹크와 함께 구멍에 들어가고 싶지 않다. 그들은 스컹크가 쓸 사다리를 만든다. 멀둔 씨가 구멍에 빠진다. 스컹크는 밖으로 나온다. 에디가 멀둔 씨가 있는 구멍 속으로 스컹크를 다시 빠뜨린다. 멀둔 씨는 스컹크 사다리를 두고 경쟁을 한다.

Hmong

Skunk Tus Ntaiv

Eddie Muldoon thiab nws tus phooj ywg xav tswv yim saib yuav ua yam khoom dab tsi. Eddie txiv hais rau nkawv hais tias kom nkawv tsis txhob ua ib yam dab tsi li.

Eddie thiab nws tus phooj ywg khawb ib lub qhov. Lub qhov mas loj kawg lis, nkawv yuav tsum tau siv hlua thiaj nce tau tawm. Nkawv txiav txim siab phaus lub qhov ntawv rau taig kis vim tias tsam nyuj ho los poob rau.

Nyob rau hmo ntawv, Tus skunk nkag los rau lub qhov. Ob tug me nyuam tub ntawv tsis kam mus rau hauv lub qhov nrog rau tus skunk. Nkawv ua tau ib tug ntaiv rau tus skunk siv. Mr. Muldoon poob rau hauv lub qhov lawm. Tus skunk nce tawm los lawm. Eddie muab tus skunk pov rov qab rau hauv lub qhov nrog rau Mr. Muldoon. Mr. Muldoon muab tus skunk tus ntaiv tshum tawm los.

Name _____

- **Read** *A Backyard Adventure* again.
- Use the information in the book to **answer** the questions.

pages 2–3

1. How does Matt feel about his younger sister Amanda?

_____

_____

2. Why do you think that he feels that way?

_____

_____

pages 4–6

3. What does Amanda do to protect the nest from the cat?

_____

4. How do Amanda and Matt help the mother bird?

_____

_____

pages 7–8

5. How else do you know that Matt and Amanda want to take care of the birds?

_____

6. Why do you think that the author feels that life in the country can be exciting?

_____

Family Link

Ask family members if they have ever watched wild birds and their babies. Have them describe how the baby birds were taken care of by their parents.

Weekly Resources Guide for English Language Learner Support

For this week's content and language objectives, see p. 155e.

Instructional Strand	Day 1	Day 2
Concept Development/Academic Language	TEACHER'S EDITION • Academic Language, p. DI•41 • Concept Development, p. DI•41 • Anchored Talk, pp. 198j—198–199 • Preteach Academic Vocabulary, p. 201a • Concept Talk Video ELL HANDBOOK • Hear It, See It, Say It, Use It, pp. xxxvi–xxxvii • ELL Poster Talk, Concept Talk, p. 155c ELL POSTER 22 • Day 1 Activities	TEACHER'S EDITION • Academic Language, p. DI•41 • Concept Development, p. DI•41 • Anchored Talk, p. 202a • Concept Talk Video ELL HANDBOOK • ELL Poster Talk, Concept Talk, p. 155c • Concept Talk Video Routine, p. 477 ELL POSTER 22 • Day 2 Activities
Phonics and Spelling	TEACHER'S EDITION • Phonics and Spelling, p. DI•45	TEACHER'S EDITION • Phonics and Spelling, p. DI•45
Listening Comprehension	TEACHER'S EDITION • Modified Read Aloud, p. DI•44 • Read Aloud, p. 199b • Concept Talk Video ELL HANDBOOK • Concept Talk Video Routine, p. 477	TEACHER'S EDITION • Modified Read Aloud, p. DI•44 • AudioText of *The Unsinkable Wreck of the R.M.S.* Titanic • Concept Talk Video ELL HANDBOOK • AudioText CD Routine, p. 477 • Time Line, p. 491
Reading Comprehension	TEACHER'S EDITION • Preteach Graphic Sources, p. DI•46	TEACHER'S EDITION • Reteach Graphic Sources, p. DI•46 • Frontloading Reading, p. DI•47 ELL HANDBOOK • Picture It! Skill Instruction, pp. 156–156a • Multilingual Summaries, pp. 157–159
Vocabulary **Basic and Lesson Vocabulary** **Word Analysis: Acronyms**	TEACHER'S EDITION • Basic Vocabulary, p. DI•42 • Preteach Lesson Vocabulary, p. DI•42 • Acronyms, p. DI•45 ELL HANDBOOK • Word Cards, p. 155 • ELL Vocabulary Routine, p. 471 ELL POSTER 22 • Day 1 Activities	TEACHER'S EDITION • Basic Vocabulary, p. DI•42 • Reteach Lesson Vocabulary, p. DI•43 • Acronyms, p. DI•45 ELL HANDBOOK • Word Cards, p. 155 • Multilingual Vocabulary List, p. 431 ELL POSTER 22 • Day 2 Activities
Grammar and Conventions	TEACHER'S EDITION • Teach Adjectives and Articles, p. DI•49	TEACHER'S EDITION • Reteach Adjectives and Articles, p. DI•49
Writing	TEACHER'S EDITION • Paraphrase, p. DI•50 • Introduce Notes, pp. 201e–201f	TEACHER'S EDITION • Writing Trait: Organization, pp. 211d–211e

The Unsinkable Wreck of the R.M.S. Titanic

This symbol indicates leveled instruction to address language proficiency levels.

Day 3	Day 4	Day 5
TEACHER'S EDITION • Academic Language, p. DI•41 • Concept Development, p. DI•41 • Anchored Talk, p. 212a • Concept Talk Video **ELL HANDBOOK** • ELL Poster Talk, Concept Talk, p. 155c **ELL POSTER 22** • Day 3 Activities	**TEACHER'S EDITION** • Academic Language, p. DI•41 • Concept Development, p. DI•41 • Anchored Talk, p. 220a • Concept Talk Video **ELL HANDBOOK** • ELL Poster Talk, Concept Talk, p. 155c **ELL POSTER 22** • Day 4 Activities	**TEACHER'S EDITION** • Academic Language, p. DI•41 • Concept Development, p. DI•41 • Concept Talk Video **ELL HANDBOOK** • ELL Poster Talk, Concept Talk, p. 155c **ELL POSTER 22** • Day 5 Activities
		TEACHER'S EDITION • Phonics and Spelling, p. DI•45
ELL HANDBOOK • Phonics Transition Lesson, pp. 301, 306	**ELL HANDBOOK** • Phonics Transition Lesson, pp. 301, 306	
TEACHER'S EDITION • AudioText of *The Unsinkable Wreck of the R.M.S. Titanic* • Concept Talk Video **ELL HANDBOOK** • AudioText CD Routine, p. 477	**TEACHER'S EDITION** • Concept Talk Video	**TEACHER'S EDITION** • Concept Talk Video
TEACHER'S EDITION • Sheltered Reading, p. DI•47 **ELL HANDBOOK** • Multilingual Summaries, pp. 157–159	**TEACHER'S EDITION** • ELL/ELD Reader Guided Reading, p. DI•48 **ELL HANDBOOK** • ELL Study Guide, p. 160	**TEACHER'S EDITION** • ELL/ELD Reader Guided Reading, p. DI•48 **ELL HANDBOOK** • ELL Study Guide, p. 160
		TEACHER'S EDITION • Acronyms, p. 227i
ELL HANDBOOK • High-Frequency Words Activity Bank, p. 446 **ELL POSTER 22** • Day 3 Activities	**ELL HANDBOOK** • High-Frequency Words Activity Bank, p. 446	**ELL HANDBOOK** • High-Frequency Words Activity Bank, p. 446
TEACHER'S EDITION • Grammar Jammer **ELL HANDBOOK** • Grammar Transition Lesson, pp. 370, 373–374 • Grammar Jammer Routine, p. 478	**TEACHER'S EDITION** • Grammar Jammer **ELL HANDBOOK** • Grammar Transition Lesson, pp. 370, 373–374	**TEACHER'S EDITION** • Grammar Jammer **ELL HANDBOOK** • Grammar Transition Lesson, pp. 370, 373–374
TEACHER'S EDITION • Let's Write It!, p. 218–219 • Writing Trait: Focus/Ideas, pp. 219a–219b	**TEACHER'S EDITION** • Revising Strategy, pp. 227d–227e	**TEACHER'S EDITION** • Adjectives and Articles, pp. 227p–227q

Question of the Week
How does technology help adventurers reach new places?

Throughout the week, use the ELL Poster to help students produce and comprehend language, understand the concept, and build English vocabulary. Use the Question of the Week and other questions to help students share ideas in pairs, small groups, or the large group. Sample questions are shown, with examples of possible responses by students.

ELL Poster 22

Weekly Concept and Language Goals

• Identify different kinds of technology

• Tell how scientists use technology

• Discuss how technology can help people explore new places

By the end of the lesson, students should be able to talk about and write sentences about how technology helps to reach new places.

Daily Team Talk

Day 1	Day 2	Day 3	Day 4	Day 5
After Day 1 activities on Poster, ask questions such as	After Day 2 activity on Poster, ask questions such as	After Day 3 activity on Poster, ask questions such as	After Day 4 activity on Poster, ask questions such as	After Day 5 activity on Poster, ask questions such as
What technology can you see in the poster picture?	*How do people control the probe in the poster picture if they cannot get inside it?*	*The scientists on the boat are using sonar to map the ocean floor. What is sonar?*	*How does sonar help the scientists find debris from a shipwreck?*	*How does technology help the scientists explore?*
Beginning A probe. **Intermediate** There is a probe that goes underwater. **Advanced** The scientists are using an underwater probe to find the ocean floor. **Advanced High** The scientists are using an underwater probe that uses sonar to map the ocean floor. There is also a building with a satellite dish in the background.	**Beginning** People run it. **Intermediate** People on a boat control it. **Advanced** A probe is attached by a rope to a boat. People on the boat operate it. **Advanced High** The probe is attached by a tether to the boat, where scientists operate it.	**Beginning** It is sound waves. **Intermediate** Sonar uses sound waves. **Advanced** Sonar uses sound waves bouncing off the ocean floor. **Advanced High** Sonar is a system that bounces sound waves off the ocean floor. Scientists use the sound waves to determine the distance to the ocean floor.	**Beginning** Sound waves hit it. **Intermediate** Sound waves hit the debris. **Advanced** Sonar sends sound waves to the ocean floor. They hit the debris first. **Advanced High** The scientists use sonar to send sound waves toward the ocean floor, but they hit the shipwreck debris first.	**Beginning** They can see underwater. **Intermediate** It helps them find things underwater. **Advanced** Technology helps the scientists find the shipwreck underwater. **Advanced High** Without technology, such as sonar and a probe, the scientists would have had to search a lot longer to find the shipwreck debris.

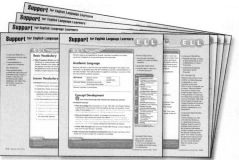

Teacher's Edition pages 198j–227q

See the support for English language learners throughout the lesson, including ELL strategies and scaffolded activities at points of use.

Teacher's Edition pages DI•41–DI•50

Differentiated Instruction for English language learners provides daily group activities that "frontload," or preteach, core instruction.

ELL Handbook pp. 155a–160

Find additional lesson materials that support the core lesson and the ELL instructional pages.

ELL Poster 22

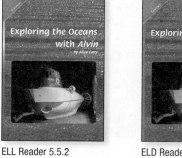

ELL Reader 5.5.2

ELD Reader 5.5.2

Concept Literacy Reader

ELD, ELL Reader Teaching Guide

Concept Literacy Reader Teaching Guide

Technology

Online Teacher's Edition Use the digital version of the core Teacher's Edition for planning and instruction.

eReaders
This week's ELL and ELD Readers and Concept Literacy Reader are also available in digital format.

This Week's Content and Language Objectives by Strand

Concept Development/ Academic Language How does technology help adventurers reach new places?	**Content Objective** • Use concept vocabulary related to the idea of finding adventure. **Language Objective** • Express ideas in response to art and discussion.
Phonics and Spelling Related Words	**Content Objective** • Understand related words. **Language Objective** • Apply phonics and decoding skills to vocabulary.
Listening Comprehension Modified Read Aloud: "Inside the Treasure Chest"	**Content Objective** • Monitor and adjust oral comprehension. **Language Objectives** • Discuss oral passages. • Use a graphic organizer to take notes.
Reading Comprehension Graphic Sources	**Content Objectives** • Interpret information from graphic sources. • Take notes to build comprehension. • Monitor and adjust comprehension. **Language Objectives** • Discuss the graphic sources in a story. • Cite content from graphic sources.
Vocabulary Basic and Lesson Vocabulary	**Language Objectives** • Understand and use basic vocabulary. • Learn meanings of grade-level vocabulary. • Produce drawings, phrases, or short sentences to show understanding of Lesson Vocabulary. • Understand the general meaning of spoken language.
Word Analysis Acronyms	**Content Objective** • Understand acronyms. **Language Objective** • Correctly use acronyms.
Grammar and Conventions Adjectives and Articles	**Content Objective** • Use adjectives and articles correctly. **Language Objectives** • Speak using adjectives and articles correctly. • Write sentences using adjectives and articles correctly.
Writing Paraphrase	**Content Objectives** • Paraphrase written material. • Use paraphrasing techniques in note taking. **Language Objectives** • Paraphrase spoken language. • Share feedback for editing and revising.

Word Cards for Vocabulary Activities

cramped

debris

interior

ooze

robotic

sediment

sonar

Teacher Note: Beginning Teach two to three words. **Intermediate** Teach three to four words. **Advanced** Teach four to five words. **Advanced High** Teach all words.

Name _____

Look at the picture. **Read** the story.

- **Number** the three locations the ship visited. Start with the beginning of the trip.

- **Draw** a line to show the path on the map.

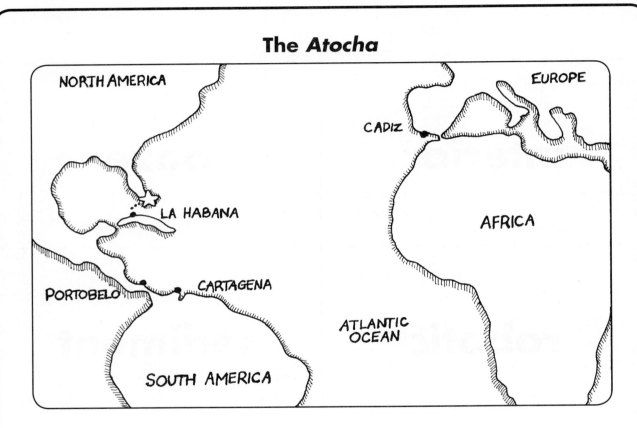

The *Atocha*

NORTH AMERICA

EUROPE

CADIZ

LA HABANA

AFRICA

PORTOBELO

CARTAGENA

ATLANTIC OCEAN

SOUTH AMERICA

The *Atocha* was a Spanish treasure ship. On March 23, 1622, it left Cádiz, Spain. It went to Cartagena, South America, to pick up gold, silver, and other treasures. Then it stopped in La Habana, Cuba. On September 5, the *Atocha* started its trip back to Spain. A hurricane crossed its path and sunk the ship. The shipwreck was lost until 1985. Searchers found the ship and a fortune in gold and silver.

Graphic Sources

Use this lesson to supplement or replace the skill lesson on page 199c of the Teacher's Edition. Display the Skill Points (at right) and share them with students.

Teach/Model

Beginning Draw a compass on the board. Read a description of a compass from a children's dictionary or encyclopedia. Ask: *How does my drawing help you understand the text?* (It shows what a compass looks like. It makes the text clearer.)

Intermediate Tell students how to get from the classroom to the school's library or media center. Ask: *What is a good way to show this information?* (make a map of the school) Have students make a map of the school and draw a line that shows how they can get from the classroom to the school's library or media center.

Advanced Discuss the parts of a boat, including sail, anchor, bow, and stern. Talk about where each is located on a boat. Ask: *What is a good way to show this information?* Have students draw a diagram of a boat and label its parts. Ask them why the graphic source helps them understand the information better.

Advanced High Display a map of the United States. Ask: *Which places have you visited?* Have each student write his or her name on a sticky note and then place it on the map. Ask: *How does this map now help you understand the information? What other information can we learn from the notes on the map?* Have students write their responses.

Then distribute copies of Picture It! page 156.

- Point to the map. Ask students to tell what the map shows.
- Read the paragraph aloud. Ask: *What do the dots mean?* (They show where the cities are located.) Tell students to use the map to help them track where the ship travels.
- Review the Skill Points with students.

Practice

Read aloud the directions on page 156. Then reread the paragraph aloud. Then have students use the events in the paragraph as they complete the map.

Beginning Students can point to each location on the page and say what they want to write near each before writing the numbers. Provide help with labeling and drawing the line.

Intermediate Students can first orally answer before writing numbers and drawing a line connecting the cities in order.

Advanced Students can write the numbers and draw the line and then check their answers by comparing them with a partner's.

Advanced High Students can write the numbers and draw the line and then explain how the map makes the paragraph easier to understand.

Answers for page 156: Line begins at 1. Cádiz, Spain; proceeds to 2. Cartagena, South America; continues to 3. La Habana, Cuba; and ends somewhere in the Atlantic Ocean.

> ### Skill Points
> - ✔ Pictures, diagrams, maps, and time lines are **graphic sources.**
> - ✔ Preview graphic sources before you read. Use the graphic sources to predict what the text will be about.

Multilingual Summaries

The Unsinkable Wreck of the R.M.S. *Titanic*

Scientists went underwater to study the wreck of the *Titanic*. They traveled in a submarine called *Alvin*. The *Titanic* was the largest, finest ship ever built. On its first trip to sea in 1912, it hit an iceberg and sank. There were not enough lifeboats. There were 2,200 people on the ship; 1,500 of them drowned.

The scientists in *Alvin* were the first to see the *Titanic* in more than seventy years. *Alvin* moved past the front part of the ship. One of the crew remembered the story of two little boys who survived the sinking.

The crew saw debris on the ocean floor. The ship broke into two parts when it sank. Objects fell everywhere when it split. The crew returned to the surface after only two hours. They will go back again to study the wreck.

Spanish

Los restos del *Titanic* que nunca se hunden

Los científicos fueron debajo del agua para estudiar los restos del *Titanic*. Viajaron en un submarino llamado *Alvin*. El *Titanic* fue el barco más grande y elegante que se ha construido. En su primer viaje por mar, en 1912, chocó contra un iceberg y se hundió. No había suficientes botes salvavidas. Había 2,200 personas en el barco. Se ahogaron 1,500 de ellas.

Los científicos en el *Alvin* fueron los primeros en ver el *Titanic* después de más de setenta años. Uno de los tripulantes recordó la historia de dos niños que sobrevivieron el hundimiento.

Los tripulantes vieron escombros en el fondo del océano. El barco se partió en dos partes cuando se hundió. Los objetos cayeron en todas direcciones cuando éstas se separaron. Los tripulantes volvieron a la superficie después de sólo dos horas. Ellos regresarán de nuevo para estudiar los restos.

Multilingual Summaries

泰坦尼克號的殘骸

科學家乘坐阿爾文號潛艇，到達深海研究泰坦尼克號的殘骸。泰坦尼克號是歷史上最大、最豪華的輪船。可是在1912年第一次出海時，就撞上了冰山永遠沈入海底。由於沒有足夠的救生艇，船上2,200乘客中有1,500人不幸溺斃了。

科學家乘坐阿爾文號，七十多年來首次看到泰坦尼克。潛艇駛過沈船前端時，一名考察隊隊員清楚地記得，當年兩個小男孩逃生的故事。

他們還看見海底有許多碎片。泰坦尼克沈沒時斷成了兩段，因此在裂開時有許多東西散落到外面。科學家結束了兩小時的考察，回到海面，將來還會再回來仔細研究。

Xác Chiếc Tàu Không Chìm
R.M.S *Titanic*

Các nhà khoa học đã lặn xuống nước để nghiên cứu xác chiếc tàu Titanic. Họ du hành trong một chiếc tàu ngầm tên Alvin. Tàu Titanic là chiếc tàu lớn nhất, đẹp nhất được xây từ trước đến nay. Trong chuyến khởi hành ra biển đầu tiên vào năm 1912, tàu đụng một tảng băng và bị chìm. Không có đủ thuyền cứu đắm trên tàu. Có 2,200 người ở trên tàu. 1,500 người trong số họ bị chết đuối.

Các nhà khoa học trên chiếc Alvin là những người đầu tiên được thấy chiếc Titanic trong hơn bảy mươi năm. Alvin đi qua phần phía trước của chiếc tàu. Một người trong đoàn nhớ lại câu chuyện về hai cậu bé sống sót qua kỳ đắm tàu.

Những người này thấy các mảnh vụn dưới đáy đại dương. Chiếc tàu gẫy ra làm đôi khi bị chìm. Các đồ vật rơi rớt khắp nơi khi chiếc tàu vỡ. Chỉ sau hai giờ đồng hồ những người này trở lên mặt nước. Họ sẽ trở xuống lần nữa để nghiên cứu xác tàu.

Multilingual Summaries

침몰하지 않는 R.M.S. 타이타닉 호의 잔해

과학자들은 타이타닉 호의 잔해를 연구하기 위해 앨빈이라는 잠수정을 타고 해저로 들어갔다. 타이타닉 호는 사상 최대 크기의 가장 훌륭한 선박이었는데 1912년 첫 항해 때 빙산에 부딪혀 가라앉게 되었다. 배에는 구명보트가 충분하지 않았고 배에 탄 2,200명 중 1,500명이 익사했다.

사고 후 70년도 더 지나서 잠수정 앨빈 호를 탄 과학자들이 최초로 타이타닉 호를 조사했다. 앨빈 호는 타이타닉 호의 앞부분을 지나 이동했다. 선원 중 한 명이 침몰에서 살아남은 어린 두 남자아이에 대한 이야기를 기억해냈다.

선원들은 바다 밑바닥에서 파편들을 발견했다. 타이타닉 호가 가라앉을 때 두 부분으로 부러졌고 그 때 배에 있는 물건들이 사방으로 떨어진 것이었다. 선원들은 두 시간 동안만 탐색 한 후 수면 위로 돌아왔다. 그들은 잔해를 연구하기 위해 바다 밑으로 되돌아갈 것이다.

Kev Puas Tsuaj ntawm lub RMS Titanic uas Tsis Txawj Tog

Cov tub kawm txog dej tau mus hauv qab nruab deg mus kawm txog kev puas tsuaj ntawm lub nkoj Titanic. Lawv tau caij ib lub nkoj submarine hu uas Alvin uas yog ib lub mus rau hauv qab nrug dej. Lub Titanic thaum ub yog lub nkoj loj tshaj plaws thiab zoo tshaj plaws uas tau txua los. Thawj zaug luag tau caij lub nkoj ntawd nyob rau xyoo ib txhiab cuaj pua kaum ob, nws tau mus tsoo raug ib thooj nas kuab loj thiab tau tog lawm. Tsis muaj cov nkoj me cawm neeg txaus. Ob phav ob puas leej neeg caij nkoj. Ib txhiab tsib puas leej tau poob dej tuag lawm.

Cov tub kawm txog dej uas tau caij Alvin yog thawj cov uas tau pom lub Titanic tau muaj li xya caum xyoo no. Alvin mus dhau thawj feem ua ntej ntawm lub nkoj. Lawv ib tug nco qab txog zaj dab neeg piav txog ob tug menyuam tub uas nyob dhau lub nkoj tog.

Pab tub kawm ntawd pom khib nyiab nyob puas hauv qab thus dej. Lub nkoj tau tu nrho ua ob ya thaum nws tog ntawd. Khoom ub khoom no poob qhov txhia qhov chaws thaum lub nkoj tu nrho. Pab tub kawm rov qab mus rau saum nplaim dej tom qab ob xuab moo. Lawv yuav rov qab mus kawm txog kev puas tsuaj ntawd ntxiv.

Name ______________________

Exploring the Oceans with *Alvin*

- **Read** *Exploring the Oceans with* Alvin again.
- **Find** details that support the conclusion shown below.
- **Write** them in the *Supporting Detail* boxes.

Conclusion: The submersible *Alvin* has helped scientists study the oceans.

Supporting Detail

Supporting Detail

Supporting Detail

Family Link

Tell your family members what you learned about *Alvin*. Ask them to tell you what they know about the ocean.

Weekly Resources Guide for English Language Learner Support

For this week's content and language objectives, see p. 161e.

Instructional Strand	Day 1	Day 2
Concept Development/Academic Language	**TEACHER'S EDITION** • Academic Language, p. DI•66 • Concept Development, p. DI•66 • Anchored Talk, pp. 228j—228–229 • Preteach Academic Vocabulary, p. 231a • Concept Talk Video **ELL HANDBOOK** • Hear It, See It, Say It, Use It, pp. xxxvi–xxxvii • ELL Poster Talk, Concept Talk, p. 161c **ELL POSTER 23** • Day 1 Activities	**TEACHER'S EDITION** • Academic Language, p. DI•66 • Concept Development, p. DI•66 • Anchored Talk, p. 232a • Concept Talk Video **ELL HANDBOOK** • ELL Poster Talk, Concept Talk, p. 161c • Concept Talk Video Routine, p. 477 **ELL POSTER 23** • Day 2 Activities
Phonics and Spelling	**TEACHER'S EDITION** • Phonics and Spelling, p. DI•70	**TEACHER'S EDITION** • Phonics and Spelling, p. DI•70
Listening Comprehension	**TEACHER'S EDITION** • Modified Read Aloud, p. DI•69 • Read Aloud, p. 229b • Concept Talk Video **ELL HANDBOOK** • Concept Talk Video Routine, p. 477	**TEACHER'S EDITION** • Modified Read Aloud, p. DI•69 • AudioText of *Talk with an Astronaut* • Concept Talk Video **ELL HANDBOOK** • AudioText CD Routine, p. 477 • Three Column Chart, p. 494
Reading Comprehension	**TEACHER'S EDITION** • Preteach Author's Purpose, p. DI•71	**TEACHER'S EDITION** • Reteach Author's Purpose, p. DI•71 • Frontloading Reading, p. DI•72 **ELL HANDBOOK** • Picture It! Skill Instruction, pp. 162–162a • Multilingual Summaries, pp. 163–165
Vocabulary **Basic and Lesson Vocabulary** **Word Analysis: Greek and Latin Roots**	**TEACHER'S EDITION** • Basic Vocabulary, p. DI•67 • Preteach Lesson Vocabulary, p. DI•67 • Greek and Latin Roots, p. DI•70 **ELL HANDBOOK** • Word Cards, p. 161 • ELL Vocabulary Routine, p. 471 **ELL POSTER 23** • Day 1 Activities	**TEACHER'S EDITION** • Basic Vocabulary, p. DI•67 • Reteach Lesson Vocabulary, p. DI•68 • Greek and Latin Roots, p. DI•70 **ELL HANDBOOK** • Word Cards, p. 161 • Multilingual Vocabulary List, p. 431 **ELL POSTER 23** • Day 2 Activities
Grammar and Conventions	**TEACHER'S EDITION** • Preteach *This, That, These,* and *Those,* p. DI•74	**TEACHER'S EDITION** • Reteach *This, That, These,* and *Those,* p. DI•74
Writing	**TEACHER'S EDITION** • Writing with Quotations, p. DI•75 • Introduce Biographical Sketch, pp. 231e–231f	**TEACHER'S EDITION** • Writing Trait: Focus/Ideas, pp. 241d–241e

This symbol indicates leveled instruction to address language proficiency levels.

Day 3	Day 4	Day 5
TEACHER'S EDITION • Academic Language, p. DI•66 • Concept Development, p. DI•66 • Anchored Talk, p. 242a • Concept Talk Video **ELL HANDBOOK** • ELL Poster Talk, Concept Talk, p. 161c **ELL POSTER 23** • Day 3 Activities	**TEACHER'S EDITION** • Academic Language, p. DI•66 • Concept Development, p. DI•66 • Anchored Talk, p. 250a • Concept Talk Video **ELL HANDBOOK** • ELL Poster Talk, Concept Talk, p. 161c **ELL POSTER 23** • Day 4 Activities	**TEACHER'S EDITION** • Academic Language, p. DI•66 • Concept Development, p. DI•66 • Concept Talk Video **ELL HANDBOOK** • ELL Poster Talk, Concept Talk, p. 161c **ELL POSTER 23** • Day 5 Activities
		TEACHER'S EDITION • Phonics and Spelling, p. DI•70
ELL HANDBOOK • Phonics Transition Lesson, pp. 299, 304	**ELL HANDBOOK** • Phonics Transition Lesson, pp. 299, 304	
TEACHER'S EDITION • AudioText of *Talk with an Astronaut* • Concept Talk Video **ELL HANDBOOK** • AudioText CD Routine, p. 477	**TEACHER'S EDITION** • Concept Talk Video	**TEACHER'S EDITION** • Concept Talk Video
TEACHER'S EDITION • Sheltered Reading, p. DI•72 **ELL HANDBOOK** • Multilingual Summaries, pp. 163–165	**TEACHER'S EDITION** • ELL/ELD Reader Guided Reading, p. DI•73 **ELL HANDBOOK** • ELL Study Guide, p. 166	**TEACHER'S EDITION** • ELL/ELD Reader Guided Reading, p. DI•73 **ELL HANDBOOK** • ELL Study Guide, p. 166
		TEACHER'S EDITION • Greek and Latin Roots, p. 255i
ELL HANDBOOK • High-Frequency Words Activity Bank, p. 446 **ELL POSTER 23** • Day 3 Activities	**ELL HANDBOOK** • High-Frequency Words Activity Bank, p. 446	**ELL HANDBOOK** • High-Frequency Words Activity Bank, p. 446
TEACHER'S EDITION • Grammar Jammer **ELL HANDBOOK** • Grammar Transition Lesson, pp. 371, 376 • Grammar Jammer Routine, p. 478	**TEACHER'S EDITION** • Grammar Jammer **ELL HANDBOOK** • Grammar Transition Lesson, pp. 371, 376	**TEACHER'S EDITION** • Grammar Jammer **ELL HANDBOOK** • Grammar Transition Lesson, pp. 371, 376
TEACHER'S EDITION • Let's Write It!, p. 248–249 • Writing Trait: Sentences, pp. 249a–249b	**TEACHER'S EDITION** • Revising Strategy, pp. 255d–255e	**TEACHER'S EDITION** • *This, these, that,* and *those,* pp. 255p–255q

Question of the Week
What is life like for an astronaut?

Throughout the week, use the ELL Poster to help students produce and comprehend language, understand the concept, and build English vocabulary. Use the Question of the Week and other questions to help students share ideas in pairs, small groups, or the large group. Sample questions are shown, with examples of possible responses by students.

ELL Poster 23

Weekly Concept and Language Goals

• Share details about space

• Explain how life is different in space

• Name specific differences between Earth and space

By the end of the lesson, students should be able to talk about and write sentences about life in space.

Daily Team Talk

Day 1	Day 2	Day 3	Day 4	Day 5
After Day 1 activities on Poster, ask questions such as *Where are the astronauts in the poster picture? How do you know?*	After Day 2 activity on Poster, ask questions such as *In the poster picture, what is the astronaut on the left doing?*	After Day 3 activity on Poster, ask questions such as *How would life inside the spacecraft be different if the astronauts were in space?*	After Day 4 activity on Poster, ask questions such as *In* Talk with an Astronaut, *how does Ellen Ochoa describe eating in space?*	After Day 5 activity on Poster, ask questions such as *In* Talk with an Astronaut, *how does Ellen Ochoa describe sleeping in space?*
Beginning They are on Earth. **Intermediate** They are at a training center. **Advanced** They are in a flight simulator. I know because there is an astronaut outside. **Advanced High** These astronauts are in a flight simulator in Texas. I can tell they are not in space because one astronaut is standing outside the spacecraft.	**Beginning** Moving a robot. **Intermediate** He is controlling a robot. **Advanced** The astronaut is controlling a robot outside the spacecraft. **Advanced High** The astronaut is operating a robot outside the flight simulator.	**Beginning** They float. **Intermediate** There is no gravity. **Advanced** There would be no gravity in space. **Advanced High** There would be no gravity in space, so the astronauts would float.	**Beginning** The food is different. **Intermediate** The food is freeze-dried. **Advanced** The food astronauts eat in space is freeze-dried. **Advanced High** In space, astronauts eat food that has been freeze-dried. They have to add water to it before eating.	**Beginning** They have to hook in. **Intermediate** They have to hook their sleeping bags in. **Advanced** They have to use a hook to secure their sleeping bags to the spacecraft. **Advanced High** In space, astronauts secure their sleeping bags to the spacecraft using hooks, or they sleep in coffin-like beds that keep them from floating away.

This Week's Materials

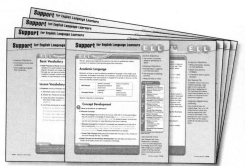

Teacher's Edition pages 228j–255q

See the support for English language learners throughout the lesson, including ELL strategies and scaffolded activities at points of use.

Teacher's Edition pages DI•66–DI•75

Differentiated Instruction for English language learners provides daily group activities that "frontload," or preteach, core instruction.

ELL Handbook pp. 161a–166

Find additional lesson materials that support the core lesson and the ELL instructional pages.

ELL Reader 5.5.3

ELD Reader 5.5.3

Concept Literacy Reader

ELL Poster 23

ELD, ELL Reader
Teaching Guide

Concept Literacy Reader
Teaching Guide

Technology

Online Teacher's Edition Use the digital version of the core Teacher's Edition for planning and instruction.

eReaders
This week's ELL and ELD Readers and Concept Literacy Reader are also available in digital format.

This Week's Content and Language Objectives by Strand

Concept Development/ Academic Language What is life like for an astronaut?	**Content Objective** • Use concept vocabulary related to adventures in space. **Language Objectives** • Express ideas in response to art and discussion. • Respond orally to media.
Phonics and Spelling Greek Word Parts	**Content Objective** • Identify and define Greek and Latin roots. **Language Objective** • Apply phonics and decoding skills to vocabulary.
Listening Comprehension Modified Read Aloud: "The Successful Failure"	**Content Objective** • Monitor and adjust oral comprehension. **Language Objectives** • Discuss oral passages. • Use a graphic organizer to take notes.
Reading Comprehension Author's Purpose	**Content Objectives** • Identify author's purpose to aid comprehension. • Monitor and adjust comprehension. **Language Objectives** • Discuss evidence for author's purpose. • Read grade-level text with accuracy.
Vocabulary Basic and Lesson Vocabulary	**Language Objectives** • Understand and use basic vocabulary. • Learn meanings of grade-level vocabulary. • Produce drawings, phrases, or short sentences to show understanding of Lesson Vocabulary. • Speak using learning strategies.
Word Analysis Greek and Latin Roots	**Content Objective** • Identify and define Greek and Latin roots. **Language Objective** • Discuss meanings of words with Greek and Latin roots.
Grammar and Conventions *This*, *That*, *These*, and *Those*	**Content Objective** • Identify and use demonstrative pronouns *this*, *that*, *these*, and *those*. **Language Objectives** • Speak and write using demonstrative adjectives. • Speak using grammatical structures.
Writing Writing with Quotations	**Content Objective** • Identify quotations in a text. **Language Objectives** • Use informal English. • Respond to questions. • Write paragraphs using quotations.

Word Cards for Vocabulary Activities

accomplishments

focus

gravity

monitors

role

specific

Teacher Note: Beginning Teach two to three words. **Intermediate** Teach three to four words. **Advanced** Teach four to five words. **Advanced High** Teach all words.

Name _____

Read the paragraph. **Study** the chart. Then **write** answers to the questions that follow.

Mission	Years of Mission
Sputnik 1	1957–1958
Apollo 11	1969
Pathfinder	1996–1997
Spirit	2003–2004
Cassini-Huygens	1997–2005

Space Exploration

Space exploration began in 1957. That was the year Russia put *Sputnik 1* into orbit. In 1969, the United States put the first man on the moon. Since then, *Pathfinder* and *Spirit* have brought rocks back to Earth from Mars. Those missions showed that water probably existed on Mars at one time. More recently, the *Cassini-Huygens* mission took photos of Titan, Saturn's largest moon. Titan may also have frozen ice. Many more discoveries await us. Who knows what we will learn from future missions?

1. What is the purpose of this paragraph?

_____

_____

2. How can you tell?

_____

_____

3. What is the paragraph mainly about?

_____

_____

ELL Handbook

Author's Purpose

Use this lesson to supplement or replace the skill lesson on page 229c of the Teacher's Edition. Display the Skill Points (at right) and share them with students.

Teach/Model

Beginning Write and read aloud: *Astronauts learn new things every time they travel in space. Space exploration costs a lot of money. What is the author's purpose?* (to inform)

Intermediate Say: *If you ever get a chance, you should take a trip in space. Better yet, you should try the space ride at the amusement park. It's just like the real thing.* Ask: *What is the author's purpose?* (to persuade) Guide students in identifying words that show the author's purpose. (should, like)

Advanced Say: *Joy is an astronaut. She has taken many trips to space. When she returns home, she tells her family exciting stories about her adventures. What do you think is Joy's purpose for sharing those stories?* (to entertain)

Advanced High Assign each student a purpose for writing (to inform, to entertain, to persuade, to express feelings). Have students write a three-sentence paragraph about space that uses their assigned purpose.

Then distribute copies of Picture It! page 162.
- Point to the chart at the top left of the page. Ask students to predict what the paragraph is about, based on the chart.
- Review the Skill Points with students.
- Read the paragraph aloud. Ask: *What is the author's purpose, or reason, for writing this paragraph?* (to inform)
- Have students discuss the author's purpose and how the author achieves it.

Practice

Read aloud the directions on page 162. Then reread the paragraph aloud. Have students use the chart and the paragraph as they answer the questions.

Beginning Students can first say what they want to write before writing their answers on the lines. Provide help with English writing and spelling.

Intermediate Students can orally answer and then write their answers. Provide help with English writing and spelling.

Advanced Students can answer the questions and then check them by comparing them with a partner's.

Advanced High Students can answer the questions and then explain how the chart supports the author's purpose.

Answers for page 162: 1. The purpose is to give information. 2. Possible answers: It contains a lot of facts. It does not tell a made-up story or express personal feelings. 3. It is about the history of space exploration.

Multilingual Summaries

English

Talk with an Astronaut

Fifth-grade students interviewed Ellen Ochoa. She decided to become an astronaut during graduate school and after the first six women astronauts were chosen.

Ellen is thankful for her hard training. It helps prevent problems during missions. Ellen thinks that floating in zero gravity is fun! The astronauts sleep in floating beds attached to hooks in the wall. Most of their food is freeze-dried, and they just add water.

Ellen misses her family while she is in space. She is able to e-mail them daily. Sometimes they can have a video conference. Ellen thinks space travel is exciting, not scary. Ellen suggests that if students want to be astronauts, they should study math and science. Students should also get involved in team activities. This is helpful because the astronauts work closely in teams.

Spanish

Conversación con un astronauta

Los estudiantes de quinto grado entrevistaron a Ellen Ochoa. Ella les contó que decidió hacerse astronauta durante su postgrado y después que ya habían sido elegidas las primeras seis mujeres astronautas.

Ellen está agradecida por el fuerte entrenamiento que se recibe. Esto ayuda a prevenir problemas durante las misiones. ¡Ellen piensa que flotar cuando no hay gravedad es muy divertido! Los astronautas duermen en camas flotantes amarradas con ganchos a las paredes. La mayor parte de la comida es congelada y seca, y ellos sólo le agregan agua.

Ellen extraña a su familia cuando está en el espacio. Ella puede enviarles un correo electrónico todos los días. Algunas veces, ellos tienen videoconferencias. Ellen piensa que los viajes en el espacio son emocionantes, no aterradores. Ellen sugiere que si los estudiantes quieren ser astronautas deben estudiar matemáticas y ciencias. Los estudiantes también deben participar en trabajos de equipo. Esto ayuda mucho porque los astronautas con frecuencia trabajan en equipos.

Multilingual Summaries

Chinese

訪問宇航員

　　五年級學生一起去拜訪埃倫‧奧喬亞。她在研究院時，就立志當一名宇航員。第一批女宇航員挑選了六人，她就是其中一個。

　　埃倫說艱苦訓練非常重要，它可以防止執行任務時出現差錯。她還說體驗零重力漂浮很有趣！宇航員睡在漂浮的床裏，兩邊繫在墻壁的勾子上。許多食物是乾凍的，吃的時候要加水。

　　在太空時，埃倫很想念家人，因此每天給他們發電子郵件，有時還通過電視交談。埃倫認為太空旅行很有意思，一點也不可怕。她告訴同學們，如果要當宇航員，必須學好數學與科學，還要積極參加團隊活動，這非常必要，因為宇航員需要密切的合作。

Vietnamese

Nói Chuyện Với Một Phi Hành Gia Vũ Trụ

　　Các học sinh lớp năm phỏng vấn Ellen Ochoa. Cô quyết định làm phi hành gia vũ trụ khi học ở trường cao học và sau khi sáu nữ phi hành gia vũ trụ đầu tiên được chọn.

　　Ellen mừng là đã được khổ công huấn luyện. Việc này giúp ngăn ngừa những vấn đề xảy ra trong các lần bay. Ellen nghĩ là lơ lửng vì không có trọng lực là điều vui! Các phi hành gia vũ trụ ngủ trong những cái giường treo lơ lửng gắn vào những cái móc trên tường. Hầu hết những thức ăn của họ đã được đông khô, và họ chỉ cần để nước vào.

　　Ellen nhớ gia đình khi bay trong không gian. Cô có thể "email" cho họ mỗi ngày. Thỉnh thoảng họ có thể có buổi hội đàm bằng "video". Ellen nghĩ là du hành vũ trụ là hứng thú, chứ không đáng sợ. Ellen đề nghị là nếu học sinh muốn trở thành những phi hành gia vũ trụ, thì các em nên học toán và khoa học. Học sinh cũng nên tham gia vào những sinh hoạt đồng đội. Điều này hữu ích vì các phi hành gia vũ trụ làm việc chặt chẽ với nhau trong đội.

Multilingual Summaries

우주 비행사와의 대화

5학년 학생들이 엘렌 오코어와 인터뷰를 했다. 그녀는 대학원을 다니는 동안 여섯 명의 최초 여성 우주 비행사가 선출되자 우주 비행사가 되기로 마음먹었다.

엘렌은 힘든 훈련 기간에 대해 감사해한다. 그 덕분에 임무를 수행하는 동안 문제들을 예방할 수 있었기 때문이다. 엘렌은 무중력 상태에서 떠 다니는 것을 재미있어 한다! 우주 비행사들은 벽의 고리에 연결되어 있는 떠다니는 침대에서 잠을 잔다. 그들이 먹는 음식의 대부분은 동결 건조되어 있어 물만 부어 먹는다.

엘렌은 우주에 있는 동안 가족을 그리워하며 매일 이메일을 보낸다. 그들은 가끔 비디오 회의도 한다. 엘렌은 우주 여행은 무서운 것이 아니라 아주 신나는 것이라고 생각한다. 엘렌은 학생들에게 우주 비행사가 되고 싶으면 수학과 과학 공부를 해야 한다고 얘기해준다. 우주 비행사들은 그룹으로 긴밀히 활동하기 때문에 학생들은 그룹 활동에도 참여해야 한다.

Nrog ib tug Astronaut Tham

Cov tub kawm ntawv nyob qib tsib tau nrog Ellen Ochoa tham. Nws tau txiav txim siab kawm los ua ib tug astronaut, ib tug ua ya ub rau saum nruab ntug, thaum nws kawm ntawv qib siab thiab tom qab rau leej poj niam astronaut tau nruag xaiv los lawm.

Ellen txaus siab rau nws txoj kev kawm uas nyuaj heev. Kev kawm ntawd pab lawm tiv thaiv teeb meem thaum lawv ua hauj lwm. Ellen xav tias thaum yus ya thaum tsis muaj kev nqus mas lom zem kawg nkaus li. Cov astronauts pw saum ib co txaj uas nta saum ib ya thiab uas luag siv nqe lauj muab pav rau tim phab ntsa. Feem ntau ntawm lawm cov zoo mov khov qhuav qhuav lawm ces lawv tsuas ntxiv ntej rau xwb.

Ellen nco nws tsev neeg thaum nws nyob saum ntuab nrug. Nws sau tau ntawv hauv kosputawj (computer) tuaj rau lawv txhua txhua hnub. Muaj tej zaum uas lawv sib koob thaij duab los sib tham (video conference) tau thiab. Ellen xav tias kev tau nchim ntuab nrug lom zem heev, tsis muaj kev ntshai li. Ellen xav tias yog cov tub kawm ntawv leej twg xav mus ua ib tug astronaut, kom lawv yuav tsum kawm leeb thiab tswvyim txawj ntse (science). Cov tub kawm ntawv yuav tsum koom tes nrog tej pab neeg ua ub ua no uake thiab. Qhov ntawd yuav pab lawv heev vim tias cov astronaut sawvdaws ua hauj lwm uake heev.

Name _____

- **Read** *Fixing Hubble's Troubles* again.
- **Find** details that support the author's purpose shown below.
- **Write** them in the *Supporting Detail* boxes.

> **Author's Purpose:** To give a history of how the Hubble Space Telescope was repaired.

Supporting Detail	**Supporting Detail**	**Supporting Detail**

Family Link

Tell your family what you learned about the Hubble telescope. What do your family members know about outer space? Take notes so that you can tell your classmates what you learned.

Weekly Resources Guide for English Language Learner Support

For this week's content and language objectives, see p. 167e.

Instructional Strand	Day 1	Day 2
Concept Development/Academic Language	TEACHER'S EDITION • Academic Language, p. DI•91 • Concept Development, p. DI•91 • Anchored Talk, pp. 256j—256–257 • Preteach Academic Vocabulary, p. 259a • Concept Talk Video ELL HANDBOOK • Hear It, See It, Say It, Use It, pp. xxxvi–xxxvii • ELL Poster Talk, Concept Talk, p. 167c ELL POSTER 24 • Day 1 Activities	TEACHER'S EDITION • Academic Language, p. DI•91 • Concept Development, p. DI•91 • Anchored Talk, p. 260a • Concept Talk Video ELL HANDBOOK • ELL Poster Talk, Concept Talk, p. 167c • Concept Talk Video Routine, p. 477 ELL POSTER 24 • Day 2 Activities
Phonics and Spelling	TEACHER'S EDITION • Phonics and Spelling, p. DI•95	TEACHER'S EDITION • Phonics and Spelling, p. DI•95
Listening Comprehension	TEACHER'S EDITION • Modified Read Aloud, p. DI•94 • Read Aloud, p. 257b • Concept Talk Video ELL HANDBOOK • Concept Talk Video Routine, p. 477	TEACHER'S EDITION • Modified Read Aloud, p. DI•94 • AudioText of *Journey to the Center of the Earth* • Concept Talk Video ELL HANDBOOK • AudioText CD Routine, p. 477 • Three Column Chart, p. 494
Reading Comprehension	TEACHER'S EDITION • Preteach Cause and Effect, p. DI•96	TEACHER'S EDITION • Reteach Cause and Effect, p. DI•96 • Frontloading Reading, p. DI•97 ELL HANDBOOK • Picture It! Skill Instruction, pp. 168–168a • Multilingual Summaries, pp. 169–171
Vocabulary **Basic and Lesson Vocabulary** **Word Analysis: Complex Spelling Patterns -*ous*, -*ious*, -*eous***	TEACHER'S EDITION • Basic Vocabulary, p. DI•92 • Preteach Lesson Vocabulary, p. DI•92 • Complex Spelling Patterns -*ous*, -*ious*, -*eous*, p. DI•95 ELL HANDBOOK • Word Cards, p. 167 • ELL Vocabulary Routine, p. 471 ELL POSTER 24 • Day 1 Activities	TEACHER'S EDITION • Basic Vocabulary, p. DI•92 • Reteach Lesson Vocabulary, p. DI•93 • Complex Spelling Patterns -*ous*, -*ious*, -*eous*, p. DI•95 ELL HANDBOOK • Word Cards, p. 167 • Multilingual Vocabulary List, p. 431 ELL POSTER 24 • Day 2 Activities
Grammar and Conventions	TEACHER'S EDITION • Teach Comparative and Superlative Adjectives, p. DI•99	TEACHER'S EDITION • Reteach Comparative and Superlative Adjectives, p. DI•99
Writing	TEACHER'S EDITION • Know Your Audience and Purpose, p. DI•100 • Writing for Tests: Letter to the Editor, pp. 259e–259f	TEACHER'S EDITION • Writing for Tests: Letter to the Editor, pp. 269d–269e

Unit 5, Week 4 *Journey to the Center of the Earth*

This symbol indicates leveled instruction to address language proficiency levels.

Day 3	Day 4	Day 5
TEACHER'S EDITION • Academic Language, p. DI•91 • Concept Development, p. DI•91 • Anchored Talk, p. 270a • Concept Talk Video **ELL HANDBOOK** • ELL Poster Talk, Concept Talk, p. 167c **ELL POSTER 24** • Day 3 Activities	**TEACHER'S EDITION** • Academic Language, p. DI•91 • Concept Development, p. DI•91 • Anchored Talk, p. 278a • Concept Talk Video **ELL HANDBOOK** • ELL Poster Talk, Concept Talk, p. 167c **ELL POSTER 24** • Day 4 Activities	**TEACHER'S EDITION** • Academic Language, p. DI•91 • Concept Development, p. DI•91 • Concept Talk Video **ELL HANDBOOK** • ELL Poster Talk, Concept Talk, p. 167c **ELL POSTER 24** • Day 5 Activities
		TEACHER'S EDITION • Phonics and Spelling, p. DI•95
ELL HANDBOOK • Phonics Transition Lesson, pp. 300, 305 **TEACHER'S EDITION** • AudioText of *Journey to the Center of the Earth* • Concept Talk Video **ELL HANDBOOK** • AudioText CD Routine, p. 477	**ELL HANDBOOK** • Phonics Transition Lesson, pp. 300, 305 **TEACHER'S EDITION** • Concept Talk Video	**TEACHER'S EDITION** • Concept Talk Video
TEACHER'S EDITION • Sheltered Reading, p. DI•97 **ELL HANDBOOK** • Multilingual Summaries, pp. 169–171	**TEACHER'S EDITION** • ELL/ELD Reader Guided Reading, p. DI•98 **ELL HANDBOOK** • ELL Study Guide, p. 172	**TEACHER'S EDITION** • ELL/ELD Reader Guided Reading, p. DI•98 **ELL HANDBOOK** • ELL Study Guide, p. 172
		TEACHER'S EDITION • Complex Spelling Patterns *-ous, -ious, -eous*, p. 283i
ELL HANDBOOK • High-Frequency Words Activity Bank, p. 446 **ELL POSTER 24** • Day 3 Activities	**ELL HANDBOOK** • High-Frequency Words Activity Bank, p. 446	**ELL HANDBOOK** • High-Frequency Words Activity Bank, p. 446
TEACHER'S EDITION • Grammar Jammer **ELL HANDBOOK** • Grammar Transition Lesson, pp. 371, 375 • Grammar Jammer Routine, p. 478	**TEACHER'S EDITION** • Grammar Jammer **ELL HANDBOOK** • Grammar Transition Lesson, pp. 371, 375	**TEACHER'S EDITION** • Grammar Jammer **ELL HANDBOOK** • Grammar Transition Lesson, pp. 371, 375
TEACHER'S EDITION • Let's Write It!, p. 276–277 • Writing for Tests: Evaluation, pp. 277a–277b	**TEACHER'S EDITION** • Writing for Tests, pp. 283d–283e	**TEACHER'S EDITION** • Writing for Tests, pp. 283p–283q

Question of the Week
How do we explore places underground?

Throughout the week, use the ELL Poster to help students produce and comprehend language, understand the concept, and build English vocabulary. Use the Question of the Week and other questions to help students share ideas in pairs, small groups, or the large group. Sample questions are shown, with examples of possible responses by students.

Weekly Concept and Language Goals

• Share ideas about underground places

• Describe what an underground mine is like

• Discuss an underground journey

By the end of the lesson, students should be able to talk about and write sentences about exploring underground places.

ELL Poster 24

Daily Team Talk

Day 1	Day 2	Day 3	Day 4	Day 5
After Day 1 activities on Poster, ask questions such as *What are the miners in the poster picture looking for?*	After Day 2 activity on Poster, ask questions such as *Why do you think the miners in the poster picture go all the way to the Earth's mantle?*	After Day 3 activity on Poster, ask questions such as *How do you think the miners felt as they traveled down to this mine?*	After Day 4 activity on Poster, ask questions such as *What do the miners see on the walls of the mine?*	After Day 5 activity on Poster, ask questions such as *How does the make-believe center of the Earth in* Journey to the Center of the Earth *compare to the underground coal mine in the poster picture?*
Beginning For coal. **Intermediate** They are looking for coal. **Advanced** The miners are looking for coal and other minerals. **Advanced High** The miners go far underground to look for coal and other minerals.	**Beginning** To find coal. **Intermediate** That's where coal is. **Advanced** They go to the mantle because that's where coal is. **Advanced High** The miners know that they can find coal in the Earth's mantle.	**Beginning** Scared. **Intermediate** They felt excited. **Advanced** I think the miners felt scared and excited. **Advanced High** The miners took an elevator ride two miles underground. I think this trip made them feel nervous but excited.	**Beginning** They see fossils. **Intermediate** They see fossils of animals. **Advanced** They see fossils of animals that don't live anymore. **Advanced High** The miners see fossils of extinct animals, such as serpents and fish.	**Beginning** It is dry. **Intermediate** It is dry and there are no monsters. **Advanced** The real center is not wet and light. There are no monsters. **Advanced High** Jules Verne's story tells of a wet center that is always light and filled with monsters. The real center is dry and dark and has no animals.

This Week's Materials

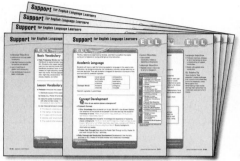

Teacher's Edition pages 256j–283q

See the support for English language learners throughout the lesson, including ELL strategies and scaffolded activities at points of use.

Teacher's Edition pages DI•91–DI•100

Differentiated Instruction for English language learners provides daily group activities that "frontload," or preteach, core instruction.

ELL Handbook pp. 167a–172

Find additional lesson materials that support the core lesson and the ELL instructional pages.

ELL Poster 24

ELL Reader 5.5.4

ELD Reader 5.5.4

Concept Literacy Reader

ELD, ELL Reader Teaching Guide

Concept Literacy Reader Teaching Guide

Technology

Online Teacher's Edition Use the digital version of the core Teacher's Edition for planning and instruction.

eReaders
This week's ELL and ELD Readers and Concept Literacy Reader are also available in digital format.

This Week's Content and Language Objectives by Strand

Concept Development/ Academic Language How do we explore places underground?	**Content Objective** • Use concept vocabulary related to exploring underground. **Language Objective** • Express ideas in response to art and discussion.
Phonics and Spelling Latin Roots	**Content Objective** • Identify Latin roots in related words. **Language Objectives** • Apply phonics and decoding skills to vocabulary. • Discuss meanings of related words with Latin roots.
Listening Comprehension Modified Read Aloud: "The Cave Mappers"	**Content Objective** • Monitor and adjust oral comprehension. **Language Objectives** • Discuss oral passages. • Use a graphic organizer as visual support to understand spoken language.
Reading Comprehension Cause and Effect	**Content Objectives** • Distinguish between cause and effect. • Monitor and adjust comprehension. **Language Objectives** • Discuss evidence for cause and effect. • Write causes and effects from personal experience.
Vocabulary Basic and Lesson Vocabulary	**Language Objectives** • Understand and use basic vocabulary. • Speak and learn meanings of grade-level vocabulary. • Use techniques to acquire basic vocabulary.
Word Analysis Complex Spelling Patterns -ous, -ious, -eous	**Content Objective** • Spell and pronounce words with the complex spelling patterns -ous, -ious, and -eous. **Language Objective** • Monitor written language and self-correct.
Grammar and Conventions Comparative and Superlative Adjectives	**Content Objective** • Use and form comparative and superlative adjectives. **Language Objective** • Speak and write sentences with comparative and superlative adjectives.
Writing Know Your Audience and Purpose	**Content Objective** • Identify audience and purpose. **Language Objectives** • Write paragraphs, considering alternatives and using proper punctuation. • Use informal English appropriately.

Word Cards for Vocabulary Activities

armor

encases

extinct

hideous

plunged

serpent

Teacher Note: Beginning Teach two to three words. **Intermediate** Teach three to four words. **Advanced** Teach four to five words. **Advanced High** Teach all words.

Name _____

Look at the picture. **Read** the paragraph.

• **Complete** the chart below to show each cause-and-effect relationship.

Mount St. Helens

Mount St. Helens is an active volcano in Washington. On May 18, 1980, an earthquake started an avalanche. The avalanche tore open the side of the mountain. Steam blasted sideways from the volcano in a strong wind. The steam melted ice and snow at the top of the mountain, which caused mud to flow down the mountain. Together, the steam blast and mudflow flattened the forest at the bottom of the mountain. It took many years for the forest to grow back.

Cause	**Effect**
An earthquake started an avalanche.	
	The steam melted the ice and snow.
Mud flowed down the mountain.	

Cause and Effect

Use this lesson to supplement or replace the skill lesson on page 257c of the Teacher's Edition. Display the Skill Points (at right) and share them with students.

Teach/Model

Beginning Say: *Lightning hits the tree. The tree splits.* Have students identify the cause (lightning hitting the tree) and the effect (the tree splits). Show students how to combine the sentence using the clue word *because.* (The tree splits because lightning hits it.)

Intermediate Say and write on the board: *The wind blows. I zip up my jacket.* Have students copy the sentences and label the cause (the wind) and the effect (I zip up my jacket). Have students combine the sentences using a clue word.

Advanced Say: *There was a thunderstorm last night. Today, some branches are in the street.* Ask students to identify the cause and the effect. Ask: *What are some other possible effects of a thunderstorm?* (floods, trees knocked down, no electricity)

Advanced High Pair students. Have one partner write a cause-and-effect sentence about the weather. Then have the other partner read the sentence and label the cause and effect. Then have partners trade roles.

Then distribute copies of Picture It! page 168.

- Point to the picture and ask students if they know what it shows. (a volcano)
- Tell students they are going to learn about Mount St. Helens, a volcano in the state of Washington.
- Read the paragraph aloud. Ask: *What effect do you think a volcanic eruption has on the animals in the area?* (They move away.)
- Review the Skill Points with students.

Practice

Read aloud the directions on page 168. Have students reread the paragraph aloud. Explain the word *avalanche.* Then have them use the picture and the paragraph as they complete the chart.

Beginning Students can first say what they want to write in each box and then write their answers. Provide help with writing.

Intermediate Students can first orally answer before writing the cause and effects in the chart.

Advanced Students can write their answers in the boxes and then check them by comparing their answers with a partner's.

Advanced High Students can write their answers in the chart and then check their answers by rereading the paragraph and making any necessary corrections.

Answers for page 168: *Effect:* The avalanche tore open the side of the mountain. *Cause:* Steam blasted sideways from the volcano. *Effect:* The forest was flattened.

> **Skill Points**
> ✔ A **cause** is why something happens. An **effect** is what happens.
> ✔ Words such as *because* and *since* are clues. They tell you that you are reading about a cause-and-effect relationship.
> ✔ A cause may have several effects. An effect may have several causes.

Multilingual Summaries

Journey to the Center of the Earth

Three men take a trip to explore the center of the Earth. They are floating on a raft on an underground sea. The travelers see many huge animals that look like monsters. The animals are fighting each other in the sea. The men fear that their raft will turn over from the crashing waves. They feel tiny compared to the monsters.

Then the animals disappear. After a short time, one animal rises to the surface and slowly dies. The men realize that the monsters are really dinosaurs. The men hope the other dinosaur has gone to hide. They worry that it will come back.

Spanish

Viaje al centro de la Tierra

Tres hombres hacen un viaje al centro de la Tierra. Ellos están flotando en una balsa en un mar debajo de la superficie. Los viajeros ven muchos animales enormes. Estos animales parecen monstruos. Los animales están luchando unos contra otros en el mar. Los hombres temen que las olas al estrellarse le den vuelta a su balsa. Ellos se sienten pequeños comparados con los monstruos.

Luego, los animales desaparecen. Después de poco tiempo, uno de los animales emerge en la superficie y muere lentamente. Los hombres se dan cuenta de que los monstruos son realmente dinosaurios. Los hombres tienen la esperanza de que el otro dinosaurio se haya ido a esconderse. Ellos se preocupan de que él regrese.

Multilingual Summaries

Chinese

地心曆險記

故事要說的是，三個朋友出發去地心探險，乘著皮筏，漂浮在地下海洋。他們看見許多巨獸，像是可怕的怪物，在海裏互相搏鬥。三個人害怕洶涌的海浪會把皮筏打翻。與巨獸相比，人簡直像小小的螞蟻。

這時所有巨獸突然消失了。過了不久，有一頭巨獸浮出水面，掙扎著慢慢死了。三個人這才發現，巨獸原來是恐龍。他們希望另一隻恐龍已經離開，擔心它隨時會回來。

Vietnamese

Đi Vào Tâm Điểm Địa Cầu

Trong câu chuyện này, có ba ông đi thám hiểm tâm điểm Địa Cầu. Họ đi trên một chiếc thuyền bè trên biển ở dưới lòng đất. Những người du hành thấy có nhiều thú vật đồ sộ. Chúng trông giống như quái vật. Các con thú này đang đánh nhau dưới biển. Ba ông này sợ là chiếc thuyền bè của họ sẽ bị lật vì những cơn sóng đập mạnh. Họ cảm thấy mình bé nhỏ so với những con quái vật.

Rồi cả hai quái vật biến mất. Sau chốc lát, một con nổi lên mặt nước, và từ từ chết. Ba ông nhận ra rằng những con quái vật thật ra là những con khủng long. Ba ông này hy vọng là con khủng long kia đã đi trốn. Họ lo sợ là nó sẽ quay lại.

Multilingual Summaries

지구 중심으로의 여행

세 남자가 지구의 중심부를 탐사하기 위해 여행을 떠난다. 그들은 지하의 바다에서 뗏목을 타고 떠다니고 있다. 그들은 괴물같이 생긴 큰 동물들을 많이 만나게 된다. 동물들이 바다에서 서로 싸우는 바람에 뗏목이 파도에 부딪혀 뒤집힐까봐 세 남자는 두려워한다. 이들은 자신이 괴물에 비해 아주 작다고 느낀다.

그때 동물들이 사라진다. 잠시 후 동물 한 마리가 표면으로 떠올라 천천히 죽는다. 세 남자는 괴물이 진짜 공룡이라는 것을 알게 되고 다른 공룡이 숨어버렸기를 바라며 공룡이 다시 돌아올까봐 걱정한다.

Nchim mus txog hauv Plawv Ntiaj Teb

Zaj dab neeg no piav txog peb tug txiv neej uas mus ncig txog hauv plaws ntiaj teb no. Lawv ntab sau ib phuaj ntoo nyob hauv ib lub hiavtxwv nyob sab hauv av. Cov neeg ncig ntawd pom ib cov tsiaj loj loj kawg. Lawv ntxim zoo li dab. Cov tsiaj ntawd sib ntaus hauv dej. Cov txiv neej ntshai tsam lawv lub phuaj ntoo ntxeev vim dej txaws ntxhee. Lawv txim li lawv me heev thaum muaj lawv piv nrog rau cov dab ntawd.

Ces ob tug tsiaj ntawd cia li ploj lawm. Ib me ntsis tom qab, ib tug tsiaj maj mam tshwm los saum nplaim dej ces cia li maj mam tuag lawm. Cov txiv neej ntawd pom tau tias cov dab ntawd yog daisnausxauj (dinosaurs) tiag xwb. Cov txiv neej ntawd cia siab tias lwm cov daisnausxauj ib mus nkaum lawm. Cov neeg ncig ntawd ntshai tsam nws yuav rov qab los.

Name _____

- **Read** *Exploring the Sonora Caverns* again.
- As you read the story, **look** for causes and effects.
- **Fill in** the graphic organizer below.

In the table, write the cause or effect that is missing.
The first example is done for you. Use information from your reading.

Cause	Effect
Stanley Mayfield's dog chased a raccoon.	The dog discovered Sonora Caverns.
_____	People give the formations names like Butterfly and Angel's Wings.
Rain moved through limestone.	_____
Water and minerals drip down formations on the top of the cavern.	_____
_____	Stalagmites form.
Water flows over parts of a cavern and leaves minerals behind.	_____
Sonora Caverns have lights, paths, and stairs.	_____
_____	Cavers need hats.
_____	People must protect caverns.

Family Link

Suppose you discovered a cave. No one had explored it. Write a story about your explorations. Include what equipment you bring and what formations you see. Then, read your story to your family. Answer any questions they may have about caverns.

Weekly Resources Guide for English Language Learner Support

For this week's content and language objectives, see p. 173e.

Instructional Strand	Day 1	Day 2
Concept Development/Academic Language	**TEACHER'S EDITION** • Academic Language, p. DI•116 • Concept Development, p. DI•116 • Anchored Talk, pp. 284j—284–285 • Preteach Academic Vocabulary, p. 287a • Concept Talk Video **ELL HANDBOOK** • Hear It, See It, Say It, Use It, pp. xxxvi–xxxvii • ELL Poster Talk, Concept Talk, p. 173c **ELL POSTER 25** • Day 1 Activities	**TEACHER'S EDITION** • Academic Language, p. DI•116 • Concept Development, p. DI•116 • Anchored Talk, p. 288a • Concept Talk Video **ELL HANDBOOK** • ELL Poster Talk, Concept Talk, p. 173c • Concept Talk Video Routine, p. 477 **ELL POSTER 25** • Day 2 Activities
Phonics and Spelling	**TEACHER'S EDITION** • Phonics and Spelling, p. DI•120	**TEACHER'S EDITION** • Phonics and Spelling, p. DI•120
Listening Comprehension	**TEACHER'S EDITION** • Modified Read Aloud, p. DI•119 • Read Aloud, p. 285b • Concept Talk Video **ELL HANDBOOK** • Concept Talk Video Routine, p. 477	**TEACHER'S EDITION** • Modified Read Aloud, p. DI•119 • AudioText of *Ghost Towns of the American West* • Concept Talk Video **ELL HANDBOOK** • AudioText CD Routine, p. 477 • Three Column Chart, p. 494
Reading Comprehension	**TEACHER'S EDITION** • Preteach Generalize, p. DI•121	**TEACHER'S EDITION** • Reteach Generalize, p. DI•121 • Frontloading Reading, p. DI•122 **ELL HANDBOOK** • Picture It! Skill Instruction, pp. 174–174a • Multilingual Summaries, pp. 175–177
Vocabulary **Basic and Lesson Vocabulary** **Word Analysis: Morphemes**	**TEACHER'S EDITION** • Basic Vocabulary, p. DI•117 • Preteach Lesson Vocabulary, p. DI•117 • Morphemes, p. DI•120 **ELL HANDBOOK** • Word Cards, p. 173 • ELL Vocabulary Routine, p. 471 **ELL POSTER 25** • Day 1 Activities	**TEACHER'S EDITION** • Basic Vocabulary, p. DI•117 • Reteach Lesson Vocabulary, p. DI•118 • Morphemes, p. DI•120 **ELL HANDBOOK** • Word Cards, p. 173 • Multilingual Vocabulary List, p. 431 **ELL POSTER 25** • Day 2 Activities
Grammar and Conventions	**TEACHER'S EDITION** • Teach Adverbs, p. DI•124	**TEACHER'S EDITION** • Reteach Adverbs, p. DI•124
Writing	**TEACHER'S EDITION** • Summarize, p. DI•125 • Introduce Summary, pp. 287e–287f	**TEACHER'S EDITION** • Writing Trait: Focus/Ideas, pp. 297d–297e

This symbol indicates leveled instruction to address language proficiency levels.

Day 3	Day 4	Day 5
TEACHER'S EDITION • Academic Language, p. DI•116 • Concept Development, p. DI•116 • Anchored Talk, p. 298a • Concept Talk Video **ELL HANDBOOK** • ELL Poster Talk, Concept Talk, p. 173c **ELL POSTER 25** • Day 3 Activities	**TEACHER'S EDITION** • Academic Language, p. DI•116 • Concept Development, p. DI•116 • Anchored Talk, p. 306a • Concept Talk Video **ELL HANDBOOK** • ELL Poster Talk, Concept Talk, p. 173c **ELL POSTER 25** • Day 4 Activities	**TEACHER'S EDITION** • Academic Language, p. DI•116 • Concept Development, p. DI•116 • Concept Talk Video **ELL HANDBOOK** • ELL Poster Talk, Concept Talk, p. 173c **ELL POSTER 25** • Day 5 Activities
		TEACHER'S EDITION • Phonics and Spelling, p. DI•120
ELL HANDBOOK • Phonics Transition Lesson, pp. 299, 304 **TEACHER'S EDITION** • AudioText of *Ghost Towns of the American West* • Concept Talk Video **ELL HANDBOOK** • AudioText CD Routine, p. 477	**ELL HANDBOOK** • Phonics Transition Lesson, pp. 299, 304 **TEACHER'S EDITION** • Concept Talk Video	**TEACHER'S EDITION** • Concept Talk Video
TEACHER'S EDITION • Sheltered Reading, p. DI•122 **ELL HANDBOOK** • Multilingual Summaries, pp. 175–177	**TEACHER'S EDITION** • ELL/ELD Reader Guided Reading, p. DI•123 **ELL HANDBOOK** • ELL Study Guide, p. 178	**TEACHER'S EDITION** • ELL/ELD Reader Guided Reading, p. DI•123 **ELL HANDBOOK** • ELL Study Guide, p. 178
		TEACHER'S EDITION • Morphemes, p. 311i
ELL HANDBOOK • High-Frequency Words Activity Bank, p. 446 **ELL POSTER 25** • Day 3 Activities	**ELL HANDBOOK** • High-Frequency Words Activity Bank, p. 446	**ELL HANDBOOK** • High-Frequency Words Activity Bank, p. 446
TEACHER'S EDITION • Grammar Jammer **ELL HANDBOOK** • Grammar Transition Lesson, pp. 372, 378 • Grammar Jammer Routine, p. 478	**TEACHER'S EDITION** • Grammar Jammer **ELL HANDBOOK** • Grammar Transition Lesson, pp. 372, 378	**TEACHER'S EDITION** • Grammar Jammer **ELL HANDBOOK** • Grammar Transition Lesson, pp. 372, 378
TEACHER'S EDITION • Let's Write It!, p. 304–305 • Writing Trait: Transitional Words, pp. 305a–305b	**TEACHER'S EDITION** • Revising Strategy, pp. 311d–311e	**TEACHER'S EDITION** • Adverbs, pp. 311p–311q

Question of the Week
What adventures helped drive westward expansion?

Throughout the week, use the ELL Poster to help students produce and comprehend language, understand the concept, and build English vocabulary. Use the Question of the Week and other questions to help students share ideas in pairs, small groups, or the large group. Sample questions are shown, with examples of possible responses by students.

ELL Poster 25

Weekly Concept and Language Goals

• Participate in a discussion about westward expansion

• Explain why people moved westward

• Describe how people traveled to California during the Gold Rush

By the end of the lesson, students should be able to talk about and write sentences about westward expansion.

Daily Team Talk

Day 1	Day 2	Day 3	Day 4	Day 5
After Day 1 activities on Poster, ask questions such as *How do you know the poster picture took place a long time ago?*	After Day 2 activity on Poster, ask questions such as *How do you think the people in the poster picture will get food now that the store owner went to California?*	After Day 3 activity on Poster, ask questions such as *Why does the man in front of the store want to go to California?*	After Day 4 activity on Poster, ask questions such as *How could the man who wants to go to California get there?*	After Day 5 activity on Poster, ask questions such as *In Ghost Towns of the American West, how did the building of railroad tracks affect westward expansion?*
Beginning Old clothes. **Intermediate** The clothes are from a long time ago. **Advanced** The picture took place during the Gold Rush, which was a long time ago. **Advanced High** The picture shows 1861 during the Gold Rush, about 150 years ago. You can tell from the buildings and the clothes people wear that it is a long time ago.	**Beginning** A new person. **Intermediate** A person will run the store. **Advanced** Another person will run the store so they can get food. **Advanced High** I think someone else will work in the store now that the owner has left.	**Beginning** To find gold. **Intermediate** He wants to make money. **Advanced** He wants to find gold so he will be rich. **Advanced High** The man wants to join the Gold Rush. He will look for gold that could make him rich.	**Beginning** Ride a horse. **Intermediate** He could ride a horse. **Advanced** He could ride in a horse-drawn wagon. **Advanced High** The man could drive a Conestoga wagon to California.	**Beginning** Many new towns. **Intermediate** People built new towns. **Advanced** Towns moved closer to the tracks. **Advanced High** Towns were created along the railroad tracks. Towns that already existed actually moved closer to the tracks.

This Week's Materials

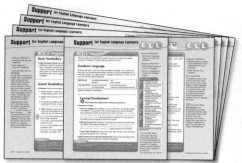

Teacher's Edition pages 284j–315a

See the support for English language learners throughout the lesson, including ELL strategies and scaffolded activities at points of use.

Teacher's Edition pages DI•116–DI•125

Differentiated Instruction for English language learners provides daily group activities that "frontload," or preteach, core instruction.

ELL Handbook pp. 173a–178

Find additional lesson materials that support the core lesson and the ELL instructional pages.

ELL Poster 25

ELL Reader 5.5.5

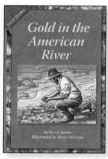

ELD Reader 5.5.5

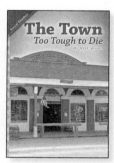

Concept Literacy Reader

ELD, ELL Reader Teaching Guide

Concept Literacy Reader Teaching Guide

Technology

Online Teacher's Edition Use the digital version of the core Teacher's Edition for planning and instruction.

eReaders
This week's ELL and ELD Readers and Concept Literacy Reader are also available in digital format.

ELL Handbook

This Week's Content and Language Objectives by Strand

Concept Development/ Academic Language What adventures helped drive westward expansion?	**Content Objective** • Use concept vocabulary related to the California Gold Rush. **Language Objectives** • Express ideas in response to art and discussion. • Use prior experiences to understand meanings in English.
Phonics and Spelling Greek Word Parts	**Content Objective** • Identify Greek word parts in words. **Language Objectives** • Apply phonics and decoding skills to vocabulary. • Discuss meanings of related words with Greek word parts.
Listening Comprehension Modified Read Aloud: "Cold!"	**Content Objective** • Monitor and adjust oral comprehension. **Language Objectives** • Discuss oral passages. • Use a graphic organizer to take notes. • Ask for information.
Reading Comprehension Generalize	**Content Objectives** • Learn what it means to generalize. • Monitor and adjust comprehension. **Language Objectives** • Generalize about a selection. • Understand the main points of spoken language. • Read with appropriate rate.
Vocabulary Basic and Lesson Vocabulary	**Language Objectives** • Understand and use basic vocabulary. • Learn meanings of grade-level vocabulary. • Produce drawings, phrases, or short sentences to show understanding of Lesson Vocabulary.
Word Analysis Morphemes	**Content Objective** • Identify and use morphemes. **Language Objective** • Monitor oral language to employ self-corrective techniques.
Grammar and Conventions Adverbs	**Content Objectives** • Identify adverbs of frequency and amount. • Use and form comparative and superlative adverbs. **Language Objective** • Speak and write sentences with comparative and superlative adverbs.
Writing Summarize	**Content Objective** • Identify main points. **Language Objectives** • Summarize material to show comprehension. • Edit writing for verb tenses.

ELL Handbook

Word Cards for Vocabulary Activities

economic

independence

overrun

scrawled

vacant

Teacher Note: Beginning Teach two to three words. **Intermediate** Teach three to four words. **Advanced** Teach four to five words. **Advanced High** Teach all words and review one word from an earlier lesson.

Name _____

Look at the map, and **read** the paragraph. **Complete** the graphic organizer.

- In the first box, **write** a generalization about the Transcontinental Railroad.
- In the three smaller boxes, **write** examples from the text that support your generalization.

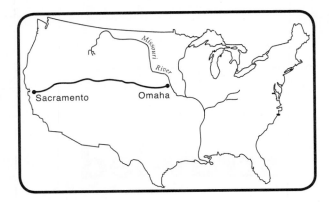

The Transcontinental Railroad

The Transcontinental Railroad was completed in 1869. It went from Nebraska to California. Leaders and business people invested their money in the project. Surveyors and engineers planned how to build the railroad over mountains and across rivers. Thousands of Irish and Chinese workers laid hundreds of miles of tracks for the railroad. The Transcontinental Railroad gave people a faster, cheaper way to travel across the United States. It opened up the West.

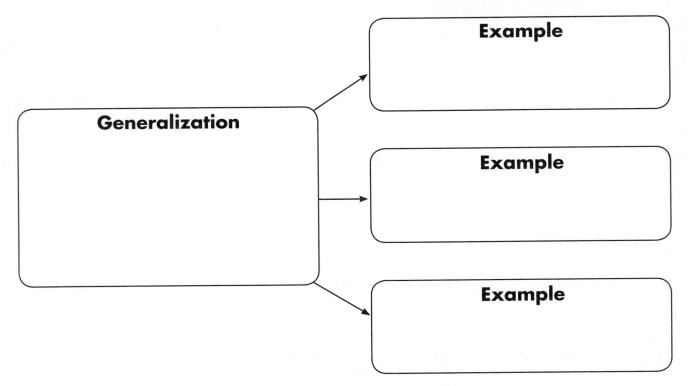

Generalization

Example

Example

Example

Generalize

Use this lesson to supplement or replace the skill lesson on page 285c of the Teacher's Edition. Display the Skill Points (at right) and share them with students.

Teach/Model

Beginning Say: *Most trains had more than one train car. A train is one way of traveling in the United States. Which sentence can apply to many examples?* (the first one) *Which sentence is a generalization?* (the first one) Point out that the word *most* is a clue word for recognizing a generalization.

Intermediate Write and read aloud: *Many people travel to work by train.* Ask: *What makes this sentence a generalization?* (It tells a way many people are alike. It uses the word *many.*) Have students think of how they can support the generalization.

Advanced Write a generalization on the board. For example: *All trucks need a steering wheel.* Ask students why this is a generalization. Have them write a fact that supports the generalization. Explain that the reason why trucks need steering wheels supports the generalization: *Steering wheels help a truck turn.*

Advanced High Pair students. Have partners write a generalization about a topic such as forms of transportation. Say: *Use a clue word such as* always, usually, *or* many *in your generalization.* Have partners write a fact that supports their generalization.

Then distribute copies of Picture It! page 174.

- Point to the map. Ask students to tell what they think the map is showing.
- Read the paragraph aloud. Ask: *What is the Transcontinental Railroad?* (a railroad built in 1869 that went from Nebraska to California)
- Review the Skill Points with students.

Practice

Read aloud the directions on page 174. Reread the paragraph aloud. Then have students use the picture and the paragraph as they complete the graphic organizer.

Beginning Students can say their generalization and examples before writing them in the boxes. Provide help with writing and spelling English words.

Intermediate Students can first orally answer and then write their answers in the boxes. Provide help with writing.

Advanced Students can write their answers in the graphic organizer and then check their answers by comparing them with a partner's.

Advanced High Students can write their answers in the graphic organizer and then orally explain how their generalization is supported by the information in the paragraph.

Answers for page 174: *Generalization:* Many different groups of people helped complete the Transcontinental Railroad. *Examples:* Leaders and business people invested money. Surveyors and engineers planned how to build it. Irish and Chinese workers laid the tracks.

Skill Points

✔ To **generalize** means to make a broad statement that applies to several examples.

✔ Words such as *always, never, generally, all, many,* and *most* signal a generalization.

Multilingual Summaries

Ghost Towns of the American West

Ghost towns were once busy mining camps or cowboy towns. Thousands of people moved to the West when gold was discovered there in 1848.

Towns were built where gold, silver, and copper were discovered. Towns were also built near the railroad and railroad stations. Most of these towns' people were men. Some towns put ads in the newspapers. The ads asked for women to come and live there.

Some towns became big cities. Other towns failed because the mines closed. Some failed because they were too far from the railroad when it came. People moved away to be nearer to more gold and closer to the railroad. They left empty towns behind. The towns that were once full of people are the ghost towns of today.

Spanish

Los pueblos fantasmas del Oeste estadounidense

Los pueblos fantasmas fueron alguna vez activos campamentos mineros o pueblos de vaqueros. Miles de personas se mudaron al Oeste cuando oro fue descubierto allí en 1848.

Los pueblos se construyeron donde se había encontrado oro, plata y cobre. Además se construyeron cerca de los ferrocarriles y de las estaciones ferroviarias. La mayoría de la gente que vivía en esos pueblos eran hombres. Algunos pueblos ponían avisos en los periódicos. Los avisos les pedían a las mujeres que fueran a vivir allí.

Unos pueblos se convirtieron en grandes ciudades. Otros fracasaron porque las minas cerraron. Algunos fracasaron porque estaban muy lejos de los ferrocarriles cuando estos se construyueron. La gente se fue para estar más cerca del oro y de los ferrocarriles. Los pueblos que antes estaban llenos de personas, ahora son pueblos fantasmas.

Multilingual Summaries

Chinese

美國西部無人鎮

無人鎮曾經住著繁忙的礦工和嘈雜的牛仔。1848年西部發現金礦後，許多人來到這裏。

哪里發現金礦、銀礦或銅礦，哪里就有村莊。哪里靠近鐵路與車站，哪里就有城鎮。來這裏的大都是男人。有些村鎮就在報紙做廣告，吸引女人搬到這些地方。

有些村鎮後來變成大城市，有些卻因為礦場關閉、離通車的鐵路太遠而衰落。人們都搬到金礦和鐵路附近，只留下一些空城。原來這裏有許多居民，現在卻成了荒涼的無人鎮。

Vietnamese

Những Thị Trấn Bỏ Hoang ở Miền Tây Hoa Ky

Các thị trấn bỏ hoang đã từng là những trại khai thác hầm mỏ nhộn nhịp hoặc là những phố thị của các tay chăn bò. Hàng ngàn người đã dọn đến miền Tây khi vàng được tìm thấy ở đó vào năm 1848.

Các thị trấn được dựng lên ở nơi nào vàng, bạc, và đồng được tìm thấy. Thị trấn cũng được dựng lên gần đường rày xe lửa và trạm xe lửa. Đa số dân sinh sống ở những thị trấn này là đàn ông. Một vài thị trấn đăng quảng cáo trên báo. Các quảng cáo này mời gọi phụ nữ đến và sinh sống ở đó.

Một vài thị trấn trở thành những thành phố lớn. Vài thị trấn khác bị bỏ vì các hầm mỏ đóng cửa. Vài thị trấn bị bỏ vì cách đường rày xe lửa quá xa khi đường rày được xây. Người ta dọn đến ở gần nơi nào có nhiều vàng hơn và gần với đường rày xe lửa hơn. Họ bỏ lại sau lưng những thị trấn không người. Những thị trấn đã có một thời đông đúc thì ngày nay là những thị trấn bỏ hoang.

Copyright © Pearson Education, Inc., or its affiliates. All Rights Reserved. 5

ELL Handbook   Unit 5, Week 5 *Ghost Towns of the American West* **176**

Multilingual Summaries

미국 서부의 유령 도시

유령 도시는 한때 금광 캠프 또는 카우보이 마을로 분주한 곳이었다. 1848년 서부에서 금이 발견되자 수천 명의 사람들이 서부로 몰려 왔다.

도시는 금, 은 또는 구리가 발견된 곳이나 기찻길 근처와 기차역 주변에 만들어졌다. 이런 도시에 사는 사람들은 대부분 남자여서 어떤 도시에서는 여자들에게 와서 살라는 광고를 신문에 내기도 했다.

몇몇 도시는 대도시가 되었고 몇몇 도시는 금광이 문을 닫거나 처음부터 기찻길에서 너무 멀리 떨어진 곳에 있어서 쇠퇴했다. 사람들은 금이 더 많이 나는 곳이나 기찻길에서 더 가까운 곳으로 가기 위해 빈 도시를 남겨두고 떠나갔다. 한때 사람들로 가득했던 도시는 이제 유령 도시가 되었다.

Zos Dab nyob rau Amiskas Teb Sab Hnub Poob

Puag thaum ub mas cov zos dab niaj hnub niam no yog ib co zos ua neeg khawb nyiaj khawb kub los khawb tooj khawb hlau tau nyob lossis lawv yog zos cowboy. Tshej phav leej neeg tau tsiv mus nyob rau sab hnub poob thaum luag nrhiav tau nyiaj kub ntawd nyob rau xyoo ib txhiab yim puas plaub caug yim.

Qhov twg luag nrhiav tau nyiaj tau kub los tau tooj liab ces qhov ntawd luag tau ua zos nyob. Luag kuj tau ua zos nyob ze kev tshe ciav hlau thiab ntawm tej chaws nres tshe ciav hlau. Feem coob ntawm cov neeg nyob tej zos ntawd yog txiv neej. Ib txhia zos kuj khu xab nas hauv ntawv xov xwm thiab. Cov ntawv khu xas nas ntawd thov kom poj niam tuaj nyob ntawd.

Ib txhia zos kuj loj tuaj ua zos loj kawg li. Ib txhia kuj poob lawm vim cov qhov khawb nyiaj kub thiab tooj ntawd tau raug kaw lawm. Ib txhia ho poob lawm vim lawv nyob deb kev tsheb ciav hlau dhau lawm thaum lawv tuaj. Tib neeg tsiv mus nyob kom ze nyiaj kub thiab ze kev tsheb ciav hlau tshaj. Lawv cia li tseg tej zos ntawd tseg xwb. Cov zos uas thaum ub muaj neeg nyob coob coob niaj hnub no tsuas yog zos dab lawm xab.

Name _____

- **Read** *Gold in the American River* again.
- **Summarize** each section of the book. Follow the example.

---

pages 3–5
"Gold in the American River!"

1. James Marshall finds gold at Sutter's sawmill. Sam Brannan runs through the streets telling everybody about it. Everyone runs to the river.

---

pages 6–7
The Gold Rush

2. _____

_____

---

page 8
Reaching California

3. _____

_____

---

pages 9–10
Impact of the Gold Rush

4. _____

_____

---

pages 11–12
The Gold Rush Spirit Lives On

5. _____

_____

Family Link

Share what you learned about the Gold Rush with your family. Ask family members to tell you about things that are made out of gold.

Weekly Resources Guide for English Language Learner Support

For this week's content and language objectives, see p. 179e.

Instructional Strand	Day 1	Day 2
Concept Development/Academic Language	**TEACHER'S EDITION** • Academic Language, p. DI•16 • Concept Development, p. DI•16 • Anchored Talk, pp. 318j—318–319 • Preteach Academic Vocabulary, p. 321a • Concept Talk Video **ELL HANDBOOK** • Hear It, See It, Say It, Use It, pp. xxxvi–xxxvii • ELL Poster Talk, Concept Talk, p. 179c **ELL POSTER 26** • Day 1 Activities	**TEACHER'S EDITION** • Academic Language, p. DI•16 • Concept Development, p. DI•16 • Anchored Talk, p. 322a • Concept Talk Video **ELL HANDBOOK** • ELL Poster Talk, Concept Talk, p. 179c • Concept Talk Video Routine, p. 477 **ELL POSTER 26** • Day 2 Activities
Phonics and Spelling	**TEACHER'S EDITION** • Phonics and Spelling, p. DI•20	**TEACHER'S EDITION** • Phonics and Spelling, p. DI•20
Listening Comprehension	**TEACHER'S EDITION** • Modified Read Aloud, p. DI•19 • Read Aloud, p. 319b • Concept Talk Video **ELL HANDBOOK** • Concept Talk Video Routine, p. 477	**TEACHER'S EDITION** • Modified Read Aloud, p. DI•19 • AudioText of *The Truth About Austin's Amazing Bats* • Concept Talk Video **ELL HANDBOOK** • AudioText CD Routine, p. 477 • Problem and Solution, p. 490
Reading Comprehension	**TEACHER'S EDITION** • Preteach Draw Conclusions, p. DI•21	**TEACHER'S EDITION** • Reteach Draw Conclusions, p. DI•21 • Frontloading Reading, p. DI•22 **ELL HANDBOOK** • Picture It! Skill Instruction, pp. 180–180a • Multilingual Summaries, pp. 181–183
Vocabulary **Basic and Lesson Vocabulary** **Word Analysis: Prefix *dis-***	**TEACHER'S EDITION** • Basic Vocabulary, p. DI•17 • Preteach Lesson Vocabulary, p. DI•17 • Prefix *dis-*, p. DI•20 **ELL HANDBOOK** • Word Cards, p. 179 • ELL Vocabulary Routine, p. 471 **ELL POSTER 26** • Day 1 Activities	**TEACHER'S EDITION** • Basic Vocabulary, p. DI•17 • Reteach Lesson Vocabulary, p. DI•18 • Prefix *dis-*, p. DI•20 **ELL HANDBOOK** • Word Cards, p. 179 • Multilingual Vocabulary List, p. 431 **ELL POSTER 26** • Day 2 Activities
Grammar and Conventions	**TEACHER'S EDITION** • Preteach Modifiers, p. DI•24	**TEACHER'S EDITION** • Reteach Modifiers, p. DI•24
Writing	**TEACHER'S EDITION** • Writing a Journal Entry, p. DI•25 • Introduce Journal Entry, pp. 321e–321f	**TEACHER'S EDITION** • Writing Trait: Voice, pp. 329d–329e

ELL Handbook

Unit 6, Week 1 The Truth About Austin's Amazing Bats

Day 3	Day 4	Day 5
TEACHER'S EDITION • Academic Language, p. DI•16 • Concept Development, p. DI•16 • Anchored Talk, p. 330a • Concept Talk Video **ELL HANDBOOK** • ELL Poster Talk, Concept Talk, p. 179c **ELL POSTER 26** • Day 3 Activities	**TEACHER'S EDITION** • Academic Language, p. DI•16 • Concept Development, p. DI•16 • Anchored Talk, p. 340a • Concept Talk Video **ELL HANDBOOK** • ELL Poster Talk, Concept Talk, p. 179c **ELL POSTER 26** • Day 4 Activities	**TEACHER'S EDITION** • Academic Language, p. DI•16 • Concept Development, p. DI•16 • Concept Talk Video **ELL HANDBOOK** • ELL Poster Talk, Concept Talk, p. 179c **ELL POSTER 26** • Day 5 Activities
		TEACHER'S EDITION • Phonics and Spelling, p. DI•20
ELL HANDBOOK • Phonics Transition Lesson, pp. 288, 295	**ELL HANDBOOK** • Phonics Transition Lesson, pp. 288, 295	
TEACHER'S EDITION • AudioText of *The Truth About Austin's Amazing Bats* • Concept Talk Video **ELL HANDBOOK** • AudioText CD Routine, p. 477	**TEACHER'S EDITION** • Concept Talk Video	**TEACHER'S EDITION** • Concept Talk Video
TEACHER'S EDITION • Sheltered Reading, p. DI•22 **ELL HANDBOOK** • Multilingual Summaries, pp. 181–183	**TEACHER'S EDITION** • ELL/ELD Reader Guided Reading, p. DI•23 **ELL HANDBOOK** • ELL Study Guide, p. 184	**TEACHER'S EDITION** • ELL/ELD Reader Guided Reading, p. DI•23 **ELL HANDBOOK** • ELL Study Guide, p. 184
		TEACHER'S EDITION • Compound Words, p. 343i
ELL HANDBOOK • High-Frequency Words Activity Bank, p. 446 **ELL POSTER 26** • Day 3 Activities	**ELL HANDBOOK** • High-Frequency Words Activity Bank, p. 446	**ELL HANDBOOK** • High-Frequency Words Activity Bank, p. 446
TEACHER'S EDITION • Grammar Jammer **ELL HANDBOOK** • Grammar Transition Lesson, pp. 370–372, 374–378 • Grammar Jammer Routine, p. 478	**TEACHER'S EDITION** • Grammar Jammer **ELL HANDBOOK** • Grammar Transition Lesson, pp. 370–372, 374–378	**TEACHER'S EDITION** • Grammar Jammer **ELL HANDBOOK** • Grammar Transition Lesson, pp. 370–372, 374–378
TEACHER'S EDITION • Let's Write It!, p. 338–339 • Writing Trait: Voice, pp. 339a–339b	**TEACHER'S EDITION** • Revising Strategy, pp. 343d–343e	**TEACHER'S EDITION** • Modifiers, pp. 343p–343q

Question of the Week
How can unplanned situations have positive outcomes?

Throughout the week, use the ELL Poster to help students produce and comprehend language, understand the concept, and build English vocabulary. Use the Question of the Week and other questions to help students share ideas in pairs, small groups, or the large group. Sample questions are shown, with examples of possible responses by students.

Weekly Concept and Language Goals

- Explain how unplanned situations can be positive
- Describe the possible outcomes of an unplanned situation
- Discuss situations they have found themselves in that were unplanned

By the end of the lesson, students should be able to talk about and write sentences about how unplanned situations can be positive.

ELL Poster 26

Daily Team Talk

Day 1	Day 2	Day 3	Day 4	Day 5
After Day 1 activities on Poster, ask questions such as *How is this situation unplanned for two of the hikers in the poster picture?*	After Day 2 activity on Poster, ask questions such as *How do you think the hikers in the poster picture got lost?*	After Day 3 activity on Poster, ask questions such as *How do you think the lost hikers feel about the location they found by accident?*	After Day 4 activity on Poster, ask questions such as *Where is the eagle's planned destination?*	After Day 5 activity on Poster, ask questions such as *When were you in a situation that was not planned? How did it turn out?*
Beginning They got lost. **Intermediate** They planned a different hike. **Advanced** They had planned a different hike but got lost. **Advanced High** Two of the hikers had planned a different destination, but they got lost.	**Beginning** Did not use the map. **Intermediate** They didn't read the map right. **Advanced** They probably read the map incorrectly. **Advanced High** The hikers may have read their map incorrectly, or the map may be outdated.	**Beginning** It is pretty. **Intermediate** It is a very pretty place. **Advanced** They are happy that they found such a pretty location. **Advanced High** The hikers are happy that they found such a beautiful location, but they also may be sad that they did not reach their planned destination.	**Beginning** The nest. **Intermediate** It plans to go to its nest. **Advanced** The eagle plans to go to its nest. **Advanced High** The eagle's planned destination is its nest, where its hungry babies wait.	**Beginning** At a baseball game. Fun. **Intermediate** We went to a baseball game. It was fun. **Advanced** At the last minute, my cousin said we should go to a baseball game. It was fun. **Advanced High** For my cousin's birthday, she decided just before the game started that we should go to a baseball game. We ended up having a lot of fun.

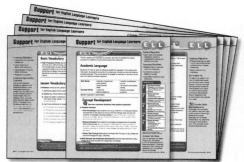

Teacher's Edition pages 318j–343q

Teacher's Edition pages DI•16–DI•25

ELL Handbook pp. 179a–184

See the support for English language learners throughout the lesson, including ELL strategies and scaffolded activities at points of use.

Differentiated Instruction for English language learners provides daily group activities that "frontload," or preteach, core instruction.

Find additional lesson materials that support the core lesson and the ELL instructional pages.

ELL Poster 26

ELL Reader 5.6.1

ELD Reader 5.6.1

Concept Literacy Reader

ELD, ELL Reader
Teaching Guide

Concept Literacy Reader
Teaching Guide

Technology

Online Teacher's Edition Use the digital version of the core Teacher's Edition for planning and instruction.

eReaders
This week's ELL and ELD Readers and Concept Literacy Reader are also available in digital format.

This Week's Content and Language Objectives by Strand

Concept Development/ Academic Language How can unplanned situations have positive outcomes?	**Content Objective** • Use concept vocabulary related to unexpected situations with positive outcomes. **Language Objective** • Express ideas in response to art and discussion.
Phonics and Spelling Suffixes *-sion, -tion, -ation*	**Content Objective** • Identify suffixes in words. **Language Objectives** • Apply phonics and decoding skills to vocabulary. • Use English spelling rules and patterns with accuracy.
Listening Comprehension Modified Read Aloud: "A Sweet Treat"	**Content Objective** • Monitor and adjust oral comprehension. **Language Objectives** • Discuss oral passages. • Use a graphic organizer to take notes.
Reading Comprehension Draw Conclusions	**Content Objectives** • Form opinions and make decisions about text. • Monitor and adjust comprehension. **Language Objectives** • Demonstrate and expand comprehension with inferential skills. • Use details from text to write a conclusions.
Vocabulary Basic and Lesson Vocabulary	**Language Objectives** • Understand and use basic vocabulary. • Learn meanings of grade-level vocabulary. • Produce drawings, phrases, or short sentences to show understanding of Lesson Vocabulary.
Word Analysis Prefix *dis-*	**Content Objective** • Identify prefixes in words. **Language Objective** • Discuss meaning of words with the prefix *dis-*.
Grammar and Conventions Modifiers	**Content Objective** • Identify modifiers as adjectives and adverbs. **Language Objectives** • Speak using modifiers. • Write phrases and sentences with adjectives and adverbs.
Writing Writing a Journal Entry	**Content Objective** • Express the writer's personality through relating feelings about a personal experience. **Language Objectives** • Write a journal entry about a personal experience. • Distinguish between formal and informal English.

Word Cards for Vocabulary Activities

bizarre	breathtaking
headline	high-pitched
roost	vital

Teacher Note: Beginning Teach two to three words. **Intermediate** Teach three to four words. **Advanced** Teach four to five words. **Advanced High** Teach all words.

Name _____

Read the story. Then **fill in** the four boxes that follow to show what the story is about.

- Write details from the text in the first two boxes.
- Write something from your own knowledge in the third box.
- Write a conclusion about the story in the fourth box.

The Emperor Who Had No Clothes

There once lived an emperor who liked clothes. He heard that two men could make the finest suit in the world. The men said people who were stupid could not see the clothes. The emperor dressed in this suit for a parade. He didn't say that he could not see what he was wearing. He was afraid the people in town would think that he was stupid. Of course, everyone praised the emperor's new clothes, afraid to say that they couldn't see them. Then a child said: "But he has nothing on!" Soon everyone was shouting that the emperor had nothing on. The emperor heard this. The people were right, but he went on marching.

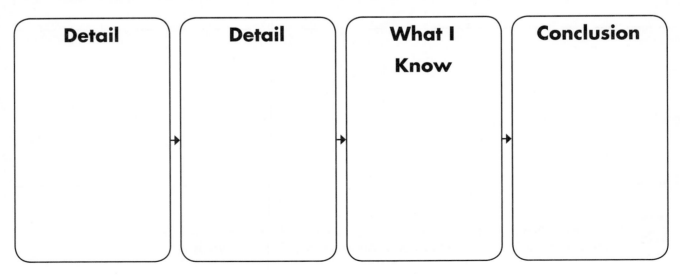

Detail	**Detail**	**What I Know**	**Conclusion**

Draw Conclusions

Use this lesson to supplement or replace the skill lesson on page 319c of the Teacher's Edition. Display the Skill Points (at right) and share them with students.

Teach/Model

Beginning Say: *A good leader listens to all people. A good leader tries to be fair. Sometimes not everyone is happy with a leader's decisions.* Have students tell what they know about leadership. Say: *Draw a conclusion about leaders.* (Possible answer: It is hard to be a good leader.)

Intermediate Say: *President Lincoln led our country during war. He fought to keep the country together. He wanted all people to be free.* Have students use these details and prior knowledge to write a conclusion. (Possible answer: Lincoln was a great leader.)

Advanced Write on the board: *Rosa and Jon are running for class president. Rosa wants to help her classmates. She talks to them about many issues. Jon just puts up a lot of posters.* Have students write a conclusion about the story. (Possible answer: Rosa puts in more effort to be class president.) Have them explain how they reached their conclusions.

Advanced High Have students write a short paragraph about a familiar leader. Pair students and have them share paragraphs. Have each partner draw a conclusion about the other partner's selected leader.

Then distribute copies of Picture It! page 180.

• Have students look at the picture and read the title of the story.
• Review the Skill Points with students.
• Read the story aloud. Ask: *What details do you know about the emperor's clothes? What conclusion can you make based on the details of this story?* Discuss students' ideas.

Practice

Read aloud the directions on page 180. Have students reread the story silently. Have them look at the picture and the story as they answer the questions.

Beginning Students can tell what they want to write before filling in the boxes. Provide help with writing.

Intermediate Students can look for the details in the story and then write sentences to fill in the graphic organizer.

Advanced Students can write sentences to fill in the graphic organizer and then check them by silently rereading the story and making any necessary corrections.

Advanced High Students can write sentences to fill in the graphic organizer and then orally explain how details from the story helped them draw the conclusions.

Answers for page 180: Possible answers: *Detail:* The emperor believed he was wearing clothes that some people could not see. *Detail:* He dressed in the suit for a parade. *What I Know:* Clothes like these do not exist. *Conclusion:* The emperor was tricked.

Skill Points

✔ When you **draw conclusions,** you think about details in the text. Together, the details tell you something that might not be actually said in the text.

✔ A conclusion is an idea or decision you make after combining details from the text and your personal knowledge.

Multilingual Summaries

The Truth About Austin's Amazing Bats

Every summer, 1.5 million bats visit the city of Austin, Texas. They live under a large bridge in Austin. Many people come to see them. Long ago, the people of Austin were afraid of the bats. They thought bats hurt people. They tried to get rid of the bats.

Ecologists at Bat Conservation International (BCI) try to teach people the truth about bats. Bats do not attack humans. They use sounds to find their way at night. They eat harmful insects. Bats also help pollinate flowers. The bats in Austin are also a thrill to see!

La verdad sobre los sorprendentes murciélagos de Austin

Cada verano, 1.5 millones de murciélagos visitan la ciudad de Austin, Texas. Viven bajo un puente en Austin. Muchas personas van a verlos. Hace mucho, los habitantes de Austin les tenían miedo. Pensaban que les atacaban a las personas. Trataron de deshacerse de ellos.

Ecologistas de la organización Conservación Internacional del Murciélago (BCI) trataron de mostrar la verdad sobre los murciélagos. Los murciélagos no atacan a las personas. Usan sonidos para moverse durante la noche. Comen insectos que son nocivos para las personas. También ayudan a polinizar las flores. Además, ¡son un gran espectáculo!

Multilingual Summaries

Chinese

奥斯汀的奇妙蝙蝠

每一年的夏天都有一百五十万的游客来到得克萨斯州的奥斯汀；它们住在奥斯汀的一条大桥底下，很多人都来看它们。很久以前，奥斯汀的人很害怕蝙蝠；他们以为蝙蝠会伤害人，所以就想灭绝它们。

国际蝙蝠保育组织的生态学家教育人们有关蝙蝠的生态：蝙蝠不会袭击人类；它们用声波在晚间导航；它们吃有害的昆虫；它们帮助传播花粉；观赏奥斯汀的蝙蝠也很有意思。

Vietnamese

Sự thật về những con dơi lạ lùng ở Austin

Mỗi mùa Hè, 1 triệu rưởi con dơi đến viếng thăm thành phố Austin, Texas. Chúng sống dưới gầm một cây cầu lớn ở Austin. Nhiều người đến xem chúng. Đã lâu rồi, người dân Austin sợ dơi. Họ nghĩ rằng dơi làm hại người. Họ cố trừ khử dơi.

Những nhà sinh thái học tại Hội Bảo tồn Quốc tế (BCI) cố dạy cho dân chúng biết sự thật về loài dơi. Dơi không tấn công người. Chúng dùng âm thanh để tìm đường trong đêm. Chúng ăn những côn trùng có hại. Dơi cũng giúp cho hoa thụ phấn. Dơi ở Austin cũng khiến người ta háo hức đến xem !

Multilingual Summaries

오스틴의 놀라운 박쥐에 관한 진실

매년 여름 150 만 마리의 박쥐가 오스틴 시를 찾아온다. 박쥐들은 오스틴의 큰 다리 밑에서 산다. 많은 사람들은 박쥐들을 보러 온다. 오래 전에, 오스틴 시 주민들은 박쥐를 무서워했다. 박쥐가 사람을 해친다고 생각했다. 그래서 박쥐를 없애려고 했다.

박쥐 보전 국제 연구소 (BCI)의 생태학자들은 사람들에게 박쥐에 관한 진실을 가르치려고 노력한다. 박쥐는 사람을 공격하지 않는다. 박쥐는 밤에 길을 찾으려고 소리를 이용한다. 해충을 잡아먹는다. 또 꽃 이수분하는 것을 돕는다. 오스틴의 박쥐들은 흥미만점의 구경거리이다!

Hmong

Qhov Tseeb Txog Austin Cov Puav uas Muaj Peevxwm

Txhua txhia caij ntuj kub, 1.5 lab tus puav mus rua nrag Austin, Texas. Lawv nyob hauvqab ib tus choj loj loj hauv Austin. Tibneeg coob coob tuaj saib lawv. Yav tag los, cov tibneeg nyob hauv Austin ntshai puav kawg li. Lawv xav tias puav ua rau tibneeg raug mob. Lawv sim tua kom tag cov puav.

Cov tub txawg ntse kawm txog tsiaj tom Bat Convservation International (BCI) siv zog qhia cov tibneeg qhov tseeb txog puav. Puav tsi caum tua tibneeg. Lawv siv lawv lub suab qw nrhiav lawv txoj kev thaus mo ntuj. Lawv noj cov kab uas muaj taug. Lawv pab ywg moov paj rau cov paj. Cov puav nyob hauv Austin mas mus saib lomzem kawg.

Name _____

- **Read** *An Unexpected Friend* again.
- Think about David's feelings in the book. **Write** sentences to describe five of his feelings. Follow the example. Then **write** sentences about how you know this from the story.

Pages	David's Feelings	How Do You Know?
2–3	**1.** David is feeling bored. **2.** _____	**1.** _____ **2.** _____
4–6	**3.** _____ **4.** _____	**3.** _____ **4.** _____
7–8	**5.** _____	**5.** _____

Family Link

Ask family members to talk about their feelings. Have them tell about a time when they had good feelings and a time when they had bad feelings.

Weekly Resources Guide for English Language Learner Support

For this week's content and language objectives, see p. 185e.

Instructional Strand	Day 1	Day 2
Concept Development/Academic Language	**TEACHER'S EDITION** • Academic Language, p. DI•41 • Concept Development, p. DI•41 • Anchored Talk, pp. 344j—344–345 • Preteach Academic Vocabulary, p. 347a • Concept Talk Video **ELL HANDBOOK** • Hear It, See It, Say It, Use It, pp. xxxvi–xxxvii • ELL Poster Talk, Concept Talk, p. 185c **ELL POSTER 27** • Day 1 Activities	**TEACHER'S EDITION** • Academic Language, p. DI•41 • Concept Development, p. DI•41 • Anchored Talk, p. 348a • Concept Talk Video **ELL HANDBOOK** • ELL Poster Talk, Concept Talk, p. 185c • Concept Talk Video Routine, p. 477 **ELL POSTER 27** • Day 2 Activities
Phonics and Spelling	**TEACHER'S EDITION** • Phonics and Spelling, p. DI•45	**TEACHER'S EDITION** • Phonics and Spelling, p. DI•45
Listening Comprehension	**TEACHER'S EDITION** • Modified Read Aloud, p. DI•44 • Read Aloud, p. 345b • Concept Talk Video **ELL HANDBOOK** • Concept Talk Video Routine, p. 477	**TEACHER'S EDITION** • Modified Read Aloud, p. DI•44 • AudioText of *The Mystery of Saint Matthew Island* • Concept Talk Video **ELL HANDBOOK** • AudioText CD Routine, p. 477 • Time Line, p. 491
Reading Comprehension	**TEACHER'S EDITION** • Preteach Main Idea and Details, p. DI•46	**TEACHER'S EDITION** • Reteach Main Idea and Details, p. DI•46 • Frontloading Reading, p. DI•47 **ELL HANDBOOK** • Picture It! Skill Instruction, pp. 186–186a • Multilingual Summaries, pp. 187–189
Vocabulary **Basic and Lesson Vocabulary** **Word Analysis: Homophones**	**TEACHER'S EDITION** • Basic Vocabulary, p. DI•42 • Preteach Lesson Vocabulary, p. DI•42 • Homophones, p. DI•45 **ELL HANDBOOK** • Word Cards, p. 185 • ELL Vocabulary Routine, p. 471 **ELL POSTER 27** • Day 1 Activities	**TEACHER'S EDITION** • Basic Vocabulary, p. DI•42 • Reteach Lesson Vocabulary, p. DI•43 • Homophones, p. DI•45 **ELL HANDBOOK** • Word Cards, p. 185 • Multilingual Vocabulary List, p. 431 **ELL POSTER 27** • Day 2 Activities
Grammar and Conventions	**TEACHER'S EDITION** • Teach Conjunctions, p. DI•49	**TEACHER'S EDITION** • Reteach Conjunctions, p. DI•49
Writing	**TEACHER'S EDITION** • Writing a Paraphrase, p. DI•50 • Introduce Mystery, pp. 347e–347f	**TEACHER'S EDITION** • Writing Trait: Focus/Ideas, pp. 355d–355e

The Mystery of Saint Matthew Island

This symbol indicates leveled instruction to address language proficiency levels.

Day 3	Day 4	Day 5
TEACHER'S EDITION • Academic Language, p. DI•41 • Concept Development, p. DI•41 • Anchored Talk, p. 356a • Concept Talk Video **ELL HANDBOOK** • ELL Poster Talk, Concept Talk, p. 185c **ELL POSTER 27** • Day 3 Activities	**TEACHER'S EDITION** • Academic Language, p. DI•41 • Concept Development, p. DI•41 • Anchored Talk, p. 364a • Concept Talk Video **ELL HANDBOOK** • ELL Poster Talk, Concept Talk, p. 185c **ELL POSTER 27** • Day 4 Activities	**TEACHER'S EDITION** • Academic Language, p. DI•41 • Concept Development, p. DI•41 • Concept Talk Video **ELL HANDBOOK** • ELL Poster Talk, Concept Talk, p. 185c **ELL POSTER 27** • Day 5 Activities
ELL HANDBOOK • Phonics Transition Lesson, pp. 302, 307	**ELL HANDBOOK** • Phonics Transition Lesson, pp. 302, 307	**TEACHER'S EDITION** • Phonics and Spelling, p. DI•45
TEACHER'S EDITION • AudioText of *The Mystery of Saint Matthew Island* • Concept Talk Video **ELL HANDBOOK** • AudioText CD Routine, p. 477	**TEACHER'S EDITION** • Concept Talk Video	**TEACHER'S EDITION** • Concept Talk Video
TEACHER'S EDITION • Sheltered Reading, p. DI•47 **ELL HANDBOOK** • Multilingual Summaries, pp. 187–189	**TEACHER'S EDITION** • ELL/ELD Reader Guided Reading, p. DI•48 **ELL HANDBOOK** • ELL Study Guide, p. 190	**TEACHER'S EDITION** • ELL/ELD Reader Guided Reading, p. DI•48 **ELL HANDBOOK** • ELL Study Guide, p. 190
ELL HANDBOOK • High-Frequency Words Activity Bank, p. 446 **ELL POSTER 27** • Day 3 Activities	**ELL HANDBOOK** • High-Frequency Words Activity Bank, p. 446	**TEACHER'S EDITION** • Russian Word Origins, p. 369i **ELL HANDBOOK** • High-Frequency Words Activity Bank, p. 446
TEACHER'S EDITION • Grammar Jammer **ELL HANDBOOK** • Grammar Transition Lesson, pp. 379, 381 • Grammar Jammer Routine, p. 478	**TEACHER'S EDITION** • Grammar Jammer **ELL HANDBOOK** • Grammar Transition Lesson, pp. 379, 381	**TEACHER'S EDITION** • Grammar Jammer **ELL HANDBOOK** • Grammar Transition Lesson, pp. 379, 381
TEACHER'S EDITION • Let's Write It!, p. 362–363 • Writer's Craft: Details, pp. 363a–363b	**TEACHER'S EDITION** • Revising Strategy, pp. 369d–369e	**TEACHER'S EDITION** • Conjunctions, pp. 369p–369q

Question of the Week
What unexpected effects can humans have on nature?

Throughout the week, use the ELL Poster to help students produce and comprehend language, understand the concept, and build English vocabulary. Use the Question of the Week and other questions to help students share ideas in pairs, small groups, or the large group. Sample questions are shown, with examples of possible responses by students.

ELL Poster 27

Weekly Concept and Language Goals

• Understand the unexpected effects humans have on nature

• Name ways humans help and hurt nature

• Discuss how humans impact nature

By the end of the lesson, students should be able to talk about and write sentences about the unexpected effects humans have on nature.

Daily Team Talk

Day 1	Day 2	Day 3	Day 4	Day 5
After Day 1 activities on Poster, ask questions such as *How do humans affect the reindeer in the poster picture?*	After Day 2 activity on Poster, ask questions such as *Why do you think people brought reindeer to the island?*	After Day 3 activity on Poster, ask questions such as *How can humans help the reindeer on the island?*	After Day 4 activity on Poster, ask questions such as *What are some other ways that people hurt nature?*	*After Day 5 activity on Poster, ask questions such as What are some ways that people can help nature?*
Beginning They moved them. **Intermediate** They brought them to a new place. **Advanced** People brought the reindeer to a new place where there was not enough food. **Advanced High** Humans moved the reindeer to an island where there is not enough food for them to survive. They are stranded on the island and cannot find food.	**Beginning** To live there. **Intermediate** They want the reindeer to live on the island. **Advanced** People wanted more kinds of animals to live on the island. **Advanced High** People probably wanted to make the animals living on the island more diverse.	**Beginning** Bring food. **Intermediate** They can bring them shrubs and plants. **Advanced** People can bring the reindeer plants to eat or move them back. **Advanced High** People can introduce plants that the reindeer can eat or move them back to their original habitat.	**Beginning** We throw trash. **Intermediate** We throw trash on the ground. **Advanced** People throw trash on the ground that animals can get stuck in. **Advanced High** Some people litter, rather than put garbage where it belongs. Animals can get stuck in the garbage and it can pollute natural habitats.	**Beginning** We can clean up litter. **Intermediate** We can recycle and reuse. **Advanced** People can recycle and reuse products. That way trash is saved from landfills. **Advanced High** People can recycle and reuse products to avoid adding more garbage to landfills. They can also clean up litter when they see it.

This Week's Materials

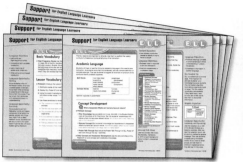

Teacher's Edition pages 344j–369q

See the support for English language learners throughout the lesson, including ELL strategies and scaffolded activities at points of use.

Teacher's Edition pages DI•41–DI•50

Differentiated Instruction for English language learners provides daily group activities that "frontload," or preteach, core instruction.

ELL Handbook pp. 185a–190

Find additional lesson materials that support the core lesson and the ELL instructional pages.

Poster 27

ELL Reader 5.6.2

ELD Reader 5.6.2

Concept Literacy Reader

ELD, ELL Reader Teaching Guide

Concept Literacy Reader Teaching Guide

Technology

Online Teacher's Edition Use the digital version of the core Teacher's Edition for planning and instruction.

eReaders
This week's ELL and ELD Readers and Concept Literacy Reader are also available in digital format.

This Week's Content and Language Objectives by Strand

Concept Development/ Academic Language What unexpected effects can humans have on nature?	**Content Objective** • Use concept vocabulary related to effects humans have on nature. **Language Objectives** • Express ideas in response to art and discussion. • Use prior experiences to understand ideas.
Phonics and Spelling Final Syllable -ance, -ence	**Content Objectives** • Distinguish syllables in multi-syllabic words. • Listen for vowel sounds in individual syllables. **Language Objectives** • Apply phonics and decoding skills to vocabulary. • Discuss intonation patterns of English.
Listening Comprehension Modified Read Aloud: "A Place for the Animals"	**Content Objective** • Monitor and adjust oral comprehension. **Language Objectives** • Discuss oral passages. • Use a graphic organizer to take notes.
Reading Comprehension Main Idea and Details	**Content Objectives** • Identify main ideas and details that aid comprehension. • Monitor and adjust comprehension. **Language Objectives** • Discuss how to identify the most important idea of a topic. • Identify details that support the main idea. • Use details from text to write a conclusion.
Vocabulary Basic and Lesson Vocabulary	**Language Objectives** • Understand and use basic, grade-level and high-frequency vocabulary. • Write using content-based vocabulary. • Produce drawings, phrases, or short sentences to show understanding of Lesson Vocabulary.
Word Analysis Homophones	**Content Objective** • Identify homophones. **Language Objective** • Discuss the pronunciation and meaning of homophones.
Grammar and Conventions Conjunctions	**Content Objectives** • Identify conjunctions. • Explain the purpose of coordinating and subordinating conjunctions. **Language Objectives** • Speak using modifiers. • Use conjunctions to connect ideas meaningfully.
Writing Writing a Paraphrase	**Content Objective** • Identify the features of a paraphrase. **Language Objective** • Write a paraphrase of a mystery, including clues to reveal what happened, how it happened, and why.

Word Cards for Vocabulary Activities

bleached	**carcasses**
decay	**parasites**
scrawny	**starvation**
suspicions	**tundra**

Teacher Note: Beginning Teach three to four words. **Intermediate** Teach four to six words. **Advanced** Teach six to seven words. **Advanced High** Teach all words.

Name _____

Read the passage. **Answer** the questions that follow.

The Mystery of Stonehenge

Stonehenge is a mysterious place in southern England. It consists of a circle of very large stone slabs. The stones were erected thousands of years ago, before people had machines to help them build and lift. The stones weigh as much as 50 tons (100,000 pounds) each. Even more amazing, the stones were brought from places up to 240 miles away! Nobody is sure why the stones were placed here. But one thing is certain: Stonehenge must have been very important to the ancient people who built it.

1. What is the main idea?

_____

_____

2. What are three examples that support the main idea?

_____

_____

_____

_____

_____

ELL Handbook

Main Idea and Details

Use this lesson to supplement or replace the skill lesson on page 345c of the Teacher's Edition. Display the Skill Points (at right) and share them with students.

Teach/Model

Beginning Say: *There are many ways to learn about past cultures. You can look at their artwork or their writings to learn about how they lived.* Help students identify which sentence is the main idea (first sentence) and which sentence tells details that support the main idea (second sentence).

Intermediate Write: *England has many ancient stone structures. Stonehenge and Avebury are sites of famous stone circles. Standing stones are found in northern England.* Ask: *Which sentence tells the main idea?* (the first sentence) *Which sentences tell details?* (the second and third sentences)

Advanced Write on the board: *There are many historic places in our country.* Say: *This is the main idea of a paragraph I am writing. Write a detail that supports this main idea.* Allow students to use reference materials, if needed.

Advanced High Read aloud information about the Great Pyramids from an encyclopedia. Have students use the information to write a main idea about ancient Egypt. For example: *The ancient Egyptians were master builders.* Then have them write two details that support their main idea.

Then distribute copies of Picture It! page 186.

- Point to the illustration. Tell students that it shows Stonehenge, an ancient place in England. If necessary, point to England on a map.
- Review the Skill Points with students.
- Read the passage aloud. Ask: *What are some details about Stonehenge?*

Practice

Read aloud the directions on page 186. Have volunteers take turns reading the paragraph aloud. Have students look at the picture and the paragraph as they answer the questions.

Beginning Students can say what main idea and supporting details they want to write before writing words and phrases. Provide help with English words and writing.

Intermediate Students can first answer orally and then write their answers. Provide help with spelling.

Advanced Students can write their answers and then check them by rereading the paragraph and comparing what they wrote to the information in the paragraph.

Advanced High Students can write their answers and then orally explain how the details tell more about the main idea.

Answers for page 186: Possible answers: 1. Stonehenge is a mysterious place. 2. It was built thousands of years ago, before people had machines to help them. The stones came from places up to 240 miles away. Nobody is sure why the stones were placed here.

Skill Points

✔ The **main idea** is the most important idea in a paragraph or passage. The author often states the main idea at the beginning or the end of the paragraph.

✔ Sometimes the main idea is not directly stated.

✔ **Details** are small pieces of information that tell more about the main idea.

Multilingual Summaries

The Mystery of Saint Matthew Island

Scientists released twenty-nine reindeer on Saint Matthew Island in 1944. There were no predators on the island. Saint Matthew Island had plenty of food for the reindeer. The herd quickly expanded. By 1963, there were more than six thousand reindeer.

The reindeer began to die. No one knew why. A scientist named David Klein went to the island to investigate. He knew the reindeer had not been exposed to parasites. There were no predators on the island. Why did they die?

Dr. Klein examined the bones. They had no fat in their bone marrow. Dr. Klein realized that the animals had too little to eat. They had died during a hard winter. The herd had grown too fast. They had eaten all the food on the island and died of starvation.

Spanish

El misterio de la isla de Saint Matthew

En 1944, los científicos llevaron veintinueve renos a la isla de Saint Matthew y los dejaron en libertad. No había depredadores en la isla. La isla de Saint Matthew tenía suficiente comida para los renos. La manada se expandió rápidamente. Para 1963, había más de seis mil renos.

Los renos comenzaron a morir. Nadie sabía por qué. Un científico llamado David Klein fue a la isla para investigar. Él sabía que los renos no estaban expuestos a los parásitos. No había depredadores en la isla. Entonces, ¿por qué murieron?

El Dr. Klein examinó los huesos. No tenían grasa en la médula. El Dr. Klein se dio cuenta de que ellos habían tenido muy poco que comer. Habían muerto durante un duro invierno. La manada había crecido muy rápido. Los renos se habían comido toda la comida de la isla y murieron de hambre.

Multilingual Summaries

Chinese

聖馬修島的秘密

　　1944年，科學家把29頭馴鹿放到聖馬修島上。那裏沒有凶猛的食肉動物，而且食物充足，因此馴鹿急劇增長。到1963年，島上的馴鹿數目已經超過6000多。

　　可是馴鹿開始莫名其妙地死去，沒有人知道原因。科學家克萊因去島上研究。他知道這裏沒有寄生蟲，也沒有食肉動物。為什麼馴鹿會神秘地死亡？

　　克萊因仔細研究馴鹿殘骸，發現骨髓中沒有脂肪。他終於明白，原因是食物太少，在嚴寒的冬天，就會造成死亡。馴鹿繁殖迅速，吃光島上所有食物，活活餓死了。

Vietnamese

Điều Bí Ẩn ở Đảo Saint Matthew

　　Các nhà khoa học đã thả hai mươi chín con nai tuyết trên Đảo Saint Matthew vào năm 1944. Không có những con dã thú săn bắt mồi trên đảo này. Đảo Saint Matthew có nhiều thức ăn cho các con nai tuyết này. Đàn nai gia tăng mau chóng. Đến năm 1963, đã có trên sáu ngàn con nai tuyết.

　　Những con nai tuyết bắt đầu chết. Không ai biết vì lý do gì. Một nhà khoa học tên David Klein đi đến đảo này để điều tra. Ông biết là các con nai tuyết này không có bị ký sinh trùng. Trên đảo cũng không có dã thú săn mồi. Tại sao những con nai này chết?

　　Klein khám nghiệm những mảnh xương. Các mảnh xương không có chất mỡ trong tủy xương. Bác sĩ Klein hiểu ra là những con thú này đã không có đủ ăn. Chúng chết trong một mùa đông khắc nghiệt. Đàn nai đã gia tăng quá nhanh. Chúng đã ăn hết mọi thức ăn trên đảo, và chết vì đói.

Multilingual Summaries

Korean

세인트 매튜섬의 미스터리

1944년 과학자들은 세인트 매튜섬에 순록 29마리를 풀어주었다. 섬에는 어떤 맹수도 없었으며 먹을 것도 풍부했다. 순록 무리는 빠른 속도로 성장했다. 1963년까지 그곳엔 6천마리 이상의 순록이 있었다.

그런데 순록이 죽기 시작했고 누구도 그 이유를 알지 못했다. 데이비드 클라인이라는 한 과학자가 섬에 들어가 조사를 시작했다. 그는 순록이 기생충에 노출되지 않았고 섬에는 맹수도 없었다는 사실을 알게 되었다. 그렇다면 순록들은 왜 죽은 것일까?

클라인은 순록의 뼈를 조사했는데 그들의 골수에는 지방이 하나도 없었고, 섬에 먹을 것이 너무나 없었다는 것을 알아냈다. 이들은 혹독한 겨울에 죽었다. 즉 순록 무리가 너무도 빨리 늘어나 섬의 모든 먹을 것을 먹어 치우고는 굶어 죽었던 것이다.

Hmong

Txoj Kev Xav Tsis Thoob Txog Lub Koog Povtxwv Saint Matthew

Nyob xhoo ib txhiab cuaj puas plaub caug plaub cov kws Scientists tso nees nkaum cuaj cov muas lwj tom lub koog pov txwv Saint Matthew. Nyob lub koog povtxwv ntawd tsis tau muaj lwm cov tsiaj txhu zoo li lawv. Lub koog povtxwv Saint Matthew tau muaj cov mov txaus rau cov muas lwj noj. Lub pab muas lwj tau loj hlob sai sai li. Txog xyoo ib txhiab cuaj puas rau caum peb, tau muaj rau hav cov muas lwj.

Cov muas lwj pib tas sim neej. Tsis tau muaj leejtwg paub ua li cas. Ib tug kws scientisit hu ua David Klein mus xyuas lub koog pov txwv nrhiav kawm saib. Nws twb paub tias cov muas lwj tsis tau ntsib kab mob hlo li. Tsis tau muaj lwm cov tsiaj txhu sib twv tom lub koog pov txwv. Ua licas lawv tuag?

Klein kawm saib cov pob txha. Cov muas lwj tsis muaj cov roj rau hauv lawv pob txha hlwb. Tus kws Klein twb tau nrhiav cov tsiaj txhu tsis muaj cov mov txaus rau lawv noj. Lawv tau tam sim neej thaum lub ciaj nyuj no no heev. Lub pab tau loj hlob sai sai dhau lawm. Lawv tau hoj txhua yam mov nyob rau lub koog pov txwv, lawv thiaj li tau tuag.

- **Read** *All Things in Balance* again.
- **Draw** animals or plants in each level of a food chain.
- **Write** a sentence about each level of the food chain you drew.

1._____

_____

2._____

_____

3._____

_____

4._____

_____

Family Link
Share the food chain with your family. Ask family members to help you create another food chain.

Weekly Resources Guide for English Language Learner Support

For this week's content and language objectives, see p. 191e.

Instructional Strand	Day 1	Day 2
Concept Development/Academic Language	**TEACHER'S EDITION** • Academic Language, p. DI•66 • Concept Development, p. DI•66 • Anchored Talk, pp. 370j—370–371 • Preteach Academic Vocabulary, p. 373a • Concept Talk Video **ELL HANDBOOK** • Hear It, See It, Say It, Use It, pp. xxxvi–xxxvii • ELL Poster Talk, Concept Talk, p. 191c **ELL POSTER 28** • Day 1 Activities	**TEACHER'S EDITION** • Academic Language, p. DI•66 • Concept Development, p. DI•66 • Anchored Talk, p. 374a • Concept Talk Video **ELL HANDBOOK** • ELL Poster Talk, Concept Talk, p. 191c • Concept Talk Video Routine, p. 477 **ELL POSTER 28** • Day 2 Activities
Phonics and Spelling	**TEACHER'S EDITION** • Phonics and Spelling, p. DI•70	**TEACHER'S EDITION** • Phonics and Spelling, p. DI•70
Listening Comprehension	**TEACHER'S EDITION** • Modified Read Aloud, p. DI•69 • Read Aloud, p. 371b • Concept Talk Video **ELL HANDBOOK** • Concept Talk Video Routine, p. 477	**TEACHER'S EDITION** • Modified Read Aloud, p. DI•69 • AudioText of *King Midas and the Golden Touch* • Concept Talk Video **ELL HANDBOOK** • AudioText CD Routine, p. 477 • K-W-L Chart, p. 480
Reading Comprehension	**TEACHER'S EDITION** • Preteach Compare and Contrast, p. DI•71	**TEACHER'S EDITION** • Reteach Compare and Contrast, p. DI•71 • Frontloading Reading, p. DI•72 **ELL HANDBOOK** • Picture It! Skill Instruction, pp. 192–192a • Multilingual Summaries, pp. 193–195
Vocabulary **Basic and Lesson Vocabulary** **Word Analysis: Complex Spelling Patterns** *ous* = /us/, *ci* = /sh/, *ti* = /sh/	**TEACHER'S EDITION** • Basic Vocabulary, p. DI•67 • Preteach Lesson Vocabulary, p. DI•67 • Complex Spelling Patterns *ous* = /us/, *ci* = /sh/, *ti* = /sh/, p. DI•70 **ELL HANDBOOK** • Word Cards, p. 191 • ELL Vocabulary Routine, p. 471 **ELL POSTER 28** • Day 1 Activities	**TEACHER'S EDITION** • Basic Vocabulary, p. DI•67 • Reteach Lesson Vocabulary, p. DI•68 • Complex Spelling Patterns *ous* = /us/, *ci* = /sh/, *ti* = /sh/, p. DI•70 **ELL HANDBOOK** • Word Cards, p. 191 • Multilingual Vocabulary List, p. 431 **ELL POSTER 28** • Day 2 Activities
Grammar and Conventions	**TEACHER'S EDITION** • Teach Commas, p. DI•74	**TEACHER'S EDITION** • Teach Commas, p. DI•74
Writing	**TEACHER'S EDITION** • Point of View, p. DI•75 • Introduce Parody, pp. 373e–373f	**TEACHER'S EDITION** • Writing Trait: Plot, pp. 383d–383e

This symbol indicates leveled instruction to address language proficiency levels.

Day 3	Day 4	Day 5
TEACHER'S EDITION • Academic Language, p. DI•66 • Concept Development, p. DI•66 • Anchored Talk, p. 384a • Concept Talk Video **ELL HANDBOOK** • ELL Poster Talk, Concept Talk, p. 191c **ELL POSTER 28** • Day 3 Activities	**TEACHER'S EDITION** • Academic Language, p. DI•66 • Concept Development, p. DI•66 • Anchored Talk, p. 398a • Concept Talk Video **ELL HANDBOOK** • ELL Poster Talk, Concept Talk, p. 191c **ELL POSTER 28** • Day 4 Activities	**TEACHER'S EDITION** • Academic Language, p. DI•66 • Concept Development, p. DI•66 • Concept Talk Video **ELL HANDBOOK** • ELL Poster Talk, Concept Talk, p. 191c **ELL POSTER 28** • Day 5 Activities
		TEACHER'S EDITION • Phonics and Spelling, p. DI•70
ELL HANDBOOK • Phonics Transition Lesson, pp. 300, 305 **TEACHER'S EDITION** • AudioText of *King Midas and the Golden Touch* • Concept Talk Video **ELL HANDBOOK** • AudioText CD Routine, p. 477	**ELL HANDBOOK** • Phonics Transition Lesson, pp. 300, 305 **TEACHER'S EDITION** • Concept Talk Video	**TEACHER'S EDITION** • Concept Talk Video
TEACHER'S EDITION • Sheltered Reading, p. DI•72 **ELL HANDBOOK** • Multilingual Summaries, pp. 193–195	**TEACHER'S EDITION** • ELL/ELD Reader Guided Reading, p. DI•73 **ELL HANDBOOK** • ELL Study Guide, p. 196	**TEACHER'S EDITION** • ELL/ELD Reader Guided Reading, p. DI•73 **ELL HANDBOOK** • ELL Study Guide, p. 196
		TEACHER'S EDITION • Complex Spelling Patterns: *ci*/sh/, *ti*/sh/, *ous*/us/, p. 401i
ELL HANDBOOK • High-Frequency Words Activity Bank, p. 446 **ELL POSTER 28** • Day 3 Activities	**ELL HANDBOOK** • High-Frequency Words Activity Bank, p. 446	**ELL HANDBOOK** • High-Frequency Words Activity Bank, p. 446
TEACHER'S EDITION • Grammar Jammer **ELL HANDBOOK** • Grammar Transition Lesson, pp. 346, 359 • Grammar Jammer Routine, p. 478	**TEACHER'S EDITION** • Grammar Jammer **ELL HANDBOOK** • Grammar Transition Lesson, pp. 346, 359	**TEACHER'S EDITION** • Grammar Jammer **ELL HANDBOOK** • Grammar Transition Lesson, pp. 346, 359
TEACHER'S EDITION • Let's Write It!, p. 396–397 • Writing Trait: Voice, pp. 397a–397b	**TEACHER'S EDITION** • Revising Strategy, pp. 401d–401e	**TEACHER'S EDITION** • Commas, pp. 401p–401q

Question of the Week
How can we learn from the results of our actions?

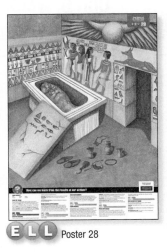

ELL Poster 28

Throughout the week, use the ELL Poster to help students produce and comprehend language, understand the concept, and build English vocabulary. Use the Question of the Week and other questions to help students share ideas in pairs, small groups, or the large group. Sample questions are shown, with examples of possible responses by students.

Weekly Concept and Language Goals

• Discuss things that we can learn from the results of actions

• Describe how we can learn from the results of our actions

• Explain how we can learn from the results of others' actions

By the end of the lesson, students should be able to talk about and write sentences about how we can learn from the results of actions.

Daily Team Talk

Day 1	Day 2	Day 3	Day 4	Day 5
After Day 1 activities on Poster, ask questions such as *In the poster picture, whose actions help us learn about Egyptian culture?*	After Day 2 activity on Poster, ask questions such as *Why do you think the Egyptians left shoes and other treasures on the floor of the tomb?*	After Day 3 activity on Poster, ask questions such as *What can we learn about Egyptian culture by studying the tomb in the poster picture?*	After Day 4 activity on Poster, ask questions such as *In* King Midas and the Golden Touch, *what was the result of Midas's actions?*	After Day 5 activity on Poster, ask questions such as *In* King Midas and the Golden Touch, *what can we learn from Midas's actions?*
Beginning The people of Egypt.	**Beginning** So he can have them.	**Beginning** About their life.	**Beginning** His daughter was gold.	**Beginning** Turning things to gold is bad.
Intermediate The people who made the tomb.	**Intermediate** That way he can still enjoy them.	**Intermediate** We can learn how people in Egypt lived.	**Intermediate** His daughter turned to gold.	**Intermediate** We shouldn't wish for the golden touch.
Advanced We can learn from the people who made the tomb.	**Advanced** They buried him with his treasures so he could enjoy them after death too.	**Advanced** We can learn about Egyptian life, language, and gold.	**Advanced** Everything he touched turned to gold.	**Advanced** We should be careful what we wish for.
Advanced High We can learn about Egyptian culture from the Egyptian people who made the prince's tomb.	**Advanced High** The Egyptian people left treasures important to the prince in his tomb so that he would have them with him even in death.	**Advanced High** By studying the tomb and the hieroglyphics in it, we can learn about Egyptian life and culture. We can see the products they treasured.	**Advanced High** King Midas wished that everything he touched be turned to gold. When he touched his beloved daughter, even she turned to gold.	**Advanced High** We should be happy with what we have and not wish for more.

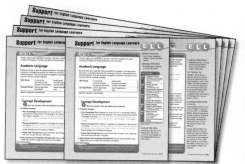

Teacher's Edition pages 370j–401q

See the support for English language learners throughout the lesson, including ELL strategies and scaffolded activities at points of use.

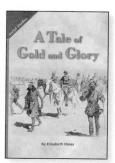

Teacher's Edition pages DI•66–DI•75

Differentiated Instruction for English language learners provides daily group activities that "frontload," or preteach, core instruction.

ELL Handbook pp. 191a–196

Find additional lesson materials that support the core lesson and the ELL instructional pages.

ELL Poster 28

ELL Reader 5.6.3

ELD, ELL Reader Teaching Guide

ELD Reader 5.6.3

Concept Literacy Reader Teaching Guide

Concept Literacy Reader

Technology

Online Teacher's Edition Use the digital version of the core Teacher's Edition for planning and instruction.

eReaders
This week's ELL and ELD Readers and Concept Literacy Reader are also available in digital format.

This Week's Content and Language Objectives by Strand

Concept Development/ Academic Language How can we learn from the results of our actions?	**Content Objective** • Use concept vocabulary related to actions and their results. **Language Objective** • Express ideas in response to art and discussion.
Phonics and Spelling Words with Latin Roots	**Content Objectives** • Recognize words with Latin roots. • Use knowledge of Latin roots to determine word meanings. **Language Objective** • Use context to understand spoken language.
Listening Comprehension Modified Read Aloud: "A Precious Fossil"	**Content Objective** • Monitor and adjust oral comprehension. **Language Objectives** • Discuss oral passages. • Ask for information in academic contexts. • Use a graphic organizer to take notes.
Reading Comprehension Compare and Contrast	**Content Objectives** • Compare and contrast people and things. • Use a Venn diagram to map similarities and differences. • Monitor and adjust comprehension. **Language Objectives** • Derive meaning from environmental print. • Comprehend routine classroom English. • Talk and write about similarities and differences.
Vocabulary Basic and Lesson Vocabulary	**Language Objectives** • Understand and use basic vocabulary. • Learn meanings of grade-level vocabulary. • Internalize new basic language. • Produce drawings, phrases, or short sentences to show understanding of Lesson Vocabulary.
Word Analysis Complex Spelling Patterns *ous = /us/, ci = /sh/, ti = /sh/*	**Content Objective** • Spell words with complex spelling patterns. **Language Objectives** • Pronounce words with complex spelling patterns. • Discuss the meaning of words with the ending *–ous.*
Grammar and Conventions Commas	**Content Objectives** • Use commas in a series. • Name items in a category. **Language Objectives** • Speak using sentences that contain commas in a series. • Ask questions that contain commas in a series.
Writing Point of View	**Content Objective** • Identify the point of view from which a story is told. **Language Objective** • Write a paragraph telling what they can learn from the results of their actions.

Word Cards for Vocabulary Activities

adorn	**cleanse**
lifeless	**precious**
realm	**spoonful**

Teacher Note: Beginning Teach two to three words. **Intermediate** Teach three to four words. **Advanced** Teach four to five words. **Advanced High** Teach all words.

Name _____

Read the paragraph and study the pictures. Then complete the chart.

• **Write** what the Parthenon was like in ancient times in the *Then* column.
• **Write** what it is like today in the *Now* column.
• **Write** how it is the same in both times in the *Then and Now* column.

The Parthenon

The Parthenon is an ancient Greek temple. The building was completed more than 2,400 years ago. It has gone through many changes since then. Originally, it had a pointed roof, but the roof is gone now. Most of the statues are gone too. In ancient times, teachers gave lectures on the front steps. Boys and young men came to listen. These days you will not see anybody taking classes at the Parthenon. But you can see many tourists taking pictures.

The Parthenon		
Then	Now	Then and Now

ELL Handbook

Compare and Contrast

Use this lesson to supplement or replace the skill lesson on page 371c of the Teacher's Edition. Display the Skill Points (at right) and share them with students.

Teach/Model

Beginning Have students think about what they liked to do in first grade and what they like to do now. Ask: *What activity or game did you play when you were in first grade?* (possible answer: blocks) *What activity or game do you play now that you didn't play in first grade?* (kickball) *What activities or games do you still play now like you did in first grade?* (tag)

Intermediate Say: *In the 1890s, many students studied in one-room schoolhouses. Now, most students study in large school buildings.* Have students write a sentence that tells how school has changed. Then discuss ways in which school has stayed the same.

Advanced Tell students about early televisions of the past, and show a picture if available: small screens, black and white images, and families watching at home or elsewhere. Have them write ways in which televisions of the past and present are alike and different.

Advanced High Pair students. Assign partners an activity topic, such as traveling. Have one partner write a sentence about how the activity was done in the past, and have the other partner write a sentence telling how it is done in the present. Then have partners work together to find ways that the activity is the same.

Then distribute copies of Picture It! page 192.

- Direct students' attention to the two pictures. One shows the Parthenon in ancient times. The other shows the Parthenon as it is today. Have students describe the pictures.
- Review the Skill Points with students.
- Read the paragraph aloud. Ask: *How has the Parthenon changed over time?*

Practice

Read aloud the directions on page 192. Reread the paragraph aloud, explaining the words *temple* and *lecture*. Have students look at the pictures and the paragraph as they complete the chart.

Beginning Students can say how the Parthenon has changed and how it has stayed the same before writing their answers in the chart. Provide help with English words.

Intermediate Students can first state orally what they will write in each section of the chart and then write their answers on the page. Provide help with writing.

Advanced Students can write their answers in the chart and then check them by comparing them to a partner's.

Advanced High Students can write their answers in the chart and then use the information to discuss how the Parthenon has changed over time.

Answers for page 192: *Then:* The Parthenon had a pointed roof and many statues. Teachers gave lectures. Boys and young men came to listen. *Now:* The roof and most of the statues are gone. Tourists come to take pictures. *Then and Now:* It has columns. It is rectangular. People visit the Parthenon.

> ### Skill Points
> ✔ When you **compare and contrast,** you show how things are similar and how they are different.
>
> ✔ You can compare and contrast two separate things, or you can compare and contrast the same thing in the past and in the present, showing how it has changed.
>
> ✔ You can use clue words to tell when an author is comparing (*like* or *as*) or contrasting (*but* or *unlike*).

Multilingual Summaries

King Midas and the Golden Touch

King Midas loved gold. His daughter was the only thing he loved more.

One day, the guards brought in a man they found. He had been sleeping in the garden. King Midas asked the man to stay for dinner.

To thank the king, the man offered him a wish. King Midas wished for all he touched to turn to gold. The next day, the king woke up to find his wish had come true. The king was happy with his wish until he touched his daughter. She turned to gold. King Midas begged for the wish to be undone. He got that wish too. King Midas restored everything he had turned to gold. He saved one gold rose to always remember the curse.

Spanish

El rey Midas y su don del oro

Al rey Midas le fascinaba el oro. Su hija era lo único que él amaba más.

Un día, los guardias llevaron a su presencia a un hombre que habían encontrado durmiendo en el jardín. El rey Midas le pidió al hombre que se quedara a cenar con él.

Para agradecerle al rey, el hombre se ofreció a concederle un deseo. El rey Midas deseaba que todo lo que él tocara se convirtiera en oro. Al día siguiente, el rey se levantó y supo que su deseo se había hecho realidad. El rey estaba feliz con el don que había adquirido hasta que tocó a su hija y ella también se convirtió en oro. El rey Midas suplicó que su deseo fuera anulado. Ese deseo también le fue concedido. El rey Midas restableció todo lo que él había convertido en oro a su estado original. Sólo dejó una rosa de oro para recordar siempre la maldición.

Multilingual Summaries

Chinese

邁達斯國王的金手

邁達斯國王著迷金子，女兒是他唯一的珍愛。

有一天，警衛發現有人在花園裏睡覺，把他帶到國王面前。邁達斯不但沒處罰他，而且邀他共進晚餐。

那個人為了感謝國王，說可以滿足他的願望。邁達斯希望，能把碰到的東西都變成金子。第二天醒來，發現他的夢想真的實現了。他非常高興，可是一擁抱女兒，把她也變成了金子。邁達斯國王懊悔萬分，希望收回所說的話。於是，所有東西變回原來的樣子。國王保留了一朵金玫瑰，他要永遠記住這個教訓。

Vietnamese

Vua Midas và Phép Hóa Vàng

Vua Midas yêu vàng. Con gái của ông là điều duy nhất mà ông yêu hơn vàng.

Một ngày nọ, quân cảnh vệ dẫn vào một người đàn ông mà họ tìm gặp. Ông này đang ngủ trong vườn của vua. Vua Midas mời ông này ở lại dùng bữa ăn tối.

Để cám ơn nhà vua, ông này ban cho vua một điều ước. Vua Midas ước là mọi thứ mà ngài đụng vào sẽ biến thành vàng. Qua ngày sau, nhà vua thức giấc và thấy là điều ước của mình trở nên sự thật. Nhà vua vui mừng vì lời ước của mình đến khi ngài đụng vào con gái của mình. Cô con gái trở thành vàng. Vua Midas khẩn xin cho điều ước được xóa bỏ. Nhà vua được điều ước này. Vua Midas phục hồi lại mọi vật mà ngài đã biến thành vàng. Ngài để lại một hoa hồng bằng vàng để luôn nhớ đến lời nguyền.

Multilingual Summaries

마이다스 왕과 황금 손길

마이다스 왕은 황금을 사랑했고 그가 금보다 더 사랑하는 유일한 것은 그의 딸이었다.

하루는 경비병들이 정원에서 잠을 자고 있던 한 남자를 발견하고 궁으로 데리고 왔다. 마이다스 왕은 그 남자에게 남아서 저녁을 먹자고 청했다.

왕에게 감사를 전하기 위해 남자는 왕의 소원을 들어주겠다고 말했다. 마이다스 왕은 그가 만지는 모든 것이 금으로 변하게 해달라고 빌었다. 그 다음날 왕은 잠에서 깨어나 자신의 소원이 실현되었다는 것을 알게 되었다. 왕은 자신의 딸에게 손을 갖다 대서 딸이 금으로 변하기 전까지는 자신의 소원에 대해 행복해했다. 마이다스 왕은 자신의 소원을 되돌리길 간청했고 그 소원 역시 이루어졌다. 왕은 자신이 황금으로 바꾸어 놓았던 모든 것을 되돌려 놓았지만 그 저주를 항상 기억하기 위해 황금 장미 하나를 남겨두었다.

Vaj ntxwv Midas thiab Kev Kov Kub

Vaj ntxwv Midas nyiam nyiam kub. Nws tus ntxhais yog tib tug nws nyiam nyiam tshaj.

Muaj ib hnub, cov tiv thaiv tau coj ib tug txiv neeg hauv tsev lawv nrhiav. Nws mas pw tom teb. Vaj ntxwv tau caw tus no los noj hmo.

Kom ua kev zoo siab ua tsaug rau tus vaj ntxwv, tus txiv neej hais tias nws mam foom ib yam dabtsi los xij raws li tus vaj ntxwv lub siab xav. Tus vaj ntxwv Midas lub siab xav tau ib lub txiaj ntsim uas pub hwj chim kom ib puas yam tsav nws kov mam txi los ua kub. Hnub tom qab, tus vaj ntxwv sawv los mus nrhiav hais tias nws qhov lub siab xav no twb muaj lawm. Vaj ntxwv zoo zoo siab txog thaum nws kov nws tus ntxhais. Nws ho txi los ua kub. Vaj ntxwv Midas thov thov kom nws qhov lub siab xav no cia ploj mus lawm. Nws txawm tau raws li nws lub siab xav no thiab. Vaj ntxwv Midas rov qab kov ib puas yam tsav nws kov thaum ib kom txhob ua kub ntxiv li lawm. Nws tau ceev ib lub paj kub kom nco ntsoov qhov foom tsis zoo no xawb mawm.

Name _____

- **Read** *A Tale of Gold and Glory* again.
- What did you learn about Christopher Columbus, Marcos de Niza, and Francisco Vasquez de Coronado? **Complete** the chart.
- Then **answer** the questions below.

Pages	Person	What I Learned About Him
2–3	**1. Christopher Columbus**	
5–9	**2. Marcos de Niza**	
9–11	**3. Francisco Vasquez de Coronado**	

4. What did Christopher Columbus, Marcos de Niza, and Francisco Vasquez de Coronado have in common?

_____

5. What was different about these three people?

_____

Family Link

Tell your family what you have learned. Ask your family members what they know about Native Americans.

Weekly Resources Guide for English Language Learner Support

For this week's content and language objectives, see p. 197e.

Instructional Strand	Day 1	Day 2
Concept Development/Academic Language	**TEACHER'S EDITION** • Academic Language, p. DI•91 • Concept Development, p. DI•91 • Anchored Talk, pp. 402j—402–403 • Preteach Academic Vocabulary, p. 405a • Concept Talk Video **ELL HANDBOOK** • Hear It, See It, Say It, Use It, pp. xxxvi–xxxvii • ELL Poster Talk, Concept Talk, p. 197c **ELL POSTER 29** • Day 1 Activities	**TEACHER'S EDITION** • Academic Language, p. DI•91 • Concept Development, p. DI•91 • Anchored Talk, p. 406a • Concept Talk Video **ELL HANDBOOK** • ELL Poster Talk, Concept Talk, p. 197c • Concept Talk Video Routine, p. 477 **ELL POSTER 29** • Day 2 Activities
Phonics and Spelling	**TEACHER'S EDITION** • Phonics and Spelling, p. DI•95	**TEACHER'S EDITION** • Phonics and Spelling, p. DI•95
Listening Comprehension	**TEACHER'S EDITION** • Modified Read Aloud, p. DI•94 • Read Aloud, p. 403b • Concept Talk Video **ELL HANDBOOK** • Concept Talk Video Routine, p. 477	**TEACHER'S EDITION** • Modified Read Aloud, p. DI•94 • AudioText of *The* Hindenburg • Concept Talk Video **ELL HANDBOOK** • AudioText CD Routine, p. 477 • Story Map A, p. 483
Reading Comprehension	**TEACHER'S EDITION** • Preteach Fact and Opinion, p. DI•96	**TEACHER'S EDITION** • Reteach Fact and Opinion, p. DI•96 • Frontloading Reading, p. DI•97 **ELL HANDBOOK** • Picture It! Skill Instruction, pp. 198–198a • Multilingual Summaries, pp. 199–201
Vocabulary **Basic and Lesson Vocabulary** **Word Analysis: Word Families**	**TEACHER'S EDITION** • Basic Vocabulary, p. DI•92 • Preteach Lesson Vocabulary, p. DI•92 • Word Families, p. DI•95 **ELL HANDBOOK** • Word Cards, p. 197 • ELL Vocabulary Routine, p. 471 **ELL POSTER 29** • Day 1 Activities	**TEACHER'S EDITION** • Basic Vocabulary, p. DI•92 • Reteach Lesson Vocabulary, p. DI•93 • Word Families, p. DI•95 **ELL HANDBOOK** • Word Cards, p. 197 • Multilingual Vocabulary List, p. 431 **ELL POSTER 29** • Day 2 Activities
Grammar and Conventions	**TEACHER'S EDITION** • Preteach Quotations and Quotation Marks, p. DI•99	**TEACHER'S EDITION** • Reteach Quotations and Quotation Marks, p. DI•99
Writing	**TEACHER'S EDITION** • Include Important Details, p. DI•100 • Writing for Tests: Review, pp. 405e–405f	**TEACHER'S EDITION** • Writing for Tests: Review, pp. 417d–417e

This symbol indicates leveled instruction to address language proficiency levels.

Day 3	Day 4	Day 5
TEACHER'S EDITION • Academic Language, p. DI•91 • Concept Development, p. DI•91 • Anchored Talk, p. 418a • Concept Talk Video **ELL HANDBOOK** • ELL Poster Talk, Concept Talk, p. 197c **ELL POSTER 29** • Day 3 Activities	**TEACHER'S EDITION** • Academic Language, p. DI•91 • Concept Development, p. DI•91 • Anchored Talk, p. 428a • Concept Talk Video **ELL HANDBOOK** • ELL Poster Talk, Concept Talk, p. 197c **ELL POSTER 29** • Day 4 Activities	**TEACHER'S EDITION** • Academic Language, p. DI•91 • Concept Development, p. DI•91 • Concept Talk Video **ELL HANDBOOK** • ELL Poster Talk, Concept Talk, p. 197c **ELL POSTER 29** • Day 5 Activities
		TEACHER'S EDITION • Phonics and Spelling, p. DI•95
ELL HANDBOOK • Phonics Transition Lesson, pp. 301, 306	**ELL HANDBOOK** • Phonics Transition Lesson, pp. 301, 306	
TEACHER'S EDITION • AudioText of *The* Hindenburg • Concept Talk Video **ELL HANDBOOK** • AudioText CD Routine, p. 477	**TEACHER'S EDITION** • Concept Talk Video	**TEACHER'S EDITION** • Concept Talk Video
TEACHER'S EDITION • Sheltered Reading, p. DI•97 **ELL HANDBOOK** • Multilingual Summaries, pp. 199–201	**TEACHER'S EDITION** • ELL/ELD Reader Guided Reading, p. DI•98 **ELL HANDBOOK** • ELL Study Guide, p. 202	**TEACHER'S EDITION** • ELL/ELD Reader Guided Reading, p. DI•98 **ELL HANDBOOK** • ELL Study Guide, p. 202
		TEACHER'S EDITION • Word Families, p. 433i
ELL HANDBOOK • High-Frequency Words Activity Bank, p. 446 **ELL POSTER 29** • Day 3 Activities	**ELL HANDBOOK** • High-Frequency Words Activity Bank, p. 446	**ELL HANDBOOK** • High-Frequency Words Activity Bank, p. 446
TEACHER'S EDITION • Grammar Jammer **ELL HANDBOOK** • Grammar Transition Lesson, pp. 347, 360 • Grammar Jammer Routine, p. 478	**TEACHER'S EDITION** • Grammar Jammer **ELL HANDBOOK** • Grammar Transition Lesson, pp. 347, 360	**TEACHER'S EDITION** • Grammar Jammer **ELL HANDBOOK** • Grammar Transition Lesson, pp. 347, 360
TEACHER'S EDITION • Let's Write It!, p. 426–427 • Writing for Tests: Evaluation, pp. 427a–427b	**TEACHER'S EDITION** • Writing for Tests, pp. 433d–433e	**TEACHER'S EDITION** • Quotations, pp. 433p–433q

Question of the Week
How can unexpected encounters reveal hidden dangers?

Throughout the week, use the ELL Poster to help students produce and comprehend language, understand the concept, and build English vocabulary. Use the Question of the Week and other questions to help students share ideas in pairs, small groups, or the large group. Sample questions are shown, with examples of possible responses by students.

ELL Poster 29

Weekly Concept and Language Goals

• Understand how unexpected encounters can reveal hidden dangers

• Name ways to avoid hidden dangers

• Describe safe travel

By the end of the lesson, students should be able to talk about and write sentences about how unexpected encounters can reveal hidden dangers.

Daily Team Talk

Day 1	Day 2	Day 3	Day 4	Day 5
After Day 1 activities on Poster, ask questions such as *What hidden dangers are in the science lab in the poster picture?*	After Day 2 activity on Poster, ask questions such as *How are the students in the poster picture avoiding hidden dangers in their science lab?*	After Day 3 activity on Poster, ask questions such as *Which student will be most prepared for hidden dangers during the experiment? Why?*	After Day 4 activity on Poster, ask questions such as *In The Hindenburg, how did the airship's engineers try to make it safe?*	After Day 5 activity on Poster, ask questions such as *Why is air travel safer today than it was when the* Hindenburg *was flying?*
Beginning There are chemicals. **Intermediate** Chemicals are hidden dangers. **Advanced** Experimenting with chemicals is dangerous. **Advanced High** Doing experiments and working with chemicals can be dangerous.	**Beginning** They wear glasses. **Intermediate** They wear gloves and goggles. **Advanced** The students are wearing rubber gloves and goggles. **Advanced High** The students in the science lab are wearing rubber gloves and protective goggles. They are also listening to their teacher and reading the warning poster.	**Beginning** The boy on the right. **Intermediate** The boy on the right is ready. **Advanced** The boy on the right is most prepared. He is taking notes. **Advanced High** The boy sitting down will be most prepared because he is listening to his teacher and taking notes.	**Beginning** They were careful. **Intermediate** They warned people not to have sparks. **Advanced** The engineers tried to avoid any sparks, which could cause an explosion. **Advanced High** The *Hindenburg's* engineers understood that hydrogen could explode if it came in contact with a spark so they tried to avoid all sparks on board.	**Beginning** Airplanes are safe. **Intermediate** Airplanes don't use hydrogen. **Advanced** Airplanes are safer to fly in than zeppelins, which were filled with hydrogen. **Advanced High** Zeppelins were filled with hydrogen, which caught fire easily. Today's airplanes run on gasoline, which is not as dangerous.

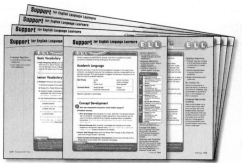

Teacher's Edition pages 402j–433q

See the support for English language learners throughout the lesson, including ELL strategies and scaffolded activities at points of use.

Teacher's Edition pages DI•91–DI•100

Differentiated Instruction for English language learners provides daily group activities that "frontload," or preteach, core instruction.

ELL Handbook pp. 197a–202

Find additional lesson materials that support the core lesson and the ELL instructional pages.

ELL Poster 29

ELL Reader 5.6.4

ELD Reader 5.6.4

Concept Literacy Reader

ELD, ELL Reader Teaching Guide

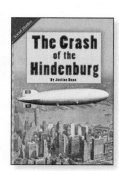

Concept Literacy Reader Teaching Guide

Technology

Online Teacher's Edition Use the digital version of the core Teacher's Edition for planning and instruction.

eReaders
This week's ELL and ELD Readers and Concept Literacy Reader are also available in digital format.

This Week's Content and Language Objectives by Strand

Concept Development/ Academic Language How can unexpected encounters reveal hidden dangers?	**Content Objective** • Use concept vocabulary related to dangers of some experiences. **Language Objectives** • Understand implicit ideas in spoken language. • Respond orally to art. • Use visual support to confirm spoken language.
Phonics and Spelling Related Words	**Content Objective** • Understand use of related words. **Language Objective** • Discuss how understanding the meaning of related words can help comprehension.
Listening Comprehension Modified Read Aloud: "The Clever Inventor of Wings"	**Content Objective** • Monitor and adjust oral comprehension. **Language Objectives** • Discuss oral passages. • Use a graphic organizer to take notes.
Reading Comprehension Fact and Opinion	**Content Objectives** • Guide students in understanding the difference between fact and opinion. • Allow students to identify fact and opinion in the text. • Monitor and adjust comprehension. **Language Objectives** • Discuss importance of fact and opinion. • Summarize text using visual support.
Vocabulary Basic and Lesson Vocabulary	**Language Objectives** • Understand and use basic vocabulary. • Learn meanings of grade-level vocabulary. • Produce drawings, phrases, or short sentences to show understanding of Lesson Vocabulary.
Word Analysis Word Families	**Content Objective** • Understand word families.
Grammar and Conventions Quotations and Quotation Marks	**Content Objectives** • Correctly use quotation marks with titles. • Correctly capitalize the title within the quotation marks. **Language Objective** • Write using quotation marks correctly.
Writing Include Important Details	**Content Objective** • Understand the importance of including important details in writing. **Language Objectives** • Write sentences that include important details. • Use connecting words.

Word Cards for Vocabulary Activities

criticizing

cruised

drenching

era

explosion

hydrogen

Teacher Note: Beginning Teach two to three words. **Intermediate** Teach three to four words. **Advanced** Teach four to five words. **Advanced High** Teach all words.

Name _____

Read the paragraph. Then **complete** the chart.
- **Find** information that can be proved. **Write** it in the *Facts* column.
- **Find** information that expresses the writer's thoughts or opinions.
  Write it in the *Opinions* column.

The Grand Canyon by Balloon

The best way to see the Grand Canyon is by balloon. Airplanes and helicopters fly too fast for you to see details. If you hike on foot or ride on horseback, you can see only part of the canyon. If you ride in a balloon, you can take a tour of the whole canyon in a day. Balloons are quiet too. Sometimes you can hear the wind whistling through the canyon.

Facts	Opinions

Fact and Opinion

Use this lesson to supplement or replace the skill lesson on page 403c of the Teacher's Edition. Display the Skill Points (at right) and share them with students.

Teach/Model

Beginning Say: *Many people visit the Grand Canyon each year. It has the best scenery.* Ask students to identify the fact (the first sentence) and the opinion (the second sentence). Ask: *How do you know the first sentence is a fact?* (It can be proven true.)

Intermediate Write: *The Grand Canyon is the most important landmark in our country. It is located in Arizona.* Have students copy the sentences and label the fact (the second sentence) and the opinion (the first sentence). Then have them circle the clue words in the opinion (most important), and explain how they can prove the fact (look on a map).

Advanced Provide background information on the Grand Canyon Skywalk. Write: *The Skywalk was completed in 2007.* Ask: *How can we prove this is a fact?* (look on the Internet or in reference materials) Ask: *What is your opinion about the Grand Canyon Skywalk?* Have each student write a statement of opinion.

Advanced High Ask each student to write a fact and opinion about a park they have visited. Then have them trade sentences with a partner. Tell the partner to identify the fact and opinion and explain how he or she chose the fact and the opinion.

Then distribute copies of Picture It! page 198.

- Have students look at the picture and describe what is happening. Provide background information on the Grand Canyon, if needed.
- Review the Skill Points with students.
- Read the paragraph aloud. Ask: *What are some of the author's opinions? How can you tell they are opinions?*

Practice

Read aloud the directions on page 198. Have volunteers reread the paragraph aloud. Have students look at the picture and the paragraph as they fill in the chart.

Beginning Students can say facts and opinions from the paragraph before writing them in the chart. Provide help with writing and spelling.

Intermediate Students can first orally answer and then write their answers on the lines in the chart. Provide help with writing.

Advanced Students can write their answers on the lines and then check their answers by comparing them with a partner's.

Advanced High Students can write their answers on the lines and then orally explain how they decided which sentences were facts and which were opinions.

Answers for page 198: *Facts:* If you hike on foot or ride on horseback, you can see only part of the canyon. If you ride in a balloon, you can take a tour of the whole canyon in a day. Sometimes you can hear the wind whistling through the canyon. *Opinions:* The best way to see the Grand Canyon is by balloon. Airplanes and helicopters fly too fast for you to see details. Balloons are quiet too.

Skill Points

✔ A **fact** is a true statement. You can prove that a fact is true by looking in reference materials, looking on the Internet, or asking an expert.

✔ An **opinion** is not true or false. It is a personal thought or belief. Opinions cannot be proved.

✔ You can look for clue words *(think, believe, too, best, most)* to identify opinions.

Multilingual Summaries

The *Hindenburg*

Hugo Eckener began to make airships in Germany in 1900. Airships were huge, hollow structures. Gas-filled balloons inside made them float. The gas was very explosive. Sparks and flames could easily set the airship on fire. People traveled across the Atlantic Ocean in the airships.

The biggest airship ever made was the *Hindenburg*. It first flew in 1936. It took two and a half days to cross the Atlantic Ocean. On May 3, 1937, the *Hindenburg* left Germany for what would be its last flight.

When the airship reached the United States, thunderstorms kept it from landing right away. The airship circled and came back. Suddenly, the airship was on fire. No one knew how the fire started. Of the ninety-seven people on the ship, sixty-seven survived. Airships were never again used for travel.

Spanish

El *Hindenburg*

Hugo Eckener empezó a hacer dirigibles en Alemania en 1900. Un dirigible era una estructura hueca enorme. Se llenaba con globos de gas y estos lo hacían flotar. El gas era muy explosivo. Las chispas y las llamas podían provocar un incendio. La gente viajaba a través del océano Atlántico en estos dirigibles.

El dirigible más grande que se había hecho era el *Hindenburg*. Voló por primera vez en 1936. Le tomó dos días y medio atravesar el océano Atlántico. El 3 de mayo de 1937, el *Hindenburg* salió de Alemania en un vuelo que sería el último.

Cuando el dirigible se acercaba a Estados Unidos, una tormenta eléctrica le impidió aterrizar de inmediato. El dirigible daba vueltas y regresaba. De repente se incendió. Nadie sabía cómo había comenzado el fuego. De las noventa y siete personas que estaban a bordo, sobrevivieron sesenta y siete. Los dirigibles nunca más fueron usados para viajar.

Multilingual Summaries

Chinese

興登堡號飛船

　　1900年，埃克納開始在德國造飛船。飛船頂上是非常大的氣球，裏面充滿易燃氣體，這樣才能飛行。氫氣很容易爆炸，碰到火星就會著火。但人們駕駛飛船，橫越了大西洋。

　　最大的飛船叫興登堡號，第一次飛行是在1936年，它用兩天半時間就飛過了大西洋。1937年5月3日，興登堡號飛離德國，這是它最後一次飛行。

　　飛船到達美國時，因為有雷雨不能降落。它慢慢地盤旋來回，不知道為什麼，突然著火了。飛船上有97人，只有67人生還。從此以後，飛船不再用作載人旅行。

Vietnamese

Tàu Khinh Khí Cầu *Hindenburg*

　　Hugo Eckener bắt đầu chế tạo những chiếc tàu khinh khí cầu ở Đức Quốc vào năm 1900. Các chiếc tàu khinh khí cầu là những kiến trúc rỗng, khổng lồ. Những quả cầu bơm đầy khinh khí giữ cho chiếc tàu bay trên không. Khinh khí rất dễ nổ. Những tia lửa và lửa ngọn có thể dễ dàng làm cháy chiếc tàu. Người ta du lịch ngang Đại Tây Dương trong những chiếc tàu khinh khí cầu này.

　　Chiếc tàu khinh khí cầu lớn nhất được chế tạo là chiếc Hindenburg. Chiếc này bay lần đầu vào năm 1936. Phải mất hai ngày rưỡi để băng qua Đại Tây Dương. Vào ngày 3 tháng Năm, năm 1937, chiếc Hindenburg rời Đức Quốc kể như chuyến bay cuối cùng.

　　Khi chiếc tàu khinh khí cầu đến Hoa Kỳ, mưa bão làm cho chiếc tàu không đáp xuống liền được. Chiếc tàu bay một vòng và quay trở lại. Thình lình, chiếc tàu bị cháy. Không ai biết làm thế nào mà lửa đã bốc cháy. Trong số chín mươi bảy người đi trên tàu, có sáu mươi bảy người sống sót. Tàu khinh khí cầu từ đó không còn được dùng để du lịch nữa.

Multilingual Summaries

힌덴버그 호

휴고 에케너는 1900년 독일에서 비행선을 만들기 시작했다. 그 비행선은 거대했고 속이 빈 구조로 만들어졌다. 내부에 가스를 채운 풍선이 비행선을 뜨도록 만들었는데 그 가스는 폭발성 물질로 불꽃과 화염이 비행선을 쉽사리 태울 수 있었다. 사람들은 비행선을 타고 대서양을 횡단했다.

그때까지 제작된 비행선 중 가장 큰 것은 힌덴버그 호였다. 힌덴버그 호는 1936년 처녀비행을 했는데 대서양을 건너는 데 이틀 반이나 걸렸다. 1937년 5월 3일 힌덴버그 호는 독일을 향해 떠났고 그것이 마지막 비행이 되었다.

비행선이 미국에 도착했을 때 심한 뇌우로 곧바로 착륙하는 것이 어려웠다. 비행선은 선회하다 다시 돌아왔는데 갑자기 선체에 불이 났다. 하지만 아무도 그 불이 어떻게 나게됐는지 알지 못했다. 비행선에 타고 있던 97명 중 67명이 살아 남았다. 그 이후로 비행선은 여행을 목적으로 사용되지 않았다.

Lub *Hindenburg*

Thaum xyoo ib txhiab cuaj puas (1900) hauv teb chaws Yelemes Hugo Eckner pib txua cov zais nyob hoom. Cov zais nyob hoom no yog khoob thiab loj kawg nkaus. Lawv muaj cov zais loj rau hauv kom thiaj ntab saum cua. Cov roj rau hauv hlaws tau yoojyim. Cov txim taws, thiab cov nplaim taws muaj peevxwm kom lub zais nyob hoom raug hluavtaws. Cov neeg caij nyob hoom no, hla lub dej hiav txwv Atlantic.

Lub zais nyob hoom loj tshaj yog lub Hindenburg. Ib txhiab cuaj puas peb caug rau (1936) yog thawj thawj zaug lub no ya ya. Nws siv sijhawm npaum li ob thiab ib nrag hnub hla lub hiav txwv Atlantic. Thaum lub tsib hlis ntuj, hnub tim peb, xyoo ib txhiab cuaj puas peb caug xya (1937) Lub Hindenburg tau ncaim tebchaws Yelemees zaum kawg.

Thaum lub zais nyob hoom tuaj txog tebchaws Ameslikas, nag xob nag cua tiv thaiv Lub ntawd kom nws tsaws tsis tau zaum. Lub zais nyob hoom sim tsaws ib zaug ntxiv. Lub zais nyob hoom txawm raug hluav taws. Tsis muaj leejtwg paub lub zais nyob hoom ntawd raug hluavtaws li cas. Cuaj kaum xya neeg caij lub zais nyob hoom ntawd, tau muaj peb caug neeg tuag.

- **Read** *Lighter Than Air* again.
- **Tell** about each of these airships. **Write** details you learned about each kind of airship.

page 5
LZ1: The first airship built by Count Zeppelin. It was only a little faster than other airships. _____

page 6
LZ10: _____

_____

page 8
The USS *Macon:* _____

_____

page 9
R34: _____

_____

pages 9–10
Graf Zeppelin: _____

_____

page 11
The *Hindenburg:* _____

_____

Family Link

Tell your family what you learned about airships. Ask them whether they have ever flown. Did they fly in an airplane, airship, or something else? Ask them to tell you about it.

Weekly Resources Guide for English Language Learner Support

For this week's content and language objectives, see p. 203e.

Instructional Strand	Day 1	Day 2
Concept Development/Academic Language	**TEACHER'S EDITION** • Academic Language, p. DI•116 • Concept Development, p. DI•116 • Anchored Talk, pp. 434j—434–435 • Preteach Academic Vocabulary, p. 437a • Concept Talk Video **ELL HANDBOOK** • Hear It, See It, Say It, Use It, pp. xxxvi–xxxvii • ELL Poster Talk, Concept Talk, p. 203c **ELL POSTER 30** • Day 1 Activities	**TEACHER'S EDITION** • Academic Language, p. DI•116 • Concept Development, p. DI•116 • Anchored Talk, p. 438a • Concept Talk Video **ELL HANDBOOK** • ELL Poster Talk, Concept Talk, p. 203c • Concept Talk Video Routine, p. 477 **ELL POSTER 30** • Day 2 Activities
Phonics and Spelling	**TEACHER'S EDITION** • Phonics and Spelling, p. DI•120	**TEACHER'S EDITION** • Phonics and Spelling, p. DI•120
Listening Comprehension	**TEACHER'S EDITION** • Modified Read Aloud, p. DI•119 • Read Aloud, p. 435b • Concept Talk Video **ELL HANDBOOK** • Concept Talk Video Routine, p. 477	**TEACHER'S EDITION** • Modified Read Aloud, p. DI•119 • AudioText of *Sweet Music in Harlem* • Concept Talk Video **ELL HANDBOOK** • AudioText CD Routine, p. 477 • Story Map A, p. 483
Reading Comprehension	**TEACHER'S EDITION** • Preteach Sequence, p. DI•121	**TEACHER'S EDITION** • Reteach Sequence, p. DI•121 • Frontloading Reading, p. DI•122 **ELL HANDBOOK** • Picture It! Skill Instruction, pp. 204–204a • Multilingual Summaries, pp. 205–207
Vocabulary **Basic and Lesson Vocabulary** **Word Analysis: Compound Words**	**TEACHER'S EDITION** • Basic Vocabulary, p. DI•117 • Preteach Lesson Vocabulary, p. DI•117 • Compound Words, p. DI•120 **ELL HANDBOOK** • Word Cards, p. 203 • ELL Vocabulary Routine, p. 471 **ELL POSTER 30** • Day 1 Activities	**TEACHER'S EDITION** • Basic Vocabulary, p. DI•117 • Reteach Lesson Vocabulary, p. DI•118 • Compound Words, p. DI•120 **ELL HANDBOOK** • Word Cards, p. 203 • Multilingual Vocabulary List, p. 431 **ELL POSTER 30** • Day 2 Activities
Grammar and Conventions	**TEACHER'S EDITION** • Preteach Punctuation, p. DI•124	**TEACHER'S EDITION** • Reteach Punctuation, p. DI•124
Writing	**TEACHER'S EDITION** • Writing Topic Sentences, p. DI•125 • Introduce Personal Narrative, pp. 437e–437f	**TEACHER'S EDITION** • Writer's Craft: Topic Sentences, pp. 449d–449e

Unit 6, Week 5 *Sweet Music in Harlem*

This symbol indicates leveled instruction to address language proficiency levels.

Day 3	Day 4	Day 5
TEACHER'S EDITION • Academic Language, p. DI•116 • Concept Development, p. DI•116 • Anchored Talk, p. 450a • Concept Talk Video **ELL HANDBOOK** • ELL Poster Talk, Concept Talk, p. 203c **ELL POSTER 30** • Day 3 Activities	**TEACHER'S EDITION** • Academic Language, p. DI•116 • Concept Development, p. DI•116 • Anchored Talk, p. 462a • Concept Talk Video **ELL HANDBOOK** • ELL Poster Talk, Concept Talk, p. 203c **ELL POSTER 30** • Day 4 Activities	**TEACHER'S EDITION** • Academic Language, p. DI•116 • Concept Development, p. DI•116 • Concept Talk Video **ELL HANDBOOK** • ELL Poster Talk, Concept Talk, p. 203c **ELL POSTER 30** • Day 5 Activities
		TEACHER'S EDITION • Phonics and Spelling, p. DI•120
ELL HANDBOOK • Phonics Transition Lesson, pp. 301, 306	**ELL HANDBOOK** • Phonics Transition Lesson, pp. 301, 306	
TEACHER'S EDITION • AudioText of *Sweet Music in Harlem* • Concept Talk Video **ELL HANDBOOK** • AudioText CD Routine, p. 477	**TEACHER'S EDITION** • Concept Talk Video	**TEACHER'S EDITION** • Concept Talk Video
TEACHER'S EDITION • Sheltered Reading, p. DI•122 **ELL HANDBOOK** • Multilingual Summaries, pp. 205–207	**TEACHER'S EDITION** • ELL/ELD Reader Guided Reading, p. DI•123 **ELL HANDBOOK** • ELL Study Guide, p. 208	**TEACHER'S EDITION** • ELL/ELD Reader Guided Reading, p. DI•123 **ELL HANDBOOK** • ELL Study Guide, p. 208
		TEACHER'S EDITION • Compound Words, p. 467i
ELL HANDBOOK • High-Frequency Words Activity Bank, p. 446 **ELL POSTER 30** • Day 3 Activities	**ELL HANDBOOK** • High-Frequency Words Activity Bank, p. 446	**ELL HANDBOOK** • High-Frequency Words Activity Bank, p. 446
TEACHER'S EDITION • Grammar Jammer **ELL HANDBOOK** • Grammar Transition Lesson, pp. 345, 357 • Grammar Jammer Routine, p. 478	**TEACHER'S EDITION** • Grammar Jammer **ELL HANDBOOK** • Grammar Transition Lesson, pp. 345, 357	**TEACHER'S EDITION** • Grammar Jammer **ELL HANDBOOK** • Grammar Transition Lesson, pp. 345, 357
TEACHER'S EDITION • Let's Write It!, p. 460–461 • Writing Trait: Voice, pp. 461a–461b	**TEACHER'S EDITION** • Revising Strategy, pp. 467d–467e	**TEACHER'S EDITION** • Punctuation, pp. 467p–467q

Question of the Week
What unexpected influence do we have on those around us?

Throughout the week, use the ELL Poster to help students produce and comprehend language, understand the concept, and build English vocabulary. Use the Question of the Week and other questions to help students share ideas in pairs, small groups, or the large group. Sample questions are shown, with examples of possible responses by students.

Weekly Concept and Language Goals

• Understand the concept of influence

• Explain the unexpected influence we can have on those around us

• Share ways people have unexpected influence

By the end of the lesson, students should be able to talk about and write sentences about the unexpected influence we have on those around us.

E L L Poster 30

Daily Team Talk

Day 1	Day 2	Day 3	Day 4	Day 5
After Day 1 activities on Poster, ask questions such as *What are the musicians in the poster picture doing?*	After Day 2 activity on Poster, ask questions such as *How do the musicians in the poster picture influence the people watching them?*	After Day 3 activity on Poster, ask questions such as *Why do you think the girl is looking at the saxophone that is for sale?*	After Day 4 activity on Poster, ask questions such as *Why is the influence the musicians have over the girl unexpected?*	After Day 5 activity on Poster, ask questions such as *How has someone had an unexpected influence over you?*
Beginning Playing music. **Intermediate** They are playing music at night. **Advanced** The musicians are playing music on the street. **Advanced High** The jazz band is playing their music on the street corner, like they did every night that week.	**Beginning** They enjoy it. **Intermediate** The people enjoy their music. **Advanced** Some people are clapping, and everyone looks like they enjoy the music. **Advanced High** Some people are clapping along with the music. One boy is dancing. Everyone is smiling, so I think they enjoy the music.	**Beginning** She wants to play. **Intermediate** She wants to learn how to play it. **Advanced** She likes the music and wants to learn how to play an instrument. **Advanced High** She likes the music the jazz band is playing so much that it has influenced her. She wants to learn to play music too.	**Beginning** They did not know. **Intermediate** They did not know she would do that. **Advanced** The musicians play their music for fun and to entertain people. **Advanced High** The jazz band plays their music because they enjoy entertaining people. They did not know the girl would want to learn because of them.	**Beginning** I saw children playing a soccer game. **Intermediate** I saw my brother play soccer and I wanted to play too. **Advanced** When I saw my older brother play soccer, I thought it looked fun. I wanted to play too. **Advanced High** I watched my older brother play in a soccer game, and I thought it looked fun. I asked my mom if I could play soccer too.

Teacher's Edition pages 434j–471a

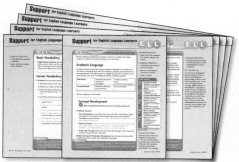

Teacher's Edition pages DI•116–DI•125

ELL Handbook pp. 203a–208

See the support for English language learners throughout the lesson, including ELL strategies and scaffolded activities at points of use.

Differentiated Instruction for English language learners provides daily group activities that "frontload," or preteach, core instruction.

Find additional lesson materials that support the core lesson and the ELL instructional pages.

ELL Poster 30

ELL Reader 5.6.5

ELD Reader 5.6.5

Concept Literacy Reader

ELD, ELL Reader Teaching Guide

Concept Literacy Reader Teaching Guide

Technology

Online Teacher's Edition Use the digital version of the core Teacher's Edition for planning and instruction.

eReaders
This week's ELL and ELD Readers and Concept Literacy Reader are also available in digital format.

This Week's Content and Language Objectives by Strand

Concept Development/ Academic Language What unexpected influence do we have on those around us?	**Content Objective** • Use concept vocabulary related to the influence people have on others. **Language Objectives** • Understand main points of spoken language. • Use prior knowledge to understand meaning.
Phonics and Spelling Easily Confused Words	**Content Objective** • Identify, spell, and define easily confused words. **Language Objective** • Apply phonics and decoding skills to vocabulary.
Listening Comprehension Modified Read Aloud: "Learning from the Best"	**Content Objective** • Monitor and adjust oral comprehension. **Language Objectives** • Discuss oral passages. • Use a graphic organizer to take notes.
Reading Comprehension Sequence	**Content Objectives** • Identify a sequence of events. • Monitor and adjust comprehension. **Language Objectives** • Use analytical skills to infer the sequence. • Internalize new academic language for sequence. • Retell a sequence of events in the order they occurred from a reading. • Write a sequence of events from a personal experience.
Vocabulary Basic and Lesson Vocabulary	**Language Objectives** • Understand and use basic vocabulary. • Learn meanings of grade-level vocabulary. • Produce drawings, phrases, or short sentences to show understanding of Lesson Vocabulary.
Word Analysis Compound Words	**Content Objective** • Identify and define words in compound words. **Language Objectives** • Discuss meaning of compound words. • Learn new language structures. • Learn relationships between sounds and letters.
Grammar and Conventions Punctuation	**Content Objective** • Use colons and other forms of punctuation correctly. **Language Objective** • Write using colons correctly.
Writing Writing Topic Sentences	**Content Objective** • Identify topic sentences in a text. **Language Objective** • Write paragraphs using topic sentences.

Word Cards for Vocabulary Activities

bass

clarinet

fidgety

forgetful

jammed

nighttime

secondhand

Teacher Note: Beginning Teach two to three words. **Intermediate** Teach three to four words. **Advanced** Teach four to six words. **Advanced High** Teach all words.

Name _____

Read the story of Harlem's Apollo Theater. **Write** an important event from the history of the Apollo Theater at each year listed under the time line.

Harlem's Apollo Theater

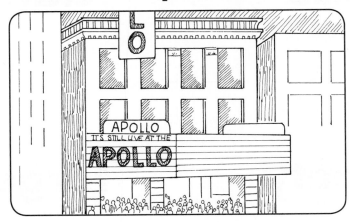

"We are now turning onto 125th Street in Harlem," the tour guide explained as the bus turned the corner. "In a moment we will pass the Apollo Theater, one of New York City's most popular tourist attractions. When it opened in 1913, only white people could see shows here. But in 1934 a new owner invited African American artists to perform there. For the first time, blacks and whites sat together in the same audience. Many world-famous performers began their careers at the Apollo Theater. In 1978, the theater closed. In 1983 the theater became a landmark and reopened a few years later. You can go there to see both new and experienced performers. You might even bring your talent to the Apollo Theater stage someday!"

1910	1925	1940	1955	1970	1985	2000

1913   1934   1978

_____ _____   _____

_____ _____   _____ 1983

_____ _____   _____

                                       _____

Sequence

Use this lesson to supplement or replace the skill lesson on page 435c of the Teacher's Edition. Display the Skill Points (at right) and share them with students.

Teach/Model

Beginning Write: *Last spring, I started training for a race. In August, I ran ten miles without stopping.* Have students tell what happened before you ran ten miles. (You started training.) Ask: *What clue words helped you find the sequence?* (Last spring, August)

Intermediate Display a time line from a history textbook. Read the information aloud. Point out three sequential events. Ask: *Which event happened first? Then what happened? What happened after that event?* Have students write their answers.

Advanced Display a time line of events in your state's history. Say: *How can we use clue words to show this information in a paragraph?* (We can use dates and time words.) Have students use the time line to write brief paragraphs with clue words.

Advanced High Pair students. Have one partner write a brief autobiography using time order clue words *(When I was seven, last summer, In 2008)* to indicate sequence of events. Have the other partner read the paragraph and use the time order words to make a time line. Then have the partners switch roles.

Then distribute copies of Picture It! page 204.

- Point to the picture. Explain that the picture shows the Apollo Theater in New York City. Tell students they will read about the history of the Apollo Theater.
- Review the Skill Points with students.
- Read the paragraph aloud. Ask: *What did you find out about the history of the Apollo Theater?*

Practice

Read aloud the directions on page 204. Reread the paragraph aloud, explaining the terms *tourist, attraction,* and *landmark*. Have students look at the picture and the paragraph as they complete the graphic organizer.

Beginning Students can orally describe the events they want to write before writing them on the time line. Provide help with writing English words.

Intermediate Students can tell what they want to write before filling in the time line.

Advanced Students can write the events on the time line and check their work by rereading the paragraph and making necessary corrections.

Advanced High Students can write the events on the time line and orally explain how they determined the order of events.

Answers for page 204: *1913:* Apollo Theater opened; *1934:* African American artists perform; *1978:* Theater closed; *1983:* Theater became a landmark.

Skill Points

✔ The **sequence** is the order in which events happen.
✔ Look for clue words such as *first, next, then, last,* or dates and times of day.
✔ You can use a time line to keep track of the events.

Multilingual Summaries

Sweet Music in Harlem

C.J.'s Uncle Click is a jazz musician. C.J. wants to be one too. One afternoon, a photographer comes to take Uncle Click's picture for a magazine. Uncle Click cannot find his special hat.

C.J. goes to look for the hat. It's not at the barbershop, but the barber wants to be in the picture. It's not at the diner, but the diner's waitress wants to be in the picture. It's not at the music club, but the club's singer wants to be in the picture too.

C.J. goes home without the hat. He is sorry he did not find it. The photographer comes. His uncle is happy that so many people came to be in the picture. That night, Uncle Click gave C.J. his birthday present a week early. Inside the box was a new clarinet and also Uncle Click's hat!

Spanish

La dulce música de Harlem

El tío de C.J., tío Click, es un músico de jazz. C.J. también quiere ser músico. Una tarde, un fotógrafo llega a tomarle una foto al tío Click para una revista. Tío Click no puede encontrar su sombrero especial.

C.J. va a buscar el sombrero. No está en la barbería, pero el barbero quiere salir en la foto. No está en el restaurante, pero la mesera quiere salir en la foto. No está en el club de música, pero el cantante del club también quiere salir en la foto.

C.J. se va a casa sin el sombrero. Está triste porque no lo encontró. El fotógrafo llega. Su tío está feliz de que viniera tanta gente para salir en la foto. Esa noche, una semana antes de su cumpleaños, el tío Click le da a C.J. su regalo. Dentro de la caja había un clarinete nuevo, ¡y también el sombrero del tío Click!

Multilingual Summaries

Chinese

哈萊姆的動聽樂曲

克裏克的叔叔是個爵士音樂家，克裏克很想和叔叔一樣。有一天下午，攝影師要來為叔叔拍照，登在雜誌上。叔叔怎麼也找不到他那頂特別的帽子。

克裏克四處去找叔叔的帽子。理髮店裏沒有帽子，可理髮師說，他也想拍照。餐館裏沒有帽子，可女招待員說，她也想拍照。音樂俱樂部也沒有帽子，可歌手說，他也想拍照。

克裏克沒有找到帽子，心裏非常抱歉。攝影師來了，叔叔看到有這麼多人一起拍照，非常開心。那天晚上，叔叔特意提前一個星期，把生日禮物送給克裏克。禮盒裏有全新的單簧管，還有叔叔的帽子！

Vietnamese

Nhạc Du Dương Ở Harlem

Chú Click của C.J. là một nhạc sĩ nhạc jazz. C.J. cũng muốn được là một nhạc sĩ như vậy. Một buổi chiều nọ, một nhiếp ảnh gia đến chụp ảnh Chú Click để đăng lên một tạp chí. Chú Click không tìm thấy chiếc nón đặc biệt của mình.

C.J. đi tìm chiếc nón. Chiếc nón không có ở tiệm hớt tóc, nhưng ông thợ hớt tóc muốn được chụp trong ảnh. Nón không có ở tiệm ăn, nhưng cô hầu bàn ở tiệm ăn muốn được chụp trong ảnh. Nón không có ở câu lạc bộ âm nhạc, nhưng ca sĩ của câu lạc bộ cũng muốn được chụp trong ảnh nữa.

C.J. về nhà mà không có nón. Cậu bé hối tiếc là cậu không tìm được chiếc nón. Nhiếp ảnh gia đến. Chú của cậu bé vui mừng là nhiều người đã đến để được chụp trong ảnh. Tối hôm đó, Chú Click tặng C.J. món quà sinh nhật sớm đến một tuần. Trong hộp là cây kèn clarinet mới, và cả chiếc nón của Chú Click nữa!

Multilingual Summaries

할렘의 달콤한 음악

C.J.의 삼촌인 클릭은 재즈 음악가다. C.J.는 자신도 재즈 음악가가 되고 싶어한다. 어느 날 오후 잡지에 실을 클릭 삼촌 사진을 찍으러 사진사 하나가 온다. 클릭 삼촌은 사진 촬영 때 쓸 그의 특별한 모자를 찾을 수가 없다.

C.J.는 그 모자를 찾으러 간다. 이발소에서 모자를 찾을 수 없었지만 이발사는 사진을 같이 찍고 싶어한다. 식당에서도 모자를 찾을 수 없었지만 식당의 웨이트리스도 사진을 같이 찍고 싶어한다. 음악 클럽에서도 모자를 찾을 수 없었지만 클럽의 가수 역시 사진을 같이 찍고 싶어한다.

C.J.는 모자를 찾지 못하고 집으로 돌아왔고 그 점에 대해 미안해 한다. 이제 사진사가 온다. 삼촌은 많은 사람들이 사진을 같이 찍으려고 온 것을 보고 기뻐한다. 그날 밤, 클릭 삼촌은 C.J.에게 생일 선물을 1주일이나 먼저 준다. 상자 안에는 새 클라리넷이 있었고 클릭 삼촌의 모자도 있는 것이 아닌가!

Kev Hu Nkauj Zoo Mloog Hauv Harlem

C.J.'s tus dab laug Click yog ib tug kws nkauj jazz. C.J. xav ua ntawd thiab. Muaj ib tav su ib tug thaij koob los thaij tus dab laug Click duab kom ntxiv tau rau hauv phau ntawv magazine. Dab laug Click nrhiav tsi laib nws kaub mom tshwj xeeb.

C.J. tau mus nrhiav kaub mom. Nws tsi nyob tim lub tsev txiav plaub hau, tiam si tu txiav plaub hau xav kom nws lub duab nyob ntawm daim duab. Nws tsi nyob hauv tsev ua mov noj, tiam si tu muab mov noj xav kom nws lub duab nyob ntawm daim duab. Nws tsi nyob hauv tsev ua nkauj, tiam si tsev nkauj tus hu nkauj xav kom nws lub duab nyob ntawm daim duab thiab.

C.J. mus tsev tsis muaj lub kaub mom. Nws tu siab nws nrhiav tsis laib. Tus thaij duab tuaj lawm. Nws tus dab laug zoo siab tias neeg coob xav tuaj kom lawv cov duab nyob ntawm daim duab thiab. Hmo ntawd, dab laug Click tau pub C.J. nws hnub yug khoom plig ib as thiv ntxov. Nyob hauv lub thawb muaj ib lub tshuaj clarinet, thiab kuj muaj tus dab laug lub kaub mom thiab.

Name _____

- **Read** *What Do You See, James Van Der Zee?* again.
- **Write** about the photographs in the book. **Describe** the people in each photograph. The first one has been done.

page 2
1. "Future Expectations"

A man and woman are in their house on their wedding day. A little girl sits by their feet. The girl is a "picture" of their future.

page 3
2. "Do Tell"

_____

_____

page 6
3. "Victory Parade of the 369th Regiment"

_____

_____

pages 8–9
4. "A Couple With Raccoon Fur Coats"

_____

_____

page 11
5. "Mother and Daughter"

_____

_____

Family Link

Tell your family members about the photos in this book. Then look at a family photo album with someone in your family and talk about the pictures.

Answer Key

page 30, Picture It!
Characters: Ana, Mr. Lopez, Mai; problem: Mai, the star, was sick. Solution: Mr. Lopez takes the role of stage manager, and Ana plays Mai's part.

page 34, ELL Reader Study Guide
What? Molly goes to war.
When? During the Revolutionary War
Where? Pennsylvania
Why? To help her husband and country

page 36, Picture It!
Cause: The rain stops.
Effect: Insects and plants die.
Cause: there is no more food.

page 40, ELL Reader Study Guide
Effect: Christopher had to babysit Tommy.
Cause: Tex saw a storm coming.
Effect: They could be safe from the tornado.

page 42, Picture It!
1. C **2.** B **3.** A

page 46, ELL Reader Study Guide
Check to make sure students have labeled each item. The path should go from Anacapa's village to the beach.

page 48, Picture It!
Facts: She was born in1940. She won three gold medals in 1960. When she was five, she became very ill. In 1956, she won a bronze medal.
Opinions: Wilma was a great athlete. The story of her life is more interesting than any other athlete's story. If she were alive today, she would be able to win more gold medals.

page 52, ELL Reader Study Guide
4; 6; 2; 1; 3; 5

page 54, Picture It!
Cause: He studied and practiced;
Effect: graduated top of his class, going to college

page 58, ELL Reader Study Guide
Cause: It was Enid's first day at a new school in a new country.
Effect: Enid cooks dinner for her.
Cause: It is very cold in Milwaukee.

page 60, Picture It!
Alike: They are identical twins, so they look alike. They are both nine and in the fourth grade. They both like school. They both take dance lessons.
Different: Maria loves to write stories; Marisa loves to read books. Maria takes piano lessons; Marisa takes violin lessons. Maria keeps her things neat and clean; Marisa does not.

page 64, ELL Reader Study Guide
Sophie: brown hair and blue eyes; Katie: looks similar to Sophie but with a different hairstyle. Sophie likes driftwood; Katie likes shells. Sophie found driftwood and a wallet; Katie found broken shells. Sophie and Katie wanted to keep the money at first; Both decide to send it back to its owner.

page 66, Picture It!
2, 1, 3

page 70, ELL Reader Study Guide
Why did the Danish king agree not to fight the Germans?
Who was George F. Duckwitz?
Where did the Jewish people hide?
How many Jewish Danes escaped to Sweden?
Which country kept the Jewish homes in good condition?

page 72, Picture It!
Similarities: fireworks and parades
Differences: dragons, ball dropping in Times Square; date new year begins

page 76, ELL Reader Study Guide
Before Katrina: People had their own homes; they lived near their families and friends.
After Katrina: People lost their homes; they moved away from their families and friends.

page 78, Picture It!
1. A; **2.** C

page 82, ELL Reader Study Guide
1. They need love, medicine, and care to heal.
2. They are all places were animals are safe.
3. When you sponsor a horse, you pay for things it needs, but the sanctuary keeps the horse. When you adopt a horse, you take care of it yourself.
4. To inform readers about different ways to care

page 84, Picture It!
1. B
2. The author provides facts and information about the Boston Tea Party. The author does not give opinions or use persuasive language.

page 88, ELL Reader Study Guide
3, 5, 4, 1, 6, 2

page 90, Picture It
1. 2, 3, 1   2. 3, 1, 2

page 94, ELL Reader Study Guide
1. He used the scientific method as a doctor.
2. Ben Franklin wanted to solve the problem of lightning causing damages to houses.
3. If lightning was electricity, an iron rod would attract it.
4. Pointed rods worked better than blunt rods.

page 96, Picture It!
Main Idea: It's a mixture of two metals. Details: One of the metals is copper, the other is zinc; Brass is use to make many things, including jewelry and musical instruments.

page 100, ELL Reader Study Guide
Michelangelo: decorated walls of buildings with paintings.
Copernicus: discovered things about the sun and planets
Descartes: wrote about right and wrong
Leonardo da Vinci: planned new inventions
Shakespeare: wrote and performed plays

page 102, Picture It!
Facts: *T. rex* was 18 feet tall and weighed 6 tons. Its teeth were sharp and pointed. They could cut through bone and meat. Opinions: *T. rex* was the "king" of dinosaurs. No other dinosaur can compare. People will always think of *T. rex* as the biggest and scariest.

page 106, ELL Reader Study Guide
1. F 2. F 3. O 4. F 5. F 6. O

page 108, Picture It!
Main Idea: Rhythm is an important part of soul music. *Details:* The drumbeat starts the rhythm; the bass builds on the rhythm; even the singer must have rhythm.

page 112, ELL Reader Study Guide
1. He interviewed Marie Dixon, Willie's wife.
2. First they met at a club. Two years later, they met again at a drug store where Marie worked.
3. They could play in small places, and a lot of people said they would make more money in Chicago.
4. Nobody was listening to his music in Chicago.
5. They are both about pain and disappointment.
6. Possible response: Her grandfather taught her music at an early age, and she has learned from many accomplished blues musicians.

page 114, Picture It!
1. Possible response: Costumes or makeup.
2. Special effects makeup.
3. masks, wigs, and makeup

page 118, ELL Reader Study Guide
1. They can do things real actors can't do. They do not get hurt. They do not have to be people at all.
2. They have feelings. They are more expressive than animated characters. Movie watchers know the difference between real characters and animated characters.

page 120, Picture It!
Details: Veronica is at the starting line. Somebody says, "ready, set, go!"
What I know: That's what people say to start a race.
Conclusion: Veronica must be in a race.

page 124, ELL Reader Study Guide
Drawings should review conclusions and details and allow students to compare ancient dwellings to the dwellings of today.

page 126, Picture It!
Generalization: Many kinds of people helped enslaved people through the Underground Railroad. Supporting details: Some were formerly enslaved people. Some were free African Americans. Some were white abolitionists.

page 130, ELL Reader Study Guide
Students should include details that support the author's viewpoint about how people adapt to challenges.

page 132, Picture It!
In clockwise order from the top: eggs, caterpillar, pupa or cocoon, butterfly

page 136, ELL Reader Study Guide
2. A praying mantis looks like a stick or a twig.
3. A katydid looks like leaves and stems.
4. A syrphid fly looks like a wasp or bee.
5. A walking stick looks like a wooden stick.

page 138, Picture It!
Generalization: The students at Hugo's school are friendly.
Support: One student showed him the way to the office. Another student took him to all of his classes. At lunch, a girl offered to share her sandwich.

page 142, ELL Reader Study Guide
1. The poet wonders what her old place is like now that she's gone.
2. The poet compares the way English is taught to the way it is really spoken.
3. The poet's new home is not perfect, but it is hers.
4. This is a funny poem about the unfamiliar names of American food.
5. This poem lists both the practical things and the character traits you need when you move to a new school.

page 144, Picture It!
Details: You have to be flexible enough to bend over backward and touch the floor; You have to be strong enough to hang from bars and lift your own weight.
Conclusion: Gymnastics is not an easy sport.

page 148, ELL Reader Study Guide
Detail: Betty won a gold medal at the 1928 Olympics.
Detail: Betty could not go to the 1932 Olympics because of an injury.
Detail: Betty helped her team win a relay at the 1936 Olympics.

page 150, Picture It!
Traits: focused, determined, smart; Supporting facts: she climbed a mountain, she kept going when other people quit, she took off her

backpack to make hiking easier; Plot: Sonja climbs to the top of Mount Washington.

page 154, ELL Reader Study Guide
1. He feels that having a younger sister can be a lot of work.
2. Because his sister always wants him to play with her.
3. She waves her arms and yells at the cat.
4. They hang a bird feeder filled with seeds near the nest.
5. They want to help the baby bird that fell from the nest.
6. Because even things that happen all the time can be interesting.

page 156, Picture It!
Line beginning in 1. Cadiz, Spain, 2. Cartagena, South America, 3. La Habana, Cuba

page 160, ELL Reader Study Guide
Supporting details should list facts that *Alvin* has discovered about the ocean.

page 162, Picture It!
1. The purpose is to gain information.
2. It contains many facts. It does not tell a story or express personal feelings.
3. It is about the history of space exploration.

page 166, ELL Reader Study Guide
Details in the graphic organizer should come directly from the text and support the main idea.

page 168, Picture It!
Effect: The avalanche tore open the side of the mountain. Cause: Steam blasted sideways from the volcano.
Effect: The forest was flattened.

page 172, ELL Reader Study Guide
Causes: The formations look like other objects; Water and minerals drip from the top of the cavern; Rocks can fall inside caves; Caverns tell us a lot about changes to Earth over time.
Effects: Stalactites form; Caverns form; Flowstone forms; More people can explore the caverns safely.

page 174, Picture It!
Generalization: Many different groups of people

helped complete the Transcontinental Railroad. Examples: Leaders and business people invested money. Surveyors and engineers planned how to build it. Irish and Chinese workers laid the track.

page 178, ELL Reader Study Guide
2. News about the Gold Rush spread around the world. People came from far away, even though travel was difficult.
3. Travelers overran John Sutter's ranch and set up camps along the American River.
4. The Gold Rush caused pollution and destruction, but it also brought people together and inspired new businesses.
5. The Gold Rush has ended, but California is still a place of opportunity for newcomers.

page 180, Picture It!
The emperor wanted to wear the finest suit in the world.
He believed he was wearing a suit that stupid people could not see.
These is no such thing as cloth that some people can see and others cannot.
The emperor was tricked and too proud to admit it.

page 184, ELL Reader Study Guide
Students should list feelings that David portrays in the book and include details that prove each of the feelings.

page 186, Picture It!
Main idea: Stonehenge is a mysterious place in England; Details: Stonehenge is a circle of large stones; the stones weigh as much as 50 tons; the stones were brought from up to 240 miles away.

page 190, ELL Reader Study Guide
1. Carnivores eat other animals.
2. Herbivores eat only plants.
3. Plants get nutrients from decaying matter, water, and sunshine.
4. Each living thing provides food for another.

page 192, Picture It!
Then: The Parthenon had a roof and many statues. Teachers gave lectures. Boys and young men came to listen.
Now: The roof and most of the statues are gone. Tourists come to take pictures.

page 196, ELL Reader Study Guide
1. He sailed to find an easy way to get to India and China. Instead, he found the New World. He went there four times.
2. He was a Spanish monk. He traveled north from Mexico City almost 600 miles. He eventually turned back.
3. In 1540, he left New Spain with many people. They conquered a Zuni village. He sent scouts east and west, but returned without finding the Seven Cities of Cibola.
4. and 5. Answers will vary.

page 198, Picture It!
Facts: If you hike on foot or ride on horseback, you can see only part of the canyon. If you ride in a balloon, you can take a tour of the whole canyon in a day. Sometimes you can hear the wind whistling through the canyon.
Opinions: The best way to see the Grand Canyon is by balloon. Airplanes and helicopters fly too fast for you to see details. Balloons are quiet too.

page 202, ELL Reader Study Guide
The following information should be included:
LZ10: It made more than 100 flights in 1911.
USS Macon: A "mother ship" for the US Navy that could carry airplanes.
R34: The first airship to cross the Atlantic Ocean, in 1919
Graf Zeppelin: A grand airship that went around the world in 1929
Hindenburg: One of the largest airships ever built; it exploded over New Jersey in 1937.

page 204, Picture It!
1913: Apollo Theater opened; 1934: African American artists perform; 1978: Theater closes; 1983: Theater becomes a landmark

page 208, ELL Reader Study Guide
2. Two young women in dresses smile happily.
3. African American soldiers march through New York City. They look proud and happy.
4. A couple poses for the camera by their Cadillac. They look proud and happy.
5. A little girl and her mother share a quiet moment.

Part 3
Phonics Instruction for English Language Learners

Contents

Introduction to the Phonics Transition Lessons

Phonological and phonemic awareness, phonics, and word study are critical components of literacy instruction for English learners. The core lessons in *Reading Street* provide the explicit, systematic instruction that all children need to become fluent readers and writers. The following Phonics Transition Lessons and Practice Pages will supplement the core instruction with customized lessons that meet the particular needs of English learners. Lessons and Practice Pages are divided into three sections:

- **Phonological Awareness and Concepts of Print** English learners may not have learned to distinguish word boundaries, syllables, rhymes, or phonemes within words in English, or even in their home languages. Some children also may be unfamiliar with English print conventions such as the alphabet and left-to-right directionality. This section provides activities that can be used at any time to develop phonological awareness and concepts of print.

- **Problem Sounds in English** These lessons cover the phonemes that are typically the most challenging for English learners, such as easily confused consonants and short vowel sounds. In some cases, a Model Lesson is provided along with notes for using the same lesson format with related phonics skills. Lessons in this section include Pronunciation Tips that teachers can use to help children produce the target phonemes. A Practice Page for every lesson provides strong visual support for instruction and offers additional practice.

- **Word Study** An understanding of word parts and word origins is a powerful tool for English learners. The Word Study Lessons reinforce the core instruction and include suggestions for making connections with the home language. The Practice Pages provide visual support and context for the target skills.

Throughout the Phonics Transition Lessons, a **Transfer Skills** feature identifies specific challenges faced by English language learners as they acquire the target skills.

In addition to the Phonics Transition Lessons and Practice Pages, you can supplement core phonics instruction with routines such as the following:

- **Strengthen oral language skills.** Allow beginning speakers to work with partners when completing phonics activities. Encourage children to talk about their work with English, and provide other oral language opportunities with the target words.

- **Teach word meanings.** Before teaching the phonics skills, introduce the target words orally to children by using them in activities such as riddle games, songs, chants, or asking and answering questions that use the words.

- **Provide alternate instruction.** If children have limited literacy skills, use resources such as the *Reading Street Intervention Kit* or *Early Reading Intervention (ERI)* to provide literacy instruction at the level where children can participate and learn.

- **Relate to the home language.** Whenever possible, help children build on what they already know by making connections between each target phonics skill and the home language. Use available resources such as bilingual staff members, bilingual dictionaries, and language Web sites to gather information about the home language.

- **Engage children as active learners.** Children who are acquiring English may have a stronger awareness of language than monolingual speakers. Build their knowledge with engaging activities that explicitly show the patterns and structures of language. Consider using games such as **Phonics Four** and **Word Hunt** on the next page.

Four by Four

Make and distribute copies of page 217. Work with students to generate a class list of twenty or more words that reflect the target phonics or word study skills that students have recently studied—for example, words that begin with the prefixes *im-* and *in-*. Write each word on a card. Have students choose sixteen words from the list and write them in random order in the squares on page 217. Have students cut out the star markers at the

Use with page 217.

bottom of the page. Shuffle the cards, and read aloud one card at a time. Students should look for each word on their paper and cover it with a star marker. The first one to have four marked words in a row (horizontally, vertically, or diagonally) calls out "Four by Four!" Note: For students in early stages of literacy, write consonants in the squares, and have students listen for words that begin with the consonants.

Word Hunt

Use with page 218.

Choose a target phonics or word study skill, such as "Words with long *a*" or "Words with the suffix *-ly*," and list it at the top of page 218. Make and distribute copies to individuals, partners, or small groups. Have students look around the classroom and school, in books and magazines, and perhaps at home, for

words that have the particular phonics feature. They can list the words in the chart on page 218, and either draw or attach (with glue or tape) pictures that illustrate the words. Conclude by having students share the words they find.

Name _____

Four by Four

- **Write** the words that your teacher gives you. Write one word in each square.
- **Listen** to the words. When you hear a word that is in a square, **cover** it with a star marker.
- When you have four covered words in a row, **say** "Four by Four!"

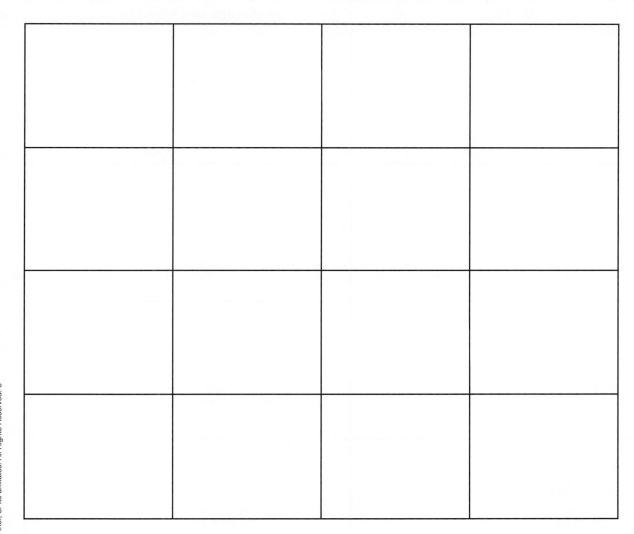

- **Cut out** the star markers. **Use** them in the game.

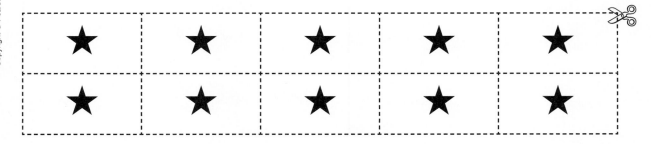

Name _____

Word Hunt: Words with _____

- **Find** words that share a sound or a spelling pattern.
- **Write** the words. **Add** pictures or definitions for the words.
- **Tell** your words to a friend.

Word	Picture or Definition

Transfer Skills

Many factors can influence students' understanding of print conventions. The students may be emergent readers of non-alphabetic languages or languages with alphabets similar to or different from the English alphabet. Some English learners may be familiar with reading left to right and top to bottom, as in English. Others may be accustomed to reading text from right to left, or from the bottom to the top of the page. Some have little experience with printed text. For students who are unfamiliar with English print conventions, activities such as these will help develop print awareness and strengthen literacy skills.

Print Awareness Activities

Parts of a Book Show students how to hold a book. Point out and explain the title, author byline, and illustrator's name. Turn to the selection pages and read a sentence or two. Discuss how the illustrations go with the text. Page through the book, and show how the narrative continues. Point to the text on each page. Then have students practice holding the book correctly, finding the title and author's name, turning the pages, and pointing to the text on each page.

Words, Sentences, Paragraphs Display a few paragraphs of printed text in a large format or on an overhead transparency. Frame one word with your fingers, and read it aloud. Explain that it is a word, and point out the spacing before and after the word. Then read aloud a sentence, running your finger under each word as you read. Point out the sentence boundaries: a capital letter at the beginning of the sentence and the end punctuation. Then circle a paragraph with your finger, and explain that a paragraph is a group of related sentences. Point out the indent at the beginning of the paragraph. Have students practice finding words, sentences, and paragraphs in other texts.

Directionality As you read a book aloud, put your finger on the starting point in the text on each page. Show that you read from left to right and from top to bottom by moving your finger along lines of text. Use your finger to show how to sweep back from the end of a line to the beginning of another, and how to move to the next page. Then have students use their fingers to show the correct movement as you read the text aloud again.

Writing the Alphabet Students should be introduced systematically to all the letters of the English alphabet, in manuscript and cursive writing. Students can practice writing letters, punctuation marks, and numbers, using pages 220, 221, and 222 as handwriting guides.

The Alphabet

- **Practice** writing the letters of the alphabet.
- **Write** more of the letters on other paper.

The D'Nealian™ Alphabet

- **Practice** writing the letters of the alphabet.
- **Write** more of the letters on other paper.

a b c d e f g h i j k

l m n o p q r s t

u v w x y z

A B C D E F G H I J K

L M N O P Q R S T

U V W X Y Z

1 2 3 4 5 6 7 8 9 10

Name _____

The D'Nealian™ Cursive Alphabet

- **Practice** writing the letters of the alphabet in cursive.
- **Write** more of the letters on other paper.

a b c d e f g h i j k

l m n o p q r s t

u v w x y z

A B C D E F G H I J K

L M N O P Q R S T

U V W X Y Z

1 2 3 4 5 6 7 8 9 10

Transfer Skills

The phonemes of certain English consonants may be unfamiliar to English language learners or easily confused with other phonemes. For example, consonant digraphs such as /th/, /sh/, and /ch/ may sound alike to some English language learners. Spanish speakers may hear and write /n/ at the end of words ending with /m/. The following lessons provide practice with certain consonant pairs that English language learners may find troublesome. You can develop similar lessons for other consonant sounds that are difficult for your students. This model lesson gives you a pattern for teaching.

☆ Model Lesson:
Words with *b* and *v*   Use with page 226.

Preteach Copy and distribute page 226. Have students point to the picture of the box at the top of the page. Say: *This is a box. The word* box *begins with /b/. Say it with me: /b/, /b/, /b/, box.* Repeat the procedure with the word *van*, using the other picture at the top of the page.

Teach/Model Guide students to distinguish between /b/ and /v/, using the Pronunciation Tip. Then, direct students' attention to Row 1. Name each of the items shown, one by one: *boat, vest, bat, vase.* Continue: *I'll say each word one more time. If the word starts with the letter* b, *circle* b *under the picture. If the word starts with the letter* v, *circle* v. Read the words aloud once more, giving students enough time to circle the corresponding letter.

Repeat the process for Row 2, omitting the directions: *violin, vine, basketball, bike.*

Practice Have students look at the pictures in Row 3. Ask them to tell what the pictures show *(box, van)* and then write those words on the appropriate blank line.

Read the practice sentence aloud and have students find the words with *b* and *v (Val, Billy, dove, wave).* After they've had a chance to repeat the sentence several times, challenge students to say it as quickly as they can.

Assess Make letter cards for *b* and *v*, and give one of each to each student. Tell students: *I will say some words. Hold up the card that matches the sound you hear at the beginning of each word:* boat, vote, bolt, volt, vanilla, basket, very, berry, bent, vent, best, vest, vane. Then have students repeat the contrasting word pairs after you, striving for the correct pronunciation of /b/ and /v/. Keep in mind that students who have difficulty distinguishing /b/ and /v/ may still be able to comprehend words they hear or read that start with these consonants.

> **Pronunciation Tip**
> **b and v** *When you say /b/, your lips start out together. Then they open and a tiny puff of air comes out of your mouth. If you touch your throat, you can feel it move because your voice box is on. Can you hold a /b/ sound? Try it: /b/, /b/. No, you can't hold it. When you say /v/, you can hold it: /vvvv/. Your voice box is still on. Your top teeth touch your bottom lip. Say /v/ and feel your teeth touch your bottom lip. Hold the sound. Try it: /vvvv/, /vvvv/. Try both sounds: /b/, /vvvv/.*

Adapting the ☆ **Model Lesson**

Use the same lesson format above to teach the following consonants and digraphs: /ch/, /sh/, /d/, /th/, /l/, /r/, /m/, /n/, and /s/. The following information will help you to customize each lesson.

Notes for Additional Lessons

Words with *ch* and *sh*
Use with page 227.

Teach/Model Use these words: *child, shop.* Row 1 of page 227: *shoe, cherry, chair, sheep.*

Practice Row 2: *shark, shell, chicken, chalk.* Row 3: *child, shop.* Practice sentence: *Sherry the Shark chewed and chewed on a shiny shoe.*

Assess Use these words: *chew, shoe, chin, shin, chomp, cherry, Sherry, shell, chain, chair, share.*

> **Pronunciation Tip**
> ***ch* and *sh*** *When you say /ch/, your lips are open and your teeth are close together. Your tongue moves as you make the sound. Can you hold a /ch/ sound? Try it: /ch/, /ch/. No, you can't hold it. When you say /sh/, your lips are also open and your teeth are close together. But your tongue doesn't move, and you can hold the sound: /shhhhh/. Try it: /shhhhh/, /shhhhh/. Try both sounds: /ch/, /shhhhh/.*

Words with *d* and *th*
Use with page 228.

Teach/Model Use these words: *desk, third.* Row 1 of page 228: *door, thorn, thirty, dinosaur.*

Practice Row 2: *thermos, thumb, dish, dog.* Row 3: *third, desk.* Practice sentence: *Think a thought about a daring dog walking through thick grass.*

Assess Use these words: *thigh, dye, think, thirty, dirty, duck, though, dough, there, dare.*

> **Pronunciation Tip**
> ***d* and *th*** *When you say /d/, the tip of your tongue touches above your top teeth. Say /d/ and feel the tip of your tongue touch above your top teeth: /d/. Is your voice box on? Yes, you can feel your throat move when you say /d/. Can you hold a /d/ sound? Try it: /d/, /d/. No, you can't hold it. When you say /ŦH/ in a word like this, your voice box is also on: /ŦH/. But your tongue is between your teeth, and you can hold the sound. Try it: /ŦHHHHH/, /ŦHHHHH/. Try both sounds: /d/, /ŦHHHHH/. When you say /th/ in a word like thin, your voice box is off, and you can hold the sound: /thhhhh/. The tip of your tongue comes out between your teeth and air comes out, but no sound. Try it: /thhhhh/, /thhhhh/. Try both th sounds: /ŦHHHHH/, /thhhhh/.*

Notes for Additional Lessons

Words with *l* and *r*

Use with page 229.

Teach/Model Use these words: *leg, ring.*
Row 1 of page 229: *radio, lake, light, ruler.*

Practice Row 2: *rose, lizard, leaf, river.*
Row 3: *leg, ring.* Practice sentence: *The red river runs into a little lake.*

Assess Use these words: *rake, lake, rip, lip, red, rice, late, rate, load, road, loud, lean.*

> **Pronunciation Tip**
> *l* and *r* *When you say /l/, the tip of your tongue touches above your top teeth and stays there. Say /l/ and feel your throat move. Your voice box is on when you say /l/. Try it: /l/, /l/. When you say /r/, your voice box is on again. The tip of your tongue goes toward the roof of your mouth, but doesn't touch it. Try it: /r/, /r/. Try both sounds: /l/, /r/.*

Words with *m* and *n*

Use with page 230.

Teach/Model Use these words: *mask, nest.*
Row 1 of page 230: *nose, net, mouse, match.*

Practice Focus on ending sounds for Row 2: *jam, pen, stem, fan.*
Row 3: *mask, nest.* Practice sentence: *The man in the moon eats ice cream with a spoon.*

Assess Use these words: *meat, neat, mole, next, moat, note, Pam, pan, tone, time, some, sun.*

> **Pronunciation Tip**
> *m* and *n* *When you say /m/, your lips come together and a little air comes out of your nose. Can you hold the sound /m/? Try it: /mmmm/, /mmmm/. Yes, you can hold the sound. You can also hold the /n/ sound. Try it: /nnnn/. But when you say /n/, your lips are open. Your tongue is behind your top teeth. Say it again: /n/, /n/. Try both sounds: /m/, /n/.*

Words with *s* and *th*

Use with page 231.

Teach/Model Use these words: *sun, thorn.*
Row 1 of page 231: *saw, thumb, thermos, soap.*

Practice Row 2: *sandwich, soup, thigh, thirteen.*
Row 3: *sun, thorn.* Practice sentence: *Sara sipped thick soup.*

Assess Use these words: *some, thumb, so, think, sink, sock, thin, thing, sing, thank.*

> **Pronunciation Tip**
> *s* and *th* *When you say /s/, the tip of your tongue touches above your top teeth. It makes a snake sound, and you can hold the sound. Try it: /ssss/, /ssss/. When you say /th/ in a word like thick, the tip of your tongue comes out between your teeth. You can feel air come out of your mouth. Try it: /thhhh/, /thhhh/. Try both sounds: /ssss/, /thhhh/.*

Name _____

Words with *b* and *v*

- If the word begins with the sound of *b* in *box*, **circle** the *b*.
- If the word begins with the sound of *v* in *van*, **circle** the *v*.

ROW 1

  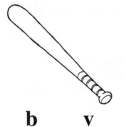 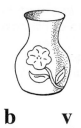

b   v   b   v   b   v   b   v

ROW 2

 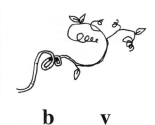  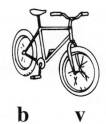

b   v   b   v   b   v   b   v

- **Look** at each picture. **Say** its name. **Write** the word.

ROW 3

_____   _____

Find *b* and *v* in this sentence. Then **practice** chanting or singing the sentence.

Val and Billy dove into the wave.

Name _____

Words with *ch* and *sh*

- If the word begins with the sound of *ch* in *child*, **circle** the *ch*.
- If the word begins with the sound of *sh* in *shop*, **circle** the *sh*.

ROW 1

ch   sh   ch   sh   ch   sh   ch   sh

ROW 2

ch   sh   ch   sh   ch   sh   ch   sh

- **Look** at each picture. **Say** its name. **Write** the word.

ROW 3

 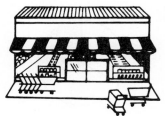

_____   _____

Find *ch* and *sh* in this sentence. Then **practice** chanting or singing the sentence.

Sherry the Shark chewed and chewed on a shiny shoe.

Name _____

Words with *d* and *th*

- If the word begins with the sound of *d* in *desk*, **circle** the *d*.
- If the word begins with the sound of *th* in *third*, **circle** the *th*.

ROW 1

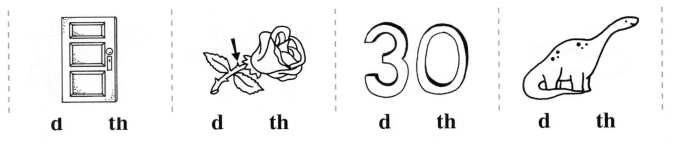

| d   th | d   th | d   th | d   th |

ROW 2

| d   th | d   th | d   th | d   th |

- **Look** at each picture. **Say** its name. **Write** the word.

ROW 3

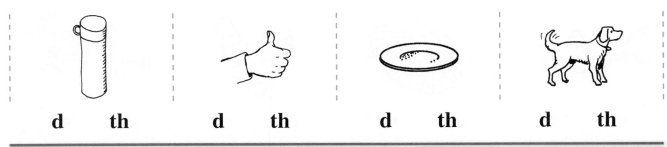

_____   _____

Find *th* and *d* in this sentence. Then **practice** chanting or singing the sentence.

Think a thought about a daring dog walking through thick grass.

Name _____

Words with *l* and *r*

- If the word begins with the sound of *l* in *leg*, **circle** the *l*.
- If the word begins with the sound of *r* in *ring*, **circle** the *r*.

ROW 1

l   r   l   r   l   r   l   r

ROW 2

l   r   l   r   l   r   l   r

- **Look** at each picture. **Say** its name. **Write** the word.

ROW 3

_____   _____

Find *l* and *r* in this sentence. Then **practice** chanting or singing the sentence.

The red river runs into a little lake.

Name _____

Words with *m* and *n*

- If the word has the sound of *m* in *mask*, **circle** the *m*.
- If the word has the sound of *n* in *nest*, **circle** the *n*.

ROW 1

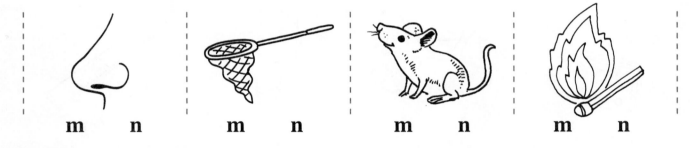

| m   n | m   n | m   n | m   n |

ROW 2

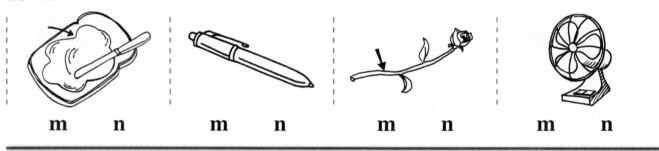

| m   n | m   n | m   n | m   n |

- **Look** at each picture. **Say** its name. **Write** the word.

ROW 3

_____   _____

Find *m* and *n* in this sentence. Then **practice** chanting or singing the sentence.

The man in the moon eats ice cream with a spoon.

Name _____

Words with *s* and *th*

- If the word begins with the sound of *s* in *sun*, **circle** the *s*.
- If the word begins with the sound of *th* in *thorn*, **circle** the *th*.

ROW 1

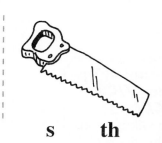         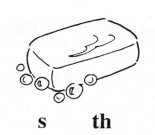

| s   th | s   th | s   th | s   th |

ROW 2

| s   th | s   th | s   th | s   th |

- **Look** at each picture. **Say** its name. **Write** the word.

ROW 3

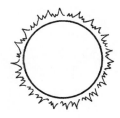   

_____   _____

Find *s* and *th* in this sentence. Then **practice** chanting or singing the sentence.

Sara sipped thick soup.

Transfer Skills

The writing systems of languages such as Arabic and Hebrew focus on consonant sounds and long vowels. Short vowels are indicated with separate marks that are often optional. Speakers of these languages may need extra help in spelling words with short vowels or multiple vowel sounds.

Syllables V/CV and VC/V   Use with page 236.

Preteach Write the word *lemon* on the board and draw a small picture or point to the picture of a lemon on page 236. Say: *This is a lemon, /l/ /e/ /m/ /ə/ /n/. How many vowel sounds do you hear in the word* lemon? *Say it with me, /l/ /e/ /m/ /ə/ /n/,* lemon. *That's right, there are two vowel sounds.* Cover the *mon.* Say: *If the syllable ended after the* e, *I would pronounce the word with a long* e: lē mon. *This does not make a word that I know.* Cover the *on,* then say: *I will try it with a short* e, */l/ /e/ /m/ /ə/ /n/. Now I pronounce the word* lemon, *and I recognize it. The short vowel sound is correct.* Repeat with the words *broken* and *finish,* emphasizing the short or long vowel sound in the first syllable.

Teach/Model Write the word *pupil* on the board. Draw a line between the two syllables and tell students: *When you hear a word with more than one vowel sound, divide it into parts.* Explain that when there is one consonant between two vowels, it is important to figure out if the first vowel has a short or long sound in order to know where to divide the syllable.

Point out that because the first syllable in *pupil* has a long vowel sound, it ends after the first vowel. Then write *finish* on the board. Draw a line between the *n* and the second *i* and then say: *This word also has one consonant between two vowels. The first vowel sound in* finish *is short, so we know that the first syllable ends with a consonant. Say it with me:* finish, fin/ish.

Practice Copy and distribute page 236. Help students read the words in the box on page 236. Clap as you read each word to emphasize the syllable break in the word. Say: *I am going to read the words again. This time, circle each word with a long vowel sound in the first syllable. Underline each word with a short vowel sound in the first syllable.* Review the answers as a class *(Circle: broken, frozen, music, tulip; Underline: salad, lemon).*

Assess Make word cards with these word parts: *bro, ken, si, lent, sev, en, fe, male, rap, id.* In pairs, give students the pile of word cards. Have students put the various word parts together to create complete words. If necessary, list the words *broken, silent, seven, female,* and *rapid* on the board.

> **Pronunciation Tip**
> **Syllables V/CV and VC/V**
> When a syllable ends with a single vowel, the vowel sound is usually long. When a syllable ends with a consonant, the vowel sound is usually short.

Transfer Skills

Speakers of monosyllabic languages such as Cantonese, Hmong, Khmer, Korean, and Vietnamese may pronounce a two-syllable word as two separate words. Have students practice saying multisyllabic words.

Syllables CV/VC   Use with page 237.

Preteach Write the word *violin* on the board and draw a small picture or point to the picture of a violin on page 237. Say: *This is a violin, /v/ /ī/ /ə/ /l/ /i/ /n/. How many vowel sounds do you hear in the word* violin? *Say it with me, /v/ /ī/ /ə/ /l/ /i/ /n/,* violin. *That's right, there are three vowel sounds.* Explain that if a word in English has three vowel sounds, it must also have three syllables. Repeat with the words *computer* and *calendar*, emphasizing vowel sounds and reviewing what students have learned about breaking words into syllables.

Teach/Model Write the word *create* on the board. Draw a line between the first *e* and *a* and tell students: *When you hear a word with more than one vowel sound, divide it into parts.* Explain that when there are two vowels side by side, you must put a syllable break between the two vowels.

Practice breaking multisyllabic words with the CV/VC syllable pattern into meaningful parts. Write the word *reorganize*. Point out the prefix *re-* and say: *We know that the prefix* re- *is its own syllable and means "again."* Then cover up the prefix so that only *organize* is visible. Say: Organize *means "to put in order." We know that* organize *has three vowel sounds, so it has three syllables.* Uncover the prefix, draw lines between the syllables, and blend the word. Have students repeat the word after you. Have them explain the meaning of *reorganize*. Repeat this exercise with the words *reunite, deactivate,* and *scientists*.

Practice Copy and distribute page 237. Read the directions aloud, and help students read the words if necessary. After students complete the activities, practice saying the multisyllabic words aloud. (See answers on page 308.)

Assess Make word cards with the word parts in Part 2 of page 237. Put students in pairs. Give one student the word parts from column 1. Give the second student word parts from column 2. Once students have pieced the words together, have them write out the words and draw lines between each syllable.

> **Pronunciation Tip Syllables CV/VC**
> Remind students that a word has as many syllables as it has vowel sounds.

Syllables

Speakers of monosyllabic languages such as Cantonese, Hmong, Khmer, Korean, and Vietnamese may pronounce a two-syllable word as two separate words. Have students practice saying multisyllabic words.

Syllables VCCCV
Use with page 238.

Preteach Write *dolphin* on the board and draw a small picture. Say: *This is a dolphin, /d/ /o/ /l/ /f/ /i/ /n/.* Point out that there are two vowel sounds in *dolphin,* and therefore two syllables. Say: *How many consonants do you see between the vowels o and i in the word* dolphin? Point to the *l, p,* and *h* as you say: *That's right, there are three consonants between the vowels.* Remind students that when two consonants, such as the *ph* in *dolphin* make one sound, those letters stay together when you divide the word into syllables. Say: *Now let's break the word* dolphin *into syllables: dol/phin, dolphin.* Repeat with the words *huddle* and *contract,* emphasizing vowel sounds and reviewing what students have learned about breaking words into syllables.

Teach/Model Write *surprise* on the board. Underline the three consonants between the vowels *u* and *i* and tell students: *There are three consonants between two vowels in this word. Each vowel means that there is a syllable, so we know that there are two syllables in this pattern.* Since it is hard to generalize where the syllable break comes in a word with the VCCCV syllable pattern, help students understand that they must look at each word separately to find its syllable breaks.

Practice breaking words with the VCCCV syllable pattern. Distribute several copies of a dictionary and point out how each word is divided into syllables. Write the word *complain* on the board. Ask: *How many syllables does this word have?* (2) *What is the first syllable?* (com) *What's the second syllable?* (plain) Repeat this exercise with the words *explore, sample, enclose,* and *hundred.*

Practice Copy and distribute page 238. Read the directions aloud, and have students look at the sample answer to help them get started. After students complete the activity, have them break each of the words into syllables. (See answers on page 308.)

Assess Write the following words on the board: *address, district, substance, complete,* and *control.* Have students write the words on a piece of paper, showing the syllable divisions. Students should use what they know about dividing words into syllables. If they have difficulty with a word, they may use a dictionary to see how a word is divided into syllables.

> **Pronunciation Tip**
> **Syllables VCCCV**
> Remind students that a word has as many syllables as it has vowel sounds.

Transfer Skills

Many languages do not have the schwa /ə/ sound, so English learners may have difficulty pronouncing and spelling the unstressed syllable in words such as *table* and *apple*. Provide additional practice pronouncing these words.

C + -*le*   **Use with page 239.**

Preteach Say the word *candle* and draw a small picture of it or point to the picture of a candle on page 239. Say: *This is a candle, /k/ /a/ /n/ /d/ /əl/. How many syllables do you hear in the word* candle? *That's right, there are two syllables.* Sound out and blend the following words with -*le: bubble, puddle, table.* Point out that the first syllable in each word carries more stress than the second syllable.

Teach/Model Write *candle* on the board. Draw a line between the two syllables and tell students: *When you hear a word with more than one vowel sound, divide it into parts.* Cover *can.* Say: *If a word ends with* -le, *then the consonant before the* -le *is part of the last syllable.* Show that in the word *candle,* the letter *d* comes right before the -*le* and is part of the second syllable. Now write *double* on the board. Draw a line between the *u* and the *b* and say: *In the word* double, *the letter* b *comes before the* -le *and is part of the second syllable. Say it with me: double, dou/ble.*

Practice Copy and distribute page 239. Help students name the words that are pictured on the top half of page 239. Then read the words in the box. Clap as you read each word to emphasize the syllable break in the word. Say: *I am going to read the words again. This time write the word below the correct picture.* Review the answers as a class (*bubble, puddle, eagle, candle*) and then tell students to break the words into syllables.

Assess Tell students: *I will say some words. Put your thumb up if you hear a consonant with* -le *at the end of the word. Put your thumb down if you do not:* purple, bubble, puppy, people, softball, broken, noodle. Then have students repeat the C + -*le* words back to you.

> **Pronunciation Tip**
> **C + -*le***
> When a word ends in -*le*, the consonant that comes before the -*le* must be part of the last syllable.

Name _____

Syllables V/CV and VC/V

- **Read** the words in the box. **Circle** each word with a **long vowel sound** in the first syllable. **Underline** each word with a **short vowel sound** in the first syllable.
- **Write** a word on the line by each picture.

music	tulip
lemon	broken
frozen	salad

_____

_____

_____

ELL Handbook

Name _____

Syllables CV/VC

PART 1
- **Read** the words.
- **Find** the syllables in each word. **Draw** a line between each syllable.

scientist

piano

violin

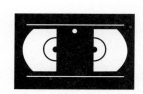

video

stadium

radio

rodeo

meteor

PART 2
- **Read** the two lists of words.
- **Connect** word parts from each list to make words.

studi-	-neer
cre-	-onic
ide-	-o
me-	-ate
pio-	-dium
immedi-	-ance
bi-	-a
reli-	-ate

Name _____

Syllables VCCCV

- **Read** the words in the box.
- **Look** at the pictures. **Read** the meanings.
- **Write** the correct word on each blank line.

1.  ___**purchase**___ = to buy something

2.  _____ = to look closely at something

3.  _____ = something unexpected

4.  _____ = more than one child

5.  _____ = blow apart with a loud noise

6. 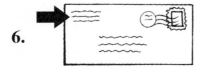 _____ = the street where someone lives

ELL Handbook

Name _____

C + -le

PART 1
- **Look** at the pictures.
- **Read** the words in the box.
- **Write** the word on the line.

_____ _____ _____ _____

| puddle | bubble | candle | eagle |

PART 2
- **Read** the word.
- **Write** the two syllable parts that make up the word.

_____ + _____ = marble

_____ + _____ = middle

_____ + _____ = double

_____ + _____ = little

_____ + _____ = title

_____ + _____ = handle

Consonant Blends

Consonant blends in English words often are challenging for English language learners because their home languages may not combine consonant phonemes in similar ways at the beginnings and ends of words. For example, consonant blends with *l* and *r* can be particularly difficult for speakers of Asian languages such as Chinese, Korean, and Vietnamese. Speakers of Arabic may insert vowel sounds between the consonants within a blend. The following lessons provide practice with consonant blends. If your students are struggling with particular blends, you can develop similar lessons targeted to those blends.

Initial Consonant Blends   Use with page 242.

Preteach Copy and distribute page 242. Have students point to the picture of the crib at the top of the page. Say: *This is a crib. The word* crib *begins with /kr/.* Write *crib* on the board. Say: *Usually, when two letters come before a vowel* (underline the *cr*), *we blend the sounds of the letters: /k/ /r/... /kr/ /i/ /b/. Say it with me: /kr/ /i/ /b/,* crib. Repeat for *clap.*

Teach/Model Direct students' attention to Row 1. Name each of the items shown, one by one: *crab, crown, clock, cloth.* Continue: *I'll say each word one more time. If the word starts with the letters* cr, *circle* cr *under the picture. If the word starts with the letters* cl, *circle* cl. Read the words aloud once more, giving students enough time to circle the corresponding letter.

   Tell students that there are many beginning blends in English. Write a 10-column chart on the board with the headings: *br, cr, cl, fl, gr, pr, pl, sn, sp, st.* List the words *crib* and *clap* in the columns where they belong. Add the words from Row 1 to the chart. Give several more examples. Invite children to suggest other words that begin with these blends that can be added to the chart.

Practice Have students look at the pictures in Row 2. Name the items shown *(princess, plant, price, plug),* and pause to let students circle their answer choices. Repeat the procedure for Row 3 *(straw, string, steak, starfish).*

   Read the practice sentence aloud, and have students find the words with beginning blends *(clock, struck, students, snapped).* After they've had a chance to repeat the sentence several times, challenge students to say it as quickly as they can.

Assess Prepare sets of cards with a blend written on each one: *cr, cl, pr, pl, tr, dr, st, str.* Give each student a set of cards. Say a list of words, and have students display the correct initial blends: *crawl, please, claw, preen, tree, street, draw, stall.* Then have students repeat the words after you, striving for the correct pronunciation of the initial blends. Keep in mind that students who have difficulty pronouncing the initial blends may still be able to comprehend words they hear or read that start with these consonants.

**Pronunciation Tip
Initial Consonant
Blends** *When a word begins with two consonants such as* c and r, *you blend the sounds of the two consonants together. In the word* crib, *take the /k/ sound and /r/ sound and put them together: /kr/. Try it: /kr/, /kr/, /kr/ /i/ /b/,* crib.

Final Consonant Blends   Use with page 243.

Preteach Copy and distribute page 243. Have students point to the picture of the pond at the top of the page. Say: *This is a pond. The word* pond *ends with /nd/. Usually, when two letters come after a vowel* (underline the *nd*), *we blend the sounds of the letters: /n/ /d/.../p/ /o/ /nd/. Say it with me: pond, /p/ /o/ /nd/.* Repeat for *sink.*

Teach/Model Direct students' attention to Row 1. Name each of the items shown, one by one: *(band, trunk, hand, bank).* Continue: *I'll say each word one more time. If the word ends with the letters* nd, *circle* nd *under the picture. If the word ends with the letters* nk, *circle* nk. Read the words aloud once more, giving students enough time to circle the corresponding letter.

Tell students that there are many ending blends in English. Write a 9-column chart on the board with the headings *lt, mp, nch, nd, nk, nt, sk, sp, st.* List the words *pond* and *sink* in the columns where they belong. Add the words from Row 1 to the chart. Give several more examples. Invite children to suggest other words that end with these blends that can be added to the chart.

Practice Have students look at the pictures in Row 2. Name the items shown *(ant, paint, branch, inch),* and pause to let students circle their answer choices. Repeat the procedure for Row 3 *(desk, vest, cast, mask).*

Read the practice sentence aloud, and have students find the words with ending blends *(must, ask, band, paint, bench).* After they've had a chance to read the sentence several times, challenge students to say it from memory.

Assess Prepare sets of cards with a blend written on each one: *nd, nk, nt, nch, sk, st.* Give each student a set of cards. Say a list of words, and have students display the correct final blends: *sink, cinch, bank, band, inch, ink, dusk, dust, ant, and, paint, pond.* Then have students repeat the words after you, striving for the correct pronunciation of the final blends. Keep in mind that students who have difficulty pronouncing the final blends may still be able to comprehend words they hear or read that end with these consonants.

> **Pronunciation Tip**
> **Final Consonant Blends** *When a word ends with two consonants such as* s *and* k, *you blend the sounds of the two consonants together. In the word* desk, *take the /s/ sound and /k/ sound and put them together: /sk/. Try it: /sk/, /sk/, desk.*

Name _____

Initial Consonant Blends

- If the word begins with the sound of *cr* in *crib*, **circle** the *cr*.
- If the word begins with the sound of *cl* in *clap*, **circle** the *cl*.

ROW 1

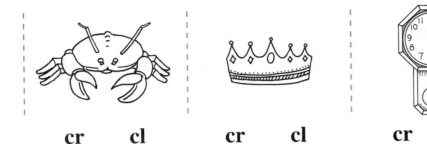 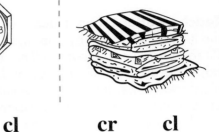

| cr cl | cr cl | cr cl | cr cl |

- If the word begins with the sound of *pl* in *plum*, **circle** the *pl*.
- If the word begins with the sound of *pr* in *prize*, **circle** the *pr*.

ROW 2

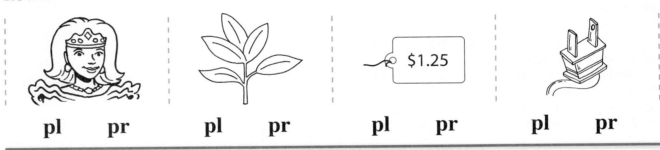

| pl pr | pl pr | pl pr | pl pr |

- If the word begins with the sound of *str* in *stripe*, **circle** the *str*.
- If the word begins with the sound of *st* in *stick*, **circle** the *st*.

ROW 3

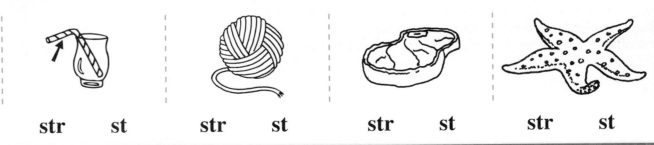

| str st | str st | str st | str st |

Find the beginning blends in this sentence. Then **practice** chanting or singing the sentence.

When the clock struck one, the students snapped their fingers.

ELL Handbook

Name _____

Final Consonant Blends

- If the word ends with the sound of *nd* in *pond*, **circle** the *nd*.
- If the word ends with the sound of *nk* in *sink*, **circle** the *nk*.

ROW 1

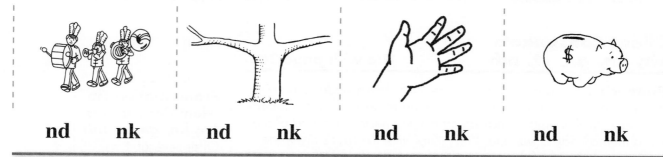

| nd nk | nd nk | nd nk | nd nk |

- If the word ends with the sound of *nt* in *cent*, **circle** the *nt*.
- If the word ends with the sound of *nch* in *bench*, **circle** the *nch*.

ROW 2

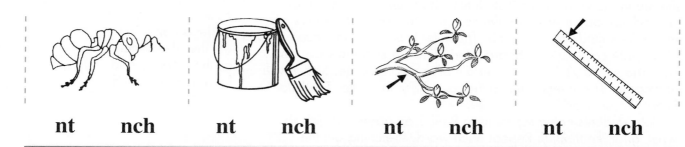

| nt nch | nt nch | nt nch | nt nch |

- If the word ends with the sound of *st* in *nest*, **circle** the *st*.
- If the word ends with the sound of *sk* in *tusk*, **circle** the *sk*.

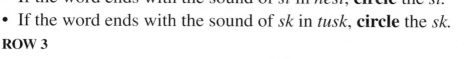

ROW 3

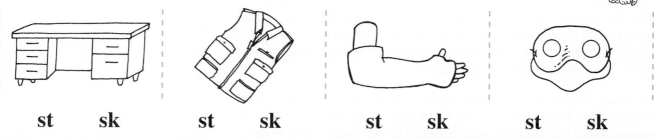

| st sk | st sk | st sk | st sk |

Find the ending blends in this sentence. Then **practice** chanting or singing the sentence.

You must ask the band to paint the bench.

Silent Consonants

Transfer Skills

Students who are literate in their home language(s) may be familiar with the concept of silent letters. In Spanish, the letter *h* is always silent, and the letter *u* is silent when it follows a *q*. In French, the letter *s* at the end of a word is often silent. Discuss students' awareness of silent letters in their home languages before introducing *wr, kn, gn, st,* and *mb*.

Silent Consonants
wr, kn, gn, st, mb   Use with page 245.

Preteach Copy and distribute page 245. Have students point to the picture of a thumb at the top of the page. Say: *This is a thumb, /th/ /u/ /m/, thumb. What sound do you hear at the end of the word* thumb? *Say it with me: /m/, /m/, thumb. That's right, the ending sound is /m/.* Now point to the *castle.* Ask: *What sound do you hear in the middle of the word? Listen: /k/ /a/ /s/ /əl/. Yes, the middle sound is /s/.*

Teach/Model Write the word *thumb* on the board. Underline the *mb* in the word and tell students: *The sound /m/ in* thumb *is spelled* mb. *Say it with me: thumb, /th/ /u/ /m/. The letters* mb *make the sound /m/ in* thumb. *The letter* b *is not pronounced.* Now write *castle* on the board. Underline the *st* in the word and say: *The sound /s/ is in the middle of the word* castle. *Say it with me:* castle. *The letters* st *make the sound /s/ in* castle. *The letter* t *is not pronounced.*

Help students name the items in Row 1 on page 245 *(climb, wrist, gnat, knot, knit).* Repeat each word, stretching out the sounds. Say: *I am going to read the words again. This time, circle the silent consonants in each word.* Review the answers as a class *(mb, wr, gn, kn, kn).*

Practice Have students name the items in the chart on page 245 *(write, wrench, knee, knot, gnat, sign, listen, castle, thumb, crumb).* Repeat each word and then say: *The chart shows several words with silent consonants. Look at each picture and write its name. Underline the silent consonants (write, wrench, knee, knot, gnat, sign, listen, castle, thumb, crumb).*

Assess Create word cards containing the silent consonant letter patterns *wr, kn, gn, st,* and *mb.* Give each student a pile of word cards. Read the following words aloud to the class: *knob, knock, knit, write, wrist, wreath, sign, gnat, design, listen, hustle, bustle, lamb, comb,* and *numb.* Pause after each word so students can find and hold up the card that contains the silent consonant letter pattern that corresponds to each word.

> **Pronunciation Tip**
> **Silent Consonants**
> ***wr, kn, gn, st, mb***
> Offer several examples of words containing letter patterns with silent consonants *(knee, knob, wrist, sign, castle, lamb).* See if students can point out the silent letter as they look at and listen to each word.

Silent Consonants *wr, kn, gn, st, mb*

- **Listen** for the beginning and ending sounds.
- **Circle** the correct letters.

ROW 1

| mb   gt | kr   wr | gn   gr | mn   kn | kn   wr |

- **Look** at the pictures in each column. **Write** the word for each picture.

Silent Consonants				
wr	kn	gn	st	mb

Short Vowels

Short vowel sounds may be challenging for many English language learners because in many languages, short vowel sounds may not exist or may only have approximations. For example, English language learners from various language backgrounds may pronounce short *i* like the *ee* in *see*. The following lessons provide practice for hearing and producing short vowel sounds. This model lesson gives you a pattern for teaching.

☆ Model Lesson: Short *a* Use with page 248.

Preteach Copy and distribute page 248. Have students point to the apple at the top of the page. Say: *This is an apple. Apple begins with /a/. Say it with me: /a/, /a/, /a/, apple.*

Teach/Model Tell students: *The /a/ sound is one sound of the letter a. We call this sound the short a. Repeat these /a/ words after me: cap, am, mat, pan.*

    Ask students to name the items in Row 1 on page 248 *(acrobat, mop, bat, ant)*. Repeat each word, clearly pronouncing the vowel each time. Then say: *I'll say these words again. If you hear the /a/ sound, circle the picture: acrobat, mop, bat, ant.* Students should circle the *acrobat, bat,* and *ant* pictures—but not the *mop*.

Practice Have students look at the pictures in Row 2 on page 248. Have them read the words below each picture and circle the word that names it *(cap, man, map, can)*. Then have them look at the pictures in Row 3, say the name of each picture, and write the names *(man, bat, ant, hat)*.

    Read the practice sentence aloud, and have students find the short *a* words *(acrobat, an, apple, bat, act)*. Invite students to chant the sentence together, clapping each time they hear short *a*.

Assess Tell students: *I will say some word pairs. Raise your hand when you hear the /a/ sound:* pat, pet; hot, hat; bad, bed; man, main; tug, tag. Then have students repeat the word pairs after you, striving for the correct pronunciation of /a/. Keep in mind that students who have difficulty pronouncing /a/ may still be able to comprehend short a words that they hear or read.

Adapting the ☆ **Model Lesson**

Use the same lesson format above to teach the short vowels /e/, /i/, /o/, and /u/. The following information will help you to customize each lesson.

> **Pronunciation Tip**
> **short *a*** *When you say /a/, your jaw and tongue are down. Say /a/ and feel your jaw and tongue go down.*

Notes for Additional Lessons

Short *e*

Use with page 249.

Teach/Model Use these /e/ words: *enter, exit, elephant, elk.* Row 1 of page 249: *vest, elephant, tiger, tent.*

Practice Row 2: *pen, web, bell, bed;* Row 3: *ten, bell, nest, web.* Practice sentence: *The elephant entered the tent with an elegant step.*

Assess Use these word pairs: *set, sat; ten, tan; net, not; sell, sale.*

> **Pronunciation Tip**
> **short e** *When you say /e/, your mouth is open. Your tongue is behind your bottom teeth. Say /e/. Did your mouth open? Say /e/ again.*

Short *i*

Use with page 250.

Teach/Model Use these /i/ words: *it, sit, if, thin, with.* Row 1 of page 250: *dinner, gift, ice, inch.*

Practice Row 2: *pin, zip, dig, sit;* Row 3: *zip, gift, pig, six.* Practice sentence: *Six pigs with bibs grinned and did a jig in a minute.*

Assess Use these word pairs: *tin, ten; six, socks; pig, pine; trip, trap.*

> **Pronunciation Tip**
> **short i** *When you say /i/, your mouth is open and your tongue is slightly lowered. Say /i/. Is your mouth open, and is your tongue slightly lowered? Practice: /i/. In Spanish, the letter i is pronounced /ē/. Point out that this letter has different sounds in English.*

Short *o*

Use with page 251.

Teach/Model Use these /o/ words: *on, olive, Oscar, opposite.* Row 1 of page 251: *elephant, dog, octopus, box.*

Practice Row 2: *lock, rock, fox, hop;* Row 3: *box, dog, lock, mop.* Practice sentence: *I opened the lock and a fox jumped out of the box.*

Assess Use these word pairs: *hop, hope; top, tape; dog, dig; lock, lake.*

> **Pronunciation Tip**
> **short o** *When you say /o/, your mouth is open and your jaw drops. Put your hand under your chin and say /o/. See, your mouth opened and your jaw dropped. In Spanish, the sound of letter a is similar to /o/ in English. Examples mami/mom; mapa/mop.*

Short *u*

Use with page 252.

Teach/Model Use these /u/ words: *up, bump, slump, plug.* Row 1 of page 252: *truck, plane, puppy, train.*

Practice Row 2: *bus, duck, tub, rug;* Row 3: *bus, truck, duck, sun.* Practice sentence: *A bug on a rug jumped up and landed on a pup.*

Assess Use these word pairs: *bug, bag; tub, tube; cup, cap; cub, cube.*

> **Pronunciation Tip**
> **short u** *When you say /u/, your mouth is open and your tongue is down. Say /u/ again. Is your mouth open? Is your tongue down?*

Name _____

Words with Short *a*

- **Listen** for the sound of *a* in *apple*.
- **Circle** the pictures of words that have this sound.

ROW 1

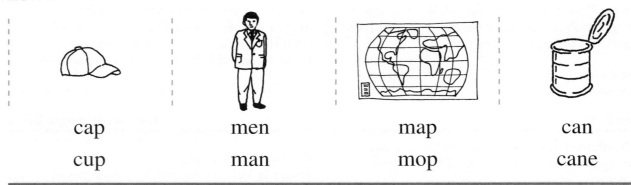

- **Look** at each picture. **Say** its name.
- **Circle** the word that names each picture.

ROW 2

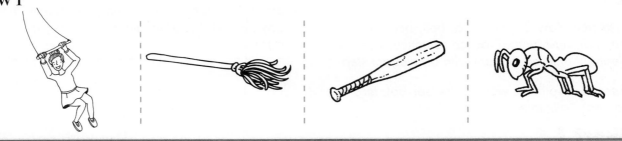

cap	men	map	can
cup	man	mop	cane

- **Look** at each picture. **Say** its name.
- **Write** the name of the picture.

ROW 3

_____ _____ _____ _____

Find short *a* in this sentence. Then **practice** chanting or singing the sentence.

The acrobat hit an apple with a bat in the middle of her act.

Name _____

Words with Short e

- **Listen** for the sound of *e* in *elbow*.
- **Circle** the pictures of words that have this sound.

ROW 1

- **Look** at each picture. **Say** its name.
- **Circle** the word that names each picture.

ROW 2

| pine | web | ball | bed |
| pen | weed | bell | bead |

- **Look** at each picture. **Say** its name.
- **Write** the name of the picture.

ROW 3

   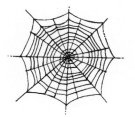

_____ _____ _____ _____

Find short *e* in this sentence. Then **practice** chanting or singing the sentence.

The elephant entered the tent with an elegant step.

Name _____

Words with Short *i*

- **Listen** for the sound of *i* in *pig*.
- **Circle** the pictures of words that have this sound.

ROW 1

- **Look** at each picture. **Say** its name.
- **Circle** the word that names each picture.

ROW 2

pin   zip   dog   set

pine   zap   dig   sit

- **Look** at each picture. **Say** its name.
- **Write** the name of the picture.

ROW 3

_____ _____ _____ _____

Find short *i* in this sentence. Then **practice** chanting or singing the sentence.

Six pigs with bibs grinned and did a jig in a minute.

Name _____

Words with Short *o*

- **Listen** for the sound of *o* in *ox*.
- **Circle** the pictures of words that have this sound.

ROW 1

- **Look** at each picture. **Say** its name.
- **Circle** the word that names each picture.

ROW 2

| lick | rock | fox | hop |
| lock | rack | fix | hope |

- **Look** at each picture. **Say** its name.
- **Write** the name of the picture.

ROW 3

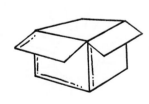  

_____ _____ _____ _____

Find short *o* in this sentence. Then **practice** chanting or singing the sentence.

I opened the lock and a fox jumped out of the box.

Name _____

Words with Short *u*

- **Listen** for the sound of *u* in *sun*.
- **Circle** the pictures of words that have this sound.

ROW 1

- **Look** at each picture. **Say** its name.
- **Circle** the word that names each picture.

ROW 2

bus	dock	tub	rug
boss	duck	tube	rag

- **Look** at each picture. **Say** its name.
- **Write** the name of the picture.

ROW 3

_____ _____ _____ _____

Find short *u* in this sentence. Then **practice** chanting or singing the sentence.

A bug on a rug jumped up and landed on a pup.

🧩 Transfer Skills

Long vowels and the vowel digraphs that produce long vowel sounds can be confusing for English language learners. For example, some long vowel sounds in English are similar to the sounds made by different vowels or vowel combinations in Spanish. As a result, Spanish speakers may spell long *a* words with an *e*, or long *i* words with *ai*. The following lessons provide practice for hearing, producing, and spelling long vowel sounds. This model lesson gives you a pattern for teaching.

☆ **Model Lesson: Long *a***   Use with page 255.

Preteach Copy and distribute page 255. Have students point to the bunch of grapes at the top of the page. Say: *These are grapes. Grapes has the sound of /ā/. Say it with me: /ā/, /ā/, grapes.* Repeat for *rain* and *tray.*

Teach/Model Tell students: *The /ā/ sound is one sound of the letter* a. *We call this sound the long* a. *Repeat these /ā/ words after me: age, name, make, place, state.*

Ask students to name the items in Row 1 on page 255 *(rake, cat, train, plate).* Repeat each word, clearly pronouncing the vowel each time. Then say: *I'll say these words again. If you hear the /ā/ sound, circle the picture:* rake, cat, train, plate. Students should circle the *rake, train,* and *plate* pictures—but not the *cat.*

Point out that there are different ways of spelling long *a* words. Write a 3-column chart on the board with the headings *a_e, ai,* and *ay.* List the words *grapes, rain,* and *tray* in the columns where they belong. Add the long *a* words from Row 1 to the chart. Invite students to suggest other long *a* words they know that can be added to the chart.

Practice Have students look at the pictures in Row 2 on page 255. Have them read the words below each picture and circle the word that names it *(snake, chain, plane, hay).* Then have them look at the pictures in Row 3, say the name of each picture, and write the names *(grapes, tray, rake, rain).*

Read the practice sentence aloud, and have students find the long *a* words *(came, gate, cave, waited, Dave).* Invite students to chant the sentence together, clapping each time they hear long *a.*

Assess Tell students: *I will say some word pairs. Raise your hand if both words have the /ā/ sound:* sell, sale; cage, rage; ate, late; gate, get; rack, rake. Then have students repeat the word pairs after you, striving for the correct pronunciation of /ā/. Keep in mind that students who have difficulty pronouncing /ā/ may still be able to comprehend long *a* words that they hear or read.

> **Pronunciation Tip**
> **long *a*** *When you start to say /ā/, your mouth is open. Your tongue is in the middle of your mouth. To finish the sound /ā/, your tongue and your jaw move up a little. Try it: /ā/, /ā/, ape. The long* a *sound is similar to the Spanish digraph* ei. *Example: rain/reina (queen).*

Adapting the ☆ **Model Lesson**

Use the same lesson format above to teach the long vowels /ē/, /ī/, /ō/, and /ū/. The following information will help you to customize each lesson.

Long Vowels

Notes for Additional Lessons

Long e
Use with page 256.

Teach/Model Use these /ē/ words: *bee, beaver, me, team.* Row 1 of page 256: *eagle, teeth, eye, feet.* Make a 4-column chart for long e words.

Practice Row 2: *he, wheel, thirty, leaf.* Row 3: *tree, leaf, me, bee.* Practice sentence: See the leaves on the trees on our street.

Assess Use these word pairs: *team, Tim; meat, met; leaf, lean; seen, seat; wheat, wet.*

> **Pronunciation Tip**
> **long e** *When you say /ē/, your lips are stretched wide. Your mouth has a little smile when you say /ē/. Try it: /ē/, /ē/, /ē/. The long e sound is similar to the sound of i in Spanish. Examples:* need/nido *(nest);* see/sí *(yes).*

Long i
Use with page 257.

Teach/Model Use these /ī/ words: *kite, five, sky, why.* Row 1 of page 257: *bike, night, mice, fish.* Make a 5-column chart for long i words.

Practice Row 2: *ice, child, tie, light.* Row 3: *five, kite, light, sky.* Practice sentence: Five kites in the sky are flying high.

Assess Use these word pairs: *fight, fit; sky, sly; mice, miss; rice, price; light, lit.*

> **Pronunciation Tip**
> **long i** *When you say /ī/, your mouth is open and your jaw drops. Your tongue is down. To finish the sound /ī/, your tongue and your jaw move up. Try it: /ī/, /ī/, /ī/. The long i sound is similar to the Spanish digraphs* ai *and* ay. *Examples:* I/hay *(there is/are);* bike/baile *(dance).*

Long o
Use with page 258.

Teach/Model Use these /ō/ words: *rose, goat, pillow, smoke.* Row 1 of page 258: *rope, lock, nose, bone.* Make a 4-column chart for long o words.

Practice Row 2: *robe, gold, bow, boat.* Row 3: *goat, rose, snow(man), gold.* Practice sentence: Joan wrote a note and rode on a boat.

Assess Use these word pairs: *boat, bought; globe, lobe; low, blow; hose, toes; coat, cot.*

> **Pronunciation Tip**
> **long o** *When you say /ō/, your mouth is round. Try it: /ō/, /ō/, /ō/. The long o sound is similar to the sound of o in Spanish. Example:* no/no.

Long u
Use with page 259.

Teach/Model Use these /ū/ words: *flute, balloon, cube, use, news, true, blue.* Row 1 of page 259: *boat, boot, suitcase, foot.* Make a 5-column chart for long u words.

Practice Row 2: *glue, stool, fruit, mule.* Row 3: *fruit, flute, moon, cube.* Practice sentence: Sue used blue when she drew the moon.

Assess Use these word pairs: *tune, ton; rule, tool; soon, son; glue, blue; too, toe.*

> **Pronunciation Tip**
> **long u** *When you say /ū/ in a word like* rule, *your mouth is round and the opening is small. Try it: /ū/, /ū/. When you say /ū/ in a word like* use, *your lips start out in a line. Then they move into a circle. Try it: /ū/, /ū/. The long u sound in* tube *is similar to the sound of u in Spanish:* tube/tubo. *The long u sound in* unit *is similar to the sound of* iu *or* yu *in Spanish:* unit/yugo.

Name _____

Words with Long a

- **Listen** for the sound of *a* in *grapes*.
- **Circle** the pictures of words that have this sound.

ROW 1

- **Look** at each picture. **Say** its name.
- **Circle** the word that names each picture.

ROW 2

| snack | chin | plan | hay |
| snake | chain | plane | hat |

- **Look** at each picture. **Say** its name.
- **Write** the name of the picture.

ROW 3

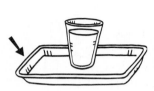

_____ _____ _____ _____

Find long *a* in this sentence. Then **practice** chanting or singing the sentence.

We came to a gate by the cave and waited for Dave.

Name _____

Words with Long e

- **Listen** for the sound of *e* in *bee*.
- **Circle** the pictures of words that have this sound.

ROW 1

   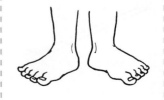

- **Look** at each picture. **Say** its name.
- **Circle** the word that names each picture.

ROW 2

| he | well | thirst | leaf |
| hi | wheel | thirty | loaf |

- **Look** at each picture. **Say** its name.
- **Write** the name of the picture.

ROW 3

_____ _____ _____ _____

Find long *e* in this sentence. Then **practice** chanting or singing the sentence.

See the leaves on the trees on our street.

Words with Long *i*

- **Listen** for the sound of *i* in *kite*.
- **Circle** the pictures of words that have this sound.

ROW 1

   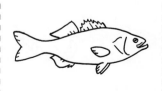

- **Look** at each picture. **Say** its name.
- **Circle** the word that names each picture.

ROW 2

| ice | child | tie | lit |
| ace | chill | tea | light |

- **Look** at each picture. **Say** its name.
- **Write** the name of the picture.

ROW 3

_____ _____ _____ _____

Find long *i* in this sentence. Then **practice** chanting or singing the sentence.

Five kites in the sky are flying high.

Name _____

Words with Long o

- **Listen** for the sound of *o* in *goat*.
- **Circle** the pictures of words that have this sound.

ROW 1

- **Look** at each picture. **Say** its name.
- **Circle** the word that names each picture.

ROW 2

   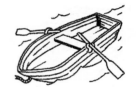

rob	gold	bow	bat
robe	good	box	boat

- **Look** at each picture. **Say** its name.
- **Write** the name of the picture.

ROW 3

_____ _____ _____ _____

Find long *o* in this sentence. Then **practice** chanting or singing the sentence.

Joan wrote a note and rode on a boat.

Words with Long *u*

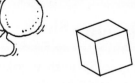

- **Listen** for the sound of *u* in *flute*.
- **Circle** the pictures of words that have this sound.

ROW 1

  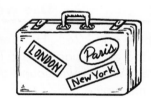 

- **Look** at each picture. **Say** its name.
- **Circle** the word that names each picture.

ROW 2

glue	stole	fright	mole
glow	stool	fruit	mule

- **Look** at each picture. **Say** its name.
- **Write** the name of the picture.

ROW 3

_____ _____ _____ _____

Find long *u* in this sentence. Then **practice** chanting or singing the sentence.

Sue used blue when she drew the moon.

Vowel Diphthongs

Vowel Diphthongs   Use with page 261.

Preteach Copy and distribute page 261. Have students point to the picture of a *voice* at the top of the page. Say: *This child has a voice, /v/ /oi/ /s/, voice. What vowel sound do you hear in the word* voice? *Say it with me: voice, /oi/, /oi/, voice. That's right, the sound is /oi/. Now point to the* cloud. Ask: *What vowel sound do you hear in the word* cloud? *Listen: /k/ /l/ /ou/ /d/. Yes, the sound is /ou/. Repeat this drill for the words* royal *and* plow.

> **Pronunciation Tip**
> **Vowel Diphthongs**
> In a diphthong, each vowel contributes to the sound that is produced or heard.

Teach/Model Write the word *voice* on the board. Underline the *oi* and tell students: *The sound /oi/ in* voice *is spelled* oi. Now write *royal* on the board. Underline the *oy* in the word and say: *The sound /oi/ in* royal *is spelled* oy. Then write *cloud* on the board. Underline the *ou* and say: *The sound /ou/ in* cloud *is spelled* ou. Repeat for the word *plow*.

Help students name the items in Row 1 on page 261 *(soil, boy, coin, box)*. Repeat each name, clearly pronouncing the vowel sound in each word. Say: *I am going to say these words again:* soil, boy, coin, box. *Circle the pictures of words that have the /oi/ sound as in* voice. (Students should circle *soil, boy,* and *coin,* but not *box.*)

Practice Have students look at the pictures in Row 2 on page 261. Help students name each picture *(crowd, count, towel, plow)*. Have them choose and circle the word that correctly names each picture. Have students look at the pictures in Row 3, say the name of each picture, and write the names *(cow, toy, voice, cloud)*.

Assess Tell students: *I will say some word pairs. Raise your hand when you hear the /ou/ sound:* plow, blow; grow, how; owl, snow; goose, south. Then have students repeat the word pairs after you. Then tell the class: *Here are more word pairs. Raise your hand when you hear the /oi/ sound:* soy, soon; enjoy, rock; choice, short; toil, coat; join, born. Have the class repeat the word pairs after you, striving for the correct pronunciation of /oi/.

Name _____

Vowel Diphthongs

- **Listen** to the sound of *oi* in *voice* and *oy* in *royal*.
- **Circle** the pictures of words that have this sound.

ROW 1

   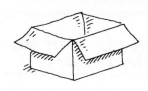

- **Look** at each picture. **Say** its name.
- **Circle** the word that names the picture.

ROW 2

  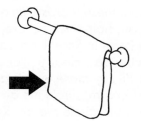 

crowd	cob	towel	plow
crop	count	toil	pot

- **Look** at each picture. **Say** its name.
- **Write** the name of the picture.

ROW 3

 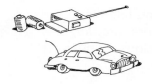  

_____   _____   _____   _____

Find the vowel diphthongs in this sentence. Then **practice** chanting or singing the sentence.

The boy will count his toy cows.

Transfer Skills

The sound of /r/ is flapped or rolled in languages such as Spanish, Polish, Farsi, and Arabic, so speakers of these languages may have difficulty pronouncing words with r-controlled vowels, especially in words such as *part* and *turn*, when r is followed by a consonant. Also, Spanish does not have a sound that is equivalent to /ėr/, so Spanish speakers may pronounce *bird* as *beerd* or *later* as *la-tair*. The following lessons provide practice for hearing and pronouncing words with r-controlled vowels.

Words with *ar, are, air, or, ore*

Use with page 264.

Preteach Copy and distribute page 264. Have students point to the picture of the arm at the top of the page. Say: *This is an arm. Arm has the sound of /är/. Say it with me: /är/, /är/, arm.* Repeat the procedure for the sound of /âr/ in the word *chair*, and the sound of /ôr/ in the word *horn*.

Teach/Model Tell students: *The sound of a vowel changes when it is followed by the sound of r. We say that these kinds of vowels are r-controlled vowels. Repeat these words with r-controlled vowels:* barn, harp, jar, care, stare, air, hair, thorn, chore, more, core.

Ask students to name the items in Row 1 on page 264 *(stair, shark, car, fair)*. Repeat each word, clearly pronouncing the vowel each time. Then say: *I'll say these words again. If you hear the r-controlled vowel sound in* arm, *circle the* ar. *If you hear the r-controlled vowel sound in* chair, *circle the* air. Repeat the words one more time, pausing as you go to give students time to circle their choice. Then ask students to name the items in Row 2 *(corn, horse, car, fork)*. Repeat each word, clearly pronouncing the vowel each time. Then say: *I'll say these words again. If you hear the r-controlled vowel sound in* horn, *circle the picture.* Students should circle the pictures of the corn, horse, and fork.

Practice Have students look at the pictures in Row 3 on page 264. Have them name the pictures *(star, hair, store, porch)*. Then ask them to circle the correct word below each picture. Finally, have them write the words.

Read the practice sentence aloud, and have students find the words with r-controlled vowels *(chairs, forks, corn, more, are, for, store)*. Invite students to chant the sentence together, clapping each time they hear the r-controlled vowels.

Assess Tell students: *I will say some words. Put your thumb up if you hear an r-controlled vowel. Put your thumb down if you do not:* chair, chew, chore, far, feet, stare, stand, store, car, more. Then have students repeat the r-controlled words after you, striving for the correct pronunciation of the r-controlled vowels. Keep in mind that students who have difficulty pronouncing the r-controlled vowels may still be able to comprehend words with r-controlled vowels that they hear or read.

> **Pronunciation Tip**
> **Words with *ar, are, air, or, ore***
> When you say words like *far, dare,* and *more, you make the vowel sound first. Then you bring your lips together for the /r/ sound. Try:* far, dare, more.

Words with *er, ir, or, ur, eer, ear*

Use with page 265.

Preteach Copy and distribute page 265. Have students point to the picture of the purse at the top of the page. Say: *This is a purse. Purse has the sound /ėr/. Say it with me: /ėr/, /ėr/, purse.* Repeat the procedure for the sound of /ir / in the word *tear.*

Teach/Model Tell students: *The sound of a vowel changes when it is followed by the sound of r. We say that these kinds of vowels are* r-controlled vowels. *Repeat these words with r-controlled vowels: fern, third, curve, dear, cheer, clear.*

Ask students to name the items in Row 1 on page 265 *(nurse, ear, surf, spear).* Repeat each word, clearly pronouncing the vowel each time. Then say: *I'll say these words again. If you hear the* r-controlled vowel sound in purse, *circle the* ur. *If you hear the* r-controlled vowel sound in tear, *circle the* ear. Repeat the words one more time, pausing as you go to give students time to circle their choice.

Practice Have students look at the pictures in Row 2 on page 265 *(bird, deer, fern, skirt)* and circle the pictures of words that have the sound of *-ir* in *shirt*. Students should circle the pictures of the bird, fern, and skirt. Then have them look at the pictures in Row 3. Have them read the words below each picture, circle the correct words *(worm, deer, purse, shirt)*, and write the words.

Read the practice sentence aloud, and have students find the words with *r*-controlled vowels *(dear, girl, tear, purse, near, here)*. Invite students to chant the sentence together, clapping each time they hear the *r*-controlled vowels.

Assess Tell students: *I will say some word pairs. Raise your hand when you hear a sound with er, eer, or ear: cheer, chair; steer, stare; her, hair; deer, door; fear, for.* Then have students repeat the word pairs after you, striving for the correct pronunciation of the *r*-controlled vowels. Keep in mind that students who have difficulty pronouncing the *r*-controlled vowels may still be able to comprehend words with *r*-controlled vowels that they hear or read.

Pronunciation Tip
Words with *er, ir, or, ur, eer, ear*
When you say words like sir and word, you put your lips close together and hold them: /ėr/, /ėr/. When you say a word like fear, your lips start out in a line. Then you bring your lips together for the /ir/ sound. Try it: /ir/, /ir/, fear.

Words with *ar, are, air, or, ore*

- If the word has the sound of *ar* in *arm*, **circle** the *ar*.
- If the word has the sound of *air* in *chair*, **circle** the *air*.

ROW 1

ar **air**   **ar** **air**   **ar** **air**   **ar** **air**

- If the picture has the sound of *or* in *horn*, **circle** it.

ROW 2

 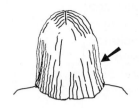  

- **Look** at each picture. **Say** its name.
- **Circle** the correct word. **Write** the name of the picture.

ROW 3

stair
star

hair
here

stare
store

porch
perch

_____ _____ _____ _____

Find words with *r* in this sentence. Then **practice** chanting or singing the sentence.

Chairs, forks, corn, and so much more are all for sale in the store.

Name _____

Words with *er, ir, or, ur, eer, ear*

- If the word has the sound of *ur* in *purse*, **circle** the *ur*.
- If the word has the sound of *ear* in *tear*, **circle** the *ear*.

ROW 1

| ear | ur | ear | ur | ear | ur | ear | ur |

- If the picture has the sound of *ir* in *shirt*, **circle** it.

ROW 2

- **Look** at each picture. **Say** its name.
- **Circle** the correct word. **Write** the name of the picture.

ROW 3

| warm | deer | purse | short |
| worm | door | pass | shirt |

_____ _____ _____ _____

Find words with *r* in this sentence. Then **practice** chanting or singing the sentence.

"Oh, dear," said the girl with a tear. "My purse is not near here."

The Schwa and Unstressed Syllables

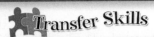 **Transfer Skills**

Some languages are "syllable-timed" languages: the syllables within words are each pronounced in the same amount of time. In English, by contrast, vowels in stressed syllables are pronounced more distinctly. Vowels in unstressed syllables often take a more neutral schwa sound. This lesson provides practice with the schwa sound, which English learners may have difficulty pronouncing and spelling.

The Schwa and Unstressed Syllables   Use with page 267.

Preteach Copy and distribute page 267. Have students point to the picture of the pretzel. Say: *This is a pretzel. Say the two syllables of pretzel with me: PRET-zel. Which syllable sounds louder? Yes, the first syllable. It is called the stressed syllable. The second syllable is the unstressed syllable, and it sounds quieter. Look at Row 1. Listen to the vowel sound in the unstressed syllables of these words: a-LARM, a-FRAID, BOT-tle, DRAG-on. The vowel sound in the unstressed syllables sounds like this: /ə/. We call this the schwa sound. Say the schwa sound in these words: PRET-zel, a-FRAID.*

Teach/Model Tell students: *In English, unstressed syllables often have a schwa sound. The schwa sound can be at the beginning, middle, or end of a word:* about, alone, animal, avenue, ribbon, table.

Have students look at Row 1. Repeat each word. Say: *Circle the words that have the /ə/ sound in the first syllable. Underline the words that have the /ə/ sound in the last syllable.* Read the words aloud one more time. Students should circle *alarm* and *afraid.* They should underline *bottle* and *dragon.*

Tell students: *It can be hard to know how to spell syllables that have a schwa sound, because this sound can be spelled with any vowel. It can also be spelled with a consonant +* le, *as in* table.

Practice Ask students to name the items in the chart on page 267 (medal, sandal, nickel, shovel, table, apple, wagon, button). Repeat each word and then say: *The chart shows some of the ways that the schwa sound can be spelled at the end of words. Look at each picture and write its name.*

Read the practice sentence aloud, and have students find the words with the schwa sound (apples, bagels, alarm, a, pretzel, table). Invite students to chant the sentence together, raising a finger each time they hear the schwa sound.

Assess Tell students: *I will say a list of words. Put your hand up when you hear a word with the /ə/ sound:* asleep, asking, final, panel, pancake, cradle, crazy, lesson, ribbon, backbone. Then have students repeat the words with a schwa sound: *asleep, final, panel, cradle, lesson,* and *ribbon.* Keep in mind that students who have difficulty pronouncing the schwa may still be able to comprehend words with /ə/.

> **Pronunciation Tip**
> **schwa** *When you say the schwa sound, it sounds a little like the /u/ sound in up. But you say it quickly and without any stress on the syllable: /ə/, /ə/, /ə/. Try these words with a schwa sound:* about, around, final, little, taken, pencil, jungle, able.

The Schwa and Unstressed Syllables

- **Say** each word. If you hear the schwa sound in the first syllable, **circle** the word.
- If you hear the schwa sound in the last syllable, **underline** the word.

ROW 1

| alarm | afraid | bottle | dragon |

- **Look** at the pictures in each column. **Write** the word for each picture.

Final Syllables with Schwa			
-al	-el	-le	-on

Find words with a schwa sound in this sentence. Then **practice** chanting or singing the sentence.

There are three apples, two bagels, one alarm clock, and a pretzel on the table.

Inflected Endings

Inflected endings may be challenging for English language learners. For example, languages such as Chinese, Hmong, and Vietnamese do not use inflected endings to form verb tenses. Students may need help understanding that adding -ed to a verb indicates that the action happened in the past. Spelling changes in inflected verbs may also be difficult for English language learners to master. The following lessons provide practice with the inflected endings of nouns and verbs.

Plurals and Possessives   Use with page 270.

Preteach Write the following pair of sentences on the board, and ask students how they are different: *A chair and a table are in the room. Chairs and tables are in the room.* Students will probably notice that the nouns in the first sentence are in the singular form, whereas the nouns in the second sentence are in the plural form.

Next, write these two sentences on the board, again asking students what they notice about them: *The pen of the teacher is red. The teacher's pen is red.* Both sentences mean the same, but they use different ways to show possession, or ownership.

Teach/Model Copy the following chart on the board, and use it to teach students how to form plurals and possessives in English.

	Rules	Examples
Plurals	• Add -s to the singular form of most nouns. • Add -es to words that end with sh, ch, x, s, and z. • For words that end with a consonant and y, change the y to i before adding -es.	• *boys, girls, pens, balls, teachers* • *boxes, classes, brushes, dishes* • *cities, stories, candies*
Possessives with an apostrophe	• Add an apostrophe and s to most singular nouns. • Add an apostrophe to plural nouns that end in s.	• Juana's idea, Kin's report, Carlos's dog • the girls' uniforms, the boys' team

Practice Copy and distribute page 270. Read the directions aloud, and direct students' attention to the pictures of the children and their pets. Have students complete the sentences by writing each word in parentheses in the plural or possessive form, as appropriate. (See answers on page 310.)

Assess Tell students to write pairs of sentences about a friend and a family member. The first sentence should introduce the person, and the second sentence tells about something that person has or owns. Write this example on the board: *My friend's name is Samuel. Samuel's wheelchair can go fast.*

Verb Endings *-s, -ed, -ing*   Use with page 271.

Preteach Write these verbs on the board and read them aloud for the class, asking students to pay close attention to the sound at the end of each word: *washes, cleans, writes, sleeps, fixes, plays, swims, talks.* Ask students if they noticed a difference in the way the final *-s* was pronounced in certain words. Confirm for them that *writes, sleeps,* and *talks* are pronounced with the sound of /s/ at the end, and that *washes, cleans, fixes, plays,* and *swims* are pronounced with the sound of /z/.

In a similar way, ask students to determine if the following words end with the sound of /d/ or /t/: *walked, enjoyed, liked, talked, played, measured.*

Finally, have students practice saying the following gerunds aloud, modeling correct pronunciation as necessary: *playing, cleaning, jogging, talking, washing, swimming.*

Teach/Model The following rules may help students know which pronunciation to use with words that end in *-s* and *-ed.* Remind students that these are general guidelines, and that they should listen carefully to native speakers for further guidance.

For words that end in *-s,*
- use the sound of /s/ if the letter before it is *k, p,* or *t.*
- use the sound of /z/ if the letter before it is *b, f, g, m, n,* or a vowel.

Note: If a word ends in silent *e,* the sound of *-s* depends on the letter before the *e.*

For words that end in *-ed,*
- use the sound of /d/ if the letter before it is *b, l, m, n,* or a vowel.
- use the sound of /t/ if the letter before it is *ch, k, p, s, sh,* or *x.*

To make the *-ing* form of a verb,
- add *-ing* to the simple verb.
- double final *b, g, m, n,* or *p* before adding *-ing.*
- drop silent *e* before adding *-ing.*

Practice Copy and distribute page 271. Read the directions aloud, and have students look at the sample answers to help them get started. After students complete the activities, practice saying the verbs in each chart aloud. (See answers on page 310.)

Assess Ask students to write three sentences using a verb from each of the three charts on page 271, keeping the verb in the same form as in the chart.

Name _____

Plurals and Possessives

- **Look** at the pictures. **Read** the children's names.
- **Complete** each sentence. Use the word in parentheses. Make the word possessive or plural.

Martin

Miho

Mia

Carlos

1. The children's (pet) _____ are nice and friendly.

2. (Martin) _____ lizard is very tame.

3. The (birds) _____ cage is open.

4. (Mia) _____ cat likes to sit on her lap.

5. (Carlos) _____ dog is still a puppy.

6. When dogs are (puppy) _____, they like to play.

Name _____

Verb Endings -s, -ed, -ing

Part 1
- **Read** the verbs in the box.
- **Write** the *-s* form of the verb in the correct column of the chart.

ask	call	help	write
play	run	walk	see

/s/	/z/
asks	

Part 2
- **Read** the verbs in the box.
- **Write** the *-ed* form of the verb in the correct column of the chart.

call	fix	help	open
play	rub	walk	wash

/d/	/t/
called	

Part 3
- **Read** the words in the chart.
- **Write** the correct *-ing* form of the verb in the second column.

Verb	*-ing* Form
call	
hope	
play	
run	

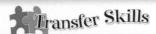

Transfer Skills

English learners may benefit from extra practice distinguishing between /j/ and /ch/ sounds. Have students pronounce the sounds while placing their hands on their throats. Have them feel how the sound /j/ is voiced from their throats and the /ch/ sound is unvoiced and originates in their mouth.

Spellings of /j/, /s/, /k/   Use with page 275.

Preteach Copy and distribute page 275. Have students point to the picture of a bridge at the top of the page. Say: *This is a bridge, /b/ /r/ /i/ /j/. Where do you hear the /j/ sound in the word? Say it with me: /j/, /j/, bridge. That's right, the sound /j/ comes at the end of the word.* Now point to the *sailboat.* Ask: *Do you hear the /s/ sound in this word? Where? Listen: /s/ long ā /l/ /b/ /ō/ /t/. Yes, the /s/ sound is at the beginning of the word.* Repeat this drill for the word *kick.*

Teach/Model Write *bridge, jump,* and *judge* on the board. Say the words aloud, and point to the letters that make the /j/ sound in each. Write *bus* and *mice* on the board. Say the words aloud, and point to the letters that make the /s/ sound in each. Then write *care, back, kite,* and *chrome.* Say the words aloud, and point to the letters that make the /k/ sound. Review each set of words. Have students repeat the words after you.

Practice Help students name the items in Row 1 on page 275 *(jet, cage, tree, jam).* Say: *I will say the words again. This time, circle the picture if the word has the sound of j, as in* bridge. Repeat each name, stretching out the sound of each letter so students can hear the /j/ sound in each word. Students should circle *jet, cage, jam,* but not *tree.* Repeat the process for Rows 2 and 3.

Read the practice sentence aloud and have students find the words with /j/, /s/, and /k/ sounds *(Jessica, checks, crossing, bridge).* After they have repeated the sentence several times, challenge students to say it as quickly as they can.

Assess Make another copy of page 275 and cut out all of the pictures. Prepare a sheet of paper with three columns that are labeled with the letters *j, k,* and *s.* Give each student the pile of pictures. Have students say the names of the pictures and place each one under the sound that the word contains.

> **Pronunciation Tip**
> **Spellings of /j/, /s/, /k/** The sound /j/ can be spelled *g, j,* or *dge.* The sound /s/ can be spelled *s* or *c.* The sound /k/ can be spelled *c, k, ck,* or *ch.*

Transfer Skills

In Spanish, each vowel has only one sound. Spanish speakers may benefit from extra practice pronouncing and spelling words with variant vowel sounds in English. Let students practice saying and writing groups of words that have the /ȯ/ sound in *ball* and *walk: all, fault, awe, scald.*

Spellings of /ȯ/ (Vowel Sound in ball): a, au, aw, al
Use with page 276.

Preteach Copy and distribute page 276. Have students point to the picture of a ball at the top of the page. Say: *This is a ball, /b/ /ȯ/ /l/. What vowel sound do you hear in the word* ball? *Say it with me: /ȯ/, /ȯ/,* ball.

Teach/Model Write *call, sauce, yawn,* and *talk* on the board. Underline the *a, au, aw,* and *al* sound spellings in the words. Tell students: *The sound /ȯ/ can be spelled* a, au, aw, *and* al. *When* a *is followed by* u, l, *or* w, *it usually stands for the sound you hear in* ball. Point out the sound spellings for /ȯ/ in the words *call, sauce, yawn,* and *talk.* Segment and blend each of the words as a class.

Help students name the items in Row 1 on page 276 *(saw, sausage, fence, straw).* Repeat each name, stretching out the sound of each letter so students can hear the vowel sound in each word. Read the words again. This time, tell students to circle the pictures for words that contain the /ȯ/ sound. Review the answers as a class *(saw, sausage, straw).*

Practice Have students look at the pictures in Row 2 on page 276. Help them read the words in the box. Have them write the word that names each picture *(applause, lawn, walnut, salt).* Then, students can work with a partner to fill in the chart at the bottom of the page. When they are finished, share answers, and teach any new words students do not know.

Assess Have students write the /ȯ/ sound spellings *a, au, aw,* and *al* on index cards. Then read the following words aloud to the class: *all, fault, raw, bald, talk, sauce, yawn, saw, crawl, call.* Pause after each word so students can find and hold up the card that contains the sound-spelling pattern that corresponds to the word.

> **Pronunciation Tip**
> **Spellings of /ȯ/ in a, au, aw, al**
> When words end in the sound /ȯ/, the /ȯ/ sound is usually spelled *aw.*

Spellings

Transfer Skills

Students may need assistance with words spelled *augh* and *ough* as in *caught* and *fought*, in which the *gh* is silent. Practice the words along with words containing the vowel patterns *aw, au,* and *al* as in *claw, jaunt,* and *call*. Display the words on the board as you practice.

Spellings of /ȯ/ as in *thought: augh, ough*
Use with page 277.

Preteach Display and say the word *thought*. Ask: *What vowel sound do you hear in the word* thought? *Say it with me:* /ȯ/, /ȯ/, *thought*. Display and say the word *caught*. Ask: *What vowel sound do you hear in the word* caught? *Say it with me:* /ȯ/, /ȯ/, *caught. In the words* thought *and* caught, *the vowel sound is* /ȯ/.

Teach/Model Write *thought* and *caught* on the board. Underline the *ough* and *augh* sound spellings in the words. Tell students: *The sound* /ȯ/ *can be spelled* ough *and* augh. *When you see the spellings* ough *and* augh, *you know the word will have the* /ȯ/ *vowel sound*. Point out the sound spellings for /ȯ/ in the words *thought* and *caught*. Segment and blend each of the words as a class.

Write two columns on the board, labeled *ough* and *augh*. As a class, brainstorm a list of words with *ough* and *augh* sound spellings such as *sought, ought, brought, taught, daughter,* and *fraught*. Have students repeat the words after you, and then have them practice saying the words with a partner.

Practice Copy and distribute page 277. Read the directions aloud, and discuss the meanings of the words in the box. Then do the first example together. Have students choose and write a logical word in the blank. Then have students read the sentences aloud with a partner. (See answers on page 310.)

Assess Have students write the /ȯ/ sound spellings *ough* and *augh* on index cards. Then read the following words aloud to the class: *brought, caught, daughter, fraught, taught, thought, fought*. Pause after each word so students can hold up the card that contains the sound-spelling pattern that corresponds to the word.

Name _____

Sounds of j, s, k

- If the word has the sound of *j* as in *bridge*, **circle** it.

ROW 1

- If the word has the sound of *s* as in *sail*, **circle** it.

ROW 2

- If the word has the sound of *k* as in *kick*, **circle** it.

ROW 3

Find the sounds of *j*, *s*, and, *k* in this sentence. Then **practice** chanting it.

Jessica checks both ways before crossing the bridge.

Name _____

Vowel Sound in *ball*

- **Listen** for the vowel sound in *ball*. This sound can be spelled *a, au, aw,* or *al*.
- **Circle** the pictures of words that have this sound.

ROW 1

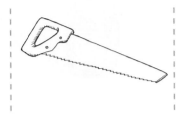  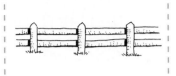 

- **Look** at each picture. **Read** the words in the box.
- **Write** the word that names each picture.

| lawn | walnut | salt | applause |

ROW 2

_____ _____ _____ _____

- **Write** the words with the same vowel sound as in *ball* spelled *a, au, aw,* and *al* in the chart below. **Use** a dictionary to **find** more words.

a	au	aw	al

ELL Handbook

Name _____

Vowel Sound in *thought: augh, ough*

- **Read** the sentences.
- **Choose** the correct word from the box to complete each sentence.
- **Write** the word on the blank line.

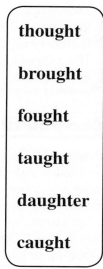

thought

brought

fought

taught

daughter

caught

1. We _____ sandwiches for lunch today.

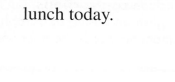

2. My neighbor has a new baby

_____ .

3. The boy _____ he locked the door.

4. The two puppies _____ over a ball.

5. I _____ the ball at the baseball game.

6. My mom _____ me how to plant a tree.

Compound Words, Homophones, and Contractions

Transfer Skills

Compound words exist in many languages, including Spanish, Vietnamese, Haitian Creole, German, and Russian. Children may readily understand the concept of compound words, but may need additional help with decoding to break English compound words into their parts. **Homophones** are also common in other languages, but English learners may not recognize that English homophone pairs have the same pronunciation despite their different spellings. They may need to learn to use their knowledge of word meaning to choose the correct spelling of homophones. Some languages, such as the Romance languages, include **contractions**, but English learners may need help recognizing them in English and using apostrophes correctly. The following lessons provide practice with compound words, homophones, and contractions.

Compound Words   Use with page 281.

Preteach On two separate index cards, write the words *story* and *teller*. Ask students to define each word. If necessary, define *teller* as "a person who talks or tells something" (as opposed to a teller at a bank). Then hold the cards side by side, ask students what *storyteller* means, and confirm that it means "a person who tells stories." Explain that the new word is a compound word. It is made up of two smaller words.

Teach/Model Tell students: *When you make a compound word, you put two words together to make a new word. Usually, there isn't any change to the spellings of the two smaller words.*

Write the following pairs of words on separate index cards: *butter, fly; day, light; hand, writing; sun, flower.* Discuss the meaning of each separate word, and then show how the words can be combined to create a new word. Point out that neither of the smaller words has a spelling change. The words are simply put together to create a new word. Ask students to share any other compounds that they know. Spanish examples include *abrelatas* (can opener), *rascacielos* (skyscraper), and *parasol* (parasol).

Practice Copy and distribute page 281. Read the directions aloud, and help students read the words if necessary. After students complete the activities, practice saying the compound words aloud. (See answers on page 310.)

Assess Form pairs of students, and provide partners with a set of word cards with words from page 281. Challenge students to match the cards to create a complete set of compound words. To check comprehension, ask each pair to make an oral sentence with three words from their set.

Homophones

Use with page 282.

Preteach Tell students this joke in the form of a question and answer: *What is black and white and read all over? A newspaper!* Explain to students that the question seems to be asking about colors (black, white, and red), but there is a play on the word *red.* The color red sounds the same as *read,* a past tense form of the verb *read.* Explain that this joke is based on a pair of homophones *(red* and *read),* two words that sound the same but are spelled differently and mean completely different things.

Teach/Model Write the following homophone pairs on the board: *pair, pear; flour, flower; ceiling, sealing; week, weak.* Explain the meaning of each word and point out the two different spellings. Model the pronunciation, emphasizing that the two words in each pair are pronounced in exactly the same way. Invite students to share any other homophones that they know. Spanish examples include *casa/caza* (house/hunt), *hola/ola* (hello/wave), and *ciento/siento* (one hundred/I feel).

Practice Copy and distribute page 282. Read the directions aloud, and help students answer the first item in each exercise. Help students read the words if necessary. When they are finished, invite volunteers to write their answers on the board. Review the meanings of the words. Make corrections as necessary, and tell students to correct their own work as well. (See answers on page 310.)

Assess Ask students to write three sentences that include a pair of homophones, such as: *Our English class is an hour long.* Encourage students to make simple jokes with the homophones; they can also write sentences that are fanciful or silly, as in: *On Monday, I was too weak to make it through the whole week.* Alternatively, you can dictate pairs of sentences using homophones from page 282; for example: *Mo threw the ball. The ball went through the window.* Check students' work to make sure that they used the correct homophone in each sentence.

Compound Words, Homophones, and Contractions

Contractions

Use with page 283.

Preteach Write the following sentences on the board, and ask students to tell you how they are different:

I am sorry for being late to class. → I'm sorry for being late to class.

Confirm that *I am* has been shortened to *I'm* in the second sentence. Tell students that this is a contraction. Summarize: *The pronoun* I *and the verb* am *are put together with an apostrophe to form one word,* I'm. *The letter* a *is dropped from the word* am, *and the apostrophe takes its place.*

Teach/Model Write the following chart on the board, asking students to tell you how to write each contraction as you go:

The Verb "be"	The Verb "have"	Negatives
I am → I'm	I have → I've	has not → hasn't
You are → You're	You have → You've	have not → haven't
He is → He's	He has → He's	are not → aren't
She is → She's	She has → She's	is not → isn't
It is → It's	It has → It's	should not → shouldn't
We are → We're	We have → We've	can not → can't
They are → They're	They have → They've	will not → won't
		do not → don't
		did not → didn't

Conclude by showing how the future tense marker *will* can be shortened and connected to a pronoun using *'ll: I'll, you'll, she'll,* etc.

Practice Copy and distribute page 283. Read the directions aloud, and complete the first line together. Help students read the dialogue if necessary. After students complete the activities, have them practice the dialogue. (See answers on page 310.)

Assess Form pairs of students, and have partners create their own dialogue between a parent and child. Tell them to include a contraction in each line of dialogue. Circulate as they work to provide assistance. When they are finished, invite students to read their dialogues aloud for the class.

280 *Phonics Transition Lessons*

ELL Handbook

Copyright © Pearson Education, Inc., or its affiliates. All Rights Reserved. 5

Name _____

Compound Words

PART 1
- **Read** the compound words.
- **Draw** a line between the two words in each compound.

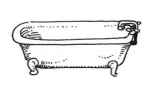

bathtub

flashlight

keyboard

mailbox

spaceship

starfish

toothpaste

waterfall

PART 2
- **Read** the two lists of words.
- **Connect** words from each list to make compounds.

back	boat
book	bow
class	brush
finger	mark
hair	nail
rain	pack
sail	room
side	walk

Name _____

Homophones

- **Read** each pair of words aloud.
- Do the words sound the same? **Check** "Same."
- Do the words sound different? **Check** "Different."

		Same	**Different**
1. knew	new	_____	_____
2. meal	mail	_____	_____
3. hour	our	_____	_____
4. week	weak	_____	_____
5. plate	played	_____	_____
6. best	beast	_____	_____

- **Look** at the pictures. **Read** the words aloud.
- **Draw** a line from each word to its picture.

  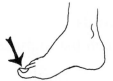 

flour   tow

flower   toe

sun   through

son   threw

Contractions

- **Read** the dialogue.
- **Choose** the correct word from the box to complete each sentence.
- **Write** the correct word on the blank line.

Dad: Hi, Grace. Where are you going?

Grace: _____ going to soccer practice.

Dad: _____ soccer practice on Thursday night?

Grace: Yes, _____ usually on Thursday, but tonight

_____ having a special practice because of

the game on Saturday.

Dad: You finished your homework, _____ you?

Grace: _____ done my math and English. The science

teacher _____ give us homework.

Dad: OK. Have a good practice.

Grace: Thanks, Dad. _____ be home by six o'clock.

didn't
doesn't
I'll
I'm
I've
isn't
it's
we're

Choose four contractions. **Write** the two words that make up each one.

_____ _____ _____ _____

Prefixes and Suffixes

 **Transfer Skills**

Some English prefixes and suffixes have equivalent forms in the Romance languages. For example, the prefix *dis-* in English *(disapprove)* corresponds to the Spanish *des-* *(desaprobar)*, the French *des-* *(desapprouver)*, and the Haitian Creole *dis-* or *dez-* *(dezaprouve)*. Students who are literate in these languages may be able to transfer their understanding of prefixes and suffixes by using parallel examples in the home language and in English. Some suggestions for Spanish are provided below. The following lessons provide additional practice with prefixes and suffixes.

Prefixes *un-* and *re-*   Use with page 291.

Preteach Write these word pairs on the board: *happy, unhappy; safe, unsafe; lucky, unlucky.* Read the words aloud with students, and discuss their meanings. Ask: *What do you notice about these words?* Guide students to see that each word pair is a set of opposites, and that one word in each pair begins with *un-*. Circle the prefix *un-* in each word and say: *This syllable,* un-, *is a prefix. A prefix is a word part that is added to the beginning of a word. Adding a prefix changes the meaning of a word. A new word is made.*

Teach/Model Present the prefixes *un-* and *re-*. Use these examples to explain how the prefixes can change the meanings of words.

Prefix	Meaning	Examples	Spanish Examples
un-	not	happy → unhappy safe → unsafe locked → unlocked	*feliz → infeliz* *seguro → inseguro*
re-	again	tell → retell do → redo write → rewrite	*contar → recontar* *hacer → rehacer*

Practice Copy and distribute page 291. Read the directions aloud, and read the first example together. Have volunteers say the words they wrote in each column of the chart. (See answers on page 310.)

Assess Have students write these prefixes and base words on cards: *un-, re-, afraid, lock, run, unite.* Have students use the cards in different combinations to make words that have prefixes. Have students show you a base word without a prefix, add a prefix, say the new word, and tell what it means.

Prefixes *im-, in-, mis-, over-*

Use with page 292.

Preteach Write these word pairs on the board: *patient, impatient; polite, impolite; proper, improper; pure, impure.* Read the words aloud with students, and discuss their meanings. Ask students what they notice about these words. Guide students to see that each word pair is a set of opposites, and that one word in each pair begins with *im-*. Circle the prefix *im-* in each word and explain: *This word part,* im-, *is a prefix. It usually changes the meaning of a word to its opposite.*

Teach/Model Present the prefixes *im-, in-, mis-,* and *over-*. Use these examples to explain how the prefixes can change the meanings of words. Tell Spanish speakers that the Spanish prefixes *im-* and *in-* have similar meanings *(impaciente, intolerante)*. The Spanish prefix *sobre-* is sometimes used like the English prefix *over- (sobrecarga)*.

Prefix	Meaning	Examples
im-	not	*impatient, imperfect, impossible*
in-	not	*insecure, intolerant, indestructible*
mis-	wrong	*misunderstood, misbehave, mismatch*
over-	beyond, more than	*overcook, overpay, overweight*

Practice Copy and distribute page 292. Read the directions aloud, and help students fill in the first blank line. After students complete the activity, have pairs of students practice the dialogue. (See answers on page 311.)

Assess Have students write these prefixes and base words on index cards: *im-, in-, mis-, over-, correct, interpret, load, coat, mature, take, use.* Tell students to use the cards to make words with prefixes. Circulate as they work, asking students to show you a base word and a prefix that goes with it. Ask advanced students to tell you what the word means and to use it in an oral sentence.

Transfer Skills

Point out to Spanish speakers that the prefix *mid-* is related in meaning to the Spanish word *medio*, which means *half* or *middle*. Display cognates such as *midnight/ medianoche* and *midday/mediodía* as examples.

Prefixes *pre-, mid-, over-, out-, bi-*   **Use with page 293.**

Preteach Write these word pairs on the board: *test, pretest; air, midair; time, overtime; side, outside; monthly, bimonthly*. Read the words aloud with students and discuss their meanings. Ask: *What do you notice about these words?* Explain that the second word in each pair has a prefix that changes the meaning of the first word. Circle the prefix *pre-* and say: *This syllable*, pre-, *is a prefix. A prefix is a word part that is added to the beginning of a word to change its meaning. When you add a prefix, a new word is made. The prefix* pre- *means "before." So,* prepay *means "to pay before."*

Teach/Model Present the prefixes *pre-, mid-, over-, out-,* and *bi-*. Using the chart below, explain how adding prefixes to base words changes the meaning of the word.

Prefix	Meaning	Examples
pre-	before	paid → prepaid view → preview
mid-	in the middle of	day → midday night → midnight
over-	more than normal, too much	grown → overgrown cooked → overcooked
out-	outward; or to a greater degree	side → outside run → outrun
bi-	two	cycle → bicycle

Practice Copy and distribute page 293. Read the directions aloud, and complete the first example together. Have students choose a prefix to add to the base word and write a new word that makes sense in the blank. Then have them read the story aloud with a partner. (See answers on page 311.)

Assess Have students write these prefixes and base words on index cards: *pre-, mid-, over-, out-, bi-, paid, air, time, field, weekly*. Have them use the cards in different combinations to make words with prefixes. As an additional challenge, have students show a base word without a prefix, add a prefix, say the new word, and tell what it means.

Suffixes -ly, -ful, -less, -ness
Use with page 294.

Preteach Write the following words on the board: *careful, carefully, careless, carelessness*. Ask students what these words have in common and what makes them different from each other. They will notice that they all have the same base, *care*. But each successive word also has a different word part at the end. Explain that each of these word parts is a *suffix*. Say: *A suffix is a word part that is added to the end of a word. Adding a suffix changes the meaning of a word.*

Teach/Model Present the suffixes *-ly, -ful, -less,* and *-ness*. Write the following chart on the board, asking students to provide additional examples for the last column. Tell Spanish speakers that *-ly* is similar to the Spanish suffix *-mente*. The Spanish suffix *-dad (felicidad)* is similar to *-ness*.

Suffix	How and Why to Use It	Part of Speech	Examples
-ly	Add it to an adjective to tell how an action is done.	Adverb	*quickly calmly completely*
-ful	Add it to a noun to mean "full of" the noun.	Adjective	*thoughtful colorful helpful*
-less	Add it to a noun to mean "without" the noun.	Adjective	*spotless joyless flawless*
-ness	Add it to an adjective to describe a state of being.	Noun	*darkness happiness carelessness peacefulness*

Practice Copy and distribute page 294. Read the directions aloud, and have students look at the sample answer to help them get started. After students complete the activity, invite volunteers to take turns reading the passage aloud. (See answers on page 311.)

Assess Have students write these suffixes and base words on index cards: *-ly, -ful, -less, -ness, slow, quiet, perfect, fear, rude.* Tell students to use the cards to make words with suffixes. Circulate as they work, asking students to show you a base word and a suffix that goes with it. Ask advanced students to tell you what the word means and to use it in an oral sentence.

Suffixes -tion, -sion, -able, -ible
Use with page 295.

Introduce Write the following words on the board: *perfection, decision, walkable, sensible.* Tell students that each of these words is made up of a base word and a suffix. Circle the suffix *-tion* in the first word and explain: *This word part, -tion, is a suffix.* Ask volunteers to find the suffixes in the other three words. Point out that the base word might need a spelling change before the suffix is added. The word *decide,* for example, drops the final *-de* before adding *-sion.* The reason for these spelling changes has to do with pronunciation, and the rules are hard to generalize, as there are many exceptions to the rules. Students will learn the different spellings with practice.

Teach/Model Present the suffixes *-tion, -sion, -able,* and *-ible.* Explain that *-tion* and *-sion* have the same meaning, as do *-able* and *-ible.* Write the following chart on the board, asking students to provide additional examples for the last column. Spanish examples of these suffixes are *-ción (reacción), -sión (decisión), -able (confortable),* and *-ible (sensible).*

Suffix	How and Why to Use It	Part of Speech	Examples
-tion, -sion	Add it to a verb to describe an action or a state of being.	Noun	*perfection imagination reaction decision admission confusion*
-able, -ible	Add it to a verb to add the meaning "can be."	Adjective	*walkable comfortable dependable sensible reversible flexible*

Practice Copy and distribute page 295. Read the directions aloud, and do the first example together. Tell students that they can use the chart on the board to check spellings. After students complete the activity, review the answers together. (See answers on page 311.)

Assess Have students write these suffixes and base words on index cards: *-tion, -sion, -able, -ible, sense, comfort, confuse, react.* Tell students to use the cards to make words with suffixes. Circulate as they work, asking students to show you a base word and a suffix that goes with it. Ask advanced students to tell you what the word means and to use it in an oral sentence.

Suffixes -er, -or, -ess, -ist Use with page 296.

Preteach Write the following words on the board: *swimmer, actor, hostess,* and *tourist.* Tell students that each of these words is made up of a base word and a suffix. Remind students that a suffix is a word part added to the end of a word to change its meaning. Circle the suffix *-er* in the first word and explain: *This word part,* -er, *is a suffix.* Ask individuals to find suffixes in the other three words. Explain that the base word may require a spelling change before a suffix is added. For example, the word *swimmer* adds an *m* before the suffix. Point out that some spelling changes are related to pronunciation. Explain to students that they will become familiar with different spellings as they practice using the words.

Teach/Model Present this chart to practice the suffixes *-er, -or, -ess,* and *-ist.* Ask students for additional examples of words with these suffixes.

Suffix	What It Means	Examples
-er -or	a person or thing that does something	teacher opener editor tutor
-ess	a female who does something as a job; a female	actress lioness
-ist	a person who has studied something or does something as a job	artist dentist

Practice Copy and distribute page 296. Read the directions to students, and complete the first example together. Tell students that they can use the chart on the board to check spellings. After students complete the activity, review the answers together. (See answers on page 311.)

Assess Have students write these suffixes and base words or word parts on index cards: *-er, -or, -ess, -ist, act, sell, host, dent, tour, teach, lion.* Have students use the cards in different combinations to make words that have suffixes. As an additional challenge, have students show a base word without a suffix, add a suffix, say the new word, and tell what it means.

Suffixes -y, -ish, -hood, -ment

Use with page 297.

Preteach Write the following words on the board: *rocky, foolish, parenthood,* and *shipment.* Tell students that each of these words is made up of a base word and a suffix. Remind students that a suffix is a word part that is added to the end of a word to change its meaning. Circle the suffix *-y* in *rocky* and explain: *This word part -y is a suffix. The base word in* rocky *is* rock. Ask students to find base words in the other three words. Have them tell you what each base word means.

Teach/Model Present this chart to practice the suffixes *-y, -ish, -hood,* and *-ment.* Have students identify each base word and suffix in the examples. Ask students for additional examples of words with these suffixes.

Suffix	What It Means	Examples
-y	having the quality of	*cloudy* *rainy* *thirsty*
-ish	describing nationality or language; somewhat	*Spanish* *brownish* *foolish*
-hood	a state or condition of	*childhood* *fatherhood*
-ment	a state, action, or quality	*excitement* *movement*

Practice Copy and distribute page 297. Read the directions aloud, and have students look at the sample answer to help them get started. After students complete the activity, have individuals take turns reading the passage aloud. (See answers on page 311.)

Assess Have students write these suffixes and base words on index cards: *-y, -ish, -hood, -ment, smell, Brit, mother, excite, wind, brown, false, ship.* Have students use the cards in different combinations to make words that have suffixes. As an additional challenge, have students show you a base word without a suffix, add a suffix, say the new word, and tell what it means.

Name _____

Prefixes *un-* and *re-*

- **Read** each group of words.
- **Use** *un-* or *re-* to make one new word.
- **Write** the new word.

1. read again   _____reread_____

2. appear again   _____

3. not believable   _____

4. not familiar   _____

5. heat again   _____

6. not interested   _____

7. not like   _____

8. start again   _____

9. use again   _____

10. not kind   _____

- **Write** all the new words in the chart.

un-	re-

Name _____

Prefixes *im-, in-, mis-, over-*

- **Read** the conversation. **Finish** the sentences with words from the box.
- Then **practice** the conversation.

Alex: This game costs too much. It is _____.
(1)

Tanya: This ball doesn't cost too much. It is _____.
(2)

Alex: The price on that sign is wrong. It is not correct.

Tanya: You're right! The price must be _____.
(3)

Alex: Let's tell someone that the sign has a _____.
Then they can fix the sign. (4)

Tanya: OK, but let's hurry. I want to go.

Alex: Why are you so _____? We have a lot of time!
(5)

| impatient |
| incorrect |
| inexpensive |
| misprint |
| overpriced |

Write one more word for each prefix. You may **use** a dictionary to **find** the words.

im-   in-   mis-   over-

_____   _____   _____   _____

Name _____

Prefixes *pre-*, *mid-*, *over-*, *out-*, *bi-*

- **Read** the story.
- **Add** *pre-*, *mid-*, *over-*, *out-*, or *bi-* to the beginning of each word in parentheses.

Today is the worst day ever! Yesterday I took a _____ (test) in
(1)

class. I did not do well. I have a hard time with _____ (fixes). My
(2)

teacher said that I need to study hard for the next test. She said that I should make an

_____ (line) to help me study.
(3)

Last night I studied until _____ (night). I also have a report that is
(4)

_____ (due). I am going to have to work _____ (time) to
(5)   (6)

finish all of my homework.

My friends are _____ (side) having fun. But I am still in my room.
(7)

My mom and dad said that I could go outside and ride my _____ (cycle)
(8)

when I finish. I hope I can finish all my work soon!

Name _____

Suffixes -ly, -ful, -less, -ness

- **Read** the story.
- **Add** -ly, -ful, -less, or -ness to each word in parentheses.

Yesterday I took Domingo, my dog, to my grandmother's house. As usual, her

house was ____spotless____ (spot). We had milk and cookies in the kitchen while

Domingo sat _____ (quiet) in the living room. In fact, he was *too* quiet.
(1)

I went to check on him. He had _____ (complete) chewed a pillow into
(2)

bits and pieces. There were feathers everywhere!

My grandmother came in the room and said, "Oh my _____!" (good)
(3)

"I'm sorry, Grandma," I said. "I should have been more _____." (care)
(4)

_____ (lucky) for me, my grandmother laughed. She
(5)

_____ (playful) threw a pillow at me and we had a pillow fight. We had
(6)

so much fun it was easy to forget Domingo's _____. (frisky)
(7)

Name _____

Suffixes -*tion*, -*sion*, -*able*, -*ible*

- **Read** the sentences. Look at the underlined word.
- **Add** -*tion, -sion, -able,* or -*ible* to make a new word. Write the word.

1.

Yasmin <u>imagined</u> being a princess.

She used her _____.

2.

We can <u>walk</u> on this path.

The path is _____.

3.

I can <u>depend</u> on Pablo.

Pablo is _____.

4.

Aisha <u>decided</u> which book to read.

She made a _____.

5.

I can <u>reverse</u> this shirt.

The shirt is _____.

Name _____

Suffixes -*er*, -*or*, -*ess*, -*ist*

- **Read** the sentences. **Look** at the underlined word.
- **Add** -*er*, -*or*, -*ess*, or -*ist* to **make** a new word. **Write** the word.

1.

Olivia and her mother went to the <u>pharmacy</u>.

They spoke to the _____.

2.

It is a long <u>commute</u> to my dad's office.

My dad is a _____.

3.

I like to <u>invent</u> things.

I am an _____.

4.

We saw a male <u>lion</u> on our safari.

He was sitting next to a _____.

Name _____

Suffixes -y, -ish, -hood, -ment

- **Read** the story.
- **Add** *-y, -ish, -hood,* or *-ment* to the end of each word in parentheses.

Emma looked outside. She was happy because it was not a ___rainy___ (1)

(rain) day. It was sunny. She liked to walk outside in her _____ (2)

(neighbor). She had a lot of energy. She did not feel _____ (sleep) (3)

at all.

Emma skipped happily down the sidewalk. She saw _____ (move) (4)

ahead of her. She wondered what it was. But then she felt _____ (fool). (5)

It was just her brother, John, trying to surprise her. He can be so _____ (6)

(child) sometimes!

Cognates and Word Roots

Cognates are words that share origins and appear in similar forms in different languages. For example, the English word *school* is of Greek origin, and it is similar to the Spanish *escuela,* the French *école,* the Polish *szkoła,* and the German *Schule.* For speakers of languages that share word origins with English, the study of cognates can be a powerful vocabulary-building tool. The following lessons provide practice for working with cognates and words with Greek and Latin roots.

Cognates   Use with page 303.

Preteach Present a chart like the one below. Read the words with students, and note the similarities across various languages. Tell students that when words look similar and have a similar meaning in different languages, they are called *cognates.* Invite students to suggest other cognates they know in English and another language. Tell students that cognates can help them understand more words in English.

English	Spanish	French	Haitian Creole	Polish
telephone	teléfono	téléphone	telefonn	telefon

> Use this lesson with students who are literate in languages that have many cognates of English words, such as Spanish, Portuguese, French, and, to a lesser extent, Haitian Creole, Polish, and Russian.

Teach/Model Explain to students that cognates in different languages usually have the same origins. For example, the different words for *telephone* are all based on the Greek word parts *telē,* which means "far off", and *phōnē,* which means "sound" or "voice". Explain that because many scientific words have Greek or Latin origins, they often are cognates.

   Then point out that sometimes words in different languages are "false friends"—they look almost the same, but they don't mean the same thing. For example, the Spanish word *sopa* looks and sounds similar to the English word *soap,* but it means "soup". Ask students to give other examples of "false friends," words that are not cognates.

Practice Copy and distribute page 303. Have students look for English cognates of home-language words in an English text they are currently reading. (A nonfiction science or social studies text is likely to offer more examples.) Help them decide whether or not the words really are cognates. Suggest that students consult resources such as bilingual dictionaries, other students, or the Internet (with your guidance) to find translations and word meanings. Students might make a class chart showing words for *computer* in various languages. (See answers on page 311.)

Assess Ask students to say or write five examples of cognate pairs in English and their home language, and one example of "false friends."

Words with Greek Roots   Use with page 304.

Preteach Write the following words on the board: *autograph, phonograph, photograph, paragraph.* Ask students what all these words have in common. Confirm for them that they all have the word part *graph.* Tell students that this word part comes from the Greek language. It means "written." Conclude by saying: *Many other words in English have Greek roots, too. Learning these roots can help you learn more words.*

Teach/Model Write the following chart on the board, asking students to provide additional examples for the last column.

Greek Root	Meaning	Sample Words
biblio	book	bibliography
bio	life	biography
crac, crat	rule, govern	democrat
demos	people	democracy
geo	earth	geology
graph, gram	written, drawn, describe, record	photograph
log	idea, word, speech, study	biology
meter	measure	perimeter
phono	sound	symphony
scope	to see	telescope

Show students how different word parts can be combined. The root *bio*, for example, can be combined with *graph* to form *biography*, and it can also be combined with *logy* to form *biology*. Knowing this, students can conclude that any word with the root *bio* has to do with life. Tell Spanish speakers that many Spanish words have these same Greek roots. Ask them to provide translations for the sample words in the chart (*bibliografía, biografía, demócrata, democracia, geología, fotografía, biología, perímetro, sinfonía, telescopio*).

Practice Copy and distribute page 304. Read the directions aloud, and have students look at the sample answer to help them get started. After students complete the activity, invite volunteers to take turns forming other words with the Greek roots in the word box. (See answers on page 311.)

Assess Write the following words on the board: *autobiography, phonology, geography,* and *telescope.* Ask students to copy these words and to write their definitions, based on what they've learned. When they've finished, have a volunteer write his or her answers on the board, and model corrections as necessary. You can collect students' work for later assessment.

Cognates and Word Roots

Words with Latin Roots   Use with page 305.

Preteach Write the following words on the board: *animal, animation, animated.* Ask students what all these words have in common. Confirm for them that they all have the word part *anima.* Tell students that this word part is from Latin, an ancient language that was originally spoken in Italy. *Anima* means "living." Conclude by saying: *Many other words in English have Latin roots, too. Learning these roots can help you learn more words.*

Teach/Model Write the following chart on the board, asking students to provide additional examples for the last column. Tell Spanish speakers that Spanish comes from Latin, so these roots should be familiar.

Latin Root	Meaning	Sample Words
aqua	water	aquarium
aud	to hear	auditorium
cent	one hundred	century
cert	sure, to trust	certificate
circ	around	circle
compute	to compute	computer
dic, dict	to say, to speak	dictionary
fin	to end	finish
grad	step, degree	graduate
scrib	to write	scribble

Practice Copy and distribute page 305. Read the directions aloud, and have students look at the sample answer to help them get started. After students complete the activity, invite volunteers to take turns forming other words with the Latin roots in the answer box. (See answers on page 311.)

Assess Write the following words on the board: *certain, final, audition, gradual,* and *dictate.* Ask students to copy these words and to identify their Latin roots. To check comprehension, ask students to make a sentence with each of these words.

Related Words   Use with page 306.

Preteach On the board, write *breath, breathe,* and *breathless.* Ask students what these words have in common. Confirm for them that they all have the word *breath* as the base. The endings on the other two words change their part of speech and meaning. *Breathe* is a verb and *breathless* is an adjective. Many other words are closely related in the same way. Tell students that it will help them expand their vocabulary if they try to learn new words in groups with other related words.

Teach/Model Write the following chart on the board, asking students to provide additional examples for the last column. Spanish examples include *planeta/planetario, horizonte/ horizontal,* and *salud/saludable.*

Base Word	Related Words
jewel	jeweler, jewelry
planet	planetary, planetarium
paint	painter, painting
act	action, actor, active
sign	signature
compute	computer, computation
horizon	horizontal
pot	potter, pottery
bank	banker, banking
heal	health, healthy
relate	relative, relationship
produce	product, production
please	pleasant, pleasure

Practice Copy and distribute page 306. Read the directions aloud, and have students look at the sample answer to help them get started. (See answers on page 311.)

Assess Ask students to take turns thinking of other words that are related to the words in the word box on page 306 or the words in the above chart.

Cognates and Word Roots

Reading Multisyllabic Words

Use with page 307.

Preteach On the board, write the word *dic/tion/ar/y*, dividing it into syllables, as indicated. Sound it out, pausing between each syllable, and then blend the syllables together. Ask students how many syllables it has (4). Follow the same procedure for *en/cy/clo/pe/di/a*, which has 6 syllables. Tell students: *Pay attention to the syllables in a word. This will help you spell the word, and it will help you pronounce it, too.*

Teach/Model Distribute multiple copies of a dictionary, and point out how each entry word is divided into syllables. Ask students to find the word *brontosaur*, for example. Ask: *How many syllables does this word have?* (3) *What's the first syllable?* (bron) *What are the other syllables?* (*to* and *saur*) Repeat the procedure with the following words: *mystery, parentheses, enthusiasm, personality.*

Practice Copy and distribute page 307. Read the directions aloud, and have students look at the sample answer to help them get started. Help students read the words if necessary. (See answers on page 311.)

Assess Write the following words on the board: *relative, warrior, mathematical, magnificent, principal.* Have students use a dictionary to find out how many syllables each word has. Tell students to write the words on a piece of paper, showing the syllable divisions.

Name _____

Cognates

- **Read** a few pages of a book or article. **Find** English words that look like words in another language you know.
- **Write** the words in both languages on the chart.
- **Write** the meaning of each word, using dictionaries if necessary. Then **tell** if the two similar words are cognates.

English	_____ (language)	Cognates? (yes/no)
Word: Meaning:	Word: Meaning:	
Word: Meaning:	Word: Meaning:	
Word: Meaning:	Word: Meaning:	
Word: Meaning:	Word: Meaning:	
Word: Meaning:	Word: Meaning:	

- **Find out** how to say *computer* in at least two different languages. **Use** sources such as dictionaries, the Internet, and people you know. **Write** the words.
- **Decide** which words are cognates of *computer*.

Words with Greek Roots

- **Read** the word parts in the box.
- **Look** at the pictures. **Put** one word part from each box together to make a word.
- **Write** the correct word on each blank line.

auto = self	**photo** = light	**scope** = to see
mega = large	**tele** = from a distance	**phone/phono** = sound
micro = very small		**graph** = written

1.  _____megaphone_____ = a tool used to make sound "larger"

2.  _____ = a tool for seeing very small things

3.  _____ = a machine that allows two people in different places to talk

4.  _____ = a person's signature

5.  _____ = a tool for seeing the planets and stars

6.  _____ = an image taken by a camera

Words with Latin Roots

- **Study** the word parts in the box.
- **Read** the sentences.
- **Complete** each sentence. **Write** the correct word in the blank space.

aqua = water	**herba** = plant	**terr** = earth
carn = meat	**mill** = thousand	**tract** = pull
cent = one hundred	**ject** = throw	

1.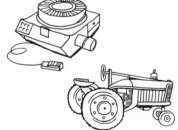

A _____carnivore_____ is an animal that eats meat, and

an _____ is an animal that eats plants.

(herbivore, carnivore)

2.

A _____ is one hundred years, and a

_____ is one thousand years.

(century, millenium)

3.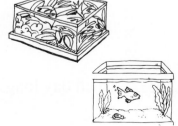

A _____ is a machine that "throws light,"

and a _____ is a machine that pulls heavy

loads. (tractor, projector)

4.

Small plants are grown in a _____, and

fish are kept in an _____.

(terrarium, aquarium)

Name _____

Related Words

- **Look** at the words in the box.
- **Read** the sentences.
- **Complete** each sentence. **Write** the correct word in the blank space.

| desert | dirt | mask | painter | volcanic |
| deserted | dirty | masquerade | painting | volcano |

1.  The _____volcano_____ exploded with a huge blast.

   _____ ash rose into the air and then

   settled on the ground.

2.  The _____ is finishing a pretty

   _____.

3.  This part of the _____ is quiet

   and _____.

4.  Everybody at the _____ wore a

   _____.

5.  After playing in the _____ all day long,

   Cory's shirt was completely _____.

ELL Handbook

Reading Multisyllabic Words

- **Read** the words. **Sound out** the number of syllables.
- **Write** each word in the correct column of the chart.

ROW 1

baseball

binoculars

champion

envelope

ROW 2

mushroom

pineapple

watermelon

meditation

ROW 3

barbecue

harmonica

telescope

zipper

Two Syllables	Three Syllables	Four Syllables
baseball		

pages 223–225:
Confusing Consonants, Assess
b and *v:* b, v, b, v, v, b, v, b, b, v, b, v, v
ch and *sh:* ch, sh, ch, sh, ch, ch, sh, sh, ch, ch, sh
d and *th:* th, d, th, th, d, d, th, d, th, d
l and *r:* r, l, r, l, r, r, l, r, l, r, l, l
m and *n:* m, n, m, n, m, n, m, n, n, m, m, n
s and *th:* s, th, s, th, s, s, th, th, s, th

page 226: Words with *b* and *v*
Row 1: b, v, b, v
Row 2: v, v, b, b
Row 3: box, van
Sentence: Val, Billy, dove, wave

page 227: Words with *ch* and *sh*
Row 1: sh, ch, ch, sh
Row 2: sh, sh, ch, ch
Row 3: child, shop
Sentence: Sherry, Shark, chewed, shiny, shoe

page 228: Words with *d* and *th*
Row 1: d, th, th, d
Row 2: th, th, d, d
Row 3: third, desk
Sentence: Think, thought, daring, dog, through, thick

page 229: Words with *l* and *r*
Row 1: r, l, l, r
Row 2: r, l, l, r
Row 3: leg, ring
Sentence: red, river, runs, little, lake

page 230: Words with *m* and *n*
Row 1: n, n, m, m
Row 2: m, n, m, n
Row 3: mask, nest
Sentence: man, in, moon, cream, spoon

page 231: Words with *s* and *th*
Row 1: s, th, th, s
Row 2: s, s, th, th
Row 3: sun, thorn
Sentence: Sara, sipped, thick, soup

page 236: Syllables V/CV and VC/V
Long: *broken, frozen, music, tulip;* Short: *salad, lemon*

page 237: Syllables CV/VC
Part 1: sci/en/tist; pi/an/o; vi/o/lin; vid/e/o; sta/di/um; ra/di/o; ro/de/o; me/te/or
Part 2: studio, create, idea, medium, pioneer, immediate, bionic, reliance

page 238: Syllables VCCCV
1. purchase; **2.** inspect; **3.** surprise; **4.** children; **5.** explode; **6.** address

page 239: C + *-le*
Part 1: bubble, puddle, eagle, candle
Part 2: mar/ble, mid/dle, dou/ble, lit/tle, ti/tle, han/dle

pages 240–241:
Consonant Blends, Assess
Initial Consonant Blends: cr, pl, cl, pr, tr, str, dr, st
Final Consonant Blends: nk, nch, nk, nd, nch, nk, sk, st, nt, nd, nt, nd

page 242: Initial Consonant Blends
Row 1: cr, cr, cl, cl
Row 2: pr, pl, pr, pl
Row 3: str, str, st, st
Sentence: clock, struck, students, snapped

page 243: Final Consonant Blends
Row 1: nd, nk, nd, nk
Row 2: nt, nt, nch, nch
Row 3: sk, st, st, sk
Sentence: must, ask, band, paint, bench

page 244: Silent Consonants *wr, kn, gn, st, mb*, Assess
Silent Consonants: kn, kn, kn, wr, wr, wr, gn, gn, gn, st, st, st, mb, mb, mb

page 245: Silent Consonants *wr, kn, gn, st, mb*
Row 1: mb, wr, gn, kn, kn
Chart: write, knee, gnat, listen, thumb; wrench, knot, sign, castle, crumb

pages 246–247:
Short Vowels, Assess
Short *a:* pat, hat, bad, man, tag
Short *e:* set, ten, net, sell
Short *i:* tin, six, pig, trip
Short *o:* hop, top, dog, lock
Short *u:* bug, tub, cup, cub

page 248: Words with Short *a*
Row 1: acrobat, bat, ant
Row 2: cap, man, map, can
Row 3: man, bat, ant, hat
Sentence: acrobat, an, apple, bat, act

page 249: Words with Short *e*
Row 1: vest, elephant, tent
Row 2: pen, web, bell, bed
Row 3: ten, bell, nest, web
Sentence: elephant, entered, tent, elegant, step

page 250: Words with Short *i*
Row 1: dinner, gift, inch
Row 2: pin, zip, dig, sit
Row 3: zip, gift, pig, six
Sentence: Six, pigs, with, bibs, grinned, did, jig, in, minute

page 251: Words with Short *o*
Row 1: dog, octopus, box
Row 2: lock, rock, fox, hop
Row 3: box, dog, lock, mop
Sentence: lock, fox, box

page 252: Words with Short *u*
Row 1: truck, puppy
Row 2: bus, duck, tub, rug
Row 3: bus, truck, duck, sun
Sentence: bug, rug, jumped, up, pup

**pages 253–254:
Long Vowels, Assess**
Long *a*: cage, rage; ate, late
Long *e*: leaf, lean; seen, seat
Long *i*: sky, sly; rice, price
Long *o*: globe, lobe; low, blow; hose, toes
Long *u*: rule, tool; glue, blue

page 255: Words with Long *a*
Row 1: cake, train, plate
Row 2: snake, chain, plane, hay
Row 3: grapes, tray, rake, rain
Sentence: came, (a), gate, cave, waited, Dave

page 256: Words with Long *e*
Row 1: eagle, teeth, feet
Row 2: he, wheel, thirty, leaf
Row 3: tree, leaf, me, bee
Sentence: See, leaves, trees, street

page 257: Words with Long *i*
Row 1: bike, night, mice
Row 2: ice, child, tie, light
Row 3: five, kite, light, sky
Sentence: Five, kites, sky, flying, high

page 258: Words with Long *o*
Row 1: rope, nose, bone
Row 2: robe, gold, bow, boat
Row 3: goat, rose, snow(man), gold
Sentence: Joan, wrote, note, rode, boat

page 259: Words with Long *u*
Row 1: boot, suitcase
Row 2: glue, stool, fruit, mule
Row 3: fruit, flute, moon, cube
Sentence: Sue, blue, drew, moon

page 260: Vowel Diphthongs, Assess
/ou/: plow, how, owl, south
/oi/: soy, enjoy, choice, toil, join

page 261: Vowel Diphthongs
Row 1: soil, boy, coin
Row 2: crowd, count, towel, plow
Row 3: cow, toy, voice, cloud
Sentence: boy, count, toy, cows

**pages 262–263:
r-Controlled Vowels, Assess**
Words with *ar, are, air, or, ore*: thumbs up: chair, chore, far, stare, store, car, more; thumbs down: chew, feet, stand
Words with *er, ir, or, ur,* and *eer, ear*: cheer, steer, her, deer, fear

**page 264:
Words with *ar, are, air, or, ore***
Row 1: air, ar, ar, air
Row 2: corn, horse, fork
Row 3: star, hair, store, porch
Sentence: Chairs, forks, corn, more, are, for, store

**page 265:
Words with *er, ir, or, ur, eer, ear***
Row 1: ur, ear, ur, ear
Row 2: bird, butter, skirt
Row 3: worm, deer, purse, shirt
Sentence: dear, girl, tear, purse, near, here

Answer Key

page 266: The Schwa and Unstressed Syllables, Assess
asleep, final, panel, cradle, lesson, ribbon

page 267:
The Schwa and Unstressed Syllables
Row 1: circle: alarm, afraid; underline: bottle, dragon
Chart: medal, nickel, table, wagon, sandal, shovel, apple, button
Sentence: apples, bagels, alarm, (a), pretzel, table

pages 268–269:
Inflected Endings, Assess
Plurals and Possessives: Answers will vary, but will include possessives.
Verb Endings -s, -ed, -ing: Answers will vary.

page 270: Plurals and Possessives
1. pets; **2.** Martin's; **3.** birds'; **4.** Mia's; **5.** Carlos's; **6.** puppies

page 271: Verb Endings -s, -ed, -ing
Part 1: /s/: helps, writes, walks; /z/: calls, plays, runs, sees
Part 2: /d/: opened, played, rubbed; /t/: fixed, helped, walked, washed
Part 3: calling, hoping, playing, running

page 275: /j/, /s/, /k/
Row 1: jet, cage, jam
Row 2: bus, dancing
Row 3: back, cat, knock(ing)
Sentence: Jessica, checks, crossing, bridge

page 276: /ȯ/ spelled a, au, aw, al
Row 1: saw, sausage, straw
Row 2: applause, lawn, walnut, salt
Chart: au: sausage, applause; aw: saw, straw, lawn; al: walnut, salt

page 277: /ȯ/ spelled augh, ough
1. brought; **2.** daughter; **3.** thought; **4.** fought; **5.** caught; **6.** taught

pages 278–280:
Compound Words, Homophones, and Contractions, Assess
Compound Words: Answers may include any of

the words on page 221.
Homophones: Answers will vary.
Contractions: Answers will vary.

page 281: Compound Words
Part 1: bath/tub; flash/light; key/board; mail/box; space/ship; star/fish; tooth/paste; water/fall
Part 2: backpack, bookmark, classroom, fingernail, hairbrush, rainbow, sailboat, sidewalk

page 282: Homophones
1. same; **2.** different; **3.** same; **4.** same; **5.** different; **6.** different
Students will match pictures to words.

page 283: Contractions
I'm, Isn't, it's, we're, didn't, I've, doesn't, I'll
Answers will vary, but will be four of the following: *did not, does not, I will, I am, I have, is not, it is, we are.*

pages 284–290: Prefixes and Suffixes, Assess
Prefixes *un-* and *re-:* unafraid, not afraid; unlock, open the lock; rerun, run again; reunite, unite again
Prefixes *im-, in-, mis-, over-:* incorrect, misinterpret, overload, overcoat, intake, mistake, overtake, misuse, overuse
Prefixes *pre-, mid-, over-, out-, bi-:* prepaid, midair, overtime, outfield, biweekly
Suffixes *-ly, -ful, -less, -ness:* slowly, slowness, quietly, quietness, perfectly, fearful, fearless, rudely, rudeness
Suffixes *-tion, -sion, -able, -ible:* sensible, comfortable, confusion, reaction
Suffixes *-er, -or, -ess, -ist:* actor, seller, hostess, dentist, tourist, teacher, lioness
Suffixes *-y, -ish, -hood, -ment:* smelly, British, motherhood, excitement, windy, brownish, falsehood, shipment

page 291: Prefixes *un-* and *re-*
2. reappear; **3.** unbelievable; **4.** unfamiliar; **5.** reheat; **6.** uninterested; **7.** unlike; **8.** restart; **9.** reuse; **10.** unkind
un-: unbelievable, unfamiliar, uninterested, unlike, unkind; *re-:* reread, reappear, reheat, restart, reuse

310 Answer Key

ELL Handbook

page 292: Prefixes *im-, in-, mis-, over-*
1. overpriced; **2.** inexpensive; **3.** incorrect;
4. misprint; **5.** impatient
Additional words: Answers will vary. Words
may include *impolite, insecure, mismatch,* and
overcook.

**page 293: Prefixes *pre-, mid-, over-,
out-, bi-***
1. pretest; **2.** prefixes; **3.** outline; **4.** midnight;
5. overdue; **6.** overtime; **7.** outside; **8.** bicycle

page 294: Suffixes *-ly, -ful, -less, -ness*
1. quietly; **2.** completely; **3.** goodness;
4. careful; **5.** Luckily; **6.** playfully; **7.** friskiness

**page 295:
Suffixes *-tion, -sion, -able, -ible***
1. imagination; **2.** walkable; **3.** dependable;
4. decision; **5.** reversible

page 296: Suffixes *-er, -or, -ess, -ist*
1. pharmacist; **2.** commuter; **3.** inventor;
4. lioness

page 297: Suffixes *-y, -ish, -hood, -ment*
1. rainy; **2.** neighborhood; **3.** sleepy;
4. movement; **5.** foolish; **6.** childish

**pages 298–302: Cognates and Word
Roots, Assess**
Cognates: Answers will vary.
Words with Greek Roots: autobiography: a book
about yourself; phonology: the study of sounds;
geography: description of the Earth; telescope:
something that lets you see far away
Words with Latin Roots: certain, cert; final, fin;
audition, aud; gradual, grad; dictate, dict
Related Words: Answers will vary.
Reading Multisyllabic Words: Syllabication may
vary among dictionaries. rel/a/tive; war/ri/or;
math/e/mat/i/cal; mag/ni/fi/cent; prin/ci/pal

page 303: Cognates
Chart: Answers will vary. The Spanish word for
computer, computadora, is a cognate.

page 304: Words with Greek Roots
2. microscope; **3.** telephone; **4.** autograph;
5. telescope; **6.** photograph

page 305: Words with Latin Roots
1. carnivore, herbivore; **2.** century, millennium;
3. projector, tractor; **4.** terrarium, aquarium

page 306: Related Words
1. volcano, Volcanic; **2.** painter, painting;
3. desert, deserted; **4.** masquerade, mask;
5. dirt, dirty

page 307: Reading Multisyllabic Words
Two Syllables: baseball, mushroom, zipper;
Three Syllables: champion, envelope, pineapple,
barbecue, telescope; Four Syllables: binoculars,
watermelon, meditation, harmonica

Part 4
Grammar Instruction for English Language Learners

Contents

ELL Handbook

Introduction to the Grammar Transition Lessons

English language learners may have experience mainly with their home languages, and the grammars of different languages vary widely. As these students encounter English, keep in mind that their home languages may differ in aspects such as the following:

- The languages may use different word order than English does.

- They may not use the same parts of speech as English does.

- Their tense structures may be simpler or more complex than English tense structure.

- Nouns and adjectives that are neutral in English may be masculine or feminine in a child's home language.

For teachers, it is vitally helpful to remember that grammar is much more than a set of rules for saying and writing sentences correctly. Grammar primarily consists of the ways that speakers and writers of a language communicate ideas, mainly in sentences. As students learn the meanings of new words and how English sentences work, they become able to successfully communicate their ideas. They will gradually learn rules, read and write punctuation, and eventually become proficient in standard English usage.

The core grammar and writing lessons in Scott Foresman *Reading Street* provide the systematic instruction that students need to write. The following Grammar Transition Lessons and Practice Pages will supplement the core instruction with customized lessons that meet the particular needs of English learners.

Each group of grammar lessons covers a topic, such as Nouns, Verbs, or Sentences. Each lesson is supported by a reproducible Practice Page that provides strong context for the skill. Throughout the Grammar Transition Lessons, a **Transfer Skills** feature identifies challenges faced by English learners, based on the grammar of their home languages, as well as language knowledge that can transfer to English. Each lesson also includes a **Grammar in Action** feature to reinforce the skill through active learning.

In addition to the Grammar Transition Lessons and Practice Pages, you can further support grammar instruction with routines such as the following:

- **Emphasize sentence meaning.** Encourage children to try to understand and convey ideas rather than focusing only on separate words. Build their knowledge by presenting many examples that show how English sentences convey meaning. Include sentences that the children say or write.

- **Strengthen oral language skills.** Allow beginning English speakers to work with partners when completing grammar activities, talking about what English words and sentences mean. Encourage students to make up new phrases and sentences together.

- **Engage students as active learners.** Students who are acquiring English will make mistakes. They need encouragement rather than constant correction. Let students sing, chant, and play language games together. Allow them to communicate freely and have fun with English.

- **Relate to the home language.** Whenever possible, help students build on what they already know by making connections between a target grammar skill and the home language. Use available resources, such as bilingual staff members, language Web sites, and the students themselves, to gather information about the home language.

Nouns

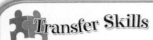

Transfer Skills

Common Nouns
In languages such as Spanish and French, nouns are masculine or feminine. You can point out that while some nouns in English refer to males or females *(boy, girl, uncle, aunt),* English nouns do not have masculine and feminine endings.

Grammar *in Action*

Noun Hunt Have partners look through picture books and make a list of nouns they find in the pictures or texts.

Common Nouns

Preteach Point to objects in the room, and have students name them. Tell students: *We have names for the things around us. A noun is a word that names something or somebody.*

Teach/Model Present the concept and provide examples:
• A noun names a person, a place, an animal, or a thing.

person	place	animal	things
girl	yard	dog	box, music

Practice/Assess Copy and distribute page 318. Read the directions aloud, and name the items in the picture before students complete the page. (See answers on page 382.)

Transfer Skills

Proper Nouns
Students who are literate in nonalphabetic languages such as Chinese, Korean, and Japanese may not be familiar with capitalizing proper nouns.

Grammar *in Action*

Use capital letters On chart paper, have students draw pictures and write or dictate the names of people and places that are special to them. Remind them to use capital letters.

Proper Nouns

Special Names

Preteach Have students practice writing each other's names. Point out that each student's name begins with a capital letter. Tell students: *Each of us has our own special name. A proper noun is the special name of a person, place, animal, or thing. Proper nouns begin with capital letters.*

Teach/Model Present the concept and provide examples:
• A proper noun names a special person, place, animal, or thing.
• A proper noun begins with a capital letter.

special person	special place	special animal	special thing
Sandra	Africa	Fifi	Statue of Liberty

Practice/Assess Copy and distribute page 319. Read the directions aloud. Help students name the people and animals in the picture before they complete the page. (See answers on page 382.)

Titles and Abbreviations

Preteach Write the names of various school staff members on the board, including titles such as *Mr., Mrs.,* and *Dr.* Read the names aloud with students, and underline the titles as you say them. Point out the titles that are abbreviations, or shortened forms of words.

Teach/Model Present the concept and provide examples:
• Proper names may begin with a title such as *Mrs.* or *Dr.*
• A title begins with a capital letter. If a title is an abbreviation, it ends with a period.

Title	Example
Mr. *(mister)*	Mr. Garza
Ms. *(miz)*	Ms. Prince
Mrs. *(missus)*	Mrs. Dexter
Miss *(miss)*	Miss Wong
Dr. *(doctor)*	Dr. Marco

Practice/Assess Copy and distribute page 320. Read the directions aloud before students complete the page. (See answers on page 382.) Have students read their own answers aloud.

Days, Months, and Holidays

Preteach Ask students to name today's day and date. Write them on the board, and point out that the day and month begin with capital letters.

Teach/Model Present the concept and provide examples:
• The names of the days of the week, months of the year, and holidays begin with capital letters.

Days of the Week	Months of the Year		Holidays (Examples)
Sunday	January	July	Memorial Day
Monday	February	August	Labor Day
Tuesday	March	September	Thanksgiving
Wednesday	April	October	
Thursday	May	November	
Friday	June	December	
Saturday			

Practice/Assess Copy and distribute page 321. Read the directions aloud. Go through the sample calendar with students before they complete the page. (See answers on page 382.)

Transfer Skills

Titles
• Students may not realize that, in English, the title *Doctor* is used for both men and women.
• In some countries, the word *Teacher* is used as a title. Point out that in the U.S., teachers are addressed with a title such as *Mr., Ms., Mrs.,* or *Miss.*

Grammar *in Action*

Oral Language Have students practice introducing adult staff members to each other, using the correct titles.

Transfer Skills

Days and Months
• In languages including Spanish, French, Polish, and Vietnamese, the names of days and months are not usually capitalized.
• In languages such as Chinese, Vietnamese, and Portuguese, the names of the days are formed by counting from the first day of the week.

Grammar *in Action*

Word Origins Have students use dictionaries that show etymologies to find out the origins of the English names for days of the week.

Transfer Skills

Plural Nouns
- Spanish speakers use -s and -es endings for nouns.
- In some languages, including Chinese, Hmong, and Vietnamese, nouns do not have plural forms. Instead, the plural is indicated with an adjective.

Grammar *in Action*

Noun Sort Have students make a 3-column chart with the headings "add -s," "add -es," and "change y to i and add -es." Invite students to look through magazines to find nouns that fit each category.

Singular and Plural Nouns

Preteach Point to one book and say: *book.* Point to two books and say: *books.* Repeat with *(lunch)box* and *(lunch)boxes.* Have students name other singular and plural nouns as you point to them. Say: *A singular noun names one thing. A plural noun names more than one thing.* Plural *means "more than one."*

Teach/Model Present the concept and provide examples:
- Add -s to most nouns to form the plural.
- If the noun ends in -ch, -sh, -s, -ss, or -x, add -es.
- If the noun ends in a consonant + y, change the y to i and add -es.

Add -s	Add -es	Change y → i and add -es
girl/girls	box/boxes	berry/berries

Practice/Assess Copy and distribute page 322 after teaching *Irregular Plural Nouns.*

Transfer Skills

Irregular Plurals
English learners may add -s to irregular nouns in sentences or to nouns for which English uses the singular for a quantity: *sheeps, mens, clothings.*

Grammar *in Action*

Concentration Have partners create "singular noun" word cards: *child, tooth, leaf, foot, man,* and "irregular plural noun" cards, including incorrect forms: *childs, children, teeth, tooths, leafs, leaves, feet, feets, men, mans.* Partners place the "singular" and "plural" cards face down in two separate groups, then take turns drawing correct pairs.

Irregular Plural Nouns

Preteach Write this sentence on the board: The <u>children</u> brushed their <u>teeth.</u> Ask a volunteer to name the singular of the underlined nouns *(child, tooth).* Tell students: *Most nouns add -s or -es to form the plural. Some nouns form the plural in a special way. They are called* irregular plural nouns.

Teach/Model Present the concept and provide examples:
- Most nouns add -s or -es: *books, girls, boxes, brushes.*
- Irregular plural nouns have special forms. Here are some examples:

Irregular Plural Nouns			
child/children	foot/feet	life/lives	man/men
ox/oxen	tooth/teeth	leaf/leaves	woman/women

Practice/Assess Copy and distribute page 322. Help students name the singular and plural nouns in the picture. (See answers on page 382.) Have students name the irregular plural nouns. As an extension, have students list the singular of the plural nouns.

Singular Possessive Nouns

Preteach Display these sentences, gesturing as appropriate: *This is* <u>Maya</u>. *This is* <u>Maya's</u> *desk.* Explain: *The first sentence is about Maya. The second sentence says that Maya has something. To show that a person, place, or thing has or owns something, add an apostrophe* (point to apostrophe) *and the letter* s. *The word* Maya's *is called a singular possessive noun.*

Teach/Model Present the concept and provide examples:
• A singular possessive noun ends in *'s.*

Singular Nouns	Singular Possessive Nouns	Examples
Sam	Sam's	Sam's mom
friend	friend's	friend's house
class	class's	class's pet
child	child's	child's jacket

Practice/Assess Copy and distribute page 323 after teaching *Plural Possessive Nouns.*

Plural Possessive Nouns

Preteach Display these sentences: *All my* <u>students</u> *have desks. These are my* <u>students'</u> *desks.* Encourage students to discuss the meaning of the two sentences. Explain: *To show that two or more people, places, or things have or own something, use a plural possessive noun.*

Teach/Model Present the concept and provide examples:
• If the plural noun ends in *-s, -es,* or *-ies,* add an apostrophe (')
to make it possessive.
• If the plural noun does **not** end in *-s, -es,* or *-ies,* add *'s* to make it possessive.

Plural Nouns	Plural Possessive	Examples
friends	friends'	friends' houses
classes	classes'	classes' teachers
puppies	puppies'	puppies' tails
children	children's	children's jackets

Practice/Assess Copy and distribute page 323. Make sure students understand the directions. Have students read their completed sentences aloud. (See answers on page 382.)

ELL Handbook

🧩 Transfer Skills

Possessive Nouns
In many languages, speakers show possession in phrases rather than noun endings. Show students how to change phrases such as *the tail of the cat* and *the nest of the bird* to *the cat's tail* and *the bird's nest,* in order to show possession in English.

Grammar *in Action*

Oral Language Have students place school supplies on their desks. Then have students point to and name a friend's things. For example: *This is Lin's book. This is Lin's calculator.*

🧩 Transfer Skills

Plural Possessive Nouns
An apostrophe after the letter s may seem incorrect to many students. Explain the difference between clear examples such as *a cat's tail* and *cats' tails* or *a bird's nest* and *birds' nests.* Use pictures or simple drawings to help students understand.

Grammar *in Action*

Use Plural Possessive Nouns Provide sentences such as these, and ask students to rewrite or rephrase them using plural possessive nouns: *This cake belongs to the students. (This is the students' cake.) These chairs belong to the children. (These are the children's chairs.)*

Name _____

Common Nouns

Practice
- **Look** at the picture.
- **Name** the people, places, animals, and things in the picture.

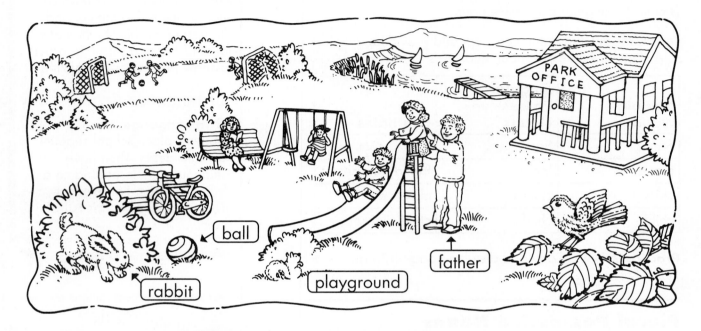

People	Places	Animals	Things
girl	pond	bird	slide

Assess
- **Look** around the room. What do you **see**?
- **Write** six nouns. **Name** things that you see.

_____

_____

Name _____

Special Names

Practice
- **Look** at the picture.
- **Find** the children, animals, and places that have special names.
- **Write** the names. Remember to **begin** the names with a capital letter.

Names of Children	Names of Animals	Names of Places
Maya		

Assess
- **Write** the names of two people you know.

_____

- **Write** the names of two special places you know.

_____

Name _____

Titles and Abbreviations

Practice
- **Look** at the pictures.
- **Write** the name of each person.
- **Include** a title for each person.

Title	Use with:
Mr.	a man
Ms.	a woman
Mrs.	a married woman
Miss	an unmarried girl or woman
Dr.	a doctor (male or female)

Mark Tanaka

Mr. Turner

Eva Santos
8 p.m.
Tonight!

Eva Santos

Lisa Johnson

1. Who is the teacher? _____

2. Who is the doctor? _____

3. Who is the dancer? _____

4. Who is the carpenter? _____

Assess
- **Write** the names of four adults you know. **Include** their titles.

_____

_____

Days, Months, and Holidays

Practice
- Use this class calendar to **answer** the questions.
- Remember to **begin** the names of days, months, and holidays with capital letters.

November						
Sunday	Monday	Tuesday	Wednesday	Thursday	Friday	Saturday
				1	2	3
4	5	6 Election Day	7 LIBRARY VISIT	8	9	10
11 Veterans Day	12	13	14 LIBRARY VISIT	15	16	17
18	19	20	21 LIBRARY VISIT	22 Thanksgiving	23	24
25	26	27	28 LIBRARY VISIT	29	30 BOOK FAIR	

1. What holiday is on Thursday, November 22? _____

2. What holiday is on Sunday, November 11? _____

3. When is the Book Fair? _____

4. When is Election Day? _____

5. When does the class visit the library? _____

Assess
- **Write** the names of the seven days of the week.

_____

- **Write** the name of a holiday or another day that is important to you. **Tell** the date of the holiday, or when it takes place.

_____   _____
           Name of the holiday   Date of the holiday

Name _____

Singular and Plural Nouns

Practice

• **Look** at the picture.
• **Write** three singular nouns. **Write** three plural nouns.

Singular Nouns	Plural Nouns
tree	flowers

Assess

• **Look** around the room. What do you **see**?
• **Write** three singular nouns and three plural nouns.

_____

_____

Singular and Plural Possessive Nouns

Practice
- **Look** at the picture. **Read** the sentences.
- **Circle** the correct possessive noun to complete each sentence.

1. (Today, Today's) date is May 19.
2. It is time for the (childrens', children's) story hour.
3. The (reader's, readers) name is Ed.
4. The (lady's, ladies') book club chooses a book.

Assess
- **Choose** a singular possessive noun from the sentences above. **Use** it in another sentence here.

_____

- **Choose** a plural possessive noun from the sentences above. **Use** it in another sentence here.

_____

Verbs

 Transfer Skills

Present Tense

English verb endings differ from verb endings in languages such as Spanish and Polish, which use different endings for person and number. However, students may need practice adding -s or -es to present-tense verbs with third-person singular subjects.

Grammar *in Action*

Present Tense Practice

Write these subjects on index cards: *The baby, The girls, Sam, My brother, I*. Write these verbs on another set: *work, sleep, jump, run, play*. Have students draw a card from each set and create a sentence.

 **Transfer Skills**

Past Tense

- Explain that regular past-tense verbs in English always have an -ed ending.
- In Chinese, Hmong, and Vietnamese, verbs do not change to show the tense. Adverbs or expressions of time indicate when an action has taken place.

Grammar *in Action*

Oral Language Display a list of verbs: *walk, play, jump, call, move, push, listen, watch*. Begin to tell a story: *Yesterday I walked to the park with my friend*. Have students add to the story, using the verbs from the list in the past tense.

Verbs in Present Tense

Preteach Perform these actions as you narrate: *I walk to the front of the room. I point to the board. The words* walk *and* point *are verbs. The tense of a verb tells when something happens. A verb in present tense, like* walk *or* point, *tells what happens now. To talk about one other person or thing, add* -s: *He walks. She points.*

Teach/Model Present the concept and provide examples:
- Verbs in present tense tell what happens now.

	Verb	Example
I, you, we, they	see	I <u>see</u> my sister.
he, she, it	sees	She <u>sees</u> me.

Practice/Assess Copy and distribute page 330. Help students describe the picture. (See answers on page 382.)

Verbs in Past Tense

Preteach Display these sentences: *I <u>walked</u> to the front of the room. I <u>pointed</u> to the board.* Explain: *I did these things in the past. Many verbs in past tense end with* -ed. *If a verb ends in* e, *like* move, *drop the* e *and then add* -ed: *moved. If a verb has one syllable and ends with a vowel followed by a consonant, such as* shop, *double the consonant before adding* -ed: *shopped.*

Teach/Model Present the concept and provide examples:
- Verbs in past tense tell what happened in the past.

	Verbs in Past Tense
Add -ed	He <u>jumped</u> over the chair.
Drop the final e and add -ed	I <u>moved</u> the chair.
Double the consonant and add -ed	He <u>slipped</u> on the rug.

Practice/Assess Copy and distribute page 331 after teaching *Irregular Verbs*, page 325.

Irregular Verbs

Preteach Display these sentences: *I _think_ about you. I _write_ a note. I _thought_ about you. I _wrote_ a note.* Explain: *Usually, you add* -ed *to a verb to form the past tense. But here, I didn't use* thinked *or* writed. *Some verbs are not regular verbs. They are called* irregular verbs. *An irregular verb has a different spelling in the past tense.*

Teach/Model Present the concept and provide examples:
- Irregular verbs do not add -ed to form the past tense.
- Irregular verbs have different spellings in the past tense.

Irregular Verbs	Past Tense
write	I _wrote_ a poem yesterday.
sing	I _sang_ a song last night.
eat	I _ate_ an apple earlier today.

Practice/Assess Copy and distribute page 331. Explain that some answers will be irregular verbs. (See answers on page 382.)

Transfer Skills

Irregular Verbs
Many English learners need extra practice with the variety of irregular verbs that also feature unfamiliar phonics elements, such as *catch/caught, buy/ bought,* and *can/could.*

Grammar *in Action*

Oral Language
Prepare index cards with irregular verbs. On one side, write the present tense. On the other side, write the past tense: *write/wrote; sing/sang; make/made; give/gave; eat/ ate; have/had.* Have partners dictate sentences to each other using the words on both sides.

Verbs in Future Tense

Preteach Say: *What will I do after school today? I _will go_ home. I _will eat_ a snack. I _will read_ my e-mail.* Explain: *To talk about the future, we use verbs in future tense. The future may be later today, next week, or even next year.* Write one of the statements and point out the word *will.* Say: *Use the helping verb* will *to form the future tense.*

Teach/Model Present the concept and provide examples:
- Verbs in future tense tell what will happen in the future.

Verbs in Future Tense
I _will go_ home.
I _will eat_ a snack.
I _will do_ my homework.

Practice/Assess Copy and distribute page 332. Help students describe the picture. Review the meanings of the verbs. (See answers on page 382.)

Transfer Skills

Future Tense
Spanish, Haitian Creole, and Hmong speakers may use present tense in places where English calls for future tense. Help students practice verbs in statements such as *I will read later* and *After we hear the story, we will write a new story.*

Grammar *in Action*

Oral Language Have partners tell each other what they will do when they get home from school or at some other time. If students can pantomime the action, have them act out the verb.

Transfer Skills

Verb Tenses

Speakers of several languages, including Arabic, may find the English distinction between the past and present perfect tenses unfamiliar. Show contrasting examples, and explain how the sense of time differs.

Grammar *in Action*

Present Participle Practice

Say and display these verbs: *jump, walk, talk, wave, laugh.* Have students give the present participle of each verb, with the subjects *I, you, she,* and *they.* Have them pantomime the actions and point to the corresponding subject.

Transfer Skills

Learning Verb Forms

Spanish, like English, has irregular verbs (such as *ser,* which means "to be," and *ir,* "to go"). Challenge students who are literate in Spanish to identify irregular Spanish verbs, and see whether English verbs with the same meanings are irregular.

Grammar *in Action*

Find the Parts

Write the principal parts of *go, sing, take,* and *write* on index cards. Give each student a card. Students circulate to find others with principal parts of the same verb.

Principal Parts of Regular Verbs

Preteach Display these sentences: *I talk to you. I am talking to you. I talked to you. I have talked to you many times.* Explain: *A verb's tenses are made from four basic forms: Present, Present Participle, Past, and Past Participle. These are called the verb's principal parts. The present form is used in the first sentence. The second sentence uses the present participle form. The third sentence uses the past form, which is the -ed form of the regular verb. The fourth sentence uses the past participle.*

Teach/Model Present the concept and provide examples:
- The four basic forms are called the principal parts.
- The present participle can use *am, is,* or *are* and the *-ing* form.
- The past participle uses *has, have,* or *had* and the *-ed* form.

	Principal Parts: Regular Verbs
Present	The baby plays all day.
Present Participle	The baby is playing now.
Past	You helped me yesterday.
Past Participle	You have helped me before.

Practice/Assess Copy and distribute page 333. Have students share their sentences. (See answers on page 382.)

Principal Parts of Irregular Verbs

Preteach Display these sentences: *You grow every day. You are growing so much! You grew an inch last year. You have grown an inch every year.* Point out the past and past participle: *Irregular verbs change spelling in these forms.*

Teach/Model Present the concept and provide examples:
- The principal parts of irregular verbs are the same four kinds as the principal parts of regular verbs. The *-ing* form is made the same way, such as *growing* or *going.*
- But irregular verbs do not use the *-ed* ending for the past and the past participle. For example, we do not say "growed"; we say "grew." We do not say "have growed"; we say "have grown."

> I go. I am going. I went. I have gone.
> He sees it. He is seeing it. He saw it. He has seen it.

Practice/Assess Copy and distribute page 334. Remind students that irregular verbs have their own spellings of the past and past participle. (See answers on page 383.)

Helping Verbs

Preteach Display these sentences: *I am planting* seeds. *They will grow* fast. *I have planted* seeds before. Explain: *The underlined parts are called* verb phrases. *The main verbs—*planting, grow, *and* planted*—show action. The helping verbs—*am, will, *and* have*—tell more about the action. The helping verb* am *tells what I am doing now.* Will *tells what the seeds will do in the future.* Have *tells what I have done that started in the past.*

Teach/Model Present the concept and provide examples:
• Helping verbs can tell the time of the action.

	Helping Verbs
Present	The dog **is** wagging his tail.
Past	He **was** barking last night.
Future	He **will** stay inside tonight.
Started in the Past	You **have** helped me before.

Practice/Assess Copy and distribute page 335. Have students read their sentences aloud. (See answers on page 383.)

Linking Verbs

Preteach Display these sentences: *I am tired. I feel sick. She seems sad. He is the leader. The car was new.* Explain: *In these sentences, the underlined words are called* linking verbs. *They tell what the subject is or what the subject is like.*

Teach/Model Present the concept and provide examples:
• Linking verbs do not show actions.
• They tell what the subject is or what the subject is like.

Linking Verbs	**Examples**
is	Summer is here.
are	The days are longer.
feels	The sun feels warmer.

Practice/Assess Copy and distribute page 336. Help students describe what is happening in the picture. (See answers on page 383.)

Transfer Skills

Helping Verbs
The uses of *have* and *had* as helping verbs may be familiar to Spanish-speaking students once they learn the English words. The Spanish verb *haber* is used similarly.

Grammar *in Action*

Time to Listen Have each student create three index cards labeled *present, past,* and *future.* Say these sentences and have students hold up the corresponding card: *You were playing basketball yesterday. You are listening to me now. You will go to the library later.* Encourage students to say other sentences with helping verbs.

Transfer Skills

Linking Verbs
• In languages including Chinese and Korean, linking verbs often are not required: *She tired. They sad.* Help students practice English sentences with linking verbs.
• Vietnamese speakers may use the English verb *have* in place of *There are* or *is,* as in "Inside the box have a gift." Help students practice with sentences using forms of *be.*

Grammar *in Action*

Oral Language Have partners tell each other three nice things they observe about each other: *You seem happy. You are smart. You are funny.*

Transfer Skills

Contractions

Ask students if there are contractions in their home languages. (In Spanish, *a + el = al* and *de + el = del;* in Portuguese, *de + as = das.*) Explain that an English contraction uses an apostrophe to replace the missing letters.

Grammar *in Action*

Contraction Substitution
Say these sentences, and have students rephrase them using contractions: *You are hiding. I do not see you. I am going to find you. I will not stop looking.* If necessary, help students learn *you're, don't, I'm,* and *won't.*

Transfer Skills

Negatives

In Spanish, Haitian Creole, and some other languages, double negatives (similar to *We did not do nothing*) are correct. Tell students that standard English does not use double negatives.

Grammar *in Action*

Double Negatives Write these sentences on the board. Invite students to come up and show how they would fix the double negative. Ask them to read the new sentence. *I can't never tell you. I won't say nothing. I don't want nobody to hear.*

Contractions

Preteach Display these sentences: <u>You're</u> *calling me.* <u>I'm</u> *far away. I* <u>can't</u> *hear you.* Explain: *The underlined words are contractions. A contraction is a shortened form of two words. An apostrophe* (point to an apostrophe) *takes the place of one or more letters. Look at these contractions: you and are become you're, I and am become I'm, can and not become can't.*

Teach/Model Present the concept and provide examples:
- A contraction is a shortened form of two words.
- An apostrophe takes the place of a letter or letters that are removed when you write a contraction.

	Contractions
I *and* have	<u>I've</u> eaten breakfast.
Should *and* not	You <u>shouldn't</u> run in the hall.
Can *and* not	She <u>can't</u> come to my party.

Practice/Assess Copy and distribute page 337 after teaching *Negatives.*

Negatives

Preteach Display these sentences: *I* <u>never</u> *eat fish. I* <u>don't</u> *ever eat fish.* Explain: *The underlined words are negatives. They mean "no" or "not." Contractions with* n't *are negatives. In English, we use only one negative with one verb. I* <u>don't</u> <u>never</u> *eat fish has a double negative. Take away one negative.* (See the first two examples.)

Teach/Model Present the concept and provide examples:
- Use only one negative with one verb.
- Use a positive word in a sentence with *not.*

	Examples
Negative	<u>Nothing</u> is on the table.
Positive	I don't see <u>anything</u> there.
Negative	They went <u>nowhere</u>.
Positive	We didn't go <u>anywhere</u>.

Practice/Assess Copy and distribute page 337. Remind students to watch for double negatives. (See answers on page 383.)

Troublesome Verbs, Lie/Lay, Sit/Set

Preteach Write and say: *The boy lays his book on the table. Then he lies down on his bed to take a nap.* Explain that in the first sentence, the boy puts his book down on a table. In the second sentence, he goes to bed to rest. Write and say: *Miguel sets the plates on the table. Then he sits at the table.* Show the difference between *set* and *sit* in these sentences by pantomiming the actions.

Teach/Model Present the concept and provide examples:
- Some verbs look similar or have similar meanings.
- Think of the meanings and the main parts of verbs.

Troublesome Verb	Past	Past Participle
Lie: "rest" or "recline"	lay	(has, have, had) lain
Lay: "put" or "place"	laid	(has, have, had) laid
Sit: "sit down"	sat	(has, have, had) sat
Set: "put something somewhere"	set	(has, have, had) set

Practice/Assess Copy and distribute page 338. Read the directions aloud and discuss the picture with students before they complete the activity. Then ask students to read their original sentence aloud. (See answers on page 383.)

Troublesome Verbs, Leave/Let, Rise/Raise

Preteach Write and say: *The girl will leave with her friends. Her mother let her go.* Explain that first the girl is going away. Her mother allows, or permits, her to go. Write and say: *The sun will rise every day. The children raise their hands in class.* Use pantomime or pictures to discuss the differences between *rise* and *raise* in these sentences.

Teach/Model Present the concept and provide examples:
- Some verbs look similar or have similar meanings.
- Think of the meanings and the principal parts of the verbs to use them correctly.

Practice/Assess Copy and distribute page 339. Read the directions aloud. Discuss the picture. Have students complete page 339. Then ask them to read their original sentence aloud. (See answers on page 383.)

Transfer Skills

Troublesome Verbs
Tell students that the verbs *set* and *lay* usually take a direct object. Display the sentences: *She set her keys on the counter. He lays his wallet on the table.* Use the sentences to show students that a direct object (keys, wallet) is a noun or pronoun that receives the action of a verb (set, lays) or shows the result of the action.

Grammar *in Action*

My Turn, Your Turn
In pairs, have students take turns creating sentences that include troublesome verbs. The partner accepts a correct example and offers a new example.

Transfer Skills

Troublesome Verbs
Have English learners study the meanings and principal parts of troublesome verbs. Then provide additional examples of the verbs used correctly.

Grammar *in Action*

Incomplete Sentences
Display several incomplete sentences, asking students to complete each sentence with a troublesome verb. For example, say: *The teacher _____ (let) the children go home. The children _____ (left) quickly.*

Name _____

Verbs in Present Tense

Practice
- **Look** at the picture. **Read** the sentences.
- **Write** the correct verb in present tense to complete each sentence.

bench

1. At 8:00, we _____ (wait, waits) for the bus.

2. Liz _____ (talk, talks) to her mom.

3. Adam _____ (sit, sits) on the bench.

4. I _____ (see, sees) the bus!

Assess
- **Look** at the picture. **Write** a sentence about the dog. **Use** a verb in present tense.

_____

ELL Handbook

Verbs in Past Tense

Practice
- **Look** at the picture. **Read** the sentences.
- **Circle** the correct verb in past tense.

Yesterday was my little sister's first day of school. We (celebrated, celebrates) with

a picnic. I (gived, gave) her a soccer ball. She (play, played) with it all day. My mom

(maked, made) snacks. We (haved, had) a good time!

Assess
- **Look** at the picture again. **Write** another sentence about the picnic. Use the verb *ate*.

Name _____

Verbs in Future Tense

Practice
- **Look** at the picture. **Read** the story. **Read** the verbs in the box.
- **Write** the correct verb in future tense to complete each sentence.

The mother bird _____ food for the babies.

In a few days, she _____ them to fly. Soon,

the baby birds _____ big and strong. They

_____ away from the nest.

| **will find** | **will fly** | **will teach** | **will grow** |

Assess
- What do you think the mother bird will do when the baby birds fly away? **Write** a sentence about it.

_____

ELL Handbook

Principal Parts of Regular Verbs

Practice
- **Look** at the picture. **Read** the sentences.
- **Circle** the verb in each sentence. **Write** *present*, *present participle*, *past*, or *past participle* to name the principal part of the verb.

1. The concert has started. _____

2. We listen to Sofia, Ben, and Ray. _____

3. Sofia and Ben are playing violins. _____

4. Sofia has played the violin for three years. _____

5. Ray plays the flute well. _____

Assess
- **Write** a sentence about the concert. **Use** the present participle *playing*.

_____

Principal Parts of Irregular Verbs

Practice
- **Look** at the picture. **Read** the sentences.
- **Circle** the verb in each sentence. **Write** *present*, *present participle*, *past*, or *past participle* to name the principal part of each irregular verb.

1. Yesterday I went to the doctor's office. _____

2. I go every year. _____

3. I have grown two inches this year. _____

4. I am growing very fast. _____

Assess
- **Write** a sentence to say what the doctor did. Use the past tense verb *wrote*.

_____

Helping Verbs

Practice
- **Look** at the picture. **Read** the sentences.
- **Circle** the verb phrase in each sentence. **Underline** the helping verb.

computer

DOLPHINS

1. We are learning about dolphins in class.

2. We have seen dolphins at the zoo.

3. I am using the Internet now.

4. I will give my report tomorrow.

Assess
- **Write** a sentence about the girl's report. Use the verb phrase *will tell*.

Linking Verbs

Practice

- **Look** at the picture. **Read** the sentences.
- **Circle** the linking verb in each sentence.

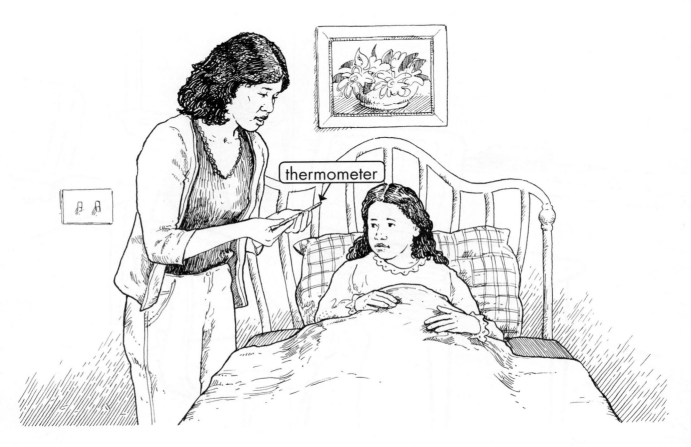

thermometer

1. I am sick today.

2. I feel tired and cold.

3. Mom seems worried.

4. My temperature is 102°F.

Assess

- **Write** a sentence about the girl. Use the linking verb *is*.

_____

Name _____

Contractions and Negatives

Practice

- **Look** at the picture. **Read** the sentences.
- **Circle** the correct word to complete each sentence.

baseball
glove

backpack

1. Dad, (I'm, I'll) going out to play baseball.

2. (Shouldn't, Should'nt) you do your homework first?

3. Oh, (I've, I'm) already done it.

4. (You're, Your) such a good student!

5. I won't (ever, never) forget to do my schoolwork.

Assess

- **Write** a sentence about the girl's dad. Use a contraction with *not*.

_____

Troublesome Verbs Lie/Lay, Sit/Set

Practice
- **Look** at the picture. **Read** the sentences.
- **Circle** the correct verb in each sentence.

1. Judy (lays / lies) on the chair by the pool.

2. She likes to (set / sit) on the edge of the pool.

3. The little girl (set / sit) her goggles on the table.

4. My mom (lays / lies) her towel on the chair.

Assess
- **Look** at the picture again. **Write** and then **say** a sentence about it. Use the verbs *lie, lay, sit,* or *set.*

Troublesome Verbs Leave/Let, Rise/Raise

Practice
- **Look** at the picture. **Read** the sentences.
- **Circle** the correct verb in each sentence.

1. Marcos, do not (let / leave) class without your music!

2. (Leave / Let) me play this song for you.

3. The teacher told us to (raise / rise) our hand when we have a question.

4. We want to (let / leave) a gift for our teacher.

5. We watched the balloons (raise / rise) into the air.

Assess
- **Look** at the picture again. **Write** and **say** a sentence about it. Use the verbs *leave, let, rise,* or *raise.*

_____

Transfer Skills

Subjects and Predicates
The typical English sequence of subject then predicate is not standard in some languages. For example, in Spanish the verb often appears before the subject, while in Korean and Hindi the verb typically appears at the end of a sentence.

Grammar *in Action*

Sentence Scramble Write these sentences onto strips: *My friend rides a bike. My dog barks at cats. The fish smells good. The clown is funny.* Cut each strip into subject and predicate. Have students scramble the sentence parts to form new sentences such as *The fish rides a bike.*

Transfer Skills

Verbs and Subjects
Students of various language backgrounds may add *-s* to both the nouns and verbs in sentences: *The robots walks.* Point out that, in English, verbs add *-s* for singular nouns *(A robot walks)*, not for verbs with plural nouns *(The robots walk).*

Grammar *in Action*

Subject-Verb Agreement
Encourage students to scour the day's headlines for examples of subject-verb agreement. For example: *Schools Close; Teams Win; Gas Prices Rise; Dog Saves Girl.*

Subjects and Predicates

Preteach Display this sentence: <u>The girl</u> walks to school. Explain that "The girl" is the subject of the sentence. The sentence is about the girl. A sentence is about its subject. Explain that "walks to school" is the predicate. What does the girl do? (walks to school) A predicate tells something about the subject.

Teach/Model Present the concept and provide examples:
- The subject of a sentence tells whom or what the sentence is about.
- The predicate of a sentence tells what the subject is or what the subject does.

Subject	Predicate
Sam	went to the store.
The students	write a paper.
The vegetables	are fresh.
My dog	had puppies.

Practice/Assess Copy and distribute page 348. Look at the picture after students complete the page. Have students contribute other sentences and identify the subjects and predicates. (See answers on page 383.)

Subject-Verb Agreement

Preteach Display these sentences: *The <u>bird</u> <u>sings</u> a song. The <u>birds</u> <u>sing</u> a song.* Encourage students to discuss the differences between the underlined parts. Explain: *The first sentence has a singular subject: bird. The second sentence has a plural subject: birds. The subject and the verb must work together, or agree. That's why the first sentence uses* sings *and the second sentence uses* sing.

Teach/Model Present the general concept and provide examples:
- If the subject is singular, add *-s* to the verb.
- If the subject is plural, do not add *-s* to the verb.

Subject	Verb
man	dances
Mom	works
friends	play
both feet	hurt

Practice/Assess Copy and distribute page 349. Help students describe the picture, emphasizing subject-verb agreement. (See answers on page 383.)

Word Order

Preteach Display these sentences and read them aloud, gesturing: *The bird flies. Flies the bird.* Ask: *What is the subject of the first sentence? (The bird) The second sentence does not sound right. The words are not in the right order to make a statement. In an English statement, the subject usually comes first. The predicate usually follows.*

Teach/Model Present the concept and provide examples:
- Sentences need to have words in the right order.
- In a statement, the subject usually comes first. The predicate usually follows.

| In the right order: | Pablo is my friend. |
| Not in the right order: | Is friend my Pablo. |

Practice/Assess Copy and distribute page 350. Help students describe what is happening in the picture. (See answers on page 383.)

Transfer Skills

Word Order
- Help students see that word order strongly affects meaning in English. *Lee thanked Tony* has a different meaning from *Tony thanked Lee.*
- See the Transfer note about the sequence of subjects and predicates on page 340.

Grammar *in Action*

Oral Language Say these groups of words: *The food is good. Is good the food. My friend rides a bike. Rides a bike my friend. Plays the dog. The dog plays.* Have students say which sentences are in correct word order.

Complete Sentences and Sentence Fragments

Preteach Write this sentence and fragment on the board: *Tom went to the library. Went to the library.* Ask: *Who went to the library? (Tom) Which sentence tells you this? The first sentence tells a complete idea. It says who did something. The second set of words (went to the library) is called a* sentence fragment. *It does not tell a complete idea. It does not say who went to the library. How would you make this fragment a complete sentence? (Add a subject.)*

Teach/Model Present the concept and provide examples:
- A sentence tells a complete idea.
- A fragment is a piece of a sentence. It does not tell a complete idea.

| Sentence | Cheny eats her lunch. |
| Fragment | Her lunch in a bag. |

Practice/Assess Copy and distribute page 351. As an extension, have students choose a fragment from the Practice and create a sentence from it. (See answers on page 383.)

Transfer Skills

Sentence Fragments
Spanish- and Chinese-speaking students may omit some pronouns as sentence subjects because in their home languages the pronoun may be unnecessary. For example, the Spanish equivalent of *Am reading* is a complete sentence.

Grammar *in Action*

Time to Listen Say these groups of words. Have students call out *sentence* or *fragment* after each one: *My brother. We walk to school. We ride on the bus. In the car. After school.* Invite students to contribute other sentences.

Transfer Skills

Statements
Children who have begun to read in Spanish and other alphabetic languages may recognize that sentences begin with capital letters and end with periods.

Grammar *in Action*

Fix the Statements Write groups of words such as these on the board, including the mistakes: *my friends are funny. / They tell me jokes / I laugh every day* Have volunteers come up and fix the statements by adding correct punctuation and a capital letter at the beginning.

Transfer Skills

Questions
Speakers of Chinese, Vietnamese, and other Asian languages often form questions by adding words to statements, comparable to *The food is hot, no?* or *You see or not see the bird?* Provide model English questions for students to understand and to follow the patterns.

Grammar *in Action*

Oral Language Have pairs of students ask each other questions about what they did yesterday. For example, *What did we do in school yesterday? What is your favorite subject?*

Types of Sentences

Statements

Preteach Display these sentences: *I went to the library. My brother went too. We both found good books.* Say: *Let's look at these sentences. Each one starts with a capital letter and ends with a period. Each one tells something. A sentence that tells something is called a* statement.

Teach/Model Present the concept and provide examples:
- A sentence that tells something is called a *statement.*
- It begins with a capital letter and ends with a period.

Statements
I had a party yesterday.
All of my friends came to my house.
You ate pizza.

Practice/Assess Copy and distribute page 352 after teaching *Questions.*

Questions

Preteach Display these sentences: *What is your name? Where do you live? How old are you? Do you have any brothers?* Ask: *How are these sentences different from statements? They each ask something, and they end with question marks. A sentence that asks something is called a* question. Model the difference in intonation between these two sentences: *That is your dog. Is that your dog?*

Teach/Model Present the general concept and provide examples:
- A sentence that asks something is called a *question.*
- It starts with a capital letter and ends with a question mark.

Questions
How are you?
Did you go to Sam's party?
Does Ami like pizza?

Practice/Assess Copy and distribute page 352. Help students describe the picture. (See answers on page 383.)

Exclamations and Interjections

Preteach Write and say in an excited voice: *I am so happy!* Have students repeat, and then ask: *What feeling does that sentence express? (excitement; happiness) Whenever you say something with strong feeling, you are saying an exclamation. A written exclamation ends with an exclamation mark.* Next, write and say: *Hooray!* Explain: *This word also shows strong feeling and ends in an exclamation mark. However, it is <u>not</u> a complete sentence. It is called an* interjection.

Teach/Model Present the concept and provide examples:
- An exclamation is a sentence that shows strong feeling. It ends with an exclamation mark.
- An interjection is a word or group of words that shows strong feeling. It ends with an exclamation mark, but it is not a complete sentence.

Exclamation	I have a new baby brother!
Interjection	Wow!

Practice/Assess Copy and distribute page 353. Remind students that exclamations are complete sentences. (See answers on page 384.)

Commands

Preteach Give students various commands such as these: *Please stand up. Walk to the front of the class. Say hello. Sit down.* Ask: *How are these sentences the same? Sentences that tell someone to do something are called* commands.

Teach/Model Present the concept and provide examples:
- A command is a sentence that tells someone to do something.
- It begins with a capital letter and ends with a period.

Commands
Open the door. Turn on the light. Sweep the floor.

Practice/Assess Copy and distribute page 354. Have students use it as a model for writing another recipe. (See answers on page 384.)

Transfer Skills

Exclamations
Speakers of Russian, Polish, and other languages may need to practice correct word order in exclamations. Have students make and use sentence strips, correcting exclamations such as *We enjoy very much movies!*

Grammar *in Action*

Interjection Charades
Write these interjections on index cards: *Ouch! Wow! Oh, no! Hooray!* Display them. Have a volunteer secretly choose an interjection and pantomime a scene that would elicit that interjection. Whoever guesses correctly takes the next turn.

Transfer Skills

Commands
Vietnamese speakers may recognize commands when they include an adverb or another clue word: *Go to school now. Take this to the office; go now.*

Grammar *in Action*

Oral Language Teach students the jump rope chant "Teddy Bear," in which the jumper obeys these commands while jumping rope: *Teddy Bear, Teddy Bear, turn around. Teddy Bear, Teddy Bear, touch the ground. Teddy Bear, Teddy Bear, stomp your feet. Teddy Bear, Teddy Bear, show your teeth.* Invite students to play.

Transfer Skills

Compound Sentences
Students may have difficulty distinguishing the clauses in a compound sentence in English. Give them additional practice finding the subject and verb within each independent clause.

Grammar *in Action*

Oral Language Say several pairs of simple sentences. Have students say compound sentences, keeping in mind the differences among *and, but,* and *or: I want to buy juice. I do not have a dollar. / I can drink water. I can borrow a dollar. / Tom is my friend. He gave me a dollar.*

Transfer Skills

Combining Sentences
Speakers of Indonesian and some other Asian languages may need practice combining sentences.

Grammar *in Action*

Form Sentences Make a set of sentence cards: *Mari wrote a poem. David sings. Rita went home.* Make a second set and distribute: *Mari read it to the class. David plays the guitar. Simón went home.* Read a sentence from the first set. The student holding a sentence with the same subject or predicate reads it. Have a volunteer form a combined sentence.

Simple and Compound Sentences

Preteach Display these sentences: *I went to Sal's house. We watched a movie.* Ask students to tell the subjects and predicates. Explain: *A simple sentence has one subject and one predicate. You can join the two simple sentences this way: I went to Sal's house, and we watched a movie. The new sentence is called a* compound sentence. *The two simple sentences are joined with the word* and.

Teach/Model Present the concept and provide examples:
- A simple sentence has one subject and one predicate.
- A compound sentence has two simple sentences joined by a comma and one of these words: *and, but,* or *or.*

Simple Sentences	Lena is my sister. I love her. I like peanuts. They make me sick. You can walk to school. I can drive you.
Compound Sentences	Lena is my sister, and I love her. I like peanuts, but they make me sick. You can walk to school, or I can drive you.

Practice/Assess Copy and distribute page 355. In the first compound sentence, help students see the two simple sentences. (See answers on page 384.)

Combining Sentences

Preteach Display these sentences: *I ate a sandwich. I drank some milk.* Ask: *What is the subject of both sentences? You can combine two sentences that have the same subject: I ate a sandwich and drank some milk.* Display these sentences: *Max went to the beach. I went to the beach. What is the predicate of both sentences? You can combine two sentences that have the same predicate: Max and I went to the beach.*

Teach/Model Present the concept and provide examples:
- Combine two sentences that have the same subject.
- Combine two sentences that have the same predicate.

Same Subject	Dan sat down. Dan did his homework. Dan sat down and did his homework.
Same Predicate	Miguel walked to school. I walked to school. Miguel and I walked to school.

Practice/Assess Copy and distribute page 356. Help students describe the picture. (See answers on page 384.)

Complex Sentences

Preteach Review compound sentences. Then present these complex sentences: _When I run, I feel good. I feel good when I run._ Explain: _This type of sentence is called a complex sentence. It has two parts, called clauses. The underlined part cannot stand alone as a sentence. If it comes first in the sentence, use a comma. The other part_ (I feel good) _can stand alone as a complete sentence._

Teach/Model Present the concept and provide examples:
• A complex sentence is made of two clauses.
• The two clauses are joined together with words such as _because, when, since, if,_ or _until._

Complex Sentences	When I grow up, I will be a teacher. I will be a teacher when I grow up.

Practice/Assess Copy and distribute page 357. Remind students that a complex sentence has two clauses. (See answers on page 384.)

Independent and Dependent Clauses

Preteach Present this complex sentence: _We cross the street when the light is green._ Explain: _The underlined part cannot stand alone as a sentence. It is a dependent clause. It depends on another part. The other part_ (we cross the street) _can stand alone. It is an independent clause._

Teach/Model Present the concept and provide examples:
• A complex sentence is made of an independent clause and a dependent clause.
• The dependent clause cannot stand alone.
• The independent clause can stand alone.

Independent Clause	Dependent Clause
I am happy	because I passed the test.

Practice/Assess Copy and distribute page 358. Remind students that dependent clauses often start with words such as _since, although, when, if,_ or _until._ (See answers on page 384.)

Transfer Skills

Complex Sentences Functional words such as _if, that, so,_ and _because_ are often used somewhat differently in English than how their equivalents are used in other languages. Help students practice and understand usages of these words.

Grammar _in Action_

Identify Complex Sentences Have students write these sentences and tell whether they are complex or not: _My sister's name is Lupe._ (no) _Since she is little, I help her with homework._ (yes) _I also tie her shoes._ (no) _When I was little, my mom helped me._ (yes)

Transfer Skills

Dependent Clauses Provide models of dependent clauses that begin with words such as _after, although, as, because, before, if, since, then, until, when,_ and _while._ These words may have uses that are unfamiliar to students of many language backgrounds.

Grammar _in Action_

Write Complex Sentences Say these dependent clauses. Have students add independent clauses to form complex sentences: _Since I was little / When I grow up / Because it was raining / If you help me / Until my alarm clock rings._ Have students write the complex sentences.

Grammar *in Action*

Oral Language On the board, write menu items such as *soup, salad, sandwich, milk, tea, juice.* Have pairs play the roles of server and customer at a café. The server starts with *"May I take your order?"* The customer names three items, such as: *I want soup, salad, and milk.* The server says and writes the order: *"He wants soup, salad, and milk."* Have students switch roles.

Grammar *in Action*

Comma Practice

Brainstorm names of school staff. Write their names and job titles, such as *Mrs. Olson, the bus driver.* Have students use this information to write sentences with appositives.

Commas

In a Series and in Direct Address

Preteach Display this sentence: *My favorite colors are red, blue, and yellow.* Point out the commas. Say: *Commas help you understand a sentence. They tell you when to pause, or rest. Put commas after items in a series of words such as red, blue, and yellow.* Display these sentences: *Kim, may I use your pen? Yes, Lucas, you may.* Say: *When we write a sentence in which a person is directly addressed by name, we use a comma.*

Teach/Model Present the concept and provide examples:
- Use commas to separate items in a series.
- Use commas with direct address.

Commas in a Series	I like baseball, basketball, and soccer. I play Monday, Wednesday, and Friday.
Commas in Direct Address	Lori, would you come here? Yes, Mom, I'm coming. I need your help, Lori.

Practice/Assess Copy and distribute page 359 after the lesson on commas with appositives and introductory phrases.

With Appositives and Introductory Phrases

Preteach Display these sentences: *Mr. Hays, <u>my teacher</u>, speaks Spanish. <u>Yes</u>, I know.* Explain: *The underlined part of the first sentence is called* an appositive. *It is a noun phrase that describes another noun. Use a comma before and after an appositive. The underlined part of the second sentence is called an* introductory word. *Put a comma after an introductory word or phrase such as* well, no, oh, *and "in other words."*

Teach/Model Present the concept and provide examples:
- Use a comma before and after an appositive.
- Use a comma after an introductory word or phrase.

Appositives	Mr. Sims, <u>my neighbor</u>, has a dog. The dog, <u>a poodle</u>, barks all night.
Introductory Words or Phrases	<u>Oh</u>, I am very sorry. <u>In other words</u>, you cannot sleep.

Practice/Assess Copy and distribute page 359. Read the sentences, pausing where commas belong. (See answers on page 384.)

Quotations

Preteach Display and read the following dialogue: *"Do you have homework?" my mother asked. "Yes, I have to read a book," I said. "What is the name of the book?" my mother wanted to know.* Point out the position of the quotation marks in the dialogue.

Teach/Model Present the concept and provide examples:
- A quotation shows the exact words of a speaker.
- Quotation marks enclose a quotation.
- Use a comma to separate the speaker's exact words from the rest of the sentence when the quotation doesn't end with a question mark or exclamation mark.
- Quotation marks are also used for poetry, song titles, and story titles.

Quotation	Story Title
"Mr. Chung is my favorite teacher," said Joy.	"The Cat Has a Hat"

Practice/Assess Copy and distribute page 360. Have students add quotation marks in the sentences where appropriate. (See answers on page 384.)

Parentheses

Preteach Write and say the following sentence: *Jin has several pets (dog, bird, fish), but he is allergic to cats.* Ask: *What information is provided in the parentheses of this sentence?* Explain: *The information in the parentheses tells us more about Jin's pets.*

Teach/Model Present the concept and provide examples:
- Words in parentheses give an explanation or a comment in an already complete sentence.
- The information in parentheses is not necessary but adds detail to the sentence.

Sentence Without Parentheses	Sentence With Parentheses
Some subjects are very hard for me.	Some subjects (especially math and science) are very hard for me.

Practice/Assess Copy and distribute page 361. Have students add parentheses in the sentences where appropriate. (See answers on page 385.)

Transfer Skills

Quotation Marks
Help students use quotation marks by having them complete the following sentence frame in English: *My favorite song is " _____ ."* Model an answer and write it with quotation marks. Have students repeat. Ask about writing song titles in home languages.

Grammar *in Action*

Correct or Incorrect?
Display correct and incorrect examples of quotation use within a sentence. Write the sentences *"He plays soccer"* (incorrect) and *He said, "I am going to play soccer."* (correct). Offer several examples and ask students to identify correct and incorrect usage.

Transfer Skills

Parentheses
The writing systems of students' home languages may have different conventions for parentheses. Have students practice finding parentheses in classroom texts.

Grammar *in Action*

Oral Language Have students give extra details about a friend by completing the following sentence: *My friend likes to do many things after school (such as _____).*

Name _____

Subjects and Predicates

Practice

- **Look** at the picture. **Read** the sentences.
- **Circle** the complete subject of each sentence. **Underline** the complete predicate of each sentence.

1. The farmer's market is a busy place.

2. The sun shines brightly today.

3. A man sells big, red tomatoes.

4. A woman puts carrots into her bag.

Assess

- **Look** at the picture again. **Write** a subject to begin this sentence.

_____ sells flowers at the market.

Subject-Verb Agreement

Practice

- **Look** at the picture. **Read** the sentences.
- **Circle** the correct verb to complete each sentence.

sandwiches

skate

1. Mom (give, gives) the children sandwiches.

2. The children (enjoy, enjoys) a day at the park.

3. The boys (throw, throws) a ball.

4. The girl (like, likes) to skate.

Assess

- **Write** a sentence about one person or two people doing something at the park. Make sure that the subject and the verb work together.

_____

Word Order

Practice
- **Look** at the picture. **Read** the sentences.
- **Circle** the sentences with the words in the right order.

Welcome to the
ZOO

giraffes

elephants

1. We went to the zoo.
   Went to the zoo we.

2. Elephants I saw the.
   I saw the elephants.

3. Were tall the giraffes.
   The giraffes were tall.

Assess
- **Look** at the picture again. **Write** another sentence about it.

Name _____

Complete Sentences and Sentence Fragments

Practice
- **Look** at the picture. **Read** the groups of words.
- **Write** each group of words that is a complete sentence.

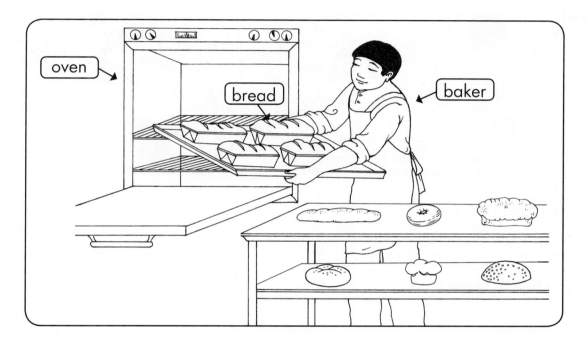

1. How the baker bakes.   The baker bakes bread.

_____

2. He puts the bread into the oven.   Many different breads.

_____

3. Makes delicious bread.   He makes delicious bread.

_____

Assess
- **Choose** one of the fragments. **Add** more words and **make** a complete sentence.

_____

Statements and Questions

Practice
- **Look** at the picture. **Read** the sentences.
- **Write** each sentence correctly. If it is a statement, **end** it with a period. If it is a question, **end** it with a question mark.

1. This is Raquel's party

_____

2. Do you like to dance

_____

3. Raquel's mom takes pictures

_____

4. Len eats pizza

_____

5. What time is it

_____

Assess
- **Look** at the picture again. **Write** another question about Raquel's party. **Start** with one of these words: *did, was, when, how.*

_____

Exclamations and Interjections

Practice
- **Look** at the picture. **Read** the sentences.
- **Write** the exclamation or interjection that each person says.

I am running fast!

Hooray! You will win!

I want to go home!

Assess
- What would you say if you won a contest? **Write** it here.

_____

Name _____

Commands

Practice
- **Look** at the pictures. **Read** the sentences.
- **Circle** the sentences that are commands.

1. Lemonade is easy to make.

2. Squeeze lemon juice into the pitcher.

3. Add water, sugar, and ice.

4. This lemonade is so good!

Assess
- **Write** how to make lemonade. Use only commands. Use these words: *find, cut, squeeze, add.*

_____

_____

Name _____

Simple and Compound Sentences

Practice
- **Look** at the picture. **Read** the compound sentences.
- **Write** the two simple sentences in each compound sentence.

bowl of cereal

1. Mom needs to go to work, but Jon is still eating his cereal.

_____

_____

2. Jon needs to hurry, or Mom will be late for work.

_____

_____

3. Jon finishes his cereal, and they both run out the door.

_____

_____

Assess
- Do you think Jon's mom will be late for work? **Write** a compound sentence about it.

_____

_____

Name _____

Combining Sentences

Practice

- **Look** at the picture. **Read** the sentences.
- **Combine** each pair of sentences. Use the underlined words only once in the new sentence.

1. Dad <u>went to the park</u>. I <u>went to the park</u>.

_____

2. <u>Dad</u> sat on a bench. <u>Dad</u> read his book.

_____

3. <u>I</u> found a stick. <u>I</u> threw it.

_____

4. <u>My dog</u> ran far. <u>My dog</u> got the stick.

_____

Assess

- **Write** another sentence using one of the underlined parts.

_____

_____

Name _____

Complex Sentences

Practice
- **Look** at the picture.
- **Read** the sentences. **Check** the circle next to the ones that are complex sentences.

painting

painter

1. ○ I watch Tran because she is a good painter.
   ○ She is making a big, beautiful painting!

2. ○ I want a painting for my room.
   ○ Since this painting is big, Tran will put it in Mom's room.

3. ○ Tran will make a smaller painting.
   ○ She will start it when she finishes this one.

Assess
- **Write** another complex sentence about the girl who is painting.

_____

_____

Independent and Dependent Clauses

Practice
- **Look** at the picture. **Read** the sentences.
- **Circle** the dependent clause in each sentence.

basketball

1. After I do my homework, I play basketball.

2. When David is there, he plays with me.

3. We play until we are very tired.

4. David goes home because he has homework.

Assess
- **Write** a sentence that starts with *When David goes home.*

_____

_____

Name _____

Commas

Practice

- **Look** at the picture.
- **Read** the sentences. **Add** commas where they are needed.

1. Gino's the new Italian restaurant has great food.

2. Mom thank you for buying us dinner.

3. I want soup salad pizza and lemonade.

4. Well I hope you can eat all that!

Assess

- **Write** three things you would order at your favorite restaurant. Then **read** your sentence to a partner. Remember to **pause** after each comma.

_____

_____

Quotation Marks

Practice
- **Read** the sentences.
- **Add** quotation marks.

1. I am excited about our skating lesson, said Aunt Beverly.

2. David said, I think you will be great.

3. What if I fall down on the ice? Aunt Beverly asked.

4. I fell down the first time too, David said. But you should keep trying.

5. I will feel better if you stay close to me, Aunt Beverly said.

6. Don't worry, David said, I will.

Parentheses

Practice

- **Read** the sentences.
- **Add** parentheses.

1. Anita and her father are making dinner. They need different cooking utensils pan, spoons, cups, knife for their dish.

2. Anita put the food eggs, sausage, cheese, bread on the counter.

3. Her father showed her how to prepare cutting, pouring, stirring the dish.

4. When they were finished, Anita and her father put the rest of the meal vegetables, potatoes on the table.

5. Anita told the rest of her family mother, sister, brother that dinner was ready.

Assess

- **Write** another sentence with parentheses about the picture.

_____

_____

Pronouns

Copyright © Pearson Education, Inc., or its affiliates. All Rights Reserved. 5

Subject Pronouns

Preteach Point to yourself and say *I am a teacher.* Point to the students and say *You are students.* Point to a boy and say *He is a student.* Point to a girl and say *She is a student.* Indicate everyone in the room and say *We are at school.* Explain: *Pronouns such as* I, you, he, she, we, *and* they *are used in place of nouns or noun phrases such as people's names. These pronouns are used for subjects of sentences. We do not say "Me am a teacher" or "Him is a student."*

Teach/Model Present the concept and provide examples:
* A subject pronoun is used as the subject of a sentence.

	Subject Pronouns
Singular	I, you, he, she, it
Plural	we, you, they

Practice/Assess Copy and distribute page 365. Review gender and number of subject pronouns. (See answers on page 385.)

Transfer Skills

Subject Pronouns
* In Spanish, unlike English, speakers may omit subject pronouns because Spanish verbs can indicate the subjects.
* Korean speakers may add a subject pronoun after the noun, reflecting a pattern in Korean: *Nathan, he is my brother.*

Grammar *in Action*

Oral Language Say these sentences, and have students rephrase them using subject pronouns: <u>Ana</u> *sits in the third row.* <u>Max</u> *sits here.* <u>Ana and Max</u> *are cousins.* <u>The sandwich</u> *is the teacher's lunch.*

Object Pronouns

Preteach Display these sentences: *Give the book to* <u>me</u>. *Mom made* <u>us</u> *a snack. They talked with* <u>Tom and her</u>. Explain: *Pronouns such as* me, you, him, her, us, *and* them *are used after verbs, or after words such as* for, at, with, *or* to. *We do not say "Give the book to I" or "Mom made we a snack."*

Teach/Model Present the concept and provide examples:
* An object pronoun is used in the predicate, after an action verb or preposition.

	Object Pronouns
Singular	me, you, him, her, it
Plural	us, you, them

Practice/Assess Copy and distribute page 366. Help students describe the picture. (See answers on page 385.)

Transfer Skills

Object Pronouns
Spanish, Chinese, and Vietnamese speakers and other English learners may use subject pronouns as objects *(Give the book to she.)* until practice in English clarifies the different pronoun forms.

Grammar *in Action*

Oral Language Pose open-ended sentences, cueing object pronoun endings by gesturing to different people in the room: *I will help....* [gesture toward a girl]. Students should finish the sentence: *her.*

Possessive Pronouns

Preteach Hold a book and say: *This is my book. This book is mine.* Explain: *The words* my *and* mine *are possessive pronouns. They show that I have this book. Possessive pronouns show who or what has or owns something.*

Teach/Model Present the concept and provide examples:
- Use *my, your, her, our,* and *their* before nouns.
- Use *mine, yours, hers, ours,* and *theirs* alone.
- *His* and *its* can be used before nouns and alone.

Possessive Pronouns
Before nouns: This is your pen. It is her doll.
Alone: The shoes are mine. The doll is hers.
Both: The pen is his. This is his home.

Practice/Assess Copy and distribute page 367. Have students read their sentences aloud. (See answers on page 385.)

Pronouns and Antecedents

Preteach Display these sentences: *Sam says he will go.* Explain: *In this sentence, the pronoun* he *replaces the name Sam. The sentence does not have to say, "Sam says Sam will go." Sam, the noun being replaced, is called the* antecedent. *A pronoun must agree in number and gender with the noun or noun phrase it replaces. Sam is one person, a boy. So we use the pronoun* he, *which is singular and masculine. The pronoun for a girl is feminine:* she. *Lisa says she will go.*

Teach/Model Present the concept and provide examples:
- A pronoun and its antecedent must agree in number and gender.

Pronouns and Antecedents
Laura knows what she wants.
Bobi and Ben call me when they get home.
The parrot repeats what it hears.

Practice/Assess Copy and distribute page 368. Remind students that singular antecedents are either masculine, feminine, or neuter. (See answers on page 385.)

Transfer Skills

Possessive Pronouns
Students who speak Asian languages may try various forms for possessive pronouns—*the hat of her, you hat*—or may not always state the pronoun (*Mo Yun took off hat*). Provide practice with possessive pronouns.

Grammar *in Action*

Oral Language Have students look around the room and identify objects that belong to them or to someone else. Have them use each item in a sentence with a possessive pronoun: *Here is my pencil. This calculator is yours.*

Transfer Skills

Third-Person Pronouns
Some Asian languages emphasize distinctions such as older and younger people rather than gender pronouns. At first, students may use pronouns that do not match the antecedents—*Joanne and his family; throw the ball to it* (rather than *him*).

Grammar *in Action*

Antecedent Agreement
Display this sentence: *The cat eats what it likes.* Write the following on cards and distribute to students: *The girl; My brother; The children; The teacher; she; he; they.* Invite students to substitute antecedents and pronouns in the sentence using the cards.

Pronouns

Indefinite Pronouns

Preteach Display this sentence: <u>Someone</u> *wrote you a note.* Ask: *Who is this someone? If we don't know, then we can use an indefinite pronoun:* someone. *Other singular indefinite pronouns are:* anybody, everyone, everything, either, each. *Some plural indefinite pronouns are:* few, several, both, others, many, all, some.

Teach/Model Present the concept and provide examples:
- Indefinite pronouns may not refer to specific nouns.
- Use the correct verb forms with singular indefinite pronouns and with plural indefinite pronouns.

	Indefinite Pronouns
Singular	<u>Everyone</u> is clapping. <u>Somebody</u> has sung very well.
Plural	<u>Some</u> are standing. <u>Others</u> are sitting.

Practice/Assess Copy and distribute page 369 after teaching *Reflexive Pronouns.*

Reflexive Pronouns

Preteach Display these sentences: *I will write a note to <u>myself</u>. She will buy <u>herself</u> a snack. Explain:* Myself *and* herself *are reflexive pronouns.*

Teach/Model Present the concept and provide examples:
- Reflexive pronouns reflect the action back on the subject: *They gave themselves a chance to rest.*
- Reflexive pronouns end in *-self* or *-selves.*

	Reflexive Pronouns
Singular	himself, herself, myself, itself, yourself
Plural	ourselves, yourselves, themselves

Practice/Assess Copy and distribute page 369. Have students read the completed sentences aloud. (See answers on page 385.)

Subject Pronouns

Practice

- **Look** at the picture. **Read** each sentence.
- **Circle** the correct pronoun in parentheses.

1. David and (I, me) are good friends.

2. (Us, We) ride the bus together every morning.

3. Today there were many cars. (Them, They) moved very slowly.

4. David had a phone, so (he, him) called the school.

Assess

- **Write** a sentence about the students on the bus. **Start** with the subject pronoun *They.*

Object Pronouns

Practice
- **Look** at the picture. **Read** the sentences.
- **Circle** the correct pronoun to complete each sentence.

The Spanish Club is having a book sale. Mrs. Ruiz asked Jen and (me, I) to collect

books. Many students bought books from (we, us). I had fun selling (them, they).

How many books are left? I will count (it, them).

Assess
- **Write** another sentence about the book sale. Use *him* or *her.*

_____

Possessive Pronouns

Practice

- **Look** at the picture. **Read** the sentences.
- **Circle** the correct possessive pronoun in parentheses.

1. Mr. Sims is (our, ours) neighbor.

2. (His, Her) bird flew out of (it's, its) cage.

3. Did you find a yellow bird in (yours, your) tree?

4. That bird is (his, theirs).

Assess

- **Write** a sentence about the yellow bird. Use the possessive pronoun *its*.

_____

Name _____

Pronouns and Antecedents

Practice
- **Look** at the picture. **Read** the sentences.
- **Circle** the correct pronoun in each sentence. The antecedent is underlined for you.

1. Cecilia wanted to surprise <u>Ali</u> in (her, their) new home.

2. Cecilia bought <u>balloons</u> and gave (they, them) to Ali.

3. <u>Ali</u> said, "(I, We) am so surprised!"

4. <u>Balloons</u> are fun, and (them, they) make people happy.

Assess
- **Look** at the picture again. **Write** another sentence about the balloons. Use the word *they* or *them*.

_____

Name _____

Indefinite and Reflexive Pronouns

Practice

- **Look** at the picture. **Read** the sentences.
- **Circle** the correct pronoun in parentheses to complete each sentence.

1. (Other, Someone) left a note on my desk.

2. I read it out loud to (myself, itself).

3. It said that (everyone, either) thinks I am a good writer.

4. (Somethings, No one) heard me read the note.

5. Maybe the writer of the note will identify (himself, ourselves).

Assess

- **Write** a sentence about yourself. Use a reflexive pronoun.

Articles, Adjectives, and Adverbs

Transfer Skills

Articles

- Spanish speakers may use the word *one* in place of the article *a* (or *an*), just as *un/una* is used in Spanish. Students may use *ones* as a plural article.
- English learners may use (or omit) the article *the* differently from native English speakers—*I like the science; my cousin is nurse.*

Grammar *in Action*

Time to Listen Copy and distribute a simple newspaper article. Read it aloud and have students follow along, highlighting the articles they encounter.

Articles

Preteach Say: *I need a pencil.* Hold up a pencil and say: *Here is a pencil with an eraser. The pencil is yellow.* Show some pencils: *The pencils are new.* Explain that *a*, *an*, and *the* are called *articles*: *Articles are these words that come before nouns: A pencil, the paper, an ink pen. Use a or an before a singular noun. You can use the before singular nouns or plural nouns.*

Teach/Model Present the concept and provide examples:
- *A*, *an*, and *the* are articles.
- Use *a* before a singular noun that begins with a consonant sound; use *an* before a singular noun that begins with a vowel sound.

Articles
I want <u>a</u> banana. Sue wants <u>an</u> apple.
<u>The</u> fruit salad was good. <u>The</u> girls ate it all.

Practice/Assess Copy and distribute page 373. Explain that *an* is used before a word beginning with silent *h*. (See answers on page 385.)

Transfer Skills

Adjectives

- Spanish adjectives have endings that match the gender and number of nouns they modify. Assure students that English adjectives do not have these endings.
- In Spanish and Vietnamese, adjectives often follow nouns.

Grammar *in Action*

Oral Language Have a student describe a classmate: *She is smart. She is quiet. She is wearing a blue sweater.* Whoever correctly guesses the classmate gives the next clues.

Adjectives

Size, What Kind, How Many

Preteach Say: *You know that nouns are words that name people, places, animals, or things—for example,* girls *and* house. *Adjectives are words that tell more about the nouns:* small house, four girls, blue car, long hair. *Which words are the adjectives?* (small, four, blue, long)

Teach/Model Present the concept and provide examples:
- An adjective tells more about a noun or pronoun.

	Adjectives
What Kind?	a <u>good</u> friend; The food is <u>spicy.</u>
How Many?	<u>two</u> men; <u>many</u> apples
Size	a <u>big</u> hat; The school was <u>small</u>.

Practice/Assess Copy and distribute page 374. Explain the chart to students. (See answers on page 385.)

Comparative and Superlative Adjectives

Preteach Draw three long lines of different lengths on the board. Point to the different lines and say: *This line is long. This line is longer. This line is the longest.* Say: *Long is an adjective. Longer compares two nouns, like two lines. To compare two nouns, add -er to most adjectives. Longest compares three or more nouns. To make a superlative adjective, add -est to most adjectives.*

Teach/Model Present the concept and provide examples:
* Many comparative adjectives end in *-er: faster, thinner, tinier.* Change the spelling of some adjectives, like *tiny,* when you add *-er.*
* Many longer adjectives use the word *more* instead of *-er: more exciting, more beautiful.*
* Many superlative adjectives end in *-est: brightest, loudest, tallest.* Use *most* with longer adjectives: *most beautiful.*
* Some adjectives have irregular forms, such as *good, better, best.*

Comparative	Superlative
bigger; more important	fastest; most difficult

Practice/Assess Copy and distribute page 375. Discuss the completed sentences. (See answers on page 385.)

Demonstrative Adjectives

Preteach Present three girls and three boys, with the boys farther away. Ask: *Which students are girls? These students are girls. Those students are boys. Which girl is Tina? This girl is Tina. That boy is Ben. These, those, this, and that are called* demonstrative adjectives. *They help you demonstrate, or show, which one or which ones. Use* this *and* these *when things are close. Use* that *and* those *when things are far.*

Teach/Model Present the concept and provide examples:
* Demonstrative adjectives: *this, that, these, those*

	Demonstrative Adjectives
Singular	<u>This</u> book is longer than <u>that</u> book.
Plural	<u>These</u> shoes are bigger than <u>those</u> shoes.

Practice/Assess Copy and distribute page 376. Remind students that *this* and *that* are used with singular nouns. (See answers on page 385.)

Transfer Skills

Comparative and Superlative Adjectives
Speakers of African and Asian languages may use English adjectives in patterns from their first languages: *She was the most fastest runner. My story is less longer than yours.*

Grammar *in Action*

Classroom Comparisons
Have pairs of students find pairs or sets of objects in the classroom to compare. For example, one pencil might be longer than another, while one book might be the heaviest of three. Have pairs present their findings.

Transfer Skills

This and That
In certain languages, including Korean, the relationship between expressing *this* and *that* and *here* and *there* does not correspond exactly to the way these terms are used in English. Clarify that the words *this* and *that* can modify nouns.

Grammar *in Action*

Oral Language Provide two sets of word cards for a game of Concentration. Place both sets face down, and have students find matching pairs. As they play, they should say: *I want this card, I want that card,* or *These cards match.*

Transfer Skills

Adverbs

- English learners may use adjectives as adverbs. Help students use adverbs.
- Point out to Spanish speakers that the adverb suffix -ly is like the ending -mente in Spanish. Give examples with cognates such as *rapidly/rápidamente*.

Grammar *in Action*

Time to Listen Write adverbs on slips of paper: *slowly, quickly, loudly, sleepily*. Display them. Have a volunteer choose one. Give a command, such as *Walk to the door*. The volunteer must walk in the manner of the adverb. The student who guesses the adverb takes the next turn.

Transfer Skills

Comparative Adverbs
English phrases can be challenging for students whose home languages use different phrasing, and students may say or write: *running quickly more than you* or *studying more hard than you*. Model sentences with comparative adverbs.

Grammar *in Action*

Oral Language Display 3 pictures of athletes. Have students compare them, using *well, better, best* or *fast, faster, fastest* with verbs *run, play*, or *swim*.

Adverbs

Adverbs for When, Where, and How

Preteach Say and act out this chant: *Slowly I turn. Loudly I clap! I walk here and there. I end with a tap.* Say: Slowly, loudly, here, and there *are adverbs. They tell how, when, or where something happens.*

Teach/Model Present the concept and provide examples:
- Adverbs tell more about the actions of verbs.
- Adverbs that tell *how* something happens often end in *-ly*.

	Adverbs
When?	I <u>always</u> walk to school.
Where?	I like to walk <u>outside</u>.
How?	I walk <u>quickly</u>.

Practice/Assess Copy and distribute page 377. Explain that an adverb can come before or after the verb. (See answers on page 386.)

Comparative and Superlative Adverbs

Preteach Say each sentence: *I speak quietly. Katya speaks more quietly. Raúl speaks most quietly.* More quietly *is a comparative adverb. It compares two actions:* I speak, Katya speaks. Most quietly *is a superlative adverb. It compares three or more actions. If an adverb does not end in* -ly, *add* -er *or* -est *to compare.*

Teach/Model Present the concept and provide examples:
- A comparative adverb compares two actions.
- A superlative adverb compares three or more actions.
- Some adverbs are irregular: *well, better, best.*

Comparative and Superlative Adverbs
Julia runs <u>fast</u>. Anil sings <u>beautifully</u>.
Pat runs <u>faster</u>. Kenji sings <u>more</u> <u>beautifully</u>.
Tere runs the <u>fastest</u>. Ivan sings <u>most</u> <u>beautifully</u>.

Practice/Assess Copy and distribute page 378. Remind students that *more* or *most* are not added to an adverb that already has an -er or -est ending. (See answers on page 386.)

Name _____

Articles

Practice

- **Look** at the picture. **Read** the sentences.
- **Circle** the article in parentheses that completes each sentence.

1. Cali, Beth, and Lyn found (an, a) rope in their garage.

2. (An, The) rope was six feet long.

3. Beth knew (a, an) song for jumping rope.

4. (The, A) girls jumped rope for (a, an) hour.

Assess

- What can you do for an hour? **Write** about it here. Use articles.

_____

Name _____

Adjectives for Size, What Kind, How Many

Practice
- **Look** at the picture. **Read** the story.
- **Circle** the adjectives in the story.

My two brothers and I have a small garden. We have three plants. The plants have many

tomatoes that are big and red. They are delicious!

Assess
- **Write** the adjectives from the story in the chart.

Size	What Kind	How Many

ELL Handbook

Comparative and Superlative Adjectives

Practice
- **Look** at the picture. **Read** the sentences.
- **Write** the correct adjective to complete each sentence.

Buffy   Max   Chico

1. Buffy is _____ than Chico. (smaller, smallest)

2. Chico is the _____ of the three dogs. (largest, larger)

3. Max is _____ than Buffy. (more beautiful, beautifulest)

4. The big dog should have a _____ name. (gooder, better)

5. Buffy has the _____ name of all. (funniest, funnier)

Assess
- **Write** your own sentence that compares one of the dogs to another dog.

_____

Name _____

Demonstrative Adjectives

Practice
- **Look** at the picture. **Read** the sentences.
- **Circle** the correct adjective to complete each sentence.

1. (These, This) flowers are called poppies.

2. Each spring, (this, these) field is full of poppies.

3. (That, Those) tree on the hill looks like a person.

4. People ride their bikes in (those, this) hills.

5. Many people take pictures of (this, these) place.

Assess
- **Look** at the picture again. **Write** another sentence about the field. Use *this, that, these,* or *those.*

ELL Handbook

Name _____

Adverbs for When, Where, and How

Practice
- **Look** at the picture. **Read** the sentences.
- **Circle** the correct adverb for each sentence.

1. My sister sings (loudly, neatly).

2. I stand (outside, below) and listen.

3. She sings (beautifully, safely)!

4. I (always, yesterday) like listening to my sister sing.

Assess
- **Write** a sentence that tells how, when, or where you do something. Use an adverb.

_____

Name _____

Comparative and Superlative Adverbs

Practice
- **Look** at the picture. **Read** the sentences.
- **Circle** the correct adverb to complete each sentence.

1. The stars shine (more brightly, brightly) in the country than in the city.

2. The dogs bark (louder, more louder) here.

3. I sleep (better, goodly) with the window closed.

4. People walk (more faster, faster) in the city.

5. This is the place I like to visit the (later, most).

Assess
- Do you like the city or the country better? **Write** a sentence about it.
  Include an adverb.

_____

Prepositions and Prepositional Phrases

Preteach Stand behind a chair, and have students do the same. Say: *Behind the chair,* and have students repeat. Continue moving and speaking with *beside, around,* and *on* (sit). Explain: Behind, beside, around, *and* on *are prepositions.* Behind the chair *and* on it *are prepositional phrases.* Behind *is a preposition, and* chair *is a noun.* On *is a preposition, and* it *is a pronoun.*

Teach/Model Present the concept and provide examples:
- A prepositional phrase can tell where, when, how, or which one.
- A prepositional phrase begins with a preposition (*above, across, at, behind, for, from, in, near, with,* and so on).
- It ends with a noun or pronoun.

Preposition	around
Prepositional Phrase	around the chair

Practice/Assess Copy and distribute page 380. Help students describe the picture. (See answers on page 386.)

Conjunctions

Preteach Use colored pens or markers to illustrate: *I have a red pen <u>and</u> a green pen.* The word *and joins two similar things: two colors of pens. Do you like red <u>or</u> green better? The word* or *gives a choice: red or green. You can use the green pen, <u>but</u> don't use the red pen right now. The word* but *joins two different ideas: use and don't use. Or, but, and and are called* conjunctions.

Teach/Model Present the concept and provide examples:
- A conjunction joins words, phrases, and sentences.

Related ideas: *Pak <u>and</u> I are friends.*
Different ideas: *We live far apart, <u>but</u> we talk often.*
Choice: *We talk on the phone <u>or</u> we send e-mail.*

Practice/Assess Copy and distribute page 381. Help students name the items in the picture. (See answers on page 386.)

Transfer Skills

Prepositional Phrases
Prepositional phrases will be familiar to speakers of various langues, but students may choose prepositions based on home-language usage or meanings: *in Friday; on April; until there.*

Grammar *in Action*

Following Directions
Model as you give students directions to follow: *Walk to this side of the room. Walk across the room. Stand by a desk. Look under the desk.* Have volunteers take turns giving directions that include prepositional phrases.

Transfer Skills

Conjunctions
Speakers of Chinese and some other languages may build sentences using two conjunctions where English typically uses one: *Because the sun came up, so I could see the clock.* Help students practice English patterns.

Grammar *in Action*

Common Phrases Share these common phrases with conjunctions: *salt and pepper; thanks, but no thanks; stop-and-go traffic; left or right; boy or girl.* Invite students to say them while using gestures to help show the meanings.

Name _____

Prepositions

Practice

- **Look** at the picture. **Read** the sentences.
- **Circle** the correct preposition to complete each sentence.

1. We are (behind, at) the lake.

2. I play a game called "catch" (with, over) my dad.

3. Jeff walks (after, near) the water.

4. Mom sits (under, on) a chair and reads.

5. Ducks swim (in, from) the water.

Assess

- **Write** a sentence about the lake. Use a prepositional phrase.

_____

ELL Handbook

Name _____

Conjunctions

Practice

- **Look** at the picture. **Read** the sentences.
- **Circle** the correct conjunction to complete each sentence.

1. Are you ready to order, (but, or) do you want me to come back later?

2. I want a tuna sandwich, (and, or) the young lady wants soup.

3. Do you want a roll, (or, but) do you want a salad with your lunch?

4. I would like a salad, (or, but) please do not put salad dressing on it.

Assess

- What do you think the waiter said next? **Write** a sentence that has one of these words: *and, but, or.*

_____

Answer Key

page 318: Common Nouns

Practice

People: father, boys, woman; **Places:** soccer field, playground, park office; **Animals:** rabbit; **Things:** swing, ball, bike

Assess

Answers will vary. Students should write the names of items found in the classroom.

page 319: Special Names

Practice

Names of Children: Alex, Karen, Tuan; **Names of Animals:** Spot, Lulu, Speedy, Goldie; **Names of Places:** Greenview School, Hope Garden, Barton Library

Assess

Answers will vary. Students should write the names of specific places and people, beginning each name with a capital letter.

page 320: Titles and Abbreviations

Practice

1. Mr. Turner; **2.** Dr. Lisa Johnson; **3.** Miss Eva Santos; **4.** Mr. Mark Tanaka

Assess

Answers will vary. Verify that students include a title such as Mr., Ms., Mrs., Miss, and Dr. when writing each names of adults they know.

page 321: Days, Months, and Holidays

Practice

1. Thanksgiving; **2.** Veterans Day; **3.** Friday, November 30; **4.** Tuesday, November 6; **5.** on Wednesdays

Assess

Sunday, Monday, Tuesday, Wednesday, Thursday, Friday, Saturday; Answers will vary. Students should begin the name of each holiday and each month with a capital letter.

page 322: Singular and Plural Nouns

Practice

Singular Nouns: nest, bird, sun; **Plural Nouns:** men, butterflies, feet, leaves, benches

Assess

Answers will vary but should include three singular and three plural nouns. Students should write the names of items found in the classroom.

page 323: Singular and Plural Possessive Nouns

Practice

1. Today's; **2.** children's; **3.** reader's; **4.** ladies'

Assess

Answers will vary. For sentences using singular possessive nouns, students may choose *reader's* or *today's*. For sentences using plural possessive nouns, students may choose *children's* or *ladies'*.

page 330: Verbs in Present Tense

Practice

1. wait; **2.** talks; **3.** sits; **4.** see

Assess

Answers will vary, but students may write a sentence such as *The dog barks.*

page 331: Verbs in Past Tense

Practice

celebrated; gave; played; made; had

Assess

Answers will vary, but students may write *We ate apples at the picnic.*

page 332: Verbs in Future Tense

Practice

The mother bird <u>will find</u> food for the babies. In a few days, she <u>will teach</u> them to fly. Soon, the baby birds <u>will grow</u> big and strong. They <u>will fly</u> away from the nest.

Assess

Answers will vary, but students may write a sentence such as *The mother bird will go too.*

page 333: Principal Parts of Regular Verbs

Practice

1. *has started*, past participle; **2.** *listen*, present; **3.** *are playing*, present participle; **4.** *has played*, past participle; **5.** *plays*, present

Assess

Answers will vary, but students may write a sentence such as *Ray is playing the flute.*

page 334: Principal Parts of Irregular Verbs

Practice

1. *went*, past; **2.** *go*, present; **3.** *have grown*, past participle; **4.** *am growing*, present participle

Assess

Answers will vary, but students may write a sentence such as *The doctor wrote on the chart.*

page 335: Helping Verbs

Practice

1. <u>are</u> learning; **2.** <u>have</u> seen; **3.** <u>am</u> using; **4.** <u>will</u> give

Assess

Answers will vary, but students may write a sentence such as *She will tell her friends about dolphins.*

page 336: Linking Verbs

Practice

1. *am;* **2.** *feel;* **3.** *seems;* **4.** *is*

Assess

Answers will vary, but students may write *The girl is sick.*

page 337: Contractions and Negatives

Practice

1. *I'm;* **2.** *Shouldn't;* **3.** *I've;* **4.** *You're;* **5.** *ever*

Assess

Answers will vary, but students may write *The dad didn't know she already did her homework.*

page 338: Troublesome Verbs Lie/Lay, Sit/Set

Practice

1. lies; **2.** sit; **3.** set; **4.** lays

Assess

Answers will vary, but students may write *The cat lies on the bed.*

page 339: Troublesome Verbs Leave/Let, Rise/Raise

Practice

1. leave; **2.** Let; **3.** raise; **4.** leave; **5.** rise

Assess

Answers will vary, but should include *leave, let, rise,* or *raise.*

page 348: Subjects and Predicates

Practice

1. The farmer's market / is a busy place;
2. The sun / shines brightly today;
3. A man / sells big, red tomatoes;
4. A woman / puts carrots into her bag.

Assess

Answers will vary, but students may begin the sentence with *A woman.*

page 349: Subject-Verb Agreement

Practice

1. gives; **2.** enjoy; **3.** throw; **4.** likes

Assess

Answers will vary. Check for subject-verb agreement.

page 350: Word Order

Practice

1. We went to the zoo. **2.** I saw the elephants. **3.** The giraffes were tall.

Assess

Answers will vary, but make sure students start sentences with the subject or use another word order that makes sense.

page 351: Complete Sentences and Sentence Fragments

Practice

1. The baker bakes bread. **2.** He puts the bread into the oven. **3.** He makes delicious bread.

Assess

Answers will vary but should be complete sentences.

page 352: Statements and Questions

Practice

1. This is Raquel's party. **2.** Do you like to dance? **3.** Raquel's mom takes pictures. **4.** Len eats pizza. **5.** What time is it?

Assess

Answers will vary; possible questions: *Did you go to Raquel's party? Was it fun? When did people dance?*

page 353: Exclamations and Interjections

Practice

Runner would think: "I am running fast!"
Friend would say: "Hooray! You will win!"
Crying boy would say: "I want to go home!"

Assess

Answers will vary. Encourage students to imagine themselves winning at a school or sports competition. Some suggestions: *Hooray! Wow! I worked so hard!*

page 354: Commands

Practice

Sentences 2 and 3 are commands.

Assess

Answers will vary, but students may write *First, find a pitcher and some lemons. Cut the lemons. Squeeze the lemons. Add water, sugar, and ice.*

page 355: Simple and Compound Sentences

Practice

1. Mom needs to go to work. Jon is still eating his cereal. **2.** Jon needs to hurry. Mom will be late for work. **3.** Jon finishes his cereal. They both run out the door.

Assess

Answers will vary, but students may write *Jon will not be late for school, and Mom will not be late for work.*

page 356: Combining Sentences

Practice

1. Dad and I went to the park. **2.** Dad sat on a bench and read his book. **3.** I found a stick and threw it. **4.** My dog ran far and got the stick.

Assess

Answers will vary, but sample answers include: *My friend and I went to the park. Dad drove us there and read his book. I played with my friend and with my dog. My dog was happy and playful.*

page 357: Complex Sentences

Practice

1. I watch Tran because she is a good painter; **2.** Since this painting is big, Tran will put it in Mom's room; **3.** She will start it when she finishes this one.

Assess

Answers will vary, but students may write sentences such as *When Tran finishes this painting, she will make another one. Since Tran's sister wants a painting, Tran will make one.*

page 358: Independent and Dependent Clauses

Practice

1. After I do my homework; **2.** When David is there; **3.** until we are very tired; **4.** because he has homework

Assess

Answers will vary, but sample answers include: *When David goes home, I go home also. When David goes home, he does his homework.*

page 359: Commas

Practice

1. Gino's, the new Italian restaurant, has great food. **2.** Mom, thank you for buying us dinner. **3.** I want soup, salad, pizza, and lemonade. **4.** Well, I hope you can eat all that!

Assess

Answers will vary, but make sure students use a comma after each menu item in the series.

page 360: Quotation Marks

Practice

1. "I am excited about our skating lesson," said Aunt Beverly. **2.** David said, "I think you will be great." **3.** "What if I fall down on the ice?" Aunt Beverly asked. **4.** "I fell down the first time too," David said. "But you should keep trying." **5.** "I will feel better if you stay close to me," Aunt Beverly said. **6.** "Don't worry," David said, "I will."

page 361: Parentheses

Practice
1. They need different cooking utensils (pan, spoons, cups, knife) for their dish. **2.** Anita put the food (eggs, sausage, cheese, bread) on the counter. **3.** Her father showed her how to prepare (cutting, pouring, stirring) the dish. **4.** When they were finished, Anita and her father put the rest of the meal (vegetables, potatoes) on the table. **5.** Anita told the rest of her family (mother, sister, brother) that dinner was ready.

Assess
Answers will vary, but make sure students use parentheses correctly.

page 365: Subject Pronouns

Practice
1. I; **2.** We; **3.** They; **4.** he

Assess
Answers will vary, but students may write a sentence such as *They were late for school.*

page 366: Object Pronouns

Practice
me; us; them; them

Assess
Answers will vary, but students may write a sentence such as *Jen gave the book to him.*

page 367: Possessive Pronouns

Practice
1. our; **2.** His, its; **3.** your; **4.** his

Assess
Answers will vary, but students may write a sentence such as *The bird will fly to its cage.*

page 368: Pronouns and Antecedents

Practice
1. her; **2.** them; **3.** I; **4.** they

Assess
Answers will vary, but students may write a sentence such as *Ali loved the balloons because they were from her friend.*

page 369: Indefinite and Reflexive Pronouns

Practice
1. Someone; **2.** myself; **3.** everyone; **4.** No one; **5.** himself

Assess
Answers will vary, but students may write a sentence such as *I like to teach myself English words.*

page 373: Articles

Practice
1. a; **2.** The; **3.** a; **4.** The, an

Assess
Answers will vary, but students may write a sentence such as *I can play baseball for an hour.*

page 374: Adjectives for Size, What Kind, How Many

Practice
two; small; three; many; big; red; delicious

Assess
Size: small, big; **What Kind:** red, delicious; **How Many:** two, three, many

page 375: Comparative and Superlative Adjectives

Practice
1. smaller; **2.** largest; **3.** more beautiful; **4.** better; **5.** funniest

Assess
Answers will vary, but students may write a sentence such as *Max is larger than Buffy.*

page 376: Demonstrative Adjectives

Practice
1. These; **2.** this; **3.** That; **4.** those; **5.** this

Assess
Answers will vary, but students may write a sentence such as *This field is beautiful.*

page 377: Adverbs for When, Where, and How

Practice
1. loudly; **2.** outside; **3.** beautifully; **4.** always

Assess
Answers will vary, but students may write a sentence such as *I run quickly.*

page 378: Comparative and Superlative Adverbs

Practice
1. more brightly; **2.** louder; **3.** better; **4.** faster; **5.** most

Assess
Answers will vary, but students may write a sentence such as *I like the city better.*

page 380: Prepositions

Practice
1. at; **2.** with; **3.** near; **4.** on; **5.** in

Assess
Answers will vary, but students may write a sentence such as *Ducks live near the lake.*

page 381: Conjunctions

Practice
1. or; **2.** and; **3.** or; **4.** but

Assess
Answers will vary, but students may write a sentence such as *Thank you for your order, and I will be back soon.*

Part 5
Workshops for English Language Learners

Contents

Introduction to Workshops for English Language Learners

To develop their skills in English, English language learners need instruction that integrates speaking, listening, reading, and writing. While core lesson content encourages the development of these skills, English language learners need targeted instruction to navigate listening and speaking in situations that, for native speakers, come naturally. Students who are first using spoken English may have difficulty in areas such as the following:

- knowing appropriate times to use formal and informal English.
- using the correct syntax patterns for sentences, including placement of nouns, verbs, adjectives, and prepositions
- expressing opinions and feelings
- using the transactional language of the classroom
- retelling or summarizing a message in English

In addition, students who are newcomers or who have not interacted with instructional materials in English may have difficulty with the following:

- interacting with environmental print and understanding what information they can get from reading the words around them
- using classroom resources
- expanding their knowledge and use of academic vocabulary words
- using graphic organizers to record ideas and organize information

Each one of these lessons covers a particular topic with a lesson for the teacher and a reproducible blackline master for students. The lessons are designed to be fluid and needs-based. Some of the lessons will correspond to your teaching with the core program, while others can be introduced when students have a need for the instruction. The workshop on group discussion, for example, can be introduced when you notice that students are struggling to use the transactional give-and-take language in group discussions.

All Workshops follow the same format:

- A **Preteach** section provides simple scripted language that allows you to introduce the strategy or skill.
- The **Teach/Model** section involves students while you carefully scaffold instruction in the skill or strategy.
- In the **Practice** section, students begin to take ownership of the skill, sometimes through practice with a blackline master, and sometimes through interaction with peers.
- Each workshop includes an **Assess** section, with ideas for both assessment and corrective feedback.
- **Leveled Support** suggestions allow students to practice the skills at their individual levels of proficiency and progress from level to level.
- An accompanying **blackline master** allows for practice with the skill. The master often includes a rubric for self-assessment or a word bank to which students can add their ideas throughout the year.

Many of the blackline masters can be used multiple times. Based on students' needs, consider how to integrate the workshops into your instruction and use them multiple times to measure students' growth as users of classroom and conversational English.

In addition to the workshops, support students' development of spoken English with activities such as the following:

- **Answering questions**. Have students answer questions that you pose, first with yes/no questions and then with longer answers. Supply sentence frames and models as necessary.
- **Have dialogues**. Use various scenarios to have dialogues with students before having them pair up to have conversations of their own.
- **Picture the conversation**. Show students a photograph of people immersed in conversation in a familiar setting. Have them talk about what the people in the picture might be saying. Encourage them to role-play.

Use Informal English

Preteach Model informal language for students and explain: *The words I use depend on who I am talking to and why I am speaking. When I am talking with my friends in casual situations, I use informal language. I might use slang words. I might speak in sentences that are not complete. I usually don't organize my ideas before I speak. It's more like having a conversation.*

Teach/Model With a volunteer, act out the scene on the right side of the page. Model using informal language, such as sentence fragments. Then model rating your knowledge using the rubric.

Practice Direct students to look at the second picture. Explain that in the picture, two teammates are talking about a soccer game. *Why would their language be informal?* (They are teammates in a game. They do not need to speak formally.) *What phrases might the friend say?* (Hey! Let's go! Good job!) For additional practice, students can draw another scenario that calls for informal English and use that drawing as the basis for role play. As students role-play, work with them to create a bank of words and phrases that they use when they speak informally with their friends or family.

Assess Assess students' conversations to clear up any misconceptions about informal English. Review students' ratings. Revisit the workshop so that students can reevaluate their progress in recognizing speaking situations in which informal language is acceptable and using appropriate language.

Beginning Have students do a simple role-play activity in which one student acts as a student in class and the other acts as a new student who is trying to find a certain room in the building. The students may use informal English.

Intermediate Ask students to work with partners to role-play a conversation with a sibling that would use informal English. Remind students that informal English is "relaxed," but it should also be appropriate.

Advanced/Advanced High Have students create new scenarios where they might use informal language and model appropriate language they might use and hear.

Name _____

  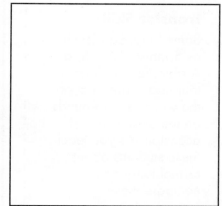

Act out what is happening in the picture. **Say** what the people would be saying.

Draw a situation in which you could use informal English.

Circle the rating for each sentence. **Tell** how you use informal English.

1 I need help to do this better.

2 I do this sometimes.

3 I know how to do this.

I understand when to use informal English.	1	2	3
I am respectful of others when I use informal English.	1	2	3
I use slang that is appropriate.	1	2	3
I listen to others before I speak.	1	2	3

Use Formal English

Preteach Model formal language for students and explain: *The words I use depend on who I am talking to and why I am speaking. When I am talking with older people or to bigger groups, I use formal language. For example, I use titles for people, such as Mrs. or Mr. I don't use slang in formal language. I might say* Hello *instead of* Hey. *My speech may be slower. I might take more time to organize my thoughts before I speak.*

Teach/Model With a volunteer, act out the scene on the right side of the page. Model using formal language, such as titles. Then model rating your knowledge using the rubric. *When I speak to a teacher or other adult, I use titles such as Miss, Mr., and Mrs. I ask questions using more formal words, such as* please.

Practice Direct students to look at the second picture. Explain that in the picture, a girl is introducing a friend to her grandparents. *Why would she use formal language?* (to show respect for her grandparents) *What phrases might the friend say?* (Pleased to meet you.) For additional practice, students can draw another scenario that calls for formal English and use that drawing as the basis for role play. As students role-play, work with them to create a bank of words and phrases used in formal English for their reference.

Assess Assess students' conversations to clear up any misconceptions about formal language. Review students' ratings. Revisit the workshop so that students can reevaluate their progress in recognizing formal speaking situations and using appropriate language.

Beginning Have students do a simple role-play activity in which one student acts as a student and the other as the principal. The student should use formal language in greeting the principal.

Intermediate Ask students to work with partners to role-play introducing themselves in a formal situation, such as a club meeting. Write out the students' introductions and have them read them back to you. Identify phrases that make the speech formal, such as *It's nice to meet you.*

Advanced/Advanced High Have students create new scenarios where they might use formal language and model appropriate language they might use and hear.

Name _____

Act out what is happening in the picture. **Say** what the people would be saying.

Circle the rating for each sentence. **Tell** how you use formal language.

1 I need help to do this better.

2 I do this sometimes.

3 I know how to do this.

When speaking formally with adults:

I do not use slang.	1	2	3
I use titles and formal names such as *Mr., Mrs., Ms.,* and *Miss.*	1	2	3
I use polite words such as *please* and *thank you.*	1	2	3

When speaking formally to a big group:

I think about and organize what I will say.	1	2	3
I slow down my speech.	1	2	3

Distinguish Between Formal and Informal English

Preteach *Informal language is casual or relaxed. Formal language does not use casual language, such as slang.* Have students name differences between formal and informal language. Then write these examples of informal English on the board. Have students say the same phrases in more formal English. Examples: *Hi, teach! How are ya'? What's up?*

Teach/Model With a volunteer, act out the first scene of the child shaking hands with an adult. Ask students to identify if they would use formal or informal English. Why would they use that type of English? What words or phrases would they use? *When I speak to a teacher or other adult, I use titles such as Miss, Mr., and Mrs. If I am meeting them for the first time, I might say things like* How do you do? *or* It is nice to meet you.

Practice Direct students to look at the second picture. Have them identify if this is a formal or informal speaking situation. With partners, have them take turns telling what the friends might say to each other when skating. Model using informal language or slang, such as referring to a friend as *dude* or talking about *grinding* on their skateboards.

Assess Have students use the T-chart to record situations in which they would use formal or informal English in the correct columns. Assess their placements of the situations to see if they need more support in distinguishing between when to use formal and informal English. Have them choose situations to role-play and add other situations to the chart.

Beginning Show students magazine pictures of various settings (e.g., a business meeting, family watching television). Ask the students to indicate whether the people in the situation would use formal or informal English.

Intermediate Write an informal conversation on the board. (Sample: *Hey John. Wanna play a game?*) Have the students work with partners to repeat the conversation. Then have them role-play the conversation again, this time substituting formal language for the informal.

Advanced/Advanced High Have students work with partners to talk about a soccer game. The first conversation should be telling a friend about a game. The second conversation should be a recap of the game for the school announcements.

Name _____

Act out what is happening in the picture. **Say** what the people would be saying.

Decide if the language you used was formal or informal.

Read each situation below. **Write** each situation in the chart under Formal English or Informal English.

Write and **share** your own situations. Have others decide if they are formal or informal.

a family dinner
playing a game with friends
giving a speech at school
meeting a new teacher
asking for help at the store
helping a younger brother

Formal English	Informal English

Preteach *I am going to give you directions for making a cheese sandwich: Last, eat the sandwich. Next, put the bread slices together. Second, put the cheese on the bread. First, take out two pieces of bread and some cheese. Did those directions make sense? What was wrong? They did not make sense because they are out of order! When we give directions, we need to be sure the steps are clear. The steps need to be in order.*

Teach/Model Provide a simple scenario for students, such as *I want to give directions for getting from our classroom to the lunchroom.* Ask students to provide steps as you write them on the board. Help them to use sequence words and clear directions. Read the directions back. Can students use the directions to find the lunchroom? As students form the directions with you, write order words on the board for students' reference.

Practice Place students in groups and ask them to give directions orally for a simple task, such as sharpening a pencil or folding a sheet of paper. One student can give directions while the others complete the task. Do the directions make sense? Guide practice as needed. Have volunteers share the best examples with the class.

Assess Listen in as students give directions. Assess their ability to provide clear steps and use sequence words.

Beginning On index cards, write steps or draw simple pictures for a simple process. Write one step per card. Give the cards to groups of students and have them work together to place the cards in order. Then students can say or read the directions aloud.

Intermediate/Advanced Provide out-of-order directions without order words. Have students place the directions in order and say them aloud, inserting sequence words to add organization.

Advanced High Have students work with partners to create a list of sequence words they can use in giving directions. Then have them give directions for a simple task, using words from their list.

Name _____

Use the sentence starters to give directions for a task, such as tying your shoe.

First, you should . . .

Second, . . .

Next, . . .

After that, . . .

Finally, . . .

Ask a friend to follow your directions. Were the directions clear? How could you improve them?

Circle the rating for each sentence. **Tell** how you give directions.

1 I need help to do this better.

2 I do this sometimes.

3 I know how to do this.

I can give directions with more than one or two steps.	1	2	3
I use order words when I give directions.	1	2	3
My directions are clear. People can follow them.	1	2	3

Follow Directions

Preteach *I have to follow directions every day. This morning, I followed directions for making breakfast in the microwave. I follow directions when I drive to school. I had to read the directions for using the DVD player when I showed you a video. And my teacher books have directions for teaching lessons. It is important to look at the steps in directions and read them (or listen) carefully to follow them.*

Teach/Model *Listen as I give you directions.* Give students directions for drawing things on sheets of paper, such as *First, draw a star in the upper right corner. Next, draw a circle in the middle.* After students have followed your directions, have them compare their drawings to the "answer." Point out important features of directions: time-order words that organize directions, and steps that need to be completed in order. If students had trouble following the directions, what made them difficult?

Practice Have students work in pairs to answer the questions on the student worksheet. Discuss and identify what makes the directions easy to follow (details in the steps and the numbers in order). Then have pairs read the directions for making a healthy snack to each other. One student can listen and the other student can gesture to show understanding.

Assess Assess students' oral and written work to check their ability to follow directions. Be sure that students understand they need to look for important details in directions and follow steps in order. Help them to understand that restating directions helps to clarify understanding.

Beginning Give simple one- or two-step directions for students to follow. Ask them to restate the most important details of each step before they follow it.

Intermediate Gather directions for students, such as recipes or directions for making or building simple things at home. Have them look for sequence words or other clues to order as well as the important details in the steps. Discuss in small groups, and then practice giving each other directions.

Advanced/Advanced High Provide directions for making or doing something. Have students work in small groups to discuss the directions and complete the tasks.

Name _____

Read the directions.

Answer the questions.

Make a healthy snack!

You will need: one red or green pepper, carrot sticks, celery sticks, salad dressing, a sharp knife, an adult helper

1. Have an adult cut the pepper in half across the middle.
2. Scoop out the seeds and material from inside the pepper.
3. Wash the inside and outside of each pepper. Each half of the pepper is a bowl!
4. Put salad dressing in each bowl.
5. Dip carrots and celery into the salad dressing. Eat them.
6. When you finish eating the celery and carrots, you can eat the bowl!

How many pepper bowls does this recipe make?

_____

What do you do with the salad dressing in step 5?

_____

_____

What does the adult helper do? Why do you need an adult helper? _____

_____

Draw the steps on the back of this sheet.

Use Classroom Language

Preteach *Every day in class, we communicate with each other. We ask questions and give directions. We work in groups. Students listen and ask for help from classmates and from the teacher. We have some words and sentences that we use often in the classroom. It's important for us to know how to use classroom language to get help, work with others, and understand what is happening around us in class.*

Teach/Model Ask several students to assist you in a role play. *Please take out your books. Open your books to page 15.* Assist students as needed to open their books to the correct page. *I used classroom language. You hear your teacher ask all the time to open your books to a certain page. That means that you can see that page in front of you.* Pairs can role-play, taking turns saying the classroom language and opening their books to the correct page.

Practice Help students gather examples of classroom language to record in the chart on the student worksheet. Some examples are already included on the chart. Have students role-play using the language. As students think of more examples of classroom language, add the examples to a large chart displayed on the wall.

Assess As students role-play and use classroom language, listen to the conversations and clear up any misconceptions. Continue to have students add examples to the worksheet and the chart in the classroom.

Beginning Give simple examples of classroom language for students to use, role-playing a scenario such as a student asking another student or the teacher to repeat what he or she said.

Intermediate/Advanced Have students role-play a scenario in which they are trying to understand a new word. They can use classroom language such as *What does _____ mean? How do you say _____ in English?*

Advanced High Have students create reference sheets or posters to use in the classroom that capture various examples of classroom language. Students can illustrate the posters to show the situations in which they use the classroom language and teach those words and phrases to others.

Name _____

Read the examples of classroom language.
Use them in conversations with classmates.

Is this right?
What are we supposed to do?
Put this in your own words.
Can you say it again, please?
How do you say it in English?
How do you spell it in English?
What does . . . . mean?
What do you think?
I agree with you.
I disagree. Here's why.
Let's ask the teacher about this.
Open your book to page . . .
Copy this into your notes.
Listen and repeat.
The homework is . . .
Work in pairs.
Work in groups.

Circle the rating for each sentence. **Tell** how you use
classroom language.

1 I need help to do this better.
2 I do this sometimes.
3 I know how to do this.

I ask for help in English.	1	2	3
I use classroom language with classmates.	1	2	3
I use classroom language with the teacher.	1	2	3
I understand the directions my teacher gives me.	1	2	3

Learn New Words

Teaching Tip

Make multiple copies of the student master. As you introduce words tied to the reading selections, as well as words from content areas, students can add to their own dictionaries of new words. Challenge students to refer to their dictionaries and use the new words twelve times in their writing and speaking to internalize meaning.

Preteach Copy the student blackline master on chart paper or display on an overhead. *When I read or hear a word I don't know, I think about what I do know about the word. Does it have a cognate I know to give a clue to meaning? Then I try to describe what the word means in a way that makes sense to me. I think about how the word relates to something in my own life. I try to remember where I've seen this word before. Sometimes I even draw a picture to help me remember what the word means. Then I use the word many times so I don't forget the meaning.*

Teach/Model Model how to use the chart with a word from a reading selection or from content-area studies, such as *weather*. Write the word on the line. Then model rating your knowledge: *A 1 means that I don't know this word at all. A 4 means I know it well enough to explain it to someone else. I understand what weather is, but I'm not sure I could define it. I'll give it a 3.* Then explain or describe weather and write a description. Be sure that your description uses simple language that all students understand.

Practice Write a word for students to copy on the chart. Pronounce the word, and then have students say it three times. Ask students to rate their knowledge of the word. Then guide students to describe the word to build understanding. Give an example of how the word relates to a class experience, tell a story that includes the word, or show a picture that defines the word. After you have defined the word, students should create their own descriptions of the word on their charts. Students can work in pairs or small groups.

Assess Assess students' word descriptions to clear up any misconceptions about the words. Look over word understanding ratings and periodically have students reevaluate their understandings of the words. Give students multiple opportunities to listen, speak, read and write with the new words, to internalize meaning.

Beginning Rather than write word meanings, students can draw and label pictures of the words.

Intermediate Have students use the words in simple spoken sentences that they share with partners. Listen in for correct word use.

Advanced/Advanced High Students can use a dictionary or glossary to reinforce their understandings of the words.

Name _____

Write the word on the line.

Rate how well you understand the word.

1 I don't know the word.

2 I think I know what the word means.

3 I know the word. I can use it in a sentence.

4 I can teach this word to someone else.

Describe the word in a way that helps you understand it.

Word: _____ My Understanding   1   2   3   4

Describe the word: _____

_____

Word: _____ My Understanding   1   2   3   4

Describe the word: _____

_____

Word: _____ My Understanding   1   2   3   4

Describe the word: _____

_____

Ask Clarifying Questions

Preteach *If I don't understand something, I need to ask the person speaking to repeat what they said. Then I can understand it. That is called* clarifying. *I ask questions to clarify, or be sure I understand. I also ask questions when I am reading. I ask questions before I read, while I read, and after I read. That helps me understand what I am reading.*

Teach/Model Work with a student to role-play a situation in which you would ask a clarifying question. Have the student give you simple directions for doing something. As the student speaks, find an opportunity to ask a question such as *What does that mean? Can you repeat that, please?* or *How do you do that?*

Practice Share the worksheet with students and talk about situations in which students would use each of the clarifying questions. Then point out the question starters. Have students use the question starters to ask questions about a selection you have recently read.

Assess As students role-play asking clarifying questions, assess their ability to ask the questions in appropriate situations. Provide multiple opportunities to practice using question starters. Assess students' ability to use those question words to form questions that make sense.

Beginning Have students role-play situations with you in which they ask for assistance for completing a math problem or other classroom task.

Intermediate/Advanced Have students work in small groups to identify questions they would ask the teacher, their parents, other students in a group, and so on to clarify their understanding.

Advanced High Have student use the "5Ws and an H" to ask and answer questions about a reading selection.

Name _____

Read the examples of clarifying questions.

Use them in conversations with classmates and your teachers.

Use the question starters to ask questions about what you read or hear.

Is this right?
Can you say it again, please?
Can you speak slower, please?
How do you say it in English?
How do you spell it in English?
What does . . . mean?
What do I need to do?
What should I do next?

Use these sentence frames to ask questions. Use the sentence frames to answer questions, too.

Who is _____? That person is _____.

What is _____? That is _____.

When did _____ happen? It happened _____.

Where is _____? The _____ is _____.

Why did _____ happen? It happened because _____.

Use Classroom Resources

Teaching Tip
Place labels on various classroom resources (maps, dictionaries, thesaurus, and others you may have in the room) to help students remember the names of the resources. Model using various resources as you read, write, and look for locations. Think aloud to demonstrate how to use these resources.

Preteach *I was reading a story, and I found a word I didn't know. I tried to figure out what the word meant from reading the words around it, but I still needed help. I asked my friend, but she didn't know either. So I used this.* (Show a dictionary.) *A dictionary is a classroom resource. It's a tool that I can use to find out word meanings.* Model how to use a dictionary and its features: guide words, pronunciations, and so on.

Teach/Model Draw attention to the student worksheet with the list of classroom resources. Start with the first one. *A map shows the locations of things. I'll write that in the chart. Why would I use a map? I'd use a map to find the capital of our state. I'd use a map to figure out how to get somewhere. I'd use a map to locate natural features. I'll write one of these uses in the chart.*

Practice As you use various resources with students, have students consider how and why to use the resources. The worksheet can be completed as an ongoing activity. Be sure to think aloud as you use various resources and demonstrate how and why to use them. Students can add resources that are particular to your classroom.

Assess Assess students' ability to choose appropriate resources. They would use a thesaurus, for example, to make writing more interesting. Other examples would be to use a DVD to get information in a visual way and to use a computer to find out information for presentations.

Beginning Have students work in pairs to use a picture dictionary to find a word from a reading selection. Help them restate the definition in their own words.

Intermediate/Advanced Have small groups of students use a classroom resource such as a map to locate directions, cities, and physical features.

Advanced High Ask students to add more classroom resources to the chart and explain to other students how to use those resources.

Name _____

Read the name of the resource.
Explain what the resource is like.
Tell why you would use it.
Add more resources to the chart.

Classroom Resources

Resource	What's it like?	Why would I use it?
Dictionary	a book of words and definitions; words are in alphabetical order	to find out the meaning of a word; to find out how to say a word
Map		
Thesaurus		
Almanac		
Encyclopedia		
Computer		

Retell or Summarize

Preteach *I saw a movie yesterday. When my friends asked me about it, I didn't tell every detail from the beginning to end. Instead, I told the most important things. This is called summarizing. I summarize things I see, things I read, and things I hear. When I summarize, I know that I have sorted out the most important details. A summary includes important things, not everything. Retelling is a little different. When you retell something, you listen to or read the message, and then say it in your own words to show you understand it.*

Teach/Model Ask students to listen carefully as you read a short passage aloud. After you read, ask students to contribute to a summary of the passage. Help frame their thinking as you list their ideas to create a summary. Have pairs of students read the complete summary together. Then reread the passage. Have pairs decide if the summary lists the most important details. What should be added or changed? Discuss and clarify answers.

Practice Have students use the graphic organizer on the student worksheet to list details from a written or spoken passage. In the box at the bottom, students can write their summaries. Encourage them to keep their summaries short and to the point. Ask them to read their summaries aloud and compare them with classmates' summaries.

Assess Assess students' summaries to be sure that students have included only important details. Ask questions to guide their thinking, (e.g., *Why is this detail important? Does your summary match what the author wanted us to remember?*).

Beginning Have students orally summarize a simple spoken message or a simple text, such as a comic strip. They can work in pairs to practice, then share oral summaries with the group.

Intermediate Provide a simple text and a sample summary that is missing some information and provides too many details about the text. Ask students to read and discuss the summary in pairs. *What details are missing? What details don't need to be included?*

Advanced/Advanced High Ask students to work in pairs to create directions for summarizing. Have them share their directions and sample summaries with other students.

Name _____

Use the graphic organizer to list important details.

Write a summary in the box.

Say the summary aloud.

Use the summary starters if you need to.

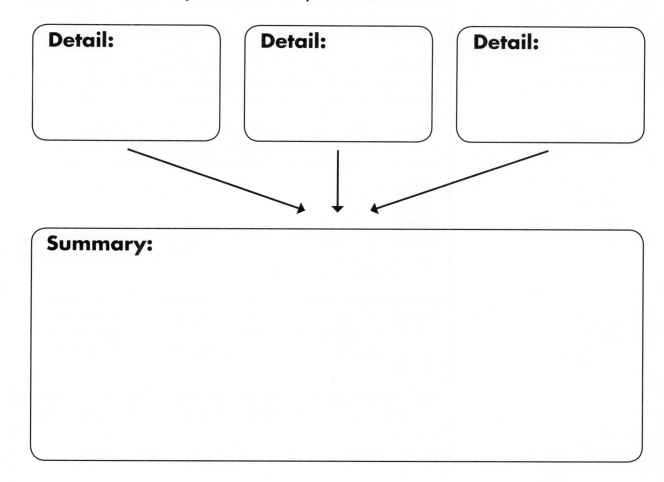

Detail:

Detail:

Detail:

Summary:

Summary language:

In summary, . . .

The most important ideas are . . .

What we need to remember is . . .

Take Notes/ Create an Outline

Preteach *When I am in a meeting, I listen for important ideas and take notes. You do the same thing in class. When you listen, you write down important ideas. When you read, you write down important ideas too. Writing down ideas, or taking notes, helps you remember them later.*

Teach/Model Model using the web graphic organizer and the outline on the student worksheet. Tell students that the web organizer is great for writing down details about one idea. Then model using the outline form to record main details and subdetails from a reading selection. Think aloud as you differentiate between main details and subdetails and place them on the outline.

Practice Have students work in pairs to copy one of the organizers and use it to record ideas from a spoken message or a short passage you provide. Provide assistance as needed.

Assess Assess students' organizers for understanding of main ideas and details from spoken and written messages. Collect samples to show progress. Provide additional support as necessary.

Beginning Guide pairs to create a web organizer about a simple passage. Have them use the organizer to retell the important ideas of the passage to a partner.

Intermediate Write important details and subdetails from a familiar passage on index cards. Have students sort the cards before they record details in the outline. Then they can use their outlines to summarize the important ideas of the passage for a partner.

Advanced/Advanced High Ask students to work on organizers independently. They can share with partners and summarize their notes.

Name _____

Choose a graphic organizer to take notes.

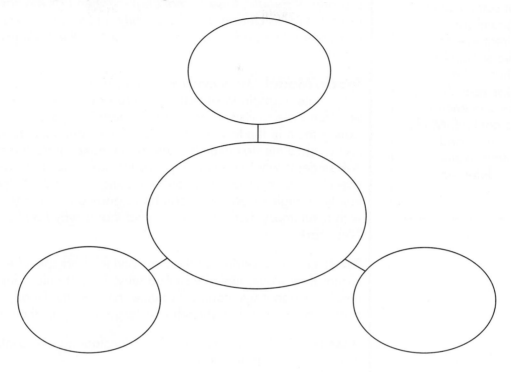

Outline

I. _____

    A. _____

    B. _____

II. _____

    A. _____

    B. _____

III. _____

    A. _____

    B. _____

Give a Speech

Preteach *A speech is a planned talk that you give in front of a group of people. I use formal English when I give a speech. I express ideas clearly, speaking firmly and loudly enough so everyone in the audience can hear. I look at the audience when I speak.*

Teach/Model Use a classroom map of the United States to pick out a state. Explain to students three reasons why you think it would be a fun state to visit. Then, model organizing your ideas and stating them in the form of a speech. Give your speech two times. As you give the first, mumble and don't make much eye contact. Ask students what you can improve for next time. Then deliver the speech correctly. Call attention to making eye contact, speaking loudly enough so everyone can hear, and concluding your speech with a summary. For example: *...and that is why I'd like to visit New York.*

Practice Have partners take turns giving short speeches about places they would like to visit and why. They should offer corrective feedback about eye contact, volume, and clarity. Finally, have each student give his or her speech to a larger group or the entire class.

Assess Assess students' speeches, considering eye contact, volume, and organization.

Beginning Have students work on delivering speeches by answering simple questions, speaking aloud. Because speeches are planned, give students a chance to plan what they will say. Tell them the questions first so they can think through their answers.

Intermediate Have students work on elaborating. Lead them by explaining that sentences that add more details include words such as *because, as a result,* etc.

Advanced/Advanced High Give students time to plan, then have them speak on a topic for two minutes. Speakers should elaborate with details and avoid using *um, uh,* and *you know.*

Name _____

Use the planner to organize ideas for your speech.

Write your topic.

Explain how you will introduce your speech.

List details to include in the speech.

End with a conclusion, or a final thought for your audience to remember.

Topic:

_____

To **introduce** my topic, I will:

_____

_____

Details I will include:

_____

_____

I will **end** my speech by:

_____

Evaluate your speech.

1 I need to practice more to do this.

2 I did this sometimes.

3 I did this during my whole speech.

I spoke loudly enough for my audience to hear.	1	2	3
I looked at the audience when I spoke.	1	2	3
I spoke clearly.	1	2	3
I used formal English.	1	2	3
I organized my ideas with a clear beginning and end.	1	2	3

ELL Handbook

Express Opinions

Preteach *We express opinions to show what we think or believe. We cannot prove if an opinion is true or false. If I say, It is raining outside, that's a fact. I can look outside and see rain falling. If I say, Rainy weather is the best weather, that's an opinion. I like rainy weather because it helps my flowers grow in the garden. But some people don't like rain. They have a different opinion.*

Teach/Model Display the words and phrases from the student page. *We use these words to give our opinions. These words tell what we think or believe.* Model creating an opinion using one of the words or phrases.

Practice Have students work with partners to state opinions about sports, food, television shows, books, or movies. Have them use the words in the box on the student page. Refer them to the sentence frames as needed. Point out that these frames will help them correctly express opinions in English. For additional practice, have students write statements of opinion and then say them aloud with partners. Have students elaborate by giving reasons for their opinions.

Assess As students state opinions, assess understanding. Do students state ideas that cannot be proven true or false and express feelings or beliefs? Do students use words or phrases from the box? Correct students as necessary.

Beginning Write sentence frames on index cards and distribute them to students. Have them work in pairs to state opinions using the frames.

Intermediate When calling on students to give oral opinions, have them use phrases such as *I like* or *I do not like* rather than single words. Have pairs ask each other why they have that opinion. Report answers to the class.

Advanced/Advanced High Challenge students to add other opinion words or phrases to the box and write additional sentence frames. They can use the frames to state opinions.

Name _____

> ### Opinion Words
>
> | | | | |
> |---|---|---|---|
> | I think | I believe | my opinion is | I agree |
> | I disagree | I like | I do not like | |
> | best | worst | good | bad |

Complete opinions using these sentence frames:

I like _____.

I think _____.

I believe _____.

I do not like _____.

My opinion is _____.

Statements of opinion:

_____

_____

_____

Challenge! Add more details to your sentence.

I like _____ because _____.

Her opinion is _____ because _____.

Express Feelings

Preteach *If you see someone with a frown on his or her face* (demonstrate for students), *you know that person might be sad or angry. Anger and sadness are feelings. We often express our feelings with our facial expressions and our actions, but we can also use words to express feelings. Finding the right words isn't always easy!*

Teach/Model Use exaggerated facial expressions and body language to express a feeling, such as happiness or confusion. Model by speaking: *I am happy. I feel happy.* Model another feeling and have students use the frames after you model:

You feel _____. *You are* _____.

Practice Explain a situation to students that would elicit a feeling, such as *Your favorite cousin is coming to a family party. You haven't seen your cousin in a long time. How do you feel?* (excited, happy) *You came to school without your homework. You know your teacher is going to ask for it.* (worried, guilty) Have students gesture to show the emotion and then work with partners to express that feeling in words. As students suggest more feeling words, write them on a chart for reference so that students can include them on their worksheets.

Assess As students express their feelings, assess the sentences they use as well as their ability to identify feelings. Correct any misconceptions as students use sentence frames to express feelings.

Beginning Have students draw or make faces to show a facial expression that expresses a feeling. Partners can identify the feeling and create a sentence: *He/she feels* _____.

Intermediate Have students look for pictures in magazines or newspapers that show a situation that would elicit feelings. Have them speak about the picture.

Advanced/Advanced High Challenge students to think of specific words for feelings, such as *joyful, ecstatic, lively, overjoyed, pleased, thrilled,* or *upbeat* instead of *happy.*

Name _____

Record words that express feelings in the box. A few words are already in the box. **Add** more.

> ### Feeling Words
>
> glad   afraid   proud   angry
>
> lonely   confused   surprised

Speak a sentence using one of the frames below.
Choose words from the box.

I feel   _____.

I am   _____.

He/She is   _____.

They felt   _____.

They are   _____.

He/She was   _____.

They were   _____.

Challenge! Add more details to your sentence.

I feel _____ because _____.

They felt _____ when _____.

Discuss with Classmates

Teaching Tips

Consider setting roles for class discussions, such as a time keeper, a leader (keeps the group on track), a note taker, and a summarizer. Model how to do each of these roles and provide guided practice before assigning these roles for students to do independently.

Preteach *When do we have discussions? I discuss work with students. I talk with my family at the dinner table. I discuss ideas with other teachers at school. In a discussion, we speak and we listen. We respect other people's ideas.*

Teach/Model Create a fishbowl, in which you and a few students are in the center while others are around you watching. Introduce an easy discussion topic such as a question about a selection you have just read. Model the discussion behaviors from the rubric on the next page. As you model these behaviors, pause to think aloud. You might say *I repeated back what Tommy said to me. He knows that I have understood him. He also knows I was listening. Now it is my turn to speak. It is important to take turns being a good listener and a good speaker.*

Practice Have students work in small groups. Introduce a topic such as: *What is your favorite thing to do after school?* As students discuss, monitor and encourage the positive behaviors you observe. Share these positive behaviors with the class and have students identify others they know.

Assess Use the rubric on the student page to have students assess their discussion skills. Follow up with your own observations of student discussions.

Beginning Offer students examples of nonverbal communication skills that a good listener uses: nodding, making eye contact, and making appropriate expressions. Have them mimic you as you model them.

Intermediate Offer students an example of a conversation that could occur at the lunch table. Have the students mimic you, each partner playing another role. Stress the importance of active listening and behaviors that go with it.

Advanced/Advanced High Have students model discussion scenarios and demonstrate behaviors of listening and speaking for other groups.

Name _____

Rate what you do during discussions with your classmates.

1 I need to practice this skill.
2 I do this sometimes.
3 I almost always do this.

I share my ideas with others.	1	2	3
I answer questions when classmates ask.	1	2	3
I give a lot of facts or details when I speak.	1	2	3
I respect other people in the group.	1	2	3
I listen to other people's ideas.	1	2	3
I look at the person speaking.	1	2	3
I repeat back what other people say to show I understand.	1	2	3
I support other people's ideas.	1	2	3

What topics would you like to discuss with classmates?
List them here. Then discuss!

_____

_____

_____

_____

Act Out or Draw Meaning

Preteach Choose a content-area or lesson word that students recently learned. *When I learn new words, I want to remember them. Drawing a picture of a word's meaning or acting out the meaning of a word helps me remember a word, what it means, and how it is used. I just learned a new word in science:* fault. *A fault is a place in the earth where an earthquake takes place. I drew a picture of a circle to show the Earth and drew a line on it. I put arrows to show how the Earth shifts at the fault line.* (Show picture.) *I can also act out the meaning by taking two blocks and rubbing them together to show what happens at a fault to make an earthquake.*

Teach/Model Introduce words from a recent story or from content-area studies. Place students in small groups, and give each group a word. Have students work together to create a picture and/or gestures to demonstrate meanings of the words. Groups can share with other groups as you monitor for understanding.

Practice Play a guessing game with students. Distribute words on index cards that students have learned in class. Students can take turns drawing pictures or acting out word meanings for other classmates to guess. Use the student worksheet for students to create "dictionaries" of word meanings. Distribute copies of the drawing frames when students learn new words. Have students keep and add to their own personal word books.

Assess Assess students' drawings to clear up any misconceptions about the words. Discuss with students how drawing words may help them remember word meanings.

Beginning Ask students to follow up their drawings or gestures by explaining word meanings orally.

Intermediate Ask students to use each word in a sentence to describe what they drew or acted out.

Advanced/Advanced High Have students look up the definitions of words in a dictionary to supplement their understanding of the words. They can write definitions in their own words to show understanding.

Name _____

Word: _____

Drawing

This word means _____

Word: _____

Drawing

This word means _____

Read the Words Around You

Preteach Before starting, draw a stop sign on the board and ask what it means. Students may answer *stop. We are surrounded by words and signs that can be useful. We need to learn what these signs tell us.* Point out that the name of the school is on the front of the building. *The sign tells people what this building is. It helps people find the school.* Then, point out that the classrooms have numbers. *These help students find their way around the school.*

Teach/Model Walk around the classroom until you find an example of instructional environmental print. Model reading the word, and figuring out what it means: *A sign on this door reads P-U-L-L. I know that word is* pull. *This sign tells me how to open the door.* Then, model opening the door.

Practice Tell students that their task is to keep a log of the signs they notice and can read throughout the school day. They must keep track of the words in the table on their worksheets. At the end of the day, have students share one word they recognized in a sign, and one they did not. Discuss as a class. Help them understand the meanings of words they did not recognize. As you discuss students' examples, talk about the information they get from reading the signs or other environmental print. Students can keep a running log of environmental print they see and learn. Discuss the words regularly.

Assess Assess students' understandings of environmental print by questioning them as they share their results, for example: *Why do you think the sign "gymnasium" was placed in that spot?* (The sign tells us where the gym is.) Explain the meanings of unknown words to students.

Beginning Have beginning students only keep track of words they recognize and know.

Intermediate Have students organize their words by category, such as *foods, signs, rooms, clubs,* and so on.

Advanced/Advanced High Provide environmental print for students, such as store advertisements, posters, and additional signs. Students can discuss with partners what they learn from reading the signs and texts.

Name _____

Write the words you see around you.

Practice saying each word aloud.

Date	Words I Know	Words I Do Not Know Yet

Use Nouns in Your Speaking

Preteach *Nouns are words that name people, places, or things. Nouns can name one thing, or they can name more than one thing. I can count these pencils: one, two, three, four. But the word* weather *is a noun, too. I can't count weather, though: one weather, two weathers, three weathers? That doesn't make sense! There must be different kinds of nouns, with different rules for how we say them and write them.*

Teach/Model Write *desks* and *furniture* on the board and draw a quick sketch under each: three desks under *desks* and a desk, chair, and couch under *furniture. Let's make sentences with these words. I see three desks. I can count them: one, two, three. I see that furniture. I used the word* that *because I cannot count furniture and say* one furniture, two furnitures, three furnitures. *Nouns that you can count, such as* desk, *are called* count nouns. *Nouns that you cannot count, such as* furniture, weather, *or* anger, *are called* noncount nouns.

Practice Have students complete the student worksheet. Focus on the ability to count some nouns and ask questions to frame as necessary. For the first sentence, for example, you might say: *You can count the apples. One, two, three, four. Write the word* four *on the line.* For the second sentence: *When I drink the water, I can't count how many waters. So I'll complete the sentence with* the. As students complete the exercise, point out that some noncount nouns might have the word *a* or *an* in front of them.

Assess As students complete their worksheets, circulate to assess their work and clear up any misconceptions.

Beginning Say a count noun, such as *bird.* Ask students to use the word in a sentence. Then say a noncount noun, such as *music.* Have students use the word in a sentence. Check for understanding.

Intermediate Write words on index cards, one word per card. Have students work together to sort the words into count and noncount nouns. They can choose one count noun and one noncount noun to use in a sentence.

Advanced/Advanced High Challenge students to find sentences in magazines or newspapers and underline the nouns. Have them work in pairs to classify nouns as count or noncount nouns. Then have them speak using those nouns as you check for understanding.

Name _____

Look at the picture.

Read the sentence.

Complete the sentence by writing a number OR by writing the word *the.*

Say the sentences aloud.

1. We need _____ apples for our pie.

2. Hold up _____ fingers.

3. _____ weather is hot.

4. We heard _____ music.

5. There are _____ houses on this block.

6. Please put those _____ books on the shelf.

Circle the count nouns in the sentences above.

Explain the difference between a count and a noncount noun to a partner.

Listen for other count and noncount nouns you hear in conversations.

Teaching Tip

Follow a similar routine for teaching adjectives. Focus on adjectives that are troublesome for your students. You might, for example, focus on position of adjectives (before the nouns they describe or as predicate adjectives). You might also focus on comparative and superlative adjectives to help students avoid speaking sentences like *This is more better* or *That was most crunchiest.*

Preteach Demonstrate as you describe prepositions. *I push the chair under the table. I put my coat on the hook. When I was describing where I put things, I used special words to tell where. These words,* on *and* under, *are called prepositions. We can use prepositions to tell locations. We can also use prepositions to tell when things happen. We eat lunch after our math class. In that sentence,* after *is a preposition that helps us tell time.*

Teach/Model Use a preposition in a sentence that shows location, such as *I walk between the rows of desks.* Demonstrate by walking between the desks. Say the sentence again and ask students to raise their hands when they hear the preposition. Then pair students. Assign each a preposition. Have students say and demonstrate a sentence using the preposition.

Practice Have students use the space on the bottom of the worksheet to draw a picture. They can write about the picture using prepositions. Model if necessary: *I drew a picture of myself riding my bicycle. I put my helmet on my head. I was careful when I rode across the street.* Students can also use this sheet to work with adjectives. Have them list adjectives in the second column. They can use adjectives to describe the picture they drew.

Assess Assess students' pictures and sentences for understanding of how to use prepositions. Provide extra support as necessary.

Beginning Write prepositions on index cards, one preposition per card. Demonstrate putting books *on* the table or putting your pencil *into* a desk. As you model and say the prepositional phrases, students can repeat the prepositions and hold up the cards with the corresponding prepositions. Then have students use gestures to demonstrate prepositions, while other students guess the prepositions they are demonstrating.

Intermediate/Advanced Share photographs from magazines. Ask students to describe locations of items in the photographs using prepositions. They can use adjectives to describe the photos as well.

Advanced High Challenge students to find prepositions and adjectives from their reading or from other sources. They can add them to the worksheet and to a chart for class reference. Have them practice using prepositions that tell time in addition to location.

Name _____

Write prepositions in the first column.

Write adjectives in the second column.

Prepositions	Adjectives

Draw a picture.

Write about it. **Use** prepositions and adjectives.

Use Verbs in Your Speaking

Preteach *Verbs are words that show action. I look before I cross the street.* (Model turning your head to look both ways before crossing the street.) *The word* look *is a verb. It describes something I do. If I said, Please look up a word in the dictionary, does that mean that you would really look up?* (Model looking up toward the ceiling.) *Look up is a group of words that has a different meaning as a group of words than if you say each word individually. The phrase* Look up *is called a phrasal verb. It's a verb with a preposition or an adverb. The phrase makes a meaning different from the verb's meaning.*

Teach/Model Choose a phrasal verb from the chart for modeling. *Let's focus on the phrase* go over. *A car can go over a hill. But* go over *can have a different meaning. What does it mean if I say* Let's go over your homework? *That means that we are going to review and check your answers.* Guide students by choosing another phrasal verb and explaining and modeling its meaning.

Practice Have students work in pairs to complete the worksheet by choosing the correct phrase to complete each sentence.

Assess Assess students' answers on the worksheet. Correct any errors, and explain misconceptions students may have.

Beginning Assist students by reading the sentence and inserting the meaning of the correct answer. After students use the chart to choose the correct answer, they can reread the sentence to reinforce their understanding of the concept in English.

Intermediate/Advanced Ask students to choose a phrase and work in pairs to write a sentence that includes the phrase. They can illustrate their sentences to show meaning.

Advanced High Have students search for phrasal verbs in their reading selections or other printed material, share them in small groups, and discuss their meanings.

Name _____

Read each phrasal verb in the chart.

Phrasal Verb	Meaning
show up	arrive
make up	create or invent something
run into	meet
look up	find
back up	support an idea
come across	find something
come up with	think of an idea
do over	do something again
give up	stop doing something
go over	check something; review
hold on	wait for a short time
keep up	go at the same speed
make up one's mind	decide something
turn in	give something to someone

Circle the phrasal verb that fits the sentence.

1. Let's _____ the correct answers.

go over   give up

2. I want to make a better drawing. I'll _____.

give up   do it over

3. Did you _____ that story?

keep up   make up

4. Please _____. I am almost ready to go.

hold on   back up

5. I cannot _____ my mind about lunch.

make up   give up

Role-play conversations with phrasal verbs. Share them.

Part 6
Multilingual Vocabulary

Introduction to Multilingual Vocabulary

The lesson words are arranged by unit and week to coincide with the reading selections. Each lesson word is translated into Spanish, Chinese, Vietnamese, Korean, and Hmong. Use the translated lesson words to build students' background knowledge before reading a selection. Frontloading the vocabulary will allow students to access the content and will aid their comprehension of the text.

The multilingual thinking words, also translated into the same languages, are process words, such as *analyze, compare, describe, illustrate, list,* and *predict.* Students can use these words to discuss the strategies they use as they read various selections, including content-area texts.

Table of Contents

Multilingual Vocabulary
Unit 1

English	Spanish	Chinese	Vietnamese	Korean	Hmong
Week 1: Red Kayak					
compressions	compresiones	壓抑	sức ép	압박	puab tau me me lawm
grumbled	refunfuñé	發牢騷	càu nhàu	불평했다	vaus tas
insistently	insistentemente	堅持地	nài nỉ	끈질기게	yeej yog muaj li
intentionally	intencionalmente	故意地	cố ý	계획적으로	thoob ntiaj teb li
minute	minuto	分	phút	1분	nathis
neutral	neutral	中立	trung hòa	중립의	nws yeej muaj nws
normally	normalmente	正常地	bình thường	보통	nws yog li qub
Week 2: Thunder Rose					
branded	marcados	烙印	được đóng dấu	상표를 붙이다, 낙인을 찍다	ci npe, ntau npe
constructed	construyó	修建	đã xây dựng	세우다	txiav
daintily	con elegancia	精緻	một cách xinh đẹp	우아하게	ntxim nyiam
devastation	devastación	破壞	sự tàn phá	황폐하게 함	tu siab
lullaby	nana	催眠曲	bài hát ru em	자장가	zaj nkauj rau me nyuam ab
pitch	brea	瀝青	mức giọng	던지다	lub suab
resourceful	ingeniosa	機智勇敢	tháo vát	자원이 풍부한	muaj tswv yim heev
thieving	(hábitos de) robar	竊取	trộm cắp	도둑질의	nyiag
veins	venas	靜脈	những đường gân, tĩnh mạch	성질, 경향	leeg
Week 3: Island of the Blue Dolphins					
gnawed	royeron	咬	gặm nhấm	갉아먹다	tom, xov
headland	promontorio	陸岬	mũi đất	돌출부	pob tsuas
kelp	algas	海帶	loại rong biển lớn	켈프	nroj hiav txwv

English	Spanish	Chinese	Vietnamese	Korean	Hmong
lair	guarida	穴	hang ổ	짐승의 굴	tsiaj chaw sov
ravine	barranco	山溝	khe núi	협곡	qhov dej
shellfish	mariscos	貝類	động vật có vỏ như cua, tôm, sò, hào, chem chép	갑각류 동물	pias deg
sinew	tendón	精力	sợi gân nối cơ với xương	힘줄	leeg

Week 4: Satchel Paige

English	Spanish	Chinese	Vietnamese	Korean	Hmong
confidence	confianza	信心	sự tin tưởng	자신감	muaj peev xwm
fastball	bola rápida	快球	quả bóng thần tốc	속구	pob txawb muaj zog heev
mocking	burlón	嘲笑	chế giễu	비웃는	thuam
outfield	jardines	外野	khu vực cách xa người ném hoặc bắt bóng nhất trên sân chơi bóng chày/dã cầu	외야	tshav ntau pob
unique	único	獨特	đặc biệt nhất, độc nhất vô nhị	독특한	zoo txawv
weakness	debilidad	弱點	khuyết điểm	약함	tsis muaj zog
windup	movimiento para lanzar	纏繞	mưu toan khiêu khích	종결, <야구> 와인드업	thaj thaum tus neeg yuav txawb baseball

Week 5: Ten Mile Day

English	Spanish	Chinese	Vietnamese	Korean	Hmong
barren	inhabitada	荒地	trơ trụi	메마른	tsis tuaj plaub
deafening	ensordesedor	震耳欲聾的	chát tai	귀청이 터질 것 같은	tsis hnov lus li
lurched	dan tumbos	蹣跚的	nghiêng qua một bên	갑자기 기울어 졌다	hem mus
previous	anterior	先前的	trước đây	이전의	yav tas los
prying	atornillando	撬動	tò mò	살피는	thov ntuj
surveying	cintas de medir	測量	quan sát	측량	nug

Unit 2

English	Spanish	Chinese	Vietnamese	Korean	Hmong
Week 1: At the Beach					
algae	algas	海藻	rong rêu	조류	nroj tsuag hauv dej hiav txwv
concealed	ocultos	隱瞞	bị che giấu	숨기다	zais
driftwood	madera flotante	漂流木頭	gỗ trôi dạt trên nước	쓰레기	ntoo ua dej tshoob los
hammocks	hamacas	吊床	những chiếc võng	해먹	txaj hlua pw
lamented	lamentó	哀嘆	đã than khóc	유감스러운	los yas tshooj
sea urchins	erizos de mar	海膽	các con nhím biển	성게	yam ntsev nyob dej hiav txwv
sternly	severamente	嚴厲地	nghiêm nghị	엄격하게	nyaum li
tweezers	pinzas	鑷子	cây nhíp	족집게, 핀셋	rab koob nrho pos
Week 2: Hold the Flag High					
canteen	cantina	水罐	chai nước	수통	taub dej
Confederacy	Confederación	南方联盟军	phe lien kết	(남부)연맹	cov xeev qab teb
glory	gloria	荣耀	vinh quang	영광	hwjchim
quarreling	riña	争论	gây gỗ	언쟁	pheej sis tshe
rebellion	rebelión	反抗	phiến loạn	반란, 폭동	tawm tsam
stallion	semental	公马	ngựa giống:	종마	neeg (tus txiv)
Union	Unión	北方联盟军	phe thống nhất	(북부)연합	cov xeev qaum teb
Week 3: Ch'i-lin Purse					
astonished	asombrada	吃驚	kinh ngạc	놀라다	ceeb
behavior	comportamiento	行為	hành vi	행동	yeeb yam
benefactor	benefactora	恩人	người được hưởng	은인	tus pab nyiaj txiag
distribution	distribución	分配	việc phân phát	배급	faib

English	Spanish	Chinese	Vietnamese	Korean	Hmong
gratitude	gratitud	謝意	lòng biết ơn	감사	(nyiaj) tshav ntuj
procession	procesión	隊伍	đoàn người, đám rước	행진, 행렬	mus (tom ntej)
recommend	recomendar	推薦	giới thiệu	추천하다	qhuas
sacred	sagrado	神聖	thiêng liêng, sùng kính	신성한	muaj nuj nqis
traditions	tradiciones	傳統	truyền thống	전통	kab lig kev cai

Week 4: A Summer's Trade

English	Spanish	Chinese	Vietnamese	Korean	Hmong
bandana	pañuelo	头巾	khăn quàng cổ	큰 손수건	phuam qhwv taubhau
bracelet	brazalete	手镯	vòng đeo tay	팔찌	paug
hogan	hogan	荷根	nhà người indian	호건	tsev khab
jostled	empujar	碰撞	chen lấn	떠밀다, 부딪히다	mus phoom
mesas	mesetas	台地	vùng bình nguyên	메사, 대지	roob ncov tiaj tiaj
Navajo	Navajo	纳瓦霍	Navajo	나바호	cov khab Navajo
turquoise	turquesa	绿松石	màu ngọc lam	터키옥, 청록색의	xim xiavntsuab

Week 5: The Midnight Ride of Paul Revere

English	Spanish	Chinese	Vietnamese	Korean	Hmong
fate	destino	命運	định mệnh	운명	txoj hmoo
fearless	intrépido	無畏的	can đảm	용감한	tsis ntshai
glimmer	destello	微光	le lói	깜박이는 빛, 반짝거리다	ci
lingers	se entretiene	徘徊	chần chừ, nán lại	꾸물거리다, 오래 끌다	nyob luj loos
magnified	ampliado	放大	được phóng đại	확대하다	ua kom loj tuaj
somber	sombrías	微暗	nghiêm nghị	어두컴컴한, 흐린	tsaus ntuj
steed	corcel	駿馬	con ngựa hùng dũng	말	nees

Unit 3

English	Spanish	Chinese	Vietnamese	Korean	Hmong
Week 1: The Fabulous Perpetual Motion Machine					
applauds	aplaude	稱讚	khen ngợi	박수치다	npuaj teg
browsing	mirando	瀏覽	nhìn sơ qua	검색하는	rub mus
fabulous	fabulosa	傑出的	tưởng tượng	전설적인	zoo zoo
inspecting	inspeccionando	檢查	kiểm soát	점검하는	khuaj
project	proyecto	計劃	đồn án	연구 과제	tsom
Week 2: Leonardo's Horse					
achieved	logrado	達到	đạt được	이룩하다	ua tau
architect	arquitecto	建築師	kiến trúc	건축가	ua vaj ua tsev
bronze	bronce	古銅	(về kim loại) đồng	청동	tooj liab
cannon	cañón	大炮	súng đại bác	대포	phom loj
depressed	deprimido	壓平的	buồn trầm uất	낙담한	nyuj siab
fashioned	elaboró	塑造	đã làm theo mẫu	~을 만들다	ua raws li
midst	(en) medio (de)	中間	ở giữa	한가운데	nruab nrab
philosopher	filósofo	哲學家	triết gia	철학자	tus neeg soj tsum neeg lub leej
rival	rival	對手	đối thủ	경쟁자	tus neeg nyiam sib tw
Week 3: The Dinosaurs of Waterhouse Hawkins					
erected	erigió	豎起	dựng lên	직립하다	sawv tseg
foundations	cimientos	基礎	nền tảng	토대	qhov txheem
mold	molde	模具	khuôn	틀, 뼈대	puab
occasion	ocasión	場合	dịp	경우	sij hawm

English	Spanish	Chinese	Vietnamese	Korean	Hmong
proportion	proporción	比例	tỷ lệ, cân xứng	비율	sib txig
tidied	ordenó	整理	đã dọn gọn gàng	정돈된	huv
workshop	taller	工場	xưởng nhỏ	연수회	hoob sib tham

Week 4: Mahalia Jackson

English	Spanish	Chinese	Vietnamese	Korean	Hmong
appreciate	apreciar	讚賞	hiểu và biết ơn, thưởng thức	감사하다	saib muaj nuj nqis
barber	barbero	理髮師	thợ hớt tóc	이발사	tus txiav plaub hau
choir	coro	唱詩班	ban hợp ca	합창단	ib pab hu nkauj
released	se publicó	釋放	đã phát hành	해방하다	tso ntawm
religious	religiosa	宗教	sùng đạo	종교적인	ntseeg ntuj
slavery	esclavitud	奴隸	chế độ nô lệ	노예의	ua qhev
teenager	adolescente	少年	thanh thiếu niên tuổi từ 13 đến 19	10대의 청소년	tub ntxhais hluas

Week 5: Special Effects in Film and Television

English	Spanish	Chinese	Vietnamese	Korean	Hmong
background	fondo	背景	nền, hậu cảnh	배경	nyob tom qab
landscape	paisaje	場景	cảnh vật	풍경	toj roob hauv pes
miniature	miniatura	縮影	hình, vật được rút nhỏ	소형 모형	tej yam me me
prehistoric	prehistórico	史前	tiền sử	선사 시대의	puag thaum ub
reassembled	reensamblados	重新組裝	lắp ráp lại	다시 모으다	rov sib dhos

Unit 4

English	Spanish	Chinese	Vietnamese	Korean	Hmong
Week 1: Weslandia					
blunders	tropezones	錯誤	những sai lầm vụng về	큰 실수	dig muag, tsis kag siab
civilization	civilización	文明	nền văn minh	문명	cov neeg muaj txuj ci tsim kho lub neej
complex	complejo	複雜	phức tạp	복잡한	ib pawg
envy	envidia	妒嫉	ghen tỵ	부러워하다	khib
fleeing	huir	逃走	chạy trốn	벗어나는	khiav
inspired	inspiró	啟發	được gợi cảm	영감을 주다, 고무하다	ua rau yus xav heev
rustling	susurrando	沙沙聲	xào xạc	바스락 소리나는	txav ub no
strategy	estrategia	策略	kế hoạch, chiến lược	전략, 방법	tswv yim
Week 2: Tripping Over the Lunch Lady					
Dalmatian	dálmata	大麦町斑点犬	loài chó lông ngắn	달마티아종의	aub dawb uas dub tej tee
frilly	escarolado	虛飾的	có nếp gấp	주름장식이 달린	tsi tseem ceeb
promenading	pasear	散步	dạo chơi	산책하는	mus taug kev
sprained	dislocado	扭伤	bị bong gân	삐었다	qes
substitute	sustituto	代课老师	thay thế	대리	hloov
Week 3: Exploding Ants					
critical	críticos	重要	quan trọng, then chốt	비판적인	nyaum, tseem ceeb
enables	permite	使能夠	làm cho có thể	가능하게 하다	ua tau
mucus	mucus	黏液	đờm dãi	점액	quav ntswg
scarce	escaso	缺乏	khan hiếm	부족한	tsawg tsawg

English	Spanish	Chinese	Vietnamese	Korean	Hmong
specialize	se especializan	專門研究	chuyên môn về	특수화하다	ua ib yam khoom kaws xwb
sterile	estériles	不育	vô trùng	불임의, 살균한, 헛된	muaj tsis tau me nyuam

Week 4: The Stormi Giovanni Club

English	Spanish	Chinese	Vietnamese	Korean	Hmong
cavities	caries	洞	sâu răng	구멍	qhov
combination	combinación	組合	sự phối hợp	결합	ob peb yam los ua ke
demonstrates	demuestra	展示	biểu diễn	증명, 설명하다	ua piv txwv
episode	episodio	情節	một giai đoạn	에피소드	ib zag
profile	(mantenerse en) segundo plano	外形	tiểu sử sơ lược	특성	sab ntsej muag
strict	estricto	嚴密	nghiêm khắc, gắt gao	엄격한	nkhaws

Week 5: The Gymnast

English	Spanish	Chinese	Vietnamese	Korean	Hmong
bluish	azulados	帶藍色的	có chút màu xanh da trời	푸르스름한	xiav loos
cartwheels	volteretas laterales	側手翻	lộn nhào	옆으로 재주넘기	tis lis kas
gymnastics	gimnástica	體操	môn thể dục	체조의	txawj siv tes taw
hesitation	duda	猶疑	sự do dự	주저	ua ob peb lub siab, ua siab deb
limelight	centro de atención	石灰光	ánh đèn pha	조명, 스포트라이트	teem ci ntsa
skidded	patinó	滑動	trượt	미끄러지다	kiv, ya
somersault	dar saltos mortales	筋斗	lộn mèo	공중제비	somersault
throbbing	latía	跳動	nhức nhối	두근두근하는, 떨리는	od od
wincing	haciendo una mueca de dolor	畏縮	nhăn mặt	주춤하는	quaj txhawj

Unit 5

English	Spanish	Chinese	Vietnamese	Korean	Hmong
Week 1: The Skunk Ladder					
abandoned	cambió	放任不管的	bỏ không	그만 뒀다	tso tseg
attempt	intento	試圖	toan tính	시도	npaj tseg
bellow	grito	吼叫	rống	고함소리	poob qis
cavern	caverna	洞穴	hang lớn	땅굴	qhov tsua
feat	hazaña	事蹟	việc làm hiển hách	묘기	ua tiav
immensely	inmensamente	極大地	bao la	막대하게	loj tshaj
savage	salvaje	野性的	dã man	사나운	ua cia
Week 2: The Unsinkable Wreck of the R.M.S. *Titanic*					
cramped	estrecho	偪促	đã nhét vào; chật chội	답답한	ti
debris	restos	殘骸	mảnh vỡ	파편	khib nyiab
interior	interior	內部	nội thất, bên trong	내부의	sab hauv tsev
ooze	limo	滲流	chảy rỉ	배어 나오다, 새 다	av nkos
robotic	robótico	機器人的	về người máy	로봇의	raws li robots
sediment	sedimento	沉積	đất sạn ở dưới đáy	침전물	tej yam khoom tog rau qab deg
sonar	sonar	聲波導航測距儀	về mặt trời	수중 음파 탐 지기	sonar

English	Spanish	Chinese	Vietnamese	Korean	Hmong
Week 3: Talk with an Astronaut					
accomplishments	logros	成就	sự thành công	성취	yam ua tau
focus	atención	焦點	tiêu điểm	초점	saib meej
gravity	gravedad	重力	trọng lực	중력	gravity
monitors	monitores	顯示器	theo dõi	모니터	saib
role	ejemplo	角色	vai trò	역할	yus txoj hauj lwm
specific	específico	特殊的	đặc biệt, cụ thể	특정한	meej, tseeb
Week 4: Journey to the Center of the Earth					
armor	armadura	裝甲	áo giáp	갑옷	tub rog cev khaub ncaws hnav thaib ib ce
encases	reviste	裝箱	bao bọc	싸다	ntim
extinct	extintas	絕種	tiệt chủng	멸종하다	tuag tag
hideous	horrorosas	醜陋	xấu xí	무서운	dab tuag
plunged	sumergido	浸入	lao vào	밀어 넣다	dhia rau
serpent	serpiente	大蛇	con rắn	큰 뱀	nab
Week 5: Ghost Towns of the American West					
economic	económico	經濟	về kinh tế	경제의	kev nrhiav nyiaj txiag
independence	independencia	獨立	sự độc lập	독립	nyob ib leeg (tsis tso leej twg)
overrun	rebosante	超出量	chạy nhanh hơn	침략하다	khiav tshaj
scrawled	garabateó	潦草地寫	vẽ nguệch ngoạc	낙서하다	sau ntawv nyeem tsis tau
vacant	vacantes	空置	bỏ trống	공허한	chav khoom

Unit 6

English	Spanish	Chinese	Vietnamese	Korean	Hmong
Week 1: The Truth About Austin's Amazing Bats					
bizarre	raro	毛虫	kỳ lạ	별난	txawv txawv
breathtaking	asombroso	非凡的	hấp dẫn	숨막히는, 기가 막히는	txaus siab heev
headline	encabezado	头条新闻	đề mục	표제, 헤드라인	tis npe rab ntawv
high-pitched	agudo	尖锐的	âm cao	고음의	suab soob soob
roost	percha	栖息	nơi chim đậu	홰, 닭장	mus so los siav
vital	vital	有活力	thiết yếu	굉장히 중요한	tseem ceeb
Week 2: The Mystery of Saint Matthew Island					
bleached	decolorados	漂白	bị bạc màu	탈색되다	ntxhua tshuaj dawb
carcasses	animales muertos	屍體	những bộ xương	시체	lub cev
decay	descomposición	腐朽	hư thối	부식하다	lwj
parasites	parásitos	寄生生物	ký sinh trùng	기생충	kab mob uas nyob hauv
scrawny	escuálido	骨瘦如柴	ốm khẳng khiu	수척한	nka tawv
starvation	inanición	飢餓	sự đói khát	기아	tshaib plab
suspicions	sospechas	懷疑	những nghi ngờ	의심	tsis ntseeg lwm tus
tundra	tundra	寒帶草原	bình nguyên ở vùng bắc cực hoặc vùng núi; lãnh nguyên	툰드라	toj
Week 3: King Midas and the Golden Touch					
adorn	adornar	裝飾	làm tăng vẻ đẹp	꾸미다	ua rau zoo nkauj
cleanse	(te) bañas	洗滌	làm sạch	깨끗이 하다	ntxuav kom hu
lifeless	inanimada	無生命	không có sinh lực	생명이 없는	tsis muaj sia
precious	precioso	珍貴	quý báu	귀중한	muaj nuj nqis

English	Spanish	Chinese	Vietnamese	Korean	Hmong
realm	reino	領土	vương quốc	범위	lub vaj loog
spoonful	cucharada	一匙	đầy một muỗng	소량	diav puv nkaus, diav puv npo

Week 4: The *Hindenburg*

criticizing	criticando	批評	chỉ trích	비판하는	hais taus
cruised	navegó	巡航	đã bay ở tốc độ hiệu quả về nhiên liệu	유람 항해하다	caij cig
drenching	empapándolo	脫灰	ướt sũng	가득 채운	ntub dej tag, tsau dej
era	era	時代	thời kỳ	시대	lub sij hawm
explosion	explosión	爆炸	sự bùng nổ	폭발	tawg
hydrogen	hidrógeno	氫	khí hy-đrô	수소	pa hydrogen

Week 5: Sweet Music in Harlem

bass	bajo	低音	đàn bass	저음의	lub suab laus
clarinet	clarinete	單簧管	kèn clarinet	클라리넷	raj nplaim
fidgety	inquieto	坐立不安的	bồn chồn	안절부절 못하는	nti nti
forgetful	olvidadizo	健忘	hay quên	잊기 쉬운	hnov qab heev, hnov qauj heev
jammed	improvisé	阻塞	bị ép chặt; đầy ních người	[장소 따위를] 메운	daig
nighttime	noche	夜間	ban đêm	야간에	hmo ntuj
secondhand	de segunda mano	第二手的	cũ, đã có người dùng trước	중고의	tus tes ntev nyob ntawm lub moos

Multilingual Thinking Words

English	Spanish	Chinese	Vietnamese	Korean	Hmong
Analyze	Analizar	分析	Phân tích	분석하다	Xam pom
Apply	Aplicar	应用	Áp dụng	응용하다	Tso rau
Assess	Calcular	估值	Lượng định	평가하다, 감정하다	Ntsuam xyuas
Categorize	Categorizar	分类	Phân loại	분류하다	Teev uake tej pawg
Clarify Information	Clarificar la información	阐明信息	Nói rõ thông tin	정보를 분명히 하다	Ntaub ntawv meej zog ntxiv
Classify	Clasificar	分类	Xếp loại	분류하다	Xaiv uake tej pawg
Combine Information	Combinar la información	拼合信息	Kết hợp thông tin	정보를 합치다	Ntaub ntawv sis dhos
Compare	Comparar	比较	So sánh	비교하다	Sis piv
Conclude	Concluir	归纳	Kết luận	마무리짓다	Xaus
Connect	Conectar	联系	Kết nối	연결하다	Txuas
Construct	Construir	建构	Xây dựng	건축하다, 구성하다	Ua txuas
Contrast	Contrastar	对比	Đối chiếu	대조하다	Tsi sib thooj
Define	Definir	限定	Định nghĩa	정의하다	Txhais
Demonstrate	Demostrar	示范	Chứng minh	증명하다	Nthauv tawm
Describe	Describir	描述	Mô tả	묘사하다	Piav
Determine Importance	Determinar la importancia	判断重要性	Thẩm định tầm quan trọng	중요성을 결정하다	Xam tseem ceeb
Determine Main Idea	Determinar la idea principal	判断要旨	Thẩm định Ý Chính	주제를 정하다	Xam ntsiab lus
Diagram	Diagrama	图表	Lập biểu đồ	그림, 도표	Kos duab
Differentiate	Diferenciar	辨别	Phân biệt	구별하다	Qhia qhov txawv
Elaborate	Abundar	阐述	Tạo lập	상세히 말하다	Piav meej zog
Evaluate	Evaluar	评估	Lượng giá	평가하다	Soj ntsuam
Examine	Examinar	核查	Khảo sát	조사하다	Tshuaj xyuas

English	Spanish	Chinese	Vietnamese	Korean	Hmong
Explain	Explicar	辩解	Giải thích	설명하다	Piav
Generalize	Generalizar	概括	Tổng quát hóa	일반화하다	Hais dav dav
Identify Characteristics	Identificar características	辨认特征	Nhận diện các Đặc tính	특징을 밝히다	Qhia yam ntxwv
Identify Pattern	Identificar patrones	辨认规律	Nhận diện Khuôn mẫu	형태를 밝히다	Qhia tus qauv
Identify Relationships	Identificar relaciones	辨认关系	Nhận diện Tương quan	관계를 밝히다	Qhia kev txheeb ze
Illustrate	Ilustrar	说明	Minh họa	설명하다	Taw qhia
Infer	Inferir	推论	Luận ra	추론하다	Txhais
Judge	Juzgar	判定	Xét thấy	판단하다	Txiav txim
Label	Etiquetar	命名	Dán nhãn	(-라는) 딱지를 붙이다	Lo ntawv
List	Hacer una lista	列表	Liệt kê	열거하다	Teev
Match	Igualar	相配	Tương xứng	-에 어울리다, 필적하다, 대등하다	Sib phim
Observe	Observar	观察	Quan sát	관찰하다	Saib
Organize	Organizar	组织	Tổ chức	정리, 조직구성하다	Sis sau
Outline	Esbozar	概述	Phác thảo	윤곽을 그리다	Teev cov ntsiab
Predict	Predecir	预计	Đoán trước	예측하다	Kwv yees
Recall	Recordar	回想	Nhớ lại	기억하다	Xam txog
Record	Grabar	纪录	Ghi lại	기록, 녹음하다	Teev tseg
Restructure	Reestructurar	重构	Tái cấu trúc	재구성, 구조조정하다	Teeb dua
Sequence	Secuenciar	次序	Xếp thứ tự	순서대로 나열하다	Teev cov ntsiab sis dhos
Show	Mostrar	展示	Chìra	보여주다	Qhia
Solve a Problem	Resolver un problema	解决一个问题	Giải quyết	문제를 풀다, 해결하다	Kho teeb meem
Summarize	Resumir	概括	Tóm tắt	요점정리하다	Piav zuaj zog uake
Verify	Verificar	查证	Kiểm lại	확인하다, 입증하다	Kuaj kos meej

Part 7
High-Frequency Words, Linguistic Contrastive Analysis, ELL Teaching Routines, and Graphic Organizers

Contents

High-Frequency Words

The high-frequency words section includes activities and word cards that allow students to use these words in speaking and writing to build their competency and fluency.

Linguistic Contrastive Analysis

Use these pages to find out more about challenges in pronunciation and grammar that your English language learners may face as they produce spoken English. The linguistic contrastive analysis chart equates sounds in English with sounds in Spanish, Vietnamese, Cantonese, Hmong, Filipino, Korean, and Mandarin.

English Language Learner Teaching Routines

These routines support systematic and scaffolded instruction in using core lesson materials.

Graphic Organizers

Graphic organizers provide visual support important to English language learners' comprehension.

High-Frequency Words

The high-frequency words are words that appear most often in written English, words of the greatest general service to English language learners. Many of the words are part of word families that are useful for students to know as they learn English.

Each week, provide the list of high-frequency words for students' reference for speaking and writing. Choose strategies from this bank of activities to ensure students' mastery.

Cloze Activity

Create a passage that includes high-frequency words. Display the passage covering high-frequency words with sticky notes. Ask students to read the passage with you, substituting the missing words. Have them explain how they figured out which words to use.

Play Bingo

After students have learned at least 25 words, provide a 5×5 grid with a high-frequency word written in each square. Read aloud high-frequency words as you draw them randomly. Students cover words they hear with markers to create a row. When a student has created a row, have him or her read the words aloud.

Semantic Map

For words with richer meanings, create semantic maps. Place the word in the middle of a web and ask students to supply related words for the "arms." Discuss word relationships.

High-Frequency Scavenger Hunt

Have students keep the word lists on their desks for the week. Ask them to tally how many times they see each word in their reading selections, science or social studies books, magazine articles, and so on. They can tally how often they say the word.

Realia and Visuals

Use both hands-on experiences and visuals to reinforce meanings of the words.

- Provide realia that evokes meanings of high-frequency words. For *year,* for example, you might show a calendar. For *see,* you might show a pair of eyeglasses. Discuss the items, using the high-frequency words.
- Use visuals to teach abstract high-frequency words. For *of,* for example, you could show pictures: a basket of laundry, a slice of bread, a glass of water.

Word Sorts

Have students sort the words. Provide index cards with words, one word per card. Students can sort them into categories you provide (*words that show action, words that name things, words in the same family,* and so on) or sort them and explain the rationale behind their categories.

Flashcard Activities

- Post high-frequency words on a word wall as you introduce them. From time to time, hand students flashcards with the words on them, one word per card. Students match the card to the word on the wall, and then use the word in a sentence.
- Hand out flashcards, one word to each pair of students. Students work together to create two sentences using the word.
- Make up simple sentences using the high-frequency words. Write the sentences on cards, one word per card. Hand the cards out to students. Have them unscramble the words to make a sentence and read it aloud chorally.
- Pair students and give one student in each pair a card. The student with the card gives clues about the word for the other student to guess.

Unit 1 Week 1	Unit 1 Week 2	Unit 1 Week 3
1 the	11 that	21 by
2 be	12 for	22 this
3 of	13 they	23 we
4 and	14 I	24 you
5 a	15 with	25 do
6 to	16 as	26 but
7 in	17 not	27 from
8 he	18 on	28 or
9 have	19 she	29 which
10 it	20 at	30 one

Unit 1 Week 4	Unit 1 Week 5	Unit 2 Week 1
31 would	41 if	51 about
32 all	42 no	52 than
33 will	43 man	53 into
34 there	44 out	54 could
35 say	45 other	55 state
36 who	46 so	56 only
37 make	47 what	57 new
38 when	48 time	58 year
39 can	49 up	59 some
40 more	50 go	60 take

Unit 2 Week 2	Unit 2 Week 3	Unit 2 Week 4
61 come	71 work	81 day
62 these	72 now	82 also
63 know	73 may	83 after
64 see	74 such	84 way
65 use	75 give	85 many
66 get	76 over	86 must
67 like	77 think	87 look
68 then	78 most	88 before
69 first	79 even	89 great
70 any	80 find	90 back

Unit 2 Week 5	Unit 3 Week 1	Unit 3 Week 2
91 through	101 because	111 little
92 long	102 good	112 world
93 where	103 each	113 very
94 much	104 those	114 still
95 should	105 feel	115 nation
96 well	106 seem	116 hand
97 people	107 how	117 old
98 down	108 high	118 life
99 own	109 too	119 tell
100 just	110 place	120 write

Unit 3 Week 3	Unit 3 Week 4	Unit 3 Week 5
121 become	131 under	141 begin
122 here	132 last	142 while
123 show	133 right	143 number
124 house	134 move	144 part
125 both	135 thing	145 turn
126 between	136 general	146 real
127 need	137 school	147 leave
128 mean	138 never	148 might
129 call	139 same	149 want
130 develop	140 another	150 point

Unit 4 Week 1	Unit 4 Week 2	Unit 4 Week 3
151 form	161 interest	171 again
152 off	162 large	172 hold
153 child	163 person	173 govern
154 few	164 end	174 around
155 small	165 open	175 possible
156 since	166 public	176 head
157 against	167 follow	177 consider
158 ask	168 during	178 word
159 late	169 present	179 program
160 home	170 without	180 problem

Unit 4 Week 4	Unit 4 Week 5	Unit 5 Week 1
181 however	191 fact	201 city
182 lead	192 group	202 put
183 system	193 play	203 close
184 set	194 stand	204 case
185 order	195 increase	205 force
186 eye	196 early	206 meet
187 plan	197 course	207 once
188 run	198 change	208 water
189 keep	199 help	209 upon
190 face	200 line	210 war

Unit 5 Week 2	Unit 5 Week 3	Unit 5 Week 4
211 build	221 side	231 study
212 hear	222 try	232 woman
213 light	223 provide	233 member
214 unite	224 continue	234 until
215 live	225 name	235 far
216 every	226 certain	236 night
217 country	227 power	237 always
218 bring	228 pay	238 service
219 center	229 result	239 away
220 let	230 question	240 report

Unit 5 Week 5	Unit 6 Week 1	Unit 6 Week 2
241 something	251 though	261 better
242 company	252 young	262 big
243 week	253 less	263 boy
244 church	254 enough	264 cost
245 toward	255 almost	265 business
246 start	256 read	266 value
247 social	257 include	267 second
248 room	258 president	268 why
249 figure	259 nothing	269 clear
250 nature	260 yet	270 expect

Unit 6 Week 3

271 family

272 complete

273 act

274 sense

275 mind

276 experience

277 art

278 next

279 near

280 direct

Unit 6 Week 4

281 car

282 law

283 industry

284 important

285 girl

286 food

287 several

288 matter

289 usual

290 rather

Unit 6 Week 5

291 per

292 often

293 kind

294 among

295 white

296 reason

297 action

298 return

299 foot

300 care

How People Speak

All languages have consonant and vowel sounds. Consonants are made with some obstruction of the vocal tract, either a complete stoppage of air or enough constriction to create friction. Vowels are produced with a more open vocal tract; there is no constriction that might cause friction.

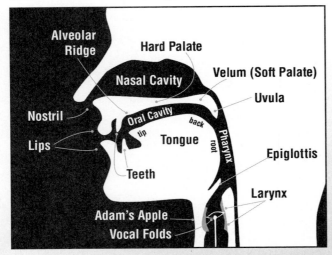

Figure 1: The human vocal tract makes the sounds of speech.

Consonants

Every consonant can be described by noting three characteristics: voicing, place of articulation, and manner of articulation.

Voicing

Many sounds of language, including all vowels, employ vibration of the vocal folds in the larynx. This creates more resonance and energy for the sound. All speech sounds are characterized as either voiced (with vocal fold vibration) or voiceless (with no vocal fold vibration). Feeling the vibration around the Adam's apple can help you understand this difference. If you say "sssss" and then "zzzzz," you can feel the distinction: /s/ is voiceless and /z/ is voiced.

Place of Articulation

This is the location in the vocal tract where the air stream may be constricted. The /s/ sound, for example, is made with the tongue tip close to the alveolar ridge (see Figure 1).

Place of Articulation Terms

Alveolar: tongue tip and ridge behind teeth

Bilabial: using both lips

Glottal: produced at the larynx

Interdental: tongue tip between upper and lower teeth

Labio-dental: upper teeth and lower lip

Labio-velar: rounding of lips; tongue body raised toward velum

Palatal: body of tongue and high part of palate

Palato-alveolar: tongue tip and palate behind alveolar ridge

Velar: body of tongue and velum (soft palate)

Manner of Articulation

This is the type or degree of constriction that occurs in an articulation. For example, the /t/ sound completely stops the airflow with the tongue tip at the alveolar ridge, but /s/ allows air to pass noisily through a small opening.

Manner of Articulation Terms

Affricate: complete constriction followed by slow separation of the articulators resulting in friction

Approximant: close constriction, but not enough for friction

Fricative: narrow constriction; turbulent airflow causing friction

Glottal: produced at the larynx

Lateral: air passes over sides of tongue

Nasal: lowered velum to let air escape through the nose

Stop: complete constriction, closure so that air cannot escape through the oral cavity

Tap: brief contact between tongue tip and alveolar ridge

Vowels

Vowels are open, sonorous sounds. Each vowel can be uniquely described by noting the position of the tongue, the tension of the vocal tract, and the position of the lips. Vowels are described by ***height,*** where the tongue is relative to the roof of the mouth. They can be high, mid, or low. Tongue backness tells if the tongue articulation is in the front or back of the mouth.

Tense vowels are more common around the world. In English, they are longer and include an expansion of the throat at the pharynx. Lax vowels are shorter with a more neutral pharynx. An example is the tense long *e* as in *meet*

Speaking English

versus the lax short *i* as in *mitt.* The lips either can be in a spread or neutral position, or they can be rounded and protrude slightly.

English is the third most widely spoken native language in the world, after Mandarin and Spanish. There are about 330 million native speakers of English and 600 million who speak it as a foreign language.

English Consonant Sounds

The following chart gives the International Phonetic Alphabet (IPA) symbol for each English consonant along with its voicing, place, and manner of articulation. This information can be used to understand and help identify problems that non-native speakers may encounter when learning to speak English.

CONSONANTS OF ENGLISH		
IPA	**Articulation**	**Example**
p	voiceless bilabial stop	**p**it
b	voiced bilabial stop	**b**it
m	voiced bilabial nasal stop	**m**an
w	voiced labio-velar approximant	**w**in
f	voiceless labio-dental fricative	**f**un
v	voiced labio-dental fricative	**v**ery
θ	voiceless interdental fricative	**th**ing
ð	voiced interdental fricative	**th**ere
t	voiceless alveolar stop	**t**ime
d	voiced alveolar stop	**d**ime
n	voiced alveolar nasal stop	**n**ame
s	voiceless alveolar fricative	**s**oy
z	voiced alveolar fricative	**z**eal
ɾ	voiced alveolar tap	bu**tt**er
l	voiced alveolar central approximant	**l**oop
ɹ	voiced palato-alveolar affricate	**r**ed
ʃ	voiceless palato-alveolar fricative	**sh**allow
ʒ	voiced palato-alveolar affricate	vi**si**on
tʃ	voiceless palato-alveolar affricate	**ch**irp
dʒ	voiced palato-alveolar affricate	**j**oy
j	voiced palatal approximant	**y**ou
k	voiceless velar stop	**k**ite
g	voiced velar stop	**g**oat
ŋ	voiced velar nasal stop	ki**ng**
h	voiceless glottal fricative	**h**ope

English Vowel Sounds

Most languages in the world have around five vowel sounds. English has 13 common vowel sounds, which means that many students of English must learn more vowel distinctions than there are in their native language. The lax vowels are most difficult. Some vowels are diphthongs, meaning the tongue is in one position at the beginning of the sound, and it moves to another position by the end of it.

VOWELS OF ENGLISH		
IPA	**Sound**	**Example**
i	ē	b**ea**t
ɪ	ĭ	b**i**t
e	ā	b**ai**t
ɛ	ĕ	b**e**t
æ	ă	b**a**t
u	ōō	b**oo**t
ʊ	ŏŏ	c**ou**ld
o	ō	b**oa**t
ɔ	aw	l**aw**
ɑ	ŏ	h**o**t
ə	ə	**a**bout
ʌ	ŭ	c**u**t
ɝ	er	b**ir**d
ɑ ʊ	ow	h**ou**se
ɔ ɪ	oy	b**oy**
ɑ ɪ	ī	b**i**te

Figure 2 is a schematic of the mouth. The left is the front of the mouth; the right is the back. The top is the roof of the mouth and the bottom is the floor. Placement of the vowel shows where the tongue reaches its maximum in the English articulation.

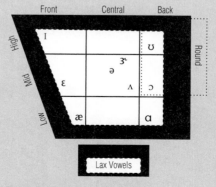

Figure 2: English vowel sounds

Transference

Pronunciation

All languages build on the same fundamentals. All languages contrast voiced and voiceless sound and have stops and fricatives. Many languages use the same places of articulation for consonants as well. The majority of sounds will easily transfer from another language to English.

However, there will always be some sounds that are not found in a person's native language that can pose a challenge to the English language learner. English has a few relatively rare sounds, such as the interdental sounds spelled with *th*, /ə/ and /ð/. The /r/ sound in English is also a very rare type of sound. Most other languages use a tap or trill articulation for an /r/ sound.

In some languages, the /l/ and /r/ sounds belong to one psychological category. This means that they count as the same sound in that language. In this case, it is not the articulation that is difficult, but the perception of the difference and consistent use of one versus the other in any word context. This type of psychological category is called a *phoneme*, and multiple speech sounds all can be categorized as the same phoneme in that language.

This is true for English as well, where, for example, the alveolar lateral /l/ as in *lob* and the velarized lateral /ł/ as in *ball* are both counted as the same sound—an *l*—to native speakers of English. It is important to keep in mind that both the phonetic articulation of a sound and its psychological, phonemic category factor into the learning of a new language.

Grammar

Pronouncing English is not the only stumbling block for English learners. The grammar and usage, or syntax, of English may present distinctions that are unique to the language. For example, English syntax requires adjectives to precede the nouns they modify, as in *the tall girl*. In other languages, such as Spanish, Hmong, and Vietnamese, adjectives follow nouns, as in *la chica alta* (literally *the girl tall* in Spanish). This may cause word-order problems, particularly for less advanced English learners.

Other syntactic differences are less obvious and may cause problems even for advanced learners. For example, many East Asian languages (such as Mandarin, Cantonese, and Korean) do not mark agreement between subject and verb. Speakers of these languages may therefore leave out agreement markers, such as the *-s* in *The girl like cats*.

The use of articles varies across languages. For instance, Spanish uses the definite article more often than English, while Mandarin and Cantonese do not have articles. A Spanish-speaking English learner might say *The girl likes the cats* instead of *The girl likes cats,* and a Mandarin or Cantonese speaker might say *Girl like cat.*

Plural marking is another potential trouble spot: Vietnamese, Filipino, Cantonese, and Mandarin do not add plural markers to nouns. Learners speaking these languages may have difficulty with English plurals, saying *cat* instead of *cats.*

> ### Grammar Hot Spots
>
> **Look for Grammar Hot Spots** on the following pages for tips on the most common syntax errors by speakers of languages other than English.

Common First Languages

In the Common First Languages section, you will find details of some common non-English languages spoken in the United States. They are:

- Spanish
- Vietnamese
- Cantonese
- Hmong
- Filipino
- Korean
- Mandarin

You can use the fundamentals of speech articulation already covered to help you understand where the languages differ from English. Differences in the spoken language and in the writing systems are explored as well. These sections pinpoint common trouble spots specific to learners of English.

Culture Clues

Look to Culture Clues for insights into the cultural differences of each language learner as well as ideas for ways to embrace students' diversity.

Linguistic Contrastive Analysis

The Linguistic Contrastive Analysis Charts provide a quick reference for comparing English sounds with those of other languages. The charts allow you to check at a glance which sounds have equivalents in other languages. For those sounds that don't have equivalents, you can find the closest sound used as a substitute and suggestions for helping someone gain a native English articulation.

In these charts, the sounds are notated using the International Phonetic Alphabet (IPA). This is the most widely recognized and used standard for representing speech sounds in any language. A guiding principle of the IPA across all languages is that each sound is uniquely represented by one symbol, and each symbol represents only one sound.

The chart has columns for each native language with rows corresponding to each English phoneme. Each cell in the chart gives an example word using that sound in the native language, a definition in parentheses, and transference tips below. If there is no sound equivalent to English, a common substitution used by speakers of that language may be provided.

Transference Tips

Transference tips give you ideas of how the sound will be produced by the learner. Cells in bold print indicate where the English learner may have particular difficulty with the English sound.

Spanish

Background
Spanish is the second most widely spoken language in the world. There are more than 400 million native Spanish speakers in 20-plus countries on three continents. Spanish vocabulary and pronunciation differ from country to country. While most dialect differences in English are in vowel sounds, Spanish dialects differ in their consonants.

Spoken
Spanish sounds are similar to those found in English, so there is a strong foundation for the native Spanish speaker learning English. However, there are three key differences between English and Spanish consonants:

1. Most of the alveolar sounds in English, such as /t/, /d/, and /n/ are produced farther forward in the mouth in Spanish. Instead of the tongue touching the alveolar ridge as in English, in Spanish it touches the back of the teeth.

2. Another difference is that the /r/ sound in English is not found in Spanish. There are two /r/ sounds in Spanish. One is the tap /ɾ/, which occurs in English as the quick sound in the middle of the name *Betty*. Psychologically, this tap sound is a kind of /t/ or /d/ sound in English, while in Spanish it is perceived as an /r/. The other /r/ sound in Spanish is a trill, or series of tongue taps on the alveolar ridge. This does not occur in English.

3. The third key difference between English and Spanish can be found in the English production of the voiceless stops /p/, /t/, and /k/. In English these sounds are aspirated, with an extra puff of air at the end, when the sound occurs at the beginning of a word or stressed syllable. So, /p/ is aspirated in *pit*. Learners can add a puff of air to such sounds to sound more like native English speakers.

There are five vowels in Spanish, which are a subset of the English vowels. Spanish vowels include tense vowel sounds a, e, i, o, u. Lax vowel sounds in English are the problematic ones for native Spanish speakers.

Written
Like English, written Spanish uses the Roman alphabet, so both writing systems are similar. There are a few orthographic differences to note, however:

- The letter *h* in Spanish is silent, but the sound /h/ is written as *j* or *g*.
- A single letter *r* in Spanish represents a tap, while the double *rr* represents a trill.
- Accents are used to show the stress on a syllable when the stress is different from the usual rules. In some cases, words change meaning according to the accents. For example, *el* means *the* while *él* means *he*.

Written Spanish vowels are pronounced like the symbols in the IPA. So, the Spanish *i* is pronounced with the long *e* as in the word *beat*. The IPA and Spanish symbol for this letter is the same: *i*.

Grammar Hot Spots

- Double negatives are part of standard grammar in Spanish. Stress the single negative construction in English.
- English prepositions are a common stumbling point for Spanish speakers.

Culture Clues

The Spanish language covers many countries, dialects, and cultures. Always encourage students to share special things about their culture, such as foods, festivals, or social customs.

Vietnamese

Background
Approximately 80 million people in Vietnam speak Vietnamese. The northern dialect is the standard, though central and southern dialects also exist. Most Vietnamese speakers in the United States are from southern Vietnam and speak the southern dialect.

Spoken
Vietnamese is a tonal language, so each syllable is pronounced with a distinctive tone that affects meaning. Vietnamese has a complex vowel system of 12 vowels and 26 diphthongs. Its consonants are simpler, but Vietnamese syllable structure allows few possibilities for final consonants.

Students may need help noticing and learning to reproduce final consonant sounds in English words and syllables. Vietnamese syllable structure allows for limited combinations of initial consonants. Students also may need help with the more complex initial consonant clusters of English words and syllables.

Culture Clues
In traditional Vietnamese education, there is a strict division between the roles of student and teacher. Students may be confused if asked to direct a part of their own study, so encourage group work.

Written
Since the 1600s, Vietnamese has used a Romanized alphabet. Many characters written in Vietnamese have sounds different from their English counterparts, such as *d, x, ch, nh, kh, g, tr, r,* and *e.*

Grammar Hot Spots
- Like English, Vietnamese uses Subject-Verb-Object (SVO) syntax, or word order.
- Vietnamese does not use affixes; instead, syntax expresses number, case, and tense.

Cantonese

Background
Cantonese is one of the seven major Chinese languages, not all of which are mutually intelligible. Cantonese is mostly spoken in China's southern provinces, Hong Kong, and Macau by about 66 million people. It is a tonal language, and the same sequence of letters can have different meanings depending on their pitch.

Spoken
Cantonese has six stops, aspirated and non-aspirated /p/, /t/, /k/; three fricatives /f/, /s/, /h/, and two affricates /ts/, /tsʰ/. Some that do not exist in Cantonese can be difficult for the English language learner. The /v/ often gets pronounced as /f/ or /w/; the /z/ is often said as /s/; the sounds spelled with *th* are often said as /t/, /d/, or /f/. Cantonese speakers have difficulty distinguishing between /l/ and /r/, since /r/ is not present in their language. They tend to produce an /l/-like sound for both English sounds in words such as *ride* and *lied.*

Cantonese has 11 vowels and 10 diphthongs. One of the major problems for Cantonese speakers is distinguishing between English tense and lax vowels because the distribution of Cantonese short and long vowels is determined by the sound context.

Syllables in Cantonese don't have consonant clusters. English consonant clusters are often deleted or broken up by vowel insertion (e.g., *list* becomes *lis*). This may be especially problematic when producing English past tense (e.g., *baked*).

Written
Cantonese is written with standard Chinese characters known as *Hànzi* where each character represents a syllable and has a meaning. Additional Cantonese-specific characters were also added. Cantonese speakers may have difficulty with sound-letter correspondences in English.

Grammar Hot Spots
- English articles and prepositions are difficult for Cantonese speakers. *In, on,* and *at,* for instance, can be translated as the same preposition in Cantonese.
- Plurals, tenses, and gerund endings are difficult for Cantonese speakers to transfer to English.

Hmong

Background
Hmong is a group of approximately 18 languages within the Hmong-Mien family. There are roughly four million speakers of Hmong, including 200,000 in the United States. They are mainly from two groups with mutually intelligible dialects—Hmong Daw and Mong Leng.

Spoken
Hmong vowels are few and simple, but its consonants are complex and differ from those of English. Notable features of Hmong phonology absent from English include consonantal pre-nasalization (the /m/n/ŋ/ sound before a consonant) and the contrast between nasalized and non-nasalized vowels. Hmong is tonal. Each syllable is pronounced with a distinctive pitch.

Culture Clues
In traditional Hmong culture, learning takes place through hands-on experience. Students may find it difficult to adjust to the use of graphics or print media. Competition, personal achievement, and self-directed instruction may be unfamiliar concepts, so students may prefer group work.

Written
The Romanized Popular Alphabet (RPA), developed in the 1950s, is the usual way of transcribing Hmong. Syllable-final consonants are absent in pronunciation but are used to orthographically represent the tonal value of a given syllable. Students may need particular help in identifying and learning to reproduce the final consonant sounds of English words and syllables.

Grammar Hot Spots
- Like English, Hmong is an SVO language. Personal pronouns are marked for number, including inflection for singular, dual, and plural, though they are not marked for case.
- Because Hmong and English prepositions often have different semantic qualities, students may need help mastering uses of English prepositions. For example, it is correct to say "think about [something]" rather than "think on [something]."

Filipino

Background
Filipino and English are the official languages of the Philippines, where 175 languages are spoken. There are about 24 million native speakers of Filipino, and more than 50 million people speak Filipino as a second language. You may hear the terms Filipino and Tagalog being used interchangeably. Another term is Pilipino.

Spoken
Filipino has many similar speech sounds to English. The notable exceptions are the lack of the consonant sounds /f/, /v/, and those spelled with *th*. Of these, the English /f/ and /v/ cause the most difficulty for learners. For /f/, they may substitute /p/. The distinction between long *e* (as in *beat*) and short *i* (as in *bit*) is also a trouble spot. Filipino does not allow consonant clusters at the end of syllables, so *detect* may be simplified to just one final consonant (*detec*).

Culture Clues
Most people from the Philippines can speak Filipino, but for many it is not their first language. Ask Filipino students about other languages they speak. Because English is used alongside Filipino as the language of instruction in the Philippines, most Filipinos are familiar with English.

Written
The Filipino alphabet has 28 letters and is based on the Spanish alphabet, so the English writing system poses little problem.

Grammar Hot Spots
- Filipino word order is Verb-Subject-Object (VSO), which does not transfer well to English.
- Inflectional verb endings, such as *-s, -en, -ed*, and *-ing* do not exist in Filipino, so it is common to leave out the third person singular verb marker (*"He walk,"* not *"He walks"*).

Korean

Background
Korean is spoken by 71 million people in North and South Korea. Standard Korean is based on the speech in and around Seoul.

Spoken
Korean does not have corresponding sounds for English /f/, /v/, /ə/, /ð/, and /dʒ/. In word-initial position, all Korean stops are voiceless. Voiced stops /b/, /d/, and /g/ are only produced between two vowels. Korean speakers may have difficulty producing /s/, /ʃ/, and /z/ in some contexts, in addition to English /r/ and /l/ sounds (e.g., *rock* and *lock*). They may have problems in producing English consonant clusters (e.g., *str-*, *sk-*). These problems can often be eliminated by vowel insertion or consonant deletion. In addition, the distinction between English tense and lax vowels (e.g., long *e* as in *beat* vs. /ɪ/ as in *bit*) may be problematic for Korean speakers.

Culture Clues
Korean uses a complex system of honorifics, so it is unusual for Korean students to use the pronoun *you* or call their teachers by their first name.

Written
Modern Korean uses the Korean alphabet *(Hangul)* or a mixed script of *Hangul* and Chinese. *Hangul* is an alphabetic script organized into syllabic blocks.

Grammar Hot Spots
- In contrast to English, Korean word order is Subject-Object-Verb (SOV). The verb always comes at the end of a sentence.
- Korean syllable stress is different, so learners may have difficulties with the rhythm of English.

Mandarin

Background
Mandarin Chinese encompasses a wide range of dialects and is the native language of two-thirds of China. There are approximately 870 million Mandarin speakers worldwide. North Mandarin, as found in Beijing, is the basis of the modern standard language.

Spoken
Mandarin Chinese and English differ substantially in their sound structure. Mandarin lacks voiced obstruent consonants (/b/, /d/, /g/, /dʒ/), causing difficulty for speakers in perceiving and producing English voiced consonants (e.g., *buy* may be pronounced and perceived as *pie*). The sounds spelled with *th* are not present in Mandarin, so they are often substituted with /s/ or /t/ causing, for example, *fourth* to be pronounced as *fours.* Mandarin Chinese has five vowels. Due to the relatively small vowel inventory and contextual effects on vowels in Mandarin, many English vowels and tense/lax distinctions present problems for speakers of Mandarin Chinese. Mandarin allows only a very simple syllable structure, causing problems in producing consonant clusters in English. Speakers may drop consonants or insert vowels between them (e.g., *film* may become /filəm/). The use of tones in Mandarin may result in the rising and falling of pitch when speaking English.

Written
Chinese is written with characters known as *Hànzi.* Each character represents a syllable and also has a meaning. A Romanized alphabet called *Pinyin* marks pronunciation of characters. Chinese speakers may have problems mastering letter-sound correspondences in written English, especially for sounds that are not present in Mandarin.

Grammar Hot Spots
- The non-inflected nature of Chinese causes Mandarin speakers to have problems with plurals, past tense markers, and gerund forms *(-s, -ed, -ing)*.
- Mastering English tenses and passive voice is difficult. Students should be familiarized with correct lexical and syntactic features as well as appropriate situations for the use of various tenses and passives.

Linguistic Contrastive Analysis Chart

The Consonants of English

IPA	ENGLISH	SPANISH	VIETNAMESE	CANTONESE
p	**p**it Aspirated at the start of a word or stressed syllable	**pa**to (duck) Never aspirated	**p**in (battery)	**p**ʰa (to lie prone) Always aspirated
b	**b**it	**ba**rco (boat) Substitute voiced bilabial fricative/ɜ/ in between vowels	**b**a (three) Implosive (air moves into the mouth during articulation)	NO EQUIVALENT Substitute /p/
m	**m**an	**m**undo (world)	**m**ot (one)	**m**a (mother)
w	**w**in	ag**u**a (water)	NO EQUIVALENT Substitute word-initial /u/	**w**a (frog)
f	**f**un	**f**lor (flower)	**ph**ương (phoenix) Substitute sound made with both lips, rather than with the lower lip and the teeth like English /f/	**f**a (flower) Only occurs at the beginning of syllables
v	**v**ery	NO EQUIVALENT Learners can use correct sound	**V**iệt Nam (Vietnam)	NO EQUIVALENT Substitute /f/
θ	**th**ing Rare in other languages. When done correctly, the tongue will stick out between the teeth.	NO EQUIVALENT Learners can use correct sound	NO EQUIVALENT Substitute /th/ or /f/	NO EQUIVALENT Substitute /th/ or /f/
ð	**th**ere Rare in other languages. When done correctly, the tongue will stick out between the teeth.	ca**d**a (every) Sound exists in Spanish only between vowels; sometimes substitute voiceless θ.	NO EQUIVALENT Substitute /d/	NO EQUIVALENT Substitute /t/ or /f/
t	**t**ime Aspirated at the start of a word or stressed syllable English tongue-touch. Is a little farther back in the mouth than the other languages.	**t**ocar (touch) Never aspirated	**t**ám (eight) Distinguishes aspirated and non-aspirated	**t**ʰa (he/she) Distinguishes aspirated and non-aspirated
d	**d**ime English tongue-touch is a little farther back in the mouth than the other languages.	**d**os (two)	**Đ**ōng (Dong = unit of currency) Vietnamese /d/ is implosive (air moves into the mouth during articulation)	NO EQUIVALENT Substitute /t/
n	**n**ame English tongue-touch is a little farther back in the mouth than the other languages.	**n**ube (cloud)	**n**am (south)	**n**a (take)
s	**s**oy	**s**eco (dry)	**x**em (to see)	**s**a (sand) Substitute *sh*– sound before /u/ Difficult at ends of syllables and words
z	**z**eal	NO EQUIVALENT Learners can use correct sound	**r**ồi (already) In northern dialect only Southern dialect, substitute /y/	NO EQUIVALENT Substitute /s/
ɾ	bu**tt**er Written 't' and 'd' are pronounced with a quick tongue-tip tap.	**r**ana (toad) Written as single *r* and thought of as a /r/ sound.	NO EQUIVALENT Substitute /t/	NO EQUIVALENT Substitute /t/
l	**l**oop English tongue-touch is a little farther back in the mouth than the other languages. At the ends of syllables, the /l/ bunches up the back of the tongue, becoming velarized /ɫ/ or dark-*l* as in the word *ball*.	**l**ibro (book)	cú **l**ao (island) /l/ does not occur at the ends of syllables	**l**au (angry) /l/ does not occur at the ends of syllables

HMONG	FILIPINO	KOREAN	MANDARIN
*p*eb (we/us/our) Distinguishes aspirated and non-aspirated	*p*aalam (goodbye) Never aspirated	*p*al (sucking)	*pʰei* (cape) Always aspirated
NO EQUIVALENT Substitute /p/	*b*aka (beef)	NO EQUIVALENT /b/ said between vowels Substitute /p/ elsewhere	NO EQUIVALENT
*m*us (to go)	*m*abuti (good)	*m*al (horse)	*m*ei (rose)
NO EQUIVALENT Substitute word-initial /u/	*w*alo (eight)	*g*we (box)	*w*en (mosquito)
*f*aib (to divide)	NO EQUIVALENT Substitute /p/	NO EQUIVALENT Substitute /p/	*f*a (issue)
*V*aj ('Vang' clan name)	NO EQUIVALENT Substitute /b/	NO EQUIVALENT Substitute /b/	NO EQUIVALENT Substitute /w/ or /f/
NO EQUIVALENT Substitute /th/ or /f/	NO EQUIVALENT Learners can use correct sound, but sometimes mispronounce voiced /ð/.	NO EQUIVALENT Substitute /t/	NO EQUIVALENT Substitute /t/ or /s/
NO EQUIVALENT Substitute /d/	NO EQUIVALENT Learners can use correct sound	NO EQUIVALENT Substitute /d/	NO EQUIVALENT Substitute /t/ or /s/
*th*em (to pay) Distinguishes aspirated and non-aspirated	*t*akbo (run) Never aspirated	*t*al (daughter)	*t*a (wet) Distinguishes aspirated and non-aspirated
*d*ev (dog)	*d*eretso (straight)	NO EQUIVALENT Substitute /d/ when said between vowels and /t/ elsewhere.	NO EQUIVALENT Substitute /t/
*n*oj (to eat)	*n*aman (too)	*n*al (day)	*n*i (you) May be confused with /l/
*x*a (to send)	*s*ila (they)	*s*al (rice) Substitute shi– sound before /i/ and /z/ after a nasal consonant	*s*an (three)
NO EQUIVALENT Learners can use correct sound	NO EQUIVALENT Learners can use correct sound	NO EQUIVALENT Learners can use correct sound	NO EQUIVALENT Substitute /ts/ or /tsʰ/
NO EQUIVALENT Substitute /t/	*r*in/din (too) Variant of the /d/ sound	Only occurs between two vowels Considered a /l/ sound	NO EQUIVALENT
*l*os (to come) /l/ does not occur at the ends of syllables	sa*l*amat (thank you)	ba*l*am (wind)	*l*an (blue) Can be confused and substituted with /r/

Linguistic Contrastive Analysis Chart

The Consonants of English (continued)

IPA	ENGLISH	SPANISH	VIETNAMESE	CANTONESE
ɹ	red Rare sound in the world Includes lip-rounding	**NO EQUIVALENT** Substitute /r/ sound such as the tap /ɾ/ or the trilled /r/	**NO EQUIVALENT** Substitute /l/	**NO EQUIVALENT** Substitute /l/
ʃ	shallow Often said with lip-rounding	**NO EQUIVALENT** Substitute /s/ or /tʃ/	sieu thị (supermarket) southern dialect only	**NO EQUIVALENT** Substitute /s/
ʒ	vision Rare sound in English	**NO EQUIVALENT** Substitute /z/ or /dʒ/	**NO EQUIVALENT** Substitute /s/	**NO EQUIVALENT** Substitute /ts/
tʃ	chirp	chico (boy)	chính phủ (government) Pronounced harder than English ch	**NO EQUIVALENT** Substitute /ts/
dʒ	joy	**NO EQUIVALENT** Sometimes substituted with /ʃ/ sound Some dialects have this sound for the ll spelling as in llamar	**NO EQUIVALENT** Substitute /ch/, the equivalent sound, but voiceless	**NO EQUIVALENT** Substitute /ts/ Only occurs at beginnings of syllables
j	you	cielo (sky) Often substitute /dʒ/	yeu (to love)	jau (worry)
k	kite Aspirated at the start of a word or stressed syllable	casa (house) Never aspirated	com (rice) Never aspirated	kʰa (family) Distinguishes aspirated and non-aspirated
g	goat	gato (cat)	**NO EQUIVALENT** Substitute /k/	**NO EQUIVALENT** Substitute /k/
ŋ	king	mango (mango)	Nguyễn (proper last name)	phaŋ (to cook)
h	hope	gente (people) Sometimes substitute sound with friction higher in the vocal tract as velar /x/ or uvular /χ/	hoa (flower)	ha (shrimp)

HMONG	FILIPINO	KOREAN	MANDARIN
NO EQUIVALENT Substitute /l/	**NO EQUIVALENT** Substitute the tap /ɾ/	**NO EQUIVALENT** Substitute the tap or /ɾ/ confused with /l/	*ran* (caterpillar) Tongue tip curled farther backward than for English /r/
sau (to write)	*siya* (s/he)	Only occurs before /i/; Considered a /s/ sound	*shi* (wet)
zos (village)	**NO EQUIVALENT** Learners can use correct sound	**NO EQUIVALENT**	**NO EQUIVALENT** Substitute palatal affricate /tɕ/
cheb (to sweep)	*tsa* (tea)	*cʰal* (kicking)	*cheng* (red)
NO EQUIVALENT Substitute *ch* sound	*Dios* (God)	**NO EQUIVALENT** Substitute *ch* sound	**NO EQUIVALENT** Substitute /ts/
Yaj (Yang, clan name)	*tayo* (we)	*je:zan* (budget)	*yan* (eye)
Koo (Kong, clan name) Distinguishes aspirated and non-aspirated	*kalian* (when) Never aspirated	*kal* (spreading)	*ke* (nest) Distinguishes aspirated and non-aspirated
NO EQUIVALENT Substitute /k/	*gulay* (vegetable)	**NO EQUIVALENT** Substitute /k/ Learners use correct sound between two vowels	**NO EQUIVALENT** Substitute /k/
gus (goose)	*angaw* (one million)	*baŋ* (room)	*tang* (gong) Sometimes add /k/ sound to the end
hais (to speak)	*hindi* (no)	*hal* (doing)	**NO EQUIVALENT** Substitute velar fricative /x/

Linguistic Contrastive Analysis Chart

The Vowels of English

IPA	ENGLISH	SPANISH	VIETNAMESE	CANTONESE
i	*beat*	*hijo* (son)	*di* (to go)	*si* (silk)
ɪ	*bit* Rare in other languages Usually confused with /i/ (*meat* vs. *mitt*)	**NO EQUIVALENT** Substitute /ē/	**NO EQUIVALENT** Substitute /ē/	*sik* (color) Only occurs before velars Substitute /ē/
e	*bait* End of vowel diphthongized—tongue moves up to /ē/ or short *e* postions	*eco* (echo)	*kê* (millet)	*se* (to lend)
ɛ	*bet* Rare in other languages. Learners may have difficulty distinguishing /ā/ and /e/ (short e): *pain* vs. *pen*	**NO EQUIVALENT** Substitute /ā/	**NO EQUIVALENT** Substitute /ā/	*seŋ* (sound) Only occurs before velars; difficult to distinguish from /ā/ in all positions
æ	*bat* Rare in other languages Learners may have trouble getting the tongue farther forward in the mouth	**NO EQUIVALENT** Substitute short *o* or short *u*	*ghe* (boat)	**NO EQUIVALENT** Hard to distinguish between /ā/ and /æ/
u	*boot*	*uva* (grape)	*mua* (to buy)	*fu* (husband)
ʊ	*could* Rare in other languages. Learners may have difficulty distinguishing the vowel sounds in *wooed* vs. *wood*	**NO EQUIVALENT** Substitute long *u*	**NO EQUIVALENT** Substitute long *u* (high back unrounded)	*suk* (uncle) Only occurs before velars Difficult to distinguish from long *u* in all positions
o	*boat* End of vowel diphthongized – tongue moves up to long *u* or ʊ position	*ojo* (eye)	*cô* (aunt)	*so* (comb)
ɔ	*law*	**NO EQUIVALENT** Substitute long *o* or short *o* Substituting long *o* will cause confusion (*low* vs. *law*); substituting short *o* will not	*cá* (fish)	*hok* (shell) Only occurs before velars Difficult to distinguish from long *o* in all positions
ɑ	*hot*	*mal* (bad)	*con* (child)	*sa* (sand)
ɑʊ	*house* Diphthong	*pauta* (guideline)	*dao* (knife)	*sau* (basket)
ɔɪ	*boy* Diphthong	*hoy* (today)	*ròi* (already)	*soi* (grill)
ɑɪ	*bite* Diphthong	*baile* (dance)	*hai* (two)	*sai* (to waste)
ə	*about* Most common vowel in English; only in unstressed syllables. Learners may have difficulty keeping it very short	**NO EQUIVALENT** Substitute short *u* or the full vowel from the word's spelling	*mua* (to buy)	**NO EQUIVALENT**
ʌ	*cut* Similar to schwa /ə/	**NO EQUIVALENT** Substitute short *o*	*giờ* (time)	*san* (new)
ɝ	*bird* Difficult articulation, unusual in the world but common in American English. Learners must bunch the tongue and constrict the throat	**NO EQUIVALENT** Substitute short *u* or /er/ with trill	**NO EQUIVALENT** Substitute /ɨ/	*hæ* (boot)

HMONG	FILIPINO	KOREAN	MANDARIN
ib (one)	*ikaw* (you) This vowel is interchangeable with /ɪ/; hard for speakers to distinguish these	ʑɩːʃaŋ (market)	*ti* (ladder) Sometimes English /i/ can be produced shorter
NO EQUIVALENT Substitute /ē/	*limampu* (fifty) This vowel is interchangeable with /ē/; hard for speakers to distinguish these	**NO EQUIVALENT** Substitute long *e*	**NO EQUIVALENT**
tes (hand)	*sero* (zero)	*be:da* (to cut)	*te* (nervous) Sometimes substitute English schwa /ə/
NO EQUIVALENT Substitute /ā/	*sero* (zero) This vowel interchanges with /ā/ like *bait;* not difficult for speakers to learn	*thɛ:do* (attitude)	**NO EQUIVALENT**
NO EQUIVALENT Substitute short *e*	**NO EQUIVALENT** Substitute short *o* as in *hot*	**NO EQUIVALENT**	**NO EQUIVALENT** Substitute /ə/ or short *u*
kub (hot or gold)	*tunay* (actual) This vowel interchanges with vowel in *could;* not difficult for speakers to learn	*zu:bag* (watermelon)	*lu* (hut) Sometimes English long *u* can be produced shorter
NO EQUIVALENT Substitute a sound like long *e* (mid central with lips slightly rounded)	*gumawa* (act) This vowel interchanges with long *u* like *boot;* not difficult for speakers to learn	**NO EQUIVALENT**	**NO EQUIVALENT**
NO EQUIVALENT	*ubo* (cough)	*bo:zu* (salary)	*mo* (sword) This vowel is a little lower than English vowel
Yaj (Yang, clan name)	**NO EQUIVALENT** Spoken as short *o*, as in *hot*	**NO EQUIVALENT**	**NO EQUIVALENT** Substitute long *o*
mov (cooked rice)	*talim* (blade)	*ma:l* (speech)	*ta* (he/she) Sometimes substitute back long *o* or *u*
plaub (four)	*ikaw* (you)	**NO EQUIVALENT**	**NO EQUIVALENT**
NO EQUIVALENT	*apoy* (fire)	**NO EQUIVALENT**	**NO EQUIVALENT**
qaib (chicken)	*himatay* (faint)	**NO EQUIVALENT**	**NO EQUIVALENT**
NO EQUIVALENT	**NO EQUIVALENT** Spoken as short *o*, as in *hot*	**NO EQUIVALENT** Difficult sound for learners	**NO EQUIVALENT**
NO EQUIVALENT	**NO EQUIVALENT** Spoken as short *o;* as in *hot*	**NO EQUIVALENT**	**NO EQUIVALENT**
NO EQUIVALENT Substitute diphthong /əɨ/	**NO EQUIVALENT** Spoken as many different vowels (depending on English spelling) plus tongue tap /ɾ/	**NO EQUIVALENT**	**NO EQUIVALENT**

ROUTINE 1 • ELL VOCABULARY ROUTINE

❶ Introduce the Word Point to the word and say it slowly. Supply a student-friendly definition and relate the word to students' prior knowledge and experience. When possible, also relate the word to the weekly concept. Have students say the word.

Example: A place is an area. Your home is a place. Your school is a place. Today we will learn about other places. Say place.

❷ Demonstrate Provide examples to show meaning. When possible, use gestures, pictures, realia, or other visuals to help convey the meaning.

Example: Look at the picture. This is a park. A park is a place. This is a building. A building is a place too.

❸ Apply Have students demonstrate understanding of the word. Include opportunities for both verbal and nonverbal responses, such as using the word in a sentence, drawing, or physical gestures to show understanding.

Example: Draw a place you know. What is this place, a house or a park?

❹ Display the Word Display the word in the classroom. Use a word wall or a graphic organizer to show meaning.

Example: Write the word place at the top of a chart. Have students write or draw examples below. When possible, have students include examples from the weekly concept.

ROUTINE 2 • WHOLE-WORD BLENDING

❶ Introduce Whole-Word Blending Write the word. When possible, use visuals or gestures to help convey the meaning.

❷ Connect Sounds to Spelling

MODEL Point to each spelling and say its sound. Remind students to watch how you move your mouth and emphasize any letter combinations.

Example: Show how the letters s and h make one sound, /sh/. Say /f/ /i/ /sh/ as you touch under f, i, and sh.

GUIDE PRACTICE Have students say the sounds as you touch under the letter(s). *When I touch under the letter(s), you say the sound.*

CORRECTIVE FEEDBACK If students say an incorrect sound, refer them to the appropriate Sound-Spelling Card. Provide examples of other words with this sound spelling and have them pronounce the words. Point out any sounds that may be different or new to students' native languages.

❸ Blend Sounds

MODEL Blend the word by saying the sound for each spelling, with no pause between sounds, as you move your hand in a continuous motion from one letter to the next. Stretch continuous sounds.

Example: Blend /f/ /i/ /sh/.

GUIDE PRACTICE Run your hand below the word as students blend the sound with you and without you.

Example: Students blend /f/ /i/ /sh/ as you run your hand under the word fish.

CORRECTIVE FEEDBACK If students stop between sounds, then model how to say the sound without stopping between them.

❹ Read the Word Display the word.

MODEL Blend the word by pronouncing it normally as you smoothly, but quickly, run your hand beneath it.

GUIDE PRACTICE Have students say the sounds quickly to read the word.

CORRECTIVE FEEDBACK If students have difficulty saying the sounds quickly, then model how to say the words first slowly and then quickly.

❶ Introduce Blending Write and say the word and use visuals and gestures to convey its meaning.

❷ Connect Sounds to Spelling

MODEL Say the first sound in the word and write the letter(s) that spell that sound. Tell students to watch your mouth and emphasize any letter combinations. Touch under the letter(s) as you say the sounds.

GUIDE PRACTICE Have students say the sound as you touch under the letter(s).

CORRECTIVE FEEDBACK If students say an incorrect sound, refer them to the appropriate Sound-Spelling Card.

❸ Add a Sound-Spelling

MODEL Say the next sound in the word and add the letter(s) for that sound. Touch under the letter(s) as you say the sound.

GUIDE PRACTICE Have students say the sound as you touch under the letter(s).

CORRECTIVE FEEDBACK Use corrective feedback as shown above.

❹ Blend Sounds

MODEL Run your hand from letter to letter as you say the sounds without pausing. Repeat until all sounds have been blended.

Example: Blend /sssaaaa/, /sssaaaannn/, and /sssaaaannnd/.

GUIDE PRACTICE Have students repeat each sound. Then have students blend the sounds with you and then without you.

CORRECTIVE FEEDBACK If students stop between sounds, then model how to say the sounds without stopping between them.

❺ Read the Word

MODEL Blend the whole word. Run your hand under the letters as you say the sounds quickly to read the word.

GUIDE PRACTICE Have students blend the sound quickly to read the word.

CORRECTIVE FEEDBACK If students have difficulty saying the sound quickly, then model how to say the sounds first slowly and then quickly.

❶ Introduce Nondecodable Words
Some English words do not sound like their spellings. We learn how to say them by remembering the letters. We will say and spell the words together.

Example: Write *we.*

❷ Connect Letters to Words

MODEL Point to and say the word. Use visuals, gestures, or examples to demonstrate the meaning of the word. Identify the letters in the word and indicate the number of letters in the word.

Example:
This is the word we.
It has two letters.
The letters are w *and* e.

GUIDE PRACTICE Have students repeat with you the word, the letters of the word, and the number of letters in the word. Then, have the students do this with a partner, then on their own.

CORRECTIVE FEEDBACK If students pronounce the word incorrectly, model again the sounds in the word. Remind students to watch how you move your mouth. Point out any letters that do not follow the standard rules or may be different from their native language patterns.

❸ Demonstrate Usage

MODEL Use the nondecodable word in a sentence to demonstrate usage of the word. Provide an example that relates to their experience and uses the word in the same context as the text.

Example: Listen to this sentence: We go to school together.

GUIDE PRACTICE Have students use the word in a sentence. Provide a sentence frame if necessary.

CORRECTIVE FEEDBACK If students are not using the word correctly, model the correct usage again.

Use this routine for multisyllabic words that do not have prefixes, suffixes, or roots.

1 **Introduce the Strategy** *We can break some words into parts. Word parts, or chunks, help us read longer words.*

Example: Write *rabbit.*

When possible, use visuals or gestures to demonstrate the meaning of the word.

2 **Connect to Sound-Spellings.** Explain that the parts of a word are called *syllables.* Break the word into syllables.

Example: Rabbit has two syllables: rab *and* bit.

MODEL *The syllables help me say the word.* Say each syllable as you run your hand from one syllable to the next. Then read the syllables together as you say the word.

GUIDE PRACTICE Have students say each syllable as you run your hand underneath the letters in that syllable. Point out any letters or syllables that may be different from the students' native language.

CORRECTIVE FEEDBACK If students have difficulty understanding syllables, have them place their hands underneath their chin. Then have the students repeat the word. Explain that each time their chin touches their hands, it indicates a syllable. Then write the words to show them how the words are divided into syllables.

3 **Read the Word**

MODEL Read the syllables as you run your hand beneath them, and then read the syllables together as you say the word.

Example: This is how I read this word. First I read each syllable, and then I read the syllables together: rab/bit—rabbit.

GUIDE PRACTICE Have students read the syllables, and then read the word as you run your hand beneath the parts.

CORRECTIVE FEEDBACK If students have difficulty using sound-spellings and syllabication to read word parts, then read one part at a time as you cover the remaining parts.

Use this routine to teach word structure skills: base words and inflected endings, prefixes, suffixes, contractions, compound words, syllables.

1 **Introduce the Strategy** *We will break longer words into smaller parts. Some word parts help us understand what a word means.*

Example: Write *shorten.*

When possible, use visuals, gestures, or examples to demonstrate the meaning of the word.

2 **Introduce the Word Parts** Discuss the word part that is the focus of the lesson, and, if appropriate, describe its relationship to the base word. Help students make any connections between suffixes or prefixes in English and their native language.

*Example: A word part added at the end of a word is called a suffix. This word has two parts—*short *and* -en. Short *is the base word, and* -en *is the suffix.*

3 **Use Word Parts for Meaning** Explain the meaning of prefixes, suffixes, and inflected endings when introducing them. For compound words, demonstrate how you can sometimes, but not always, tell the meaning from its parts. Provide examples. Then check students' understanding.

Example: The suffix -en *means "to make." When you add* -en *to the end of* short, *it changes the word. What does* shorten *mean?*

4 **Read the Word**

MODEL Read the word parts as you run your hand beneath them, and then read the parts together to say the word.

Example: First, I read the base word, short; *next, I read the suffix,* -en. *Then I read the two parts together:* short, en—shorten.

GUIDE PRACTICE Have students identify the word parts and then read the word as you run you hand beneath the parts.

CORRECTIVE FEEDBACK If students have difficulty reading word parts, then have them identify one part at a time as you cover the remaining parts. It may be necessary to have them blend the base word or individual syllables before reading the whole word.

1 Select the Text Select a text or passage that is at students' reading level. If possible, pair the ELL with a student who reads fluently.

2 First Reading Students read the selected text, switching readers at a logical breaking place—for example, at the end of a sentence, paragraph, or page. Choose a smaller segment of text for students needing more support. Reader 1 begins while Reader 2 follows along, tracking the print with his or her fingers or eyes when the partner is reading.

3 Second Reading Partners reread, but Reader 2 begins so that each child is reading different text.

4 Reread For optimal fluency, students should reread the text three or four times.

5 Provide Corrective Feedback Listen to students read and provide corrective feedback regarding their oral reading (stress, rhythm, and intonation) and use of blending strategies. Keep in mind that ELLs can read fluently in English with an accent.

1 Select a Passage Select a grade-level passage.

2 Model Have students track the print as you read. While you read, pay attention to the elements of fluency. Read at an appropriate rate and rhythm. Emphasize the correct stress and intonation for each sentence, such as phrasing a question and stressing the important words in the sentence.

3 Guide Practice Have students read along with you.

4 On Their Own
- Have the class read aloud with you.
- For optimal fluency, students should reread three or four times.

❶ Select a Passage
- Select a passage at the student's reading level.
- Have two copies of the passage. Allow the student to read the text to him or herself before beginning.

❷ Timed Reading
- Have the student read the text aloud.
- On your copy, mark any errors the student makes.
- Mark where the student is after one minute.

❸ Figure Words Correct per Minute (WCPM) To figure WCPM, subtract the number of mistakes from the number of words the student read in one minute. Tell the student his or her WCPM, and explain that by practicing, he or she will try to exceed it.

❹ Review Review with the student mistakes he or she made. Help the student reread unknown words until he or she can do so without errors.

❺ Timed Reading
- Have the student reread the passage now that he or she is comfortable with the difficult words.
- Figure out his or her WCPM during the second round. Let the student know how much he or she has improved. Point out the importance of practicing.

❻ Provide Corrective Feedback Remind students that the goal is not to read as quickly as possible, but to read accurately and quickly.

❼ Extra Time Invite students to set their own WCPM goal for another section. Help them to reach that goal.

---

❶ Introduce Retelling *When we retell a story, we tell the story in our own words. Before we can retell a story, we need to know the parts of the story.*

❷ Identify Setting and Character

MODEL *First, I think about the setting and characters. The setting is where the story takes place. The characters are the people or animals in the story.* Give an example from a familiar story. You may choose a story the student knows from his or her native culture.

> *Example:* In this story, there is a little girl named Goldilocks and three bears. The three bears live in the forest.

GUIDE PRACTICE: Help students list the characters and setting of the story. *The three bears live in the forest. What is the setting? The three bears are characters. Who is another character in the story?*

CORRECTIVE FEEDBACK If students have difficulty identifying the setting and characters, have them use the illustrations or Retelling Cards as clues.

❸ Identify Plot Help students create a three-part story map to list what happens at the beginning, middle, and end of the story. *When I retell a story, I think about the plot. The plot is what happens in a story. A plot has a beginning, middle, and an end.*

MODEL *In the first part of the story, Goldilocks was walking in the forest when she saw an empty house.*

GUIDE PRACTICE *What happens at the middle of the story? What happens at the end?* Help students draw or write their answers in each section.

❹ Retell the Story

MODEL *My story map will help me retell the story.* Model retelling the story, emphasizing the characters, setting, and the plot.

GUIDE PRACTICE Have partners take turns retelling the story using their own story map.

CORRECTIVE FEEDBACK If a student has difficulty retelling the story, have him or her reread the story or use the illustrations in the retelling.

1 Introduce Summarizing Explain to students that summarizing a passage means telling what it was about. Summarizing does not include details. It just includes the most important parts.

2 What Happened?

MODEL *When I summarize, I ask myself, what is the passage mostly about? Sometimes, I use pictures or graphic sources to remind me.*

Example: This selection is mostly about wild animals, because most of the selection tells about animals that can be found in the wild. I also see a picture of a bear in a forest.

GUIDE PRACTICE Help students make a concept web. In the center, write a few words about the selection. Then have students write or draw the most important parts in the outer circles.

CORRECTIVE FEEDBACK If students have difficulty telling the important parts, model how to find them by pointing to pictures and talking about what you see.

3 When Did It Happen?

MODEL *I can also summarize important events that happen over a period of time. I tell what happened first, next, and last. Knowing when the events happened helps me understand what I read.*

Example: First, the bird collects twigs. Next, it builds a nest. Last, the bird lays its eggs.

GUIDE PRACTICE Help students fill out a sequence chart. Write the words *first, next,* and *last* and fill in the first event. Have students write or draw to fill in the chart.

CORRECTIVE FEEDBACK If students have difficulty tracking the sequence, have them use the pictures and point to what happens first, next, and last.

1 Introduce Spelling *We will use the sounds and letters we know to spell words. First, listen to the word. Then say its sounds and write the letters.*

2 Dictate the Word Say the word, use it in a sentence, and then repeat the word.

Example: clog. The sink has a clog. clog.

3 Segment the Sounds

MODEL Sound out the word. The word is *clog.* The sounds in *clog* are /kl/ /ŏ/ /g/. Have students echo each sound.

GUIDE PRACTICE Repeat the word and have students segment the sounds.

CORRECTIVE FEEDBACK If students are having difficulty, drag each sound out: /kl/ /ŏ/ /g/. Remind students to watch how you move your mouth. Emphasize any sounds that may be different or new to the students' native languages.

4 Spell the Sounds

MODEL Say the first sound and write its spelling. Continue with each sound and spelling until the entire word has been written.

GUIDE PRACTICE Ask a volunteer what letter or letters make the first sound. Write the letter or letters. Repeat with the other sounds. Have students say each sound with you, and then write its spelling after you.

CORRECTIVE FEEDBACK If students have difficulty spelling a sound, have them refer to the Sound-Spelling Card to identify the spelling.

5 Proofread Spelling Continue the dictation until all words have been spelled. Then display the correct spelling for each word. Help students proofread their work, circle any misspelled words, and write them correctly. Help them understand any common errors by asking their reasoning for the mistake. Point out any spelling patterns that do not follow the standard rules or may be different from their native language.

ROUTINE 13 • CONCEPT TALK VIDEO

1 Introduce Talk Video Explain to students that they will be watching a video. Explain that the video will introduce the Question of the Week.

2 Assess Understanding Once the video ends, ask students, "What is the question of the week?" Have students write the answer. Then, replay the section of the video that answers this question. Pause it when done. Ask students if everyone got the answer right.

3 Access Prior Knowledge Invite students to discuss any prior knowledge they have about the weekly question or concept. Encourage them to share their experiences. Invite struggling speakers to draw a picture that illustrates their experience.

4 Summarize Begin the video again. Pause it at critical points, such as when new information is taught. Confirm that students understand what they have seen by asking them to summarize the section they just watched.

CORRECTIVE FEEDBACK If students are unable to summarize sections, rewind and watch that section again. Before they attempt to summarize, ask questions that will guide them to understand the main idea of the section.

5 Graphic Organizer Draw a two-columned graphic organizer. Title one column *What I Knew* and the next *What I Learned.* Have students fill in the columns using information about the weekly question that they already knew, and information they learned while watching the video.

CORRECTIVE FEEDBACK If students struggle when filling in the second column, allow them to watch the video again.

ROUTINE 14 • AUDIOTEXT CD

1 Before Listening Have students open their Student Edition to the selection. Explain to students that they are going to read along while listening to the selection on a CD.

2 During Listening Ask students to keep pace with the CD by moving their finger along the text of their Student Edition. Encourage students to raise their hand if they get lost or hear a phrase or word they do not understand. Pause the CD and write the problem words and phrases. Allow the selection to finish.

3 Model Replay the CD, allowing students to watch you choral read along with it. Make sure you imitate not only the words but the expression with which they are read.

4 After Listening Review any misunderstood words or phrases. For words, sound each out, calling special attention to blends before putting them all together. Have students choral read the words with you. If a phrase is an idiom, explain its meaning.

5 On Their Own Place students in pairs. Instruct them to practice reading sections of the text until they are comfortable reading them at the same pace as the CD. Encourage partners to help each other through passages they may find difficult.

CORRECTIVE FEEDBACK Make sure students do not sacrifice accuracy for speed. If there is a difficult section in the reading, replay it so students can practice.

ROUTINE 15 • GRAMMAR JAMMER

❶ Introduce Grammar Jammer Tell students that you will play a song about the weekly convention. Describe what the song is about and how it relates to the lesson.

Example: The song is about adjectives. It tells how to use adjectives to compare nouns.

❷ Display the Concept Review the concept before playing the song. Write one or more key parts from the song that is supported by the text on the screen.

Example: You can use an adjective to compare two nouns. Just add an -er.

short + er = shorter

tall + er = taller

loud + er = louder

quiet + er = quieter

MODEL Play the song for students. Pause the song at key points to review concepts. Write the text on screen and point to the visuals that support the concept. Replay these parts and model using them to understand the concept.

GUIDE PRACTICE Have students read aloud the text on screen. Prompt students to apply the grammar concepts. Ask questions, provide sentence frames, or have students give more examples.

Example: Shorter, taller, louder, quieter. These are comparative adjectives. Can you give another example?

CORRECTIVE FEEDBACK Replay any parts that students do not understand. Pause to review the text on screen and visuals. Have a volunteer explain how the song relates to the concept.

ROUTINE 16 • MODELED PRONUNCIATION AUDIO CD

❶ Before Listening Tell students that they will be listening to a CD to help with sound pronunciation. Advise them to keep their Sound-Spelling Cards ready.

❷ During Listening After each pronunciation, hit pause. Repeat the sound, exaggerating your mouth movements. Then, have students repeat the sound after you. Rewind and play the sound again. Write the letters that make the sound. Repeat it and have students do the same.

Example: The sound is /mp/. The letters that make the sound are m and p. Listen as I say the sound again: /mp/.

❸ After Listening Guide students to look at the letters you wrote. Then have them match their Sound-Spelling Cards to the sounds they learned. Once again, go through each sound, this time allowing the student to look at his or her card as you do so.

❹ Guided Practice Hold up a Sound-Spelling Card and call on a volunteer to pronounce the sound. Continue to do so until they have all been pronounced in the order they were learned. Finally, challenge students by rearranging the cards and have them repeat the exercise.

❺ On Their Own Pair students with partners. Challenge them to pronounce the sound on each card without referring to the CD.

CORRECTIVE FEEDBACK If students have difficulty recalling the sound, replay the CD and point out each example as it plays.

Graphic Organizers

Table of Contents

K-W-L Chart

Topic _____

What Do I **K** **now?**	**What Do I** **W** **ant to Learn?**	**What Did I** **L** **earn?**

ELL Handbook

Word Rating Chart

Word	Know	Have Seen	Don't Know

Story Predictions Chart

Title _____

What might happen?	What clues do I have?	What did happen?

Story Map A

Title _____

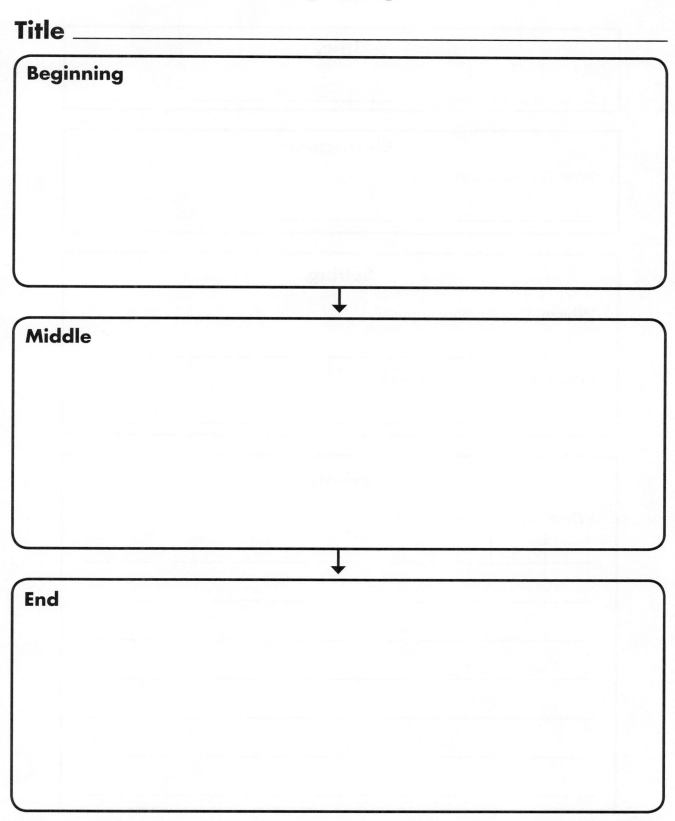

Beginning

Middle

End

Story Map B

Title

Characters
Who is in the story?

Setting
Where does the story happen?
When does the story happen?

Events
What happens in the story?

Story Comparison

Title A _____

Title B _____

_____

_____

Characters

Who is in the story?

Characters

Who is in the story?

Setting

Where and **when** does it happen?

Setting

Where and **when** does it happen?

Events

What happens in the story?

Events

What happens in the story?

Web

Main Idea

Main Idea

Details

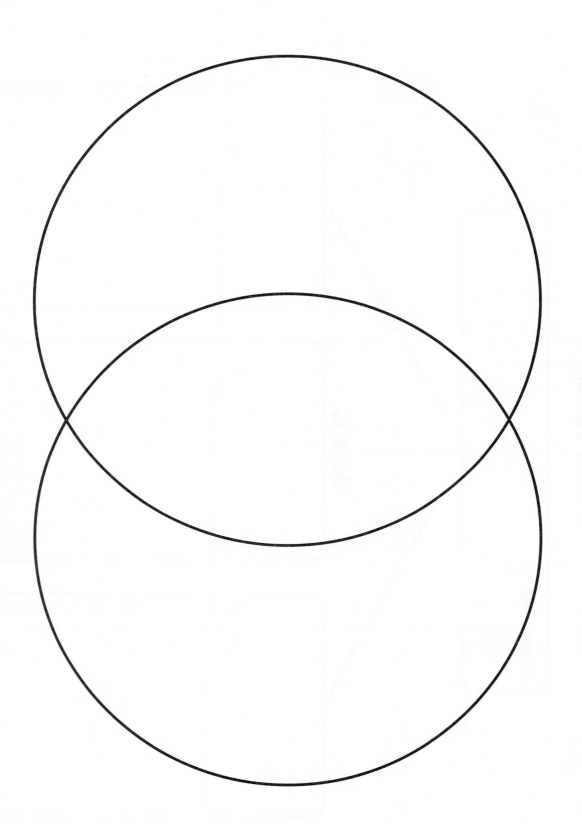

Venn Diagram

Cause and Effect

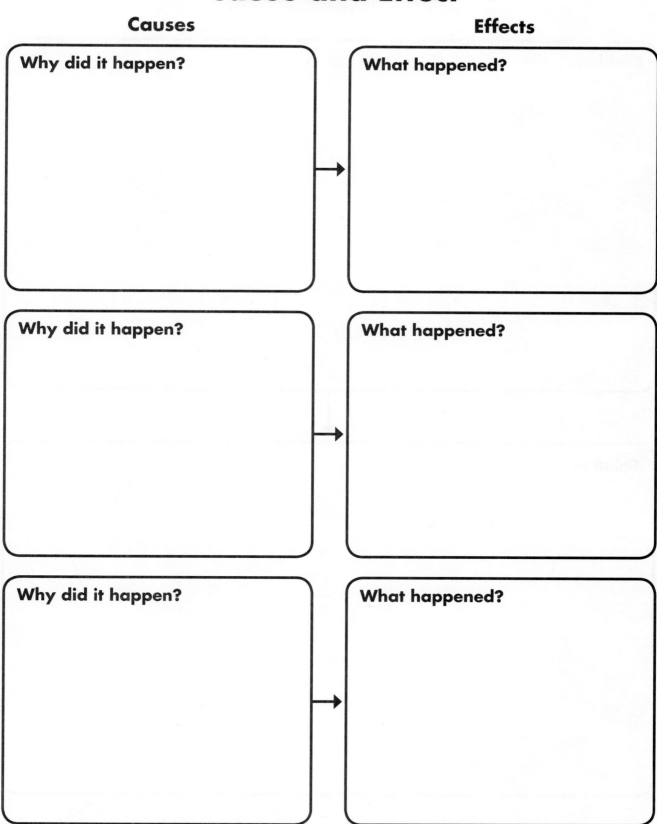

Causes

Effects

Why did it happen?

What happened?

Why did it happen?

What happened?

Why did it happen?

What happened?

Problem and Solution

Problem

Solution

Time Line

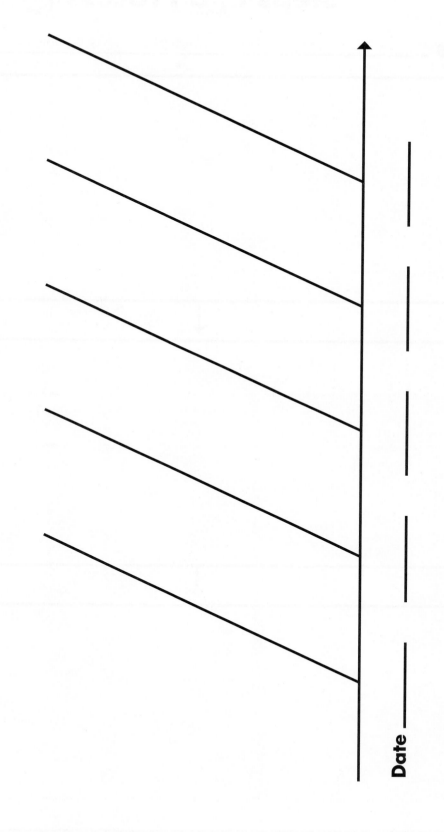

Date _____

Steps in a Process

Process _____

```
┌─────────────────────────────────────────┐
│ Step 1                                   │
│                                          │
│                                          │
│                                          │
│                                          │
└─────────────────────────────────────────┘
                    │
                    ▼
┌─────────────────────────────────────────┐
│ Step 2                                   │
│                                          │
│                                          │
│                                          │
│                                          │
└─────────────────────────────────────────┘
                    │
                    ▼
┌─────────────────────────────────────────┐
│ Step 3                                   │
│                                          │
│                                          │
│                                          │
│                                          │
└─────────────────────────────────────────┘
```

T-Chart

Three-Column Chart

Outline Form

Title _____

A _____

   1. _____

   2. _____

   3. _____

B _____

   1. _____

   2. _____

   3. _____

C _____

   1. _____

   2. _____

   3. _____

K-W-L CHART

About the Graphic Organizer

Students use what they know to explore prior knowledge about a selection, set purposes for reading, and record what they learn as they read.

Instructional Routine

The K-W-L chart works well with expository text. Display the chart for students.

○ Write the word *Know* on the board. Underline the K. Tell students that the K stands for "What Do I <u>K</u>now?" Ask students what they know about the topic and model recording their responses.

○ Write *Want* on the board and underline W. Tell students that the W stands for "What Do I <u>W</u>ant to Learn?" Ask students what they want to know about the topic. Model recording their responses in the form of questions.

○ Write *Learn* on the board. Underline the L. Tell students that the L stands for "What Did I <u>L</u>earn?" As you read, ask students what they are learning. Model recording their responses on the chart.

Teaching Tips

• After modeling, students can complete the K-W-L chart in pairs or small groups.

• Suggest that, if students are unclear about a topic they have recorded in the K column, they can turn it into a question for the L column.

• Modify the chart if necessary by changing the headings into sentence frames: *I know* _____. *I want to know* _____. *I learned* _____.

Extensions

• Create K-W-L charts that you can post in the room as you learn about different topics in content areas, such as social studies and science. Students can add to the charts as they learn more.

• Have students work in pairs to read an article at their reading level. They can use K-W-L charts to organize their thinking.

Skill and Strategies

• Activate Prior Knowledge

• Set Purpose

• Summarize

WORD RATING CHART

About the Graphic Organizer

The word rating chart helps students explore what words they already know and what words are new to them.

Instructional Routine

You can use this chart with any list of words that students are studying.

○ Display the chart for students and list words on the chart. Have students copy the chart.

○ Explain that the word *Know* means that students know and can use the word. Model placing a check in the second column for words that students know.

○ Explain that column 3, *Have Seen*, means that students have seen or heard the word, but they aren't sure what it means. Model placing a check in the third column.

○ Explain that column 4, *Don't Know*, means that students don't know the word at all. Model placing a check in the fourth column.

Teaching Tips

• After modeling, students can complete a word rating chart on their own. You might write the words in the chart and copy before distributing.

• Use the chart as a diagnostic tool to determine which words you'll focus on in classroom studies.

Extensions

• Have students revisit their chart after they have read a selection or studied the words. They can adjust their ratings.

• Consider adding a column to the chart in which students can write sentences with words they know.

• Encourage students to state meanings of words in their own words. Explain what it means to tell a meaning in your own words.

Skill and Strategies

• Activate Prior Knowledge

• Recall and Retell

• Context Clues

STORY PREDICTIONS CHART

About the Graphic Organizer

Students preview the selection title and illustrations and then predict what might happen in the selection.

Instructional Routine

This graphic organizer works well with any selection in which the title and/or pictures suggest predictions about the events in a story. Consider using it for content-area selections as well.

○ Preview the selection with students. Read the title and lead a picture walk. Ask students to predict what they think will happen in the selection. Remind them to use what they know about the topic of the story. Record their predictions in the chart.

○ Ask students how they figured out what would happen. Tell them that they used *clues*. Ask what clues they used and record those clues in the chart.

○ After reading, look back at the predictions. Write what actually happened in the third column. Ask students how their predictions were different. Why do they think their predictions were different from what really happened?

Teaching Tips

• Focus on clues in illustrations. What details in the illustrations help students make predictions?

• Provide sentence frames for predicting. *I think _____ will happen. I think this will happen because _____.*

Extensions

• After completing this activity as a class exercise, have students use the chart in pairs, small groups, or independently.

• Use the chart with content-area selections. Focus on the content, giving students a sentence frame to use: *I think I will learn about _____ because _____.*

Skill and Strategies

• Predict

• Activate Prior Knowledge

• Draw Conclusions

STORY MAP A

About the Graphic Organizer

Students use this chart to record the sequence of events in a selection.

Instructional Routine

This organizer works well with any selection with a clear sequence of events.

○ Display the organizer. Write the title of the selection.

○ Start reading. Ask students to tell you what events in the beginning of the story are important. Write them on the chart.

○ Focus on events in the middle of the story, recording them in the chart.

○ As you finish the selection, record important events from the end.

Teaching Tips

• Make a list of words that tell time order, such as *after, later, first,* or *next.* Provide sentences frames to help students use them.

• Encourage students to use story maps to retell the events to partners.

Extensions

• Have students draw pictures of events in the organizer. They can label the pictures.

• Use the story map with events in social studies or with steps in a sequence in other content area reading.

Skill and Strategies

• Sequence/Plot

• Recall and Retell

• Text Structure

• Summarize

STORY MAP B

About the Graphic Organizer

Students record the characters and setting of a story and track a sequence of events.

Instructional Routine

This graphic organizer works well with any selection that has a clear series of events. It can help students understand the relationship between the sequence of events and the outcome of the story.

- Display the organizer. Write the title of the selection on the organizer.
- Read the selection. Ask students where and when the story takes place. Record those details in the *setting* section.
- As you read, record information about characters on the organizer.
- As you read, pause to record information about the sequence of events.

Teaching Tips

- Model sentences frames for talking about characters and setting: _____ *is a person/ animal in this story. This story takes place in (the future/the past/today).*
- Help students look for clue words for sequence. Make a list of clue words to display for students' reference.
- Students may not need all the boxes, or they may need more. Help them modify the organizer depending on the story.

Extensions

- After completing this activity as a class exercise, have students use the chart in pairs, small groups, or independently.
- Students can draw events in the organizer and label those events.
- Help students think of words to use to describe characters. Make a list and have students add to it.

Skill and Strategies

- Story Elements: Character, Setting, Plot
- Recall and Retell
- Summarize

STORY COMPARISON

About the Graphic Organizer

Students use this chart to record how two selections are similar and different.

Instructional Routine

This organizer works well with selections that have something in common. It's a great tool for comparing texts by the same author or about the same topic.

- Choose two stories to compare. Write their titles on the organizer.
- Ask questions to elicit characters, setting, and plot events. Record details on the chart.

Teaching Tips

- After modeling how to use the organizer, students can work on the organizer with partners or in small groups.
- Provide sentence frames for comparison and model how to use them, such as: *The characters in this story are _____, but the characters in that story are _____.*
- Invite students to use the chart to retell stories.

Extensions

- Students can use the chart to compare a story and a nonfiction text about the same topic.
- Have students use one half the chart to plan the writing of their own story.

Skill and Strategies

- Story Elements: Character, Setting, Plot
- Text Structure
- Summarize
- Compare and Contrast

WEB

About the Graphic Organizer

Students explore their prior knowledge as they brainstorm related ideas, recognize concept relationships, and/or organize information. They can highlight a central concept and connect it to related words, ideas, or details.

Instructional Routine

This graphic organizer has multiple uses and is appropriate for all levels of learners. Use different approaches to the web as you develop the organizer with students.

○ Display the organizer. Write a central idea or topic in the middle of the web.

○ Ask students for ideas that are related to the central idea. Record those ideas in the circles attached to the middle circle.

○ You can add ideas related to the "sub ideas" in additional ovals.

Teaching Tips

• Once you have modeled how to use the organizer, have students complete the organizer independently, in pairs, or in small groups.

• Encourage students to explain how the ideas on the web are related to the central ideas. Provide sentence frames to help students talk about the web. *The main idea is* _____. *One related idea is* _____.

• Use this web to explore main ideas and details, character names along with their traits, vocabulary words and their synonyms, and so on.

Extensions

• Students can use the organizer to record ideas about a theme or about a topic in content-area reading.

• Have students use the web to record background knowledge about a topic. Use the webs to assess gaps in understanding as you plan instruction.

• Enlarge the graphic organizer so that students can draw in the circles. They can label or write sentences about their drawings.

Skill and Strategies

• Classify

• Summarize

• Main Idea and Details

MAIN IDEA

About the Graphic Organizer

Students recognize a main idea and distinguish between the main idea and the details.

Instructional Routine

This organizer works especially well with nonfiction selections that are organized around main ideas and details.

○ Record a main idea in the top box. Define *main idea* as the most important idea.

○ Model by recording a detail that supports, or tells more about, the main idea. Then have students supply additional details as you record them.

Teaching Tips

• Supply a sentence frame about main ideas: *The most important idea is* _____. Supply a sentence frame about details. *One detail about this idea is* _____.

• Model how to tell a supporting detail from a detail that is not a supporting detail. Let students know that some ideas are important to know and other ideas are interesting to know. Display part of a selection and model highlighting important ideas.

• Extend or add additional boxes if necessary to add more details.

Extensions

• Have students use the organizer to record ideas for writing pieces of their own.

• Have students use the chart in pairs or small groups to record important ideas from content area reading, such as in social studies or science.

Skill and Strategies

• Main Idea and Details

• Summarize

VENN DIAGRAM

About the Graphic Organizer

Students use this organizer to record similarities and differences between places, ideas, characters, or other elements of fiction or nonfiction.

Instructional Routine

A Venn diagram works well in any situation that lends itself to comparing and contrasting.

○ Start by comparing and contrasting something simple and familiar, such as cats and dogs. Write the subjects you are comparing over the circles of the Venn diagram.

○ Point to where the circles overlap. Let students know that in this section, you'll write similarities, or how the two things are alike. Ask how the two subjects are alike. Record students' responses.

○ Point to an individual circle and let students know that, in this section, you'll write details that describe only what is labeled at the top of the circle. Ask students to list details as you record them.

Teaching Tips

• It might help students if you ask questions that lead to details to write in the diagram, such as *Are both of these objects blue? Do both of them have four legs?* and so on.

• Help students with sentence frames: *These two things are alike because* _____. *These two things are different because* _____.

• List words that signal comparing and contrasting, such as *alike, different, but,* and so on. Students can point to those words in the text.

Extensions

• Students can create Venn diagrams to compare themselves to characters in fictional texts.

• Students can use Venn diagrams to compare topics in content areas, such as comparing two types of rock, two types of volcanoes, or two animals or plants.

Skill and Strategies

• Compare and Contrast

• Summarize

CAUSE AND EFFECT

About the Graphic Organizer

Students identify cause-and-effect relationships in either fiction or nonfiction.

Instructional Routine

This graphic organizer works well with any selection that has clear cause-and-effect relationships.

○ Tell students that something that happens is an effect. Record an effect on the graphic organizer.

○ Then ask students *Why did it happen?* Tell them the reason something happens is a cause. Record the cause on the graphic organizer.

Teaching Tips

• Remind students to ask themselves *What happened?* and *Why did it happen?* to identify effects and causes. It is usually easier to identify effects first, before the causes.

• List clue words that signal causes and effects, such as *because* and *so*. Look over the clue words with students, but remind them that not all causes and effects in selections have clue words.

Extensions

• Students can write cause and effects in their content area classes. They could record, for example, causes of thunderstorms or of events in history.

• Once students are able to use this organizer, point out that, in some cases, there are many causes for one effect or many effects for one cause. Alter the organizer with students so they can use it with multiple causes and effects.

• If students need extra assistance, fill in either causes or effects before distributing the organizer. Ask students to work in pairs to find the corresponding causes or effects.

Skill and Strategies

• Cause and Effect

• Summarize

• Text Structure

PROBLEM AND SOLUTION

About the Graphic Organizer

Students identify problems and solutions presented in fiction or nonfiction.

Instructional Routine

This graphic organizer works well with any selection with clear problems and solutions.

○ Tell students that a problem is something that needs to be solved. Give an example of a simple classroom problem. Record it in the organizer.

○ Ask students what they might do to "fix" the problem. Tell students that fixing a problem is solving a problem. Ask students how they might solve the problem. Record their ideas in the solution section.

Teaching Tips

• Once students understand how to use the organizer, focus on a problem and solution from a piece of text.

• Point out that not all solutions are "good." Sometimes the way a character solves a problem might result in an unhappy ending for the story.

• Provide sentence frames to help students discuss problems and solutions. *One problem in the text is _____. One way to solve it is _____.*

Extensions

• Write a problem in the school, classroom, or community in the first box and distribute organizers to pairs or small groups. Students can brainstorm solutions.

• Students can draw problems and solutions in the organizer and then label them with words or phrases.

Skill and Strategies

• Plot

• Summarize

• Text Structure

TIME LINE

About the Graphic Organizer

Students organize events from fiction or nonfiction in sequential order along a continuum.

Instructional Routine

This organizer works well with any selection that presents events in sequential order. It can also help students organize events in order.

○ After reading a short text, ask students what happened first. Record the first event on the chart.

○ Continue asking students to name events in order, placing them on the continuum.

Teaching Tips

• Remind students to look for clues in the text to the order in which things happen. They might find dates or clue words such as *first, next, then,* and *last.*

• If students need extra support, write events from the text on sentence strips. Have students work in pairs or small groups to place the strips in order and then write the events on the time line.

Extensions

• Students can create time lines about events in history or even things that have happened in their school or community.

• Have students interview partners and create time lines based on important events in their partners' lives.

• Share time lines from social studies texts with students. Have them discuss what the time lines have in common and identify their features.

Skill and Strategies

• Summarize

• Text Structure

• Sequence/Plot

STEPS IN A PROCESS

About the Graphic Organizer

Students break down a process into simple steps or directions.

Instructional Routine

This graphic organizer works well with any procedure that has relatively few steps. If students need more or smaller steps, help students redesign the organizer.

○ Display the organizer. Write the title on the organizer, such as *Making a Peanut Butter Sandwich.*

○ Ask students what the first step is. Record the first step in the organizer.

○ Write the remaining steps in the organizer in order as students supply them.

Teaching Tips

• Once students can contribute to a steps in a process chart, have them work in pairs or small groups to write the steps of a simple process.

• Tell students to look for clues words such as *first, next,* and *later* to help them sequence the steps.

Extensions

• Students may draw the steps in the organizer and label them with words or phrases.

• Have students use the organizer to show steps in a recipe, a science project, or in another content area.

Skill and Strategies

• Steps in a Process

• Sequence

• Visualize

T-CHART

About the Graphic Organizer

Students can explore and compare ideas, story elements, or vocabulary words. They can also chart ideas within and across texts, or between prior knowledge and new ideas.

Instructional Routine

This is a multipurpose graphic organizer that is helpful when exploring two concepts. It works well with all types of selections.

○ Model using the chart. Display the chart and write two topics being studied on the chart, one topic per column.

○ Elicit responses from students based on the topics chosen. Record responses in the chart.

Teaching Tips

• Students can write in the chart, but they can also draw and list or label.

• Students can use the T-chart to compare story elements, such as the traits of two characters.

• Use a T-chart to organize ideas gathered in a class brainstorming session.

• Use a T-chart to explore two vocabulary words. Write the words at the tops of the columns. Then under each word, list part of speech, a simple definition, and a sentence using the word in context.

Extensions

• Students can work with partners, each partner completing one half of the chart.

• Students can use T-charts to write the pros and cons of a topic for a debate or discussion.

Skill and Strategies

• Compare and Contrast

• Main Idea and Supporting Details

• Summarize

• Activate Prior Knowledge

THREE-COLUMN CHART

About the Graphic Organizer

The chart can be used to explore or classify ideas, story elements, genres, or vocabulary features. It can also help students recognize comparisons and contrasts, or chart ideas within and across texts.

Instructional Routine

This is a multi-purpose organizer that works well for exploring and organizing ideas for three concepts, words, or ideas. It works well with many selections.

○ Display the organizer. Choose three simple headings and write them on the chart, such as three different vocabulary words.

○ Ask students for details for each heading and record them on the chart. Point out that this chart helps organize information.

Teaching Tips

- Once you have modeled how to use the organizer, students can complete organizers independently or in pairs or small groups.

- Students can draw in the charts as well as list ideas.

- Students can use the three-column chart to explore story characteristics or characteristics of genre.

- Students can use the chart to organize ideas they generate during brainstorming.

- Students can use the chart to organize synonyms, antonyms, and multiple meanings of words. Create a class chart to model using the chart for vocabulary study.

Extensions

- Students can use the organizer to record ideas that follow the idea of *before, during,* and *after.*

- Students can use the chart to organize ideas in any curricular area. For example, students could organize odd numbers, even numbers, and prime numbers in math. In science, they could record details about categories of animals, such as birds, reptiles, and mammals.

Skill and Strategies

- Classify
- Summarize
- Main Idea and Details
- Activate Prior Knowledge

OUTLINE FORM

About the Graphic Organizer

Students use a simplified outline form to take notes on the organization of print materials or to organize their own thoughts before writing.

Instructional Routine

Writers can change the outline form to suit their own purposes, but this form gets students started with the basic outline organization.

○ Model using the outline form by outlining a simple text. Place the title on the top line.

○ Show students how to record the main ideas. You might display the text to point out where to find the main ideas in the text. Reread the main ideas as you record them on the form.

○ Break down the main ideas into smaller details on the secondary lines.

○ Model the same form as the basis for a class writing about something that you are currently studying.

Teaching Tips

- Depending on their English proficiency, students can use words, phrases, or sentences in their outlines. Encourage them to be consistent throughout the entire outline.

- If students use outlines for writing, point out that the outlines are tools that can be revised before and during writing if the organization will make more sense.

Extensions

- Create an outline by doing a class outline on a piece of content-area text, such as an article from a science book.

- Show students text features in a content area book, such as titles, heads, subheads, labels, and captions. Ask how these features might help them create an outline.

Skill and Strategies

- Text Structure
- Summarize
- Main Idea and Details